THE CAMBRIDGE EDITION
OF THE WORKS OF

JANE AUSTEN

LATER MANUSCRIPTS

Cambridge University Press and
Janet Todd wish to express their gratitude to the
University of Glasgow and the University of Aberdeen for
providing funding towards the creation of this edition.
Their generosity made possible the employment of
Antje Blank as research assistant during the project.

THE CAMBRIDGE EDITION
OF THE WORKS OF

JANE AUSTEN

VOLUMES IN THIS SERIES

Juvenilia edited by Peter Sabor
Northanger Abbey edited by Barbara Benedict and Deirdre Le Faye
Sense and Sensibility edited by Edward Copeland
Pride and Prejudice edited by Pat Rogers
Mansfield Park edited by John Wiltshire
Emma edited by Richard Cronin and Dorothy McMillan
Persuasion edited by Janet Todd and Antje Blank
Later Manuscripts edited by Janet Todd and Linda Bree

When stretch'd on one's bed
With a fierce-throbbing head
Which precludes alike Thought or Repose,
How little one cares
For the grandest affairs
That may busy the world as it goes.—

How little one feels
For the waltzes & reels
Of our dance-loving friends at a Ball!
How slight one's concern
To conjecture or learn
What their flounces or hearts may befall.—

How little one minds
If a company dines
On the best that the season affords!
How short is one's muse
O'er the sauces & stews,
Or the Guests, be they Beggars or Lords!—

How little the Bells,
Ring they Peels, toll they Knells
Can attract our attention or Ears!
The Bride may be married,
The Corse may be carried,
And touch nor our hopes nor our fears.

Frontispiece: First manuscript page of Jane Austen's poem 'When stretch'd on one's bed'. See p. 253.

JANE AUSTEN

LATER MANUSCRIPTS

Edited by
Janet Todd and Linda Bree

CAMBRIDGE
UNIVERSITY PRESS

CAMBRIDGE UNIVERSITY PRESS
Cambridge, New York, Melbourne, Madrid, Cape Town,
Singapore, São Paulo, Delhi, Mexico City

Cambridge University Press
The Edinburgh Building, Cambridge CB2 8RU, UK

Published in the United States of America by Cambridge University Press, New York

www.cambridge.org
Information on this title: www.cambridge.org/9781107620407

First published 2008
First paperback edition 2013

A catalogue record for this publication is available from the British Library

Library of Congress Cataloguing in Publication data
Austen, Jane, 1775–1817.
Later manuscripts / Jane Austen ; edited by Janet Todd and Linda Bree.
p. cm. – (The Cambridge edition of the works of Jane Austen)
Includes bibliographical references.
ISBN 978-0-521-84348-5 (hardback)
1. Austen, Jane, 1775–1817 – Manuscripts. I. Todd, Janet M., 1942–
II. Bree, Linda. III. Title. IV. Series.
PR4032.T63 2008
828.7 – dc22 2008035044

ISBN 978-0-521-84348-5 Hardback
ISBN 978-1-107-62040-7 Paperback

CONTENTS

ILLUSTRATIONS

GENERAL EDITOR'S PREFACE

Jane Austen wrote to be read and reread. '[A]n artist cannot do anything slovenly,' she remarked to her sister Cassandra. Her subtle, crafted novels repay close and repeated attention to vocabulary, syntax and punctuation as much as to irony and allusion; yet the reader can take immediate and intense delight in their plots and characters. As a result Austen has a unique status among early English novelists – appreciated by the academy and the general public alike. What Henry Crawford remarks about Shakespeare in *Mansfield Park* has become equally true of its author: she 'is a part of an Englishman's constitution. [Her] thoughts and beauties are so spread abroad that one touches them every where, one is intimate with [her] by instinct.' This edition of the complete oeuvre of the published novels and manuscript works is testament to Austen's exceptional cultural and literary position. As well as attempting to establish an accurate and authoritative text, it provides a full contextual placing of the novels.

The editing of any canonical writer is a practice which has been guided by many conflicting ideologies. In the early twentieth century, editors, often working alone, largely agreed that they were producing definitive editions, although they used eclectic methods and often revised the text at will. Later in the century, fidelity to the author's creative intentions was paramount, and the emphasis switched to devising an edition that would as far as possible represent the final authorial wishes. By the 1980s, however, the pursuit of the single perfected text had given way to the recording of multiple intentions of equal interest. Authors were seen to have changed, revised or recanted, or indeed to have directed various versions of their work towards different audiences. Consequently all states had validity and the text became a process rather than a fixed entity. With this approach came emphasis on the print culture in which the text appeared as well as on the social implications of authorship. Rather than being stages in the evolution of a single work, the various versions existed in their own right, all having something to tell.

The Cambridge edition describes fully Austen's early publishing history and provides details of composition, publication and publishers as well as printers and compositors where known. It accepts that many of the decisions concerning spelling, punctuation, capitalizing, italicizing and paragraphing may well have been the compositors' rather than Austen's but that others may represent the author's own chosen style. For the novels published in Jane Austen's lifetime the edition takes as its copytext the latest edition to which she might plausibly have made some contribution: that is, the first editions of *Pride and Prejudice* and *Emma* and the second editions of *Sense and Sensibility* and *Mansfield Park*. Where a second edition is used, all substantive and accidental changes between editions are shown on the page so that the reader can reconstruct the first edition, and the dominance of either first or second editions is avoided. For the two novels published posthumously together, *Northanger Abbey* and *Persuasion*, the copytext is the first published edition.

The two volumes devoted to manuscript writings divide the works between the three juvenile notebooks on the one hand and the remaining manuscript writings on the other. The juvenile notebooks and 'Lady Susan' have some resemblance to the published works, being fair copies and following some of the conventions of publishing. The other manuscript writings consist in part of fictional works in early drafts, burlesques and autograph and allograph copies of occasional verses and prayers. The possible dating of the manuscript works, as well as the method of editing, is considered in the introductions to the relevant volumes. Their features as manuscripts have been respected and changes and erasures either reproduced or noted.

In all the volumes superscript numbers in the texts indicate endnotes. Throughout the edition we have provided full annotations to give clear and informative historical and cultural information to the modern reader while largely avoiding critical speculation; we have also indicated words which no longer have currency or have altered in meaning in some way. The introductions give information concerning the genesis and immediate public reception of the texts; they also indicate the most significant stylistic and generic features. A chronology of Austen's life appears in each volume. More information about the life, Austen's reading, her relationship to publication, the print history of the novels and their critical reception through the centuries, as well as the historical, political, intellectual and religious context in which she wrote, is available in *Jane Austen in Context*, which forms part of the edition.

Janet Todd

PREFACE

This volume contains all the known manuscript works of Jane Austen's adulthood, with the exception of the cancelled chapters of *Persuasion*, which are reproduced as an Appendix in the volume of *Persuasion* in the Cambridge edition. The manuscripts exist in many forms, and each is described in detail at the appropriate point in the volume. With the exception of 'Lady Susan' and some of the poems, none exists in a fair copy in Austen's hand. Some survive only in draft form, some in versions written down by others; some have come down to us in multiple forms. Because of the 'occasional' nature of the poems in particular, where they exist in more than one version we have chosen to reproduce the earliest complete text, while noting variants between this and any other versions in Austen's handwriting.

With the exception of the reading texts of 'The Watsons' and 'Sanditon' (see below) we have not changed Jane Austen's spelling, capitalization, paragraphing or punctuation; her idiosyncrasies and inconsistencies, which form part of the texture of her work, have been carefully preserved. We have however made no attempt to represent graphic features of the manuscripts, such as lines drawn above or below titles and chapter numbers. Jane Austen occasionally uses the long 's'; throughout we have regularized this to the modern 's'. Her use of quotation marks differs from modern usage; we have followed her various systems but, when opening or closing quotation marks have been accidentally omitted, they have been inserted.

Jane Austen's handwriting is generally clear and legible, but some ambiguities in the manuscripts cause difficulties in transcription.

Since her indentations are often extremely slight, it is not always clear where a new paragraph begins. Many initial letters of words fall somewhere between upper and lower case, while commas cannot always be distinguished from periods. In such cases we have used our best editorial judgement, taking into account Jane Austen's practice in other manuscripts. The insetting of 'Lady Susan' into larger pages has sometimes resulted in the extreme right hand margin of Austen's original manuscript being no longer visible; here, and on other occasions of obvious accidental omission, we have inserted missing letters within square brackets.

'The Watsons' and 'Sanditon', her two incomplete novels, both exist in what seems to be a first-draft state. As working documents, they are very revealing of Austen's creative process. We have therefore decided that, rather than drawing an 'authoritative' text from the manuscript, with textual notes describing the revisions, additions and deletions, we would offer a line-by-line transcription of the two manuscripts: these appear as Appendices A and B. With this method, while we cannot indicate whether revisions were made at the time of first writing or later (on which one can speculate only when examining the manuscript in its material state), we can show where Austen was having difficulty working and reworking a phrase or sentence, and where she was writing smoothly in response to her first thoughts.

Because of the presence of these line-by-line transcriptions we have chosen to present, in the main body of the volume, 'reading' versions of both texts, which have been discreetly edited to reflect basic publishing conventions of the early nineteenth century, as evidenced by Austen's own published works. Accordingly, we have made the following changes:

-inserted quotation marks around speeches, except where the older convention of using brackets to indicate the speaker is used;

-inserted a line-break before and after speech, except where the speeches seem designed to run on;

-added some paragraphing when a single paragraph seems much longer than is common in the published works, and the narrative moves to a new subject; for 'Sanditon' we have usually followed the paragraph divisions suggested by Cassandra Austen in her fair copy of the manuscript made after Jane Austen's death;

-reduced Austen's heavy use of initial capital letters for nouns of all kinds;

-converted underlining into the usual printed equivalent of italics;

-normalized superscripts, so that 'M^{rs}:' becomes 'Mrs.', etc.;

-expanded grammatical contractions, so that 'tho' becomes 'though', etc.;

-expanded contractions for dates, titles and names, so that 'Oct.' becomes 'October', 'Col.' becomes 'Colonel' (as it does in most, though not all, references in the published works), 'H.' becomes 'Heywood', etc.;

-corrected idiosyncratic or old-fashioned spellings which would have been caught in any publishing process, such as 'veiw', 'freind', 'neice', 'independant', 'chearful', 'agreable', 'bason'; where the spelling was acceptable in the nineteenth century, though obsolete now, for example with 'staid' for 'stayed', 'shew' for 'show', 'stile' for 'style', 'ancle' (which appears in *Pride and Prejudice*) and Surry (in *Emma*), we have not adjusted it;

-adjusted punctuation where the text seems to require it for the sake of sense or common usage;

-harmonized Austen's inconsistent use of the apostrophe.

With one exception, we have not made consistent Austen's spelling of names, so that, just as in *Pride and Prejudice* the Bennets' aunt is either Phillips or Philips, here the keeper of the library in Sanditon remains variously Mrs. or Miss Whilby or Whitby. The exception is the spelling of Edwards/Edwardes in 'The Watsons', which we have represented throughout as Edwards, partly because of the need to expand the frequently used contraction 'E.'.

Despite clear evidence that early nineteenth-century printing practice would have insisted on extensive adjustment, we have chosen to make very few changes in Austen's use of the dash. It is clear to us that the dash is so characteristic of her style, and so closely bound up with the rhythm of her prose, that removal, or substantial reduction, would risk changing the nature of the text in a way that could not be justified in a scholarly edition.

As far as all the changes are concerned, we have made them with caution. We strongly recommend that readers compare the resulting reading text with the line-by-line transcriptions, to reach a rounder sense both of Austen's creative process as shown in these two unfinished works, and of the relationship, more generally, between her manuscripts and her published novels.

ACKNOWLEDGEMENTS

Given the very varied nature of the contents of this volume, we have been grateful for the assistance of a large number of people.

Like all editors of scholarly editions, we are indebted to those who came before us – in this instance in working on, and presenting editions of, Jane Austen's manuscripts and related works. They include Christine Alexander, R. W. Chapman, Margaret Anne Doody, Margaret Drabble, Claudia L. Johnson, Vivien Jones, David Selwyn, Brian Southam and Kathryn Sutherland.

Thanks are due to the owners of the manuscripts we have consulted and reproduced, and the libraries within which they are held: Belinda Austen, the Bath and N. E. Somerset Council, the Henry W. and Albert A. Berg Collection in the New York Public Library, the British Library, Damaris Jane Brix, Chawton House Library and Study Centre, the City Museum, Winchester, the Dean and Chapter of Winchester Cathedral, the Fondation Martin Bodmer, David Gilson, Park Honan, King's College Cambridge (in particular Patricia McGuire the Archivist), the Morgan Library in New York (in particular Christine Nelson, the Drue Heinz Curator of Literary and Historical Manuscripts), Sandy Lerner, the William H. Olin Library, Oakland, California, Queen Mary, University of London (particularly Lorraine Screene the Archivist), and Freydis Jane Welland.

We are very grateful for information, ideas and advice we have received from Kathy Atherton, Antje Blank, Marilyn Butler, Emma Clery, Edward Copeland, Jan Davies, Geoffrey Day, Alistair Duckworth, Roz Field, Heather Glen, David Hewitt, Derek Hughes, Peter Knox-Shaw, David McKitterick, James McLaverty, Claude

Rawson, Ruth Roston, David Selwyn, Tony Singleton, Margaret Smyth, Elizabeth Spearing, Fiona Sunley, Kathryn Sutherland, Mary Turner, Chris Viveash, Michael Wheeler, John Wiltshire, John Worthen and Cheryl Wilson.

The editorial and production team at Cambridge University Press – Maartje Scheltens, Audrey Cotterell, Alison Powell and Caroline Murray – have supported the volume with expertise and enthusiasm well beyond what their professional work required.

A large number of people have been particularly generous with their time, knowledge and skill. We would like to express special thanks to Tom Carpenter, David Gilson and Peter Sabor. But our greatest debt of gratitude is to Deirdre Le Faye, whose knowledge of Austen's life and family circumstances is unparalleled, and from whose intellectual generosity we have benefited hugely. This volume could not have been published in anything like its present form without her help and encouragement to us – and her stringent questioning of our conclusions – as we pursued and presented our research.

CHRONOLOGY

DEIRDRE LE FAYE

1764
26 April — Marriage of Rev. George Austen, rector of Steventon, and Cassandra Leigh; they go to live at Deane, Hampshire, and their first three children – James (1765), George (1766) and Edward (1767) – are born here.

1768
Summer — The Austen family move to Steventon, Hampshire. Five more children – Henry (1771), Cassandra (1773), Francis (1774), Jane (1775), Charles (1779) – are born here.

1773
23 March — Mr Austen becomes Rector of Deane as well as Steventon, and takes pupils at Steventon from now until 1796.

1775
16 December — Jane Austen born at Steventon.

1781
Winter — JA's cousin, Eliza Hancock, marries Jean-François Capot de Feuillide, in France.

1782

First mention of JA in family tradition, and the first of the family's amateur theatrical productions takes place.

1783

JA's third brother, Edward, is adopted by Mr and Mrs Thomas Knight II, and starts to spend time with them at Godmersham in Kent.
JA, with her sister Cassandra and cousin Jane Cooper, stays for some months in Oxford

	and then Southampton, with kinswoman Mrs Cawley.
1785	
Spring	JA and Cassandra go to the Abbey House School in Reading.
1786	
	Edward sets off for his Grand Tour of Europe, and does not return until autumn 1790.
April	JA's fifth brother, Francis, enters the Royal Naval Academy in Portsmouth.
December	JA and Cassandra have left school and are at home again in Steventon. Between now and 1793 JA writes her three volumes of 'Juvenilia'.
1788	
Summer	Mr and Mrs Austen take JA and Cassandra on a trip to Kent and London.
December	Francis leaves the RN Academy and sails to East Indies; does not return until winter 1793.
1791	
July	JA's sixth and youngest brother, Charles, enters the Royal Naval Academy in Portsmouth.
27 December	Edward Austen marries Elizabeth Bridges, and they live at Rowling in Kent.
1792	
27 March	JA's eldest brother, James, marries Anne Mathew; they live at Deane.
?Winter	Cassandra becomes engaged to Rev. Tom Fowle.
1793	
23 January	Edward Austen's first child, Fanny, is born at Rowling.
1 February	Republican France declares war on Great Britain and Holland.
8 April	JA's fourth brother, Henry, becomes a lieutenant in the Oxfordshire Militia.
15 April	James Austen's first child, Anna, born at Deane.
3 June	JA writes the last item of her 'Juvenilia'.

1794

22 February	M de Feuillide guillotined in Paris.
September	Charles leaves the RN Academy and goes to sea.
?Autumn	JA possibly writes the novella 'Lady Susan' this year.

1795

	JA probably writes 'Elinor and Marianne' this year.
3 May	James's wife Anne dies, and infant Anna is sent to live at Steventon.
Autumn	Rev. Tom Fowle joins Lord Craven as his private chaplain for the West Indian campaign.
December	Tom Lefroy visits Ashe Rectory – he and JA have a flirtation over the Christmas holiday period.

1796

October	JA starts writing 'First Impressions'.

1797

17 January	James Austen marries Mary Lloyd, and infant Anna returns to live at Deane.
February	Rev. Tom Fowle dies of fever at San Domingo and is buried at sea.
August	JA finishes 'First Impressions' and Mr Austen offers it for publication to Thomas Cadell – rejected sight unseen.
November	JA starts converting 'Elinor and Marianne' into *Sense and Sensibility*. Mrs Austen takes her daughters for a visit to Bath. Edward Austen and his young family move from Rowling to Godmersham.
31 December	Henry Austen marries his cousin, the widowed Eliza de Feuillide, in London.

1798

	JA probably starts writing 'Susan' (later to become *Northanger Abbey*).
17 November	James Austen's son James Edward born at Deane.

1799

Summer	JA probably finishes 'Susan' (*NA*) about now.

1800

	Mr Austen decides to retire and move to Bath.

1801

24 January	Henry Austen resigns his commission in the Oxfordshire Militia and sets up as a banker and army agent in London.
May	The Austen family leave Steventon for Bath, and then go for a seaside holiday in the West Country. JA's traditionary West Country romance presumably occurs between now and the autumn of 1804.

1802

25 March	Peace of Amiens appears to bring the war with France to a close.
Summer	Charles Austen joins his family for a seaside holiday in Wales and the West Country.
December	JA and Cassandra visit James and Mary at Steventon; while there, Harris Bigg-Wither proposes to JA and she accepts him, only to withdraw her consent the following day.
Winter	JA revises 'Susan' (*NA*).

1803

Spring	JA sells 'Susan' (*NA*) to Benjamin Crosby; he promises to publish it by 1804, but does not do so.
18 May	Napoleon breaks the Peace of Amiens, and war with France recommences.
Summer	The Austens visit Ramsgate in Kent, and possibly also go to the West Country again.
November	The Austens visit Lyme Regis.

1804

	JA probably starts writing 'The Watsons' this year, but leaves it unfinished.
Summer	The Austens visit Lyme Regis again.

1805

21 January	Mr Austen dies and is buried in Bath.
Summer	Martha Lloyd joins forces with Mrs Austen and her daughters.
18 June	James Austen's younger daughter, Caroline, born at Steventon.
21 October	Battle of Trafalgar.

1806	
2 July	Mrs Austen and her daughters finally leave Bath; they visit Clifton, Adlestrop, Stoneleigh and Hamstall Ridware, before settling in Southampton in the autumn.
24 July	Francis Austen marries Mary Gibson.
1807	
19 May	Charles Austen marries Fanny Palmer, in Bermuda.
1808	
10 October	Edward Austen's wife Elizabeth dies at Godmersham.
1809	
5 April	JA makes an unsuccessful attempt to secure the publication of 'Susan' (*NA*).
7 July	Mrs Austen and her daughters, and Martha Lloyd, move to Chawton, Hants.
1810	
Winter	*S&S* is accepted for publication by Thomas Egerton.
1811	
February	JA starts planning *Mansfield Park*.
30 October	*S&S* published.
?Winter	JA starts revising 'First Impressions' into *Pride and Prejudice*.
1812	
17 June	America declares war on Great Britain.
14 October	Mrs Thomas Knight II dies, and Edward Austen now officially takes surname of Knight.
Autumn	JA sells copyright of *P&P* to Egerton.
1813	
28 January	*P&P* published; JA half-way through *MP*.
?July	JA finishes *MP*.
?November	*MP* accepted for publication by Egerton about now.
1814	
21 January	JA commences *Emma*.
5 April	Napoleon abdicates and is exiled to Elba.
9 May	*MP* published.

24 December	Treaty of Ghent officially ends war with America.
1815	
March	Napoleon escapes and resumes power in France; hostilities recommence.
29 March	*E* finished.
18 June	Battle of Waterloo finally ends war with France.
8 August	JA starts *Persuasion.*
4 October	Henry Austen takes JA to London; he falls ill, and she stays longer than anticipated.
13 November	JA visits Carlton House, and receives an invitation to dedicate a future work to the Prince Regent.
December	*E* published by John Murray, dedicated to the Prince Regent (title page 1816).
1816	
19 February	2nd edition of *MP* published.
Spring	JA's health starts to fail. Henry Austen buys back manuscript of 'Susan' (*NA*), which JA revises and intends to offer again for publication.
18 July	First draft of *P* finished.
6 August	*P* finally completed.
1817	
27 January	JA starts 'Sanditon'.
18 March	JA now too ill to work, and has to leave 'S' unfinished.
24 May	Cassandra takes JA to Winchester for medical attention.
18 July	JA dies in the early morning.
24 July	JA buried in Winchester Cathedral.
December	*NA* and *P* published together, by Murray, with a 'Biographical Notice' added by Henry Austen (title page 1818).
1869	
16 December	JA's nephew, the Rev. James Edward Austen Leigh (JEAL), publishes his *Memoir of Jane Austen*, from which all subsequent biographies have stemmed (title page 1870).

1871

JEAL publishes a second and enlarged edition of his *Memoir*, including in this the novella 'LS', the cancelled chapters of *P*, the unfinished 'W', a précis of 'S', and 'The Mystery' from the Juvenilia.

1884

JA's great-nephew, Lord Brabourne, publishes *Letters of Jane Austen*, the first attempt to collect her surviving correspondence.

1922

'Volume the Second' of the Juvenilia published.

1925

The manuscript of the unfinished 'S' edited by R. W. Chapman and published as *Fragment of a Novel by Jane Austen*.

1932

R. W. Chapman publishes *Jane Austen's Letters to her sister Cassandra and others*, giving letters unknown to Lord Brabourne.

1933

'Volume the First' of the Juvenilia published.

1951

'Volume the Third' of the Juvenilia published.

1952

Second edition of R. W. Chapman's *Jane Austen's Letters* published, with additional items.

1954

R. W. Chapman publishes *Jane Austen's Minor Works*, which includes the three volumes of the *J* and other smaller items.

1980

B. C. Southam publishes *Jane Austen's 'Sir Charles Grandison'*, a small manuscript discovered in 1977.

1995

Deirdre Le Faye publishes the third (new) edition of *Jane Austen's Letters*, containing further additions to the Chapman collections.

The Austen Family

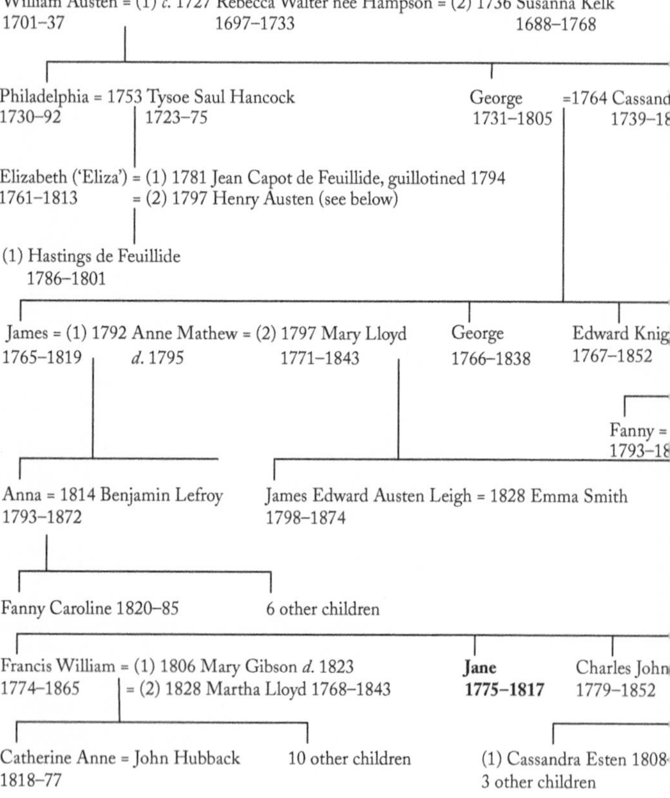

·h Leonora 1733–83

1 Elizabeth Bridges *d.* 1808

Henry 1771–1850 = (1) 1797 Eliza de Feuillide (see above) = (2) 1820 Eleanor Jackson

Cassandra Elizabeth 1773–1845

vard Knatchbull

10 other children

·oline Mary Craven ·5–80

· 1807 Frances Palmer *d.* 1814
· 1820 Harriet Palmer *d.* 1869

(2) 4 children

INTRODUCTION

Virginia Woolf famously claimed that Jane Austen was the most difficult author to catch 'in the act of greatness'.[1] If there are to be glimpses, some must come from the handwritten changes, elisions and revisions in the few prose manuscripts that survive: the small, closely written pages that form the unfinished works now entitled 'The Watsons' and 'Sanditon' and the cancelled chapters of *Persuasion*.

This volume of The Cambridge Edition of the Works of Jane Austen contains 'The Watsons', 'Sanditon', the novella 'Lady Susan', comments on fiction in a series of letters Austen wrote to her niece Anna Lefroy,[2] the burlesque 'Plan of a Novel' and the comic letter to 'Mrs. Hunter of Norwich', as well as the opinions she collected on her own novels, *Mansfield Park* and *Emma*. It also prints poems, both serious, such as 'To the Memory of Mrs. Lefroy', written in 1808, and lightly frivolous, such as 'On the Marriage of Mr. Gell of East Bourn to Miss Gill', provoked simply by the oddity of names. An appendix includes works that have been ascribed to Jane Austen but for which there is insufficient certainty to warrant placing with the texts which are securely hers. The cancelled chapters of *Persuasion*, which would otherwise have found a place in the volume, have been included with *Persuasion* in this edition.[3]

The novels published in Jane Austen's lifetime have for us now no private rehearsals – although two of them, *Sense and Sensibility*

[1] Virginia Woolf, 'Jane Austen at Sixty', *Nation*, 34 (15 December 1923), p. 433.

[2] In accordance with the usual custom of Austen scholarship, and for the sake of clarity, we refer to Anna by her married name of Lefroy throughout. Anna (1793–1872), daughter of Jane Austen's eldest brother James, married Ben Lefroy in November 1814.

[3] *Persuasion*, ed. Janet Todd and Antje Blank (Cambridge: Cambridge University Press, 2006).

and *Mansfield Park*, received small revisions between published versions[4] – and so the unfinished, fragmentary 'The Watsons' and 'Sanditon', frustrated attempts at finished works and meant in this state only for her own or her family's eyes, indicate habits of writing about which the published texts are secret. Their revisions, including the 'scratching out', may be placed beside the advice Jane Austen gave to Anna concerning descriptive minuteness, characterization, social verisimilitude and the paring down of detail when composing fiction.[5]

The two fragments of 'The Watsons' and 'Sanditon' can of course only hint at the process behind the published works. They are equally secretive about how they themselves might have looked in their final state, though the comparison between them and the printed works clearly indicates the kind of changes that Austen's publishers made to her writing. They have significance in their own right, as manuscript texts unmediated by print and compositor. They expand Jane Austen's oeuvre and indicate other directions from those taken in the six works published in or just after her lifetime. Together they suggest a greater range than the finished novels alone display.

The third substantial prose work in this volume, the novella 'Lady Susan', exists only in a fair, untitled copy probably made much later than its composition and intended, as far as we know, for readers within the circle of friends and family rather than as a prepared text for a printer to publish – we have no idea of the state of manuscripts Jane Austen or her siblings Henry and Cassandra actually sent to the printer. But, because, outside the juvenilia, 'Lady Susan' is the only example of her work in letters and because Jane Austen first composed *Sense and Sensibility* and possibly *Pride and Prejudice* in epistolary form, this also may tell us something distinctive about her creative habits in the major novels. And it too interests in its own right. The story of a designing society woman has many antecedents, English and French, but there

[4] See the volumes in the Cambridge edition for full details of the changes.
[5] See pp. 214–225.

is nothing quite like 'Lady Susan' in earlier fiction and nothing in Jane Austen's published novels prepares us for its ebulliently amoral effect.

Families often control literary remains of a famous author, feeling themselves appropriate stewards of genius. Rivalry plays a part in the withholding and delivery of items, along with discretion and sense of family honour. The Shelley family struggled hard to create a saintly image of the poet by selecting, excising, rewriting and destroying part of the surviving archive. The Austen family members were less extreme but presumably had less to hide. They did however seek to control the image of their only famous relative. It was an image that could be much affected by the manuscripts they owned.

Cassandra Austen was her sister's legatee and executrix; and to her came all Jane Austen's finished and unfinished fictional manuscripts. She was prepared to destroy letters which she did not want to leave for the eyes of her younger relatives, as being perhaps too intimate or too trivial, but she appears not to have interfered with the creative work left unpublished or unfinished at Jane Austen's death, except for small points of editing when making copies. In Cassandra's lifetime, none of the manuscripts and fragments was printed; instead they were, when she died in 1845, carefully apportioned out among those family members who, it was thought, would most appreciate them.

In a 'Biographical Notice of the Author', prefixed to the posthumous volume *Persuasion and Northanger Abbey* (published December 1817, dated 1818), Henry Austen alluded to some stanzas 'replete with fancy and vigour' which his sister had written a few days before she died; these were 'When Winchester races first took their beginning'. He later thought better – or was persuaded to think better – of the allusion and he suppressed it when he revised his 1817 'Biographical Notice' into the 'Memoir of Miss Austen', supplied to accompany Richard Bentley's 'Standard Novels' edition of *Sense and Sensibility* in 1833. No other relative of Jane Austen's generation found it appropriate to mention the completed manuscript works, including this poem, or the drafts of what she herself may have had no intention of publishing, but which, in the case of 'Lady Susan', she had kept by her through several moves over more than two decades.

In 1869, nearly twenty-five years after Cassandra's death, fifty-two years after Jane's and four years after that of the last remaining brother, Frank, James Edward Austen Leigh, son of the eldest brother, James, wrote his influential *Memoir of Jane Austen* (published 1870), in which he presented his subject as a decorous Victorian lady author.[6] In accordance with this image, Austen Leigh rejected the comic poem on the Winchester races about which Henry had been so enthusiastic. His sister Caroline Austen had been sorry her uncle had noted it in the first place; she thought it unseemly for a deathbed. To her brother she wrote, 'Tho' there are no reasons ethical or orthodox against the publication of these stanzas, there are reasons of taste—I never thought there was much of point in them—they were good enough for a passing thought, but if she had lived she would probably soon have torn them up.' Caroline was appalled at any notion that the stanzas should be published in the *Memoir*:

> there is a much stronger objection to their being inserted in any memoir, than a want of literary merit—If put in at all they must have been introduced as the latest working of her mind—They are dated July 15th—her death followed on the 18th—Till a few hours before she died, she had been feeling much better, & there was hope of amendment at least, if not of recovery—she amused herself by following a harmless fancy suggested by what was passing near her—but the joke about the dead Saint, & the Winchester races,

[6] Within family documents Francis Austen was usually called Frank and we have employed this name throughout the volume. James Edward Austen took the name 'Leigh' in 1837 soon after he inherited the estate of his great aunt Jane Leigh Perrot. For clarity we have employed the name of Austen Leigh throughout. The name is often reproduced with a hyphen, but James Edward himself did not hyphenate his surname and the hyphen in the first edition of the *Memoir* (1870) is removed in the second edition; his name is unhyphenated throughout this volume. Later generations of Austen-Leighs, however, consistently use a hyphen, and that is reflected here when they are named.

all jumbled up together, would read badly as amongst the few details given, of the closing scene—[7]

Instead of 'When Winchester races first took their beginning', Austen Leigh chose to publish in his *Memoir* five sets of verses he thought more appropriate: part of the elegy 'To the Memory of Mrs. Lefroy,' already published in a fuller version by Sir Henry Lefroy in 1868;[8] the comic poem 'On the Marriage of Mr. Gell of East Bourn to Miss Gill'; a version of a poem about Camilla Wallop's marriage to Henry Wake in 1812; burlesque stanzas probably addressed to Anna, half-sister of James Edward and Caroline; and the verses written to accompany the gift of 'a little bag' to her friend Mary Lloyd. However, an Austen admirer, the politician and man of letters, Lord Stanhope, accepting that the materials available to Austen Leigh were 'meagre' and having noted the existence of the Winchester races poem from reading Henry Austen's 'Biographical Notice', queried the omission with the publisher Richard Bentley – he hoped it 'might be set right in another edition'.[9] It was not, and 'When Winchester races first took their beginning' had to wait more than thirty years for publication in another family memoir: J. H. and E. C. Hubback's *Jane Austen's Sailor Brothers* (1906).

In the first edition of his *Memoir* Austen Leigh also included an altered and reduced version of Jane Austen's spoof 'Plan of a Novel', which mocked contemporary fiction with the ebullience of her juvenilia and was inspired in part by the incongruous advice given by the Prince Regent's librarian James Stanier Clarke in the autumn and winter of 1815 concerning a subject for her next novel. As the basis for his text Austen Leigh used his aunt's original version, by then owned by Charles Austen's daughter Cassandra (Cassy) Esten

[7] Hampshire Record Office (hereafter HRO) MS 23M93/86/3b item 73(i).

[8] *Notes and Documents relating to the Family of Loffroy . . . by a Cadet* (1868), pp. 117–18.

[9] Lord Stanhope's concern was 'probably somewhat proprietary' since Stanhope owned the Chevening estate and the rector of Chevening from 1813 was Rev. John Austen (1777–1851), Jane Austen's second cousin. Deirdre Le Faye, 'Jane Austen's Verses and Lord Stanhope's Disappointment', *The Book Collector*, 37. 1 (Spring 1988), p. 86.

Austen, Cassandra Austen's goddaughter; possibly Cassy Esten lent her copy to Austen Leigh, who modified it for publication, or she herself might have provided him with a censored version. Or possibly James Edward's sister Caroline had at some point made a copy which he used. Caroline remembered her aunt visiting Carlton House, the Prince Regent's London residence, and meeting Clarke, whose suggestions form much of the humour of the work: 'the little adventure . . . afforded some amusement'.[10]

Austen Leigh mentioned but did not include the 'condemned chapter' of *Persuasion*; 'an old copy-book containing several tales, some of which seem to have been composed while she was quite a girl'; and a few works beyond the juvenilia which were 'not without merit, but which [Jane Austen] considered unworthy of publication'.[11]

The omission of 'Lady Susan', 'The Watsons' and 'Sanditon' from the first edition of the *Memoir* followed the combined decision of Austen Leigh and his sisters, Caroline Austen and Anna Lefroy, all of whom considered 'it would be as unfair to expose preliminary processes to the world, as it would be to display all that goes on behind the curtain of the theatre before it is drawn up': 'the family have rightly, I think declined to let these early works be published,' Austen Leigh concluded.[12] The Kent branch of the Austen family, descendants of Jane's wealthy brother Edward Knight, felt less reticent, however: according to Caroline Austen, the Knights, including Edward's daughter Fanny, now Lady Knatchbull and formerly a favourite niece of the author, 'were wishing years ago to make public' 'Lady Susan' but were 'discouraged by others'.[13]

Austen Leigh and his sisters were mostly pleased with the response to the *Memoir*. Caroline recorded favourable notices,

[10] Caroline Austen, 'My Aunt Jane Austen: A Memoir', in *J. E. Austen-Leigh: A Memoir of Jane Austen and Other Family Recollections*, ed. Kathryn Sutherland (Oxford: Oxford University Press, 2002), pp. 176–7.

[11] James Edward Austen Leigh, *Memoir of Jane Austen* (1870), pp. 219, 59–60.

[12] *Ibid.*, p. 61.

[13] Copy letter from Caroline Austen to James Edward Austen Leigh, 1 April [1869], in the collection of copy letters and later correspondence deposited by R. W. Chapman with the National Portrait Gallery (hereafter NPG), fo. 6.

remarking, 'on the whole I think [James Edward] may be quite satisfied with the public voice, as it has spoken upon this occasion'; she believed the volume was 'fairly launched'.[14] She was gratified to find that many readers appreciated her brother's reticence. *The Times* for 17 January 1870 noted that Jane Austen's family 'have in their possession the manuscript of several stories written in the interval between childhood and womanhood, but have, very properly, declined to allow their publication . . . We have always thought it most culpable in the guardians of literary remains to allow a line to pass into print upon which the writer has not clearly signified his wish. The greatness of more than one name has been slurred by such remissness.' *The Quarterly Review* agreed with this stern view:

> However tantalising be the knowledge that such treasure exists, we hold the decision to be wise. In the face of the indecorous practice too largely prevalent in the present day, of exposing to common view every scrap, and relic, and incomplete essay left by those who have become famous in literature or art, it may be recommended as a wholesome truth, that a man's thoughts are as indefeasibly his own property as his acres, and that the work which he has judged discreet to withhold from public view from a sense of its incompleteness, ought to be sacred from being pored over and printed by posthumous busybodies.[15]

In reality it was too late to hide from 'busybodies'. Ever since the 1833 Bentley 'Standard Novels', with the revised notice by Henry, Jane Austen's fame had been slowly growing and by the late nineteenth century many admirers were eager to go 'behind the curtain', curious to know what the author might have left unfinished. As the reviewer in *Macmillan's Magazine* later remarked:

> The virtue of literary reticence is fast becoming extinct; we have almost indeed forgotten that it is a virtue at all. To be able to persuade oneself that the world could possibly do without information

[14] HRO MS 23M93/87/3/165, Caroline Austen to Emma Austen Leigh (James Edward's wife), n.d. (early 1870).

[15] *The Quarterly Review*, 128 (January and April 1870), pp. 199–200.

which it is in one's power to give, implies now a strength of mind so abnormal and so rare, that a modern instance of it is scarcely to be found.[16]

Caroline Austen responded to 'the vexed question between the Austens and the Public' by lamenting: 'see what it is to have a growing posthumous reputation! we cannot keep any thing to ourselves now, it seems'.[17]

In 'The Lesson of Balzac', Henry James wrote that 'Jane Austen, with all her light felicity, leaves us hardly more curious of her process, or of the experience in her that fed it, than the brown thrush who tells his story from the garden bough.' In his view her popularity had been driven up by 'the stiff breeze of the commercial bookselling spirit'; she was 'so amenable to pretty reproduction in every variety of what is called tasteful, and in what seemingly proves to be saleable'. Jane Austen was in part popular because she was unconscious of 'the extraordinary grace of her facility'.[18] Many readers disagreed and had long been curious about the author's writing methods and her consciousness of her own skill. The reviewer in *The Athenæum* noted her remark about writing on little pieces of ivory with much labour, then complained regarding the *Memoir*, 'But of this labour we hear scarcely anything.'[19] Surely some notion of her ways of composing might be obtained from the unpublished papers in the Austens' possession. Writing in *The Academy*, the feminist activist and journalist Edith Simcox also keenly felt the lack of the 'unpublished writing'. Later she remarked, 'The editor is perhaps right to avoid everything that might bear the appearance of book-making, but our faith in his judgement is rather shaken by

[16] *Macmillan's Magazine*, 51 (1885), pp. 84–91. The comments responded to the publication of Lord Brabourne's edition of Jane Austen's letters.

[17] HRO MS 23M93/86/b/73(i). R. W. Chapman, *Jane Austen: Facts and Problems* (Oxford: Clarendon Press, 1948, reprinted with corrections 1950), p. 140.

[18] Henry James, 'The Lesson of Balzac' (1905), in *The House of Fiction: Essays on the Novel*, ed. Leon Edel (1957; London: Mercury Books, 1962), pp. 62–3.

[19] *The Athenæum*, 8 January 1870, pp. 53–4.

his having waited for encouragement from without before introducing us to *Lady Susan* and *The Watsons*.'[20]

As can be deduced from Simcox's remark, Austen Leigh soon bowed to pressure, and the second edition of his *Memoir* in July 1871, which formed the sixth volume of Bentley's reissue of Austen's published work as part of the 'Favourite Novels' series, made more, although not complete, use of the unpublished writings 'with the consent and approbation of Lady Knatchbull, & my two Sisters, to whom the copies of these works respectively belong'. Austen Leigh continued, 'I felt some anxiety how these minor works might be received by the public, & a fear lest I might have lowered, rather than extended our Aunt's fame by the publication of them,' but he was pleased to report that he had 'obtained a unanimous verdict of acquittal'.[21] The title of the volume now continued: 'to which is added Lady Susan and fragments of two other unfinished tales by Miss Austen'. Within his *Memoir* Austen Leigh emended his earlier phrase, 'old copy-book containing several tales', to 'copy books', noting that these works amounted to a considerable number by the time Jane Austen was sixteen. The 'childish effusions' were still of a 'slight and flimsy texture' but he now printed an example: 'The Mystery. An Unfinished Comedy'.[22]

He understood that the reading public had not been satisfied with what he had provided from the later writings, a few poems created in a family context; they wanted signs of the great novelist. So, in this second edition, chapter 12 of the *Memoir* became the 'cancelled Chapter of "Persuasion"', and chapter 13 'The last Work' (as he referred to 'Sanditon'); 'The Watsons' and 'Lady Susan' were appended. The manuscript of 'The Watsons' had come to Caroline from her aunt Cassandra; 'Lady Susan' was taken from an inaccurate

[20] Edith Simcox, *The Academy*, 1 August 1871, in *The Academy: A Record of Literature, Learning, Science, and Art* (1871), vol. 2, p. 367. Edith Simcox wrote under the name of H. Lawrenny.

[21] James Edward Austen Leigh to Rev. George Austen junior (?), 16 August 1871, Private Collection/descendants of Admiral Charles Austen.

[22] Austen Leigh, *Memoir* (1870), p. 60; *Memoir of Jane Austen* (1871), pp. 42–5.

copy made by Fanny Knight or Anna Lefroy and now missing,[23] while Anna provided the autograph manuscript of 'Sanditon'.[24]

Austen Leigh felt that 'Lady Susan' fitted ill with the gentle, refined image of his aunt which he was eager to promote. To his disapproval, Bentley had placed its title on the spine in order to make the volume more marketable, and Jane Austen more popular, since he owned the copyright of five of the novels; Austen Leigh called the act 'perverseness' and declared it quite 'contrary to my wishes & instructions'.[25] As for those texts which existed only in foul copies, Austen Leigh did what he could to tidy them up. In 'The Watsons' he regularized punctuation and spelling and rectified 'some obscurities and inaccuracies of expression . . . which the author would probably have corrected'. For 'Sanditon' more radical intervention was required.

He conceded that some of Jane Austen's admirers desired to know something of this final work, but his sister Anna Lefroy feared that publishing it in full would be 'at the expense of the Authoresse's fame'.[26] It was one thing to write indelicately in youth as Jane Austen might have done with 'Lady Susan', another to be

[23] Fanny (1793–1882), daughter of Jane Austen's brother Edward, became Fanny Knight when her father took the name in order to inherit the Knight family estates in 1812, and is usually referred to by that name for clarity's sake. She married Sir Edward Knatchbull in 1820. In 1870 she sent a message to James Edward Austen Leigh via her daughter Louisa Knatchbull-Hugessen, that she 'begs you will make use of "Lady Susan" in yr next edition of the Memoir', but in fact Fanny had lost the manuscript in the 1860s ('I imagine she must have lent it to someone,' wrote Louisa); it was found in 1882 after her death by her son Lord Brabourne. Louisa Knatchbull-Hugessen to James Edward Austen Leigh, 15 November [1870], copy letter in NPG, fo. 21. Chapman, *Facts and Problems*, pp. 141, 144, 162 and 163.

[24] HRO, MSS 23M93/84/1/1–3, James Edward Austen Leigh to Anna Lefroy, 29 March 1845.

[25] Letter of 16 August 1871, Private Collection/descendants of Admiral Charles Austen; letter of 16 September 1873 to Lady Laura Scott (*Jane Austen Society Annual Report* (2004), pp. 70–7). William and Richard Austen-Leigh reiterated the point, 'It was far from being [James Edward's] wish that *Lady Susan* should form the title of a separate volume'; that it did was a 'mistake'. They commented, 'Strictly speaking, it is not a story, but a study', *Life and Letters of Jane Austen* (London: Smith, Elder & Co., 1913), p. 80 n.

[26] Anna Lefroy to James Edward Austen Leigh, 8 August [1862], HRO MS 23M93/86/3c/118(ii).

composing rollicking satire during a final illness. However, there was family rivalry to contend with, and Anna and her brother worried that, if they ignored the work, it would be at the mercy of their cousin Catherine Hubback, Frank Austen's daughter; she had acquired her aunt Cassandra's fair copy, newly punctuated and paragraphed – Anna declared the manuscript had been 'taken, not given'.[27] Austen Leigh's solution was to fillet the work and print the result. No heroine had yet attracted 'the sympathies of the reader', he observed, but 'some of the principal characters were already sketched in with a vigorous hand'. He – or perhaps Anna – would deliver 'Sanditon' as a series of short studies of the three 'original' characters whom he considered 'ready dressed and prepared for their parts': Mr Parker (the description taken from about a third of the way into chapter 2), Lady Denham (from chapters 3 and 6) and Diana Parker (from chapter 5). The sketches primarily used Jane Austen's words, tidied up and re-punctuated. For example, where the manuscript reads '[Mr Parker] wanted to secure the promise of a visit—to get as many of the Family as his own house would contain, to follow him to Sanditon as soon as possible—and healthy as they all undeniably were—foresaw that every one of them would be benefited by the sea.—' (ch. 2), Austen Leigh's version states, 'He wanted to secure the promise of a visit, and to get as many of the family as his own house would hold to follow him to Sanditon as soon as possible; and, healthy as all the Heywoods undeniably were, he foresaw that every one of them would be benefitted by the sea'.[28]

As this passage suggests, the extracts included words and phrases by Austen Leigh with no indication as to where he began and his aunt ended; elsewhere, excerpted sentences and paragraphs from Austen were run on with no gaps noted. All in all, 'Sanditon' was reduced to thirteen printed pages, a very small proportion of the original manuscript. The absence of any character sketch

[27] Anna Lefroy to James Edward Austen Leigh, 8 August [1862], HRO MS 23M93/86/3c/118.

[28] Austen Leigh, *Memoir* (1871), pp.182–3, 194.

of the heroine Charlotte suggests the difficulty Austen Leigh felt with this character who had perversely refused to develop the author's increasingly sophisticated experiments with inner consciousness and narrative voice. The editor was responding to what the manuscript revisions indicate: that Jane Austen was more fluent with the idiosyncratic characters than with the more sensible ones.

Austen Leigh's additions to the *Memoir* were well received. In her *Academy* piece Edith Simcox noted the coercion he had suffered: 'In obedience to the unanimous demands of his critics . . . Mr. Austen Leigh has now produced from the family storehouse nearly all the fragments of his aunt's compositions which might reasonably be supposed to be of general interest.'[29] Against Henry James's later view she concluded, from the cancelled chapters of *Persuasion*, that 'judgment had a share in [Jane Austen's] successes as well as inspiration'.[30] Anne Thackeray in *The Cornhill Magazine* welcomed 'one more glimpse of an old friend come back with a last greeting'. All lovers of Jane Austen would, she thought, 'prize this addition, small as it is, to their acquaintance with her'. Ignoring the bowdlerized 'Sanditon', she noted that 'Lady Susan' was very unlike Austen's later works 'and scarcely equal to them'. But she found 'The Watsons' 'a delightful fragment, which might belong to any of her other histories'.[31] The editor of *The Spectator* disagreed with this assessment but admitted he had anticipated being disappointed: appreciating humour and finish as the most distinguishing characteristics of Jane Austen's writing, he pointed out that the former was unlikely to be discovered in an early effort of a modest author while the latter 'could not be found in unfinished and fragmentary pieces deliberately thrown aside by her own better judgment'.[32]

[29] Simcox remarked that Austen Leigh lacked 'the courage to produce even a specimen of the many half burlesque stories written when she was little more than a child', *Academy*, p. 367.

[30] *Ibid.*, p. 368.

[31] Anne Thackeray, *The Cornhill Magazine*, 24 (July–December 1871), p. 159.

[32] *The Spectator*, 22 July 1871, p. 891.

Unexpectedly, *The Times* changed its earlier position, basing its new opinion on the work Austen Leigh and others considered most objectionable: 'Lady Susan is vain of her eloquence . . . and as she prevails over every one on whom she can use her gift, so she gains from the reader interest and almost sympathy,' the reviewer wrote. 'Generally it is a pity that posthumous works should be published if they have been deliberately consigned to oblivion by the author; but "Lady Susan" is a clear addition to the fame of the writer and the pleasure of the reader.'[33] Lord Stanhope, whose opinion Austen Leigh greatly valued, was also enthusiastic: he liked the work 'very much' and thought it 'worthy of her genius though differing very materially from her other tales'. The difference was not only generic but also substantial: 'Elsewhere she has dealt only with faults and foibles, & *ridicules*, whilst here the errors are of a far graver kind, involving an entire depravation of mind, and deriliction [*sic*] of moral principle'. But, he added with relief, 'Nowhere . . . has Miss Austen departed in the least degree from that delicacy & reserve of touch which is among her many titles to praise.'[34]

For Virginia Woolf it was 'The Watsons' that was most revelatory. After scrutinizing it, she remarked that Jane Austen, for all her 'greatness', was 'no conjuror': without the unfinished works we should never have guessed what 'pages of preliminary drudgery' she 'forced her pen to go through . . . Like other writers, she had to create the atmosphere in which her own peculiar genius could bear fruit.' Observing 'the stiffness and bareness' of 'The Watsons', Woolf judged the author to be different from what she had imagined, the kind of writer who put down the facts of her story, then returned to elaborate and flesh out: 'Those first angular chapters of *The Watsons* prove that hers was not a prolific genius.'[35]

In 1925 R. W. Chapman, Jane Austen's first scholarly editor, at last printed a full version of 'Sanditon', calling it *Fragment of a Novel*.

[33] *The Times*, 4 January 1883.

[34] Quoted by Austen Leigh in his letter of 16 August 1871, Private Collection/ descendants of Admiral Charles Austen.

[35] Virginia Woolf, 'Jane Austen', in *The Common Reader* (London: The Hogarth Press, 1925), pp. 173, 175.

He also provided a more carefully edited text of 'Lady Susan'. The following year he added 'Plan of a Novel' and the 'Two Chapters of Persuasion', along with 'Opinions' of *Mansfield Park* and *Emma*; in 1927 he finished with 'The Watsons'. In 1954 he collected all the pieces into a single volume entitled *Minor Works*, and appended it as volume six to his *Novels of Jane Austen*, which had originally appeared in 1923.

With all this labour on the part of Austen Leigh and Chapman, still some autograph and allograph manuscripts remained unpublished in family hands; gradually over the past fifty years new poems, in particular, have been identified. In this volume we are collecting as much of Jane Austen's manuscript work as is known to date. Inevitably it represents only selective evidence of her creative activity as an adult: with the exception of the cancelled chapters of *Persuasion*, the drafts and copytexts of the published novels have been lost, and there are intriguing works which were almost certainly never written down, including the stories which Aunt Jane is said to have spun to Anna 'of endless adventure and fun . . carried on from day to day or from visit to visit'.[36]

*

The manuscripts exist within a family context. The Austens and their relatives were dispersed across ranks and throughout southern England. They included the rich landowners, the Leighs of Stoneleigh Abbey and the Knights of Godmersham, as well as men and women lower in the social scale such as poorer clergy and even a milliner's apprentice. George Austen, Jane's father, was the rector of the two small Hampshire country parishes of Steventon and Deane, and her mother, Cassandra (née Leigh), came from the academic clergy of Oxford. Jane's six brothers included James, a clergyman (successor of her father as rector of Steventon), Henry, army agent, banker and later clergyman, Frank and Charles, two sailors (admirals through longevity), and Edward (heir through

[36] Fanny Caroline Lefroy, 'Family History', HRO MS 23M93/85/2, n.p.

adoption to the wealthy Knights and later owner of their estates in Kent and Hampshire).

Jane Austen interacted with three generations of this family: her parents', her own, and her nieces' and nephews'. Many of her manuscripts were copied out for them and her close friends to read and sometimes keep; to these, also, Jane Austen usually addressed her poems and burlesques. There is little evidence that she confided widely even within her family while writing the major novels. Her main confidante and critic was always her elder sister Cassandra, who remembered lively debates over the drafts of the published works, for with her alone Jane could talk 'freely of any work that she might have in hand'.[37] She also discussed her writings with the nieces with whom, as they grew up, she became intimate, Anna Lefroy and Fanny Knight, though even here she may not have been wholly open. Towards the end of her life, responding to a presumed query from Fanny concerning her present literary activities at a time when she had largely finished *Persuasion* and was close to abandoning 'Sanditon', she referred briefly to the former without naming it, and did not mention the latter at all. However, Anna later recalled 'conversations which passed between Aunt Jane & me' during the time she was writing 'Sanditon', in which they discussed the characters and situations being created.[38]

The early nineteenth century had not learned to fetishize the autograph manuscript. When in 1831 the manuscripts of the Waverley novels by Walter Scott, the most famous writer of the time, were offered for sale by auction there was little interest. Thomas Frognall Dibdin was amazed at the 'catastrophically low' prices, which included the sale of the manuscript of *The Monastery* for £18.18s.[39] In 1833 prices around £30 for Scott's manuscripts were the norm – and most were bought by Robert Cadell, who

[37] Austen Leigh, *Memoir* (1871), p. 364.

[38] Anna Lefroy to James Edward Austen Leigh, 8 August [1862], HRO MS 23M93/86/3c, item 118(ii).

[39] *Sale Catalogues of Libraries of Eminent Persons: Volume I: Poets and Men of Letters*, ed. A. N. L. Munby (London: Mansell, 1971), p. 85.

had succeeded as Scott's publisher and sole owner of Scott's copyrights.

Prose manuscripts began to fetch higher prices in the late nineteenth and early twentieth centuries when the wealthy American banker and founder of the library that bears his name, John Pierpont Morgan, began to collect. His son John Pierpont Morgan Jr., an 'ardent Austenian' according to Chapman, desired a manuscript of a published Jane Austen novel such as *Pride and Prejudice* for the library he had inherited; disappointed to learn that none existed, he set about buying letters.[40] Later, he turned to the manuscript works: in 1925 – the year in which he surrendered ownership of the library, which became an educational institution – facilitated by Chapman, he bought 'Plan of a Novel' from Charles Austen's female descendants. In the same year he purchased the first six leaves of 'The Watsons' for £317.5s.6d., much less than was asked for it. These pages had been on the market since 1915 when William Austen-Leigh, Caroline Austen's nephew, donated them to a Red Cross benefit sale in London, where they raised either £55 or £65—accounts differ.[41] In 1978 the rest of 'The Watsons', passed down through James Edward Austen Leigh's descendants, was sold for £38,000 to the British Rail Pension Fund and ten years later it went for £90,000 to Sir Peter Michael, who deposited it in Queen Mary, University of London. The first eight-page section of this material has since been lost.

'Lady Susan' remained an unbroken manuscript, inherited by Lord Brabourne from his mother Fanny Knight, Lady Knatchbull. In 1891 he wrote that he might include 'the book' of 'Lady Susan' among Austen items for sale,[42] suggesting that it was perhaps he who had the manuscript formally bound (by Robert Rivière & Son, a firm who specialized in showy bindings often for commercial sale

[40] Christine Nelson, 'Jane Austen in the Morgan Library: History of a Collection', paper presented to the New York chapter of Jane Austen Society of North America, 21 January 1995, updated 2005.

[41] *Ibid.*

[42] Copy letter from Lord Brabourne 16 January 1891, no recipient, kept with 'Lady Susan' at the Morgan Library in New York.

purposes). He sold the manuscript in 1893 and it was sold again in 1898. At the turn of the century Lord Rosebery bought it for £90; his collection was auctioned in 1933 and it went for £2,100. Then the Morgan Library purchased it for $6,750 in 1947, a lesser price considering the rate of exchange at the time.

'Sanditon' remained in the hands of the Lefroys until Anna Lefroy's granddaughter Mary Isabella Lefroy presented it to King's College, Cambridge, in 1930.

'LADY SUSAN'

'Lady Susan' survives in a fair copy in Jane Austen's handwriting, with her original sheets mounted in a larger leather-bound book. The story is never mentioned by Jane Austen in documents that survive, and the manuscript itself has no title, though it is possible that a title page was lost during the rebinding process. The story is referred to as 'Lady Susan' in a letter Anna Lefroy wrote to James Edward Austen Leigh in 1869, during the discussions about the forthcoming memoir,[43] and it was published as *Lady Susan* in the second edition of the *Memoir* itself (1871).

The manuscript consists of 79 sheets – 158 written folios – of paper of about 200 mm × 165 mm.[44] Two of the sheets (fos. 85–6 and 107–8) are watermarked 1805. In the early nineteenth century paper was expensive, and was often kept for long periods of time before use. Very rarely did Jane Austen use paper watermarked the same year as that in which she was writing (one exception was when she addressed the publisher John Murray in November 1815 on paper watermarked 1815), and she routinely wrote on paper with watermarks between two and five years old. The 1805 watermark for 'Lady Susan' might therefore suggest a copying date of any time between 1805 and 1809, including the years in which Jane Austen was living in Southampton with her mother, sister and Martha

[43] Copy letter from Anna Lefroy to James Edward Austen Leigh, 20 May [1869?], NPG, fo. 2.

[44] See *Jane Austen's Lady Susan: a Facsimile of the Manuscript in the Pierpont Morgan Library and the 1925 Printed Edition*, preface by A. Walton Litz (New York: Garland, 1989), which reproduces the pages at their actual size.

Lloyd; but it gives no clue to when, before that, the narrative was first written. Austen Leigh declared the work 'an early production' between the 'childish effusions and the composition of her living works', written in the same period as the epistolary 'Elinor and Marianne', about 1795.[45] Caroline Austen labelled the work one of the 'betweenities' 'when the nonsense was passing away, and before her wonderful talent had found it's proper channel'.[46] Like her brother, she offered no historical evidence for the dating, although the family view seems to have been a firm one.

In his preface to *Jane Austen's Lady Susan*, the critic A. Walton Litz supported Austen Leigh's dating on stylistic grounds; he too believed the work could be associated with the presumed composition of 'Elinor and Marianne'.[47] Chapman disagreed. In *Facts and Problems* (1948), he suggested that the fair copy was probably made 'at some time in, or not long after, 1805', when Jane Austen was 'still sufficiently interested in the piece to be at the trouble of making a copy of it'. In the chronology he provided for *Facts and Problems* he gave the *composition* date as '*c.* 1805'[48] and in his note before the text in *Minor Works* he wrote that it was written 'not much earlier than 1805'.[49]

Using the copying date of after 1805, Jan Fergus associated the novel with Maria Edgeworth's epistolary novel in two volumes, *Leonora* (1806). By the early years of the nineteenth century, novels in letters were less popular than in the early 1790s, but Edgeworth's successful publication in that form may have inspired Austen to think of publishing herself; hence her creation of a fair copy.[50] It is also possible, however, that Austen was prompted to make the fair copy simply for family circulation rather than for publication. After all, Edgeworth was an exception: as an established novelist

[45] Austen Leigh, *Memoir* (1870), p. 60.

[46] Copy letter from Caroline Austen to James Edward Austen Leigh, 1 April [1869?], NPG, fo. 5.

[47] Litz, preface to *Jane Austen's Lady Susan* (n. p.).

[48] Chapman, *Facts and Problems*, pp. 49–50, 178.

[49] Jane Austen, *Minor Works*, ed. R. W. Chapman (Oxford: Oxford University Press, 1954), p. 243.

[50] Jan Fergus, *Jane Austen: A Literary Life* (London: Macmillan, 1991), p. 119.

she could go against the trend for the three-volume narrated novel in the way a novice could not.

The connection with Edgeworth was more startlingly made by Marilyn Butler in her article on Jane Austen published in the new *Oxford Dictionary of National Biography* (2004).[51] Calling it one of the 'Chawton novels', she suggested that the date of composition was 1810–12, when Austen was preparing *Sense and Sensibility* and *Pride and Prejudice* for publication and beginning the composition of *Mansfield Park*. This date presupposed that Jane Austen, having embarked on her publishing career, had momentarily reverted to the epistolary form and short format of her juvenile work. Butler's primary argument rested on her assumption that Jane Austen borrowed from Maria Edgeworth for all of the six novels except *Pride and Prejudice*, and that she also borrowed for 'Lady Susan', this time from two of the satirical tales of fashionable life, 'Manoeuvring' (1809) and the earlier *Leonora*. In Butler's view Austen's work is 'a full-scale pastiche and merger' of these two tales: for example, in *Leonora* the anti-heroine Lady Olivia resembled Lady Susan in glamour, charm and playfulness, and the work furnished Austen with her opening: 'where in Edgeworth a woman of blighted reputation invites herself to become a long-resident house guest, so in Austen Lady Susan, in two similar letters, achieves the same manoeuvre'.[52] The similarities between 'Lady Susan' and 'Manoeuvring' are more marked, since both tales feature the manipulative attempts of a youngish widow to marry off her modest daughter to a foolish but wealthy man, and her eventual decision to marry the man herself. But Jane Austen avoided the heavily didactic side of Edgeworth's narratives, and in her treatment the theme of adultery and passion became romantic black comedy.

Butler's late dating has something to recommend it, perhaps less for the supposed indebtedness to Edgeworth than for the obvious sophistication of the novella's content and technique. Yet Lady

[51] The article has been revised for the ongoing online version of the *ODNB*.

[52] Marilyn Butler, 'Jane Austen', *ODNB*, 2004, and *London Review of Books*, 5 March 1998. It should be noted that, while Leonora seems at the outset rather half-heartedly trying to reform her ways, no sense of repentance is evident in Lady Susan.

Susan, the handsome selfish widow who enjoys her own energetic duplicity and has much in common with the spirited heroines of the burlesque juvenile pieces, requires no subtle inner life of the sort Jane Austen was portraying in Elinor Dashwood and Elizabeth Bennet; she has only the persona of her vivacious letters and the description of her operations in the correspondence of those surrounding her.

In contrast to Butler, B. C. Southam associated 'Lady Susan' with the failure of the early narrated story 'Catharine' (dedication dated 1792), 'to which it stands in the same relationship as "Catharine" holds to the earlier juvenilia, as an exercise in correcting technical and stylistic faults'. After 'Catharine', Southam argued, Jane Austen returned to the less demanding form of epistolary fiction, although she might have made some revision of 'Lady Susan' after 1805 at the time when she copied it out. The revision probably included the addition of the hasty conclusion to tie up loose ends.[53] Southam is not alone among critics in seeing the conclusion either as a later addition or as an admission of the failure of the epistolary method to satisfy Jane Austen's narrative requirements. However, many epistolary novels of the time ended with or included just such summary gathering by the editor/author, and Jane Austen could have been responding creatively to this established literary convention.

Disinclined to credit Jane Austen with the conception of such brisk immorality as Lady Susan reveals, her great-niece Mary Augusta Austen-Leigh could only conceive personal indignation behind the creation of the character, and she speculated on the resentment her great-aunt must have felt when learning about the cruel Mrs Craven, grandmother of her beloved friend Martha Lloyd, 'an unnatural and brutal mother', whose wicked treatment of her daughters overpowered Jane Austen's fancy 'to so great a degree that she was at last impelled to seek relief in gibbeting this repulsive creature by setting down her character in writing'. In fact, as

[53] B. C. Southam, *Jane Austen's Literary Manuscripts: A Study of the Novelist's Development through the Surviving Papers* (1964, new edition London and New York: Athlone Press, 2001), p. 46.

Elizabeth Jenkins points out in her 1938 biography of Jane Austen, Mrs Craven's cruelty speaks *against* her as a model since, unscrupulous as Lady Susan may be, 'what she does is done from a quite understandable, though entirely selfish standpoint'.[54]

A real-life source less easy to dismiss is Jane Austen's charming and cosmopolitan cousin Eliza de Feuillide. To Q. D. Leavis she appeared quite clearly the sitter for the merry widow: 'I think we can decide on internal evidence that ['Lady Susan'] was founded on events of the years 1795 to 1797, and was certainly written before the end of 1797.'[55] The events of these years included the flirtatious dealings of Eliza with Jane Austen's two brothers, James and Henry.

Eliza de Feuillide comes most alive for us now in her flighty, sophisticated letters to her more staid cousin Philadelphia (Phylly) Walter; occasionally catching the tone of Lady Susan, these depict a woman delighting in her power over men and enjoying bantering with many admirers. Jane Austen could not have seen these letters but it is unlikely that Eliza de Feuillide would entirely have repressed this side of herself when visiting the Austens in Steventon. She was there for Christmas in 1786 and fascinated young Jane, as well as her brothers, with her rakish glamour; in 1790 Jane dedicated 'Love & Freindship' to her cousin. In February 1794 Eliza's French husband was guillotined and in May 1795 James's wife died. The pair were free for more serious flirtation although Eliza was not keen to settle down to matrimony too quickly. Meanwhile, Henry, ten years Eliza's junior, was so smitten by his cousin's charms that he seems to have proposed marriage; he had to be gently rejected.[56] For a short while in 1796 Henry then attached

[54] Mary Augusta Austen-Leigh, *Personal Aspects of Jane Austen* (London, 1920), p. 104; Elizabeth Jenkins, *Jane Austen: A Biography* (1938; London: Victor Gollancz, 1961), p. 120. See also Caroline Austen's 'Reminiscences', vol. 1, n.p. (HRO MS 23M93/66/4/1).

[55] Q. D. Leavis, 'A Critical Theory of Jane Austen's Writings', first published in *Scrutiny* (1941), reprinted in *Collected Essays*, ed. G. Singh (Cambridge: Cambridge University Press, 1983), vol. 1, 'The Englishness of the English Novel', p. 88.

[56] Deirdre Le Faye, *Jane Austen: A Family Record*, 2nd edn (Cambridge: Cambridge University Press, 2004), p. 96.

himself to a Mary Pearson, described by Eliza as a 'pretty wicked looking Girl with bright Black Eyes',[57] and in January 1797 James removed himself from the fray by marrying Mary Lloyd, who may have been aware of her husband's tenderness for his cousin. One of his granddaughters recounted an occasion in 1811 when James's daughter Anna was not allowed to visit Eliza because his wife was not on good terms with her:

I believe the *ci-devant* Countess, who was an extremely pretty woman, was a great flirt, and during her brief widowhood flirted with all her Steventon cousins, our Grandfather inclusive, which was more than his after wife could stand or could ever forgive—and I think it is very probable that *he* hesitated between the fair Eliza and Miss Mary Lloyd. I can testify that to the last days of her life my Grandmother continued to dislike and speak ill of her.[58]

Henry, who had seemed too young a few years earlier and appeared to be heading unfashionably for the Church, was by May 1797 Captain Austen in the militia and a more attractive proposition: Eliza remarked, he 'bids fair to possess a considerable Share of Riches & Honours'.[59] In December 1797 Henry and Eliza de Feuillide were married.

Focusing on Eliza as a likely source of Lady Susan, William Jarvis argued that the only plausible date for the composition of the narrative would have been before Eliza had been widowed, since after that 'It would have been too cruel.'[60] However, 'Lady Susan' captures much of the tone and timbre of Eliza de Feuillide in the circumstances of 1794–5, and it could well have been written during the height of her flirtatious behaviour with both of Jane Austen's brothers and before any flirtation became serious. It would be much

[57] Deirdre Le Faye, *Jane Austen's 'Outlandish Cousin': The Life and Letters of Eliza de Feuillide* (London: The British Library, 2002), p. 129.
[58] *Ibid.*, p. 169.
[59] *Ibid.*, p. 139.
[60] William Jarvis, 'Lady Susan', The Jane Austen Society Report for the Year 1984, in *Collected Reports of the Jane Austen Society 1976–1985* (Overton, Hampshire: The Jane Austen Society, 1989), p. 302.

less appropriate once Henry and Eliza were going to marry or had married. This fact would lend support to the family's dating of about 1794–5, with which we are inclined to agree. After Henry and Eliza were married, 'Lady Susan' would not be the sort of work to circulate among the family, who might recognize the original, but it could well have been prized by Jane herself and copied out some time after 1805, when the situation had become much less sensitive. Jon Spence went rather further in this line of speculation when he argued that *Lady Susan* was in fact 'a wish-fulfilment fantasy' of a girl who feared the sway her sexy cousin held over her brothers. Quite unlike the real Henry Austen, who eventually succumbed, the novella 'shows the young man undeceived by the wicked Lady Susan', while the tale itself reveals that the author 'was never taken in by Eliza'.[61]

Eliza de Feuillide may also be concerned in a literary connection. At the end of 1786 she had come from France to Steventon, where Jane and Cassandra had recently returned from school in Reading. There is no mention of her bringing over a copy of the scandalous novel *Les Liaisons dangereuses*, as Warren Roberts speculated,[62] and in any case perhaps such a work would not have found favour in a rector's household, but it was certainly popular in England. It had been published in France in April 1782 to great acclaim; its translation into English in 1784 as *Dangerous Connections* led the *Monthly Review* to exclaim against the corrupting potential of the 'scenes of seduction and intrigue' while admiring the 'great art and address' of the execution.[63] Among other critics, Frank Bradbrook noticed resemblances between *Les Liaisons dangereuses* and 'Lady Susan' in the epistolary form, use of letters and final reversion

[61] Jon Spence, *Becoming Jane Austen: A Life* (London and New York: Hambledon, 2003, republished 2007), p. 80.

[62] Warren Roberts, *Jane Austen and the French Revolution* (1979; London: Athlone Press, 1995), p. 129: 'One suspects that it is precisely the type of novel that Eliza would have been attracted to, and one can well imagine her taking a copy to Steventon, either a French edition or the English translation, knowing that the Austens were "great novel readers" and that her cousin was an aspiring authoress.'

[63] *Monthly Review* (August, 1784), p. 149.

to narrative prose.[64] Roger Gard, however, rejected the comparison, diagnosing a 'lack of radical disquiet' and an 'absence of a concomitant voluptuousness in realisation' in Jane Austen's much slighter piece. 'Lady Susan' is, after all, 'hardly an equivalent in drastic refined debauchery' – there are plenty of intrigues in *Les Liaisons dangereuses* at which even Lady Susan would baulk – and it evinces none of the 'deeper concern about the constitution of society' which made the French *ancien régime* novel such a subversive publication.[65]

The character of the unscrupulous widow exists fully formed in *English* literature, especially in Restoration drama of the sort the Austens acted in the Steventon barn. Although this character is not usually central in William Wycherley, George Etherege and William Congreve, she becomes so for women writers of that period, especially in the novels of Eliza Haywood, Delarivier Manley and Aphra Behn: for example, in *The New Atalantis* a naïve young girl is pitted against an older skilful and scheming woman, in this case her mother. The female villain is usually unmasked and the young man gets the innocent girl, but the witty widow may or may not be thoroughly punished. The pitting of town and country, which united *Les Liaisons dangereuses* and 'Lady Susan', is also a staple of Restoration English drama; with a twist towards the country bumpkins, it becomes a strong motif in sentimental fiction on which, as her juvenilia amply testify, Jane Austen was raised.

Jane Austen was said by her brother to have recoiled from Fielding's work because of its low moral standards,[66] but the predatory Lady Bellaston from *Tom Jones* may be a model for Lady Susan; Fielding also provided, in *Jonathan Wild*, a rare eighteenth-century example of a narrative of sustained irony following the fortunes of an amoral protagonist. However, the most obvious literary context for

[64] Frank Bradbrook, 'Jane Austen and Choderlos de Laclos', *Notes and Queries*, 199 (1954), p. 75.

[65] Roger Gard, *Jane Austen's Novels: The Art of Clarity* (New Haven and London: Yale University Press, 1992), pp. 42–3.

[66] Henry Austen, 'Biographical Notice of the Author', printed in *Northanger Abbey and Persuasion* (1818).

'Lady Susan' is undoubtedly eighteenth-century English epistolary and first-person fiction. The character is replicated in Mrs Gerrarde in Frances Sheridan's *Memoirs of Miss Sidney Bidulph* (1761) for example, and in the works of the prolific Susannah Gunning, in her youth half of the Miss Minifies writing team. *The Histories of Lady Frances S—, and Lady Caroline S—* (1763) includes comparison of an innocent, tearful girl and her heartless, beautiful mother, who first packs her off to school, then laments that the 'ungrateful, designing' girl will expose her in public with her gaucheness; *Coombe Wood: a Novel in a Series of Letters* (1783) displays Lady Lucy Blank, sprightly letter-writer, who loathes the country and debates marriage to an ugly fool for the ability to spend his £200,000, the '*price* of pleasure'; while *Memoirs of Mary: A Novel* (1794) again pits a sophisticated older woman against her simple, artless charge. One final forerunner is worth mentioning, *Emily Herbert: or Perfidy Punished* (1786), possibly an early novel by Elizabeth Inchbald, adapter of Kotzebue's *Lovers' Vows*, which plays so important a role in *Mansfield Park*. It portrays a beautiful, hypocritical and sexually predatory widow who reveals herself only to a female confidante while disguising her 'true colours'; she roundly declares, ''tis the custom to wear a mask.'[67]

As Austen Leigh had anticipated, most early responses to 'Lady Susan' were unflattering. The novella was considered indecorous, more Fielding than Richardson: *The Athenæum* noted that the letter form made it difficult to vary the style, so that the narrative proceeded in a series of jerks; the reviewer called the heroine 'simply odious' and found the semi-rivalry of mother and daughter disagreeable. Eliza Quincy, a friend and admirer of Austen Leigh, writing in the New York periodical *The Nation*, found the piece 'thoroughly unpleasant in its characters and its details, and worked out with none of the skill that conceals itself which was Miss Austen's eminent gift'.[68] Anne Thackeray judged it 'very unlike'

[67] Bonnie Nelson, '*Emily Herbert*: forerunner of Jane Austen's *Lady Susan*', *Women's Writing*, 1.3 (1994), pp. 317–23.

[68] *The Athenæum*, 2281, 15 July 1871, pp. 71–2; Eliza Quincy, *The Nation*, 13 (7 September 1871), pp. 164–5.

Austen's later works and 'scarcely equal to them'.[69] R. Brimley Johnson declared confidently that it was 'most probable' that 'Miss Austen would have refused to publish, even if desired, so cold a picture, above all of a woman and a mother'.[70]

But there were other favourable or quasi-favourable notices – *The Times*, for example, in its review of the fifth issue of the *Memoir*, observed that the novella was a 'clear addition' not just to Austen's fame but to the 'pleasure of the reader'.[71] Edith Simcox, calling 'Lady Susan' a study rather than a novel, considered it more original fifty years ago than in the 1870s 'when dangerous heroines are so much in vogue', presumably a reference to such works as Mary Elizabeth Braddon's *Lady Audley's Secret* (1862). There was, Simcox asserted, 'no sensationalism in Miss Austen's sketch of such a character . . . she keeps strictly within the limits not merely of the possible, but of the real'. Her heroine 'is a clever and attractive woman far too sensible to murder anybody, and not likely even to figure in the Divorce Court, at the same time thoroughly unprincipled'.[72]

R. H. Hutton, editor of *The Spectator* and one of the nineteenth-century's ablest literary critics, devoted a detailed review to 'Lady Susan', which described the novella as a failure but for reasons very different from those of most of his contemporaries: evincing some fascination for a heroine so 'feline, velvet-pawed, cruel, false [and] licentious', he faulted Austen's narrative execution as too tame and cramped. Though she thoroughly recognized the depth of her protagonist's malice, Austen lacked 'the nerve or inclination to make her fully known'. Her choice of the epistolary genre proved detrimental, Hutton argued, since through it she not only 'voluntarily surrender[ed] the light dramatic power' of dialogue that was 'the very life of her genius' but also failed to supply descriptions of Lady Susan's relations with her daughter and her admirers in language other than her own. A young and inexperienced author, in

[69] Thackeray, *Cornhill Magazine*, p. 159.
[70] R. Brimley Johnson, *Jane Austen* (London: Sheed & Ward, 1927), p. 110.
[71] *The Times*, 4 January 1883.
[72] Simcox, *Academy*, p. 367.

Hutton's view, had committed 'the double error of choosing a subject which required a bolder style than hers, and of fettering herself in its treatment by a method which robbed her style of its greatest grace as well as power'.[73]

Writing in 1917 a centennial obituary for *The Quarterly Review*, Reginald Farrer detected more merit in the immaturity: the 'cold unpleasantness' of the protagonist, he observed, was but 'the youthful exaggeration of that irreconcileable judgement which is the very backbone of Jane Austen's power, and which, harshly evident in the first book, is the essential strength of all the later ones, finally protruding its bony structure nakedly again in "Persuasion".'[74] A reviewer of Chapman's 1925 edition thought the telling in letters a 'clumsy contrivance' and believed that the author 'scored only a partial, though an interesting success' with the form; although the work could not be 'classed with the masterpieces of Jane Austen', the reviewer observed, 'it will always engage the interest of those engaged in authorship, as showing a universality in her genius that supplements and completes what is to be found in its predecessors'.[75] Chapman demurred. He continued to regard 'Lady Susan' as unconvincing and its characters insufficiently individualized.[76]

Later twentieth- and early twenty-first-century criticism of 'Lady Susan' frequently centred on the heroine's obsession with social power, although there is considerable debate over whether she gains control by assuming male values, by exploiting feminine propriety, or through skilful manipulation of language alone. Building on Farrer's earlier arguments, Marvin Mudrick proved himself the greatest champion of 'Lady Susan' when he declared that the novella is the 'quintessence of Jane Austen's most characteristic qualities and interests', her 'first completed masterpiece'. He fervently defended the heroine as well as the work, arguing that Lady Susan's

[73] R. H. Hutton, *The Spectator*, 22 July 1871, p. 891.

[74] Reginald Farrer, 'Jane Austen, *ob.* July 1817', *The Quarterly Review*, July 1917, p. 15.

[75] P. A. G., 'Jane Austen's "Lady Susan"', *Country Life*, 18 July 1925, pp. 103–4.

[76] Chapman, *Facts and Problems*, p. 52.

objective is double: complete self-indulgence and complete social approval . . . The ultimate, tragic victim is Lady Susan, the beautiful woman who must waste her art in pretense, her passion in passing seductions, her will on invertebrates like her daughter and Reginald . . . Energy, in her immobile bounded conventional world, turns upon and devours itself. The world defeats Lady Susan, not because it recognizes her vices, but because her virtues have no room in it.[77]

LeRoy W. Smith in *Jane Austen and the Drama of Woman* (1983) accepted Mudrick's analysis but questioned the conclusion. Again, in his criticism Lady Susan appears as victim as well as predator. 'Propriety & so forth' are stacked against women, who have neither property nor status. Smith argued that the heroine is discriminated against and controlled by patriarchal culture; refusing dependence, she sustains 'self-esteem by a compensatory striving for power that takes the form of the imitation of the dominant male'. Her apparent defeat 'is not viewed so by her or her narrator. She sees herself as having preserved her freedom and, in her prompt marriage to the adoring Sir James, as having assured its continuance.'[78] In *The Historical Austen* (2003), William H. Galperin agreed with this feminist reading when he observed that, while it was 'virtually impossible to regard the recently widowed Lady Susan Vernon as a role model for a presumably female readership, it is just as impossible to perceive the cultural order, which seeks to contain and to thwart her, in a more positive light'. Marriage is a conspiracy, he continued, whose 'purpose is to remove women to a place where they are inaudible, invisible, and where their only agency is in serving the landed and patriarchal interests in which they are presumably subordinate and continually vulnerable'.[79] Yet, as Mary Favret pointed out, unlike the middle-class heroines of Austen's early juvenilia,

[77] Marvin Mudrick, *Jane Austen: Irony as Defense and Discovery* (1952; reprinted Berkeley and Los Angeles: University of California Press, 1968), pp. 129–38.

[78] LeRoy W. Smith, *Jane Austen and the Drama of Woman* (London: Macmillan, 1983), pp. 52, 55.

[79] William H. Galperin, *The Historical Austen* (Philadelphia: University of Pennsylvania Press, 2003), pp. 121–3.

'Lady Susan' begins and ends with an aristocrat, firmly established within the social order of wealth and nobility: 'She is a widow and a mother; as such, she has social authority.'[80]

Laura Fairchild Brodie disagreed with Mary Favret and observed that it is not her status that confers power on Lady Susan – in fact, as a widow with neither home nor fortune, her aggressive self-promotion emerges as an essential survival strategy that allows her to 'captivate a society that would otherwise regard her as superfluous'.[81] A psychological variation on this argument was provided by Tara Ghoshal Wallace in *Jane Austen and Narrative Authority* (1995), who claimed that 'Lady Susan' demonstrates how a woman's dominion is connected not only with evoking desire in men, but with successfully repressing her own, as is apparent from the heroine's anxious passion for Manwaring. Much as she prides herself on her manipulative articulateness, Lady Susan 'in fact desires a power based not on language but on emotional commitment'. Drawing attention to Lady Susan's anger at Reginald's misgivings over her habitually untruthful version of events, Wallace observed how Jane Austen's heroine 'allows herself to expose her longing for what neither she nor any narrator can ever have: absolute love and trust, absolute credibility based not on how well she makes her case but on faith beyond reason'.[82]

Seeing a likeness between Lady Susan's eloquence and her creator's narrative flair – perhaps 'because we admire Jane Austen's artistry with language we cannot hate Lady Susan' – Barbara Horwitz understood the novella as a sly parody on eighteenth-century educational manuals made popular by moralists such as John Gregory, Jane West and Hannah More: yet, far from representing a crude *anti*-conduct book stance, Horwitz argued, Austen's villainess 'attempts appearing to behave exactly as they recommend by

[80] Mary A. Favret, *Romantic Correspondence: Women, Politics and the Fiction of Letters* (Cambridge: Cambridge University Press, 1993), p. 142.

[81] Laura Fairchild Brodie, 'Society and the Superfluous Female: Jane Austen's Treatment of Widowhood', *Studies in English Literature, 1500–1900*, 34.4 (1994), p. 701.

[82] Tara Ghoshal Wallace, *Jane Austen and Narrative Authority* (Basingstoke: Macmillan, 1995), pp. 7, 10, 11.

using their very words to justify her behavior'.[83] Sandra M. Gilbert and Susan Gubar in *The Madwoman in the Attic* (1979) identified an even greater act of rebellion: Lady Susan is one among a series of energetic and powerful mothers in Austen's canon 'who seek to destroy their docile children'. She comes to enact the anger and revolt that the more compliant heroines in the novels – and their duplicitous author – repress so successfully: if Lady Susan's 'energy appears destructive and disagreeable', they argued, it is 'because this is the mechanism by which Austen disguises the most assertive aspect of herself as the Other'.[84]

Several critics were exercised over the place of 'Lady Susan' in literary and political culture. Bharat Tandon's reading in *Jane Austen and the Morality of Conversation* (2003) suggested that Jane Austen's novella transcended the Richardsonian sentimental ideal of transparent language: the author, Tandon argued, was 'one of the first major imaginative voices to inhabit the space left by sentimentalism – a chronicler of how one might get by in the knowledge that no language is intrinsically any more sincere than the other'.[85] Susan Allen Ford found the language of 1790s ideological debate – particularly as it invokes the family – infiltrating the work. Sir Reginald speaks of his son as 'the representative of an ancient Family', a phrase that echoes a terminology established by the conservative apologist Edmund Burke in *Reflections on the Revolution in France* (1790). This approach associated Lady Susan subversively with a perverse sentimentalism: exploiting powerful cultural ideals of affective motherhood, her 'presentation of herself as sentimental heroine attempts to clear a space for unfettered action'.[86]

[83] Barbara Horwitz, '*Lady Susan*: The Wicked Mother in Jane Austen's Work', in *Jane Austen's Beginnings: The Juvenilia and Lady Susan*, ed. J. David Grey (Ann Arbor, MI; London: UMI Research Press, 1989), pp. 184, 189.

[84] Sandra M. Gilbert and Susan Gubar, *The Madwoman in the Attic. The Woman Writer and the Nineteenth-Century Literary Imagination*, 2nd edn (New Haven and London: Yale University Press, 1984), pp. 169–70.

[85] Bharat Tandon, *Jane Austen and the Morality of Conversation* (London: Anthem, 2003), pp. 142, 144.

[86] Susan Allen Ford, '"No business with politics": Writing the Sentimental Heroine in Desmond and Lady Susan', *Persuasions online*, 26.1 (Winter 2005).

Another cultural reading set 'Lady Susan' against the background of political events, the revolutionary upheavals of the 1790s in France and their repercussions on British society. Marilyn Butler's *Jane Austen and the War of Ideas* (1975) made the heroine into 'a cruising shark in her social goldfish pond', the 'female counterpart of the male seducers of the later anti-jacobin period'.[87] Mary Favret linked the work historically with the period of Pitt's policy of national surveillance, which frequently functioned through the Post Office. 'Between the years of *Lady Susan*'s composition and final revision, Pitt's ministry in Great Britain had elevated the Post Office into a highly political – and corrupt – bureaucracy . . . These years also marked the time of the greatest intrusion into private correspondence.' In her reading, the letter as used in 'Lady Susan' emerges not so much as a dying form as an overpowering paradigm of law, 'an expression of the power of form itself, of institutions and established law'.[88]

Developing from these investigations into authorial political and moral intent is the recurring critical concern with Austen's sudden final move into third-person narration. This is often interpreted as an ideological tug-of-war between the author and her protagonist. Frequently the spirited heroine comes out on top – 'all the brains allotted to the bad side and diffused scorn directed at the good people', as Q. D. Leavis sighed.[89] Unlike most of her mature novels, where Austen controls the reader's moral point of view with irony, here she lets the energy of the character in a way defeat the morality – as she very nearly allows again in *Mansfield Park*. Leroy W. Smith considered the conclusion of 'Lady Susan' notably 'free of moralising and support for conventional social values'.[90] Tara Ghoshal Wallace went further by pointing out that the narrator, though shutting off unreliable voices, none the less eventually comes to sound remarkably like her own heroine,

87 Marilyn Butler, *Jane Austen and the War of Ideas*, 2nd edn (Oxford: Clarendon Press, 1987), p. 122.

88 Favret, *Romantic Correspondence*, p. 141.

89 Leavis, 'A Critical Theory', p. 104.

90 Smith, *The Drama of Woman*, p. 55.

suggesting that she, too, had become corrupted: her closing remarks expressing pity for Miss Manwaring are not in the voice of one who 'objectively surveys, directs, and judges, but of one who fully participates in the worldly and cynical discourse of the self-consciously sophisticated'. And this after all, Wallace concluded, is 'the voice that Austen chooses when she writes each subsequent novel'.[91]

For Susan Pepper Robbins, the conclusion embodied a 'lost parental authority'. She believed that behind the 'astringence of irony' lay 'the clear moral judgments. The narrative voice has indeed become a source of order and value.'[92] Mary Poovey saw ambivalence in Jane Austen's final narrative fiat. Since epistolarity facilitates a 'laissez-faire competition' in which those characters that know best how to entertain win the reader's sympathies, Austen needs to censure her unscrupulous widow and can effectively restore social order only by 'disrupting the epistolary narrative and ridiculing not just the correspondents but the morally anarchic epistolary form itself'. The fact that she has allowed our imaginative involvement with Lady Susan's disruptive energies until the very last is, in Poovey's reading, proof of Austen's reluctance to curb the attraction of female energy; echoing Gilbert and Gubar, she speculated that it was 'perhaps because [this energy] is too close to the creative impulse of her own wit'.[93]

Discussions of the conclusion inevitably take into account Austen's attitude to the epistolary form itself – whether or not the switch to third-person narration expressed her impatience with the letter. The early twentieth-century critic Mary Lascelles believed the hasty conclusion was written later than the original composition and showed a writer tired of the epistolary mode.[94] A. Walton Litz agreed that the conclusion represented Jane

[91] Wallace, *Narrative Authority*, p. 14.

[92] Susan Pepper Robbins, 'Jane Austen's Epistolary Fiction', in Grey, ed., *Jane Austen's Beginnings*, p. 223.

[93] Mary Poovey, *The Proper Lady and the Woman Writer: Ideology as Style in the Works of Mary Wollstonecraft, Mary Shelley and Jane Austen* (Chicago and London: University of Chicago Press, 1984), pp. 178–9.

[94] Mary Lascelles, *Jane Austen and her Art* (London: Oxford University Press, 1939), pp. 13–14.

Austen's frustration with the form: 'Lady Susan' is a 'cautious retreat' from the more mature juvenilia, especially 'Catharine', which prefigures the method of the major novels. It represents 'a move back into the more familiar world of eighteenth-century satire and comedy', growing from Jane Austen's literary rather than personal experience.[95] Deborah Kaplan challenged this view and wondered whether Austen was less disillusioned with a dying form than ambiguous about representing challenges to a patriarchal system. She understood the representation of women's correspondence in 'Lady Susan' as a fantasy of power reversal in which female networks generate authoritative versions of their selves (as Kaplan observed, this is a distinct feature of Austen's private letters to her sister Cassandra, which 'had a tendency to imagine in the shape of [legalistic and sexual] reversal'). She pointed out that, far from abandoning the letter, Jane Austen continued to experiment with the mode in early epistolary versions of 'First Impressions' and 'Elinor and Marianne'.

Possibly, however, she did begin to feel ambiguous about the appeal of this kind of unmediated access to female discourse and its concomitant challenge to patriarchal literary and social conventions; 'it may be', Kaplan mused, that Austen 'did – and did not – want to represent such challenges'.[96] Roger Gard revisited R. H. Hutton's argument of over a century earlier to present a persuasive aesthetic motive for Jane Austen's move away from the genre when he compared her economical use of letters to the unwieldy epistolary novels that preceded 'Lady Susan': classifying the non-contrapuntal nature of the correspondence in Austen's novella as bare 'reports of happenings', he admired her realistic use of the form while pointing to its drawback, a limited access to dramatic representations of public scenes, so deftly handled in her mature novels by a 'subtly directive narrative voice'.[97] Jane Austen clearly needed to move on.

[95] Litz, preface to *Jane Austen's Lady Susan*.
[96] Deborah Kaplan, *Jane Austen among Women* (Baltimore: Johns Hopkins University Press, 1992), pp. 166, 169.
[97] Gard, *Jane Austen's Novels*, p. 30.

'THE WATSONS'

'The Watsons' and 'Sanditon' come from the beginning and end of Jane Austen's adult life as a novelist but they share many material and scriptural characteristics. The manuscripts show Austen employing both sides of her paper, leaving no space for large-scale revision, as some of her contemporaries such as Walter Scott and William Godwin did. When she wanted to revise substantially, as in the cancelled chapters of *Persuasion*, she wrote on extra pieces of paper cut to the shape of the new material – women's work indeed: Jane Austen was said to have been a fine needlewoman.

The unfinished manuscripts of 'The Watsons' and 'Sanditon' share habits of punctuation, using multiple dashes instead of commas, semi-colons, colons and full stops, typical especially of women authors in the eighteenth and early nineteenth centuries. Printers presumably changed most of these before printing the finished novels, although they did not always do so for sentimental fiction of the late eighteenth century; they may also have provided paragraphing which, in the manuscripts, is economical, sometimes non-existent, with speeches and commentary run together.

In other respects the two manuscripts are rather distinct in what they suggest about Austen's method of writing. The first pages of 'Sanditon' are heavily revised but thereafter the writing is fairly fluid and untouched. 'The Watsons', however, has been subjected to considerable emendation throughout. Much of 'Sanditon' is written in a clear neat hand while 'The Watsons' contains some scrawled, hasty writing. Like the published novels and the cancellations in *Persuasion*, 'Sanditon' is divided into chapters; 'The Watsons' is not. Unlike 'Sanditon' the earlier manuscript has no date indicators.

The 'Watsons' manuscript is untitled, and the first reference to the name is given in the correspondence between James Edward Austen Leigh and his sisters during the period of preparation for the second edition of the *Memoir*, where it was reproduced with the title 'The Watsons'. The manuscript was begun on two sheets of paper of 190 mm × approximately 134 mm, written on both sides horizontally and glued to keep the four written pages together; these were followed by eleven eight-folio booklets, all cut to the same size of about 190 mm × 120 mm, marked 1–11 in the top right-hand corner of the first page, covered vertically, and originally fixed with a central pin. Individual sheets of paper containing additional text are tucked into booklets 7, 9 and 10, and were probably also originally attached with a pin. The writing of the fragment seems to be continuous: the horizontal sheets carry on to booklet 1 mid-sentence, and there is no evidence of any break in the narrative between the later booklets. Several of the pages carry a watermark of 1803.[98]

It seems very likely that these manuscript folios represent the first draft of the novel, although it is just possible that booklet 1 – which contains fewer corrections than the rest of the text and only two revisions clearly resulting from a change of mind as Austen was writing rather than revisiting the draft later – is a second version. In the rest of the manuscript, every page includes some revisions, and there are sections where Austen is clearly working very hard to find the exact words and phrases for what she wishes to say. A significant proportion of the revisions represent changes of mind in the course of writing – for example the description of the Edwards's house (f. 8r), where its elevation, the stone steps, the posts and the chain appear in several combinations, or Emma's initial reaction to Mr Howard, recording the 'quietly-chearful, gentlemanlike air' which first 'she liked', then she 'greatly approved' and which finally 'suited her' (f. 18r). Other changes could have been made only on re-reading, and for some of these a thicker pen seems to have been used.

A few generalizations may be made concerning the revisions. Jane Austen frequently refines factual detail: Penelope's Dr Harding was originally to have been afflicted with gout, but this is changed to asthma (f. 3v), perhaps because Mr Watson was later to have a gouty attack; Mr Watson recalls that he has lived in Stanton Parsonage fourteen not twelve years (f. 31v), making it the same

[98] For further observations on the paper used for the manuscript and the way it was cut, see Sutherland, *Jane Austen's Textual Lives*, p. 145.

length of time as Emma is said to have been away from home, and thus explaining her complete unfamiliarity with Stanton and its neighbourhood; Mr Edwards wins four, not all five, rubbers of whist at the assembly (f. 21v); Mrs Robert Watson boasts of seven, not nine, tables in her drawing room (f. 34r). Mrs Robert's child left at home in Croydon becomes a girl rather than a boy, entailing nine minor adjustments in a short discussion and a change of name from 'John' to 'Augusta' (f. 33v).

Some alterations may add precision, making 'tuning' into the 'Scrape' of violins (f. 12v), or they may move from it, for example causing visualization to be more rather than less difficult for the reader – as with the changes to the Edwards's townhouse, which loses colour and elevation. Some intensify, such as Mrs Edwards's offer of a carriage to take Emma home becoming what Emma 'longed' rather than 'wished' for (f. 24r); some retreat and modify like the change from Emma's 'wretchedness' to 'gloom' to 'Despondence' (f. 42v). Larger changes of mind are recorded about names: only once Jane Austen began did she decide that she would write about the town of 'D.' in 'Surry' rather than the town of 'L.' in Sussex, that Penelope was husband-hunting in Chichester rather than Southampton, that the name Charles should not be used for young Musgrave, but be kept for the little boy Charles Blake, that Captain Hunter and not Captain Carr would be the soldier who attracted Miss Edwards.

Most of the revisions are very local, and serve to adjust rather than lengthen or shorten the manuscript in any significant way. Three sections were, however, added later by means of inserted papers, all providing sections of dialogue, and one containing some of the most striking writing in the fragment. In the first, Jane Austen clearly had second thoughts about an exchange between Lord Osborne and Emma in which Lord Osborne tries to get Emma to provide a lesson on the art of giving compliments. Austen replaced this whole exchange with a section focusing rather on Emma, her circumstances and her wit: instead of 'a cold monosyllable & grave look', she now gives her heroine one of the most memorable responses in all her fiction: 'Female economy may do a great deal my Lord, but it cannot turn a small income into a large one' (f. 30ar).

The second inserted section does not require compensating deletions in the text, but amplifies the discussion between Emma and her brother Robert about Mrs Turner, and offers a greater opportunity for Robert to point out the vulnerable position in which Emma has been left and for Emma to acknowledge the change in her situation while also displaying continued affection for her aunt. The third expands the conversation with Tom Musgrave over the game of vingt-un, enabling Emma to ask Tom about Mr Howard, and Tom to reply with an account of his and Lord Osborne's view of Emma, which is interrupted by the demands of the game.

Surely it is no coincidence that the insertions in 'The Watsons' all come in the later stages of the manuscript. Although the material shows signs of extensive local revision throughout, the writing becomes significantly less confident towards the end, where Jane Austen struggles to describe to her own satisfaction Emma's feelings about her family and about her situation. The manuscript stops part-way through booklet 11, in the natural pause at the end of the visit by Robert and his wife. It is difficult to see how the narrative as a whole could have been concluded. Presumably, since we are still in comic mode, marriages would have to close the book: it was all very well to leave Nancy Steele unaccounted for in *Sense and Sensibility* but no happy ending could abandon three daughters outside matrimony, including the interesting character of the kindly eldest, Elizabeth, now a fading beauty and given rather vulgar but understandable comments. Yet how such an ending was to be brought about we cannot know. The increasing number of revisions towards the end of the fragment suggests an anxious author who may have wondered herself.

The year, or years, of composition of 'The Watsons' is not securely known, and the manuscript was not dated by Austen Leigh when he published it with the *Memoir* in 1871. However, he drew attention to paper watermarks of 1803 and 1804 – only 1803 is now visible on the extant sheets, and since Chapman also notes only 1803 it is possible Austen Leigh was in error.[99] Support for a dating of *c*. 1804 comes from a reference to 'a doubtful halfcrown' in connection with the heroine's tight-fisted brother Robert. In the late 1790s Spanish dollars taken from prize ships were overstamped with a small head of George III to compensate for the shortage of British silver for coins; counterfeiting was easy and widespread. In 1804 a new counterstamp was created and new coins were issued to replace old ones; it was noted that most old coins presented to the bank were rejected as having counterfeit stamps. So at the time Jane Austen was probably writing 'The Watsons' counterstamping and counterfeiting would have been very much in the news.[100] In more general terms it could well be that Jane Austen's decision first to accept, and then to retract her acceptance of, an offer of marriage from the wealthy Harris Bigg-Wither in December 1802 might have prompted particular thoughts about a heroine whose promise of wealth is withdrawn, and who might later be tempted by marriage to a wealthy peer whom she did not love.

Anna Lefroy's daughter, Fanny Caroline, claimed that Jane Austen began 'The Watsons' '[s]omewhere in 1804'.[101] Probably she took the date from Cassandra Austen, the owner of the manuscript after her sister's death. According to James Edward Austen Leigh, Cassandra had also known Jane's future intentions for the novel and had passed them on to her nieces: 'Mr. Watson was soon to die; and Emma to become dependent for a home on her narrow-minded sister-in-law and brother. She was to decline an offer of marriage from Lord Osborne, and much of the interest of the tale was to arise from Lady Osborne's love for Mr. Howard, and his counter affection for Emma, whom he was finally to marry.'[102]

[99] Chapman, *Facts and Problems*, p. 49.

[100] John Ashton, *Old Times: A Picture of Social Life at the End of the Eighteenth Century* (1885), pp. 235–6, and Sheila M. Hardy, compiler, *1804: That was the Year . . .* (Ipswich: Brechinset, 1984), p. 31.

[101] 'Is it Just?', *Temple Bar*, 67 (January–April 1883), pp. 270–84, p. 277. The article is anonymous but assumed to be by Fanny Caroline Lefroy.

[102] Austen Leigh, *Memoir* (1871), p. 364. Chapman, alluding to Cassandra's account, commented on the reference to Lady Osborne: 'Doubtless a slip for *Miss Osborne.* Lady O. was "nearly fifty"' (*Minor Works*, p. 363). However, the theme of an amorous

As usual, but with perhaps more difficulty, the 'pseudo-gentry' were to triumph over both aristocracy and middle class, each vulgar in its own way.[103]

Edith Brown, great-granddaughter of Frank Austen and granddaughter of Catherine Hubback, eager to appropriate the work for her branch of the family, dated 'The Watsons' much later, to 1807. In this view Austen had meant to finish the work but stopped out of delicacy, since the heroine Emma's having to live with her brother resembled too closely Jane Austen's living with her own brother Frank and his family in Southampton.[104] The date of 1807 was underpinned by the fact that Jane Austen's Tuesday 13 October, mentioned at the beginning of the fragment, occurred in that year. In fact it occurred also in 1801. Jane Austen may well have had a perpetual calendar and consulted it; or of course her chosen date, though unusually specific, may have been arbitrary.

Taking all these arguments into account, we have accepted the majority opinion of a composition date of approximately 1804; but, given any of these possible dates, 'The Watsons' follows first drafts of *Pride and Prejudice, Sense and Sensibility* and *Northanger Abbey*, and prepares for the Chawton novels, *Mansfield Park, Emma* and *Persuasion*. The fragment thus has huge significance as the only original prose work extant from the long period between the completion of a forerunner of *Northanger Abbey* in 1799 and the beginning of *Mansfield Park* in 1811.

Apart from Fanny Caroline Lefroy's, there have been many suggestions as to why the work remained unfinished. The rank-conscious Austen Leigh maintained that his aunt dropped the project once she realized she had manoeuvred herself into a corner: she saw 'the evil of having placed her heroine too low, in such a

relationship between an older woman and a younger man is a plausible one, which Austen had already deployed, in a different way, in 'Lady Susan'.

103 The term 'pseudo-gentry' was first applied to Jane Austen's world by David Spring in 'Interpreters of Jane Austen's Social World: Literary Critics and Historians', in *Jane Austen: New Perspectives*, ed. Janet Todd (New York: Holmes & Meier, 1983), pp. 59–61.

104 *The Watsons by Jane Austen Continued & Completed by Edith (Her Great Grand-Niece) & Francis Brown* (London: Elkin Mathews & Marrot, 1928), pp. 6–7.

position of poverty and obscurity as, though not necessarily connected with vulgarity, has a sad tendency to degenerate into it'. Jane Austen was like a singer who begins on too low a note, then stops because of this false start; the subject matter was 'unfavourable to the refinement of a lady'.[105] Since Austen's fiction went on to describe both the refined Fanny Price during her visit to Portsmouth and Anne Elliot during hers to Mrs Smith in situations also perilously close to vulgarity, this explanation is probably less revelatory of Jane Austen than of James Edward's mid-Victorian sensibilities.

If she was writing 'The Watsons' in 1804, external factors may also have prevented her from proceeding. In 1800, at the age of seventy, George Austen had decided to retire, handing on the Steventon rectory to his son James, who then acted as curate in the parish. He went with his wife and two unmarried daughters to reside in Bath, a still fashionable watering place. There they could live comfortably in lodgings on the tithe income from Steventon, which had appreciated during the last war-torn decade. This period in Bath is the most obscure of Jane Austen's life. Perhaps she was unhappy, perhaps not; perhaps busy with family life, perhaps falling in and out of love. Although no finished novels emerged from the time, it was not without literary activity. In spring 1803 Henry Austen and his agent William Seymour sold her novel 'Susan' for £10 to Benjamin Crosby & Co. The date suggests that she used the early part of her stay in Bath to revise the third of the novels she had drafted in Steventon. The book was not printed, however. Following the refusal of a manuscript usually assumed to be that of 'First Impressions' (later *Pride and Prejudice*), which her father had offered to a publisher and promptly had rejected sight unseen in 1797, this delay must have been disheartening. Perhaps it contributed to her putting aside 'The Watsons'.

Austen Leigh connected the interruption of the work with a thoroughly destabilizing event, George Austen's sudden death in Bath on 21 January 1805. The depression and sadness Jane and her family must have felt were not conducive to writing a story which

[105] Austen Leigh, *Memoir* (1871), p. 296.

included the death of a father and clergyman. Nor perhaps were her new (relative) poverty and insecurity. With the small annual income of £210 between them, the Austen ladies, following George's death, faced a life of dependence on Jane's brothers: 'prepare you[rself] for the sight of a Sister sunk in poverty, that it may not overcome your Spirits,' Jane wrote wryly to Cassandra.[106] The brothers noted the low sum and between them increased it to £450.

The first, relatively enthusiastic critics of 'The Watsons' ignored the probable family context of George Austen's death when they commented on the work. The reviewer of *The Athenæum* declared that 'we care very much for "The Watsons"', described as having been 'written in a moment of gay and happy inspiration'. Its unfinished state derived from its realism rather than its closeness to vulgarity: Tom Musgrave is too '*real*' a character and Jane Austen shrank 'from what she would call "an invasion of social proprieties"'.[107] Edith Simcox, who thought the work 'quite in Miss Austen's best manner', commented that it was 'not easy to account for its having been laid aside'. She speculated that perhaps Jane Austen was unhappy with the plan of the story, or could not 'get on comfortably without a leading idea of some sort or a moral to be enforced'.[108] Naming it 'only a sketch', Constance Hill felt it contained 'characters such as Jane Austen alone could have created' and with whom one parted 'after so brief an acquaintance, with great regret'.[109] Anne Thackeray saw a 'delightful fragment' that was 'bright with talk, and character, and animation', and *The Times* described it as 'full of the sparkles of Miss Austen's characteristic playfulness and humour'.[110]

In contrast to their predecessors, twentieth-century critics responded fully to the fragment's supposed connection with its author's life. They were forcibly struck by the fact that, when

[106] 24 August 1805, *Letters*, p. 108.
[107] *Athenæum*, pp. 71–2.
[108] Simcox, *Academy*, p. 367.
[109] Constance Hill, *Jane Austen: Her Homes and Her Friends* (London and New York: John Lane, 1902), p. 131.
[110] Thackeray, *Cornhill Magazine*, pp. 158–74; *The Times*, 22 July 1871.

he died, the clergyman in 'The Watsons' would leave his family of daughters in reduced circumstances. '*The Watsons*, I am convinced, was given up for other than artistic reasons,' wrote Alistair M. Duckworth; but he continued, 'the fragment we have, though admittedly somewhat "bleak" in its depiction of society, has within it the necessary thematic impulses to allow for the correction of its world'.[111] Similarly, Jan Fergus argued that, with George Austen's sudden death, Jane Austen would find her work 'imitating life too closely', a consequence of her having, probably unconsciously, used the plot of 'The Watsons' to assert her own superiority to the powerlessness and poverty that threatened her own life.[112] But Fergus went on to argue that, although the death of her father may have caused an interruption to the composition, it would not fully account for Austen's decision *never* to revise it; Margaret Drabble disagreed, suggesting that, even in her secure, settled existence at Chawton, Jane Austen dreaded the ghosts of the past: 'When she felt like writing again, the melancholy associations of the manuscript were too much for her, and she put it aside.'[113] Marilyn Butler's response was more extreme: dating the work to just after George Austen died, she characterized 'The Watsons' as 'the most depressed and bitter of [Jane Austen's] fragments', conceived in resentment over 'the arrogance and indifference of the comfortably rich and their meanness over sharing their resources when alive, or generously dispersing them after death'.[114]

Jane Austen's collateral descendants forcefully opposed the notion of her as a recycler of ideas. James Edward Austen Leigh declared that 'The Watsons' 'could not have been broken up for the purpose of using the materials in another fabric' – Mrs Robert Watson might resemble Mrs Elton but otherwise there was little to

[111] Alistair M. Duckworth, *The Improvement of the Estate* (1971; Baltimore: Johns Hopkins University Press, 1994), pp. 223–4.

[112] Fergus, *A Literary Life*, pp. 116–18.

[113] Jane Austen, *Lady Susan, The Watsons, Sanditon*, ed. Margaret Drabble (Harmondsworth: Penguin, 1974), p. 16.

[114] Marilyn Butler, *ODNB* entry on 'Jane Austen'.

remind a reader of later works, he thought; William and Richard Arthur Austen-Leigh, son and grandson of James Edward, declared that such salvaging procedures would have been 'contrary to Jane Austen's invariable practice'.[115]

Successive critics have disagreed, detecting a principle of artistic economy at work in her oeuvre. They argued that, over the years, Jane Austen let many aspects of 'The Watsons' infiltrate her later novels, a reason why she never returned to it. Early on, Anne Thackeray pointed out that, in the incomplete 'Watsons', 'vague shadows of future friends seem to be passing and repassing': 'anteghosts, if such things exist, of a Mrs Elton, of an Elizabeth Bennet, of a Darcy, meet us, only they are not ghosts at all, but very living people, with just so much resemblance to their successors as would be found no doubt between one generation and another'.[116] Chapman believed that in the Austenian narrative world '*The Watsons* may with some plausibility be regarded as a sketch for *Emma*.'[117] Noting that recycling was 'a process by which Jane Austen habitually worked', Q. D. Leavis described the transformation of 'The Watsons' in detail: the disenfranchised static and too faultless Emma turned into faulty and spoilt Emma Woodhouse, the Watson family became the Woodhouse circle, with the eldest spinster sister Elizabeth transforming into Miss Bates; Tom Musgrave begat Frank Churchill, and Emma Watson's sister-in-law with her daughter Augusta the later Augusta Elton; Mr Watson, the real invalid, became the valetudinarian Mr Woodhouse.[118]

Others detected different progeny. Following Anne Thackeray, Mary Waldron thought that much of the treatment in 'The Watsons' of economic pressures on a family of girls was incorporated into the revision of 'First Impressions' as *Pride and Prejudice*, while Kathryn Sutherland argued that Austen might not have

115 Austen Leigh, *Memoir* (1871), p. 296; Austen-Leigh, *Life and Letters*, p. 175.
116 Thackeray, *Cornhill Magazine*, p. 159.
117 Chapman, *Facts and Problems*, p. 51.
118 Leavis, 'A Critical Theory', pp. 75–82.

reached *Mansfield Park* 'without the experimental social study of *The Watsons*'.[119] Joseph Wiesenfarth cast his net a little wider and argued for an even more economical use of material from the fragmentary story:

> *The Watsons* is a pre-text – a text that comes before other texts. *The Watsons* comes before the final rewritings of *Sense and Sensibility* and *Pride and Prejudice*. Once written, these novels pre-empt characters and scenes [Mr and Mrs Robert Watson transform into the calculating Dashwoods, Lord Osborne's aloofness at the ball is pre-empted by Darcy's haughty refusal to dance with Lizzy] . . . What is left in *The Watsons* then becomes a pre-text for the creation of Jane Fairfax and for the transformation of the dance in *Emma* and for using the case of too-nice-a-mind and too-refined-a-sensibility in *Persuasion*. Almost everything that we have in *The Watsons* as a fragment, then, makes its appearance in Jane Austen's canon in some finished fashion.[120]

Like no other of Austen's works, 'The Watsons' uses as its centre the material of the lower-middle classes, much associated with Frances Burney – the Branghtons of *Evelina* for example – which Austen Leigh in his *Memoir* was at pains to declare his aunt rejected in her published novels. More than Burney, however, Austen captures the claustrophobia of a marginalized group; 'The Watsons' depicts the struggle for status of those shadowed by the upper ranks, as well as illustrating the urgency of women's need for marriage and their narrow expectations outside it. With the latter Jane Austen echoes Mary Wollstonecraft in *Thoughts on the Education of Daughters* (1787), which described the distress experienced by girls raised genteelly, then, if unmarried, reduced to dependence on unwilling brothers or forced to work as governesses and teachers.

Husband-hunting, the main career path open to the early nineteenth-century gentlewoman, was never presented as a proper pursuit by Jane Austen, but in 'The Watsons' it is downright

119 Mary Waldron, *Jane Austen and the Fiction of Her Time* (Cambridge: Cambridge University Press, 1999), p. 26; Sutherland, *Jane Austen's Textual Lives*, p. 144.

120 Joseph Wiesenfarth, '*The Watsons* as Pretext', *Persuasions*, 8 (1986), p. 109.

unappealing, if not futile: here, as John Halperin observed, the men are a 'sorry lot', proving themselves for the most part 'inconstant, unpredictable, capricious, vain, and materialistic', more concerned with 'making conquests rather than wives of women'.[121] A. Walton Litz read the Watson sisters' husband-chasing ventures as the representation of a wider existential crisis: reflecting on Jane Austen's darkening vision of herself as 'a spinster nearing thirty who has probably relinquished all hopes of an equal marriage', he saw her major artistic theme as 'the conflict between the free spirit and social-economic imperatives'. Litz argued that Emma Watson 'is deliberately pictured as an isolated and sensitive person, cut off from all expectations and trapped in an alien world'; her situation develops into 'an epitome of the dilemma faced by the free spirit in a limited world'.[122]

Anticipating this social view, Virginia Woolf responded strongly to the abrupt ending of Austen's fragment, which shows Emma by her father's sickbed assessing her new position in the world: 'from being the life and spirit of a house, where all had been comfort and elegance, and the expected heiress of an easy independence, she was become of importance to no one, a burden on those, whose affection she could not expect, an addition in an house, already overstocked, surrounded by inferior minds with little chance of domestic comfort, and as little hope of future support' (p. 135). This Emma is definitely without a room of her own or the independence that Jane Fairfax so craved. (Kathleen James-Cavan is one of the few critics who have interpreted this scene positively: she understood Emma's retreat to her father's sickroom as a refusal to emulate her sisters' husband-hunting operations and a conscious decision to find an alternative to the dilemma of her situation by becoming his 'companion in free and equal conversation'.[123] However, with

[121] John Halperin, *The Life of Jane Austen* (Baltimore: Johns Hopkins University Press, 1984, new edn 1996), p. 139.

[122] A. Walton Litz, *Jane Austen: A Study of Her Artistic Development* (London: Chatto & Windus, 1965), pp. 86–7.

[123] Kathleen James-Cavan, 'Closure and Disclosure: The Significance of Conversation in Jane Austen's The Watsons', *Studies in the Novel*, 29.4 (1997), p. 449.

Mr Watson on the verge of death, Emma's chosen release from sexual discrimination would have proved a transitory one.)

Edward Copeland also commented on Emma's sorry domestic situation, reduced from affluence to comparative poverty; he described it as 'a typical 1790s-style dislocation', which underscored the most pressing economic issue for women of the time: fear of being without money. He noted that 'The Watsons' marks its borders by material signs of wealth – types of houses, status of servants, modes of transport, all calibrated according to prosperity: 'The potential of such a rank-conscious world, with all its consequent confusions of money and place, is codified in material possessions.' He also commented on the 'distinctly hostile' relations between the classes.[124]

'The Watsons' is Austen's earliest extant work in the realist mode of the mature novels: it is about poverty, pain and reduced gentility. Several critics have discussed how this content coloured the narrative style of the fragment. Mary Lascelles commented that Jane Austen 'seems to be struggling with a peculiar oppression, a stiffness and heaviness that threaten her style' and which is also found in her letters of the time.[125] David Nokes caught a 'hard, cynical tone' in the text[126] and Kathryn Sutherland noted the work's 'cold, peculiar angularity of vision'. Emma, the youngest of the four Watson sisters, has suffered the kind of reversal of fortune that recalls the career in freefall of Burney's Cecilia, while Elizabeth, the eldest, has, unlike Emma, 'found a way of coping with the world by making her ethical expectations . . . commensurate with its limited opportunities'. Emma and the reader are 'unconfined by such pragmatism' and are simply made uncomfortable. Sutherland argued that 'The Watsons' enacts 'the moment when a new and tough realism took centre stage in Austen's art': place and setting became more than

[124] Edward Copeland, *Women Writing about Money: Women's Fiction in England, 1790–1820* (Cambridge: Cambridge University Press, 1995), pp. 99–101.

[125] Lascelles, *Jane Austen and her Art*, pp. 99–100.

[126] David Nokes, *Jane Austen: A Life* (London: Fourth Estate, 1997), p. 253.

backdrop, and small objects assumed emotional freight. It began the psychological study of banality.[127]

Bharat Tandon agreed, observing how 'The Watsons' 'narrates almost everything at the same pitch of descriptive intensity', an intensity of detail which produces, like 'Lady Susan' had earlier, a 'single effect' – though, in this case, 'of social, sexual and economic claustrophobia'.[128] Austen's uncompromising narrative focus on financial hardship entailed an equally unsentimental account of family bonds, a 'failing in generosity', as B. C. Southam termed it.[129] Austen may not be, in Juliet McMaster's words, the first author to specialize in the dramatic representation of an emotion so recognizable to a modern readership, family shame – after all, Burney's heroines are similarly burdened with mortifyingly vulgar relatives – but the Watson family certainly presents 'the hottest and most desperately disagreeable frying-pan' that any heroine in the Austen canon needs to escape. In the process refined Emma Watson closely approximates the 'regulated hatred' that D. W. Harding identified as Austen's psychological condition: she is 'bravely successful in regulating her behaviour; but she has more cause than any other heroine to judge her neighbours, and particularly her family, adversely'.[130] The 'hard, cynical tone' in which 'The Watsons' described some 'unenviable choices' in the sisters' marital prospects led David Nokes to speculate on hostile energies disrupting the sisterly bond between Jane and Cassandra, a relationship most biographers tend to perceive as blissfully harmonious. Connecting the narrative to Jane Austen's refusal of the one marriage proposal of which we know for certain, Nokes observed that there was no reason to believe that Cassandra attempted 'to supplant Jane in Harris Bigg-Wither's affections'; yet, focusing on the story's 'underlying sense of uncertainty and distrust' and drawing a link between

[127] Sutherland, *Jane Austen's Textual Lives*, pp. 136–7, 139–42.
[128] Tandon, *Jane Austen and the Morality of Conversation*, p. 192.
[129] Southam, *Jane Austen's Literary Manuscripts*, p. 63.
[130] Juliet McMaster, '"God Gave Us Our Relations": The Watson Family', *Persuasions*, 8 (1986), pp. 62–3.

Penelope Watson and Cassandra – both 'powerful off-stage presence[s]' – he conjectured: 'Could there have been rivalry – even treachery – between the Austen sisters?'[131]

The unfinished 'Watsons' provided a literary opportunity to one of Jane Austen's younger nieces, as Anna Lefroy had feared it would. Catherine Austen, later Hubback, grew up knowing Cassandra and her father's second wife Martha Lloyd, who had been close to Jane Austen at the time she was writing the work. Edith Brown claimed that 'Cassandra used to read *The Watsons* aloud to her nieces, and my grandmother Mrs Hubback, was one of them.' In 1850, needing to support herself and children after her husband suffered a mental breakdown, Catherine Hubback published a three-volume novel, *The Younger Sister*, dedicated to 'the Memory of her Aunt, the Late Jane Austen'. The first five chapters are based closely on 'The Watsons': her son John insisted they were 'a supreme effort of memory' since his mother had not seen the manuscript for seven years, while her granddaughter Edith Brown claimed that the first volume was 'Jane Austen through a haze of memory'.[132] Alternatively, Catherine Hubback may have taken a copy from Cassandra before she died: although not much of the narrative is word for word, some of the earliest dialogue is similar.

The Younger Sister was the first of many completed continuations of an Austen fragment, distinguished by the claim that its later plot was based securely on the original author's outline. A rather tedious work – the most dramatic moment is when the hero Mr Howard is wrongly declared dead – it attempted to continue Austen's bracing satire in the depiction of Robert Watson's spoiled daughter and affected Mrs Elton-like wife and it added characters reminiscent of other Austen works – one has the silly literary talk of Sir Edward in 'Sanditon', for example. At the same time it tried to give a Victorian patina to the story: the heroine's modest woes teach her that suffering is the condition of life. Taunted by her sister as 'quite a Miss Charity or Miss Meek', Hubback's Emma

[131] Nokes, *Jane Austen: A Life*, pp. 253–4.
[132] John Henry Hubback, *Cross Currents in a Long Life* (privately printed, 1935).

is remarkably priggish: a woman of forty-five should have a 'grave and gentle deportment, stately but serene', she declares; accused of scorning Lord Osborne, she responds, 'scorn cannot be a becoming quality in a young lady'. What most suggests the later period is the class inflection: while worthy rustics understand the 'true poetry of nature', the aristocratic Lord Osborne becomes ridiculous.[133] His tutor, the stuffy Mr Howard, moves from the 'pseudo gentry' of Austen's usual clergymen heroes to become the representative of the Victorian middle class in his modesty and seriousness. Ruined by easy money, the unsavoury Tom Musgrave is given a rag-merchant for a grandfather: he is forced into marriage with the peevish sister Margaret by unguarded words seized on by her lawyer brother Robert. A wicked doctor contrasts with the amiably ignorant doctors and apothecaries of Jane Austen's mature novels and in uncharacteristic style he is drowned at the end. Everyone who should gets married and the foolish aunt, whose marriage has forced Emma back on her family, obtains a separation.

Through the generations 'The Watsons' went on inspiring the Frank Austen branch of the family, and in 1928, after Chapman's published transcription appeared, Edith Brown and her husband produced another continuation using a tidied-up version of the Austen text in ten chapters and boldly entitling the whole '*The Watsons by Jane Austen Continued & Completed by Edith (Her Great Grand-Niece) & Francis Brown*'. Where her grandmother's novel was 'a long and not too faithful version', hers was, she claimed, a short work written 'in accordance with [the author's] intentions'; the dust-jacket declared that it came 'from a direct source and with the charm and flavour of Jane Austen's style recaptured in a remarkable degree'. The Preface began: 'I like my grand-aunt Jane, and she would have liked me. She would have said, "I am pleased with your notion, and expect much entertainment."' Despite noting her grandmother's deviation from the presumed Jane Austen plot, Edith and her husband availed themselves of some of her

[133] Catherine Hubback, *The Younger Sister*, 3 vols. (1850), vol. 1, p. 220, vol. 1, p. 284, vol. 1, p. 158.

additional characters, but, instead of the villainous doctor, they added a benign apothecary. Elizabeth gets a younger brother of Purvis but by the end Margaret has not managed to secure Tom Musgrave.

'SANDITON'

The manuscript of the fragment later published under the name of 'Sanditon' exists in three booklets of cut writing paper, now sewn together, though perhaps originally pinned. The first two are of 184 mm × 115 mm, with thirty-two and forty-eight pages respectively, and the third of 159 mm × 95 mm with eighty pages, of which forty-one contain text. Several pages of the first two booklets bear the watermark date of 1812 and of the third the watermark of 1815. The text of the manuscript includes three authorial dates: the first page of the first booklet is marked with the date 27 January 1817; the first page of the third booklet is marked 'Mar. 1'; and the final line of the manuscript is followed by the date 'March 18'. The precision in dating, also evident in the manuscript of the cancelled chapters of *Persuasion* but not present in the manuscript of 'The Watsons', suggests that Austen was more aware of the importance of dating her work after she had become a published novelist. Further corroborative evidence is provided by her sister Cassandra's notes dating the novels: only for *Emma* and *Persuasion* are precise start and finish dates given.[134]

The manuscript is untitled. Mrs Janet Sanders, a granddaughter of Jane Austen's brother Frank, who possessed the copy of the manuscript – also untitled – made by Cassandra long after Jane's death, informed R. W. Chapman that her father Rev. Edward Austen 'had been told, his Aunt Jane intended to name her last novel (unfinished) "The Brothers"'.[135] In a letter to James Edward Austen Leigh while he was preparing material for the *Memoir*, Anna Lefroy

134 Both notes are held at the Morgan Library, New York. One is reproduced in Chapman, *Minor Works*, opposite p. 242.

135 Letter from Janet Sanders to R. W. Chapman, 8 February 1925, King's College, Cambridge.

referred to a copy of the manuscript as of 'Sanditon';[136] however, in the *Memoir* itself, the second edition of which offers the edited extracts from the manuscript, Austen Leigh refers to it only as 'The last Work'.[137]

Like 'The Watsons', 'Sanditon' reveals much about the ways in which Jane Austen drafted and revised her work but, when compared with 'The Watsons', 'Sanditon' demonstrates a marked increase of creative confidence on Jane Austen's part. In place of the eight-page booklets in which the earlier work was drafted, she prepared for 'Sanditon' much larger ones, and of increasing size; after a tentative few pages at the beginning, the narrative – unlike 'The Watsons', neatly divided into chapters – flows smoothly without extensive deletion or revision; there are no interpolated pages containing additional or replacement material as in the earlier work; and many of the pages contain no, or very few, corrections. There is no evidence of substantial rethinking of plot, character or circumstance while the writing was actually in progress. As in the other manuscripts (and indeed in at least one of the published novels), the names of some of the characters are spelt in various ways – the owner of the circulating library at Sanditon is Miss or Mrs Whilby or Whitby, depending on Austen's mood when she was writing. Unlike in 'The Watsons' there are few revisions of names of people or places, the only significant one being the alteration of Sanditon Hall to Sanditon House, making clear that Austen wanted her readers to imagine a rather more modest, perhaps less traditional, residence. One of the few factual changes is the decision to make the interfering Diana more ridiculous by letting her claim to have rubbed somebody's ankle 'without Intermission' for six hours rather than four in order to cure a sprain (ch. 5). Cumulatively, the relatively modest level of alteration could suggest that Austen had either no time or no energy to go back for thorough revisions of her first draft; but it is equally likely that by 1817, although ill, she was

136 Copy of letter from Anna Lefroy to James Edward Austen Leigh, 20 May [1869?], NPG, fos. 2–3.

137 Austen Leigh, *Memoir* (1871), p. 181.

a much more experienced professional writer than she had been in *c*. 1804–5, and much more certain of her aims and how to achieve them before she began to write.[138]

The corrections which she did make occur in specific significant areas. She was most concerned to pin down her descriptions of places and people. Early accounts of Diana Parker and Lady Denham show great care over the phrasing and nuance of their characters and behaviour; there is extensive deliberation about how to describe Sidney Parker, and much rethinking about the descriptions of old and new Sanditon, their constituent buildings and the way the characters feel about them (ch. 4). However, the famous description of Sanditon itself in chapter 1 stands exactly as Jane Austen first wrote it, except for one second thought towards the end: Mr Parker's original 'A measured mile nearer than East Bourne. Only conceive Sir, the advantage of <u>that</u>, in a long Journey' becomes 'One complete, measured mile nearer than East Bourne. Only conceive Sir, the advantage of saving a whole Mile, in a long Journey'. It is a small change, but the comedy is increased, the Sanditon venture sounds just a little more foolish and Mr Parker's idiosyncratic enthusiasm of speech and thought is enhanced. Many of the other corrections throughout the manuscript embellish Mr Parker's speech – 'rather' weak, 'very' fine, 'by no means' for 'not' – and some highlight his fondness for speculation in all areas of life, as when Mr Heywood is said to have been induced by Mr Parker (in a bravura example of reported free indirect speech) to undertake not to spend 'even 5 shillings' at Brinshore (ch. 2). Many later critics, including Anna Lefroy, felt that the idiosyncracies of Diana and Arthur Parker should be toned down, but the revisions show Austen heightening their eccentricities: for example, Diana's declaration that 'I know where to apply' for a medical man to come to Sanditon, becomes 'I could soon put the necessary Irons in the fire'

[138] The relatively low level of correction in the 'Sanditon' manuscript throws interesting light on the much more heavily revised manuscript of the cancelled chapters of *Persuasion*, which is reproduced in the Cambridge edition of *Persuasion* (pp. 281–313).

(ch. 5). Other revisions correct infelicities or possible bad jokes, such as the removal of 'Hollies' on the land of the deceased Mr Hollis (ch. 12), or they add precision in tiny matters of rhythm and phrasing, as when the account of the Parkers' formidably large collection of medicines is altered from 'many Phials already domesticated on the Mantlepeice' to 'the several Phials already at home on the Mantlepeice' (ch. 10). Sometimes Austen just reverts to a natural preference in vocabulary, as when 'mistakes' is crossed out, to be replaced by 'blunders', her favoured word from *Emma* (ch. 11). It may be significant that, of the impressionistic phrases that critics have seen as a new departure for Austen and a sign of how her writing might have developed had she lived longer, 'dancing & sparkling in Sunshine & Freshness' (ch. 4) involved a second thought, and, while the suggestive phrase 'something White & Womanish' (ch. 12) exists in the first draft, the wording around it, including the mist which contributes to the overall effect of the sentence, was subject to revision.[139]

Throughout the manuscript, the writing, including the small section in pencil and overwritten in pen (f. 35r–f. 35v), is generally firm and legible, and, although some sections were clearly composed in more haste than others, there are no particular signs of physical or mental strain towards the end; the last pages of the manuscript are no more heavily corrected than the earlier ones, and the writing is rather neater than in some of the preceding sections. It seems nevertheless that on this occasion it was Austen's strength, rather than her imagination, that failed her, and that she knew it. She had been over-ambitious in preparing a third booklet of eighty pages, and she was able to write on only half of them. The last written page contains a single line of manuscript. Directly below it and evidently written at the same time in the same hand is the date, 'March 18'. It is, after two months and 23,500 words, a deliberate – and, to any reader of the manuscript, an affecting – signing-off.

139 See Sutherland, *Jane Austen's Textual Lives*, pp. 168–97, for an extended discussion of the 'Sanditon' manuscript.

By 18 March Jane Austen was seriously ill; four months later, on 18 July, she died, according to Cassandra wanting 'nothing but death'.[140] So 'Sanditon' became the last piece of prose fiction she wrote and, like 'Lady Susan' and to a lesser extent 'The Watsons', it hardly seems to fit the ladylike image which her nephew James Edward tried to promote for his aunt. To many it appeared a reversion to the style of the youthful parodies and caricatures, with the added poignancy that, with its jovial mockery of invalidism, it cruelly and comically recalled Jane Austen's own state. Her energetic hypochondriac Diana Parker can hardly crawl from her 'Bed to the Sofa' and is 'bilious', a fashionable term for an ailment that made a sufferer yellowish; just as Jane Austen determined that this was her own complaint she added the term 'anti-bilious' to her manuscript above the line on the list of 'antis' for which the Sanditon air was beneficial (ch. 2). Five days after abandoning her novel in its twelfth chapter, she wrote that she was turning 'every wrong colour'; several weeks later she was living 'chiefly on the sofa'.[141] No one could accuse her of the hypochondria so energetically displayed in the novel, but Mrs Edward Bridges, whose husband called at Godmersham on his way home from a summer in Ramsgate in 1813, might foreshadow the Parker sisters: 'she is a poor Honey,' wrote Austen, 'the sort of woman who gives me the idea of being determined never to be well—& who likes her spasms & nervousness & the consequence they give her, better than anything else'.[142] In a letter of 26 March 1817, mentioning her own increasing ill-health, Austen now declared, 'I am a poor Honey at present.'[143]

E. M. Forster remarked that the revisions in 'Sanditon' were 'never in the direction of vitality', so that the effect is of weakness and reminiscence, although David Gilson has suggested that Forster did not actually study the variants since the pages of notes in

[140] Cassandra Austen to Fanny Knight, 20 July 1817, *Jane Austen's Letters*, ed. Deirdre Le Faye (Oxford: Oxford University Press, 1995), p. 344. Hereafter *Letters*.

[141] JA to Fanny Knight, 23 March 1817, *Letters*, p. 335; JA to Frances Tilson (?), 28–29 May 1817, *Letters*, p. 343.

[142] 25 September 1813, *Letters*, p. 231.

[143] *Letters*, p. 338.

his review copy of Chapman's edition were unopened.[144] It is easy to assume with Forster that Jane Austen knew she was incurably or terminally ill throughout the time she was writing the novel; but this need not be the case, as Austen Leigh himself indicated when, quoting *Gil Blas*'s Archbishop, he denied that the work 'smells of apoplexy'.[145] Indeed, her letters and the external accounts clarify that Jane Austen did not realize her condition until well into the work. Just before she began her novel she composed an ebullient letter to her nephew James Edward in which she famously referred to her works as miniatures, written on little bits of ivory. She could not then walk the one and a half or so miles to his sister Anna Lefroy's house at Wyards, but otherwise she was 'very well'; a fortnight later she wrote a joke-letter in reversed spelling to her little niece Cassandra Esten.[146] A sick person might try to keep up pretences, especially for young correspondents, but there is a cheeriness in these letters that seems unforced.

The tone continued cheerful when she addressed Caroline Austen on 23 January 1817: she commented approvingly on James Edward's novel, which he had been reading to her, and declared herself stronger than half a year earlier. The walk to Alton and indeed back would soon be quite feasible and she hoped to attempt it in the coming summer. The next day she wrote more seriously to her friend Alethea Bigg: 'We are all in good health': she had 'certainly gained strength through the Winter' and now was 'not far from being well'.[147] A month later she told Fanny Knight that she was almost cured of rheumatism and showed enthusiastic interest in her niece's suitors and love life; then she sent a letter to Caroline, looking forward to receiving the four chapters of her novel.[148]

144 E. M. Forster, *Nation*, 21 (March 1925), repr. in *Abinger Harvest* (London: Edward Arnold, 1936), pp. 197–8; David Gilson, *A Bibliography of Jane Austen* (1982), reprinted with corrections (Winchester: St Paul's Bibliographies, 1997), p. 377.

145 Letter of 30 December 1870, in M. A. Dewolfe Howe, 'A Jane Austen letter', *Yale Review*, n.s. 15 (1926), p. 335.

146 16–17 December 1816, 8 January 1817, *Letters*, pp. 323, 324.

147 *Letters*, pp. 326–7.

148 *Letters*, pp. 328–31.

In mid March, she wrote again to Fanny, mainly on the subject of her suitors. When it mentioned her health, this letter was more sombre. She had clearly had a relapse. She meant to ride on the donkey when the weather became more springlike – a rather different project from her recent intention of walking to and from Alton in the summer.[149] On 23–25 March she wrote even less sanguinely to Fanny Knight, admitting, 'I certainly have not been well for many weeks, & about a week ago I was very poorly . . . I must not depend upon being ever very blooming again'; she had signed off from 'Sanditon' exactly a week earlier, on 18 March.[150] On 6 April she told her brother Charles that she had been very ill for the previous fortnight, 'too unwell . . . to write anything that was not absolutely necessary' and on the 27th of the same month she made her will.[151]

'Sanditon' eschews the country-village setting which, while she was writing *Emma*, Jane Austen had declared 'the very thing to work on' (see p. 220) and took instead an English seaside resort in the making. She was thoroughly familiar with the kind of place, since, in the years following the removal to Bath, she had visited at least Lyme Regis, Sidmouth, Dawlish and Worthing. Within her work she often mocked fashionable seaside resorts. Brighton is one of Lady Lesley's 'favourite haunts of Dissipation', while Lydia Bennet in *Pride and Prejudice* is given a vision of 'the streets of that gay bathing place covered with officers'; in Mr Knightley's formulation, Weymouth and places like it are the 'idlest haunts in the kingdom'.[152] So the attitude in 'Sanditon' comes as no surprise.

By the end of the eighteenth century seaside resorts had provoked a good deal of satiric and sardonic comment. William Cowper, reputed to be Jane Austen's favourite poet, noted that past generations had been content with Bristol, Bath and Tunbridge:

149 13 March 1871, *Letters*, p. 333.

150 JA to Fanny Knight, 23–25 March 1817, *Letters*, pp. 335–6.

151 *Letters*, pp. 338, 339.

152 'Lesley Castle', 'Juvenilia', Volume the Second, Letter the Fourth; *Pride and Prejudice*, vol. 2, ch. 18; *Emma*, vol. 1, ch. 18.

> But now alike, gay widow, virgin, wife
> Ingenious to diversify dull life,
> In coaches, chaises, caravans and hoys,
> Fly to the coast for daily, nightly joys,
> And all impatient of dry land, agree
> With one consent to rush into the sea.[153]

In the early decades of the next century seaside resorts continued to be objects of mockery: for their claims, their rivalry, their mingling visitors and their trivial amusements. William Cobbett in *Rural Rides* noted the 'morbid restlessness' communicated by such towns where there is no trade or commerce but only tourism, 'dismal to think of'.[154] Comically praising Margate, the satirist Peter Pindar wrote, 'What's Brighton, when to thee compar'd!—poor thing; / Whose barren hills in mist for ever weep; / Or what is Weymouth, though a queen and king / Wash, walk and prattle there, and wake and sleep?'[155] In 1824 Walter Scott described not a seaside resort but a new inland watering place in *Saint Ronan's Well*:

> a fanciful lady of rank in the neighbourhood chanced to recover of some imaginary complaint by the use of a mineral well about a mile and a half from the village; a fashionable doctor was found to write an analysis of the healing stream, with a list of sundry cures; a speculative builder took land in the feu, and erected lodging-houses, shops, and even streets. At length a tontine subscription was obtained to erect an inn, which, for the more grace, was called a hotel.

A resort is made rather in the manner of Sanditon; it attracts similarly silly painting- and poetry-reading tourists.[156]

Nearer to Jane Austen's moment of writing and perhaps influencing her choice of setting is a novel by the popular writer

[153] 'The Retirement,' in *Poems by William Cowper, Of the Inner Temple, Esq.* (London, 1782), p. 284.

[154] William Cobbett, *Rural Rides*, ed. G. D. H. and M. Cole (London: W. Collins, Sons & Co., 1930), vol. I (5 May 1823).

[155] 'The Praise of Margate,' *The Works of Peter Pindar* (1816), p. 9.

[156] Walter Scott, *Saint Ronan's Well*, ed. Mark Weinstein (1824; Edinburgh: Edinburgh University Press, 1995), p. 8.

T. S. Surr. *The Magic of Wealth* (1815) depicted the new seaside town of 'Flimflamton', erected by the rich and foolish banker Flimflam, who, with the help of agents Puff and Rattle and the building of hotels, a theatre, an infirmary and a grand pavilion library, makes his resort the *'magnet of Fashion'*. Flimflam's riches are associated with the 'trafficking spirit of the times'[157] which has destroyed the traditional gentry, and much of the book is an attack on capitalism, speculation and the new credit economy. This is to some extent also Jane Austen's subject, and the topic might have appealed to her for personal reasons: she had just experienced the failure in March 1816 of Henry Austen's bank – although this failure was due partly to the post-war slump and too much lending to extravagant noblemen. In the crash Jane's brothers Edward, James and Frank and her uncle James Leigh Perrot all lost considerable sums, and Jane herself lost £26.2s.0d., part of the profits on *Mansfield Park* and income from the second edition of *Sense and Sensibility*.[158] The result was a sharp diminution in the income of the Austen women, since Henry and Frank could no longer contribute to their maintenance, and James and Edward had difficulty doing so. However, from the fragment of 'Sanditon' there is no evidence that Jane Austen is attacking the whole capitalist enterprise as Surr was doing, but only the avaricious and foolish who form part of it, and the influence of *The Magic of Wealth*, with its schematic characters and melodramatic incidents, can at best have been slight.[159] The French Revolution and the long wars had put paid to the optimistic notion, associated with the Scottish Enlightenment philosophers such as James Steuart and less so with the more ambivalent Adam Smith, that money pursuits, once condemned as avarice and greed, had entirely positive effects on society, but few sensed the enormous and disturbing transformation which capitalism was bringing about. In

[157] T. S. Surr, *The Magic of Wealth* (1815), pp. 14–15.

[158] Le Faye, *Family Record*, p. 234.

[159] See B. C. Southam, 'A Source for *Sanditon*?', in *Reports of the Jane Austen Society, 1966–75* (Folkestone: Wm. Dawson & Sons, 1977), p. 122, and Edward Copeland, '*Sanditon* and "my Aunt": Jane Austen and the National Debt', *Persuasions*, 19 (16 December 1997), pp. 122–3.

'Sanditon', for all its mockery of speculation, Jane Austen seems closest to Samuel Johnson's tolerant, eighteenth-century opinion that 'There are few ways in which a man can be more innocently employed than in getting money.'[160]

Jane Austen had begun 'Sanditon' before the final touches had been put to *Persuasion* – if they ever were. In that novel Virginia Woolf found a peculiar and new beauty together with a peculiar dullness; she mused that, had the author lived, 'she would have been the forerunner of Henry James and Proust'.[161] Such an opinion cannot be supported by this last manuscript work, which failed to continue the psychological developments of the later novels in subject matter or style. It shocked and puzzled early readers, as Austen Leigh feared it would. R. Brimley Johnson thought the work skeletal, a series of notes rather than a composed narrative – it would need not revision but rewriting.[162] E. M. Forster regarded it as 'of small literary merit'; it gave 'the effect of weakness' if only because its characters feebly imitate earlier ones: 'we realize with pain that we are listening to a slightly tiresome spinster, who has talked too much in the past to be silent unaided'.[163] Terming it a precious trace of the great writer, Chapman yet noted 'a certain roughness and harshness of satire'; revision would have smoothed these but 'a degree of savagery' would have remained.[164] Mary Lascelles remarked on the enigma of 'Sanditon', noting that none of the other novels, 'if broken off short at the eleventh chapter, [would] have left us in such uncertainty as to the way in which it was going to develop'.[165]

Perhaps the only recent critic to exceed the initial shocked response is D. A. Miller, who argued in a tour de force of disapproval that, following the decadence of *Persuasion*, 'Sanditon' effects the 'formal ruination of the Austen Novel as we have come

160 *Boswell's Life of Johnson*, ed. George Birkbeck Hill, revised L. F. Powell (Oxford: Clarendon Press, 1934), vol. 2, p. 323.
161 Woolf, 'Jane Austen', pp. 180, 183.
162 Johnson, *Jane Austen*, p. 49.
163 Forster, *Abinger Harvest*, pp. 148–50.
164 Chapman, *Facts and Problems*, p. 208.
165 Lascelles, *Jane Austen and her Art*, p. 39.

to know it'.[166] Tony Tanner had called its revisions dizzying and described the excessive effect as 'a new kind of phenomenological complexity' where 'identification is deferred, vision itself is becoming narrativised': 'Sanditon' was built on and by 'careless and eroding grammar; a grammar for which the characters are responsible'.[167] Miller went a great deal further and thoroughly implicated the dying author. Mr Parker's speculation seems heading for a crash at odds with the comic marriage plot, while the proscription on the death of any major character in romantic comedy frustrates any development of the theme of foolish yet prescient hypochondria. But, Miller argued, the structural collapse pales beside 'the breakdown, registered on every page of the novel, of Austen Style'. In its bad writing, 'Sanditon' dramatizes the only death scene to be found in all Austen: 'the passing of the stylothete'. At her best she had given correctness '*a theatrical form*', but 'Sanditon' is full of repetitions and unhappy associations, such as the eliminated 'Hollies' owned by Mr Hollis; it is 'beyond the reach of correction'.[168] In direct contrast, however, Arthur Axelrad, who perceptively described Jane Austen as a 'process writer', declared of 'Sanditon': 'I remain convinced that it would have been her undoubted masterpiece.'[169]

Some readers took issue with the earlier disapproval. Clara Tuite, for example, attacked the patronizing attitude of E. M. Forster. Noting his view of a sick female body producing a sick text, she claimed that Forster pathologized 'the female-identified genre of the novel through images of female corporeality' and discredited Austen's credentials for male Augustan wit, usually associated with her writing. Forster's depreciation should be read 'in terms of the logic between the homosexual son and his mother [Austen]', she

[166] D. A. Miller, *Jane Austen, or The Secret of Style* (Princeton: Princeton University Press, 2003), p. 76.

[167] Tony Tanner, *Jane Austen* (London, Basingstoke: Macmillan, 1986), p. 260.

[168] Miller, *Jane Austen, or The Secret of Style*, pp. 80–9.

[169] Arthur M. Axelrad, *Jane Austen Caught in the Act of Greatness: A Diplomatic Transcription and Analysis of the Two Manuscript Chapters of Persuasion and the Manuscript of Sanditon* (privately printed, 2003), p. 135.

declared.[170] Reginald Hill noted that the name 'Sanditon' had 'overtones of shifting uncertainty, of grittiness, of getting in the eye and causing irritation. The fragment of the novel that we have is busier, more vibrant with nervous energy, showing greater variety of theme and a more crowded canvas than any of the other novels in their entirety let alone in their opening chapters.'[171]

While also separating themselves from his sexist disapproval, other later critics did sometimes follow Forster in associating the diseased body with the text. Litz saw 'Sanditon' as a response to the author's ill health, its 'impersonal tone' a barrier against regret and depression. Like Miller, John Halperin related Austen's bodily state to the syntax of 'Sanditon', a novel, which, had she still been developing her skill with the human psyche, 'might have been her most savagely cynical performance': 'there are no paragraph divisions, and much is abbreviated'. The whole thing seems to have been 'written fast to keep pace with the speed of composition – as if, that is, the writer, puffing and breathless, could not get it all down fast enough'. This suggested to Halperin 'both mental vivacity and physical decline'.[172]

Peter Knox-Shaw made the connection between Jane Austen's sick body and her unfinished text more positively. She had long been ill and much of 'Sanditon' must have been written 'with the inkling that it would be left incomplete', he thought. The author 'played up the comedy at the expense of narrative requirements, and turned her last piece into something of a coda. The main theme of "Sanditon" is quixotry.'[173] Seeing surreal 'gallows humour' in the text, Bharat Tandon noted that Sanditon's 'very name is repeated like a magic shibboleth' with the power to cure

[170] Clara Tuite, 'Decadent Austen Entails: Forster, James, Firbank and the "Queer Taste" of *Sanditon*', in *Janeites: Austen's Disciples and Devotees*, ed. Deidre Lynch (Princeton: Princeton University Press, 2000), p. 128.

[171] Reginald Hill, 'Jane Austen: A Voyage of Discovery,' *Persuasions*, 19 (16 December 1997), p. 89.

[172] John Halperin, 'Jane Austen's Anti-Romantic Fragment: Some Notes on *Sanditon*', *Tulsa Studies in Women's Literature*, 2.2 (1983), p. 183.

[173] Peter Knox-Shaw, *Jane Austen and the Enlightenment* (Cambridge: Cambridge University Press, 2004), p. 252.

all ills. With Knox-Shaw he saw the work as a sceptical text; he made play with the fact that the author wrote that the sea air and bathing were 'anti-spasmodic, anti-pulmonary, anti-sceptic'; it was tempting to see a suggestive misspelling in Austen's 'anti-sceptic'.[174]

Regarding less the body of the text than the hypochondriacal bodies within it, John Wiltshire noted the 'amazing inventiveness, brio and zest' with which they are presented. The characters are not covertly using illness to control others but rather allowing their bodies to fill their imaginations and direct their actions. Invalidism here is no longer merely private but the 'pivot of economic activity'; it is like sensibility a result of wealth, and a compromise formation 'between the possession of leisure and the need for outlet and activity'. The hypochondriacs' 'bodies have become the grounds of inventiveness and energy, preoccupying their imaginations and becoming the source of sufficient activity to direct the conduct of every hour of the day'. In Thomas Mann's *The Magic Mountain*, 'the medical merges in a most unnerving (so to speak) fashion with the sexual': Wiltshire wondered if something similar would happen to Charlotte, whose moralizing staidness was so persistently under siege.[175] Building on Wiltshire's work, Galperin believed that the allegorical mode of 'Sanditon' underscored 'the culture of sickness to which the status quo – as both represented and advocated by fictions of probability – is figuratively tantamount'. If there is a melancholy in a world that can be opposed or escaped only through pathological abjection, 'there is also something bracing about a possibility that, however consigned to the realm of the ridiculous, marks an alternative to the "group glossolalia" (Tanner's phrase) where, to follow Mr. Parker's own logic, "civilization" remains a homeopathic entity whose afflictions and remedies are virtually undifferentiable'.[176]

174 Tandon, *Jane Austen and the Morality of Conversation*, p. 228.
175 John Wiltshire, *Jane Austen and the Body* (Cambridge: Cambridge University Press, 1992), pp. 198–220; and 'Sickness and Silliness in *Sanditon*', *Persuasions*, 19 (16 December 1997), p. 102.
176 Galperin, *Historical Austen*, pp. 241–4.

The difference between 'Sanditon' and its predecessors provoked much comment. B. C. Southam argued that it showed Jane Austen responding to the new currents of Romanticism in her amplified subject matter, sense of place and experimental style.[177] Marilyn Butler disagreed. Far from discerning Romantic trends within its content and style, she found the work anachronistic, associated with the 1790s partisan Austen of the early novels. Its would-be seducer, Sir Edward Denham, is simply 'the bogeyman of the run-of-the-mill anti-jacobin novel' of the 1790s and his literary taste is in tune with 'the exaggerated terms of literary warfare of around 1798' when conservatives associated sentimentalism with conscious intrigue and villainy. Although this was the first time Austen had made a seaside town her subject, the depiction in symbolic terms was familiar, since Sanditon had been perverted from its original state as a fishing and agricultural community. 'The people who flock to Sanditon are of the type of gentry she always censures: urban, rootless, irresponsible, self-indulgent.' Other contemporary novelists criticized new resorts but Austen was the most conservative in her analysis, the most concerned to compare them with 'a notional older way, an inherited organic community reminiscent of the imaginative construct made by Burke'.[178]

Alistair M. Duckworth made a similar analysis but came to a different conclusion: he argued that Austen had provided 'another description of the transvaluation of social and moral attitudes in her society which she so deplored'. Sanditon is 'a world . . . so far removed from traditional grounds of moral action that its retrieval through former fictional means is no longer possible'. The heroine remains a moral figure but she cannot here be an agent of social renewal.[179]

Bringing together Charles Darwin and Austen as observers of the external world, Peter W. Graham followed Butler and Duckworth in arguing that Sanditon seems to be 'taking shape as a denunciation

[177] Southam, *Jane Austen's Literary Manuscripts*, pp. 102–24.
[178] Butler, *Jane Austen and the War of Ideas*, pp. 286–7.
[179] Duckworth, *The Improvement of the Estate*, p. 221.

of the enterprising (here, not naval officers but land developers), with the vanishing rural status quo glowing in a particularly attractive light because it's about to vanish'.[180] In turn, Edward Copeland took issue with the Duckworth and Butler view. The old method could survive, he thought. Austen would not let Sanditon, 'dancing & sparkling in Sunshine & Freshness', go under completely: although the traditional and foolish gentleman Mr Parker was out of his depth, the business man of the pseudo-gentry, Sidney Parker, would probably 'set things straight'; as Copeland suspected would happen in 'The Watsons', representatives of this social group would manage to win out. He noted the moral distinction being made in the fragment between two types of capitalism or credit economy: Lady Denham's mean-spirited, calculating commercial spirit, a kind of 'rationalized avarice', and Mr Parker's imaginative and generous speculation directed to the good of the individual and the state.[181]

Holding to his view of Jane Austen as a sceptical Enlightenment figure, Knox-Shaw was inevitably uncomfortable with the reading of 'Sanditon', stemming primarily from Marilyn Butler, in terms of a contrast between bustling improvers and worthy landed gentry. Like Copeland, he noted that the speculating Mr Parker is most concerned with stewardship and community, caring for those he set up in business and raising a subscription for an impoverished family. Butler had argued that the hypochondria of the Parker family indicated 'Sanditon's' decadence and Austen's distaste for Regency culture; Knox Shaw considered that this analysis muddles symptom and cause.[182] John Wiltshire had suggested that Austen satirizes newfangled Romantic attitudes to the body from an Augustan viewpoint; for Knox-Shaw the quackery of the Parkers is however backward-looking, and Charlotte's breezy dismissal is not so much moral as empirical. 'When Arthur complains that two cups of green tea have the effect

[180] Peter W. Graham, *Jane Austen and Charles Darwin: Naturalists and Novelists* (Aldershot: Ashgate, 2008, pp. 179–80).

[181] Copeland, *Women Writing about Money*, p. 113; '*Sanditon* and "my Aunt"', pp. 124–5.

[182] Knox-Shaw, *Jane Austen and the Enlightenment*, p. 245.

of paralysing his right side, Charlotte dryly refers the matter to "those who have studied right sides & Green Tea scientifically & thoroughly understand all the possibilities of their action on each other".'[183]

Several critics connected 'Sanditon' with *Northanger Abbey*, conceived in the 1790s; the latter was being considered and perhaps revised while the former was being composed. In both novels the subject of fiction permeating life is to the fore, but B. C. Southam noted that, in 'Sanditon', 'the state of fictional illusion is deliberately and continually violated'.[184] Responding rather differently and interested in the juxtaposition of 'realism' with a self-conscious connection with fiction displayed by several of the inhabitants of Sanditon, Tanner remarked that '*everybody* is likely to live a para-fictional life to some extent. The texture of everyday life now *includes* the texture of the fictions it produces.'[185] Kathryn Sutherland agreed: she focused on the moment when, intending to regulate herself, the heroine Charlotte takes up, then puts down, the volume of Burney's *Camilla*, which suggested to Sutherland that she submits her actions to fictional authority. The action accords with the disturbing sense running through the book 'that life is being lived at a critical distance, as a second-order reality'.[186] To Susan Allen Ford, 'Sanditon' revealed 'the very power of fiction to simultaneously serve and critique the marketplace of which it is a part'.[187]

To catch the depiction in 'Sanditon' of a speculative, rootless world, several critics concentrated on the opening: the overturned carriage. Tanner claimed that it symbolizes the overturning of established social values: 'Everything . . . represented by, and embodied in, the small, self-sealing circle of the Heywoods will

[183] Wiltshire, *Jane Austen and the Body*, pp. 215–18; Knox-Shaw, *Jane Austen and the Enlightenment*, p. 247.

[184] Southam, *Jane Austen's Literary Manuscripts*, p. 122.

[185] Tanner, *Jane Austen*, p. 279.

[186] Sutherland, *Jane Austen's Textual Lives*, p. 190.

[187] Susan Allen Ford, 'The Romance of Business and the Business of Romance: The Circulating Library and Novel-reading in *Sanditon*', *Persuasions*, 19 (16 December 1997), p. 183.

be shown to be degraded, debased, forgotten or transgressed – "overturned" – in the course even of the fragment we have.'[188] Colin Winborn remarked that the carriage fall occurs when the Parkers are toiling up a hill, half sand half rock, and he saw this as a salient image of people struggling upwards in general, socially, economically or physically, throughout the book – and inevitably facing a fall. Nature is domesticated, harnessed and prettified, and cannot any longer serve as a timely check on the lives of those living beside it.[189] Melissa Sodeman noted that as early as 1799 Hannah More had attacked mobility in modern culture and its manic restlessness; while possessing a curative value for the ill, travelling endangered the moral well-being of the healthy: 'Far from praising travel . . . *Sanditon* appears to assail it, beginning with an episode that satirizes the senselessness of wasted movement'; yet, while the work appears anxious about restless fashionable society, the heroine's own movement remains advantageous, allowing her to 'attain a definitive subjectivity' and 'learn to interpret properly the characters surrounding her and to assess value in the marketplace'.[190]

Similar to the concentration on an episode is the isolation of a particular minor character. When Anna Lefroy first considered 'Sanditon', she commented on the vibrancy of the incidental characters, and Austen Leigh had agreed with her assessment when he chose to excerpt passages describing the Parkers and Lady Denham, together with their special ways of speaking.

Two characters strike modern post-colonialist and feminist critics in a way unlikely in earlier times. The first is the West Indian visitor, the pampered pupil Miss Lambe. Considering her exploited, Elaine Jordan concluded, '*Sanditon* studies, in a comic mode, how our native frailty and mortality, our common kindness and need for both compassion and respect, are transformed and deformed

[188] Tanner, *Jane Austen*, p. 252.

[189] Colin Winborn, *The Literary Economy of Jane Austen and George Crabbe* (Aldershot: Ashgate, 2004), pp. 182–9.

[190] Melissa Sodeman, 'Domestic Mobility in *Persuasion* and *Sanditon*', *Studies in English Literature*, 45.4 (2005), pp. 787–812.

by ambitious commerce.'[191] Gabrielle D. V. White noted that it would be anachronistic to include Jane Austen in the context of imperialistic novelists, but she believed it 'a crucial part' of Austen's context 'that she writes during a transitional period between the two great events of legislation for abolition'.[192] Galperin speculated that Jane Austen might have recruited the half mulatto with her 'radical otherness' into a courtship plot with the impoverished Sir Edward Denham, though he admitted that this 'specter of miscegenation and its projected adulteration of aristocratic bloodlines is undoubtedly deflected by Miss Lambe's ambiguous constitution as someone "chilly and tender"'.[193] (In fact such a plot would not necessarily evoke such a 'specter': as Lady Denham's hopes suggest, rich West Indian mulatto offspring were routinely courted by European men for their money.[194])

The other character is Lady Denham, an interesting development from Lady Catherine de Bourgh, with just a hint, perhaps, of Lady Susan. Attitudes to her reflect changing critical fashion over a century and a half. In 1862 Anna Lefroy declared that in Jane Austen's hands she 'would have been delightful'.[195] In 1964 Southam suggested that 'the relationship between Lady Denham and her niece is open to speculation'; in 1995 Terry Castle stated that Lady Denham is 'the vulgar case for Austen's homoeroticism' – a notion roundly opposed by Southam; while in 2000 Clara Tuite declared, 'Lady Denham represents the new Gothic plot of wealthy lesbian vampirism, as she sucks her male partners dry in order to bequeath to the female favorite . . . [it] is the nonheterosexual

191 Elaine Jordan, 'Jane Austen goes to the Seaside: *Sanditon*, English Identity and the "West Indian" Schoolgirl', in *The Postcolonial Jane Austen*, ed. You-Me Park (London: Routledge, 2000), pp. 47–8.

192 Gabrielle D. V. White, *Jane Austen in the Context of Abolition* (Basingstoke: Palgrave Macmillan, 2006), pp. 152–3.

193 Galperin, *Historical Austen*, p. 239.

194 See accounts such as those of Vere Langford Oliver, *The History of the Island of Antigua . . . from the First Settlement . . . to the Present Day*, 3 vols. (1894), and novels such as Thackeray's *Vanity Fair*, where Englishmen are quite willing to marry the mixed-race Miss Swartz for her money.

195 Anna Lefroy to James Edward Austen Leigh, 8 August [1862], HRO MS 23M93/86/3c/118(ii).

romance that cuts at the nexus of property and reproduction and revises their usual standing in the Austen romance.'[196]

Like 'The Watsons', 'Sanditon' inspired the Austen family. Irritated perhaps at Catherine Hubback's continuation of the earlier work and the possibility that her cousin would publish their aunt's 'Sanditon' in the original form, Anna Lefroy began her own continuation. Her version doubled the length of Jane Austen's text without completing it. Mary Gaither Marshall, who edited the work in the late twentieth century, speculated that some of the continuation perhaps accorded with Jane Austen's aims since she may have discussed the later stages of the plot with Anna and indeed encouraged her to continue the work – a rather doubtful idea since Anna herself declared that her aunt's enigmatic 'story was too little advanced to enable one to form any idea of the plot'.[197]

Anna Lefroy knew her continuation inferior to her aunt's work but she also judged some parts of the original insufficiently subtle. For example, the Parkers, who were, she claimed, based on real-life originals and whom she believed she had discussed with Jane Austen, were, apart from Mr Parker, too 'broadly stated'.[198] For her continuation she kept the original characters but invented more townspeople – including an old fisherman, a schoolteacher and boys who run donkey rides. Perhaps she was inspired to include this last by reading 'News from Worthing' by Robert Bloomfield, which deals with the lot of a poor donkey trotting up and down Worthing beach, carrying delicate ladies to the door of the library, 'Where, nonsense preferring to sleeping, / She loads me with novels a score.'[199] She also added a sinister un-Austenian villain, Mr Tracy. The most tantalizing moment of the fragment is its ending: 'Charlotte felt a little nervous—What *could* have happened—'

[196] Southam, *Jane Austen's Literary Manuscripts*, p. 119; Terry Castle, 'Was Jane Austen Gay?', *London Review of Books*, 3 August 1995, p. 47; B. C. Southam, letter, *London Review of Books*, 7 September 1995; Tuite, 'Decadent Austen Entails', p. 134.

[197] Deirdre Le Faye, '*Sanditon*: Jane Austen's Manuscript and her Niece's Continuation', *Review of English Studies*, n.s. 38, 149 (February 1987), p. 58.

[198] *Ibid.*

[199] *The Remains of Robert Bloomfield* (1824). James Edward Austen Leigh gave Anna a copy of the ninth edition of Bloomfield's *Rural Tales, Ballads & Songs* in July 1821.

JANE AUSTEN ON FICTION

Throughout her life Jane Austen was fascinated by the craft of fiction, by her own habits of writing and by those of her contemporary authors. She read and commented on novels in her letters, and she used her responses to entertain her family, as in the burlesque 'Plan of a Novel' and the comic letter 'To Mrs. Hunter of Norwich'. In more serious vein she discussed fiction within a series of letters to her niece Anna, and, concerned with her own reputation and the effect of her novels on her readers, she collected comments on *Mansfield Park* and *Emma*.

Caroline Austen remembered her aunt as entertainer:

> The laugh she occasionally raised was by imagining for her neighbours impossible contingencies—by relating in prose or verse some trifling incident coloured to her own fancy, or in writing a history of what they had said or done, that *could* deceive nobody—As an instance I would give her description of the pursuits of Miss Mills and Miss Yates—two young ladies of whom she knew next to nothing—they were only on a visit to a near neighbour but their names tempted her into rhyme—and so *on* she went.[200]

Family enthusiasm may sometimes have enhanced memory: Constance Hill, who gained much of her information from Anna Lefroy, described Jane Austen at Godmersham waiting by the window for the arrival of brother Frank and his new wife and amusing impatient nephews and nieces 'by a poetical account of the bride and bridegroom's journey' – however, the verses concerning the Frank Austens were in fact sent in a letter to Fanny Knight at Godmersham and they empathized with Fanny's feelings in waiting; Jane Austen herself was then holidaying in Clifton, near Bristol, with her mother, sister and Martha Lloyd.[201]

Also part of family entertainment were Jane Austen's written responses to what she regarded as the continuing absurdity of the English novel. This had inspired her earliest burlesques, which

[200] Caroline Austen, *My Aunt Jane Austen*, pp. 172–3.

[201] Hill, *Jane Austen: Her Homes and Her Friends*, pp. 199–200; Le Faye, *Family Record*, p. 154.

she had copied out and kept as three notebooks, published in this edition as *Juvenilia*. In later life she could still be amused by what she regarded as seriously silly novels. During 1812, Anna and her aunt enjoyed ridiculing *Lady Maclairn, the Victim of Villany* [*sic*] (1806) by Rachel Hunter, who wrote as 'Mrs Hunter of Norwich'.[202] In 1864 Anna remembered, 'there was no harm in the book, except that in a most unaccountable manner the same story about the same people, most of whom I think had died before the real story began was repeated 3 or 4 times over'.[203] Jane Austen invented a facetious note to be sent to Mrs Hunter thanking her for a thread paper and describing how she had dissolved into tears over the story.

The reaction seems a little unfair since, although ill-constructed and featuring suicide and bigamy, the novel is not hugely melodramatic (except perhaps in the final volume) or unrealistic – people assault relatives, suffer from depression and cheat others for the usual reasons – while the work is as full of commonsense as of sentiment: the heroine writes that her 'interesting languor' and pale complexion were improved by a hearty dinner of boiled fowl[204] and that she has 'no talent at a fainting fit'.[205] However, the epistolary form of the novel is clumsily used, the same episodes from the recent Maclairn family history are told and retold from slightly different points of view, and the presentation of stories within stories has a bewildering effect: at one point in the final volume a long, involved narrative is contained within another as recounted to the person writing of it in the letter which forms part of the novel. It is also a feature of the work that almost every stranger who meets with the main characters, however concidentally, turns out to be related to them or to have a significance in the Maclairn story, past and present. Overall it is easy to see how Jane Austen and her

[202] Identified by Deirdre Le Faye in 'Jane Austen and Mrs. Hunter's Novel', *Notes & Queries*, 230 (1985), p. 335; *Letters*, p. 195.

[203] Deirdre Le Faye, 'Anna Lefroy's Original Memories of Jane Austen', *Review of English Studies*, n.s. 39.155 (August 1988), pp. 417–21.

[204] Rachel Hunter, *Lady Maclairn, the Victim of Villany: A Novel. In four volumes. By Mrs. Hunter of Norwich* (1806), vol. 3, p. 73.

[205] *Ibid.*, vol. 2, p. 64.

niece, in humorous mood, could find the failures of the novel more entertaining than its successes.

Something of what Jane Austen thought a novel should be can be gauged from the series of letters she sent to her niece Anna a little later, during the summer and autumn of 1814, which were preserved by Anna and her descendants and which are now lodged at George and James Austen's college, St John's, Oxford. At various times in the 1810s Anna and her half-siblings Caroline and James Edward were prompted by their aunt's success to write fiction of their own, and they all asked Jane Austen's views on their work. The most sustained attempt at fiction was made by Anna, and between July and November she sent her aunt draft chapters of her work, on which Jane Austen commented. Anna's marriage to Ben Lefroy in November 1814 and subsequent frequent pregnancies seem to have interrupted her writing and the advice ceased. In 1818, after her aunt's death, Anna returned to her novel, called first 'Enthusiasm' and then 'Which is the Heroine?', but finally abandoned it.[206] Her third daughter Fanny Caroline later recollected that the manuscript was thrown on to the fire towards the end of the 1820s: 'In later years when I expressed my sorrow that she had destroyed it, she said she could never have borne to finish it, but incomplete as it was Jane Austen's criticisms would have made it valuable.'[207] The criticism that does survive in the letters of 1814 is significant for the insight it provides into Jane Austen's own principles and practice as a novelist. The letters are remarkable for the fluency of the writing: on these manuscripts there are almost no additions or deletions, in striking contrast to the drafts of the fictions, 'The Watsons' and 'Sanditon'.

Some years before the letters concerning Anna's novel, Jane Austen had addressed a mock panegyric to her niece beginning, 'In measured verse I'll now rehearse / The charms of lovely Anna'. The young woman in the poem was described in the literary

[206] Deirdre Le Faye, *A Chronology of Jane Austen and Her Family* (Cambridge: Cambridge University Press, 2006), p. 596.

[207] Fanny Caroline Lefroy, 'Family History'.

terms of a popular Mary Brunton novel, her mind unexhausted by comparison with the unfathomed continent of America from the southern savannahs to Lake Ontario and Niagara Falls. Jane Austen was also reading or remembering Brunton's *Self-Control* (1811) when, probably in 1816, she composed 'Plan of a Novel according to hints from various quarters'. In October 1813, writing to Cassandra, she had described Brunton's novel as an 'excellently-meant, elegantly-written Work, without anything of Nature or Probability in it'.[208] Some of its many adventures bear a striking resemblance to those plotted for the proposed heroine of 'Plan of a Novel'. Reasonably so, since Jane Austen told Anna that she intended to write 'a close imitation of "Self-control" as soon as I can;—I will improve upon it;—my Heroine shall not merely be wafted down an American river in a boat by herself, she shall cross the Atlantic in the same way, & never stop till she reaches Gravesent'.[209] The novel described in the 'Plan' sounds like such an 'imitation'.

Two other obvious antecedents of 'Plan' are *The Heroine, or Adventures of a Fair Romance Reader* (1813) by Eaton Stannard Barrett and its predecessor Charlotte Lennox's *The Female Quixote* (1752). Lennox's novel mocked seventeenth-century heroic French romance, while Barrett ridiculed more recent English-authored sentimental fiction, which in his story turned the head of a country squire's daughter. Jane Austen was rereading *The Female Quixote* in 1807: it 'makes our evening amusement; to me a very high one, as I find the work quite equal to what I remembered it', and in March 1814 she declared herself 'very much amused' by *The Heroine* – it was 'a delightful burlesque'.[210] She probably also alluded to Barrett's work in *Emma* where Harriet Smith, whom Emma sees as just such a heroine of interestingly obscured parentage as Barrett's, reads some of the same novels as Barrett's Cherry Wilkinson. Like

[208] 11–12 October 1813, *Letters*, p. 234.
[209] 24 November 1814, *Letters*, p. 283.
[210] 7 January 1807, *Letters*, p. 116; 2 March 1814, *Letters*, pp. 255–6.

Harriet Smith, Cherry is alienated through most of the book from the proper young gentleman farmer, who, in the end, marries her and urges on her more suitable novels such as *The Vicar of Wakefield*, Hannah More's *Cœlebs in Search of a Wife* and Edgeworth's *Tales of Fashionable Life*. Like Barrett's Cherry, the heroine of 'Plan of a Novel' struggles through fantastic adventures and tumbles from high life into beggary.

People mentioned as the sources of particular suggestions in 'Plan of a Novel' are relatives – including Jane Austen's second cousin Mary Cooke, with whom she stayed in 1814 – and less expected men such as Henry Sanford, a friend and business associate of Henry Austen, and William Gifford, editor of the *Quarterly Review* for John Murray, who may have discussed novels and their plots with her in London in late 1815. Given Fanny Knight's input, and the mention of Mr Sherer, the vicar at Fanny's Godmersham home, it is possible that 'Plan' was composed when Fanny and her aunt were together during three weeks of May 1816 at Chawton Cottage, but the mention of a relative and a neighbour of Jane Austen's friends, the Fowles, raises the possibility that it might have been written in their home at Kintbury.

The immediate context of 'Plan of a Novel', which strongly suggests that it was composed some time at the end of 1815 or early 1816, is the correspondence between Jane Austen and James Stanier Clarke. The Prince Regent's Domestic Chaplain and Librarian at Carlton House, Clarke had intimated that Jane Austen should dedicate *Emma* to his master; he also suggested a fitting subject for a novel: she might like to 'delineate in some future Work the Habits of Life and Character and enthusiasm of a Clergyman— who should pass his time between the metropolis & the Country' and should be 'something like Beatties Minstrel',[211] a reference to the main figure in James Beattie's popular poem *The Minstrel: Or, The Progress of Genius* (1771 and 1774). While offering him a copy of her new novel *Emma*, Jane Austen tactfully rejected his

[211] Letter to Jane Austen, 16 November 1815, *Letters*, p. 296.

suggestion, declaring herself 'the most unlearned, & uninformed Female who ever dared to be an Authoress'.[212]

A week later, having read only a few pages of *Emma*, Clarke renewed his assault: 'Carry your Clergyman to Sea as the Friend of some distinguished Naval Character about a Court'. Now he revealed how autobiographical were his suggestions: in the 1790s he himself had been to sea as a naval chaplain. He added the advice, 'shew dear Madam what good would be done if Tythes were taken away entirely, and describe him burying his own mother—as I did—because the High Priest of the Parish in which she died—did not pay her remains the respect he ought to do', a reference to an embarrassing event in 1802 when Clarke had interrupted his mother's funeral by insisting that he himself take over conducting the ceremony.[213]

In March 1816, noting the approaching marriage of the Regent's daughter to Prince Leopold of Saxe-Coburg-Gotha, Clarke again wrote to Jane Austen, on the Regent's behalf, thanking her for the red morocco bound copy of *Emma* and proposing a new subject for her art: she should write a 'Historical Romance illustrative of the History of the august house of Cobourg'.[214] When she declared she would die laughing if she tried such a thing, he withdrew. The irony inherent in Austen's mock-demure replies to the pompous Clarke and in her 'Plan' were utterly lost on her stuffy nephew – as Margaret Oliphant, among the sharpest of the early commentators, pointed out with glee: 'Mr Austen Leigh does not seem to see the fun'; Clarke's 'clever correspondent exults over him; she gives him the gravest answers, and draws her victim out'.[215]

Jane Austen's own novels, she knew, differed substantially from those of Mary Brunton and from both the moral tale and the royal romance James Stanier Clarke would have had her write. She was

212 11 December 1815, *Letters*, p. 306.

213 21 December 1815, *Letters*, pp. 306–7. Chris Viveash, *James Stanier Clarke* (privately printed, 2006), pp. 60–4.

214 27 March 1816, *Letters*, p. 311.

215 Margaret Oliphant, 'Miss Austen and Miss Mitford', *Blackwood's Edinburgh Magazine*, 107 (January–June 1870), p. 305.

aware of her worth but was fascinated by opinions others held of her books: for *Mansfield Park* and *Emma*, the two last novels published in her lifetime, she kept a brief record of what some of her friends and relatives thought and said. She found that the majority of readers enjoyed the new works but retained *Pride and Prejudice* as the favourite. Although *Mansfield Park* prompted some criticism, it was the style and manner of *Emma* that raised most objection. Mrs Digweed, so similar in her vacuous speech to Miss Bates, declared that, 'if she had not known the Author, [she] could hardly have got through it'. Mrs Guiton 'thought it too natural to be interesting' and Mr Cockerell 'liked it so little, that Fanny wd not send me his opinion'. But her brother Charles, who was sent the book while at sea, compensated for such ill thoughts by claiming it was his favourite – he read it 'three times in the Passage'.[216]

THE POEMS

George Henry Lewes told Charlotte Brontë that Jane Austen was 'not a poetess' and that she had 'none of the ravishing enthusiasm of poetry'.[217] Certainly in the Romantic sense meant by Lewes she was no poet, but she loved words and the comedy of rhyme and she revelled in the succinctness of verse. Even after 'Sanditon' had been put aside, she continued writing or dictating, and her final production was a comic poem on Winchester races.

Apart from the stanzas in memory of Madam Lefroy, most of her verses are in similar light vein. Occasional pieces, they sometimes form part of collective rhyming games with the rest of the family, responses to poems they wrote on the same theme. Or they were reactions to absurdities she read in the newspaper or heard as gossip. Such writing was a gentry- and middle-class pastime, feeding sometimes into experimental versification; it was a tradition passing from the eighteenth into the nineteenth century, untouched by the prevailing public mode of self-absorbed Romantic poetry.

[216] See p. 239; Le Faye, *Chronology*, p. 540. Charles also mentioned the work to his diplomatic friend, Robert, later Sir Robert Liston (p. 545).

[217] *The Letters of Charlotte Brontë*, ed. Margaret Smith, 3 vols. (Oxford: Clarendon Press, 2000), vol. II, 1848–51, p. 14.

Jane's mother Cassandra was perhaps the most skilful light versifier of the family, using what she called her 'sprack wit' to write amusing comic lines on local people and events.[218] Her brother James Leigh Perrot also composed epigrams and riddles, including verses on a union of Captain Edward Foote and Miss Mary Patton in 1803 (see p. 732), which Austen Leigh reproduced in the *Memoir*; these have occasionally been attributed to Jane Austen, including in at least one posthumously revised edition of Chapman's *Minor Works*, presumably because a copy was found in her handwriting.[219] Jane's poems often sprang from similar observation of incongruous or too congruous names.

Eighteen poems, not all in Austen's hand, but which can confidently be ascribed to her, are now extant, together with three charades recorded in a family collection;[220] these undoubtedly represent only a proportion of the poems she actually wrote, many of which – including the one on Miss Mills and Miss Yates mentioned by Caroline Austen (see p. xcix) – have not survived. With the exception of a small poem created to accompany a gift in 1792, and the stanzas on the Winchester races of July 1817, the poems all derive from an eight-year period between 1805 and 1812 – a period for which we have very little original Austen prose. No fewer than five poems, more than a quarter of the whole, come from the months between February and October 1811; possibly, as she was awaiting publication of *Sense and Sensibility*, she was feeling particularly ebullient (although two of the five poems concern a headache, one of them being her own). No poems have survived from the period between November 1812 and July 1817 when she was gaining success as a published novelist, but this may be sheer accident; everything we know about Austen's versifying suggests that she continued to amuse herself and those close to her with light poetry.

218 Le Faye, *Family Record*, p. 99.

219 *Letters*, p. 523; Jane Austen, *Minor Works*, ed. R. W. Chapman, revised by B. C. Southam (Oxford: Oxford University Press, 1969, reprinted 1988), p. 452.

220 Full details of the poems and their provenance are given in the notes to each poem.

The 'Verses to rhyme with "Rose"' illustrate the difficulty of dating and placing some of the poems, along with the ways in which they are thoroughly embedded in Jane Austen's family and domestic life. The 'Verses' are a collection of four short poems, by Jane Austen, her mother Mrs Austen, Cassandra and Edward's wife Elizabeth. The series displays the inventiveness of all four women in writing verses where every line rhymes with the given word, 'rose', and bears testimony to the way in which the Austens enjoyed wordplay as a social as well as an individual recreation. (This feature of their activities is also reflected in a series of charades by various members of the family, carefully preserved in family albums.) Jane Austen evidently thought the 'Rose' poems worth keeping since she made a fair copy on a sheet of paper on to which she also copied her poem on the trial of the controversial naval hero Sir Home Popham in 1807, and two poems she wrote as alternative accompaniments to the gift of a cambric handkerchief in 1808.

The 'Rose' poems are undated, but must have been written before Elizabeth's death in October 1808. Deirdre Le Faye has identified three possible occasions when the four women were together in circumstances where they could have written such verses; the most likely of these are June–July 1805 at Godmersham, and September 1807 at Chawton House, both properties owned by Edward, with Godmersham as his main residence. Most scholars have favoured the 1807 date, and therefore the Chawton location, because Lord Brabourne, who first published the poems, had found them folded in a family letter of 1807, and – unaware that other writing on the sheet had a later date – assumed that the poems derived from that year. However, the earlier date of 1805 and the Godmersham location seem equally if not more plausible, partly because of domestic detail mentioned in the poems themselves. Mrs Austen's poem describes looking out of the window and seeing bucks and does, cows and bullocks, wethers and ewes, which might refer to the 'cattle' Jane Austen mentions in July 1806 as being in the Godmersham park ('See they come', pp. 245–246); and she describes joining the family in the library, which again suggests

Godmersham, where the library was substantial in size, and regularly used as a family parlour.[221] Elizabeth's poem may offer a more precise hint: in it she reflects on being ill in a way that suggests she had been in a poor state of health for some time. During the visit of Mrs Austen, Cassandra and Jane to Godmersham in 1805, Fanny records that a Dr Wilmot visited on 4 July; on 20 July she wrote that 'mama was well enough to come down',[222] which strongly suggests her mother had been ill in bed for an extended period. The 1805 date, unlike that in 1807, is in a season of the year when roses would have been in full bloom, possibly suggesting the topic for the poem.

Other poems also relate to the Knights, sometimes unexpectedly: 'Alas poor Brag' directly comments on family Christmas festivities at Godmersham; the verses 'Between session and session' concern moves to defer a controversial Parliamentary Bill on a subject of great interest to Edward Knight, whose Godmersham estate was directly affected by its proposal to cut a canal through the Kent countryside.

One uncharacteristically serious poem by Jane Austen is 'To the Memory of Mrs. Lefroy', written to elegize Anne Lefroy, wife of George Lefroy, rector of Ashe, two miles north west of Steventon. Known as 'Madam Lefroy' and highly respected in her parish for her good works, she had become a friend and mentor to the young Jane Austen. On 16 December 1804, Jane's twenty-ninth birthday, Madam Lefroy went shopping in the local town of Overton and, meeting Jane's brother James by chance, complained to him of the stupidity and sluggishness of her horse. On her way home, the horse bolted and she fell on to hard ground; she died a few hours later and was buried at Ashe on 21 December, with James officiating. The shocking news must have spread very quickly to Bath, where Jane was living with her family. The verses include the lines 'Beloved friend, four years have pass'd away / Since thou wert snatch'd forever

[221] Nigel Nicolson, *Godmersham Park, Kent, before, during and after Jane Austen's Time* (Chawton: Jane Austen Society, 1996), n. p.

[222] Unpublished diary entry, Centre for Kentish Studies.

from our eyes', giving a date of composition in 1808 on or around the fourth anniversary of her death.

By contrast with 'To the Memory of Mrs. Lefroy', the poem which Jane Austen wrote just before her own death has a macabre humour. 'When Winchester races first took their beginning' concerns the popular belief that, if it rained on St Swithin's Day, 15 July, the rain would continue for forty days. Jane Austen wrote her poem on 15 July 1817 in Winchester, where she had gone to seek medical attention. Possibly in earlier years she had been to the horse races there, which usually took place in July. The day before she composed the poem, the *Hampshire Chronicle* advertised the Winchester meeting forthcoming that year on 29–31 July and Jane Austen could well have seen the notice. As so often before in her life, she was being prompted by the newspaper to write light verse.[223]

Of the two extant manuscripts of this poem, one is in an unknown hand, perhaps belonging to a friend of Jane Austen. Possibly it was the result of direct authorial dictation: the word 'Venta' (the Roman name for Winchester) is spelt 'Ventar' twice, as it might be if written by someone ignorant of Latin listening to a speaker with a Hampshire accent which would lengthen and soften the last syllable, and there are cancellations which would be unlikely if the poem were being copied from a written original. Interestingly, in stanza 4, within the lines where the saint addresses Winchester, 'When once we are buried you think we are dead / But behold me Immortal', the words are roughly underlined and the word 'gone' is used instead of 'dead', which is necessary for the rhyme. Perhaps 'dead' was avoided from superstition or grief, or perhaps the substitution was a black joke between dying author and amanuensis.

Since the poems are so embedded in Jane Austen's life and quotidian events, it is not surprising that most of the few twentieth-century comments occur within biographies. 'To the Memory of

[223] *Jane Austen: Collected Poems and Verse of the Austen Family*, ed. David Selwyn (Manchester: Fyfield Books, 1996), p. 86.

Mrs. Lefroy', for example, provoked differing responses in the biographers Claire Tomalin and David Nokes, as well as the commentators Laura and Robert Lambdin and David Selwyn. Tomalin, who thought 'See they come' Austen's 'best piece of verse', found the poem on Madam Lefroy 'warm but disappointingly general in its terms' – one cannot, she thought, see a living personality through the stock phrases, 'Angelic woman', 'solid worth' and 'captivating grace'.[224] The Lambdins saw the poem as a search for connection; they called it 'a moving tribute' to a good friend while noting its 'maudlin tone'; Selwyn found in it a 'gentle acknowledgement' of Jane Austen's own lack of reason in trying to unite with her friend, conveyed 'in a tone of indulgent good sense familiar from the novels'.[225] David Nokes drew attention to the unique aspect of the verses: he wrote that Austen composed nothing similar for the wives of Edward and James or for her own father; clearly she was inspired by 'the ominous coincidence of this day'. Failing to find in the verses the tenderness, warmth and good sense caught by Tomalin and Selwyn, Nokes saw the poem as in part a response to Madam Lefroy's interference in the once budding romance between Jane and her young nephew, Tom Lefroy; it is full of 'bitter torture' and self-reproach for Austen's earlier resentment of a woman who now seemed perfect in her eyes.[226]

ATTRIBUTION

The dating of 'Lady Susan' and 'The Watsons' may be disputed, but, together with 'Sanditon', they are secure in authorship: all three are in Jane Austen's handwriting, and both 'The Watsons' and 'Sanditon' were identified as Austen's by family members with a direct knowledge of her work. We can be equally confident about the poems, riddles, charades and spoofs, and, of course, the letters,

[224] Claire Tomalin, *Jane Austen, A Life* (London: Penguin, 1997), p. 39.

[225] Laura and Robert Lambdin, 'Austen's Poems and Charades: Miniature Tonal Reverberations', in *Re-Drawing Austen: Picturesque Travels in Austenland*, ed. Beatrice Battaglia and Diego Saglia (Naples: Liguori, 2004), p. 417; David Selwyn, *Jane Austen and Leisure* (Hambledon: Continuum, 1998), p. 280.

[226] Nokes, *Jane Austen*, pp. 343–5.

which are signed. But several prose and poetic works have been ascribed to Jane Austen about which there is no such security. For these we have looked again at the evidence, including paper, watermarks and origin; the appearance of handwriting; the context of generation and reception, family tradition and biographical circumstance; style, content and manner. Where we have concluded that authorship is unlikely, or possible but not absolutely secure, we have reproduced the items in Appendices to, rather than in the main body of, the volume. The two most controversial such works are the play 'Sir Charles Grandison', a fifty-three-page manuscript in Jane Austen's hand, and the three prayers written in two manuscripts and passed down in the family of her brother Charles.

'Sir Charles Grandison'

'Sir Charles Grandison', a short play in five acts based on Samuel Richardson's seven-volume epistolary novel of 1753–4, is written on five groups of pages of different sizes: the first four pages are 95 mm × 108 mm, the next eight (which may together have originally made a 12-page booklet) 95 mm × 95 mm; there follows a booklet of twenty-eight pages, 95 mm × 153 mm, written through; a booklet of eight, 184 mm × 120 mm, with one sheet watermarked 1796, of which the first four are written on; and a booklet of twelve, 158 mm × 95 mm, with one sheet watermarked 1799, of which the first seven are written on, to complete the play. Paper used for Acts 2–5 is watermarked Portal & Co. 1796 and Sharp 1799, which suggests the play was written down some time in or shortly after 1800; this dating is supported by a reference in Act 3 to a piece of piano music deriving from the 'Grand Ballet' *Laura et Lenza*, which was performed in London in May 1800 and for which the sheet music was not available till after that. The different sorts and sizes of paper, together with the varying degrees of neatness in the handwriting within the manuscript suggest the possibility that the work, while clearly in a single hand, might have been written at different times. In addition the play might perhaps have been altered without much care for the whole, possibly while being rehearsed or performed – if it ever was performed.

The idea of reducing one of the longest of eighteenth-century novels to a short play was a humorous and audacious one, but the enterprise of abridging Richardson was not wholly original. Several abridgements had appeared in the late eighteenth century, including *The History of Sir Charles Grandison and the Hon. Miss Byron, in which is included the Memoirs of a Noble Italian Family* (*c.* 1780) and *The History of Sir Charles Grandison* (1789, in its tenth edition by 1798).

Within the family 'Sir Charles Grandison' was accepted as by Anna Lefroy. According to Anna's daughter, Fanny Caroline, 'To my mother she [Jane Austen] was especially kind writing for her the stories she invented for herself long ere she could write . . . I have still in my possession in Aunt Jane's writing a drama my mother dictated to her founded on Sir Charles Grandison a book with which she was familiar at seven years old.'[227] Constance Hill made this statement public in 1902 in *Jane Austen: Her Homes and Her Friends*.[228] Jane Austen's twentieth-century editor R. W. Chapman did not include 'Sir Charles Grandison' either in his published listing of Austen's manuscripts, or in his 1954 edition of Jane Austen's *Minor Works*. The idea that the play was, despite this secure family tradition, actually written by Jane Austen herself came from Brian Southam in 1977; on his detailed arguments first published in 1980 all later scholars who accept the attribution have relied, and so we need to rehearse them here.[229]

Southam's case is based on the assumption that the play 'bears the stamp of an adult mind' not that of 'a child of seven, too young

[227] Fanny Caroline Lefroy, 'Family History'. Some dates in her manuscript suggest that the early sections were written in 1870, and later sections after May 1871. Anna died in September 1872.

[228] Hill, *Jane Austen: Her Homes and Her Friends*, pp. 239–40.

[229] Chapman, *Facts and Problems*, pp. 161–5; *Jane Austen's 'Sir Charles Grandison'*, transcribed and ed. Brian Southam (Oxford: Oxford University Press, 1980).

to write out the play for herself'; such a child could hardly be capable of composing such 'a shrewd and amusing' work in her head. If it were composed later than 1800 by Anna (b. 1793), then she would have been old enough to write it down herself. As for the play, he judged it a 'deadly accurate' burlesque, not brilliant but 'amusing enough and highly performable'; linked to the mature novels, it suggests their strongly dramatic vein and it adds 'considerably to our understanding of Jane Austen's experience of Richardson'. Like two of the short playlets Jane Austen wrote in her juvenilia, the play's Act 1 has a laid-out title page with a formal cast list, suggesting that it might have started like them as a brief joke, in this case an 'abridgement'– especially since it has 'the same spirit of fun' as the similarly abridged 'History of England'. Act I, the opening scene of which is, Southam declared, 'wholly of Jane Austen's devising', comes in realistic mode and can be dated to about 1791–2 (before Anna was born) when Jane was moving from the extravagant burlesque of 'Love and Freindship' to the greater realism of 'Catharine', and trying her hand at *Grandison* jokes in the small prose satires. This act is 'much less amusing . . . much less accomplished dramatically' than the later acts but, Southam surmised, its 'commonplaceness and banality' could be part of the joke. The play was then put aside for some years and hurriedly finished about 1800 when the family wanted something to perform and, fully knowing the original novel, all would enjoy the style of 'allusive counterpoint'. Although firmly stating his claim for Jane Austen's authorship, Southam concedes that, if she were working intermittently on the play between 1796 and 1800, Anna, often at Steventon, might have been allowed to make some childish scribbles in pencil on the manuscript and the odd alteration in ink. 'That, almost certainly, was the extent of Anna's contribution,' he concluded. Her later claim was a 'slight and flattering misrecollection' of a woman whose memory was usually 'detailed and accurate'.[230]

With an endorsement from the distinguished Austen critic, Lord David Cecil, in 1980 Southam published the play as Jane Austen's.

[230] Introduction to *Jane Austen's 'Sir Charles Grandison'*, pp. 9, 10–11.

The excitement at the new attribution even produced a film, *Jane Austen in Manhattan* (1980), scripted by Ruth Prawer Jhabvala and directed by James Ivory. It concerned two rival producers of the new play and began with the Sotheby auction of the manuscript as definitely a work of the great novelist. (In real life the manuscript, 'officially authenticated' by Southam, was bought in 1992 for £30,800, and is now in Chawton House Library.)

Since 1980 many critics and biographers have accepted Southam's conclusion about authorship and dating. John Halperin hailed 'Grandison' (which he agreed was probably completed in 1800) as 'the last bit of sustained writing she [Jane Austen] would do for four years'. He noted 'its tendency towards burlesque and parody' and its resemblance to *Northanger Abbey*; he considered that some of its weaknesses illuminated Richardson's vulnerable sides, his 'ineptness in handling action, periodic prurience, a tendency to pursue far beyond their interest various strands of his story'. He concluded that 'The play probably was written for domestic consumption. But the Steventon household, which was soon to break up, never saw it performed so far as we know.'[231] Deirdre Le Faye raised the question of collaboration, while assuming the majority of the play to be by Jane Austen. She suggested that it was performed not at Steventon but at Godmersham, but made the point that Fanny Knight's diaries began in 1804 and included no mention of a performance of 'Grandison'; consequently Le Faye dated the work to somewhere between 1800 and 1804.[232] Margaret Anne Doody was more sceptical of Jane Austen's involvement. Noting that Southam proposed 1800 for most of the work, a date when Jane Austen was twenty-four, Doody remarked, 'she wrote better at age fourteen'.[233]

The most detailed support of the sceptical view came from Marilyn Butler in an article in the *London Review of Books*. She

[231] Halperin, *The Life of Jane Austen*, pp. 119–20.

[232] Le Faye, *Family Record*, p. 150, and private communication 31 May 2006.

[233] Margaret Anne Doody, *Nineteenth-Century Fiction*, 38.2 (September 1983), pp. 220–4.

declared the play 'a very literal transposition of the more memorable scenes' from *Sir Charles Grandison*'s main plot, 'executed by a probably young and certainly not very practical dramatist. The first act is only unembarrassing on the assumption that the author is at most 12 years old.' She called the whole a record 'of a semi-improvised production by a group of children' and asked if it could really be 'the writing of one of our greatest novelists, at a stage in her development when she had already completed versions of *Pride and Prejudice* and *Northanger Abbey*'.[234]

Judging by the variation in handwriting, Southam had considered that Act 1 was written long before the other acts. Butler however suggested that there need be little time between the two composings. She based her case on the cancelled page at the end of Act 1, intended as two possible beginnings of Act 2, where the abduction and attempted forced marriage of the heroine Harriet Byron need to be presented. The false starts follow the story as told by Richardson, but his is an epistolary novel where Harriet has to be safe before she can write her drama. However, the final Act 2 of the play, in what Butler regarded as new or different handwriting, begins by selecting a dramatic moment from the abduction: Butler speculated that this better beginning 'could in all probability signal Aunt Jane's arrival on the scene'. Concerning Act 1 she further pointed out that in Southam's hypothesis of a Steventon performance in the 1790s, the Austen family would have had only this part available. There is no record of family theatricals during this period and, in any case, Butler noted the absurdity of the child Jane writing such limp lines for her educated older brothers and their sophisticated cousin Eliza de Feuillide to act. The playlet as a whole most likely dated from the period when Jane Austen was helping her neglected niece Anna by encouraging an interest in reading and writing; most of the play has 'the awkwardness and redundancy of children wondering what to say next' with occasional 'more polite and adult lines'.[235]

234 Marilyn Butler, *London Review of Books*, 21 May–3 June 1981.
235 *Ibid.*

We have noted these arguments and examined the manuscript anew. To us the handwriting appears indeed to be Jane Austen's, and to be hers throughout. From the evidence of this handwriting, there seems no necessity to assume a gap between the writing of Act 1 and the rest. The difference in watermark dates does not necessarily suggest a difference in date of composition: 'Sanditon', for example, which we know was written in a two-month period at the beginning of 1817, uses paper watermarked 1812 and 1815, and this at a time when Austen was writing as a professional author. As for the authorship of the play, we see no compelling reason to contradict family tradition, reported by Anna's daughter, possibly during her mother's lifetime, that Anna composed the piece with her aunt writing out her words. The little plays Jane Austen invented in the juvenilia – 'The Visit', 'The Mystery' and 'The first Act of a Comedy' – are comic spoofs quite different from and far more sparkling than 'Grandison'.[236] The artefactual printing formality that Southam felt linked Act 1 of 'Grandison' with the juvenilia is certainly a habit of the child Jane Austen, but it is a common habit of young people imagining themselves writers, and of grown-ups encouraging youngsters to think seriously about the creative process. Butler's suggestion that Jane Austen or some other experienced person helped the beginning of Act 2 seems a good one, although there is perhaps no need to go further – or even perhaps so far. This scene, in which Sir Hargrave attempts to force Harriet into a marriage ceremony, is one of the most obviously dramatic in the novel, and is featured in several of the published abbreviations; each, like the version reproduced here, includes similar details from Richardson – the painful squeezing of Harriet's stomach in a slamming door, the use of a capuchin cloak (the word 'capuchin' to describe the cloak is deleted in the manuscript). In her letters to Anna concerning the novel her niece was writing, Jane Austen

[236] Anna Lefroy to James Edward Austen Leigh, December 1864, HRO MS 23M93/97/4/104. See also Deirdre Le Faye, 'Jane Austen's Nephew – A Re-identification', *RES*, n.s. 39 (1988), pp. 417–21.

suggested many devices to facilitate her niece's plot and to encourage naturalness over literariness without providing actual lines. She could have made similar suggestion for 'Grandison' while Anna was composing.

The attribution to Anna is made the more plausible since the child was much in her aunt's company: indeed, she became part of the Steventon household for two years after her mother's death in 1795 and was raised with her aunt's novels. At the age of four or five she knew *Pride and Prejudice* so well that she embarrassed Jane Austen by repeating the names of the characters when the work was still supposed to be secret.

Anna herself began writing young. Southam took the statement that Anna knew *Grandison* from the age of seven to suggest that the claim was that she *wrote* it at seven. But in fact she could have composed the work a year or two later. Anna's half sister Caroline was similarly precocious and in her old age recalled her 'wonderful facility . . . for a child of ten years old'.[237] In truth there seems little in 'Sir Charles Grandison' beyond the ability of an intelligent child between seven and ten since the few decent lines are in the original or based closely on it. For example, Harriet in the play cleverly states, 'I will not be bribed into liking your wit'; in the novel Sir Charles tells Harriet that 'Beauty shall not bribe me on your side' and Harriet says of Charlotte, 'See . . . how high this dear flighty creature bribes! But I will not be influenced, by her bribery, to take her part'. One striking Richardsonian word in Southam's transcription – 'overfrown' (Act 5, scene 2) – turns out, on close examination of the manuscript, to be the much more conventional 'overpower'. Nothing in the play signals the kind of creative engagement with Richardson that might have increased the comedy, satire or drama of the original. But, if not composing the work, a caring aunt might easily have acted as an amanuensis for it, so aiding a niece, and perhaps a group of children, who wished to write and act a little play.

[237] *Reminiscences of Jane Austen's Niece Caroline Austen* (1986), revised edition, introduced by Deirdre Le Faye (Chawton: The Jane Austen Society, 2004), p. 70.

In the mid nineteenth century the Austen family were eager to produce all bits of writing by Jane Austen and were proud to be in possession of any examples of her composing; yet this item was never presented as hers. In her letter of December 1864 to her brother James Edward Austen Leigh, about to embark on the *Memoir*, Anna Lefroy – whose memory even Southam acknowledged was 'usually detailed and accurate' – made no mention of the event of the writing of 'Grandison', which, if the play were by her aunt, one would have expected her to do. She simply remembered with affection Jane Austen's ability to create stories for her nephews and nieces – 'Ah! if but one of them could be now recovered!'[238]

Prayers

In the early 1920s two granddaughters of Jane Austen's brother Charles sold, through Sotheby's, the manuscripts of three prayers, which they, and Sotheby's, declared to be by Jane Austen. The manuscripts are now held at the F. W. Olin Library at Mills College, Oakland, California.

The prayers are written on two separate sheets of paper, each folded in half to make four pages for writing on. The first sheet, watermarked 1818, offers four manuscript pages of 235 mm × 187 mm. There are marks showing that at one time the paper was folded over into three, and fainter signs of further folds. The first page is headed 'Evening Prayer—' and the prayer itself extends over three of the four pages. On the fourth page, written sideways in what might have been the centre of the centre fold, in a different hand, is a note, 'Prayers Composed by my ever dear Sister Jane'. Beneath this, in pencil (now very faint) is, in yet another hand, the name 'Charles Austen'. The other sheet of paper is slightly larger, making four pages of 227 mm × 212 mm. The paper is watermarked with an elaborate design with plumes and fleur de lys, common at the time and not indicative of a particular year. This paper too has

238 Southam, '*Sir Charles Grandison*', p. 11; for further detail on 'Sir Charles Grandison' see Appendix C.

foldmarks, but, like the paper itself, the marks in no way match those of the other sheet. It has no title, but contains two prayers, each covering two of the four pages; the paper has been folded out both ways, but since the handwriting changes half-way through one of the prayers it is reasonable to assume that this was the one written second. All three prayers are written without correction.

In his article in the *Times Literary Supplement* of 14 January 1926, listing the Prayers among 'manuscripts by or relating to Jane Austen . . . recently . . . dispersed', R. W. Chapman, who had advised Charles Austen's granddaughters on the sale, included as item 18 '(a) 'Prayers composed by my own [*sic*] dear Sister Jane . . . in the hand of Cassandra Austen (?)' and '(b) Prayer . . . in two hands, of which the first is Henry Austen's (the author?) and the second is doubtful'. Chapman was careful therefore not to claim Jane Austen's authorship of the prayers on the second of the two sheets, and for the first he simply reproduced the annotation, with its potentially misleading plural word 'Prayers'.

This account by Chapman, concerned at the time with the sale of the manuscripts rather than with recording research about them, contains some inaccuracies, including in the wording of the annotation on the first sheet, and it does not identify the annotator; it seems clear that Chapman was working from memory rather than from direct view of the manuscripts. When he reproduced all three prayers in the *Minor Works* (1954) – implicitly as Jane Austen's, notwithstanding his earlier suggestion that the second and third prayers were by Henry – he reproduced the wording of the annotation correctly but stated that the hand in the first manuscript was 'probably – almost certainly? – Cassandra's' while the second is 'partly in a hand which I think may be Henry Austen's, partly in a hand which has been thought by experts to be JA's own'.[239] By now, in addition to his own notes from the 1920s, he had the rather doubtful advantage of the first published version of the manuscripts. These had been acquired by the Californian William Matson Roth, who published them for the first time in 1940 in a limited edition with

[239] Chapman, *Minor Works*, p. 453.

Colt Press in San Francisco (of which Roth was a director). The edition is not a scholarly one: it reproduces the prayers in a 'presentation' format, in capital letters in black and red type, and it adjusts punctuation as well as presentation. It does however reproduce the second page of the third prayer – the page it claims is in Jane Austen's own hand – in facsimile. Finally, in 2007, two separate editions of the prayers were published in more accurate versions taken from the xeroxes of the original manuscripts.[240]

In a 1996 article Bruce Stovel revisited the problem of the handwriting. He too believed the final hand was Jane Austen's, and, although he was unsure of the identity of the copyist or copyists of the rest, he thought the matter unimportant since there was no reason to doubt the attribution to Jane Austen of all three, based on what he took to be Charles Austen's words on the back of the first manuscript, applying to all; he simply assumed that 'they were copied out, at two different times, by a combination of the Austen brothers and sisters'.[241]

Deirdre Le Faye believed that, of the two hands present, the first was that of Jane Austen's eldest brother James, and the second that of Cassandra, not Jane. The very likely identification of the writing as James's is important in dating the manuscripts, since James died in December 1819 after several months of very poor health. Le Faye plausibly speculated that he had begun to copy out some of his sister's prayers in late 1818 or early 1819 (using, for the first prayer, new paper watermarked 1818) as a tribute to her after her death, and that Cassandra, ever concerned to preserve her sister's work, may have finished a task which he became too ill to complete.

Accepting the attribution to Jane Austen, as with 'Grandison' biographers and critics have used the works to comment on her other writing – though not as much as one might expect, since

[240] Brian Southam, *Jane Austen: A Students' Guide to the Later Manuscripts* (London: Concord Books, 2007), pp. 89–92; *Three Prayers and a Poem by Jane Austen* (Godmersham: The Friends of Godmersham Church, 2007).

[241] Bruce Stovel, '"The Sentient Target of Death": Jane Austen's Prayers', in *Jane Austen's Business: Her World and her Profession*, ed. Juliet McMaster and Bruce Stovel (London: Palgrave Macmillan, 1996), p. 192.

relatively few critics have addressed in detail the religious aspect of Austen's oeuvre. G. H. Tucker saw the prayers affirming the fact that, 'From her childhood until her death, Jane Austen's life and religious beliefs were governed by the rites and teachings of the Anglican church',[242] while Michael Giffin, who stressed that Austen was 'an Anglican author who wrote Christian stories', used the prayers together with the logic developed in the novels to argue that she was 'acutely aware of the fallen condition of her self and her characters'.[243] Bruce Stovel also drew attention to the relationship between the prayers and the novels. Since the prayers tell us that Jane Austen was a devout Christian, they 'suggest that the novels are more suffused with religious feelings than we might have thought': for example, Marianne's speech of contrition in *Sense and Sensibility* relates to the assumption in the prayers that religious and moral duties coincide.[244] Marilyn Butler too read the difficult (for the reader) humbling of Marianne in the light of Jane Austen's prayers for humility and self-knowledge.[245] Gene Koppel quoted the words 'we have perhaps sinned against thee and against our fellow-creatures in many instances of which we have no remembrance', noting Austen's emphasis on flawed perception.[246]

But are the prayers indisputably by Jane Austen? As we have seen, Chapman, who was recording the appearance and sale of these items, made no such claim for the two prayers on the second sheet of paper in his first account in the *TLS*; and even in *Minor Works* his language is ambiguous. In trying to reach a conclusion about authorship we have carefully inspected the original manuscripts, have considered the handwriting and the possible circumstances of composition, and have examined the internal evidence provided by the content of the prayers themselves.

242 George Holbert Tucker, *Jane Austen: The Woman* (New York: St Martin's Press, 1994), p. 199.

243 Michael Giffin, *Jane Austen and Religion: Salvation and Society in Georgian England* (Basingstoke: Palgrave, 2002), p. 27.

244 Stovel, '"The Sentient Target of Death"', p. 192.

245 Butler, *Jane Austen and the War of Ideas*, p. 192.

246 Gene Koppel, *The Religious Dimension of Jane Austen's Novels* (Ann Arbor, MI: UMI Research Press, 1988), p. 52.

We agree with Le Faye that the hand of the prayer on the first sheet, and the first three pages of the second sheet containing the second and third prayers, is likely to be that of James Austen – though written on separate occasions, with the hand of the second sheet of paper showing more haste (or less health) than the first – and also that the hand of the last part of the third prayer is that of Cassandra. And therefore we agree that the first prayer must have been copied, or written out, by James, between late 1818 (the earliest possible date given the watermark) and late 1819 (when James became too sick to undertake such a task), while the second and third prayers could have been written, and the copying begun, at any time before late 1819.

The inscription, 'Prayers composed by my ever dear Sister Jane', on the first sheet, with the pencil identification of 'Charles Austen', offers several puzzles. The inscription does seem very close, in sentiment and in the appearance of the handwriting, to a note on the back of a letter from Jane to Charles dated 6 April 1817: 'My last letter from dearest Jane – C-JA [that is, Charles-John Austen]'. However, even if we accept from this that the inscription on the first sheet of prayers is in Charles's hand, it is impossible to tell when it was made, or what authority it confers: the manuscript could have come into Charles's possession after James's death (he attended James's funeral at Steventon in December 1819) or after Cassandra's death in 1845, when Jane Austen's manuscripts were distributed around the family according to Cassandra's wishes. At this point Cassy Esten, on her father Charles's behalf, was sorting out her aunt Cassandra's effects; it was a time when memories might have been fading. Moreover, it is impossible to be sure what the inscription on the first prayer refers to: the mention of 'Prayers' in the plural suggests more than one prayer, but there is nothing other than the coincidence of handwriting to indicate that it is referring to the two sheets of paper now held together, especially since they are of different sizes, and the folds in the papers are entirely distinct. So, even if Charles did correctly identify the first prayer as the composition of his 'ever dear Sister Jane', there is only the most circumstantial evidence to associate the attribution with the second paper.

The internal evidence of the prayers is equally inconclusive. Certainly they have a lot in common with each other, but chiefly in the sense in which they are conventional variations on a familiar Church of England formula. Each prayer is followed by the beginning of the Lord's Prayer, so that worshippers are to continue in a known vein and enter or re-enter an accepted framework; each was clearly intended to form part of a longer session of evening worship.

The prayers are liberally pious, examining personal conduct and passing judgement only on the self, and, responsibly, they refer out to the wider world. They echo in simplified extemporized form aspects of the intercessional collects of the *Book of Common Prayer*. They were almost certainly written for family rather than congregational use since they do not fit into the pattern of the Church's Evensong, in which the Lord's Prayer comes early on among the said or sung responses, with intercessions occurring later.

The six novels present no examples of communal family and servant prayers, and the episode in the chapel at Sotherton in *Mansfield Park* suggests that the custom was not very common in the Regency period. In Jane Austen's surviving letters there is only one reference to home worshipping, in a letter of 24–25 October 1808 from Southampton to Cassandra in Godmersham; this mentions psalms not newly created prayers. Her two teenaged Knight nephews were on a visit after the death of their mother and on Sunday, after a church service which included a very apposite sermon for the bereaved children, Jane Austen amused them with excursions on the river and games like riddles and conundrums: 'In the evening we had the Psalms and Lessons, and a sermon at home, to which they were very attentive; but you will not expect to hear that they did not return to conundrums the moment it *was over*,' she reported.[247] Deirdre Le Faye has suggested that the prayers

[247] 24–25 October 1808, *Letters*, p. 151.

were written by Jane Austen shortly after this time: in the rainy January of 1809 when for two Sundays running the Austen ladies were unable to go to church.[248] This begs the question as to why, if they wished to worship at home together, they did not simply open the Book of Common Prayer and read psalms as they did with the Knight boys. On many other occasions after they moved to Chawton, the Austens did not attend Sunday church, usually because one or other of them was ailing, on 14 February 1813, for example. By the end of March 1817 Jane Austen was too ill to attend at all and it remains possible that she wrote the prayers at this point, although no one in the family, including Henry, who was much concerned the following year to stress her piety, made reference to such composition. Fanny Knight, who recorded her own churchgoing with some consistency, referred to *reading* prayers in her diary entry from Chawton for Sunday, 30 August 1807, at a time when Jane Austen, Cassandra and their mother were visiting from Southampton: 'We none of us went to Church but read prayers in the morning & the Psalms and lessons in the afternoon with a sermon.'

Contemporary published works on family prayers stress that they should be recited by the master of the house or, in his absence, the mistress or oldest male member. The preface in *The Family Prayer-Book: or Prayers to be used in Families* (1743, fourth edition 1797 in Bath) states: 'The Master of the Family is to read the Service himself; kneeling down in a reverent Posture', adding, 'in the Absence of a Master, let the devout Mistress . . . read the same'. In Brunton's *Self-Control* the man of the house, seating himself 'in a patriarchal-looking chair', extemporizes prayers with family and servants in attendance,[249] while in Hannah More's exemplary tract *The History of Charles Jones* (1790) the good mother assembles her children and reads 'with great solemnity' a short form of

248 30 January 1809, *Letters*, p. 171.
249 Mary Brunton, *Self-Control* (1811), ch. 22.

prayers given her by the clergyman and ending with the Lord's Prayer.

It seems unlikely that Jane Austen would have been composing prayers such as these in her father's lifetime; after his death it would still be unusual for her to compose or perhaps even read communal prayers when her mother and/or her elder sister were with her. Occasionally a daughter did read (if not compose) such prayers. In Boswell's *Tour to the Hebrides*, when he and Dr Johnson visited Inchkenneth on a Sunday, 'Miss M'Lean [Sir Allan's daughter] read the evening service, in which we all joined.' However, Johnson must have thought this was irregular practice, since, in the Latin poem he composed in praise of the experience ('Insula Sancti Kennethi'), he wrote 'Respect for the gods was here also the concern. / What though a woman handled the books of the priest— / Pure hearts make prayers lawful', which perhaps expresses some uneasiness.[250]

In terms of attribution, these are the works that most trouble us. Those poems for which we only have family evidence of authorship yet sit neatly, in style and content, into the group of verses known to be by Jane Austen. With 'Sir Charles Grandison' – a children's play based on a novel we know she admired and knew very well – a range of collaboration possibilities between Jane Austen and her niece Anna are plausible. The prayers are utterly conventional in content, and there is nothing in their context (either in terms of Jane Austen's own writings, or the habits of the Austens and their immediate contemporaries in the exercise of their religious duty) to suggest her authorship; if it had not been for the scribbled annotation probably by her brother Charles – an attribution itself unsupported by any other family evidence through to the 1920s – we would not be considering any of these prayers as even possibly by Jane Austen. Charles's note is highly significant, and it does indeed

[250] James Boswell, *The Life of Samuel Johnson*, ed. George Birkbeck Hill, revised and enlarged edition by L. F. Powell, 6 vols. (Oxford: Clarendon Press, 1964–71), vol. 5, p. 325. Translation by Derek Hughes.

raise the strong possibility that the prayer on one of the two sheets of paper is indeed hers; but, given the lack of any supporting evidence of any kind, we have decided to place all three in an Appendix, rather than in the main body of our volume.

Other attributions

Jane Austen liked to make and keep copies of poems she enjoyed, and this has caused some confusion over the years. Two of particular interest are by Lord Byron and Charlotte Smith and in both Jane Austen made small adjustments either through intention or carelessness in the phrasing of the original. For example, 'Lines of Lord Byron, in the Character of Buonaparte' substitutes 'bloom' for Byron's 'gloom' in the opening line, 'FAREWELL to the Land where the gloom of my Glory', and 'Victory' for 'Liberty' in the lines 'Farewell to thee, France—but when Liberty rallies / Once more in thy regions, remember me then'.[251] In Charlotte Smith's 'Kalendar of Flora', Smith's 'freckled cowslips' become Austen's 'pockled cowslips' (introducing a homely dialect word to accompany the country flowers), and Smith's phrase 'Sheltering the coot's' becomes Austen's 'Near the lone coot's'.[252]

These and other poems she copied out were at least never attributed to Jane Austen herself, but some less prominent verses were so until their sources were found, as has happened recently with 'Charade by a Lady', of which a manuscript in Austen's hand is held at Winchester College; it is now known to be a riddle by the occasional poet, Catherine Maria Fanshawe. 'On the Universities', the manuscript of which is held in the Henry W. and Albert A. Berg Collection at New York Public Library, was for a time considered to be by Austen and appears among Austen's poems in

[251] The poem was transcribed and described by B. C. Southam in 'Was Jane Austen a Bonapartist?', *Collected Reports of the Jane Austen Society 1949–2000* (2000), pp. 312–20; see introduction to the Cambridge *Persuasion*, p. xxviii.

[252] Deirdre Le Faye, *TLS*, 27 April 1990, p. 445; *Notes & Queries*, 244 or n.s. 46.4 (December 1999), pp. 450–1.

Minor Works (1954, p. 447). It was discovered that the lines were an anonymous epigram reproduced in a number of poetry collections from about 1790, including the often-reprinted *Elegant Extracts* (a very popular, developing collection of verse which circulated in many editions towards the end of the eighteenth century; 'On the Universities' appears from about 1790 onwards).[253] The poem 'On Captain Foote's Marriage with Miss Patton' was added by B. C. Southam to his 1967 revision of Chapman's *Minor Works* (p. 452) despite the fact that it was reproduced in the *Memoir* with the statement that the author was Jane's uncle, James Leigh Perrot. We reproduce the poem on p. 732 because of its interesting connection with Jane Austen's poem 'On the Marriage of Mr. Gell of East Bourn to Miss Gill'.

One poem remains a matter of doubt. 'Sigh Lady Sigh' was recently discovered, written in pencil, upside down, on the inside front cover and title page of a copy of Ann Murry's *Mentoria: or, The Young Ladies Instructor*, owned by Jane Austen in the 1790s and presented by her to Anna Lefroy in 1801. The title page bears the inscription 'Jane Anna Eliz:th Austen / 1801' in Jane Austen's hand, and 'From her Aunt Jane', in another hand. Anna in turn gave the book to her eldest daughter Anna Jemima Lefroy. Deirdre Le Faye has discussed the possibility that this poem was written by Austen in the late 1790s.[254] We have looked at the manuscript, which is held by the Jane Austen Memorial Trust at Chawton Cottage. Since the handwriting is difficult to identify with certainty, and the poem is written on the title page in a contrary direction to the dedication from 'Aunt Jane', we think that, while Jane Austen's authorship remains a possibility, it seems more likely that the lines were written neither by Jane Austen nor by Anna Lefroy but perhaps (since the writing seems more typical of the late eighteenth or early nineteenth

[253] *Elegant Extracts: Or Useful and Entertaining Pieces of Poetry, Selected for the Improvement of Youth, in Speaking, Reading, Thinking, Composing; and in the Conduct of Life* (1791), p. 598.

[254] Deirdre Le Faye, 'New Marginalia in Jane Austen's Books,' *The Book Collector*, 49.2 (Summer 2000), pp. 222–6.

century than of any later period) by some other contemporary, for whom the book and dedication would have had less value. Since the question remains open, however, we have included the poem in Appendix F.

There has also, over the years, been some confusion in attribution of two notes of composition of Jane Austen's novels. Both documents are now held in the Morgan Library, making comparison relatively straightforward. The longer, and probably later, of the notes is signed 'C. E. A.', indicating Cassandra Austen. The shorter, and probably earlier (in that it contains some corrections which appear in fair copy in the C. E. A. version), has been thought to be Jane Austen's own account of the dates of preparation of her novels. However, it is clear that the handwriting of both notes is the same, and the use of the word 'Persuasion' to describe Austen's last novel – a title which was not given to the novel in Austen's lifetime – seems conclusively to indicate that the note was written after her death.[255]

*

The manuscripts printed in this volume include fair copies, unfinished works, family poems, riddles, scraps and oddments, all that is left of the words of the adult Jane Austen outside the novels and letters. Most of her manuscripts she herself kept, guarding them throughout a lifetime of house moves and handing them on to Cassandra, who continued to value them as a part of the record of a remarkable sister. We have been privileged to see the originals of almost all of these manuscripts now scattered in Switzerland, the USA and Canada, as well as in Bath, Cambridge, Chawton, Leeds, London, Oxford, Swindon and Winchester, and we have personally examined every one of the copy texts for this volume.

[255] It has been suggested that Jane Austen might have contributed to a playlet of three characters concerning child-rearing (not in Austen's hand), found among the Austen-Leigh family papers, but this seems very unlikely. See Deirdre Le Faye, '"The Business of Mothering": Two Austenian Dialogues,' *The Book Collector*, 32.3 (Autumn 1983), pp. 296–314, 307, 311.

We hope that we have described the works in such a way that the sense of the documents as original artefacts remains for readers, and that in addition we have provided enough historical and cultural context to allow them to illuminate Jane Austen's life and major novels. In converting manuscript into print, we have tried to avoid over-stabilizing what are in some cases shifting texts and destroying their 'aura'.[256]

This is the last of the nine volumes of the Cambridge Jane Austen; in providing for the first time a scholarly, fully annotated edition of the manuscripts of her adult life, it completes the picture – as far as we now have it – of the work of one of the greatest of British novelists.

[256] Walter Benjamin, 'The Work of Art in the Age of Mechanical Reproduction', in *Illuminations*, ed. Hannah Arendt, trans. Harry Zohn (London: Jonathan Cape, 1970), p. 223. Originally in *Zeitschrift fur Sozialforschung*, 5.1 (1936).

The Fiction

1.

Letter 1.

Lady Susan Vernon to Mr Vernon. —

Langford, Decr —

My dear Brother

I can no longer refuse myself the pleasure of profitting by your kind invitation when we last parted, of spending some weeks with you at Churchill, & therefore if quite convenient to you & Mrs Vernon to receive me at present, I shall hope within a few days to be introduced to a Sister, whom I have so long desired to be ac:quainted with. — My kind friends here are most affectionately urgent with me to prolong my stay, but their hospitable & chearful dispositions lead them

1 The first page of 'Lady Susan'.

Lady Susan[1]

LETTER I.

Lady Susan Vernon[2] to Mr. Vernon.—

Langford, Decr.—

My dear Brother

I can no longer refuse myself the pleasure of profitting by your kind invitation when we last parted, of spending some weeks with you at Churchill,[3] & therefore if quite convenient to you and Mrs. Vernon to receive me at present, I shall hope within a few days to be introduced to a sister,[4] whom I have so long desired to be acquainted with.—My kind friends here are most affectionately urgent with me to prolong my stay, but their hospitable & chearful dispositions lead them too much into society for my present situation & state of mind;[5] & I impatiently look forward to the hour when I shall be admitted into your delightful retirement.[6] I long to be made known to your dear little Children, in whose hearts I shall be very eager to secure an interest.—I shall soon have occasion for all my fortitude, as I am on the point of separation from my own daughter.—The long illness of her dear Father prevented my paying her that attention which Duty & affection equally dictated, & I have but too much reason to fear that the Governess to whose care I consigned her, was unequal to the charge.—I have therefore resolved on placing her at one of the best Private Schools in Town,[7] where I shall have an opportunity of leaving her myself, in my way to you. I am determined you see, not to be denied admittance at Churchill.—It would indeed give me most painful sensations to know that it were not in your power to receive me.—Y[r]. most obliged & affec: Sister

S. Vernon.[8]—

LETTER 2[d].

Lady Susan to M[rs]. Johnson

Langford

You were mistaken my dear Alicia, in supposing me fixed at this place for the rest of the winter. It greives me to say how greatly you were mistaken, for I have seldom spent three months more agreably than those which have just flown away.—At present nothing goes smoothly.—The Females of the Family are united against me.—You foretold how it would be, when I first came to Langford; & Manwaring is so uncommonly pleasing that I was not without apprehensions myself. I remember saying to myself as I drove to the House, "I like this Man; pray Heaven no harm come of it!"—But I was determined to be discreet, to bear in mind my being only four months a widow, & to be as quiet as possible,—and I have been so;—my dear Creature, I have admitted no one's attentions but Manwaring's, I have avoided all general flirtation whatever, I have distinguished no Creature besides of all the Numbers resorting hither, except Sir James Martin, on whom I bestowed a little notice in order to detach him from Miss Manwaring. But if the World could know my motive <u>there</u>, they would honour me.—I have been called an unkind Mother, but it was the sacred impulse of maternal affection,

line 10: 'Alicia' written over something else, now illegible.

it was the advantage of my Daughter that led me on; & if that Daughter were not the greatest simpleton on Earth, I might have been rewarded for my Exertions as I ought.—Sir James did make proposals to me for Frederica[1]—but Frederica, who was born to be the torment of my life, chose to set herself so violently against the match, that I thought it better to lay aside the scheme for the present.—I have more than once repented that I did not marry him myself, & were he but one degree less contemptibly weak I certainly should, but I must own myself rather romantic[2] in that respect, & that Riches only, will not satisfy me. The event of all this is very provoking.—Sir James is gone, Maria highly incensed, and M^rs. Manwaring insupportably jealous;—so jealous in short, & so enraged against me, that in the fury of her temper I should not be surprised at her appealing to her Guardian if she had the liberty of addressing him—but there your Husband stands my friend, & the kindest, most amiable action of his Life was his throwing her off[3] forever on her Marriage.—Keep up his resentment therefore I charge you.—We are now in a sad state; no house was ever more altered; the whole family are at war, & Manwaring scarcely dares speak to me. It is time for me to be gone; I have therefore determined on leaving them, and shall spend I hope a comfortable day with you in Town within this week.—If I am as little in favour with M^r. Johnson as ever, you must come to me at N°. 10 Wigmore S^t.[4]—but I hope this may not be the case, for as M^r. Johnson with all his faults is a Man to whom that great word "Respectable" is always given, & I am known to be so intimate with his wife, his slighting me has an awkward Look.—I take Town in my way to that insupportable spot, a Country Village,[5] for I am really going to Churchill.—Forgive me my dear friend, it is my last resource. Were there another place in England open to me, I would prefer it.—Charles Vernon is my aversion, & I am afraid of his wife.—At Churchill however I must remain till I have something better in veiw. My young Lady accompanies me to Town, where I shall deposit her under the care of Miss Summers in Wigmore Street, till she becomes a little more reasonable. She will make good connections there, as the Girls are all of the best Families.—The price is immense, & much beyond what I can ever attempt to pay.[6]—Adeiu. I will send you a line, as soon as I arrive in Town.—Yours Ever,

S. Vernon.

LETTER 3.

Mrs. Vernon to Lady De Courcy.

Churchill

My dear Mother

I am very sorry to tell you that it will not be in our power to keep our promise of spending the Christmas with you;[1] & we are prevented that happiness by a circumstance which is not likely to make us any amends.—Lady Susan in a letter to her Brother, has declared her intention of visiting us almost immediately—& as such a visit is in all probability merely an affair of convenience, it is impossible to conjecture it's length. I was by no means prepared for such an event, nor can I now account for her Ladyship's conduct.—Langford appeared so exactly the place for her in every respect, as well from the elegant & expensive stile of Living there, as from her particular attachment to Mrs. Manwaring, that I was very far from expecting so speedy a distinction, tho' I always imagined from her increasing friendship for us since her Husband's death, that we should at some future period be obliged to receive her.— Mr. Vernon I think was a great deal too kind to her, when he was in Staffordshire.[2] Her behaviour to him, independant of her general Character, has been so inexcusably artful & ungenerous since our marriage was first in agitation, that no one less amiable & mild than himself could have overlooked it at all; & tho' as his Brother's widow & in narrow circumstances it was proper to render her pecuniary assistance, I cannot help thinking his pressing invitation to her to visit us at Churchill perfectly unnecessary.—Disposed however as he always is to think the best of every one, her display of Greif, & professions of regret, & general resolutions of prudence were sufficient to soften his heart, & make him really confide in her sincerity. But as for myself, I am still unconvinced; & plausibly as her Ladyship has now written, I cannot make up my mind, till I better understand her real meaning in coming to us.—You may guess therefore my dear Madam with what feelings I look forward to her arrival. She will have occasion for all those attractive Powers for which she is celebrated, to gain any share of my regard; & I shall certainly endeavour to guard myself against their influence, if not accompanied by something more substantial.—She expresses a most eager desire of being acquainted with me, & makes very gracious mention of my children, but I am not quite weak enough to suppose a woman who has behaved with inattention if not unkindness to her own child, should be attached to any of mine. Miss Vernon is to be placed at a school in Town before her Mother comes to us, which I am glad of, for her sake & my own. It must be to her advantage to be separated from her Mother; & a girl of sixteen who has received so wretched an education would not be a very desirable companion here.—Reginald has long wished I know to see this captivating Lady Susan, & we shall depend on his joining our party soon.—I am glad to hear that my Father continues so well, & am, with best Love &c, Cath Vernon.—

LETTER 4.

Mr. De Courcy to Mrs. Vernon.

Parklands

My dear Sister

I congratulate you & Mr. Vernon on being about to receive into your family, the most accomplished coquette[1] in England.—As a very distinguished Flirt, I have been always taught to consider her; but it has lately fallen in my way to hear some particulars of her conduct at Langford, which prove that she does not confine herself to that sort of honest flirtation which satisfies most people, but aspires to the more delicious gratification of making a whole family miserable.—By her behaviour to Mr. Manwaring, she gave jealousy & wretchedness to his wife, & by her attentions to a young Man previously attached to Mr. Manwaring's sister, deprived an amiable girl of her Lover.—I learnt all this from a Mr. Smith now in this neighbourhood—(I have dined with him at Hurst and Wilford)—who is just come from Langford, where he was a fortnight in the house with her Ladyship, & who is therefore well qualified to make the communication.—What a Woman she must be!—I long to see her, & shall certainly accept your kind invitation, that I may form some idea of those bewitching powers which can do so much—engaging at the same time & in the same house the affections of two Men who were neither of them at liberty to bestow them—& all this, without the charm of youth.—I am glad to find that Miss Vernon does not come with her Mother to Churchill, as she has not even manners to recommend her, & according to Mr. Smith's account, is equally dull & proud. Where Pride &

line 22: 'may' inserted before 'form' at beginning of MS line. // line 29: 'heavy' deleted; 'dull' inserted above line.

Stupidity unite, there can be no dissimulation worthy notice, & Miss Vernon shall be consigned to unrelenting contempt; but by all that I can gather, Lady Susan possesses a degree of captivating Deceit which it must be pleasing to witness & detect. I shall be with you very soon, & am your affec. Brother

R De Courcy.—

LETTER 5.

Lady Susan to M^rs^. Johnson

Churchill

I received your note my dear Alicia, just before I left Town, & rejoice to be assured that M^r^. Johnson suspected nothing of your engagement the evening before; it is undoubtedly better to deceive him entirely;—since he will be stubborn, he must be tricked.—I arrived here in safety, & have no reason to complain of my reception from M^r^. Vernon; but I confess myself not equally satisfied with the behaviour of his Lady.—She is perfectly well bred indeed, & has the air of a woman of fashion, but her manners are not such as can persuade me of her being prepossessed in my favour.—I wanted her to be delighted at seeing me—I was as amiable as possible on the occasion—but all in vain—she does not like me.—To be sure, when we consider that I did take some pains to prevent my Brother-in-law's marrying her, this want of cordiality is not very surprising—& yet it shews an illiberal & vindictive spirit to resent a project which influenced me six years ago, & which never succeeded at last.—I am sometimes half disposed to repent that I did not let Charles buy Vernon Castle when we were obliged to sell it, but it was a trying circumstance, especially as the sale took place exactly at the time of his marriage—& everybody ought to respect the delicacy of those feelings, which could not endure that my Husband's Dignity should be lessened by his younger brother's having possession of the Family Estate.[1]—Could Matters have been so arranged as to prevent the necessity of our leaving the Castle, could we have lived with Charles & kept him single, I should have been very far from persuading my husband to dispose of it elsewhere;—but Charles was then on the point of marrying Miss De Courcy, & the event has justified me. Here are Children in abundance, & what benefit could have accrued to me from his purchasing Vernon?—My having prevented it, may perhaps have given his wife an unfavourable impression—but where there is a disposition to dislike a motive will never be wanting; & as to money-matters, it has not with-held him from being very useful to me. I really have a regard for him, he is so easily imposed on!

The house is a good one, the Furniture fashionable, & everything announces plenty & elegance.—Charles is very rich I am sure; when a Man has once got his name in a Banking House he rolls in money.[2] But they do not know what to do with their fortune, keep very little company, & never go to Town but on business.—We shall be as stupid as possible.—I mean to win my Sister in law's heart through her Children; I know all their names already, & am going to attach myself with the greatest sensibility[3] to one in particular, a young Frederic, whom I take on my lap & sigh over for his dear Uncle's sake.—

Poor Manwaring!—I need not tell you how much I miss him—how perpetually he is in my Thoughts.—I found a dismal Letter from him on my arrival here, full of complaints of his wife & sister, & lamentations on the cruelty of his fate. I passed off the letter as his wife's, to the

Vernons, & when I write to him, it must be under cover to you.[4]—

Yours Ever, S V.—

LETTER 6.

M^rs^. Vernon to M^r^. De Courcy

Churchill

Well my dear Reginald, I have seen this dangerous creature, & must give you some description of her, tho' I hope you will soon be able to form your own judgement. She is really excessively pretty.—However you may chuse to question the allurements of a Lady no longer young, I must for my own part declare that I have seldom seen so lovely a woman as Lady Susan.—She is delicately fair, with fine grey eyes & dark eyelashes; & from her appearance one would not suppose her more than five & twenty, tho' she must in fact be ten years older.—I was certainly not disposed to admire her, tho' always hearing she was beautiful; but I cannot help feeling that she possesses an uncommon union of Symmetry, Brilliancy & Grace.[1]—Her address[2] to me was so gentle, frank & even affectionate, that if I had not known how much she has always disliked me for marrying M^r^. Vernon, and that we had never met before, I should have imagined her an attached friend.—One is apt I beleive to connect assurance of manner with coquetry, & to expect that an impudent address will necessarily attend an impudent mind;—at least I was myself prepared for an improper degree of confidence in Lady Susan; but her countenance is absolutely sweet, & her voice & manner winningly mild.—I am sorry it is so, for what is this but Deceit?—Unfortunately one knows her too well.—She is clever & agreable, has all that knowledge of the world which makes conversation easy, & talks very well, with a happy command of Language, which is too often used I beleive to make

Black appear White.—She has already almost persuaded me of her being warmly attached to her daughter, tho' I have so long been convinced of the contrary. She speaks of her with so much tenderness & anxiety, lamenting so bitterly the neglect of her education, which she represents however as wholly unavoidable, that I am forced to recollect how many successive Springs her Ladyship spent in Town,[3] while her daughter was left in Staffordshire to the care of servants or a Governess very little better,[4] to prevent my beleiving whatever she says.

If her manners have so great an influence on my resentful heart, you may guess how much more strongly they operate on M^{r}. Vernon's generous temper.—I wish I could be as well satisfied as he is, that it was really her choice to leave Langford for Churchill; & if she had not staid three months there before she discovered that her friends' manner of Living did not suit her situation or feelings, I might have beleived that concern for the loss of such a Husband as M^{r}. Vernon, to whom her own behaviour was far from unexceptionable, might for a time make her wish for retirement. But I cannot forget the length of her visit to the Manwarings, & when I reflect on the different mode of Life which she led with them, from that to which she must now submit, I can only suppose that the wish of establishing her reputation by following, tho' late, the path of propriety, occasioned her removal from a family where she must in reality have been particularly happy. Your friend M^{r}. Smith's story however cannot be quite true, as she corresponds regularly with M^{rs}. Manwaring; at any rate it must be exaggerated;—it is scarcely possible that two men should be so grossly deceived by her at once.—Yrs &c Cath Vernon.

line 19: 'not' deleted; 'far from' inserted above line. // line 30: 'ath' inserted after 'C' in 'Cath Vernon'.

LETTER 7.

Lady Susan to Mrs. Johnson

Churchill

My dear Alicia

You are very good in taking notice of Frederica, & I am grateful for it as a mark of your friendship; but as I cannot have a doubt of the warmth of that friendship, I am far from exacting so heavy a sacrifice. She is a stupid girl, & has nothing to recommend her.—I would not therefore on any account have you encumber one moment of your precious time by sending for her to Edward St.,[1] especially as every visit is so many hours deducted from the grand affair of Education, which I really wish to be attended to, while she remains with Miss Summers.—I want her to play & sing with some portion of Taste, & a good deal of assurance, as she has <u>my</u> hand & arm, & a tolerable voice. <u>I</u> was so much indulged in my infant years that I was never obliged to attend to anything, & consequently am without those accomplishments which are now necessary to finish a pretty Woman. Not that I am an advocate for the prevailing fashion of acquiring a perfect knowledge in all the Languages Arts & Sciences;[2]—it is throwing time away;—to be Mistress of French, Italian, German, Music, Singing, Drawing &c will gain a Woman some applause, but will not add one Lover to her list. Grace & Manner after all are of the greatest importance. I do not mean therefore that Frederica's acquirements should be more than superficial, & I flatter myself that she will not remain long enough at school to understand anything thoroughly.[3]—I hope to see her the wife of Sir James within a twelvemonth.—You know on what I ground my hope, & it is certainly a good foundation, for

line 15: short illegible word deleted between '<u>my</u>' and 'hand; '<u>my</u>' possibly written over other letters.

School must be very humiliating to a girl of Frederica's age;[4] & by the bye, you had better not invite her any more on that account, as I wish her to find her situation as unpleasant as possible.—I am sure of Sir James at any time, & could make him renew his application by a Line.—I shall trouble you meanwhile to prevent his forming any other attachment when he comes to Town;—ask him to your House occasionally, & talk to him about Frederica that he may not forget her.—

Upon the whole I commend my own conduct in this affair extremely, and regard it as a very happy mixture of circumspection & tenderness. Some Mothers would have insisted on their daughter's accepting so great an offer on the first overture, but I could not answer it to myself to force Frederica into a marriage from which her heart revolted; & instead of adopting so harsh a measure, merely propose to make it her own choice by rendering her thoroughly uncomfortable till she does accept him.[1] But enough of this tiresome girl.—

You may well wonder how I contrive to pass my time here—& for the first week, it was most insufferably dull.—Now however, we begin to mend;—our party is enlarged by M^rs. Vernon's brother, a handsome young Man, who promises me some amusement. There is something about him that rather interests me, a sort of sauciness, of familiarity which I shall teach him to correct. He is lively & seems clever, & when I have inspired him with greater respect for me than his sister's kind offices have implanted, he may be an agreable Flirt.— There is exquisite pleasure in subduing an insolent spirit, in making a person pre-determined to dislike, acknowledge one's superiority.—I have disconcerted him already by my calm reserve; & it shall be my endeavour to humble the Pride

line 15: 'a' inserted above line.

of these self-important De Courcies still lower, to convince M^rs. Vernon that her sisterly cautions have been bestowed in vain, & to persuade Reginald that she has scandalously belied[2] me. This project will serve at least to amuse me, & prevent my feeling so acutely this dreadful separation from You & all whom I love. Adeiu.

Yours Ever

S. Vernon.

LETTER 8.

M^rs. Vernon to Lady De Courcy.

Churchill

My dear Mother

You must not expect Reginald back again for some time. He desires me to tell you that the present open weather[1] induces him to accept M^r. Vernon's invitation to prolong his stay in Sussex[2] that they may have some hunting together.[3]—He means to send for his Horses immediately,[4] & it is impossible to say when you may see him in Kent.[5] I will not disguise my sentiments on this change from you my dear Madam, tho' I think you had better not communicate them to my Father, whose excessive anxiety about Reginald would subject him to an alarm which might seriously affect his health & spirits. Lady Susan has certainly contrived in the space of a fortnight to make my Brother like her.—In short, I am persuaded that his continuing here beyond the time originally fixed for his return, is occasioned as much by a degree of fascination towards her, as by the wish of hunting with M^r. Vernon, & of course I cannot receive that pleasure from the length of his visit which my Brother's company would otherwise give me.—I am indeed provoked at the artifice of this

line 26: 'this' deleted; 'a' inserted above line.

unprincipled Woman. What stronger proof of her dangerous abilities can be given, than this perversion of Reginald's judgement, which when he entered the house was so decidedly against her?—In his last letter he actually gave me some particulars of her behaviour at Langford, such as he received from a Gentleman who knew her perfectly well, which if true must raise abhorrence against her, & which Reginald himself was entirely disposed to credit.—His opinion of her I am sure, was as low as of any Woman in England, & when he first came it was evident that he considered her as one entitled neither to Delicacy[6] nor respect, & that he felt she would be delighted with the attentions of any Man inclined to flirt with her.

Her behaviour I confess has been calculated to do away such an idea, I have not detected the smallest impropriety in it,—nothing of vanity, of pretension, of Levity—& she is altogether so attractive, that I should not wonder at his being delighted with her, had he known nothing of her previous to this personal acquaintance;—but against reason, against conviction, to be so well pleased with her as I am sure he is, does really astonish me.—His admiration was at first very strong, but no more than was natural; & I did not wonder at his being struck by the gentleness & delicacy of her Manners;—but when he has mentioned her of late, it has been in terms of more extraordinary praise, & yesterday he actually said, that he could not be surprised at any effect produced on the heart of Man by such Loveliness & such Abilities; & when I lamented in reply the badness of her disposition, he observed that whatever might have been her errors, they were to be imputed to her neglected Education & early Marriage, & that she was altogether a wonderful Woman.—

line 9: 'as' inserted above line after 'low'. // line 17: 'pleasing' deleted; 'attractive' inserted above line.

This tendency to excuse her conduct, or to forget it in the warmth of admiration vexes me; & if I did not know that Reginald is too much at home at Churchill to need an invitation for lengthening his visit, I should regret M^r^. Vernon's giving him any.—

Lady Susan's intentions are of course those of absolute coquetry, or a desire of universal admiration. I cannot for a moment imagine that she has anything more serious in veiw, but it mortifies me to see a young Man of Reginald's sense duped by her at all.—I am &c.

Cath Vernon.—

LETTER 9.

M^rs^. Johnson to Lady Susan

Edward S^t^.—

My dearest Friend

I congratulate you on M^r^. De Courcy's arrival, & advise you by all means to marry him; his Father's Estate is we know considerable, & I beleive certainly entailed.[1]—Sir Reginald is very infirm, & not likely to stand in your way long.—I hear the young Man well spoken of, & tho' no one can really deserve you my dearest Susan, M^r^. De Courcy may be worth having.—Manwaring will storm of course, but you may easily pacify him. Besides, the most scrupulous point of honour could not require you to wait for <u>his</u> emancipation.—I have seen Sir James,—he came to Town for a few days last week, & called several times in Edward Street. I talked to him about you & your daughter, & he is so far from having forgotten you, that I am sure he would marry either of you with pleasure.—I gave him hopes of Frederica's relenting, & told him a great deal of her improvements.—I scolded him for making Love to Maria Manwaring; he protested that he had been only in joke, & we both laughed heartily at her disappointment, & in short were very agreable.—He is as silly as ever.—Yours faithfully

Alicia.—

LETTER 10.

Lady Susan to M[rs] Johnson

Churchill

I am much obliged to you my dear Friend, for your advice respecting M[r] De Courcy, which I know was given with the fullest conviction of it's expediency, tho' I am not quite determined on following it.—I cannot easily resolve on anything so serious as Marriage, especially as I am not at present in want of money, & might perhaps till the old Gentleman's death, be very little benefited by the match. It is true that I am vain enough to beleive it within my reach.—I have made him sensible of my power, & can now enjoy the pleasure of triumphing over a Mind prepared to dislike me, & prejudiced against all my past actions. His sister too, is I hope convinced how little the ungenerous representations of any one to the disadvantage of another will avail, when opposed to the immediate influence of Intellect & Manner.—I see plainly that she is uneasy at my progress in the good opinion of her Brother, & conclude that nothing will be wanting on her part to counteract me;—but having once made him doubt the justice of her opinion of me, I think I may defy her.—

It has been delightful to me to watch his advances towards intimacy, especially to observe his altered manner in consequence of my repressing by the calm dignity of my deportment, his insolent approach to direct familiarity.—My conduct has been equally guarded from the first, & I never behaved less like a Coquette in the whole course of my Life, tho' perhaps my desire of dominion was never more decided. I have subdued him entirely by sentiment & serious conversation, & made him I may venture to say at least half in Love with me, without the semblance of the most common-place flirtation. M^rs. Vernon's consciousness of deserving every sort of revenge that it can be in my power to inflict, for her ill-offices, could alone enable her to perceive that I am actuated by any design in behaviour so gentle & unpretending.—Let her think & act as she chuses however; I have never yet found that the advice of a Sister could prevent a young Man's being in love if he chose it.—We are advancing now towards some kind of confidence, & in short are likely to be engaged in a kind of platonic friendship.[1]—On my side, you may be sure of its' never being more, for if I were not already as much attached to another person as I can be to any one, I should make a point of not bestowing my affection on a Man who had dared to think so meanly of me.—

Reginald has a good figure, & is not unworthy the praise you have heard given him, but is still greatly inferior to our friend at Langford.—He is less polished, less insinuating than Manwaring, & is comparatively deficient in the power of saying those delightful things which put one in good humour with oneself & all the world. He is quite agreable enough however, to afford me amusement, and to make many of those hours pass very pleasantly which would be otherwise spent in endeavouring to overcome my sister in law's reserve, & listening to her Husband's insipid talk.—

Your account of Sir James is most satisfactory, & I mean to give Miss Frederica a hint of my intentions very soon.—Yours &c

S. Vernon.

LETTER 11.

Mrs. Vernon to Lady De Courcy.

I really grow quite uneasy my dearest Mother about Reginald, from witnessing the very rapid increase of Lady Susan's influence. They are now on terms of the most particular friendship, frequently engaged in long conversations together, & she has contrived by the most artful coquetry to subdue his Judgement to her own purposes.—It is impossible to see the intimacy between them, so very soon established, without some alarm, tho' I can hardly suppose that Lady Susan's veiws extend to marriage.—I wish you could get Reginald home again, under any plausible pretence. He is not at all disposed to leave us, & I have given him as many hints of my Father's precarious state of health, as common decency will allow me to do in my own house.—Her power over him must now be boundless, as she has entirely effaced all his former ill-opinion, and persuaded him not merely to forget, but to justify her conduct.— Mr. Smith's account of her proceedings at Langford, where he accused her of having made Mr. Manwaring & a young Man engaged to Miss Manwaring distractedly in love with her, which Reginald firmly beleived when he came to Churchill, is now he is persuaded only a scandalous invention. He has told me so in a warmth of manner which spoke his regret at having ever beleived the contrary himself.—

How sincerely do I greive that she ever entered this house!—I always looked forward to her coming with uneasiness—but very far was it, from originating in anxiety for Reginald.—I expected a most disagreable companion to myself, but could not imagine that my Brother would be in the smallest danger of being captivated by a Woman, with whose principles he was so well acquainted, & whose

Character he so heartily despised. If you can get him away, it will be a good thing.

Y^{rs} affec:^{ly},

Cath Vernon.

LETTER 12.

Sir Reginald De Courcy to his Son

Parklands

I know that young Men in general do not admit of any enquiry, even from their nearest relations, into affairs of the heart; but I hope my dear Reginald that you will be superior to such as allow nothing for a Father's anxiety, & think themselves privileged to refuse him their confidence & slight his advice.—You must be sensible that as an only son & the representative of an ancient Family, your conduct in Life is most interesting to your connections.[1]—In the very important concern of Marriage especially, there is everything at stake; your own happiness, that of your Parents, & the credit of your name.—I do not suppose that you would deliberately form an absolute engagement[2] of that nature without acquainting your Mother & myself, or at least without being convinced that we should approve your choice; but I cannot help fearing that you may be drawn in by the Lady who has lately attached you, to a Marriage, which the whole of your Family, far & near, must highly reprobate.

Lady Susan's age is itself a material objection, but her want of character is one so much more serious, that the difference of even twelve years becomes in comparison of small account.—Were you not blinded by a sort of fascination, it would be ridiculous in me to repeat the instances of great misconduct on her side, so very generally known.—Her neglect of her husband, her encouragement of other Men, her extravagance & dissipation were so gross & notorious, that no one could be ignorant of them at the time, nor can now have forgotten them.—To our Family, she has always been represented in softened colours by the benevolence of M^r. Charles Vernon; & yet inspite of his generous endeavours to excuse her, we know that she did, from the most selfish motives, take all possible pains to prevent his marrying Catherine.—

My Years & increasing Infirmities make me very desirous my dear Reginald, of seeing you settled in the world.—To the Fortune of your wife, the goodness of my own, will make me indifferent; but her family & character must be equally unexceptionable. When your choice is so fixed as that no objection can be made to either, I can promise you a ready & chearful consent; but it is my Duty to oppose a Match, which deep Art only could render probable, & must in the end make wretched.

It is possible that her behaviour may arise only from Vanity, or a wish of gaining the admiration of a Man whom she must imagine to be particularly prejudiced against her; but it is more likely that she should aim at something farther.—She is poor, & may naturally seek an alliance which must be advantageous to herself.—You know your own rights, and that it is out of my power to prevent your inheriting the family Estate.[3] My Ability of distressing you during my Life,[4] would be a species of revenge to which I should hardly stoop under any circumstances.—I honestly tell you my Sentiments & Intentions. I do not wish to work on your Fears, but on your Sense & Affection.—It would destroy every comfort of my Life, to know that you were married to Lady Susan Vernon. It would be the death of that honest Pride with which I have hitherto considered my son, I should blush to see him, to hear of him, to think of him.—

line 22: 'is' inserted above line after 'that it'.

I may perhaps do no good, but that of releiving my own mind, by this Letter; but I felt it my Duty to tell you that your partiality for Lady Susan is no secret to your friends, & to warn you against her.—I should be glad to hear your reasons for disbeleiving M^r. Smith's intelligence;[5]—you had no doubt of it's authenticity a month ago.—

If you can give me your assurance of having no design beyond enjoying the conversation of a clever woman for a short period, & of yeilding admiration only to her Beauty & Abilities without being blinded by them to her faults, you will restore me to happiness; but if you cannot do this, explain to me at least what has occasioned so great an alteration in your opinion of her.

I am &c

Reg^d. De Courcy.

LETTER 13.

Lady De Courcy to M^rs. Vernon—

Parklands

My dear Catherine,

Unluckily I was confined to my room when your last letter came, by a cold which affected my eyes so much as to prevent my reading it myself, so I could not refuse your Father when he offered to read it to me, by which means he became acquainted to my great vexation with all your fears about your Brother. I had intended to write to Reginald myself, as soon as my eyes would let me; to point out as well as I could the danger of an intimate acquaintance with so artful a woman as Lady Susan, to a young Man of his age & high expectations. I meant moreover to have reminded him of our being quite alone now, & very much in need of him to keep up our spirits these long winter evenings. Whether it would have done any good, can never be settled now; but I am excessively vexed that Sir Reginald should know anything of a matter which we foresaw would make him so uneasy.—He caught all your fears the moment he had read your Letter, & I am sure has not had the business out of his head since;—he wrote by the same post to Reginald, a long letter full of it all, & particularly asking an explanation of what he may have heard from Lady Susan to contradict the late[1] shocking reports. His answer came this morning, which I shall enclose to you, as I think you will like to see it; I wish it was more satisfactory, but it seems written with such a determination to think well of Lady Susan, that his assurances as to Marriage &c, do not set my heart at ease.—I say all I can however to satisfy your Father, & he is certainly less uneasy since Reginald's letter. How provoking it is my dear Catherine, that this unwelcome Guest of yours, should not only prevent our meeting this Christmas, but be the occasion of so much vexation & trouble.—Kiss the dear Children for me.—Your affec: Mother

C. De Courcy.—

LETTER 14.

M^r^ De Courcy to Sir Reginald—

Churchill

My dear Sir

I have this moment received your Letter, which has given me more astonishment than I ever felt before. I am to thank my Sister I suppose, for having represented me in such a light as to injure me in your opinion, & give you all this alarm.—I know not why she should chuse to make herself & her family uneasy by apprehending an Event, which no one but herself I can affirm, would ever have thought possible. To impute such a design to Lady Susan would be taking from her every claim to that excellent understanding which her bitterest Enemies have never denied her; & equally low must sink my pretensions to common sense, if I am suspected of matrimonial veiws in my behaviour to her.—Our difference of age must be an insuperable objection, & I entreat you my dear Sir to quiet your mind, & no longer harbour a suspicion which cannot be more injurious to your own peace, than to our Understandings.

I can have no veiw in remaining with Lady Susan than to enjoy for a short time (as you have yourself expressed it) the conversation of a Woman of high mental powers. If M^rs. Vernon would allow something to my affection for herself & her husband in the length of my visit, she would do more justice to us all;—but my Sister is unhappily prejudiced beyond the hope of conviction against Lady Susan.—From an attachment to her husband which in itself does honour to both, she cannot forgive those endeavours at preventing their union, which have been attributed to selfishness in Lady Susan. But in this case, as well as in many others, the World has most grossly injured that Lady, by supposing the worst, where the motives of her conduct have been doubtful.—

Lady Susan had heard something so materially to the disadvantage of my Sister, as to persuade her that the happiness of M^r. Vernon, to whom she was always much attached, would be absolutely destroyed by the Marriage. And this circumstance while it explains the true motive of Lady Susan's conduct, & removes all the blame which has been so lavished on her, may also convince us how little the general report of any one ought to be credited, since no character however upright, can escape the malevolence of slander. If my sister in the security of retirement, with as little opportunity as inclination to do Evil, could not avoid Censure, we must not rashly condemn those who living in the World & surrounded with temptation, should be accused of Errors which they are known to have the power of committing.—

I blame myself severely for having so easily beleived the scandalous tales invented by Charles Smith to the prejudice of Lady Susan, as I am now convinced how greatly they have traduced her. As to Mrs. Manwaring's jealousy, it was totally his own invention; & his account of her attaching Miss Manwaring's Lover was scarcely better founded. Sir James Martin had been drawn-in by that young Lady to pay her some attention, and as he is a Man of fortune, it was easy to see that her veiws extended to Marriage.—It is well-known that Miss Manwaring is absolutely on the catch for a husband, & no one therefore can pity her, for losing by the superior attractions of another woman, the chance of being able to make a worthy Man completely miserable.—Lady Susan was far from intending such a conquest, & on finding how warmly Miss Manwaring resented her Lover's defection, determined, inspite of Mr. and Mrs. Manwaring's most earnest entreaties, to leave the family.—I have reason to imagine that she did receive serious Proposals from Sir James, but her removing from Langford immediately on the discovery of his attachment, must acquit her on that article, with every Mind of common candour.[1]—You will, I am sure my dear Sir, feel the truth of this reasoning, & will hereby learn to do justice to the character of a very injured woman.—

I know that Lady Susan in coming to Churchill was governed only by the most honourable & amiable intentions.—Her prudence & economy[2] are exemplary, her regard for Mr. Vernon equal even to his deserts, & her wish of obtaining my sister's good opinion merits a better return than it has received.—As a Mother she is unexceptionable. Her solid affection for her Child is shewn by placing her in hands, where her Education will be properly attended to; but because she has not the blind & weak partiality of most Mothers, she is accused of wanting Maternal Tenderness.—Every person of Sense however will know how to value & commend her well directed affection, & will join me in wishing that Frederica Vernon may prove more worthy than she has yet done, of her Mother's tender cares.

I have now my dear Sir, written my real sentiments of Lady Susan; you will know from this Letter, how highly I admire her Abilities, & esteem her Character; but if you are not equally convinced by my full & solemn assurance that your fears have been most idly created, you will deeply mortify & distress me.—I am &c

R De Courcy. —

LETTER 15.

M^rs^. Vernon to Lady De Courcy.

Churchill

My dear Mother

I return you Reginald's letter, & rejoice with all my heart that my Father is made easy by it. Tell him so, with my congratulations;—but between ourselves, I must own it has only convinced me of my Brother's having no present intention of marrying Lady Susan—not that he is in no danger of doing so three months hence.—He gives a very plausible account of her behaviour at Langford, I wish it may be true, but his intelligence must come from herself, & I am less disposed to beleive it, than to lament the degree of intimacy subsisting between them, implied by the discussion of such a subject.

I am sorry to have incurred his displeasure, but can expect nothing better while he is so very eager in Lady Susan's justification.—He is very severe against me indeed, & yet I hope I have not been hasty in my judgement of her.—Poor Woman! tho' I have reasons enough for my dislike, I can not help pitying her at present as she is in real distress, &

with too much cause.—She had this morning a letter from the Lady with whom she has placed her daughter, to request that Miss Vernon might be immediately removed, as she had been detected in an attempt to run away. Why, or whither she intended to go, does not appear; but as her situation seems to have been unexceptionable, it is a sad thing & of course highly afflicting to Lady Susan.—

Frederica must be as much as sixteen, & ought to know better, but from what her Mother insinuates I am afraid she is a perverse girl. She has been sadly neglected however, & her Mother ought to remember it.—

M^r. Vernon set off for Town as soon as she had determined what should be done. He is if possible to prevail on Miss Summers to let Frederica continue with her, & if he cannot succeed, to bring her to Churchill for the present, till some other situation can be found for her.—Her Ladyship is comforting herself meanwhile by strolling along the Shrubbery[1] with Reginald, calling forth all his tender feelings I suppose on this distressing occasion. She has been talking a great deal about it to me, she talks vastly well, I am afraid of being ungenerous or I should say she talks <u>too</u> well to feel so very deeply. But I will not look for Faults. She may be Reginald's Wife—Heaven forbid it!—but why should I be quicker sighted than any body else?— M^r. Vernon declares that he never saw deeper distress than hers, on the receipt of the Letter—& is his Judgement inferior to mine?—

She was very unwilling that Frederica should be allowed to come to Churchill, & justly enough, as it seems a sort of reward to Behaviour deserving very differently. But it was impossible to take her any where else, & she is not to remain here long.—

"It will be absolutely necessary, said she, as you my dear sister must be sensible, to treat my daughter with some severity while she is here;—a most painful necessity, but I will endeavour to submit to it.—I am afraid I have been often too indulgent, but my poor Frederica's temper could never bear opposition well. You must support & encourage me—You must urge the necessity of reproof, if you see me too lenient."

All this sounds very reasonably.—Reginald is so incensed against the poor silly Girl!—Surely it is not to Lady Susan's credit that he should be so bitter against her daughter; his idea of her must be drawn from the Mother's description.—

Well, whatever may be his fate, we have the comfort of knowing that we have done our utmost to save him. We must commit the event to an Higher Power.—Yours Ever &c

Cath Vernon.

LETTER 16.

Lady Susan to Mrs. Johnson

Churchill

Never my dearest Alicia, was I so provoked in my life as by a Letter this morning from Miss Summers. That horrid girl of mine has been trying to run away.—I had not a notion of her being such a little Devil before;—she seemed to have all the Vernon Milkiness;[1] but on receiving the letter in which I declared my intentions about Sir James, she actually attempted to elope;[2] at least, I cannot otherwise account for her doing it.—She meant I suppose to go to the Clarkes in Staffordshire, for she has no other acquaintance. But she shall be punished, she shall have him. I have sent Charles to Town to make matters up if he can, for I do not by any means want her here. If Miss Summers will not keep her, you must find me out another school, unless we can get her married immediately.—Miss S. writes word that she could not get the young Lady to assign any cause for her extraordinary conduct, which confirms me in my own private explanation of it.—

Frederica is too shy I think, & too much in awe of me, to tell tales; but if the mildness of her Uncle should get anything from her, I am not afraid. I trust I shall be able to make my story as good as her's.—If I am vain of any thing, it is of my eloquence. Consideration & Esteem as surely follow command of Language, as Admiration waits on Beauty. And here I have opportunity enough for the exercise of my Talent, as the cheif of my time is spent in Conversation. Reginald is never easy unless we are by ourselves, & when the weather is tolerable we pace the shrubbery for hours together.—I like him on the whole very well, he is clever & has a good deal to say, but he is sometimes impertinent[3] & troublesome.—There is a sort of ridiculous delicacy about him which requires the fullest explanation of whatever he may have heard to my disadvantage, & is never satisfied till he thinks he has ascertained the beginning & end of everything.—

This is one sort of Love—but I confess it does not particularly recommend itself to me.—I infinitely prefer the tender & liberal spirit of Manwaring, which impressed with the deepest conviction of my merit, is satisfied that whatever I do must be right; & look with a degree of Contempt on the inquisitive & doubting Fancies of that Heart which seems always debating on the reasonableness of it's Emotions. Manwaring is indeed beyond compare superior to Reginald—superior in every thing but the power of being with me.—Poor fellow! he is quite distracted by Jealousy, which I am not sorry for, as I know no better support of Love.—He has been teizing[4] me to allow of his coming into this country, & lodging somewhere near me incog[5]—but I forbid every thing

line 30: 'been' inserted above line.

of the kind.—Those women are inexcusable who forget what is due to themselves & the opinion of the World.—

S. Vernon—

LETTER 17.

Mrs. Vernon to Lady De Courcy.

Churchill

My dear Mother

Mr. Vernon returned on Thursday night, bringing his neice with him. Lady Susan had received a line from him by that day's post informing her that Miss Summers had absolutely refused to allow of Miss Vernon's continuance in her Academy.[1] We were therefore prepared for her arrival, & expected them impatiently the whole evening.—They came while we were at Tea,[2] & I never saw any creature look so frightened in my life as Frederica when she entered the room.—

Lady Susan who had been shedding tears before & shewing great agitation at the idea of the meeting, received her with perfect self-command, & without betraying the least tenderness of spirit.—She hardly spoke to her, & on Frederica's bursting into tears as soon [as] we were seated, took her out of the room & did not return for some time; when she did, her eyes looked very red, and she was as much agitated as before.—We saw no more of her daughter.—

Poor Reginald was beyond measure concerned to see his fair friend in such distress, & watched her with so much tender solicitude that I, who occasionally caught her observing his countenance with exultation, was quite out of patience.—This pathetic[3] representation lasted the whole evening, & so

line 23: 'as' inserted above line before 'much'.

ostentatious & artful a display has entirely convinced me that she did in fact feel nothing.—

I am more angry with her than ever since I have seen her daughter.—The poor girl looks so unhappy that my heart aches for her.—Lady Susan is surely too severe, because Frederica does not seem to have the sort of temper to make severity necessary.—She looks perfectly timid, dejected & penitent.—

She is very pretty, tho' not so handsome as her Mother, nor at all like her. Her complexion is delicate, but neither so fair, nor so blooming as Lady Susan's[4]—& she has quite the Vernon cast of countenance, the oval face & mild dark eyes, & there is peculiar sweetness in her look when she speaks either to her Uncle or me, for as we behave kindly to her, we have of course engaged her gratitude.—Her Mother has insinuated that her temper is untractable, but I never saw a face less indicative of any evil disposition than her's; & from what I now see of the behaviour of each to the other, the invariable severity of Lady Susan, & the silent dejection of Frederica, I am led to beleive as heretofore that the former has no real Love for her daughter & has never done her justice, or treated her affectionately.

I have not yet been able to have any conversation with my neice; she is shy, & I think I can see that some pains are taken to prevent her being much with me.—Nothing satisfactory transpires as to her reason for running away.—Her kind hearted Uncle you may be sure, was too fearful of distressing her, to ask many questions as they travelled.—I wish it had been possible for me to fetch her instead of him;—I think I should have discovered the truth in the course of a Thirty miles Journey.[5]—

The small Pianoforté[6] has been removed within these few days at Lady Susan's request, into her Dressing room, &

Frederica spends great part of the day there;—practising it is called, but I seldom hear any noise when I pass that way.—What she does with herself there I do not know, there are plenty of books in the room, but it is not every girl who has been running wild the first fifteen years of her life, that can or will read.—Poor Creature! the prospect from her window is not very instructive, for that room overlooks the Lawn you know with the shrubbery on one side, where she may see her Mother walking for an hour together, in earnest conversation with Reginald.—A girl of Frederica's age must be childish indeed, if such things do not strike her.—Is it not inexcusable to give such an example to a daughter?—Yet Reginald still thinks Lady Susan the best of Mothers—still condemns Frederica as a worthless girl!—He is convinced that her attempt to run away, proceeded from no justifiable cause, & had no provocation. I am sure I cannot say that it had, but while Miss Summers declares that Miss Vernon shewed no sign of Obstinacy or Perverseness during her whole stay in Wigmore St. till she was detected in this scheme, I cannot so readily credit what Lady Susan has made him and wants to make me beleive, that it was merely an impatience of restraint, and a desire of escaping from the tuition of Masters which brought on the plan of an elopement.—Oh! Reginald, how is your judgement enslaved!—He scarcely dares even allow her to be handsome, & when I speak of her beauty, replies only that her eyes have no Brilliancy.[7]

Sometimes he is sure that she is deficient in Understanding, & at others that her temper only is in fault. In short when a person is always to deceive, it is impossible to be consistent. Lady Susan finds it necessary for her own justification that Frederica should be to blame, & probably has sometimes judged it expedient to accuse her of ill-nature & sometimes to lament her want of sense. Reginald is only repeating after her Ladyship.—

I am &c

Cath Vernon

LETTER 18.

From the same to the same.—

Churchill

My dear Madam

I am very glad to find that my description of Frederica Vernon has interested you, for I do beleive her truly deserving of our regard, & when I have communicated a notion that has recently struck me, your kind impression in her favour will I am sure be heightened. I cannot help fancying that she is growing partial to my brother, I so very often see her eyes fixed on his face with a remarkable expression of pensive admiration!—He is certainly very handsome—& yet more—there is an openness in his manner that must be highly prepossessing, & I am sure she feels it so.—Thoughtful & pensive in general her countenance always brightens with a smile when Reginald says anything amusing; & let the subject be ever so serious that he may be conversing on, I am much mistaken if a syllable of his uttering, escape her.—

I want to make <u>him</u> sensible of all this, for we know the power of gratitude on such a heart as his; & could Frederica's artless affection detach him from her Mother, we might bless the day which brought her to Churchill. I think my dear Madam, you would not disapprove of her as a Daughter. She is extremely young to be sure, has had a wretched Education and a dreadful example of Levity in her Mother; but yet I can pronounce her disposition to be excellent, & her natural abilities very good.—

Tho' totally without accomplishment, she is by no means so ignorant as one might expect to find her, being fond of books & spending the cheif of her time in reading. Her Mother leaves her more to herself now than she did, & I have her with me as much as possible, & have taken great pains to overcome her timidity. We are very good friends, & tho' she never opens her lips before her Mother, she talks enough when alone with me, to make it clear that if properly treated by Lady Susan she would always appear to much greater advantage. There cannot be a more gentle, affectionate heart, or more obliging manners, when acting without restraint. Her little Cousins are all very fond of her.—Y^rs^ affec:^ly^

Cath Vernon

LETTER 19.

Lady Susan to Mrs Johnson

Churchill

You will be eager I know to hear something farther of Frederica, & perhaps may think me negligent for not writing before.—She arrived with her Uncle last Thursday fortnight, when of course I lost no time in demanding the reason of her behaviour, & soon found myself to have been perfectly right in attributing it to my own letter.—The purport of it frightened her so thoroughly that with a mixture of true girlish perverseness & folly, without considering that she could not escape from my authority by running away from Wigmore Street, she resolved on getting out of the house, & proceeding directly by the stage[1] to her friends the Clarkes, & had really got as far as the length of two streets in her journey, when she was fortunately miss'd, pursued, and overtaken.—

Such was the first distinguished exploit of Miss Frederica Susanna Vernon, & if we consider that it was atchieved at the tender age of sixteen we shall have room for the most flattering prognostics of her future renown.—I am excessively provoked however at the parade of propriety which prevented Miss Summers from keeping the girl; & it seems so extraordinary a peice of nicety, considering what are my daughter's family connections, that I can only suppose the Lady to be governed by the fear of never getting her money.—Be that as it may however, Frederica is returned on my hands, & having now nothing else to employ her, is busy in pursueing the plan of Romance begun at Langford.—She is actually falling in love with Reginald De Courcy.—To disobey her Mother by refusing an unexceptionable offer is not enough; her affections must likewise be given without her Mother's approbation.—I never saw a girl of her age, bid fairer to be the sport of Mankind. Her feelings are tolerably lively, & she is so charmingly artless in their display, as to afford the most reasonable hope of her being ridiculed & despised by every Man who sees her.—

Artlessness will never do in Love matters, & that girl is born a simpleton who has it either by nature or affectation.—I am not yet certain that Reginald sees what she is about; nor is it of much consequence;—she is now an object of indifference to him, she would be one of contempt were he to understand her Emotions.—Her beauty is much admired by the Vernons, but it has no effect on him. She is in high favour with her Aunt altogether—because she is so little like myself of course. She is exactly the companion for Mrs Vernon, who dearly loves to be first, & to have all the sense and all the wit of the Conversation to herself;—Frederica will never eclipse her.—When she first came, I was at some pains to prevent her seeing much of her Aunt, but I have since relaxed, as I beleive I may

line 28: 'the' inserted above line after 'wit of'.

depend on her observing the rules I have laid down for their discourse.—

But do not imagine that with all this Lenity, I have for a moment given up my plan of her marriage;—No, I am unalterably fixed on that point, tho' I have not yet quite resolved on the manner of bringing it about.—I should not chuse to have the business brought forward here, & canvassed by the wise heads of M^r. and M^rs. Vernon; & I cannot just now afford to go to Town.— Miss Frederica therefore must wait a little.—

Yours Ever

S. Vernon.—

LETTER 20.

M^rs. Vernon to Lady De Courcy.

Churchill

We have a very unexpected Guest with us at present, my dear Mother.—He arrived yesterday.—I heard a carriage at the door as I was sitting with my Children while they dined, & supposing I should be wanted left the Nursery soon afterwards & was half way down stairs, when Frederica as pale as ashes came running up, & rushed by me into her own room.— I instantly followed, & asked her what was the matter.—"Oh! cried she, he is come, Sir James is come—& what am I to do?"—This was no explanation; I begged her to tell me what she meant. At that moment we were interrupted by a knock at the door;—it was Reginald, who came by Lady Susan's direction to call Frederica down.—"It is M^r. De Courcy, said she, colouring violently, Mama has sent for me, & I must go."—

We all three went down together, & I saw my Brother examining the terrified face of Frederica with surprise.—In the breakfast room we found Lady Susan & a young Man of genteel appearance, whom she introduced to me by the name of Sir James Martin, the very person, as you may remember, whom it was said she had been at pains to detach from Miss Manwaring.—But the conquest it seems was not designed for herself, or she has since transferred it to her daughter, for Sir James is now desperately in love with Frederica, & with full encouragement from Mama.—The poor girl however I am sure dislikes him; & tho' his person and address are very well, he appears both to M^r. Vernon & me a very weak young Man.—

Frederica looked so shy, so confused, when we entered the room, that I felt for her exceedingly. Lady Susan behaved with great attention to her Visitor, & yet I thought I could perceive that she had no particular pleasure in seeing him.—Sir James talked a good deal, & made many civil excuses to me for the liberty he had taken in coming to Churchill, mixing more frequent laughter with his discourse than the subject required;—said many things over & over again, & told Lady Susan three times that he had seen M^rs. Johnson a few Evenings before.—He now & then addressed Frederica, but more frequently her Mother.—The poor girl sat all this time without opening her lips;—her eyes cast down, & her colour varying every instant, while Reginald observed all that passed, in perfect silence.—

At length Lady Susan, weary I beleive of her situation, proposed walking, & we left the two Gentlemen together to put on our Pelisses.[1]—

As we went upstairs Lady Susan begged permission to attend me for a few moments in my Dressing room, as she was anxious to speak with me in private.—I led her thither accordingly, & as soon as the door was closed she said, "I was never more surprised in my life than by Sir James's arrival, & the suddenness of it requires some apology to You my dear

Sister, tho' to me as a Mother, it is highly flattering.—He is so warmly attached to my daughter that he could exist no longer without seeing her.—Sir James is a young Man of an amiable[2] disposition, & excellent character;—a little too much of the Rattle[3] perhaps, but a year or two will rectify that, & he is in other respects so very eligible a Match for Frederica that I have always observed his attachment with the greatest pleasure, & am persuaded that you & my Brother will give the alliance your hearty approbation.—I have never before mentioned the likelihood of it's taking place to any one, because I thought that while Frederica continued at school, it had better not be known to exist;—but now, as I am convinced that Frederica is too old ever to submit to school confinement, & have therefore begun to consider her union with Sir James as not very distant, I had intended within a few days to acquaint yourself & M^r. Vernon with the whole business.—I am sure my dear Sister, you will excuse my remaining silent on it so long, & agree with me that such circumstances, while they continue from any cause in suspense, cannot be too cautiously concealed.—When you have the happiness of bestowing your sweet little Catherine some years hence on a Man, who in connection & character is alike unexceptionable, you will know what I feel now;—tho' Thank Heaven! you cannot have all my reasons for rejoicing in such an Event.—Catherine will be amply provided for, & not like my Frederica endebted to a fortunate Establishment[4] for the comforts of Life."—

She concluded by demanding my congratulations.—I gave them somewhat awkwardly I beleive;—for in fact, the sudden disclosure of so important a matter took from me the power of speaking with any clearness.—She thanked me however most affectionately for my kind concern in the welfare of herself & her daughter, & then said,

"I am not apt to deal in professions, my dear M^rs. Vernon, & I never had the convenient talent of affecting sensations foreign to my heart; & therefore I trust you will beleive me when I declare that much as I had heard in your praise before I knew you, I had no idea that I should ever love you as I now do;—and I must farther say that your friendship towards me is more particularly gratifying, because I have reason to beleive that some attempts were made to prejudice you against me.—I only wish that They—whoever they are—to whom I am endebted for such kind intentions, could see the terms on which we now are together, & understand the real affection we feel for each other!—But I will not detain you any longer.—God bless you, for your goodness to me & my girl, & continue to you all your present happiness."

What can one say of such a woman, my dear Mother?—such earnestness, such solemnity of expression!—And yet I cannot help suspecting the truth of everything she said.—

As for Reginald, I beleive he does not know what to make of the matter.—When Sir James first came, he appeared all astonishment & perplexity. The folly of the young Man, & the confusion of Frederica entirely engrossed him; & tho' a little private discourse with Lady Susan has since had it's effect, he is still hurt I am sure at her allowing of such a Man's attentions to her daughter.—

Sir James invited himself with great composure to remain here a few days;—hoped we would not think it odd, was aware of it's being very impertinent, but he took the liberty of a relation,[5] & concluded by wishing with a laugh, that he might be really one soon.—Even Lady Susan seemed a little disconcerted by this forwardness;—in her heart I am persuaded, she sincerely wishes him gone.—

But something must be done for this poor Girl, if her feelings are such as both her Uncle & I beleive them to be.

She must not be sacrificed to Policy or Ambition, she must not be even left to suffer from the dread of it.—The Girl, whose heart can distinguish[6] Reginald De Courcy, deserves, however he may slight her, a better fate than to be Sir James Martin's wife.—As soon as I can get her alone, I will discover the real Truth, but she seems to wish to avoid me.—I hope this does not proceed from any thing wrong, & that I shall not find out I have thought too well of her.—Her behaviour before Sir James certainly speaks the greatest consciousness & Embarrassment; but I see nothing in it more like Encouragement.—

Adeiu my dear Madam,
Yrs &c Cath Vernon.—

LETTER 21.

Miss Vernon to Mr. De Courcy—
Sir,

I hope you will excuse this liberty, I am forced upon it by the greatest distress, or I should be ashamed to trouble you.—I am very miserable about Sir James Martin, & have no other way in the world of helping myself but by writing to you, for I am forbidden ever speaking to my Uncle or Aunt on the subject; & this being the case, I am afraid my applying to you will appear no better than equivocation, & as if I attended only to the letter & not the spirit of Mama's commands, but if you do not take my part, & persuade her to break it off, I shall be half-distracted, for I can not bear him.—No human Being but you could have any chance of prevailing with her.—If you will therefore have the unspeakable great kindness[1] of taking my part with her, & persuading her to send Sir James away, I shall be more obliged to you than it

line 26: 'bear him' inserted above line.

is possible for me to express.—I always disliked him from the first, it is not a sudden fancy I assure you Sir, I always thought him silly & impertinent & disagreable, & now he is grown worse than ever.—I would rather work for my bread than marry him.[2]—I do not know how to apologise enough for this Letter, I know it is taking so great a liberty, I am aware how dreadfully angry it will make Mama, but I must run the risk.—I am Sir, Your most Hum^ble. Servt.

F. S. V. —

LETTER 22.

Lady Susan to M^rs. Johnson

Churchill

This is insufferable!—My dearest friend, I was never so enraged before, & must releive myself by writing to you, who I know will enter into all my feelings.—Who should come on Tuesday but Sir James Martin?—Guess my astonishment & vexation—for as you well know, I never wished him to be seen at Churchill. What a pity that you should not have known his intentions!—Not content with coming, he actually invited himself to remain here a few days. I could have poisoned him;—I made the best of it however, & told my story with great success to M^rs. Vernon who, whatever might be her real sentiments, said nothing in opposition to mine[.] I made a point also of Frederica's behaving civilly to Sir James, & gave her to understand that I was absolutely determined on her marrying him.—She said something of her misery, but that was all.—I have for some time been more particularly resolved on the Match, from seeing the rapid increase of her affection for Reginald, & from not feeling perfectly secure that a knowledge of <u>that</u> affection might not in the end awaken a return.—Contemptible as a regard founded only on compassion, must make them both, in my eyes, I felt by no means assured that such might not be the consequence.—It is true that Reginald had not in any degree grown cool towards me;—but yet he had lately mentioned Frederica spontaneously & unnecessarily, & once had said something in praise of her person.—

He was all astonishment at the appearance of my visitor; & at first observed Sir James with an attention which I was pleased to see not unmixed with jealousy;—but unluckily it was impossible for me really to torment him, as Sir James tho' extremely gallant to me, very soon made the whole party understand that his heart was devoted to my daughter.—

I had no great difficulty in convincing De Courcy when we were alone, that I was perfectly justified, all things considered, in desiring the match; & the whole business seemed most comfortably arranged.—They could none of them help perceiving that Sir James was no Solomon,[1] but I had positively forbidden Frederica's complaining to Charles Vernon or his wife, & they had therefore no pretence for Interference, tho' my impertinent Sister I beleive wanted only opportunity for doing so.—

Everything however was going on calmly & quietly; & tho' I counted the hours of Sir James's stay, my mind was entirely satisfied with the posture of affairs.—Guess then what I must feel at the sudden disturbance of all my schemes, & that too from a quarter, whence I had least reason to apprehend it.—Reginald came this morning into my Dressing room, with a very unusual solemnity of countenance, & after some preface informed me in so many words, that he wished to reason with me on the Impropriety & Unkindness of allowing Sir James Martin to address my Daughter, contrary to her inclination.—I was all amazement.—When I found that he was not to be laughed out of his design, I calmly required an explanation, & begged to know by what he was impelled & by whom commissioned to reprimand me[.]

He then told me, mixing in his speech a few insolent compliments & ill timed expressions of Tenderness to which I listened with perfect indifference, that my daughter had acquainted him with some circumstances concerning herself, Sir James, & me, which gave him great uneasiness.—

In short, I found that she had in the first place actually written to him, to request his interference, & that on receiving her Letter he had conversed with her on the subject of it, in order to understand the particulars & assure himself of her real wishes!—

I have not a doubt but that the girl took this opportunity of making down right Love to him; I am convinced of it, from the manner in which he spoke of her. Much good, may such Love do him!—I shall ever despise the Man who can be gratified by the Passion, which he never wished to inspire, nor solicited the avowal of.—I shall always detest them both.— He can have no true regard for me, or he would not have listened to her;—And she, with her little rebellious heart & indelicate feelings to throw herself into the protection of a young Man with whom she had scarcely ever exchanged two words before. I am equally confounded at her Impudence and his Credulity.—How dared he beleive what she told him in my disfavour!—Ought he not to have felt assured that I must have unanswerable Motives for all that I had done!—Where was his reliance on my Sense or Goodness then; where the resentment which true Love would have dictated against the person defaming me, that person too, a Chit, a Child, without Talent or Education, whom he had been always taught to despise?—

line 3: 'me,' inserted above line.

I was calm for some time, but the greatest degree of Forbearance may be overcome; & I hope I was afterwards sufficiently keen.[2]—He endeavoured, long endeavoured to soften my resentment, but that woman is a fool indeed who while insulted by accusation, can be worked on by compliments.—At length he left me as deeply provoked as myself, & he shewed his anger more. —I was quite cool, but he gave way to the most violent indignation.—I may therefore expect it will the sooner subside; & perhaps his may be vanished for ever, while mine will be found still fresh & implacable.

He is now shut up in his apartment, whither I heard him go, on leaving mine.—How unpleasant, one would think, must his reflections be!—But some people's feelings are incomprehensible.—I have not yet tranquillized myself enough to see Frederica. She shall not soon forget the occurrences of this day.—She shall find that she has poured forth her tender Tale of Love in vain, & exposed herself forever to the contempt of the whole world, & the severest Resentment of her injured Mother.—Y^rs^ affec:^ly^

S. Vernon

LETTER 23.

Mrs Vernon to Lady De Courcy

Churchill

Let me congratulate you, my dearest Mother. The affair which has given us so much anxiety is drawing to a happy conclusion. Our prospect is most delightful;—and since matters have now taken so favourable a turn, I am quite sorry that I ever imparted my apprehensions to you; for the pleasure of learning that the Danger is over, is perhaps dearly purchased by all that you have previously suffered.—

I am so much agitated by Delight that I can scarcely hold a pen, but am determined to send you a few lines by James, that you may have some explanation of what must so greatly astonish you, as that Reginald should be returning to Parklands.—

I was sitting about half an hour ago with Sir James in the Breakfast parlour, when my Brother called me out of the room.—I instantly saw that something was the matter;—his complexion was raised, & he spoke with great emotion.—You know his eager manner, my dear Madam, when his mind is interested.—

"Catherine, said he, I am going home today. I am sorry to leave you, but I must go.—It is a great while since I have seen my Father & Mother.—I am going to send James forward with my Hunters immediately, if you have any Letter therefore he can take it.[1]—I shall not be at home myself till Wednesday or Thursday, as I shall go through London, where I have business.—But before I leave you, he continued, speaking in a lower voice & with still greater energy, I must warn you of one thing.—Do not let Frederica Vernon be made unhappy by that Martin.—He wants to marry her—her Mother promotes the Match—but she cannot endure the idea of it.—Be assured that I speak from the fullest conviction of the Truth of what I say.—I know that Frederica is made wretched by Sir James' continuing here.—She is a sweet girl, & deserves a better fate.—Send him away immediately. He is only a fool—but what her Mother can mean, Heaven only knows!—Good bye, he added shaking my hand with earnestness—I do not know when you will see me again. But remember what I tell you of Frederica;—you must make it your business to see justice done her. —She is an amiable girl, and has a very superior Mind to what we have ever given her credit for.—"

line 29: 'Mind' inserted above line.

He then left me & ran upstairs.—I would not try to stop him, for I knew what his feelings must be; the nature of mine as I listened to him, I need not attempt to describe.—For a minute or two I remained in the same spot, overpowered by wonder—of a most agreable sort indeed; yet it required some consideration to be tranquilly happy.—

In about ten minutes after my return to the parlour, Lady Susan entered the room.—I concluded of course that she & Reginald had been quarrelling, & looked with anxious curiosity for a confirmation of my beleif in her face.—Mistress of Deceit however she appeared perfectly unconcerned, & after chatting on indifferent subjects for a short time, said to me,

"I find from Wilson that we are going to lose M^r^ De Courcy.—Is it true that he leaves Churchill this morning?"—

I replied that it was.—

"He told us nothing of all this last night, said she laughing, or even this morning at Breakfast. But perhaps he did not know it himself.—Young Men are often hasty in their resolutions—& not more sudden in forming, than unsteady in keeping them.—I should not be surprised if he were to change his mind at last, & not go."—

She soon afterwards left the room.—I trust however my dear Mother, that we have no reason to fear an alteration of his present plan; things have gone too far.—They must have quarrelled, & about Frederica too.—Her calmness astonishes me.—What delight will be yours in seeing him again, in seeing him still worthy your Esteem, still capable of forming your Happiness!

When I next write, I shall be able I hope to tell you that Sir James is gone, Lady Susan vanquished, & Frederica at peace.—We have much to do, but it shall be done.—I am all impatience to know how this astonishing change was effected.—I finish as I began, with the warmest congratulations.—Y^{rs}. Ever,

Cath Vernon.

LETTER 24.

From the same to the same.

Churchill

Little did I imagine my dear Mother, when I sent off my last letter, that the delightful perturbation of spirits I was then in, would undergo so speedy, so melancholy a reverse!—I never can sufficiently regret that I wrote to you at all.—Yet who could have foreseen what has happened? My dear Mother, every hope which but two hours ago made me so happy, is vanished. The quarrel between Lady Susan & Reginald is made up, & we are all as we were before. One point only is gained; Sir James Martin is dismissed.—What are we now to look forward to?—I am indeed disappointed. Reginald was all but gone; his horse was ordered, & almost brought to the door!—Who would not have felt safe?—

For half an hour I was in momentary expectation of his departure.—After I had sent off my Letter to you, I went to M^{r}. Vernon & sat with him in his room, talking over the whole matter.—I then determined to look for Frederica, whom I had not seen since breakfast.—I met her on the stairs & saw that she was crying.

"My dear Aunt, said she, he is going, M^{r}. De Courcy is going, & it is all my fault. I am afraid you will be angry, but indeed I had no idea it would end so."—

"My Love, replied I, do not think it necessary to apologize to me on that account.—I shall feel myself under an obligation to any one who is the means of sending my brother home;—because, (recollecting myself) I know my Father wants very much to see him. But what is it that you have done to occasion all this?"—

She blushed deeply as she answered, "I was so unhappy about Sir James that I could not help—I have done something very wrong I know—but you have not an idea of the misery I have been in, & Mama had ordered me never to speak to you or my Uncle about it,—and"—

"You therefore spoke to my Brother, to engage his interference";—said I, wishing to save her the explanation.—

"No—but I wrote to him.—I did indeed.—I got up this morning before it was light—I was two hours about it—& when my Letter was done, I though[t] I never should have courage to give it.—After breakfast however, as I was going to my own room I met him in the passage, & then as I knew that every thing must depend on that moment, I forced myself to give it.—He was so good as to take it immediately;—I dared not look at him—& ran away directly.—I was in such a fright that I could hardly breathe.—My dear Aunt, you do not know how miserable I have been."

"Frederica, said I, you ought to have told me all your distresses.—You would have found in me a friend always ready to assist you.—Do you think that your Uncle & I should not have espoused your cause as warmly as my Brother?"—

"Indeed I did not doubt your goodness, said she colouring again, but I thought that M^r^ De Courcy could do anything with my Mother;—but I was mistaken;—they have had a dreadful quarrel about it, & he is going.—Mama will never forgive me, & I shall be worse off than ever."—

"No, you shall not, replied I.—In such a point as this, your Mother's prohibition ought not to have prevented your speaking to me on the subject. She has no right to make you unhappy, & she shall not do it.—Your applying however to

Reginald can be productive only of Good to all parties. I beleive it is best as it is.—Depend upon it that you shall not be made unhappy any longer."

At that moment, how great was my astonishment at seeing Reginald come out of Lady Susan's Dressing room. My heart misgave me instantly. His confusion on seeing me was very evident.—Frederica immediately disappeared.

"Are you going?—said I. You will find Mr. Vernon in his own room."—

"No Catherine, replied he.—I am not going.—Will you let me speak to you a moment?"

We went into my room. "I find, continued he, his confusion increasing as he spoke, that I have been acting with my usual foolish Impetuosity.—I have entirely misunderstood Lady Susan, & was on the point of leaving the house under a false impression of her conduct.—There has been some very great mistake—we have been all mistaken I fancy.—Frederica does not know her Mother—Lady Susan means nothing but her Good—but Frederica will not make a friend of her.—Lady Susan therefore does not always know what will make her daughter happy.—Besides I could have no right to interfere—Miss Vernon was mistaken in applying to me.—In short Catherine, every thing has gone wrong—but it is now all happily settled.—Lady Susan I beleive wishes to speak to you about it, if you are at leisure."—

"Certainly;" replied I, deeply sighing at the recital of so lame a story.—I made no remarks however, for words would have been vain. Reginald was glad to get away, & I went to Lady Susan; curious indeed to hear her account of it.—

line 1: 'to' deleted after 'only'; 'of' inserted above line. // line 11: 'in your own room?—' deleted; '?"' inserted after 'moment'. // line 12: 'thither directly.' deleted; 'into my room.' inserted above line.

"Did not I tell you, said she with a smile, that your Brother would not leave us after all?"

"You did indeed, replied I very gravely, but I flattered myself that you would be mistaken."

"I should not have hazarded such an opinion, returned she, if it had not at that moment occurred [to] me, that his resolution of going might be occasioned by a Conversation in which we had been this morning engaged, & which had ended very much to his Dissatisfaction from our not rightly understanding each other's meaning.—This idea struck me at the moment, & I instantly determined that an accidental dispute in which I might probably be as much to blame as himself, should not deprive you of your Brother.—If you remember, I left the room almost immediately.—I was resolved to lose no time in clearing up these mistakes as far as I could.—The case was this.—Frederica had set herself violently against marrying Sir James"—

—"And can your Ladyship wonder that she should? cried I with some warmth.—Frederica has an excellent Understanding, & Sir James has none."

"I am at least very far from regretting it, my dear Sister, said she; on the contrary, I am grateful for so favourable a sign of my Daughter's sense. Sir James is certainly under par[1]—(his boyish manners make him appear the worse)—& had Frederica possessed the penetration, the abilities, which I could have wished in my daughter, or had I even known her to possess so much as she does, I should not have been anxious for the match."

"It is odd that you alone should be ignorant of your Daughter's sense."

"Frederica never does justice to herself;—her manners are shy & childish.—She is besides afraid of me; she scarcely loves me.—During her poor Father's life she was a spoilt child; the severity which it has since been necessary for me to shew, has entirely alienated her affection;—neither has she any of that Brilliancy of Intellect, that Genius,[2] or vigour of Mind which will force itself forward."

"Say rather that she has been unfortunate in her Education."

"Heaven knows my dearest M^rs. Vernon, how fully I am aware of that; but I would wish to forget every circumstance that might throw blame on the memory of one, whose name is sacred with me."

Here she pretended to cry.—I was out of patience with her.—"But what, said I, was your Ladyship going to tell me about your disagreement with my Brother?"—

"It originated in an action of my Daughter's, which equally marks her want of Judgement, & the unfortunate Dread of me I have been mentioning.—She wrote to M^r. De Courcy."—

"I know she did.—You had forbidden her speaking to M^r. Vernon or to me on the cause of her distress:—what could she do therefore but apply to my Brother?"

"Good God!—she exclaimed, what an opinion must you have of me!—Can you possibly suppose that I was aware of her unhappiness? that it was my object to make my own child miserable, & that I had forbidden her speaking to you on the subject, from a fear of your interrupting the Diabolical scheme?—Do you think me destitute of every honest, every natural feeling?—Am I capable of consigning her to everlasting Misery, whose welfare it is my first Earthly Duty to promote?"—

"The idea is horrible.—What then was your intention when you insisted on her silence?"—

line 8: 'to' repeated as the last word on fo. 101 and the first word on fo. 102.

"Of what use my dear Sister, could be any application to you, however the affair might stand? Why should I subject you to entreaties, which I refused to attend to myself?—Neither for your sake, for hers, nor for my own, could such a thing be desireable.—Where my own resolution was taken, I could not wish for the interference, however friendly, of another person.—I was mistaken, it is true, but I beleived myself to be right."—

"But what was this mistake, to which your Ladyship so often alludes? From whence arose so astonishing a misapprehension of your Daughter's feelings?—Did not you know that she disliked Sir James?—"

"I knew that he was not absolutely the Man whom she would have chosen.—But I was persuaded that her objections to him did not arise from any perception of his Deficiency.—You must not question me however my dear Sister, too minutely on this point—continued she, taking me affectionately by the hand.—I honestly own that there is something to conceal.—Frederica makes me very unhappy.—Her applying to Mr. De Courcy hurt me particularly."

"What is it that you mean to infer said I, by this appearance of mystery?—If you think your daughter at all attached to Reginald, her objecting to Sir James could not less deserve to be attended to, than if the cause of her objecting had been a consciousness of his folly.—And why should your Ladyship at any rate quarrel with my brother for an interference which you must know, it was not in his nature to refuse, when urged in such a manner?"

"His disposition you know is warm,[3] & he came to expostulate with me, his compassion all alive for this ill-used Girl, this Heroine in distress!—We misunderstood each other. He beleived me more to blame than I really was; I considered his interference as less excusable than I now find it. I have a real regard for him, & was beyond expression mortified to find it as I thought so ill bestowed. We were both warm, & of course both to blame.—His resolution of leaving Churchill is consistent with his general eagerness;—when I understood his intention however, & at the same time began to think that we had perhaps been equally mistaken in each other's meaning, I resolved to have an explanation before it were too late.—For any Member of your Family I must always feel a degree of affection, & I own it would have sensibly[4] hurt me, if my acquaintance with M^r. De Courcy had ended so gloomily. I have now only to say farther, that as I am convinced of Frederica's having a reasonable dislike to Sir James, I shall instantly inform him that he must give up all hope of her.—I reproach myself for having ever, tho' so innocently, made her unhappy on that score.—She shall have all the retribution[5] in my power to make;—if she value her own happiness as much as I do, if she judge wisely & command herself as she ought, she may now be easy. —Excuse me, my dearest Sister, for thus trespassing on your time, but I owed it to my own Character; & after this explanation I trust I am in no danger of sinking in your opinion."

I could have said "Not much indeed";—but I left her almost in silence.—It was the greatest stretch of Forbearance I could practise. I could not have stopped myself, had I begun.—Her assurance, her Deceit—but I will not allow myself to dwell on them;—they will strike you sufficiently. My heart sickens within me.—

As soon as I was tolerably composed, I returned to the Parlour. Sir James's carriage was at the door, & he, merry as usual, soon afterwards took his leave.—How easily does her Ladyship encourage, or dismiss a Lover!—

line 9: 'hurt' inserted above line. // line 18: 'at peace.' deleted; 'easy.' inserted above line.

In spite of this release, Frederica still looks unhappy, still fearful perhaps of her Mother's anger, & tho' dreading my Brother's departure jealous, it may be, of his staying.—I see how closely she observes him & Lady Susan.—Poor Girl, I have now no hope for her. There is not a chance of her affection being returned.—He thinks very differently of her, from what he used to do, he does her some justice, but his reconciliation with her Mother precludes every dearer hope.—

Prepare my dear Madam, for the worst.—The probability of their marrying is surely heightened. He is more securely her's than ever.—When that wretched Event takes place, Frederica must belong wholly to us.—

I am thankful that my last Letter will precede this by so little, as every moment that you can be saved from feeling a Joy which leads only to disappointment is of consequence.—

Y[rs] Ever, Cath Vernon.

LETTER 25.

Lady Susan to M[rs] Johnson

Churchill

I call on you dear Alicia, for congratulations. I am again myself;—gay & triumphant.—When I wrote to you the other day, I was in truth in high irritation, & with ample cause.—Nay, I know not whether I ought to be quite tranquil now, for I have had more trouble in restoring peace than I ever intended to submit to.—This Reginald has a proud spirit of his own!—a spirit too, resulting from a fancied sense of superior Integrity which is peculiarly insolent.—I shall not easily forgive him I assure you. He was actually on the point of leaving Churchill!—I had scarcely concluded my last, when Wilson brought me word of it.—I found therefore that something must be done, for I did not chuse to have my character at the mercy of a Man whose passions were so violent &

resentful.—It would have been trifling with my reputation, to allow of his departing with such an impression in my disfavour;—in this light, condescension[1] was necessary.—

I sent Wilson to say that I desired to speak with him before he went.—He came immediately. The angry emotions which had marked every feature when we last parted, were partially subdued. He seemed astonished at the summons, & looked as if half wishing & half fearing to be softened by what I might say.—

If my Countenance expressed what I aimed at, it was composed & dignified—& yet with a degree of pensiveness which might convince him that I was not quite happy.—

"I beg your pardon Sir, for the liberty I have taken in sending to you, said I; but as I have just learnt your intention of leaving this place to day, I feel it my duty to entreat that you will not on my account shorten your visit here, even an hour.—I am perfectly aware that after what has passed between us, it would ill suit the feelings of either to remain longer in the same house.—

So very great, so total a change from the intimacy of Friendship, must render any future intercourse the severest punishment;—& your resolution of quitting Churchill is undoubtedly in unison with our situation & with those lively feelings which I know you to possess.—But at the same time, it is not for me to suffer such a sacrifice, as it must be, to leave Relations to whom you are so much attached & are so dear. My remaining here cannot give that pleasure to M^r^ & Mrs Vernon which your society must;—& my visit has already perhaps been too long. My removal therefore, which must at any rate take place soon, may with

line 1: 'To' deleted; 'It would' inserted above line. // line 18: 'of either' inserted above line.

perfect convenience be hastened;—& I make it my particular request that I may not in any way be instrumental in separating a family so affectionately attached to each other.—Where I go, is of no consequence to anyone; of very little to myself; but you are of importance to all your connection[s."]

Here I concluded, & I hope you will be satisfied with my speech.—It's effect on Reginald justifies some portion of vanity, for it was no less favourable than instantaneous.—Oh! how delightful it was, to watch the variations of his Countenance while I spoke, to see the struggle between returning Tenderness & the remains of Displeasure.—There is something agreable in feelings so easily worked on. Not that I envy him their possession, nor would for the world have such myself, but they are very convenient when one wishes to influence the passions of another. And yet this Reginald, whom a very few words from me softened at once into the utmost submission, & rendered more tractable, more attached, more devoted than ever, would have left me in the first angry swelling of his proud heart, without deigning to seek an explanation!—

Humbled as he now is, I cannot forgive him such an instance of Pride; & am doubtful whether I ought not to punish him, by dismissing him at once after this our reconciliation, or by marrying & teizing him for ever.—But these measures are each too violent to be adopted without some deliberation. At present my Thoughts are fluctuating between various schemes.—I have many things to compass.—I must punish Frederica, & pretty severely too, for her application to Reginald;—I must punish him for receiving it so favourably, & for the rest of his conduct. I must torment my Sister-in-law for the insolent triumph of her Look & Manner since Sir James has been dismissed—for in reconciling Reginald to me, I was not able to save that ill-fated young Man;—& I must make myself amends for the humiliations to which I have stooped within these few days.—To effect all this I have various plans.—I have also an idea of being soon in Town, & whatever may be my determination as to the rest, I shall probably put <u>that</u> project in execution—for London will be always the fairest field of action, however my veiws may be directed, & at any rate, I shall there be rewarded by your society & a little Dissipation for a ten weeks penance at Churchill.—

I beleive I owe it to my own Character, to complete the match between my daughter & Sir James, after having so long intended it.—Let me know your opinion on this point.—Flexibility of Mind, a Disposition easily biassed by others, is an attribute which you know I am not very desirous of obtaining;—nor has Frederica any claim to the indulgence of her whims, at the expence of her Mother's inclination.—Her idle Love for Reginald too;—it is surely my duty to discourage such romantic nonsense.—All things considered therefore, it seems encumbent on me to take her to Town, & marry her immediately to Sir James.

When my own will is effected, contrary to his, I shall have some credit in being on good terms with Reginald, which at present in fact I have not, for tho' he is still in my power, I have given up the very article by which our Quarrel was produced, & at best, the honour of victory is doubtful.—

Send me your opinion on all these matters, my dear Alicia, & let me know whether you can get Lodgings to suit me within a short distance of you.—Y[r]. most attached

S. Vernon.

line 14: 'Weakness' deleted; 'Flexibility' inserted above line.

LETTER 26.

Mrs. Johnson to Lady Susan.

Edward St.—

I am gratified by your reference, & this is my advice; that you come to Town yourself without loss of time, but that you leave Frederica behind. It would surely be much more to the purpose to get yourself well established by marrying Mr. De Courcy, than to irritate him & the rest of his family, by making her marry Sir James.—You should think more of yourself, & less of your Daughter.—She is not of a disposition to do you credit in the World, & seems precisely in her proper place, at Churchill with the Vernons;—but You are fitted for Society, & it is shameful to have you exiled from it.— Leave Frederica therefore to punish herself for the plague she has given you, by indulging that romantic tender-heartedness which will always ensure her misery enough; & come yourself to Town, as soon as you can.—

I have another reason for urging this.—Manwaring came to Town last week, & has contrived, inspite of Mr. Johnson, to make opportunities of seeing me.—He is absolutely miserable about you, & jealous to such a degree of De Courcy, that it would be highly unadvisable for them to meet at present;[1] & yet if you do not allow him to see you here, I cannot answer for his not committing some great imprudence—such as going to Churchill for instance, which would be dreadful.—Besides, if you take my advice, & resolve to marry De Courcy, it will be indispensably necessary for you to get Manwaring out of the way, & you only can have influence enough to send him back to his wife.—

I have still another motive for your coming. Mr. Johnson leaves London next Tuesday. He is going for his health to Bath, where if the waters are favourable to his constitution & my wishes, he will be laid up with the Gout many weeks.[2]—

During his absence we shall be able to chuse our own society, & have true enjoyment.—I would ask you to Edward S^t. but that he once forced from me a kind of promise never to invite you to my house. Nothing but my being in the utmost distress for Money, could have extorted it from me.—I can get you however a very nice Drawing room-apartment in Upper Seymour S^t.,[3] & we may be always together, there or here, for I consider my promise to M^r. Johnson as comprehending only (at least in his absence) your not sleeping in the House.—

Poor Manwaring gives me such histories of his wife's jealousy!—Silly woman, to expect constancy from so charming a Man!—But she was always silly; intolerably so, in marrying him at all. She, the Heiress of a large Fortune, he without a shilling!—One Title I know she might have had, besides Baronets.[4]—Her folly in forming the connection was so great, that tho' M^r. Johnson was her Guardian & I do not in general share his feelings, I never can forgive her.—

Adeiu. Yours, Alicia. —

LETTER 27.

M^rs. Vernon to Lady De Courcy.

Churchill

This Letter my dear Mother, will be brought you by Reginald. His long visit is about to be concluded at last, but I fear the separation takes place too late to do us any good.—She is going to Town, to see her particular friend, M^rs. Johnson. It was at first her intention that Frederica should accompany her for the benefit of Masters,[1] but we over-ruled her there. Frederica was wretched in the idea of going, & I could not bear to have her at the mercy of her Mother. Not all the Masters in London could compensate for the ruin of her comfort. I should have feared too for her health, & for every thing in short but her Principles; there I beleive she is not to be injured, even by her Mother, or all her Mother's friends;—but with those friends (a very bad set I doubt not) she must have mixed, or have been left in total solitude, & I can hardly tell which would have been worse for her.—If she is with her Mother moreover, she must alas! in all probability, be with Reginald—and that would be the greatest evil of all.—

Here, we shall in time be at peace.—Our regular employments, our Books & conversation, with Exercise, the Children, & every domestic pleasure in my power to procure her, will, I trust, gradually overcome this youthful attachment. I should not have a doubt of it, were she slighted for any other woman in the world, than her own Mother.—

How long Lady Susan will be in Town, or whether she returns here again, I know not.—I could not be cordial in my invitation; but if she chuses to come, no want of cordiality on my part will keep her away.—

I could not help asking Reginald if he intended being in Town this winter,[2] as soon as I found that her Ladyship's steps would be bent thither; & tho' he professed himself quite undetermined, there was a something in his Look & voice as he spoke, which contradicted his words.—I have done with Lamentation.—I look upon the Event as so far decided, that I resign myself to it in despair. If he leaves you soon for London, every thing will be concluded.—Yours affec:ly

Cath Vernon.

LETTER 28.

Mrs. Johnson to Lady Susan

Edward St.—

My dearest Friend,

I write in the greatest distress; the most unfortunate event has just taken place. Mr. Johnson has hit on the most effectual manner of plaguing us all.—He had heard I imagine by some means or other, that you were soon to be in London, & immediately contrived to have such an attack of the Gout, as must at least delay his journey to Bath, if not wholly prevent it.—I am persuaded the Gout is brought on, or kept off at pleasure;—it was the same, when I wanted to join the Hamiltons to the Lakes;[1] & three years ago when I had a fancy for Bath, nothing could induce him to have a gouty symptom.

I have received yours, & have engaged the Lodgings in consequence.—I am pleased to find that my Letter had so much effect on you, & that De Courcy is certainly your own.—Let me hear from you as soon as you arrive, & in particular tell me what you mean to do with Manwaring.—It is impossible to say when I shall be able to see you. My confinement must be great. It is such an abominable trick, to be ill here, instead of at Bath, that I can scarcely command myself at all.—At Bath, his old Aunts would have nursed him, but here it all falls upon me—& he bears pain with such patience that I have not the common excuse for losing my temper.

Y^rs Ever, Alicia.

LETTER 29.

Lady Susan to Mrs Johnson

Upper Seymour S^t

My dear Alicia

There needed not this last fit of the Gout to make me detest Mr Johnson; but now the extent of my aversion is not to be estimated.—To have you confined, a Nurse, in his apartment!—My dear Alicia, of what a mistake were you guilty in marrying a Man of his age!—just old enough to be formal, ungovernable & to have the Gout—too old to be agreable, & too young to die.

line 17: 'pain' inserted above line.

I arrived last night about five, & had scarcely swallowed my dinner when Manwaring made his appearance.—I will not dissemble what real pleasure his sight afforded me, nor how strongly I felt the contrast between his person & manners, & those of Reginald, to the infinite disadvantage of the latter.—For an hour or two, I was even stagger'd in my resolution of marrying him—& tho' this was too idle & nonsensical an idea to remain long on my mind, I do not feel very eager for the conclusion of my marriage, or look forward with much impatience to the time when Reginald according to our agreement is to be in Town.—I shall probably put off his arrival, under some pretence or other. He must not come till Manwaring is gone.

I am still doubtful at times, as to Marriage.—If the old Man would die, I might not hesitate; but a state of dependance on the caprice of Sir Reginald, will not suit the freedom of my spirit;—and if I resolve to wait for that event, I shall have excuse enough at present, in having been scarcely ten months a Widow.

I have not given Manwaring any hint of my intention—or allowed him to consider my acquaintance with Reginald as more than the commonest flirtation;—& he is tolerably appeased.—Adeiu till we meet.—I am enchanted with my Lodgings. Y^rs^ Ever,

S. Vernon.—

LETTER 30.

Lady Susan to M^r^ De Courcy.[1]—

Upper Seymour S^t^

I have received your Letter; & tho' I do not attempt to conceal that I am gratified by your impatience for the hour of meeting, I yet feel myself under the necessity of delaying that hour beyond the time originally fixed.—Do not think me unkind for such an exercise of my power, or accuse me of Instability, without first hearing my reasons.—In the course of my journey from Churchill, I had ample leisure for reflection on the present state of our affairs, & every reveiw has served to convince me that they require a delicacy & cautiousness of conduct, to which we have hitherto been too little attentive.—We have been hurried on by our feelings to a degree of Precipitance which ill accords with the claims of our Friends, or the opinion of the world.—We have been unguarded in forming this hasty Engagement; but we must not complete the imprudence by ratifying it, while there is so much reason to fear the Connection would be opposed by those Friends on whom you depend.

It is not for us to blame any expectation on your Father's side of your marrying to advantage; where possessions are so extensive as those of your Family, the wish of increasing them, if not strictly reasonable, is too common to excite surprise or resentment.—He has a right to require a woman of fortune in his daughter in law; & I am sometimes quarreling with myself for suffering you to form a connection so imprudent.—But the influence of reason is often acknowledged too late by those who feel like me.—

I have now been but a few months a widow; & however little endebted to my Husband's memory for any happiness derived from him during an Union of some years, I cannot forget that the indelicacy of so early a second marriage, must subject me to the censure of the World, & incur what would be still more insupportable, the displeasure of M^r. Vernon.—I might perhaps harden myself in time against the injustice of general reproach; but the loss of <u>his</u> valued Esteem, I am as you well know, ill fitted to endure;—and when to this,

line 4: 'posture' deleted; 'state' inserted above line.

may be added the consciousness of having injured you with your Family, how am I to support myself.—With feelings so poignant as mine, the conviction of having divided the son from his Parents, would make me, even with <u>you</u>, the most miserable of Beings.—

It will surely therefore be advisable to delay our Union, to delay it till appearances are more promising, till affairs have taken a more favourable turn.—To assist us in such a resolution, I feel that absence will be necessary. We must not meet.—Cruel as this sentence may appear, the necessity of pronouncing it, which can alone reconcile it to myself, will be evident to you when you have considered our situation in the light in which I have found myself imperiously[2] obliged to place it.—You may be, you must be well assured that nothing but the strongest conviction of Duty, could induce me to wound my own feelings by urging a lengthened separation; & of Insensibility to yours, you will hardly suspect me.—Again therefore I say that we ought not, we must not yet meet.—By a removal for some Months from each other, we shall tranquillize the sisterly fears of M^rs^. Vernon, who, accustomed herself to the enjoyment of riches, considers Fortune as necessary every where, and whose sensibilities are not of a nature to comprehend ours.—

Let me hear from you soon, very soon. Tell me that you submit to my Arguments, & do not reproach me for using such.—I cannot bear reproaches. My spirits are not so high as to need being repressed.—I must endeavour to seek amusement abroad,[3] & fortunately many of my Friends are in Town—among them, the Manwarings.—You know how sincerely I regard both Husband & Wife. — I am ever, Faithfully Yours

S. Vernon—

line 22: 'feelings' deleted; 'sensibilities' inserted above line.

LETTER 31.

Lady Susan to M^rs. Johnson

Upper Seymour S^t.

My dear Friend,

That tormenting creature Reginald is here. My Letter which was intended to keep him longer in the Country, has hastened him to Town. Much as I wish him away however, I cannot help being pleased with such a proof of attachment. He is devoted to me, heart & soul.—He will carry this note himself, which is to serve as an Introduction to you, with whom he longs to be acquainted. Allow him to spend the Evening with you, that I may be in no danger of his returning here.—I have told him that I am not quite well, & must be alone—& should he call again there might be confusion, for it is impossible to be sure of servants.—Keep him therefore I entreat you in Edward S^t.—You will not find him a heavy companion, & I allow you to flirt with him as much as you like. At the same time do not forget my real interest;—say all that you can to convince him that I shall be quite wretched if he remain here;—you know my reasons—Propriety & so forth.—I would urge them more myself, but that I am impatient to be rid of him, as Manwaring comes within half an hour.

Adeiu. S V.—

LETTER 32.

M^rs. Johnson to Lady Susan—

Edward S^t.

My dear Creature,

I am in agonies, & know not what to do, nor what you can do.— M^r. De Courcy arrived, just when he should not. M^rs. Manwaring had that instant entered the House, & forced herself into her Guardian's presence, tho' I did not know a syllable of it till afterwards, for I was out when both she &

Reginald came, or I would have sent him away at all events; but she was shut up with Mr. Johnson, while he waited in the Drawing room for me.—

She arrived yesterday in pursuit of her Husband;—but perhaps you know this already from himself.—She came to this house to entreat my Husband's interference, & before I could be aware of it, everything that you could wish to be concealed, was known to him; & unluckily she had wormed out of Manwaring's servant that he had visited you every day since your being in Town, & had just watched him to your door herself!—What could I do?—Facts are such horrid things!—All is by this time known to De Courcy, who is now alone with Mr. Johnson.—Do not accuse me;—indeed, it was impossible to prevent it.—Mr. Johnson has for some time suspected De Courcy of intending to marry you, & would speak with him alone, as soon as he knew him to be in the House.—

That detestable Mrs. Manwaring, who for your comfort, has fretted herself thinner & uglier than ever, is still here, & they have been all closeted together. What can be done?—If Manwaring is now with you, he had better be gone.—At any rate I hope he will plague his wife more than ever. —With anxious wishes, Yrs. faithfully

Alicia.

LETTER 33.

Lady Susan to Mrs. Johnson.

Upper Seymour St.

This Eclaircissement[1] is rather provoking.—How unlucky that you should have been from home!—I thought myself sure of you at 7.[2]—I am undismayed however. Do not torment yourself with fears on my account.—Depend upon it, I can make my own story good with Reginald. Manwaring is just gone; he brought me the news of his wife's arrival. Silly

Woman! what does she expect by such manouvres?[3]—yet, I wish she had staid quietly at Langford.—

Reginald will be a little enraged at first, but by Tomorrow's Dinner, every thing will be well again.—Adeiu. S V.

LETTER 34.

Mr. De Courcy to Lady Susan.

Hotel

I write only to bid you Farewell.—The spell is removed. I see you as you are.—Since we parted yesterday, I have received from indisputable authority, such an history of you, as must bring the most mortifying conviction of the Imposition I have been under, & the absolute necessity of an immediate & eternal separation from you.—You cannot doubt to what I allude;—Langford—Langford—that word will be sufficient.—I received my information in Mr. Johnson's house, from Mrs. Manwaring herself.—

You know how I have loved you, you can intimately judge of my present feelings; but I am not so weak as to find indulgence in describing them to a woman who will glory in having excited their anguish, but whose affection they have never been able to gain.

R De Courcy.

LETTER 35.

Lady Susan to Mr. De Courcy.

Upper Seymour St.

I will not attempt to describe my astonishment on reading the note, this moment received from you. I am bewilder'd in my endeavours to form some rational conjecture of what Mrs. Manwaring can have told you, to occasion so extraordinary a change in your sentiments.—Have I not explained everything to you with respect to myself which could bear a doubtful meaning, & which the illnature of the world had interpreted to my Discredit?—What can you now have heard to stagger your Esteem for me?—Have I ever had a concealment from you?—Reginald, you agitate me beyond expression.—I cannot suppose that the old story of M^rs^. Manwaring's jealousy can be revived again, or at least, be listened to again.—Come to me immediately, & explain what is at present absolutely incomprehensible.—Beleive me, the single word of Langford is not of such potent intelligence, as to supersede the necessity of more.—If we are to part, it will at least be handsome to take your personal Leave.—But I have little heart to jest; in truth, I am serious enough—for to be sunk, tho' but an hour, in your opinion, is an humiliation to which I know not how to submit. I shall count every moment till your arrival.

S. V.

LETTER 36.

M^r^. De Courcy to Lady Susan

Hotel

Why would you write to me?—Why do you require particulars?—But since it must be so, I am obliged to declare that all the accounts of your misconduct during the life & since the death of M^r^. Vernon which had reached me in common with the World in general, & gained my entire beleif before I saw you, but which you by the exertion of your perverted Abilities had made me resolve to disallow, have been unanswerably proved to me.—Nay, more[, I] am assured that a Connection, of which I had never before entertained a thought, has for some time existed, & still continues to exist between you and the Man, whose family you robbed of it's Peace, in return for the hospitality with which you were received into it!—That you have corresponded with him ever since your leaving Langford—not with his wife—but with him—& that he now visits you every day.—Can you, dare you deny it?—And all this at the time when I was an encouraged, an accepted Lover!—From what have I not escaped!—I have only to be grateful.—Far from me be all Complaint, & every sigh of regret. My own Folly had endangered me[,] my Preservation I owe to the kindness, the Integrity of another.—But the unfortunate M^rs^. Manwaring, whose agonies while she related the past, seem'd to threaten her reason—how is she to be consoled?

After such a discovery as this, you will scarcely affect farther wonder at my meaning in bidding you Adeiu.—My Understanding is at length restored, & teaches me no less to abhor the Artifices which had subdued me, than to despise myself for the weakness, on which their strength was founded.—

R De Courcy.—

LETTER 37.

Lady Susan to M^r^. De Courcy

Upper Seymour S^t^.

I am satisfied—& will trouble you no more when these few Lines are dismissed.[1]—The Engagement which you were eager to form a fortnight ago, is no longer compatible with your veiws, & I rejoice to find that the prudent advice of your Parents has not been given in vain.—Your restoration to Peace will, I doubt not, speedily follow this act of filial Obedience, & I flatter myself with the hope of surviving my share in this disappointment.

S V.

LETTER 38.

M^rs^. Johnson to Lady Susan

Edward S^t^.

I am greived, tho' I cannot be astonished at your rupture with M^r^. De Courcy;—he has just informed M^r^. Johnson of it by letter. He leaves London he says to day.—Be assured that I partake in all your feelings, & do not be angry if I say that our intercourse even by letter must soon be given up.—It makes me miserable—but M^r. Johnson vows that if I persist in the connection, he will settle in the country for the rest of his life—& you know it is impossible to submit to such an extremity[1] while any other alternative remains.—

You have heard of course that the Manwarings are to part;[2] I am afraid M^rs. M. will come home to us again. But she is still so fond of her Husband & frets so much about him that perhaps she may not live long.—

Miss Manwaring is just come to Town to be with her Aunt, & they say, that she declares she will have Sir James Martin before she leaves London again.—If I were you, I would certainly get him myself.—I had almost forgot to give you my opinion of De Courcy, I am really delighted with him, he is full as handsome I think as Manwaring, & with such an open, good humoured Countenance that one cannot help loving him at first sight.— M^r. Johnson & he are the greatest friends in the World. Adeiu, my dearest Susan.—I wish matters did not go so perversely. That unlucky visit to Langford!—But I dare say you did all for the best, & there is no defying Destiny.[3]—

Y^r. sincerely attached

Alicia.

LETTER 39.

Lady Susan to M^rs. Johnson

Upper Seymour S^t.

My dear Alicia

I yeild to the necessity which parts us. Under such circumstances you could not act otherwise. Our friendship cannot be impaired by it; & in happier times, when your situation is as independant as mine, it will unite us again in the same Intimacy as ever.—For this, I shall impatiently wait; & meanwhile can safely assure you that I never was more at ease, or better satisfied with myself & every thing about me, than at the present hour.—Your Husband I abhor—Reginald I despise—& I am secure of never seeing either again. Have I not reason to rejoice?—Manwaring is more devoted to me than ever; & were he at liberty, I doubt if I could resist even Matrimony offered by him. This Event, if his wife live with you, it may be in your power to hasten. The violence of her feelings, which must wear her out, may be easily kept in irritation.—I rely on your friendship for this.—I am now satisfied that I never could have brought myself to marry Reginald; & am equally determined that Frederica never shall. Tomorrow I shall fetch her from Churchill, & let Maria Manwaring tremble for the consequence. Frederica shall be Sir James's wife before she quits my house. She may whimper & the Vernons may storm;—I regard them not. I am tired of submitting my will to the Caprices of others—of resigning my own Judgement in deference to those, to whom I owe no Duty, & for whom I feel no respect.—I have given up too much—have been too easily worked on; but Frederica shall now find the difference.—Adeiu, dearest of Friends. May the next Gouty Attack be more favourable—& may you always regard me as unalterably Yours

S. Vernon.—

LETTER 40.

Lady De Courcy to M^rs^. Vernon

Parklands

My dear Catherine

I have charming news for you, & if I had not sent off my Letter this morning, you might have been spared the vexation of knowing of Reginald's being gone to Town, for he is returned, Reginald is returned, not to ask our consent to his marrying Lady Susan, but to tell us that they are parted forever!—He has been only an hour in the House, & I have not been able to learn particulars, for he is so very low, that I have not the heart to ask questions; but I hope we shall soon know all.—This is the most joyful hour he has ever given us, since the day of his birth. Nothing is wanting but to have you here, & it is our particular wish & entreaty that you would come to us as soon as you can. You have owed us a visit many long weeks.—I hope nothing will make it inconvenient to M^r. Vernon, & pray bring all my Grand Children, & your dear Neice is included of course; I long to see her.—It has been a sad heavy winter hitherto, without Reginald, & seeing nobody from Churchill; I never found the season so dreary before, but this happy meeting will make us young again.—Frederica runs much in my thoughts, & when Reginald has recovered his usual good spirits, (as I trust he soon will) we will try to rob him of his heart once more, & I am full of hopes of seeing their hands joined at no great distance.

Y^r. affec: Mother

C. De Courcy.

LETTER 41.

M^rs. Vernon to Lady De Courcy.

Churchill

My dear Madam

Your Letter has surprised me beyond measure. Can it be true that they are really separated—& for ever?—I should be overjoyed if I dared depend on it, but after all that I have seen, how can one be secure?—And Reginald really with you!—My surprise is the greater, because on wednesday, the very day of his coming to Parklands, we had a most unexpected & unwelcome visit from Lady Susan, looking all chearfulness & good humour, & seeming more as if she were to marry him when she got back to Town, than as if parted from him for ever.—She staid nearly two hours, was as affectionate & agreable as ever, & not a syllable, not a hint was dropped of any Disagreement or Coolness between them. I asked her whether she had seen my Brother since his arrival in Town—not as you may suppose with any doubt of the fact—but merely to see how she looked.—She immediately answered without any embarrassment that he had been kind enough to call on her on Monday, but she beleived he had already returned home—which I was very far from crediting.—

Your kind invitation is accepted by us with pleasure, & on Thursday next, we & our little ones will be with you.—Pray Heaven! Reginald may not be in Town again by that time!—

I wish we could bring dear Frederica too, but I am sorry to add that her Mother's errand hither was to fetch her away; & miserable as it made the poor Girl, it was impossible to detain her. I was thoroughly unwilling to let her go, & so was her Uncle; & all that could be urged, we *did* urge. But Lady Susan declared that as she was now about to fix herself in Town for several months she could not be easy if her Daughter were not with her, for Masters, &c.—Her Manner, to be sure, was very kind & proper—& Mr Vernon beleives that Frederica will now be treated with affection. I wish I could think so too!—

The poor girl's heart was almost broke at taking leave of us. I charged her to write to me very often, & to remember that if she were in any distress, we should be always her friends.—I took care to see her alone, that I might say all this, & I hope made her a little more comfortable.—But I shall not be easy till I can go to Town & judge of her situation myself.—

I wish there were a better prospect than now appears, of the Match, which the conclusion of your Letter declares your expectation of.—At present it is not very likely.—

Y^{rs} &c

Cath Vernon.

CONCLUSION

This Correspondence, by a meeting between some of the Parties & a separation between the others, could not, to the great detriment of the Post office Revenue,[1] be continued longer.—Very little assistance to the State[2] could be derived from the Epistolary Intercourse of Mrs Vernon & her Neice, for the former soon perceived by the stile of Frederica's Letters, that they were written under her Mother's inspection, & therefore deferring all particular enquiry till she could make it personally in Town, ceased writing minutely or often.—

Having learnt enough in the meanwhile from her open-hearted Brother, of what had passed between him & Lady Susan to sink the latter lower than ever in her opinion, she was proportionably more anxious to get Frederica removed from such a Mother, & placed under her own care; & tho' with little hope of success, was resolved to leave nothing unattempted that might offer a chance of obtaining her sister in law's consent to it.—Her anxiety on the subject made her press for an early visit to London; & Mr Vernon who, as it must have already appeared, lived only to do whatever he was desired, soon found some accomodating Business to call him thither.—With a heart full of the Matter, Mrs Vernon waited on Lady Susan, shortly after her arrival in Town; & was met with such an easy & chearful affection as made her almost turn from her with horror.—No remembrance of Reginald, no consciousness of Guilt, gave one look of embarrassment.—She was in excellent spirits, & seemed eager to shew at once, by every possible attention to her Brother & Sister, her sense of their kindness, & her pleasure in their society.—

Frederica was no more altered than Lady Susan;—the same restrained Manners, the same timid Look in the presence of her Mother as heretofore, assured her Aunt of her Situation's being uncomfortable, & confirmed her in the plan of altering it.—No unkindness however on the part of Lady Susan appeared. Persecution on the subject of Sir James was entirely at an end—his name merely mentioned to say that he was not in London; and in all her conversation she was solicitous only for the welfare & improvement of her Daughter, acknowledging in terms of grateful delight that Frederica was now growing every day more & more what a Parent could desire.—

M^rs^. Vernon surprised & incredulous, knew not what to suspect, & without any change in her own veiws, only feared greater difficulty in accomplishing them. The first hope of any thing better was derived from Lady Susan's asking her whether she thought Frederica looked quite as well as she had done at Churchill, as she must confess herself to have sometimes an anxious doubt of London's perfectly agreeing with her.—

M^rs^. Vernon encouraging the doubt, directly proposed her Neice's returning with them into the country. Lady Susan was unable to express her sense of such kindness; yet knew not from a variety of reasons how to part with her Daughter; & as, tho' her own plans were not yet wholly fixed, she trusted it would ere long be in her power to take Frederica into the country herself, concluded by declining entirely to profit by such unexampled attention.— M^rs^. Vernon however persevered in the offer of it; & tho' Lady Susan continued to resist, her resistance in the course of a few days seemed somewhat less formidable.

The lucky alarm of an Influenza,[3] decided what might not have been decided quite so soon.—Lady Susan's maternal fears were then too much awakened for her to think of any thing but Frederica's removal from the risk of infection. Above all Disorders in the World, she most dreaded the Influenza for her daughter's constitution. Frederica returned to Churchill with her Uncle & Aunt, & three weeks afterwards Lady Susan announced her being married to Sir James Martin.—

Mrs. Vernon was then convinced of what she had only suspected before, that she might have spared herself all the trouble of urging a removal, which Lady Susan had doubtless resolved on from the first.—Frederica's visit was nominally for six weeks;—but her Mother, tho' inviting her to return in one or two affectionate Letters, was very ready to oblige the whole Party by consenting to a prolongation of her stay, & in the course of two months ceased to write of her absence, & in the course of two more, to write to her at all.

Frederica was therefore fixed in the family of her Uncle & Aunt, till such time as Reginald De Courcy could be talked, flattered & finessed[4] into an affection for her—which, allowing leisure for the conquest of his attachment to her Mother, for his abjuring all future attachments & detesting the Sex, might be reasonably looked for in the course of a Twelvemonth. Three Months might have done it in general, but Reginald's feelings were no less lasting than lively.[5]—

Whether Lady Susan was, or was not happy in her second Choice—I do not see how it can ever be ascertained—for who would take her assurance of it, on either side of the question?—The World must judge from Probability.—She had nothing against her, but her Husband & her Conscience.

Sir James may seem to have drawn an harder Lot than mere Folly merited.—I leave him therefore to all the Pity that any body can give him. For myself, I confess that I can pity only Miss Manwaring, who coming to Town & putting herself to an expence in Cloathes, which impoverished her for two years, on purpose to secure him, was defrauded of her due by a Woman ten years older than herself.

Finis.

The Watsons[1]

The first winter assembly[2] in the town of D. in Surry[3] was to be held on Tuesday October the 13th,[4] and it was generally expected to be a very good one; a long list of country families[5] was confidently run over as sure of attending, and sanguine hopes were entertained that the Osbornes themselves would be there.—The Edwards's invitation to the Watsons followed of course. The Edwardses were people of fortune who lived in the town and kept their coach;[6] the Watsons inhabited a village about three miles distant, were poor and had no close carriage;[7] and ever since there had been balls in the place, the former were accustomed to invite the latter to dress, dine and sleep at their house, on every monthly return throughout the winter.[8]—On the present occasion, as only two of Mr. Watson's children were at home, and one was always necessary as companion to himself, for he was sickly and had lost his wife, one only could profit by the kindness of their friends; Miss Emma Watson, who was very recently returned to her family from the care of an aunt who had brought her up,[9] was to make her first public appearance in the neighbourhood;—and her eldest sister, whose delight in a ball was not lessened by a ten years enjoyment, had some merit in cheerfully undertaking to drive her and all her finery in the old chair[10] to D. on the important morning.—

As they splashed along the dirty lane Miss Watson thus instructed and cautioned her inexperienced sister.—

"I dare say it will be a very good ball, and among so many officers, you will hardly want partners. You will find Mrs. Edwards's maid very willing to help you, and I would advise you to ask Mary Edwards's opinion if you are at all at a loss for she has a very good taste.—If Mr. Edwards does not lose his money at cards,[11] you will stay as late as you can wish for; if he does, he will hurry you home perhaps—but you are sure of some comfortable soup.[12]—I hope you will be in good looks—. I should not be surprised if you were to be thought one of the prettiest girls in the room, there is a great deal in novelty. Perhaps Tom Musgrave may take notice of you—but I would advise you by all means not to give him any encouragement. He generally pays attention to every new girl, but he is a great flirt and never means anything serious."

"I think I have heard you speak of him before," said Emma. "Who is he?"

"A young man of very good fortune, quite independent,[13] and remarkably agreeable, an universal favourite wherever he goes. Most of the girls hereabouts are in love with him, or have been. I believe I am the only one among them that have escaped with a whole heart, and yet I was the first he paid attention to, when he came into this country,[14] six years ago; and very great attention indeed did he pay me. Some people say that he has never seemed to like any girl so well since, though he is always behaving in a particular way to[15] one or another."—

"And how came *your* heart to be the only cold one?—" said Emma smiling.

"There was a reason for that—" replied Miss Watson, changing colour.—"I have not been very well used Emma among them, I hope you will have better luck."—

"Dear sister, I beg your pardon, if I have unthinkingly given you pain."—

"When first we knew Tom Musgrave," continued Miss Watson without seeming to hear her, "I was very much attached to a young man of the name of Purvis, a particular friend of Robert's, who used to be with us a great deal. Every body thought it would have been a match."

A sigh accompanied these words, which Emma respected in silence—; but her sister, after a short pause, went on—

"You will naturally ask why it did not take place, and why he is married to another woman, while I am still single.—But you must ask him—not me—you must ask Penelope.—Yes Emma, Penelope was at the bottom of it all.—She thinks everything fair for a husband; I trusted her, she set him against me, with a view of gaining him herself, and it ended in his discontinuing his visits and soon after marrying somebody else.—Penelope makes light of her conduct, but *I* think such treachery very bad. It has been the ruin of my happiness. I shall never love any man as I loved Purvis. I do not think Tom Musgrave should be named with him in the same day.—"

"You quite shock me by what you say of Penelope—" said Emma. "Could a sister do such a thing?—Rivalry, treachery between sisters!—I shall be afraid of being acquainted with her—but I hope it was not so. Appearances were against her"—

"You do not know Penelope.—There is nothing she would not do to get married—she would as good as tell you so herself.—Do not trust her with any secrets of your own, take warning by me, do not trust her; she has her good qualities, but she has no faith, no honour, no scruples, if she can promote her own advantage.—I wish with all my heart she was well married. I declare I had rather have her well-married than myself."—

"Than yourself!—Yes I can suppose so. A heart, wounded like yours, can have little inclination for matrimony."—

"Not much indeed—but you know we must marry.[16]—I could do very well single for my own part—A little company, and a pleasant ball now and then, would be enough for me, if one could be young for ever, but my father cannot provide for us,[17] and it is very bad to grow old and be poor and laughed at.[18]—I have lost Purvis, it is true, but very few people marry their first loves.[19] I should not refuse a man because he was not Purvis—. Not that I can ever quite forgive Penelope.—" Emma shook her head in acquiescence.—

"Penelope however has had her troubles—" continued Miss Watson.—"She was sadly disappointed in Tom Musgrave, who afterwards transferred his attentions from me to her, and whom she was very fond of;—but he never means anything serious, and when he had trifled with her long enough, he began to slight her for Margaret, and poor Penelope was very wretched—. And since then, she has been trying to make some match at Chichester;[20] she won't tell us with whom, but I believe it is a rich old Dr. Harding, uncle to the friend she goes to see;—and she has taken a vast deal of trouble about him and given up a great deal of time to no purpose as yet.—When she went away the other day, she said it should be the last time.—I suppose you did not know what her particular business was at Chichester—nor guess at the object that could take her away from Stanton[21] just as you were coming home after so many years absence."—

"No indeed, I had not the smallest suspicion of it. I considered her engagement to Mrs. Shaw just at that time as very unfortunate for me. I had hoped to find all my sisters at home; to be able to make an immediate friend of each."—

"I suspect the Doctor to have had an attack of the asthma,—and that she was hurried away on that account—the Shaws are quite on her side.—At least I believe so—but she tells me nothing. She professes to keep her own counsel;

she says, and truly enough, that 'Too many cooks spoil the broth'."—

"I am sorry for her anxieties," said Emma,—"but I do not like her plans or her opinions. I shall be afraid of her.—She must have too masculine and bold a temper.—To be so bent on marriage—to pursue a man merely for the sake of situation—is a sort of thing that shocks me; I cannot understand it. Poverty is a great evil, but to a woman of education and feeling it ought not, it cannot be the greatest.—I would rather be teacher at a school[22] (and I can think of nothing worse) than marry a man I did not like.—"

"I would rather do any thing than be teacher at a school—" said her sister. "*I* have been at school,[23] Emma, and know what a life they lead; *you* never have.—I should not like marrying a disagreeable man any more than yourself,—but I do not think there *are* many very disagreeable men;—I think I could like any good-humoured man with a comfortable income.—I suppose my aunt brought you up to be rather refined."[24]

"Indeed I do not know.—My conduct must tell you how I have been brought up. I am no judge of it myself. I cannot compare my aunt's method with any other person's, because I know no other."—

"But I can see in a great many things that you are very refined. I have observed it ever since you came home, and I am afraid it will not be for your happiness. Penelope will laugh at you very much."

"*That* will not be for my happiness I am sure.—If my opinions are wrong, I must correct them—if they are above my situation, I must endeavour to conceal them.—But I doubt whether ridicule—Has Penelope much wit?"—

"Yes—she has great spirits, and never cares what she says."—

"Margaret is more gentle I imagine?"—

"Yes—especially in company; she is all gentleness and mildness when anybody is by.—But she is a little fretful and perverse among ourselves.—Poor creature!—she is possessed with the notion of Tom Musgrave's being more seriously in love with her, than he ever was with any body else, and is always expecting him to come to the point. This is the second time within this twelvemonth that she has gone to spend a month with Robert and Jane on purpose to egg him on, by her absence—but I am sure she is mistaken, and that he will no more follow her to Croydon[25] now than he did last March.—He will never marry unless he can marry somebody very great; Miss Osborne perhaps, or something in that style.—"

"Your account of this Tom Musgrave, Elizabeth, gives me very little inclination for his acquaintance."

"You are afraid of him, I do not wonder at you."—

"No indeed—I dislike and despise him."—

"Dislike and despise Tom Musgrave! No, *that* you never can. I defy you not to be delighted with him if he takes notice of you.—I hope he will dance with you—and I dare say he will, unless the Osbornes come with a large party,[26] and then he will not speak to any body else.—"

"He seems to have most engaging manners!"—said Emma.—"Well, we shall see how irresistible Mr. Tom Musgrave and I find each other.—I suppose I shall know him as soon as I enter the ball-room;—he *must* carry some of his charms in his face."—

"You will not find him in the ball-room I can tell you. You will go early that Mrs. Edwards may get a good place by the fire, and he never comes till late; and if the Osbornes are coming, he will wait in the passage, and come in with them.—I should like to look in upon you, Emma. If it was but a good day with my father, I would wrap myself up, and James should drive me over, as soon as I had made tea for him, and I should be with you by the time the dancing began."

"What! would you come late at night in this chair?"—

"To be sure I would.—There, I said you were very refined;—and *that*'s an instance of it.—"

Emma for a moment made no answer—at last she said—"I wish, Elizabeth, you had not made a point of my going to this ball, I wish you were going instead of me. Your pleasure would be greater than mine. I am a stranger here, and know nobody but the Edwardses—my enjoyment therefore must be very doubtful. Yours among all your acquaintance would be certain.—It is not too late to change. Very little apology could be requisite to the Edwardses, who must be more glad of your company than of mine, and I should most readily return to my father; and should not be at all afraid to drive this quiet old creature home. Your clothes I would undertake to find means of sending to you."—

"My dearest Emma," cried Elizabeth warmly—"do you think I would do such a thing?—Not for the universe—but I shall never forget your good nature in proposing it. You must have a sweet temper indeed!—I never met with any thing like it!—And would you really give up the ball, that I might be able to go to it!—Believe me Emma, I am not so selfish as that comes to. No, though I am nine years older than you are, I would not be the means of keeping you from being seen.—You are very pretty, and it would be very hard that you should not have as fair a chance as we have all had, to make your fortune.—No Emma, whoever stays at home this winter, it shan't be you. I am sure I should never have forgiven the person who kept me from a ball at nineteen."

Emma expressed her gratitude, and for a few minutes they jogged on in silence.—Elizabeth first spoke.—

"You will take notice who Mary Edwards dances with."—

"I will remember her partners if I can—but you know they will be all strangers to me."

"Only observe whether she dances with Captain Hunter, more than once;[27] I have my fears in that quarter. Not that her father or mother like officers,[28] but if she does, you know, it is all over with poor Sam.—And I have promised to write him word who she dances with."

"Is Sam attached to Miss Edwards?"—

"Did not you know *that*?"—

"How should I know it?—How should I know in Shropshire, what is passing of that nature in Surry?[29]—It is not likely that circumstances of such delicacy should make any part of the scanty communication which passed between you and me for the last fourteen years."

"I wonder I never mentioned it when I wrote. Since you have been at home, I have been so busy with my poor father and our great wash[30] that I have had no leisure to tell you anything—but indeed I concluded you knew it all.—He has been very much in love with her these two years, and it is a great disappointment to him that he cannot always get away to our balls—but Mr. Curtis won't often spare him, and just now it is a sickly time at Guilford—"[31]

"Do you suppose Miss Edwards inclined to like him—?"

"I am afraid not: you know she is an only child, and will have at least ten thousand pounds." —[32]

"But still she may like our brother."

"Oh! no—. The Edwardses look much higher. Her father and mother would never consent to it. Sam is only a surgeon[33] you know.—Sometimes I think she does like him. But Mary

Edwards is rather prim and reserved; I do not always know what she would be at."—

"Unless Sam feels on sure grounds with the lady herself, it seems a pity to me that he should be encouraged to think of her at all."—

"A young man must think of somebody," said Elizabeth—"and why should not he be as lucky as Robert, who has got a good wife and six thousand pounds?"

"We must not all expect to be individually lucky," replied Emma. "The luck of one member of a family is luck to all.—"

"Mine is all to come I am sure—" said Elizabeth, giving another sigh to the remembrance of Purvis.—"I have been unlucky enough, and I cannot say much for you, as my aunt married again so foolishly.—Well—you will have a good ball I dare say. The next turning will bring us to the turnpike.[34] You may see the church tower over the hedge, and the White Hart is close by it.[35]—I shall long to know what you think of Tom Musgrave."

Such were the last audible sounds of Miss Watson's voice, before they passed through the turnpike gate and entered on the pitching[36] of the town—the jumbling and noise of which made farther conversation most thoroughly undesirable.—The old mare trotted heavily on, wanting no direction of the reins to take the right turning, and making only one blunder, in proposing to stop at the milliners,[37] before she drew up towards Mr. Edwards's door.—Mr. Edwards lived in the best house in the street, and the best in the place, if Mr. Tomlinson the banker might be indulged in calling his newly erected house at the end of the town, with a shrubbery and sweep,[38] in the country.—Mr. Edwards's house was higher than most of its neighbours, with windows on each side the door, the windows guarded by posts and chain, the door approached by a flight of stone steps.[39]—

"Here we are—" said Elizabeth, as the carriage ceased moving—"safely arrived;—and by the market clock,[40] we have been only five and thirty minutes coming—which *I* think is doing pretty well, though it would be nothing for Penelope.—Is not it a nice town?—The Edwardses have a noble house, you see, and they live quite in stile. The door will be opened by a man in livery with a powdered head,[41] I can tell you."

Emma had seen the Edwardses only one morning at Stanton, they were therefore all but strangers to her, and though her spirits were by no means insensible to the expected joys of the evening, she felt a little uncomfortable in the thought of all that was to precede them. Her conversation with Elizabeth too, giving her some very unpleasant feelings with respect to her own family, had made her more open to disagreeable impressions from any other cause, and increased her sense of the awkwardness of rushing into intimacy on so slight an acquaintance.—

There was nothing in the manners of Mrs. or Miss Edwards to give immediate change to these ideas;—the mother, though a very friendly woman, had a reserved air, and a great deal of formal civility—and the daughter, a genteel looking girl of twenty two, with her hair in papers,[42] seemed very naturally to have caught something of the stile of the mother who had brought her up.—Emma was soon left to know what they could be, by Elizabeth's being obliged to hurry away—and some very, very languid remarks on the probable brilliancy of the ball, were all that broke at intervals a silence of half an hour before they were joined by the master of the house.—Mr. Edwards had a much easier and more communicative air than the ladies of the family; he was fresh from the street, and he came ready to tell whatever might interest.—After a cordial reception of Emma, he turned to his daughter with "Well Mary, I bring you good news.—The Osbornes will certainly be at the ball to night.—Horses for two carriages are ordered from the White Hart,[43] to be at Osborne Castle by nine."—

"I am glad of it—" observed Mrs. Edwards, "because their coming gives a credit to our assemblies. The Osbornes being known to have been at the first ball, will dispose a great many people to attend the second.—It is more than they deserve, for in fact they add nothing to the pleasure of the evening, they come so late, and go so early;—but great people have always their charm."—

Mr. Edwards proceeded to relate every other little article of news which his morning's lounge[44] had supplied him with, and they chatted with greater briskness, till Mrs. Edwards's moment for dressing arrived, and the young ladies were carefully recommended to lose no time.—Emma was shewn to a very comfortable apartment, and as soon as Mrs. Edwards's civilities could leave her to herself, the happy occupation, the first bliss of a ball began.—

The girls, dressing in some measure together, grew unavoidably better acquainted; Emma found in Miss Edwards the shew of good sense, a modest unpretending mind, and a great wish of obliging—and when they returned to the parlour where Mrs. Edwards was sitting respectably attired in one of the two satin[45] gowns which went through the winter, and a new cap[46] from the milliners, they entered it with much easier feelings and more natural smiles than they had taken away.—

Their dress was now to be examined; Mrs. Edwards acknowledged herself too old-fashioned to approve of every modern extravagance however sanctioned—and though complacently viewing her daughter's good looks, would give but a qualified admiration; and Mr. Edwards, not less satisfied with Mary, paid some compliments of good humoured gallantry to Emma at her expence.—The discussion led to more intimate remarks, and Miss Edwards gently asked Emma if she were not often reckoned very like her youngest brother.—Emma thought she could perceive a faint blush accompany the question, and there seemed something still more suspicious in the manner in which Mr. Edwards took up the subject.

"—You are paying Miss Emma no great compliment I think Mary," said he hastily—. "Mr. Sam Watson is a very good sort of young man, and I dare say a very clever surgeon, but his complexion has been rather too much exposed to all weathers, to make a likeness to him very flattering."[47]

Mary apologized in some confusion. "She had not thought a strong likeness at all incompatible with very different degrees of beauty.—There might be resemblance in countenance; and the complexion, and even the features be very unlike."—

"I know nothing of my brother's beauty," said Emma, "for I have not seen him since he was seven years old—but my father reckons us alike."

"Mr. Watson!—" cried Mr. Edwards. "Well, you astonish me.—There is not the least likeness in the world; your brother's eyes are grey, yours are brown, he has a long face, and a wide mouth.—My dear, do *you* perceive the least resemblance?"—

"Not the least.—Miss Emma Watson puts me very much in mind of her eldest sister, and sometimes I see a look of Miss Penelope—and once or twice there has been a glance of Mr. Robert—but I cannot perceive any likeness to Mr. Samuel."

"I see the likeness between her and Miss Watson,"[48] replied Mr. Edwards, "very strongly—but I am not sensible of the others.—I do not much think she is like any of the family *but* Miss Watson; but I am very sure there is no resemblance between her and Sam."—

This matter was settled, and they went to dinner.—

"Your father, Miss Emma, is one of my oldest friends—" said Mr. Edwards, as he helped her to wine, when they were drawn round the fire to enjoy their desert.[49]—"We must drink to his better health.—It is a great concern to me I assure you that he should be such an invalid.—I know nobody who likes a game of cards in a social way, better than he does;—and very few people that play a fairer rubber.[50]—It is a thousand pities that he should be so deprived of the pleasure. For now we have a quiet little whist club that meets three times a week at the White Hart,[51] and, if he could but have his health, how much he would enjoy it."

"I dare say he would Sir—and I wish with all my heart he were equal to it."

"Your club would be better fitted for an invalid," said Mrs. Edwards, "if you did not keep it up so late."—

This was an old grievance.—

"So late, my dear, what are you talking of?" cried the husband with sturdy pleasantry—. "We are always at home before midnight. They would laugh at Osborne Castle to hear you call *that* late; they are but just rising from dinner at midnight."[52]—

"That is nothing to the purpose—" retorted the lady calmly. "The Osbornes are to be no rule for us. You had better meet every night, and break up two hours sooner."

So far, the subject was very often carried;—but Mr. and Mrs. Edwards were so wise as never to pass that point; and Mr. Edwards now turned to something else.—He had lived long enough in the idleness of a town to become a little of a gossip, and having some curiosity to know more of the circumstances of his young guest than had yet reached him, he began with,

"I think, Miss Emma, I remember your aunt very well about thirty years ago; I am pretty sure I danced with her in the old rooms at Bath,[53] the year before I married—. She was a very fine woman then—but like other people I suppose she is grown somewhat older since that time.—I hope she is likely to be happy in her second choice."

"I hope so, I believe so, Sir—" said Emma in some agitation.—

"Mr. Turner had not been dead a great while I think?"

"About two years Sir."

"I forget what her name is now?"—

"O'Brien."

"Irish![54] Ah! I remember—and she is gone to settle in Ireland.—I do not wonder that you should not wish to go with her into *that* country Miss Emma—;[55] but it must be a great deprivation to her, poor lady!—After bringing you up like a child of her own."—

"I was not so ungrateful Sir," said Emma warmly, "as to wish to be any where but with her.—It did not suit them, it did not suit Captain O'Brien that I should be of the party.—"

"Captain!—" repeated Mrs. Edwards. "The gentleman is in the army then?"

"Yes Ma'am."—

"Aye—there is nothing like your officers for captivating the ladies, young or old.—There is no resisting a cockade[56] my dear."—

"I hope there is,"—said Mrs. Edwards gravely, with a quick glance at her daughter;—and Emma had just recovered from her own perturbation in time to see a blush on Miss Edwards's cheek, and in remembering what Elizabeth had said of

Captain Hunter, to wonder and waver between his influence and her brother's.—

"Elderly ladies should be careful how they make a second choice,"[57] observed Mr. Edwards.—

"Carefulness—discretion—should not be confined to elderly ladies, or to a second choice," added his wife. "It is quite as necessary to young ladies in their first."—

"Rather more so, my dear—" replied he, "because young ladies are likely to feel the effects of it longer. When an old lady plays the fool, it is not in the course of nature that she should suffer from it many years." Emma drew her hand across her eyes—and Mrs. Edwards, on perceiving it, changed the subject to one of less anxiety to all.—

With nothing to do but to expect the hour of setting off, the afternoon was long to the two young ladies; and though Miss Edwards was rather discomposed at the very early hour which her mother always fixed for going, that early hour itself was watched for with some eagerness.—The entrance of the tea things[58] at seven o'clock was some relief—and luckily Mr. and Mrs. Edwards always drank a dish extraordinary,[59] and ate an additional muffin[60] when they were going to sit up late, which lengthened the ceremony almost to the wished for moment. At a little before eight, the Tomlinsons' carriage was heard to go by, which was the constant signal for Mrs. Edwards to order hers to the door; and in a very few minutes, the party were transported from the quiet warmth of a snug parlour, to the bustle, noise and draughts of air of the broad entrance-passage of an inn.—

Mrs. Edwards, carefully guarding her own dress, while she attended with yet greater solicitude to the proper security of her young charges' shoulders and throats, led the way up the wide staircase, while no sound of a ball but the first scrape of one violin blessed the ears of her followers, and Miss

Edwards, on hazarding the anxious enquiry of whether there were many people come yet, was told by the waiter, as she knew she should, that "Mr. Tomlinson's family were in the room."

In passing along a short gallery to the assembly-room, brilliant in lights before them, they were accosted[61] by a young man in a morning dress and boots,[62] who was standing in the doorway of a bed chamber, apparently on purpose to see them go by.—

"Ah! Mrs. Edwards—how do you do?—How do you do Miss Edwards?—" he cried, with an easy air.—"You are determined to be in good time I see, as usual.—The candles are but this moment lit—"

"I like to get a good seat by the fire you know, Mr. Musgrave," replied Mrs. Edwards.

"I am this moment going to dress," said he—"I am waiting for my stupid fellow.—We shall have a famous ball. The Osbornes are certainly coming; you may depend upon *that* for I was with Lord Osborne this morning.—"

The party passed on—Mrs. Edwards's satin gown swept along the clean floor of the ball-room, to the fireplace at the upper end, where one party only were formally seated, while three or four officers were lounging together, passing in and out from the adjoining card-room.—A very stiff meeting between these near neighbours ensued—and as soon as they were all duly placed again, Emma, in the low whisper which became the solemn scene, said to Miss Edwards, "The gentleman we passed in the passage was Mr. Musgrave, then.—He is reckoned remarkably agreeable I understand.—"

Miss Edwards answered hesitatingly—"Yes—he is very much liked by many people.—But *we* are not very intimate."—

"He is rich, is not he?"—

"He has about eight or nine hundred pounds a year[63] I believe.—He came into possession of it when he was very young, and my father and mother think it has given him rather an unsettled turn.—He is no favourite with them."—

The cold and empty appearance of the room and the demure air of the small cluster of females at one end of it began soon to give way; the inspiriting sound of other carriages was heard, and continual accessions of portly chaperons,[64] and strings of smartly-dressed girls were received, with now and then a fresh gentleman straggler, who if not enough in love to station himself near any fair creature seemed glad to escape into the card-room.—Among the increasing numbers of military men, one now made his way to Miss Edwards, with an air of empressément,[65] which decidedly said to her companion "I am Captain Hunter"—and Emma, who could not but watch her at such a moment, saw her looking rather distressed, but by no means displeased, and heard an engagement formed for the two first dances,[66] which made her think her brother Sam's a hopeless case.—

Emma in the mean while was not unobserved, or unadmired herself.—A new face, and a very pretty one, could not be slighted—her name was whispered from one party to another, and no sooner had the signal been given, by the orchestra's striking up a favourite air, which seemed to call the young men to their duty, and people the centre of the room, than she found herself engaged to dance with a brother officer, introduced by Captain Hunter.[67]—Emma Watson was not more than of the middle height—well made and plump, with an air of healthy vigour.—Her skin was very brown, but clear, smooth and glowing—;[68] which with a lively eye, a sweet smile, and an open countenance, gave beauty to attract, and expression to make that beauty improve on acquaintance.—Having no reason to be dissatisfied with her partner, the evening began very pleasantly to her; and her feelings perfectly coincided with the re-iterated observation of others, that it was an excellent ball.—

The two first dances were not quite over, when the returning sound of carriages after a long interruption called general notice, and "the Osbornes are coming, the Osbornes are coming"[69]—was repeated round the room.—After some minutes of extraordinary bustle without, and watchful curiosity within, the important party, preceded by the attentive master of the inn to open a door which was never shut, made their appearance. They consisted of Lady Osborne, her son Lord Osborne,[70] her daughter Miss Osborne; Miss Carr, her daughter's friend, Mr. Howard, formerly tutor to Lord Osborne, now clergyman of the parish in which the castle stood,[71] Mrs. Blake, a widow-sister who lived with him, her son, a fine boy of ten years old, and Mr. Tom Musgrave; who, probably imprisoned within his own room, had been listening in bitter impatience to the sound of the music, for the last half hour. In their progress up the room, they paused almost immediately behind Emma, to receive the compliments of some acquaintance, and she heard Lady Osborne observe that they had made a point of coming early for the gratification of Mrs. Blake's little boy, who was uncommonly fond of dancing.—Emma looked at them all as they passed—but chiefly and with most interest on Tom Musgrave, who was certainly a genteel, good looking young man.—Of the females, Lady Osborne had by much the finest person;—though nearly fifty, she was very handsome, and had all the dignity of rank.—

Lord Osborne was a very fine young man; but there was an air of coldness, of carelessness, even of awkwardness about him, which seemed to speak him out of his element in a ball room. He came in fact only because it was judged expedient for him to please the Borough[72]—he was not fond of women's company, and he never danced.—Mr. Howard was an agreeable-looking man, a little more than thirty.—

At the conclusion of the two dances, Emma found herself, she knew not how, seated amongst the Osborne set; and she was immediately struck with the fine countenance and animated gestures of the little boy, as he was standing before his mother, wondering when they should begin.—

"You will not be surprised at Charles's impatience," said Mrs. Blake, a lively pleasant-looking little woman of five or six and thirty, to a lady who was standing near her, "when you know what a partner he is to have. Miss Osborne has been so very kind as to promise to dance the two first dances with him."—

"Oh! yes—we have been engaged this week," cried the boy, "and we are to dance down every couple."—[73]

On the other side of Emma, Miss Osborne, Miss Carr, and a party of young men were standing engaged in very lively consultation—and soon afterwards she saw the smartest officer of the set walking off to the orchestra to order the dance,[74] while Miss Osborne, passing before her, to her little expecting partner hastily said—"Charles, I beg your pardon for not keeping my engagement,[75] but I am going to dance these two dances with Colonel Beresford.[76] I know you will excuse me, and I will certainly dance with you after tea."[77] And without staying for an answer, she turned again to Miss Carr, and in another minute was led by Colonel Beresford to begin the set.[78]

If the poor little boy's face had in its happiness been interesting[79] to Emma, it was infinitely more so under this sudden reverse;—he stood the picture of disappointment, with crimsoned cheeks, quivering lips, and eyes bent on the floor. His mother, stifling her own mortification, tried to soothe his, with the prospect of Miss Osborne's second promise; but though he contrived to utter with an effort of boyish bravery "Oh! I do not mind it"—it was very evident by the unceasing agitation of his features that he minded it as much as ever.—

Emma did not think, or reflect;—she felt and acted—.[80]

"I shall be very happy to dance with you Sir, if you like it," said she, holding out her hand with the most unaffected good humour.—

The boy in one moment restored to all his first delight looked joyfully at his mother; and stepping forward with an honest and simple "Thank you Ma'am" was instantly ready to attend his new acquaintance.—The thankfulness of Mrs. Blake was more diffuse;—with a look, most expressive of unexpected pleasure and lively gratitude, she turned to her neighbour with repeated and fervent acknowledgements of so great and condescending[81] a kindness to her boy.—Emma with perfect truth could assure her that she could not be giving greater pleasure than she felt herself—and Charles being provided with his gloves and charged to keep them on,[82] they joined the set which was now rapidly forming, with nearly equal complacency.—[83]

It was a partnership which could not be noticed without surprise. It gained her a broad stare from Miss Osborne and Miss Carr as they passed her in the dance. "Upon my word Charles you are in luck, (said the former as she turned him[84]) you have got a better partner than me"—to which the happy Charles answered "Yes."—Tom Musgrave, who was dancing with Miss Carr, gave her many inquisitive glances; and after a time Lord Osborne himself came and under pretence of talking to Charles,[85] stood to look at his partner.—Though rather distressed by such observation, Emma could not repent what she had done, so happy had it made both the boy and his mother; the latter of whom was continually making opportunities of addressing her with the warmest civility.—

Her little partner she found, though bent chiefly on dancing, was not unwilling to speak, when her questions or remarks gave him anything to say; and she learnt, by a sort of inevitable enquiry, that "he had two brothers and a sister, that they and their mama all lived with his uncle at Wickstead,[86] that his uncle taught him Latin,[87] that he was very fond of riding, and had a horse of his own given him by Lord Osborne; and that he had been out once already with Lord Osborne's hounds."—[88]

At the end of these dances Emma found they were to drink tea;—Miss Edwards gave her a caution to be at hand, in a manner which convinced her of Mrs. Edwards's holding it very important to have them both close to her when she moved into the tea room; and Emma was accordingly on the alert to gain her proper station. It was always the pleasure of the company to have a little bustle and crowd when they thus adjourned for refreshment.—The tea room was a small room within the card room, and in passing through the latter, where the passage was straitened[89] by tables, Mrs. Edwards and her party were for a few moments hemmed in. It happened close by Lady Osborne's cassino table;[90] Mr. Howard who belonged to it spoke to his nephew; and Emma on perceiving herself the object of attention both to Lady Osborne and him, had just turned away her eyes in time, to avoid seeming to hear her young companion delightedly whisper aloud—"Oh! Uncle, do look at my partner. She is so pretty!"

As they were immediately in motion again however, Charles was hurried off without being able to receive his uncle's suffrage.[91]—On entering the tea room, in which two long tables were prepared, Lord Osborne was to be seen quite alone at the end of one, as if retreating as far as he could from the ball, to enjoy his own thoughts, and gape[92] without restraint.—Charles instantly pointed him out to Emma—

"There's Lord Osborne—let you and I go and sit by him."—

"No, no," said Emma laughing, "you must sit with my friends."[93]

Charles was now free enough to hazard a few questions in his turn. "What o'clock was it?—"

"Eleven."—

"Eleven!—And I am not at all sleepy. Mama said I should be asleep before ten.—Do you think Miss Osborne will keep her word with me, when tea is over?"

"Oh! yes.—I suppose so"—though she felt that she had no better reason to give than that Miss Osborne had *not* kept it before.—

"When shall you come to Osborne Castle?"—

"Never, probably.—I am not acquainted with the family."

"But you may come to Wickstead and see Mama, and she can take you to the Castle.—There is a monstrous curious stuffed fox there, and a badger—any body would think they were alive. It is a pity you should not see them."—

On rising from tea, there was again a scramble for the pleasure of being first out of the room, which happened to be increased by one or two of the card parties having just broken up and the players being disposed to move exactly the different way. Among these was Mr. Howard—his sister leaning on his arm—and no sooner were they within reach of Emma, than Mrs. Blake, calling her notice by a friendly touch, said

"Your goodness to Charles, my dear Miss Watson, brings all his family upon you. Give me leave to introduce my brother—Mr. Howard."

Emma curtsied, the gentleman bowed—made a hasty request for the honour of her hand in the two next dances, to which as hasty an affirmative was given, and they were immediately impelled in opposite directions.—Emma was very well pleased with the circumstance;—there was a quietly-cheerful, gentlemanlike air in Mr. Howard which suited her—and in a few minutes afterwards, the value of her engagement increased when as she was sitting in the card room somewhat screened by a door, she heard Lord Osborne, who was lounging on a vacant table near her, call Tom Musgrave towards him and say,

"Why do not you dance with that beautiful Emma Watson?—I want you to dance with her—and I will come and stand by you."—

"I was determining on it this very moment my Lord; I'll be introduced and dance with her directly.—"

"Aye do—and if you find she does not want much talking to, you may introduce me by and bye."—

"Very well my Lord—. If she is like her sisters, she will only want to be listened to.—I will go this moment. I shall find her in the tea room. That stiff old Mrs. Edwards has never done tea."—

Away he went—Lord Osborne after him—and Emma lost no time in hurrying from her corner, exactly the other way, forgetting in her haste that she left Mrs. Edwards behind.—

"We had quite lost you—" said Mrs. Edwards—who followed her with Mary, in less than five minutes.—"If you prefer this room to the other, there is no reason why you should not be here, but we had better all be together."

Emma was saved the trouble of apologizing, by their being joined at the moment by Tom Musgrave, who, requesting Mrs. Edwards aloud to do him the honour of presenting him to Miss Emma Watson, left that good lady without any choice in the business, but that of testifying by the coldness of her manner that she did it unwillingly. The honour of dancing with her, was solicited without loss of time—and Emma, however she might like to be thought a beautiful girl by lord or commoner,[94] was so little disposed to favour Tom Musgrave himself, that she had considerable satisfaction in avowing her prior engagement.—He was evidently surprised and discomposed.—The stile of her last partner had probably led him to believe her not overpowered with applications.—

"My little friend Charles Blake," he cried, "must not expect to engross you the whole evening. We can never suffer this—it is against the rules of the assembly[95]—and I am sure it will never be patronised[96] by our good friend here Mrs. Edwards; she is by much too nice[97] a judge of decorum to give her license to such a dangerous particularity."—[98]

"I am not going to dance with Master Blake Sir."

The gentleman, a little disconcerted, could only hope he might be more fortunate another time—and seeming unwilling to leave her—though his friend Lord Osborne was waiting in the doorway for the result, as Emma with some amusement perceived—he began to make civil enquiries after her family.—

"How comes it, that we have not the pleasure of seeing your sisters here this evening?—Our assemblies have been used to be so well treated by them, that we do not know how to take this neglect."—

"My eldest sister is the only one at home—and she could not leave my father—"

"Miss Watson the only one at home!—You astonish me!—It seems but the day before yesterday that I saw them all three in this town. But I am afraid I have been a very sad[99] neighbour of late. I hear dreadful complaints of my negligence wherever I go,—and I confess it is a shameful length of time since I was at Stanton.—But I shall *now* endeavour to make myself amends for the past."—

Emma's calm curtsey in reply must have struck him as very unlike the encouraging warmth he had been used to receive from her sisters, and gave him probably the novel sensation of doubting his own influence, and of wishing for more attention than she bestowed.—

The dancing now recommenced; Miss Carr being impatient to *call*,[100] everybody was required to stand up—and Tom Musgrave's curiosity was appeased, on seeing Mr. Howard come forward and claim Emma's hand—"That will do as well for *me*"—was Lord Osborne's remark, when his friend carried him the news—and he was continually at Howard's elbow during the two dances.—The frequency of his appearance there, was the only unpleasant part of her engagement, the only objection she could make to Mr. Howard.—In himself, she thought him as agreeable as he looked; though chatting on the commonest topics he had a sensible, unaffected way of expressing himself, which made them all worth hearing, and she only regretted that he had not been able to make his pupil's manners as unexceptionable as his own.—The two dances seemed very short, and she had her partner's authority for considering them so.—At their conclusion the Osbornes and their train were all on the move.

"We are off at last," said his Lordship to Tom—"How much longer do *you* stay in this heavenly place?—till sunrise?"—

"No, faith! my Lord, I have had quite enough of it I assure you—I shall not shew myself here again when I have had the honour of attending Lady Osborne to her carriage. I shall retreat in as much secrecy as possible to the most remote corner of the house, where I shall order a barrel of oysters,[101] and be famously snug."

"Let us see you soon at the Castle; and bring me word how she looks by daylight."—

Emma and Mrs. Blake parted as old acquaintance, and Charles shook her by the hand and wished her "good bye" at least a dozen times. From Miss Osborne and Miss Carr she received something like a jerking curtsey as they passed her;[102] even Lady Osborne gave her a look of complacency—and his Lordship actually came back after the others were out of the room, to "beg her pardon", and look in the window seat behind her for the gloves which were visibly compressed in his hand.—

As Tom Musgrave was seen no more, we may suppose his plan to have succeeded, and imagine him mortifying with his barrel of oysters, in dreary solitude—or gladly assisting the landlady in her bar to make fresh negus[103] for the happy dancers above.

Emma could not help missing the party, by whom she had been, though in some respects unpleasantly, distinguished, and the two dances which followed and concluded the ball were rather flat, in comparison with the others.—Mr. Edwards having played with good luck, they were some of the last in the room—

"Here we are, back again I declare—" said Emma sorrowfully, as she walked into the dining room, where the table was prepared, and the neat upper maid[104] was lighting the candles—"My dear Miss Edwards—how soon it is at an end!—I wish it could all come over again!—"

A great deal of kind pleasure was expressed in her having enjoyed the evening so much—and Mr. Edwards was as warm as herself, in praise of the fullness, brilliancy and spirit of the meeting; though as he had been fixed the whole time at the same table in the same room, with only one change of chairs, it might have seemed a matter scarcely perceived.—But he had won four rubbers out of five, and everything went well. His daughter felt the advantage of this gratified state of mind, in the course of the remarks and retrospections which now ensued, over the welcome soup.—

"How came you not to dance with either of the Mr. Tomlinsons, Mary?—" said her mother.

"I was always engaged when they asked me."

"I thought you were to have stood up with Mr. James, the two last dances; Mrs. Tomlinson told me he was gone to ask you—and I had heard you say two minutes before that you were *not* engaged.—"

"Yes—but—there was a mistake—I had misunderstood—I did not know I was engaged—I thought it had been for the two dances after, if we staid so long—but Captain Hunter assured me it was for those very two.—"—

"So, you ended with Captain Hunter Mary, did you?" said her father. "And who did you begin with?"

"Captain Hunter" was repeated, in a very humble tone.—

"Hum!—That is being constant however. But who else did you dance with?"

"Mr. Norton, and Mr. Styles."

"And who are they?"

"Mr. Norton is a cousin of Captain Hunter's."—

"And who is Mr. Styles?"

"One of his particular friends."—

"All in the same regiment," added Mrs. Edwards.—"Mary was surrounded by red coats[105] the whole evening. I should have been better pleased to see her dancing with some of our old neighbours I confess.—"

"Yes, yes, we must not neglect our old neighbours—. But if these soldiers are quicker than other people in a ball room, what are young ladies to do?"

"I think there is no occasion for their engaging themselves so many dances beforehand, Mr. Edwards."—

"No—perhaps not—but I remember my dear when you and I did the same."—

Mrs. Edwards said no more, and Mary breathed again.—A great deal of good-humoured pleasantry followed—and Emma went to bed in charming spirits, her head full of Osbornes, Blakes and Howards.—

The next morning brought a great many visitors. It was the way of the place always to call on Mrs. Edwards on the morning after a ball, and this neighbourly inclination was increased in the present instance by a general spirit of curiosity on Emma's account, as everybody wanted to look again at the girl who had been admired the night before by Lord Osborne—.

Many were the eyes, and various the degrees of approbation with which she was examined. Some saw no fault, and some no beauty—. With some her brown skin was the annihilation of every grace, and others could never be persuaded that she were half so handsome as Elizabeth Watson had been ten years ago.—

The morning passed quietly away in discussing the merits of the ball with all this succession of company—and Emma was at once astonished by finding it two o'clock, and considering that she had heard nothing of her father's chair. After this discovery she had walked twice to the window to examine the street, and was on the point of asking leave to ring the bell and make enquiries, when the light sound of a carriage driving up to the door set her heart at ease. She stepped again to the window—but instead of the convenient though very un-smart family equipage perceived a neat curricle.[106]—Mr. Musgrave was shortly afterwards announced;—and Mrs. Edwards put on her very stiffest look at the sound.—Not at all dismayed however by her chilling air, he paid his compliments to each of the ladies with no unbecoming ease, and continuing to address Emma, presented her a note, which he had "the honour of bringing from her sister; but to which he must observe that a verbal postscript from himself would be requisite."—

The note, which Emma was beginning to read rather *before* Mrs. Edwards had entreated her to use no ceremony, contained a few lines from Elizabeth importing that their father in consequence of being unusually well had taken the sudden resolution of attending the visitation[107] that day, and that as his road lay quite wide from R.[108] it was impossible for her to come home till the following morning, unless the Edwardses would send her, which was hardly to be expected, or she could meet with any chance conveyance, or did not mind walking so far.—She had scarcely run her eye through the whole, before she found herself obliged to listen to Tom Musgrave's farther account.

"I received that note from the fair hands of Miss Watson only ten minutes ago," said he—"I met her in the village of Stanton, whither my good stars prompted me to turn my horses' heads—she was at that moment in quest of a person to employ on the errand, and I was fortunate enough to convince her that she could not find a more willing or speedy messenger than myself—. Remember, I say nothing of my disinterestedness.—My reward is to be the indulgence of conveying you to Stanton in my curricle.—Though they are not written down, I bring your sister's orders for the same.—"

Emma felt distressed; she did not like the proposal—she did not wish to be on terms of intimacy with the proposer—and yet fearful of encroaching on the Edwardses, as well as wishing to go home herself, she was at a loss how entirely to decline what he offered—.[109] Mrs. Edwards continued silent, either not understanding the case, or waiting to see how the young lady's inclination lay. Emma thanked him—but professed herself very unwilling to give him so much trouble. "The trouble was of course, honour, pleasure, delight. What had he or his horses to do?"—Still she hesitated. "She believed she must beg leave to decline his assistance—She was rather afraid of the sort of carriage—. The distance was not beyond a walk.—"—

Mrs. Edwards was silent no longer. She enquired into the particulars—and then said, "We shall be extremely happy, Miss Emma, if you can give us the pleasure of your company till tomorrow—but if you can not conveniently do so, our carriage is quite at your service, and Mary will be pleased with the opportunity of seeing your sister."—

This was precisely what Emma had longed for, and she accepted the offer most thankfully; acknowledging that as Elizabeth was entirely alone, it was her wish to return home to dinner.[110]—The plan was warmly opposed by their visitor.

"I cannot suffer it indeed. I must not be deprived of the happiness of escorting you. I assure you there is not a possibility of fear with my horses. You might guide them yourself. *Your sisters* all know how quiet they are; they have none of them the smallest scruple in trusting themselves with me, even on a race-course.—Believe me—" added he lowering his voice—"*You* are quite safe, the danger is only *mine*."—Emma was not more disposed to oblige him for all this.—"And as to Mrs. Edwards's carriage being used the day after a ball, it is a thing quite out of rule I assure you—never heard of before—the old coachman will look as black as his horses—. Won't he Miss Edwards?"—No notice was taken. The ladies were silently firm, and the gentleman found himself obliged to submit.—

"What a famous ball we had last night!—" he cried, after a short pause. "How long did you keep it up, after the Osbornes and I went away?"—

"We had two dances more."—

"It is making it too much of a fatigue I think, to stay so late.—I suppose your set was not a very full one."—

"Yes, quite as full as ever, except the Osbornes. There seemed no vacancy anywhere—and everybody danced with uncommon spirit to the very last."—Emma said this—though against her conscience.—

"Indeed! perhaps I might have looked in upon you again, if I had been aware of as much;—for I am rather fond of dancing than not.—Miss Osborne is a charming girl, is not she?"

"I do not think her handsome," replied Emma, to whom all this was chiefly addressed.

"Perhaps she is not critically[111] handsome, but her manners are delightful. And Fanny Carr is a most interesting little creature. You can imagine nothing more *naive* or *piquante*; and what do you think of *Lord Osborne*, Miss Watson?"

"That he would be handsome, even though he were *not* a Lord—and perhaps—better bred; more desirous of pleasing, and shewing himself pleased in a right place.—"

"Upon my word, you are severe upon my friend!—I assure you Lord Osborne is a very good fellow."—

"I do not dispute his virtues—but I do not like his careless air."—

"If it were not a breach of confidence," replied Tom with an important look, "perhaps I might be able to win a more favourable opinion of poor Osborne.—"

Emma gave him no encouragement, and he was obliged to keep his friend's secret.—He was also obliged to put an end to his visit—for Mrs. Edwards having ordered her carriage, there was no time to be lost on Emma's side in preparing for it.—Miss Edwards accompanied her home, but as it was dinner hour at Stanton, staid with them only a few minutes.—

"Now my dear Emma," said Miss Watson, as soon as they were alone, "you must talk to me all the rest of the day, without stopping, or I shall not be satisfied. But first of all Nanny shall bring in the dinner. Poor thing!—You will not dine as you did yesterday, for we have nothing but some fried beef.—How nice Mary Edwards looks in her new pelisse![112]—And now tell me how you like them all, and what I am to say to Sam. I have begun my letter, Jack Stokes is to call for it tomorrow, for his uncle is going within a mile of Guilford the next day.—"[113]

Nanny brought in the dinner.—

"We will wait upon ourselves," continued Elizabeth, "and then we shall lose no time.—And so, you would not come home with Tom Musgrave?"—

"No. You had said so much against him that I could not wish either for the obligation, or the intimacy which the use of his carriage must have created—. I should not even have liked the appearance of it."—

"You did very right; though I wonder at your forbearance, and I do not think I could have done it myself.—He seemed so eager to fetch you, that I could not say no, though it rather went against me to be throwing you together, so well as I knew his tricks;—but I did long to see you, and it was a clever way of getting you home; besides—it won't do to be too nice.—Nobody could have thought of the Edwardses letting you have their coach,—after the horses being out so late.—But what am I to say to Sam?"—

"If you are guided by me, you will not encourage him to think of Miss Edwards.—The father is decidedly against him, the mother shews him no favour, and I doubt his having any interest with Mary. She danced twice with Captain Hunter, and I think shews him in general as much encouragement as is consistent with her disposition, and the circumstances she is placed in.—She once mentioned Sam, and certainly with a little confusion—but that was perhaps merely owing to the consciousness of his liking her, which may very probably have come to her knowledge."—

"Oh! dear! yes—she has heard enough of that from us all. Poor Sam!—He is out of luck as well as other people.—For the life of me, Emma, I cannot help feeling for those that are crossed in love.—Well—now begin, and give me an account of every thing as it happened.—"

Emma obeyed her—and Elizabeth listened with very little interruption till she heard of Mr. Howard as a partner.—

"Dance with Mr. Howard—Good heavens! You don't say so!—Why—he is quite one of the great and grand ones.—Did not you find him very high?—"[114]

"His manners are of a kind to give *me* much more ease and confidence than Tom Musgrave's."

"Well—go on. I should have been frightened out of my wits, to have had anything to do with the Osbornes' set."—Emma concluded her narration.—"And so, you really did not dance with Tom Musgrave at all?—But you must have liked him, you must have been struck with him altogether."—

"I do *not* like him, Elizabeth—. I allow his person and air to be good—and that his manners to a certain point—his address[115] rather—is pleasing.—But I see nothing else to admire in him.—On the contrary, he seems very vain, very conceited, absurdly anxious for distinction, and absolutely contemptible in some of the measures he takes for becoming so.—There is a ridiculousness about him that entertains me—but his company gives me no other agreeable emotion."

"My dearest Emma!—You are like nobody else in the world.—It is well Margaret is not by.—You do not offend *me*, though I hardly know how to believe you. But Margaret would never forgive such words."

"I wish Margaret could have heard him profess his ignorance of her being out of the country;[116]—he declared it seemed only two days since he had seen her.—"

"Aye—that is just like him. And yet this is the man, she *will* fancy so desperately in love with her.—He is no favourite of mine, as you well know, Emma;—but you must think him agreeable. Can you lay your hand on your heart, and say you do not?"—

"Indeed I can. Both hands; and spread to their widest extent.—"

"I should like to know the man you *do* think agreeable."

"His name is Howard."

"Howard! Dear me. I cannot think of *him*, but as playing cards with Lady Osborne, and looking proud.—I must own however that it *is* a relief to me, to find you can speak as you do, of Tom Musgrave; my heart did misgive me that you would like him too well. You talked so stoutly beforehand, that I was sadly afraid your brag would be punished.—I only hope it will last;—and that he will not come on to pay you much attention; it is a hard thing for a woman to stand against the flattering ways of a man, when he is bent upon pleasing her.—"

As their quietly-sociable little meal concluded, Miss Watson could not help observing how comfortably it had passed.

"It is so delightful to me," said she, "to have things going on in peace and good humour. Nobody can tell how much I hate quarrelling. Now, though we have had nothing but fried beef, how good it has all seemed.—I wish everybody were as easily satisfied as you—but poor Margaret is very snappish, and Penelope owns she had rather have quarrelling going on, than nothing at all."—

Mr. Watson returned in the evening, not the worse for the exertion of the day, and consequently pleased with what he had done, and glad to talk of it, over his own fireside.—Emma had not foreseen any interest to herself in the occurrences of a visitation—but when she heard Mr. Howard spoken of as the preacher, and as having given them an excellent sermon, she could not help listening with a quicker ear.—

"I do not know when I have heard a discourse more to my mind—" continued Mr. Watson—"or one better delivered.—He reads extremely well, with great propriety and in a very impressive manner; and at the same time without any theatrical grimace or violence.—I own, I do not like much action in the pulpit—I do not like the studied air and artificial inflexions of voice, which your very popular and most admired preachers generally have.—A simple delivery is much better calculated to inspire devotion, and shews a much better taste.[117]—Mr. Howard read like a scholar and a gentleman."—

"And what had you for dinner Sir?" said his eldest daughter.—

He related the dishes and told what he had ate himself.[118] "Upon the whole," he added, "I have had a very comfortable day; my old friends were quite surprised to see me amongst them—and I must say that everybody paid me great attention, and seemed to feel for me as an invalid.—They would make me sit near the fire, and as the partridges were pretty high,[119] Dr. Richards would have them sent away to the other end of the table, that they might not offend Mr. Watson—which I thought very kind of him.—But what pleased me as much as anything was Mr. Howard's attention.—There is a pretty steep flight of steps up to the room we dine in—which do not quite agree with my gouty foot[120]—and Mr. Howard walked by me from the bottom to the top, and would make me take his arm.—It struck me as very becoming in so young a man, but I am sure I had no claim to expect it; for I never saw him before in my life.—By the bye, he enquired after one of my daughters, but I do not know which. I suppose you know among yourselves."—

On the third day after the ball, as Nanny, at five minutes before three, was beginning to bustle into the parlour with the tray and the knife-case,[121] she was suddenly called to the front door, by the sound of as smart a rap as the end of a riding-whip could give—and though charged by Miss Watson to let nobody in, returned in half a minute, with a look of awkward dismay, to hold the parlour door open for Lord Osborne and Tom Musgrave.—The surprise of the young ladies may be imagined. No visitors would have been welcome at such a moment; but such visitors as these—such a one as Lord Osborne at least, a nobleman and a stranger, was really distressing.—He looked a little embarrassed himself,—as, on being introduced by his easy, voluble friend, he muttered something of doing himself the honour of waiting on Mr. Watson.[122]—

Though Emma could not but take the compliment of the visit to herself, she was very far from enjoying it. She felt all the inconsistency of such an acquaintance with the very humble stile in which they were obliged to live; and having in her aunt's family been used to many of the elegancies of life, was fully sensible of all that must be open to the ridicule of richer people in her present home.—Of the pain of such feelings, Elizabeth knew very little;—her simpler mind, or juster reason, saved her from such mortification—and though shrinking under a general sense of inferiority, she felt no particular shame.—Mr. Watson, as the gentlemen had already heard from Nanny, was not well enough to be down stairs.—With much concern they took their seats—Lord Osborne near Emma, and the convenient Mr. Musgrave in high spirits at his own importance, on the other side of the fireplace with Elizabeth.—*He* was at no loss for words;—but when Lord Osborne had hoped that Emma had not caught cold at the ball, he had nothing more to say for some time, and could only gratify his eye by occasional glances at his fair neighbour.—Emma was not inclined to give herself much trouble for his entertainment—and after hard labour of mind, he produced the remark of its being a very fine day, and followed it up with the question of, "Have you been walking this morning?"

"No, my Lord. We thought it too dirty."

"You should wear half-boots."[123]—

After another pause, "Nothing sets off a neat ancle more than a half-boot; nankin galoshed with black[124] looks very well.—Do not you like half-boots?"

"Yes—but unless they are so stout as to injure their beauty, they are not fit for country walking.—"

"Ladies should ride in dirty weather.—Do you ride?"

"No my Lord."

"I wonder every lady does not.—A woman never looks better than on horseback.—"

"But every woman may not have the inclination, or the means."[125]

"If they knew how much it became them, they would all have the inclination—and I fancy Miss Watson—when once they had the inclination, the means would soon follow."—

"Your Lordship thinks we always have our own way.—*That* is a point on which ladies and gentlemen have long disagreed.—But without pretending to decide it, I may say that there are some circumstances which even *women* cannot controul.—Female economy will do a great deal my Lord, but it cannot turn a small income into a large one."—[126]

Lord Osborne was silenced. Her manner had been neither sententious nor sarcastic, but there was a something in its mild seriousness, as well as in the words themselves, which made his Lordship think;—and when he addressed her again, it was with a degree of considerate propriety, totally unlike the half-awkward, half-fearless stile of his former remarks.—It was a new thing with him to wish to please a woman; it was the first time that he had ever felt what was due to a woman, in Emma's situation.—But as he wanted neither sense nor a good disposition, he did not feel it without effect.—

"You have not been long in this country I understand," said he in the tone of a gentleman. "I hope you are pleased with it."—

He was rewarded by a gracious answer, and a more liberal full view of her face than she had yet bestowed. Unused to exert himself, and happy in contemplating her, he then sat in silence for some minutes longer, while Tom Musgrave was chattering to Elizabeth, till they were interrupted by Nanny's approach, who half opening the door and putting in her head, said, "Please Ma'am, master wants to know why he be'nt to have his dinner."—

The gentlemen, who had hitherto disregarded every symptom, however positive, of the nearness of that meal, now jumped up with apologies, while Elizabeth called briskly after Nanny "to tell Betty to take up the fowls."—

"I am sorry it happens so—" she added, turning good humouredly towards Musgrave—"but you know what early hours we keep.—"

Tom had nothing to say for himself, he knew it very well, and such honest simplicity, such shameless truth rather bewildered him.—Lord Osborne's parting compliments took some time, his inclination for speech seeming to increase with the shortness of the term for indulgence.—He recommended exercise in defiance of dirt—spoke again in praise of half-boots—begged that his sister might be allowed to send Emma the name of her shoemaker—and concluded with saying,

"My hounds will be hunting this country next week—I believe they will throw off at Stanton Wood on Wednesday—at nine o'clock.[127]—I mention this, in hopes of your being drawn out to see what's going on.—If the morning's tolerable, pray do us the honour of giving us your good wishes in person."[128]

The sisters looked on each other with astonishment, when their visitors had withdrawn.

"Here's an unaccountable honour!" cried Elizabeth at last. "Who would have thought of Lord Osborne's coming to Stanton.—He is very handsome;—but Tom Musgrave looks, all to nothing, the smartest and most fashionable man of the two. I am glad he did not say anything to me; I would not have had to talk to such a great man for the world. Tom was very agreeable, was not he?—But did you hear him ask where Miss Penelope and Miss Margaret were, when he first came in?—It put me out of patience.—I am glad Nanny had not laid the cloth however, it would have looked so awkward;—just the tray did not signify.—"

To say that Emma was not flattered by Lord Osborne's visit, would be to assert a very unlikely thing, and describe a very odd young lady; but the gratification was by no means unalloyed; his coming was a sort of notice which might please her vanity, but did not suit her pride, and she would rather have known that he wished the visit without presuming to make it, than have seen him at Stanton.[129]—Among other unsatisfactory feelings it once occurred to her to wonder why

Mr. Howard had not taken the same privilege of coming, and accompanied his Lordship—but she was willing to suppose that he had either known nothing about it, or had declined any share in a measure which carried quite as much impertinence in its form[130] as good breeding.—

Mr. Watson was very far from being delighted, when he heard what had passed;—a little peevish under immediate pain, and ill-disposed to be pleased, he only replied—"Phoo! phoo!—what occasion could there be for Lord Osborne's coming. I have lived here fourteen years without being noticed by any of the family. It is some foolery of that idle fellow Tom Musgrave. I cannot return the visit.—I would not if I could." And when Tom Musgrave was met with again, he was commissioned with a message of excuse to Osborne Castle, on the too-sufficient plea of Mr. Watson's infirm state of health.—

A week or ten days rolled quietly away after this visit, before any new bustle arose to interrupt, even for half a day, the tranquil and affectionate intercourse of the two sisters, whose mutual regard was increasing with the intimate knowledge of each other which such intercourse produced.—The first circumstance to break in on this serenity was the receipt of a letter from Croydon to announce the speedy return of Margaret, and a visit of two or three days from Mr. and Mrs. Robert Watson, who undertook to bring her home and wished to see their sister Emma.—It was an expectation to fill the thoughts of the sisters at Stanton, and to busy the hours of one of them at least—for as Jane had been a woman of fortune, the preparations for her entertainment were considerable, and as Elizabeth had at all times more good will than method in her guidance of the house, she could make no change without a bustle.—An absence of fourteen years had made all her brothers and sisters strangers to Emma, but in her expectation of Margaret there was more than the awkwardness of such an alienation; she had heard things which made her dread her return; and the day which brought the party to Stanton seemed to her the probable conclusion of almost all that had been comfortable in the house.—

Robert Watson was an attorney at Croydon, in a good way of business; very well satisfied with himself for the same, and for having married the only daughter of the attorney to whom he had been clerk, with a fortune of six thousand pounds.[131]—Mrs. Robert was not less pleased with herself for having had that six thousand pounds, and for being now in possession of a very smart house in Croydon, where she gave genteel parties, and wore fine clothes.—In her person there was nothing remarkable; her manners were pert and conceited.—

Margaret was not without beauty; she had a slight, pretty figure, and rather wanted countenance[132] than good features;—but the sharp and anxious expression of her face made her beauty in general little felt.—On meeting her long-absent sister, as on every occasion of shew, her manner was all affection and her voice all gentleness; continual smiles and a very slow articulation being her constant resource when determined on pleasing.—

She was now so "delighted to see dear, dear Emma" that she could hardly speak a word in a minute.—"I am sure we shall be great friends—" she observed, with much sentiment, as they were sitting together.—

Emma scarcely knew how to answer such a proposition—and the manner in which it was spoken, she could not attempt to equal.[133] Mrs. Robert Watson eyed her with much familiar curiosity and triumphant compassion;—the loss of the aunt's fortune was uppermost in her mind, at the moment of meeting;—and she could not but feel how much better it was to be the daughter of a gentleman of property in Croydon, than the niece of an old woman who threw herself away on an Irish captain.—Robert was carelessly kind, as became a prosperous man and a brother; more intent on settling with the post-boy, inveighing against the exorbitant advance in posting,[134] and pondering over a doubtful halfcrown,[135] than on welcoming a sister, who was no longer likely to have any property for him to get the direction of.—

"Your road through the village is infamous, Elizabeth," said he; "worse than ever it was. By heaven! I would endite it if I lived near you. Who is surveyor now?"—[136]

There was a little niece at Croydon, to be fondly enquired after by the kind-hearted Elizabeth, who regretted very much her not being of the party.—

"You are very good—" replied her mother—"and I assure you it went very hard with Augusta to have us come away without her.[137] I was forced to say we were only going to church and promise to come back for her directly.—But you know it would not do, to bring her without her maid, and I am as particular as ever in having her properly attended to."

"Sweet little darling!—" cried Margaret.—"It quite broke my heart to leave her.—"

"Then why was you in such a hurry to run away from her?" cried Mrs. Robert.—"You are a sad shabby[138] girl.—I have been quarrelling with you all the way we came, have not I?—Such a visit as this, I never heard of!—You know how glad we are to have any of you with us—if it be for months together.[139]—And I am sorry, (with a witty smile) we have not been able to make Croydon agreeable this Autumn."—

"My dearest Jane—do not overpower me with your raillery.—You know what inducements I had to bring me home.—Spare me, I entreat you—I am no match for your arch sallies."[140]—

"Well, I only beg you will not set your neighbours against the place.—Perhaps Emma may be tempted to go back with us, and stay till Christmas, if you don't put in your word."—Emma was greatly obliged. "I assure you we have very good society at Croydon.—I do not much attend the balls, they are rather too mixed,[141]—but our parties are very select and good.—I had seven tables[142] last week in my drawing room.—Are you fond of the country? How do you like Stanton?"—

"Very much"—replied Emma, who thought a comprehensive answer most to the purpose.—She saw that her sister in law despised her immediately.—Mrs. Robert Watson was indeed wondering what sort of a home Emma could possibly have been used to in Shropshire, and setting it down as certain that the aunt could never have had six thousand pounds.—

"How charming Emma is!—" whispered Margaret to Mrs. Robert in her most languishing[143] tone.—

Emma was quite distressed by such behaviour;—and she did not like it better when she heard Margaret five minutes afterwards say to Elizabeth in a sharp quick accent, totally unlike the first—

"Have you heard from Penelope since she went to Chichester?—I had a letter the other day.—I don't find she is likely to make anything of it. I fancy she'll come back 'Miss Penelope' as she went.—"—

Such, she feared would be Margaret's common voice, when the novelty of her own appearance were over; the tone of artificial sensibility was not recommended by the idea.—The ladies were invited upstairs to prepare for dinner.

"I hope you will find things tolerably comfortable Jane"—said Elizabeth as she opened the door of the spare bedchamber.—

"My good creature," replied Jane, "use no ceremony with me, I intreat you. I am one of those who always take things as they find them. I hope I can put up with a small apartment for two or three nights, without making a piece of work. I always wish to be treated quite 'en famille' when I come to see you—and now I do hope you have not been getting a great dinner for us.—Remember we never eat suppers."—[144]

"I suppose," said Margaret rather quickly to Emma, "you and I are to be together; Elizabeth always takes care to have a room to herself."—

"No—Elizabeth gives me half hers."—[145]

"Oh!—(in a softened voice, and rather mortified to find that she was not ill used) I am sorry I am not to have the pleasure of your company—especially as it makes me nervous to be much alone."—

Emma was the first of the females in the parlour again; on entering it she found her brother alone.—

"So Emma," said he, "you are quite the stranger at home. It must seem odd enough to you to be here.—A pretty piece of work your aunt Turner has made of it!—By heaven! a woman should never be trusted with money. I always said she ought to have settled something on you, as soon as her husband died."

"But that would have been trusting *me* with money," replied Emma, "and *I* am a woman too.—"

"It might have been secured to your future use, without your having any power over it now.—What a blow it must have been upon you!—To find yourself, instead of heiress of eight or nine thousand pounds, sent back a weight upon your family, without a sixpence.—I hope the old woman will smart for it."[146]

"Do not speak disrespectfully of her—she was very good to me; and if she has made an imprudent choice, she will suffer more from it herself, than *I* can possibly do."

"I do not mean to distress you, but you know every body must think her an old fool.—I thought Turner had been reckoned an extraordinary sensible, clever man.—How the devil came he to make such a will?"—

"My uncle's sense is not at all impeached, in my opinion, by his attachment to my aunt. She had been an excellent wife to him. The most liberal and enlightened minds are always the most confiding.[147]—The event has been unfortunate, but my uncle's memory is if possible endeared to me by such a proof of tender respect for my aunt."—

"That's odd sort of talking!—He might have provided decently for his widow, without leaving every thing that he had to dispose of, or any part of it, at her mercy.—"

"My aunt may have erred—" said Emma warmly—"she *has* erred—but my uncle's conduct was faultless. I was her own niece, and he left to herself the power and the pleasure of providing for me."—

"But unluckily she has left the pleasure of providing for you, to your father, and without the power.—That's the long and the short of the business. After keeping you at a distance from your family for such a length of time as must do away all natural affection among us and breeding you up (I suppose) in a superior stile, you are returned upon their hands without a sixpence."

"You know," replied Emma struggling with her tears, "my uncle's melancholy state of health.—He was a greater invalid than my father. He could not leave home."

"I do not mean to make you cry—" said Robert rather softened—and after a short silence, by way of changing the subject, he added—"I am just come from my father's room, he seems very indifferent.[148] It will be a sad break-up when he dies. Pity, you can none of you get married!—You must come to Croydon as well as the rest, and see what you can do there.—I believe if Margaret had had a thousand or fifteen hundred pounds, there was a young man who would have thought of her."

Emma was glad when they were joined by the others; it was better to look at her sister in law's finery, than listen to Robert, who had equally irritated and grieved her.—Mrs. Robert, exactly as smart as she had been at her own party, came in with apologies for her dress—

"I would not make you wait," said she, "so I put on the first thing I met with.—I am afraid I am a sad figure.—My dear Mr. Watson—(to her husband) you have not put any fresh powder in your hair."—[149]

"No—I do not intend it.—I think there is powder enough in my hair for my wife and sisters."—

"Indeed you ought to make some alteration in your dress before dinner when you are out visiting, though you do not at home."

"Nonsense.—"

"It is very odd you should not like to do what other gentlemen do. Mr. Marshall and Mr. Hemmings change their dress every day of their lives before dinner. And what was the use of my putting up[150] your last new coat, if you are never to wear it."—

"Do be satisfied with being fine yourself, and leave your husband alone."—

To put an end to this altercation, and soften the evident vexation of her sister in law, Emma, (though in no spirits to make such nonsense easy) began to admire her gown.—It produced immediate complacency.—

"Do you like it?—" said she.—"I am very happy.—It has been excessively admired;—but sometimes I think the pattern too large.—I shall wear one tomorrow that I think you will prefer to this.—Have you seen the one I gave Margaret?"—

Dinner came, and except when Mrs. Robert looked at her husband's head, she continued gay and flippant, chiding Elizabeth for the profusion on the table, and absolutely protesting against the entrance of the roast turkey—which formed the only exception to "You see your dinner".—[151]

"I do beg and entreat that no turkey may be seen to day. I am really frightened out of my wits with the number of dishes we have already. Let us have no turkey I beseech you."—

"My dear," replied Elizabeth, "the turkey is roasted, and it may just as well come in, as stay in the kitchen. Besides, if it is cut, I am in hopes my father may be tempted to eat a bit, for it is rather a favourite dish."

"You may have it in my dear, but I assure you *I* shan't touch it."—

Mr. Watson had not been well enough to join the party at dinner, but was prevailed on to come down and drink tea with them.—

"I wish we may be able to have a game of cards tonight," said Elizabeth to Mrs. Robert after seeing her father comfortably seated in his arm chair.—

"Not on my account my dear, I beg. You know I am no card player. I think a snug chat infinitely better. I always say cards are very well sometimes, to break a formal circle, but one never wants them among friends."

"I was thinking of its being something to amuse my father," answered Elizabeth—"if it was not disagreeable to you. He says his head won't bear whist—but perhaps if we make a round game[152] he may be tempted to sit down with us."—

"By all means my dear creature. I am quite at your service. Only do not oblige me to chuse the game, that's all. *Speculation*[153] is the only round game at Croydon now, but I can play any thing.—When there is only one or two of you at home, you must be quite at a loss to amuse him—why do not you get him to play at cribbage?[154]—Margaret and I have played at cribbage, most nights that we have not been engaged."—

A sound like a distant carriage was at this moment caught; every body listened, it became more decided; it certainly drew nearer.—It was an unusual sound in Stanton at any time of the day, for the village was on no very public road, and contained no gentleman's family but the rector's.—The wheels rapidly approached;—in two minutes the general expectation was answered; they stopped beyond a doubt at the garden gate of the parsonage. "Who could it be?—it was certainly a postchaise.[155]—Penelope was the only creature to be thought of. She might perhaps have met with some unexpected opportunity of returning."—A pause of suspense ensued.—Steps were distinguished, first along the paved footway which led under the windows of the house to the front door, and then within the passage. They were the steps of a man. It could not be Penelope. It must be Samuel.—The door opened, and displayed Tom Musgrave in the wrap[156] of a traveller.—He had been in London and was now on his way home, and he had come half a mile out of his road merely to call for ten minutes at Stanton. He loved to take people by surprise, with sudden visits at extraordinary seasons;[157] and in the present instance had had the additional motive of being able to tell the Miss Watsons, whom he depended on finding sitting quietly employed after tea, that he was going home to an eight o'clock dinner.—

As it happened however, he did not give more surprise than he received, when instead of being shewn into the usual little sitting room, the door of the best parlour a foot larger each way than the other was thrown open, and he beheld a circle of smart people whom he could not immediately recognise arranged with all the honours of visiting round the fire, and Miss Watson sitting at the best pembroke table,[158] with the best tea things before her. He stood a few seconds, in silent amazement.—

"Musgrave!"—ejaculated Margaret in a tender voice.—

He recollected himself, and came forward, delighted to find such a circle of friends, and blessing his good fortune for the unlooked-for indulgence.—He shook hands with Robert, bowed and smiled to the ladies, and did everything very prettily; but as to any particularity of address or emotion towards Margaret, Emma, who closely observed him, perceived nothing that did not justify Elizabeth's opinions though Margaret's modest smiles imported that she meant to take the visit to herself.—

He was persuaded without much difficulty to throw off his great coat, and drink tea with them. "For whether he dined at eight or nine, as he observed, was a matter of very little consequence"—and without seeming to seek, he did not turn away from the chair close to Margaret which she was assiduous in providing him.—She had thus secured him from her sisters—but it was not immediately in her power to preserve him from her brother's claims, for as he came avowedly from London, and had left it only four hours ago, the last current report as to public news, and the general opinion of the day must be understood, before Robert could let his attention be yielded to the less national, and important demands of the women.—At last however he was at liberty to hear Margaret's soft address, as she spoke her fears of his having had a most terrible, cold, dark, dreadful journey.—

"Indeed you should not have set out so late.—"

"I could not be earlier," he replied. "I was detained chatting at the Bedford,[159] by a friend.—All hours are alike to me.—How long have you been in the country Miss Margaret?"—

"We came only this morning.—My kind brother and sister brought me home this very morning.—'Tis singular is not it?"

"You were gone a great while, were not you? a fortnight I suppose?"—

"*You* may call a fortnight a great while Mr. Musgrave," said Mrs. Robert smartly—"but *we* think a month very little. I assure you we bring her home at the end of a month, much against our will."

"A month! have you really been gone a month! 'tis amazing how time flies.—"

"You may imagine," said Margaret in a sort of whisper, "what are my sensations in finding myself once more at Stanton. You know what a sad visitor I make.—And I was so excessively impatient to see Emma;—I dreaded the meeting, and at the same time longed for it.—Do not you comprehend the sort of feeling?"—

"Not at all," cried he aloud. "I could never dread a meeting with Miss Emma Watson,—or any of her sisters." It was lucky that he added that finish.—

"Were you speaking to me?—" said Emma, who had caught her own name.—

"Not absolutely—" he answered—"but I was thinking of you,—as many at a greater distance are probably doing at this moment.—Fine open[160] weather Miss Emma!—Charming season for hunting."

"Emma is delightful, is not she?—" whispered Margaret. "I have found her more than answer my warmest hopes.—Did you ever see any thing more perfectly beautiful?—I think even *you* must be a convert to a brown complexion."—

He hesitated; Margaret was fair herself, and he did not particularly want to compliment her; but Miss Osborne and Miss Carr were likewise fair, and his devotion to them carried the day.

"Your sister's complexion," said he at last, "is as fine as a dark complexion can be, but I still profess my preference of a white skin. You have seen Miss Osborne?—She is my model for a truly feminine complexion, and she is very fair."—

"Is she fairer than me?"—

Tom made no reply.—

"Upon my honour ladies," said he, giving a glance over his own person, "I am highly endebted to your condescension for admitting me, in such dishabille,[161] into your drawing room. I really did not consider how unfit I was to be here, or I hope I should have kept my distance. Lady Osborne would tell me that I were growing as careless as her son, if she saw me in this condition."—

The ladies were not wanting in civil returns; and Robert Watson, stealing a view of his own head in an opposite glass, said with equal civility,

"You cannot be more in dishabille than myself.—We got here so late, that I had not time even to put a little fresh powder in my hair."—

Emma could not help entering into what she supposed her sister in law's feelings at that moment.—

When the tea things were removed, Tom began to talk of his carriage—but the old card table being set out, and the fish and counters with a tolerably clean pack[162] brought forward from the beaufit[163] by Miss Watson, the general voice was so urgent with him to join their party, that he agreed to allow himself another quarter of an hour. Even Emma was pleased that he would stay, for she was beginning to feel that a family party might be the worst of all parties; and the others were delighted.—

"What's your game?"—cried he, as they stood round the table.—

"Speculation I believe," said Elizabeth.—"My sister recommends it, and I fancy we all like it. I know *you* do, Tom."—

"It is the only round game played at Croydon now," said Mrs. Robert—"we never think of any other. I am glad it is a favourite with you."—

"Oh! me!" cried Tom. "Whatever you decide on, will be a favourite with *me*.—I have had some pleasant hours at Speculation in my time—but I have not been in the way of it now for a long while.—Vingt-un[164] is the game at Osborne Castle; I have played nothing but Vingt-un of late. You would be astonished to hear the noise we make there.—The fine old, lofty drawing-room rings again. Lady Osborne sometimes declares she cannot hear herself speak.—Lord Osborne enjoys it famously and he makes the best dealer without exception that I ever beheld—such quickness and spirit! he lets nobody dream over their cards.—I wish you could see him overdraw himself on both his own cards[165]—it is worth any thing in the world!"—

"Dear me!—" cried Margaret, "why should not we play at Vingt-un?—I think it is a much better game than Speculation. I cannot say I am very fond of Speculation." Mrs. Robert offered not another word in support of the game.—She was quite vanquished, and the fashions of Osborne Castle carried it over the fashions of Croydon.—

"Do you see much of the Parsonage-family at the Castle, Mr. Musgrave?—" said Emma, as they were taking their seats.—

"Oh! yes—they are almost always there. Mrs. Blake is a nice little good-humoured woman, she and I are sworn friends; and Howard's a very gentlemanlike good sort of fellow!—You are not forgotten I assure you by any of the party. I fancy you must have a little cheek-glowing now and then Miss Emma. Were not you rather warm last Saturday about nine or ten o'clock in the evening—? I will tell you how it was.—I see you are dying to know.—Says Howard to Lord Osborne—"—

At this interesting moment he was called on by the others, to regulate the game and determine some disputable point; and his attention was so totally engaged in the business and afterwards by the course of the game as never to revert to what he had been saying before;—and Emma, though suffering a good deal from curiosity, dared not remind him.—

He proved a very useful addition at their table; without him, it would have been a party of such very near relations as could have felt little interest, and perhaps maintained little complaisance, but his presence gave variety and secured good manners.—He was in fact excellently qualified to shine at a round game; and few situations made him appear to greater advantage. He played with spirit, and had a great deal to say, and though with no wit himself, could sometimes make use of the wit of an absent friend; and had a lively way of retailing a commonplace, or saying a mere nothing, that had great effect at a card table. The ways, and good jokes, of Osborne Castle were now added to his ordinary means of entertainment; he repeated the smart sayings of one lady, detailed the oversights of another, and indulged them even with a copy of Lord Osborne's stile of overdrawing himself on both cards.—

The clock struck nine, while he was thus agreeably occupied; and when Nanny came in with her master's basin of gruel,[166] he had the pleasure of observing to Mr. Watson that he should leave him at supper, while he went home to dinner himself.—The carriage was ordered to the door—and no entreaties for his staying longer could now avail,—for he well knew, that if he staid he must sit down to supper in less than ten minutes—which to a man whose heart had been long fixed on calling his next meal a dinner, was quite insupportable.—

On finding him determined to go, Margaret began to wink and nod at Elizabeth to ask him to dinner for the following day; and Elizabeth at last not able to resist hints, which her own hospitable, social temper more than half seconded, gave the invitation. "Would he give Robert the meeting,[167] they should be very happy."

"With the greatest pleasure"—was his first reply. In a moment afterwards—"That is if I can possibly get here in time—but I shoot with Lord Osborne,[168] and therefore must not engage.—You will not think of me unless you see me."—And so, he departed, delighted with the uncertainty in which he had left it.—

Margaret, in the joy of her heart under circumstances which she chose to consider as peculiarly propitious, would willingly have made a confidante of Emma when they were alone for a short time the next morning; and had proceeded so far as to say—"The young man who was here last night my dear Emma and returns to day, is more interesting to me, than perhaps you may be aware—" but Emma, pretending to understand nothing extraordinary in the words, made some very inapplicable reply, and jumping up, ran away from a subject which was odious to her feelings.—

As Margaret would not allow a doubt to be repeated of Musgrave's coming to dinner, preparations were made for his entertainment much exceeding what had been deemed necessary the day before;—and taking the office of superintendance entirely from her sister, she was half the morning in the kitchen herself directing and scolding.—After a great deal of indifferent cooking and anxious suspense, however, they were obliged to sit down without their guest.—Tom Musgrave never came, and Margaret was at no pains to conceal her vexation under the disappointment, or repress the peevishness of her temper—.

The peace of the party for the remainder of that day, and the whole of the next, which comprised the length of Robert and Jane's visit, was continually invaded by her fretful displeasure, and querulous attacks.—Elizabeth was the usual object of both. Margaret had just respect enough for her brother and sister's opinion, to behave properly by *them*, but Elizabeth and the maids could never do any thing right—and Emma, whom she seemed no longer to think about, found the continuance of the gentle voice beyond her calculation short. Eager to be as little among them as possible, Emma was delighted with the alternative of sitting above, with her father, and warmly entreated to be his constant companion each evening—and as Elizabeth loved company of any kind too well, not to prefer being below, at all risks, as she had rather talk of Croydon to Jane, with every interruption of Margaret's perverseness, than sit with only her father, who frequently could not endure talking at all, the affair was so settled, as soon as she could be persuaded to believe it no sacrifice on her sister's part.—To Emma, the exchange was most acceptable, and delightful. Her father,

… each evening. — … & Eliz.
loved company of any kind too well, not to
prefer being below, at all risks;
She had rather talk of Croydon to Jane,
with every interruption of Margt's perverse:
:ness, than sit with only her father, who
frequently cd not endure Talking at all,
the affair was so settled, as soon as she could be
persuaded to believe it no sacrifice on her
Sister's part. — To Emma, the exchange was most accep:
:table, & delightful. Her father, if ill,
required little more than gentleness & silence; & being a man
of sense & education, was if able to converse,
a welcome companion. —
In her chamber, Emma was at peace from the
dreadful mortifications of unequal Society, & family
Discord — from the immediate endurance of
Hard-hearted prosperity, low-minded Conceit,
& wrong-headed folly, engrafted on an un:
:toward Disposition. — She still suffered from them
in the contemplation of their existence; in memory & in pros:
:pect, but for the moment, she ceased to be
tortured by their effects. — She was at leisure,
she could read & think, tho' her situation was
hardly such as to make reflection very soothing,

2 'The Watsons', f. 42r.

if ill, required little more than gentleness and silence; and, being a man of sense and education, was, if able to converse, a welcome companion.—In *his* chamber, Emma was at peace from the dreadful mortifications of unequal society, and family discord—from the immediate endurance of hard-hearted prosperity, low-minded conceit, and wrong-headed folly, engrafted on an untoward disposition.—She still suffered from them in the contemplation of their existence; in memory and in prospect, but for the moment, she ceased to be tortured by their effects.—She was at leisure, she could read and think,—though her situation was hardly such as to make reflection very soothing. The evils arising from the loss of her uncle were neither trifling, nor likely to lessen; and when thought had been freely indulged, in contrasting the past and the present, the employment of mind, the dissipation of unpleasant ideas which only reading could produce, made her thankfully turn to a book.—

The change in her home society and stile of life in consequence of the death of one friend and the imprudence of another had indeed been striking.—From being the first object of hope and solicitude to an uncle who had formed her mind with the care of a parent, and of tenderness to an aunt whose amiable temper had delighted to give her every indulgence, from being the life and spirit of a house, where all had been comfort and elegance, and the expected heiress of an easy independence,[169] she was become of importance to no one, a burden on those, whose affection she could not expect, an addition in an house, already overstocked, surrounded by inferior minds with little chance of domestic comfort, and as little hope of future support.—It was well for her that she was naturally cheerful;—for the change had been such as might have plunged weak spirits in despondence.—

She was very much pressed by Robert and Jane to return with them to Croydon, and had some difficulty in getting a refusal accepted; as they thought too highly of their own kindness and situation to suppose the offer could appear in a less advantageous light to anybody else.—Elizabeth gave them her interest, though evidently against her own, in privately urging Emma to go—

"You do not know what you refuse Emma—" said she—"nor what you have to bear at home.—I would advise you by all means to accept the invitation; there is always something lively going on at Croydon. You will be in company almost every day, and Robert and Jane will be very kind to you.—As for me, I shall be no worse off without you, than I have been used to be; but poor Margaret's disagreeable ways are new to *you*, and they would vex you more than you think for, if you stay at home.—"

Emma was of course un-influenced, except to greater esteem for Elizabeth, by such representations—and the visitors departed without her.—

Sanditon[1]

Chapter 1

A gentleman and lady travelling from Tunbridge towards that part of the Sussex coast which lies between Hastings and East Bourne,[2] being induced by business to quit the high road, and attempt a very rough lane, were overturned in toiling up its long ascent—half rock, half sand. The accident happened just beyond the only gentleman's house near the lane—a house, which their driver, on being first required to take that direction, had conceived to be necessarily their object, and had with most unwilling looks been constrained to pass by—. He had grumbled and shaken his shoulders so much indeed, and pitied and cut[3] his horses so sharply, that he might have been open to the suspicion of overturning[4] them on purpose (especially as the carriage was not his master's[5]) if the road had not indisputably become considerably worse than before, as soon as the premises of the said house were left behind—expressing with a most intelligent portentous countenance that beyond it no wheels but cart wheels could safely proceed.

The severity of the fall was broken by their slow pace and the narrowness of the lane, and the gentleman having scrambled out and helped out his companion, they neither of them at first felt more than shaken and bruised. But the gentleman had in the course of the extrication sprained his foot—and soon becoming sensible of it was obliged in a few moments to cut short both his remonstrance to the driver and his congratulations to his wife and himself—and sit down on the bank, unable to stand.—

"There is something wrong here," said he—putting his hand to his ancle—"But never mind, my dear—(looking up at her with a smile)—it could not have happened, you know, in a better place.—Good out of evil—. The very thing perhaps to be wished for. We shall soon get relief.—*There*, I fancy lies my cure"—pointing to the neat-looking end of a cottage, which was seen romantically situated among wood on a high eminence at some little distance.[6]—"Does not *that* promise to be the very place?—"

His wife fervently hoped it was—but stood, terrified and anxious, neither able to do or suggest anything—and receiving her first real comfort from the sight of several persons now coming to their assistance. The accident had been discerned from a hayfield adjoining the house they had passed—and the persons who approached were a well-looking, hale, gentlemanlike man, of middle age, the proprietor of the place, who happened to be among his haymakers[7] at the time, and three or four of the ablest of them summoned to attend their master—to say nothing of all the rest of the field, men, women and children—not very far off.—Mr. Heywood, such was the name of the said proprietor, advanced with a very civil salutation—much concern for the accident—some surprise at any body's attempting that road in a carriage—and ready offers of assistance. His courtesies were received with good breeding and gratitude and while one or two of the men lent their help to the driver in getting the carriage upright again, the traveller said—

"You are extremely obliging Sir, and I take you at your word.—The injury to my leg is I dare say very trifling, but it is always best in these cases to have a surgeon's opinion[8] without loss of time; and as the road does not seem at present in a favourable state for my getting up to his house myself, I will thank you to send off one of these good people for the surgeon."

"The surgeon Sir!"—replied Mr. Heywood.—"I am afraid you will find no surgeon at hand here, but I dare say we shall do very well without him."—

"Nay Sir, if *he* is not in the way his partner will do just as well[9]—or rather better—. I would rather see his partner indeed—I would prefer the attendance of his partner.—One of these good people can be with him in three minutes I am sure. I need not ask whether I see the house (looking towards the cottage); for excepting your own, we have passed none in this place, which can be the abode of a gentleman."—

Mr. Heywood looked very much astonished and replied—

"What Sir! are you expecting to find a surgeon in that cottage?—we have neither surgeon nor partner in the parish I assure you."—

"Excuse me Sir"—replied the other. "I am sorry to have the appearance of contradicting you—but though from the extent of the parish or some other cause you may not be aware of the fact—Stay—can I be mistaken in the place?—Am I not in Willingden?[10]—Is not this Willingden?"

"Yes Sir, this is certainly Willingden."

"Then Sir, I can bring proof of your having a surgeon in the parish—whether you may know it or not. Here Sir—(taking out his pocket book—) if you will do me the favour of casting your eye over these advertisements, which I cut out myself from the Morning Post and the Kentish Gazette, only yesterday morning in London[11]—I think you will be convinced that I am not speaking at random. You will find it an advertisement, Sir, of the dissolution of a partnership in the medical line—in your own parish—extensive business—undeniable character—respectable references—wishing to form a separate establishment.—You will find it at full length Sir"—offering him the two little oblong extracts.—

"Sir"—said Mr. Heywood with a good humoured smile—"if you were to shew me all the newspapers that are printed in one week throughout the kingdom, you would not persuade me of there being a surgeon in Willingden—for having lived here ever since I was born, man and boy fifty-seven years, I think I must have *known* of such a person, at least I may venture to say that he has not *much business*.—To be sure, if gentlemen were to be often attempting this lane in post-chaises,[12] it might not be a bad speculation for a surgeon to get a house at the top of the hill.—But as to that cottage, I can assure you Sir that it is in fact—(in spite of its spruce air at this distance—) as indifferent a double tenement[13] as any in the parish, and that my shepherd lives at one end, and three old women at the other."

He took the pieces of paper as he spoke—and having looked them over, added—"I believe I can explain it Sir.—Your mistake is in the place.—There are two Willingdens in this country[14]—and your advertisements refer to the other—which is Great Willingden, or Willingden Abbots,[15] and lies seven miles off, on the other side of Battle[16]—quite down in the Weald. And *we* Sir—(speaking rather proudly) are not in the Weald."[17]—

"Not *down* in the Weald I am sure Sir," replied the traveller, pleasantly. "It took us half an hour to climb your hill.—Well Sir—I dare say it is as you say and I have made an abominably stupid blunder.—All done in a moment;—the advertisements did not catch my eye till the last half hour of our being in town[18]—; when everything was in the hurry and confusion which always attend a short stay there.—One is never able to complete anything in the way of business you know till the carriage is at the door—and accordingly satisfying myself with a brief enquiry, and finding we were actually to pass within a mile or two of a *Willingden*, I sought no farther . . . My dear—(to his wife) I am very sorry to have brought you into this scrape. But do not be alarmed about my leg. It gives me no pain while I am quiet,—and as soon as these good people have succeeded in setting the carriage to rights and turning the horses round, the best thing we can do will be to measure back our steps into the turnpike road[19] and proceed to Hailsham,[20] and so home, without attempting anything farther.—Two hours take us home, from Hailsham—and when once at home, we have our remedy at hand you know.—A little of our own bracing sea air will soon set me on my feet again.—Depend upon it my dear, it is exactly a case for the sea. Saline air and immersion[21] will be the very thing.—My sensations[22] tell me so already."—

In a most friendly manner Mr. Heywood here interposed, entreating them not to think of proceeding till the ancle had been examined, and some refreshment taken, and very cordially pressing them to make use of his house for both purposes.—

"We are always well stocked," said he, "with all the common remedies for sprains and bruises[23]—and I will answer for the pleasure it will give my wife and daughters to be of service to you and this lady in every way in their power.—"

A twinge or two in trying to move his foot disposed the traveller to think rather more as he had done at first of the benefit of immediate assistance—and consulting his wife in the few words of "Well my dear, I believe it will be better for us"—turned again to Mr. Heywood—and said—"Before we accept your hospitality Sir,—and in order to do away any unfavourable impression which the sort of wild goose-chase you find me in, may have given rise to—allow me to tell you who we are. My name is Parker.—Mr. Parker of Sanditon;—this lady, my wife Mrs. Parker.—We are on our road home from London.—*My* name perhaps—though I am by no means the first of my family, holding landed property in the parish of Sanditon, may be unknown at this distance from the coast—but Sanditon itself—everybody has heard of Sanditon,—the favourite—for a young and rising bathing-place,[24] certainly the favourite spot of all that are to be found along the coast of Sussex;[25]—the most favoured by Nature, and promising to be the most chosen by man."—

"Yes—I have heard of Sanditon," replied Mr. Heywood.—"Every five years, one hears of some new place or other starting up by the sea, and growing the fashion.[26]—How they can half of them be filled, is the wonder! *Where* people can be found with money or time to go to them![27]—Bad things for a country;—sure to raise the price of provisions and make the poor good for nothing[28]—as I dare say you find, Sir."

"Not at all Sir, not at all"—cried Mr. Parker eagerly. "Quite the contrary I assure you.—A common idea—but a mistaken one. It may apply to your large, overgrown places, like Brighton, or Worthing, or East Bourne[29]—but *not* to a small village like Sanditon, precluded by its size from experiencing any of the evils of civilization, while the growth of the place, the buildings, the nursery grounds,[30] the demand for every thing, and the sure resort of the very best company, those regular, steady, private[31] families of thorough gentility and character, who are a blessing every where, excite the industry of the poor and diffuse comfort and improvement among them of every sort.—No Sir, I assure you, Sanditon is not a place—"

"I do not mean to take exceptions to *any* place in particular Sir," answered Mr. Heywood.—"I only think our coast is too full of them altogether.—But had we not better try to get you"—

"Our coast too full"—repeated Mr. Parker.—"On that point perhaps we may not totally disagree;—at least there are *enough*. Our coast is abundant enough; it demands no more.—Everybody's taste and every body's finances may be suited—and those good people who are trying to add to the number are in my opinion excessively absurd, and must soon find themselves the dupes of their own fallacious calculations.—Such a place as Sanditon Sir, I may say was wanted, was called for.—Nature had marked it out—had spoken in most intelligible characters—the finest, purest sea breeze on the coast—acknowledged to be so—excellent bathing—fine hard sand—deep water ten yards from the shore—no mud—no weeds—no slimy rocks—never was there a place more palpably designed by Nature for the resort of the invalid—the very spot which thousands seemed in need of—the most desirable distance from London! One complete, measured mile nearer than East Bourne. Only conceive Sir, the advantage of saving a whole mile, in a long journey.[32] But Brinshore Sir, which I dare say you have in your eye—the attempts of two or three speculating people about Brinshore, this last year, to raise that paltry hamlet, lying as it does between a stagnant marsh, a bleak moor and the constant effluvia of a ridge of putrifying sea weed,[33] can end in nothing but their own disappointment. What in the name of common sense is to *recommend* Brinshore?—A most insalubrious air[34]—roads proverbially detestable—water brackish beyond example, impossible to get a good dish of tea within three miles of the place—and as for the soil—it is so cold and

~~them and~~ the Dupes of their own
fallacious Calculations.—Such a
place as Sanditon Sir, I may say was
wanted, was called for.—Nature had
marked it out—had spoken in most
intelligible Characters—The finest, purest
Sea Breeze on the Coast—acknowledged
to be so—Excellent Bathing—fine hard
Sand—Deep Water 10 yards from the Shore
—no Mud—no Weeds—no slimey rocks—
Never was there a place more palpably
designed by Nature for the resort of
the Invalid—the very Spot which
Thousands seemed in need of.—The
most desirable distance from London!
One complete
~~a measured~~ mile nearer than East
Bourne. Only conceive Sir, the ad-
saving a whole Mile
:vantage of ~~that~~, in a long Journey.
But Brinshore Sir, which I dare
say you have in your eye—the
attempts of two or three speculating
People about Brinshore, this last
Year, to raise that paltry Hamlet,
lying, as it does
~~situated~~ between a stagnant marsh,
a bleak Moor
& the constant effluvia of a ridge
of putrifying sea weed, can end in
nothing but their own Disappointment.

3 'Sanditon', f. 7v.

ungrateful that it can hardly be made to yield a cabbage.—Depend upon it Sir, that this is a faithful description of Brinshore—not in the smallest degree exaggerated—and if you have heard it differently spoken of—"

"Sir, I never heard it spoken of in my life before," said Mr. Heywood. "I did not know there was such a place in the world."—

"You did not!—There my dear—(turning with exultation to his wife)—you see how it is. So much for the celebrity of Brinshore!—This gentleman did not know there was such a place in the world.—Why, in truth Sir, I fancy we may apply to Brinshore, that line of the poet Cowper in his description of the religious cottager, as opposed to Voltaire—'*She*, never heard of half a mile from home'."[35]—

"With all my heart Sir—apply any verses you like to it—but I want to see something applied to your leg—and I am sure by your lady's countenance that she is quite of my opinion and thinks it a pity to lose any more time.—And here come my girls to speak for themselves and their mother—(two or three genteel looking young women, followed by as many maid servants, were now seen issuing from the house)—I began to wonder the bustle should not have reached *them*.—A thing of this kind soon makes a stir in a lonely place like ours.—Now Sir, let us see how you can be best conveyed into the house."—

The young ladies approached and said every thing that was proper to recommend their father's offers; and in an unaffected manner calculated to make the strangers easy—and as Mrs. Parker was exceedingly anxious for relief—and her husband, by this time, not much less disposed for it—a very few civil scruples were enough—especially as the carriage being now set up, was discovered to have received such injury on the fallen side as to be unfit for present use.—Mr. Parker was therefore carried into the house, and his carriage wheeled off to a vacant barn.—

Chapter 2

The acquaintance, thus oddly begun, was neither short nor unimportant. For a whole fortnight the travellers were fixed at Willingden, Mr. Parker's sprain proving too serious for him to move sooner.—He had fallen into very good hands. The Heywoods were a thoroughly respectable family, and every possible attention was paid in the kindest and most unpretending manner, to both husband and wife. *He* was waited on and nursed, and *she* cheered and comforted with unremitting kindness—and as every office of hospitality and friendliness was received as it ought—as there was not more good will on one side than gratitude on the other—nor any deficiency of generally pleasant manners on either, they grew to like each other in the course of that fortnight, exceedingly well.—

Mr. Parker's character and history were soon unfolded. All that he understood of himself, he readily told, for he was very open-hearted;—and where he might be himself in the dark, his conversation was still giving information, to such of the Heywoods as could observe.—By such he was perceived to be an enthusiast;[1]—on the subject of Sanditon, a complete enthusiast.—Sanditon,—the success of Sanditon as a small, fashionable bathing place was the object, for which he seemed to live. A very few years ago, and it had been a quiet village of no pretensions; but some natural advantages in its position and some accidental circumstances having suggested to himself, and the other principal land holder, the probability of its becoming a profitable speculation,[2] they had engaged in it, and planned and built, and praised and puffed,[3] and raised it to a something of young renown—and Mr. Parker could now think of very little besides.—

The facts, which in more direct communication he laid before them, were that he was about five and thirty—had been married,—very happily married seven years—and had four sweet children at home;—that he was of a respectable family, and easy though not large fortune;—no profession[4]—succeeding as eldest son to the property which two or three generations had been holding and accumulating before him;—that he had two brothers and two sisters—all single and all independent[5]—the eldest of the two former indeed, by collateral inheritance,[6] quite as well provided for as himself.—His object in quitting the high road, to hunt for an advertising surgeon, was also plainly stated;—it had not proceeded from any intention of spraining his ancle or doing himself any other injury for the good of such surgeon—nor (as Mr. Heywood had been apt to suppose) from any design of entering into partnership with him—; it was merely in consequence of a wish to establish some medical man at Sanditon, which the nature of the advertisement induced him to expect to accomplish in Willingden.—He was convinced that the advantage of a medical man at hand would very materially promote the rise and prosperity of the place—would in fact tend to bring a prodigious influx;—nothing else was wanting. He had *strong* reason to believe that *one* family had been deterred last year from trying Sanditon on that account—and probably very many more—and his own sisters, who were sad invalids, and whom he was very anxious to get to Sanditon this summer, could hardly be expected to hazard themselves in a place where they could not have immediate medical advice.—

Upon the whole, Mr. Parker was evidently an amiable family-man, fond of wife, children, brothers and sisters—and generally kind-hearted;—liberal, gentlemanlike, easy to please;—of a sanguine turn of mind, with more imagination than judgement. And Mrs. Parker was as evidently a gentle, amiable, sweet tempered woman, the properest wife in the world for a man of strong understanding, but not of capacity to supply the cooler reflection which her own husband sometimes needed, and so entirely waiting to be guided on every occasion, that whether he were risking his fortune or spraining his ancle, she remained equally useless.—Sanditon was a second wife and four children to him—hardly less dear—and certainly more engrossing.—He could talk of it for ever.—It had indeed the highest claims;—not only those of birth place, property, and home,—it was his mine, his lottery,[7] his speculation and his hobby horse;[8] his occupation, his hope and his futurity.[9]—He was extremely desirous of drawing his good friends at Willingden thither; and his endeavours in the cause were as grateful and disinterested as they were warm.—He wanted to secure the promise of a visit—to get as many of the family as his own house would contain, to follow him to Sanditon as soon as possible—and healthy as they all undeniably were—foresaw that every one of them would be benefited by the sea.—He held it indeed as certain, that no person could be really well, no person (however upheld for the present by fortuitous aids of exercise and spirits in a semblance of health) could be really in a state of secure and permanent health without spending at least six weeks by the sea every year.—The sea air and sea bathing together were nearly infallible, one or the other of them being a match for every disorder, of the stomach, the lungs or the blood; they were anti-spasmodic, anti-pulmonary, anti-sceptic, anti-bilious and anti-rheumatic.[10] Nobody could catch cold by the sea, nobody wanted appetite by the sea, nobody wanted spirits, nobody wanted strength.—They were healing, softing,[11] relaxing—fortifying and bracing—seemingly just as was wanted—sometimes one, sometimes the other.—If the sea breeze failed, the sea-bath was the certain corrective;[12]—and where bathing disagreed, the sea breeze alone was evidently designed by Nature for the cure.—

His eloquence however could not prevail. Mr. and Mrs. Heywood never left home. Marrying early and having a very numerous family, their movements had been long limited to one small circle; and they were older in habits than in age.—Excepting two journeys to London in the year, to receive his dividends,[13] Mr. Heywood went no farther than his feet or his well-tried old horse could carry him, and Mrs. Heywood's adventurings were only now and then to visit her neighbours, in the old coach which had been new when they married and fresh lined on their eldest son's coming of age ten years ago.[14]—

They had very pretty property—enough, had their family been of reasonable limits, to have allowed them a very gentlemanlike share of luxuries and change—enough for them to have indulged in a new carriage and better roads, an occasional month at Tunbridge Wells, and symptoms of the gout and a winter at Bath;[15]—but the maintenance, education and fitting out of fourteen children demanded a very quiet, settled, careful course of life—and obliged them to be stationary and healthy at Willingden. What prudence had at first enjoined, was now rendered pleasant by habit. They never left home, and they had a gratification in saying so.—But very far from wishing their children to do the same, they were glad to promote *their* getting out into the world, as much as possible. *They* staid at home, that their children *might* get out;—and while making that home extremely comfortable, welcomed every change from it which could give useful connections or respectable acquaintance to sons or daughters. When Mr. and Mrs. Parker therefore ceased from soliciting a family-visit, and bounded their views to carrying back one daughter with them, no difficulties were started. It was general pleasure and consent.—

Their invitation was to Miss Charlotte Heywood, a very pleasing young woman of two and twenty, the eldest of the daughters at home, and the one who under her mother's directions had been particularly useful and obliging to them; who had attended them most, and knew them best.—Charlotte was to go,—with excellent health, to bathe and be better if she could—to receive every possible pleasure which Sanditon could be made to supply by the gratitude of those she went with—and to buy new parasols, new gloves, and new brooches, for her sisters and herself at the library,[16] which Mr. Parker was anxiously wishing to support.—All that Mr. Heywood himself could be persuaded to promise was, that he would send everyone to Sanditon, who asked his advice, and that nothing should ever induce him (as far as the future could be answered for) to spend even five shillings at Brinshore.—

Chapter 3

Every neighbourhood should have a great lady.—The great lady of Sanditon was Lady Denham;[1] and in their journey from Willingden to the coast Mr. Parker gave Charlotte a more detailed account of her than had been called for before.—She had been necessarily often mentioned at Willingden,—for being his colleague in speculation, Sanditon itself could not be talked of long, without the introduction of Lady Denham, and that she was a very rich old lady, who had buried two husbands, who knew the value of money, was very much looked up to and had a poor cousin living with her, were facts already well known, but some further particulars of her history and her character served to lighten the tediousness of a long hill, or a heavy bit of road, and to give the visiting young lady a suitable knowledge of the person with whom she might now expect to be daily associating.—

Lady Denham had been a rich Miss Brereton, born to wealth but not to education. Her first husband had been a Mr. Hollis, a man of considerable property in the country, of which a large share of the parish of Sanditon, with manor and mansion house,[2] made a part. He had been an elderly man when she married him;—her own age about thirty.— Her motives for such a match could be little understood at the distance of forty years, but she had so well nursed and pleased Mr. Hollis, that at his death he left her everything—all his estates, and all at her disposal.[3] After a widowhood of some years, she had been induced to marry again. The late Sir Harry Denham, of Denham Park in the neighbourhood of Sanditon, had succeeded in removing her and her large income to his own domains, but he could not succeed in the views of permanently enriching his family, which were attributed to him. She had been too wary to put anything out of her own power—and when on Sir Harry's decease she returned again to her own house at Sanditon, she was said to have made this boast to a friend, "that though she had *got* nothing but her title from the family, still she had *given* nothing for it."[4]—For the title, it was to be supposed that she had married—and Mr. Parker acknowledged there being just such a degree of value for it apparent now, as to give her conduct that natural explanation.

"There is at times," said he—"a little self-importance—but it is not offensive;—and there are moments, there are points, when her love of money is carried greatly too far. But she is a good-natured woman, a very good-natured woman—a very obliging, friendly neighbour; a cheerful, independent, valuable character—and her faults may be entirely imputed to her want of education. She has good natural sense, but quite uncultivated.—She has a fine active mind, as well as a fine healthy frame for a woman of seventy, and enters into the improvement of Sanditon with a spirit truly admirable—though now and then, a littleness *will* appear. She cannot look forward quite as I would have her—and takes alarm at a trifling present expence, without considering what returns it *will* make her in a year or two.

"That is—we think *differently*, we now and then see things *differently*, Miss Heywood.—Those who tell their own story you know must be listened to with caution.—When you see us in contact, you will judge for yourself."—

Lady Denham was indeed a great lady beyond the common wants of society—for she had many thousands a year to bequeath, and three distinct sets of people to be courted by: her own relations, who might very reasonably wish for her original thirty thousand pounds[5] among them, the legal heirs of Mr. Hollis, who must hope to be more endebted to *her* sense of justice than he had allowed them to be to *his*, and those members of the Denham family, whom her second husband had hoped to make a good bargain for.—By all of these, or by branches of them, she had no doubt been long, and still continued to be, well attacked;—and of these three divisions, Mr. Parker did not hesitate to say that Mr. Hollis's kindred were the *least* in favour and Sir Harry Denham's the *most*.—The former he believed had done themselves irremediable harm by expressions of very unwise and unjustifiable resentment at the time of Mr. Hollis's death;—the latter, to the advantage of being the remnant of a connection which she certainly valued, joined those of having been known to her from their childhood and of being always at hand to preserve their interest by reasonable attention. Sir Edward, the present baronet, nephew to Sir Harry, resided constantly at Denham Park; and Mr. Parker had little doubt that he and his sister Miss Denham, who lived with him, would be principally remembered in her will. He sincerely hoped it.—Miss Denham had a very small provision—and her brother was a poor man for his rank in society.[6]

"He is a warm friend to Sanditon"—said Mr. Parker—"and his hand would be as liberal as his heart, had he the power.—He would be a noble coadjutor![7]—As it is, he does what he can—and is running up a tasteful little cottage ornée,[8] on a strip of waste ground[9] Lady Denham has granted him—which I have no doubt we shall have many a candidate for, before the end even of *this* season."[10]

Till within the last twelvemonth, Mr. Parker had considered Sir Edward as standing without a rival, as having the fairest chance of succeeding to the greater part of all that she had to give—but there was now another person's claims to be taken into the account, those of the young female relation, whom Lady Denham had been induced to receive into her family. After having always protested against any such addition, and long and often enjoyed the repeated defeats she had given to every attempt of her relations to introduce this young lady or that young lady as a companion[11] at Sanditon House,[12] she had brought back with her from London last Michaelmas[13] a Miss Brereton, who bid fair by her merits to vie in favour with Sir Edward, and to secure for herself and her family that share of the accumulated property which they had certainly the best right to inherit.—

Mr. Parker spoke warmly of Clara Brereton, and the interest of his story increased very much with the introduction of such a character. Charlotte listened with more than amusement now;—it was solicitude and enjoyment, as she heard her described to be lovely, amiable, gentle, unassuming, conducting herself uniformly with great good sense, and evidently gaining by her innate worth on the affections of her patroness.—Beauty, sweetness, poverty and dependance, do not want the imagination of a man to operate upon. With due exceptions—woman feels for woman very promptly and compassionately. He gave the particulars which had led to Clara's admission at Sanditon, as no bad exemplification of that mixture of character, that union of littleness with kindness with good sense with even liberality, which he saw in Lady Denham.—After having avoided London for many years, and principally on account of these very cousins, who were continually writing, inviting and tormenting her, and whom she was determined to keep at a distance, she had been obliged to go there last Michaelmas with the certainty of being detained at least a fortnight.—She had gone to an hotel[14]—living, by her own account, as prudently as possible, to defy the reputed expensiveness of such a home, and at the end of three days calling for her bill, that she might judge of her state.—Its amount was such as determined her on staying not another hour in the house, and she was preparing in all the anger and perturbation which a belief of very gross imposition *there*, and an ignorance of *where* to go for better usage, to leave the hotel at all hazards, when the cousins, the politic and lucky cousins, who seemed always to have a spy on her, introduced themselves at this important moment, and learning her situation, persuaded her to accept such a home for the rest of her stay as their humbler house in a very inferior part of London could offer.—

She went; was delighted with her welcome and the hospitality and attention she received from every body—found her good cousins the Breretons beyond her expectation worthy people—and finally was impelled, by a personal knowledge of their narrow income and pecuniary difficulties, to invite one of the girls of the family to pass the winter with her. The invitation was to *one*, for six months—with the probability of another being then to take her place;—but in *selecting* the one, Lady Denham had shewn the good part of her character—for passing by the actual *daughters* of the house, she had chosen Clara, a niece—more helpless and more pitiable of course than any—and dependant on poverty—an additional burden on an encumbered circle—and one who had been so low in every worldly view, as with all her natural endowments and powers to have been preparing for a situation little better than a nursery maid.[15]—

Clara had returned with her—and by her good sense and merit had now, to all appearance, secured a very strong hold in Lady Denham's regard. The six months had long been over—and not a syllable was breathed of any change, or exchange.—She was a general favourite;—the influence of her steady conduct and mild, gentle temper was felt by everybody. The prejudices which had met her at first in some quarters were all dissipated. She was felt to be worthy of trust—to be the very companion who would guide and soften Lady Denham—who would enlarge her mind and open her hand.—She was as thoroughly amiable as she was lovely—and since having had the advantage of their Sanditon breezes, that loveliness was complete.

Chapter 4

"And whose very snug-looking place is this?"—said Charlotte, as in a sheltered dip within two miles of the sea, they passed close by a moderate-sized house, well fenced and planted, and rich in the garden,[1] orchard and meadows which are the best embellishments of such a dwelling. "It seems to have as many comforts about it as Willingden."—

"Ah!"—said Mr. Parker.—"This is my old house—the house of my forefathers—the house where I and all my brothers and sisters were born and bred—and where my own three eldest children were born—where Mrs. Parker and I lived till within the last two years—till our new house was finished.—I am glad you are pleased with it.—It is an honest old place—and Hillier keeps it in very good order. I have given it up you know to the man who occupies the chief of my land.[2] *He* gets a better house by it—and I, a rather better situation!—One other hill brings us to Sanditon—modern Sanditon—a beautiful spot.—Our ancestors, you know, always built in a hole.—Here were we, pent down in this little contracted nook, without air or view, only one mile and three quarters from the noblest expanse of ocean between the South Foreland and the Land's End,[3] and without the smallest advantage from it.[4] You will not think I have made a bad exchange, when we reach Trafalgar House—which, by the bye, I almost wish I had not named Trafalgar—for Waterloo is more the thing now.[5] However, Waterloo is in reserve—and if we have encouragement enough this year for a little Crescent[6] to be ventured on—(as I trust we shall) then we shall be able to call it Waterloo Crescent—and the name joined to the form of the building, which always takes, will give us the command of lodgers—. In a good season we should have more applications than we could attend to."—

"It was always a very comfortable house"—said Mrs. Parker—looking at it through the back window with something like the fondness of regret.—"And such a nice garden—such an excellent garden."

"Yes, my love, but *that* we may be said to carry with us.—*It* supplies us, as before, with all the fruit and vegetables we want; and we have in fact all the comfort of an excellent kitchen garden, without the constant eyesore of its formalities,[7] or the yearly nuisance of its decaying vegetation.—Who can endure a cabbage bed in October?"

"Oh! dear—yes.—We are quite as well off for gardenstuff as ever we were—for if it is forgot to be brought at any time, we can always buy what we want at Sanditon House.—The gardener there is glad enough to supply us—. But it was a nice place for the children to run about in. So shady in summer!"

"My dear, we shall have shade enough on the hill and more than enough in the course of a very few years—. The growth of my plantations[8] is a general astonishment. In the mean while we have the canvas awning,[9] which gives us the most complete comfort within doors—and you can get a parasol[10] at Whitby's for little Mary at any time, or a large bonnet at Jebbs'.—And as for the boys, I must say I would rather *them* run about in the sunshine than not. I am sure we agree, my dear, in wishing our boys to be as hardy as possible."—

"Yes indeed, I am sure we do—and I will get Mary a little parasol, which will make her as proud as can be. How grave she will walk about with it, and fancy herself quite a little woman.—Oh! I have not the smallest doubt of our being a great deal better off where we are now. If we any of us want to bathe, we have not a quarter of a mile to go.—But you know (still looking back) one loves to look at an old friend, at a place where one has been happy.—The Hilliers did not seem to feel the storms last winter at all.—I remember seeing Mrs. Hillier after one of those dreadful nights, when *we* had been literally rocked in our bed, and she did not seem at all aware of the wind being anything more than common."

"Yes, yes—that's likely enough. *We* have all the grandeur of the storm,[11] with less real danger, because the wind meeting with nothing to oppose or confine it around our house, simply rages and passes on—while down in this gutter—nothing is known of the state of the air, below the tops of the trees—and the inhabitants may be taken totally unawares, by one of those dreadful currents which should do more mischief in a valley, when they *do* arise, than an open country ever experiences in the heaviest gale.—But my dear love—as to gardenstuff;—you were saying that any accidental omission is supplied in a moment by Lady Denham's gardener—but it occurs to me that we ought to go elsewhere upon such occasions—and that old Stringer and his son have a higher claim. I encouraged him to set up—and am afraid he does not do very well—that is, there has not been time enough yet.—He *will* do very well beyond a doubt—but at first it is up hill work; and therefore we must give him what help we can—and when any vegetables or fruit happen to be wanted,—and it will not be amiss to have them often wanted, to have something or other forgotten most days—just to have a nominal supply you know, that poor old Andrew may not lose his daily job—but in fact to buy the chief of our consumption of the Stringers.—"

"Very well my love, that can be easily done—and cook will be satisfied—which will be a great comfort, for she is always complaining of old Andrew now, and says he never brings her what she wants.—There—now the old house is quite left behind.—What is it, your brother Sidney says about its being a hospital?"[12]

"Oh! my dear Mary, merely a joke of his. He pretends to advise me to make a hospital of it. He pretends to laugh at my improvements.[13] Sidney says any thing you know. He has always said what he chose of and to us all. Most families have such a member among them I believe Miss Heywood.—There is a someone in most families privileged by superior abilities or spirits to say anything.—In ours, it is Sidney; who is a very clever young man, and with great powers of pleasing.—He lives too much in the world to be settled; that is his only fault.—He is here and there and every where. I wish we may get him to Sanditon. I should like to have you acquainted with him.—And it would be a fine thing for the place!—Such a young man as Sidney, with his neat equipage[14] and fashionable air.—You and I Mary, know what effect it might have: many a respectable family, many a careful mother, many a pretty daughter, might it secure us, to the prejudice of East Bourne and Hastings."—

They were now approaching the church and real village of Sanditon, which stood at the foot of the hill they were afterwards to ascend—a hill, whose side was covered with the woods and enclosures[15] of Sanditon House and whose height ended in an open down where the new buildings might soon be looked for. A branch only, of the valley, winding more obliquely towards the sea, gave a passage to an inconsiderable stream, and formed at its mouth a third habitable division, in a small cluster of fisherman's houses.[16]—

The village contained little more than cottages, but the spirit of the day had been caught, as Mr. Parker observed with delight to Charlotte, and two or three of the best of them were smartened up with a white curtain and "Lodgings to let"—, and farther on, in the little green court of an old farm house, two females in elegant white[17] were actually to be seen with their books and camp stools—and in turning the corner of the baker's shop, the sound of a harp[18] might be heard through the upper casement.—Such sights and sounds were highly blissful to Mr. Parker.—Not that he had any personal concern in the success of the village itself; for considering it as too remote from the beach, he had done nothing there—but it was a most valuable proof of the increasing fashion of the place altogether. If the *village* could attract, the hill might be nearly full.—He anticipated an amazing season.—At the same time last year (late in July) there had not been a single lodger in the village!—nor did he remember any during the whole summer, excepting one family of children who came from London for sea air after the hooping cough,[19] and whose mother would not let them be nearer the shore for fear of their tumbling in.—

"Civilization, civilization indeed!"—cried Mr. Parker, delighted—. "Look my dear Mary—Look at William Heeley's windows.—Blue shoes, and nankin boots![20]—Who would have expected such a sight at a shoemaker's in old Sanditon!—This is new within the month. There was no blue shoe when we passed this way a month ago.—Glorious indeed!—Well, I think I *have* done something in my day.—Now, for our hill, our health-breathing hill.—"[21]

In ascending, they passed the lodge-gates of Sanditon House, and saw the top of the house itself among its groves. It was the last building of former days in that line of the parish. A little higher up, the modern began; and in crossing the down, a Prospect House, a Bellevue Cottage, and a Denham Place[22] were to be looked at by Charlotte with the calmness of amused curiosity, and by Mr. Parker with the eager eye which hoped to see scarcely any empty houses.—More bills at the window[23] than he had calculated on;—and a smaller shew of company on the hill—fewer carriages, fewer walkers. He had fancied it just the time of day for them to be all returning from their airings to dinner.[24]—But the sands and the terrace always attracted some—and the tide must be flowing—about half-tide now.—He longed to be on the sands, the cliffs, at his own house and every where out of his house at once. His spirits rose with the very sight of the sea and he could almost feel his ancle getting stronger already.—

Trafalgar House, on the most elevated spot on the down, was a light elegant building, standing in a small lawn with a very young plantation round it, about an hundred yards from the brow of a steep, but not very lofty cliff—and the nearest to it, of every building, excepting one short row of smart-looking houses, called the Terrace, with a broad walk in front, aspiring to be the Mall of the place.[25] In this row were the best milliner's shop[26] and the library—a little detached from it, the hotel and billiard room.[27]—Here began the descent to the beach, and to the bathing machines[28]—and this was therefore the favourite spot for beauty and fashion.—At Trafalgar House, rising at a little distance behind the Terrace, the travellers were safely set down, and all was happiness and joy between papa and mama and their children; while Charlotte, having received possession of her apartment, found amusement enough in standing at her ample, Venetian window,[29] and looking over the miscellaneous foreground of unfinished buildings, waving linen, and tops of houses, to the sea, dancing and sparkling in sunshine and freshness.—

Chapter 5

When they met before dinner, Mr. Parker was looking over letters.—

"Not a line from Sidney!"—said he.—"He is an idle fellow.—I sent him an account of my accident from Willingden, and thought he would have vouchsafed me an answer.—But perhaps it implies that he is coming himself.—I trust it may.—But here is a letter from one of my sisters. *They* never fail me.—Women are the only correspondents to be depended on.[1]—Now Mary, (smiling at his wife)—before I open it, what shall we guess as to the state of health of those it comes from—or rather what would Sidney say if he were here?—Sidney is a saucy fellow, Miss Heywood.—And you must know, he will have it there is a good deal of imagination in my two sisters' complaints—but it really is not so—or very little.—They have wretched health, as you have heard us say frequently, and are subject to a variety of very serious disorders.—Indeed, I do not believe they know what a day's health is;—and at the same time, they are such excellent useful women and have so much energy of character that, where any good is to be done, they force themselves on exertions which, to those who do not thoroughly know them, have an extraordinary appearance.—But there is really no affectation about them. They have only weaker constitutions and stronger minds than are often met with, either separate or together.—And our youngest brother, who lives with them, and who is not much above twenty, I am sorry to say, is almost as great an invalid as themselves.—He is so delicate that he can engage in no profession.—Sidney laughs at him—but it really is no joke—though Sidney often makes me laugh at them all in spite of myself.—Now, if he were here, I know he would be offering odds, that either Susan, Diana or Arthur would appear by this letter to have been at the point of death within the last month.—"

Having run his eye over the letter, he shook his head and began:—

"No chance of seeing them at Sanditon I am sorry to say.—A very indifferent account of them indeed. Seriously, a *very* indifferent account.—Mary, you will be quite sorry to hear how ill they have been and are.—Miss Heywood, if you will give me leave, I will read Diana's letter aloud.—I like to have my friends acquainted with each other—and I am afraid this is the only sort of acquaintance I shall have the means of accomplishing between you.—And I can have no scruple on Diana's account—for her letters shew her exactly as she is, the most active, friendly, warm-hearted being in existence, and therefore must give a good impression."

He read.—

"My dear Tom, We were all much grieved at your accident, and if you had not described yourself as fallen into such very good hands, I should have been with you at all hazards the day after the receipt of your letter, though it found me suffering under a more severe attack than usual of my old grievance, spasmodic bile,[2] and hardly able to crawl from my bed to the sofa.—But how were you treated?—Send me more particulars in your next.—If indeed a simple sprain, as you denominate it, nothing would have been so judicious as friction,[3] friction by the hand alone, supposing it could be applied *instantly*.—Two years ago I happened to be calling on Mrs. Sheldon when her coachman sprained his foot as he was cleaning the carriage and could hardly limp into the house—but by the immediate use of friction alone, steadily persevered in (and I rubbed his ancle with my own hand for six hours without intermission)—he was well in three days.—Many thanks my dear Tom, for the kindness with respect to us, which had so large a share in bringing on your accident.—But pray: never run into peril again, in looking for an apothecary on our account, for had you the most experienced man in his line settled at Sanditon, it would be no recommendation to us. We have entirely done with the whole medical tribe.[4] We have consulted physician after physician in vain, till we are quite convinced that they can do nothing for us and that we must trust to our own knowledge of our own wretched constitutions for any relief.—But if you think it advisable for the interest of the *place*, to get a medical man there, I will undertake the commission with pleasure, and have no doubt of succeeding.—I could soon put the necessary irons in the fire.—As for getting to Sanditon myself, it is quite an impossibility. I grieve to say that I dare not attempt it, but my feelings tell me too plainly that in my present state, the sea air would probably be the death of me.—And neither of my dear companions will leave me, or I would promote their going down to you for a fortnight. But in truth, I doubt whether

Susan's nerves would be equal to the effort. She has been suffering much from the headache and six leeches a day for ten days together[5] relieved her so little that we thought it right to change our measures—and being convinced on examination that much of the evil lay in her gum, I persuaded her to attack the disorder there. She has accordingly had three teeth drawn,[6] and is decidedly better, but her nerves are a good deal deranged. She can only speak in a whisper—and fainted away twice this morning on poor Arthur's trying to suppress a cough. He, I am happy to say, is tolerably well—though more languid than I like—and I fear for his liver.[7]—I have heard nothing of Sidney since your being together in town, but conclude his scheme to the Isle of Wight[8] has not taken place, or we should have seen him in his way.—Most sincerely do we wish you a good season at Sanditon, and though we cannot contribute to your beau monde[9] in person, we are doing our utmost to send you company worth having; and think we may safely reckon on securing you two large families, one a rich West Indian from Surry,[10] the other a most respectable girls boarding school, or academy,[11] from Camberwell.[12]—I will not tell you how many people I have employed in the business—Wheel within wheel.[13]—But success more than repays.—Yours most affec^{ly}—&c."

"Well"—said Mr. Parker as he finished.—"Though I dare say Sidney might find something extremely entertaining in this letter and make us laugh for half an hour together, I declare *I* by myself can see nothing in it but what is either very pitiable or very creditable.—With all their sufferings, you perceive how much they are occupied in promoting the good of others!—So anxious for Sanditon! Two large families—one, for Prospect House probably, the other, for No. 2 Denham Place—or the end house of the Terrace,—and extra beds at the hotel.—I told you my sisters were excellent women, Miss Heywood—."

"And I am sure they must be very extraordinary ones,"—said Charlotte. "I am astonished at the cheerful style of the letter, considering the state in which both sisters appear to be.—Three teeth drawn at once!—frightful!—Your sister Diana seems almost as ill as possible, but those three teeth of your sister Susan's are more distressing than all the rest.—"

"Oh!—they are so used to the operation—to every operation—and have such fortitude!—"

"Your sisters know what they are about, I dare say, but their measures seem to touch on extremes.—I feel that in any illness, *I* should be so anxious for professional advice, so very little venturesome for myself, or any body I loved!—But then, *we* have been so healthy a family, that I can be no judge of what the habit of self-doctoring may do.—"

"Why to own the truth," said Mrs. Parker—"I *do* think the Miss Parkers carry it too far sometimes—and so do you my love, you know.—You often think they would be better, if they would leave themselves more alone—and especially Arthur. I know you think it a great pity they should give *him* such a turn for being ill.—"

"Well, well—my dear Mary—I grant you, it *is* unfortunate for poor Arthur, that at his time of life he should be encouraged to give way to indisposition. It *is* bad;—it *is* bad that he should be fancying himself too sickly for any profession—and sit down at one and twenty, on the interest of his own little fortune, without any idea of attempting to improve it, or of engaging in any occupation that may be of use to himself or others.—But let us talk of pleasanter things.—These two large families are just what we wanted.—But—here is something at hand, pleasanter still—Morgan, with his 'Dinner on Table.'"—

Chapter 6

The party were very soon moving after dinner. Mr. Parker could not be satisfied without an early visit to the library, and the library subscription book,[1] and Charlotte was glad to see as much, and as quickly as possible, where all was new. They were out in the very quietest part of a watering-place day, when the important business of dinner or of sitting after dinner was going on in almost every inhabited lodging;—here and there a solitary elderly man might be seen, who was forced to move early and walk for health—but in general, it was a thorough pause of company, it was emptiness and tranquillity on the Terrace, the cliffs, and the sands.—The shops were deserted—the straw hats and pendant lace[2] seemed left to their fate both within the house and without, and Mrs. Whilby at the library was sitting in her inner room, reading one of her own novels, for want of employment.—

The list of subscribers was but commonplace.[3] The Lady Denham,[4] Miss Brereton, Mr. and Mrs. Parker, Sir Edward Denham and Miss Denham, whose names might be said to lead off the season,[5] were followed by nothing better than—Mrs. Mathews—Miss Mathews, Miss E. Mathews, Miss H. Mathews.—Dr. and Mrs. Brown—Mr. Richard Pratt.—Lieutenant Smith R. N.[6] Captain Little,—Limehouse.[7]—Mrs. Jane Fisher. Miss Fisher. Miss Scroggs.—Rev. Mr. Hankins. Mr. Beard—solicitor, Grays Inn.[8]—Mrs. Davis. And Miss Merryweather.—Mr. Parker could not but feel that the list was not only without distinction, but less numerous than he had hoped. It was but July however, and August and September were the months;[9]—and besides, the promised large families from Surry and Camberwell were an ever-ready consolation.—

Mrs. Whitby came forward without delay from her literary recess,[10] delighted to see Mr. Parker again, whose manners recommended him to every body, and they were fully occupied in their various civilities and communications, while Charlotte, having added her name to the list as the first offering to the success of the season, was busy in some immediate purchases for the further good of everybody, as soon as Miss Whitby could be hurried down from her toilette,[11] with all her glossy curls and smart trinkets[12] to wait on her.—The library, of course, afforded every thing; all the useless things in the world that could not be done without, and among so many pretty temptations, and with so much good will for Mr. Parker to encourage expenditure, Charlotte began to feel that she must check herself—or rather she reflected that at two and twenty there could be no excuse for her doing otherwise—and that it would not do for her to be spending all her money the very first evening. She took up a book; it happened to be a volume of *Camilla*. She had not Camilla's youth, and had no intention of having her distress,[13]—so, she turned from the drawers of rings and brooches, repressed farther solicitation and paid for what she bought.—

For her particular gratification, they were then to take a turn on the cliff—but as they quitted the library they were met by two ladies whose arrival made an alteration necessary, Lady Denham and Miss Brereton.—They had been to Trafalgar House, and been directed thence to the library, and though Lady Denham was a great deal too active to regard the walk of a mile as anything requiring rest, and talked of going home again directly, the Parkers knew that to be pressed into their house, and obliged to take her tea with them, would suit her best,—and therefore the stroll on the cliff gave way to an immediate return home.—

"No, no," said her ladyship—"I will not have you hurry your tea on my account.—I know you like your tea late.—My early hours are not to put my neighbours to inconvenience. No, no, Miss Clara and I will get back to our own tea.—We came out with no other thought.—We wanted just to see you and make sure of your being really come—, but we get back to our own tea."—

She went on however towards Trafalgar House and took possession of the drawing room very quietly—without seeming to hear a word of Mrs. Parker's orders to the servant as they entered, to bring tea directly.

Charlotte was fully consoled for the loss of her walk, by finding herself in company with those, whom the conversation of the morning had given her a great curiosity to see. She observed them well.—Lady Denham was of middle height, stout,[14] upright and alert in her motions with a shrewd eye, and self-satisfied air—but not an unagreeable countenance—and though her manner was rather downright and abrupt, as of a person who valued herself on being free-spoken, there was a good humour and cordiality about her—a civility and readiness to be acquainted with Charlotte herself, and a heartiness of welcome towards her old friends, which was inspiring the good will she seemed to feel;—and as for Miss Brereton, her appearance so completely justified Mr. Parker's praise that Charlotte thought she had never beheld a more lovely, or more interesting[15] young woman.—Elegantly tall, regularly handsome, with great delicacy of complexion and soft blue eyes, a sweetly modest and yet naturally graceful address,[16] Charlotte could see in her only the most perfect representation of whatever heroine might be most beautiful and bewitching, in all the numerous volumes they had left behind them on Mrs. Whilby's shelves.—Perhaps it might be partly owing to her having just issued from a circulating library—but she could not separate the idea of a complete heroine from Clara Brereton. Her situation with Lady Denham so very much in favour of it!—She seemed placed with her on purpose to be ill-used.—Such poverty and dependence, joined to such beauty and merit, seemed to leave no choice in the business.[17]—These feelings were not the result of any spirit of romance in Charlotte herself. No, she was a very sober-minded young lady, sufficiently well-read in novels to supply her imagination with amusements, but not at all unreasonably influenced by them; and while she pleased herself the first five minutes with fancying the persecutions which *ought* to be the lot of the interesting Clara, especially in the form of the most barbarous conduct on Lady Denham's side,[18] she found no reluctance to admit, from subsequent observation, that they appeared to be on very comfortable terms.—She could see nothing worse in Lady Denham, than the sort of old-fashioned formality of always calling her *Miss Clara*—nor anything objectionable in the degree of observance and attention which Clara paid.—On one side it seemed protecting kindness, on the other grateful and affectionate respect.—

The conversation turned entirely upon Sanditon, its present number of visitants[19] and the chances of a good season. It was evident that Lady Denham had more anxiety, more fears of loss, than her coadjutor. She wanted to have the place fill faster, and seemed to have many harassing apprehensions of the lodgings being in some instances underlet.—Miss Diana Parker's two large families were not forgotten.

"Very good, very good," said her Ladyship.—"A West Indy family and a school. That sounds well. That will bring money."—

"No people spend more freely, I believe, than West Indians,"[20] observed Mr. Parker.—

"Aye—so I have heard—and because they have full purses, fancy themselves equal, may be, to your old country families. But then, they who scatter their money so freely, never think of whether they may not be doing mischief by raising the price of things—and I have heard that's very much the case with your West-ingines[21]—and if they come among us to raise the price of our necessaries of life, we shall not much thank them Mr. Parker."—

"My dear madam, they can only raise the price of consumable articles, by such an extraordinary demand for them and such a diffusion of money among us, as must do us more good than harm.[22]—Our butchers and bakers and traders in general cannot get rich without bringing prosperity to *us*.—If *they* do not gain, our rents must be insecure—and in proportion to their profit must be ours eventually in the increased value of our houses."

"Oh!—well.—But I should not like to have butcher's meat raised, though—and I shall keep it down as long as I can.—Aye—that young lady smiles I see;—I dare say she thinks me an odd sort of a creature,—but *she* will come to care about such matters herself in time. Yes, yes, my dear, depend upon it, you will be thinking of the price of butcher's meat in time—though you may not happen to have quite such a servants' hall to feed, as I have.—And I do believe *those* are best off, that have fewest servants.—I am not a woman of parade, as all the world knows, and if it was not for what I owe to poor Mr. Hollis's memory, I should never keep up Sanditon House as I do;—it is not for my own pleasure.—Well Mr. Parker—and the other is a boarding school, a French boarding school,[23] is it?—No harm in that.—They'll stay their six weeks.—And out of such a number, who knows but some may be consumptive and want asses' milk—and I have two milch asses[24] at this present time.—But perhaps the little Misses may hurt the furniture.—I hope they will have a good sharp governess[25] to look after them."—

Poor Mr. Parker got no more credit from Lady Denham than he had from his sisters, for the object which had taken him to Willingden.

"Lord! my dear Sir," she cried, "how could you think of such a thing? I am very sorry you met with your accident, but upon my word you deserved it.—Going after a doctor!—Why, what should we do with a doctor here? It would be only encouraging our servants and the poor to fancy themselves ill, if there was a doctor at hand.—Oh! pray, let us have none of the tribe at Sanditon. We go on very well as we are. There is the sea and the Downs and my milch-asses—and I have told Mrs. Whilby that if any body enquires for a chamber horse,[26] they may be supplied at a fair rate—(poor Mr. Hollis's chamber horse, as good as new)—and what can people want for, more?—Here have I lived seventy good years in the world and never took physic above twice—and never saw the face of a doctor in all my life, on my *own* account.—And I verily believe if my poor dear Sir Harry had never seen one neither, he would have been alive now.—Ten fees, one after another, did the man take who sent *him* out of the world.—I beseech you Mr. Parker, no doctors here."—

The tea things were brought in.—

"Oh! my dear Mrs. Parker—you should not indeed—why would you do so? I was just upon the point of wishing you good evening. But since you are so very neighbourly, I believe Miss Clara and I must stay."—

Chapter 7

The popularity of the Parkers brought them some visitors the very next morning;—amongst them, Sir Edward Denham and his sister, who having been at Sanditon House drove on to pay their compliments; and the duty of letter-writing being accomplished, Charlotte was settled with Mrs. Parker in the drawing room in time to see them all.—The Denhams were the only ones to excite particular attention. Charlotte was glad to complete her knowledge of the family by an introduction to them, and found them, the better half at least—(for while single, the *gentleman* may sometimes be thought the better half, of the pair[1])—not unworthy notice.—Miss Denham was a fine young woman, but cold and reserved, giving the idea of one who felt her consequence with pride and her poverty with discontent, and who was immediately gnawed by the want of an handsomer equipage than the simple gig[2] in which they travelled, and which their groom was leading about still in her sight.—Sir Edward was much her superior in air and manner;—certainly handsome, but yet more to be remarked for his very good address and wish of paying attention and giving pleasure.—He came into the room remarkably well, talked much—and very much to Charlotte, by whom he chanced to be placed—and she soon perceived that he had a fine countenance, a most pleasing gentleness of voice, and a great deal of conversation. She liked him.—Sober-minded as she was, she thought him agreeable, and did not quarrel with the suspicion of his finding her equally so, which *would* arise, from his evidently disregarding his sister's motion to go, and persisting in his station[3] and his discourse.—I make no apologies for my heroine's vanity.—If there are young ladies in the world at her time of life, more dull of fancy and more careless of pleasing, I know them not, and never wish to know them.—

At last, from the low French windows of the drawing room which commanded the road and all the paths across the Down, Charlotte and Sir Edward, as they sat, could not but observe Lady Denham and Miss Brereton walking by—and there was instantly a slight change in Sir Edward's countenance—with an anxious glance after them as they proceeded—followed by an early proposal to his sister—not merely for moving, but for walking on together to the Terrace—which altogether gave an hasty turn to Charlotte's fancy, cured her of her half-hour's fever, and placed her in a more capable state of judging, when Sir Edward was gone, of *how* agreeable he had actually been.—"Perhaps there was a good deal in his air and address; and his title did him no harm."

She was very soon in his company again. The first object of the Parkers, when their house was cleared of morning visitors, was to get out themselves;—the Terrace was the attraction to all;—every body who walked must begin with the Terrace, and there, seated on one of the two green benches by the gravel walk, they found the united Denham party;—but though united in the gross,[4] very distinctly divided again—the two superior ladies being at one end of the bench, and Sir Edward and Miss Brereton at the other.—

Charlotte's first glance told her that Sir Edward's air was that of a lover.—There could be no doubt of his devotion to Clara.—How Clara received it, was less obvious—but she was inclined to think not very favourably; for though sitting thus apart with him (which probably she might not have been able to prevent) her air was calm and grave.—That the young lady at the other end of the bench was doing penance, was indubitable. The difference in Miss Denham's countenance, the change from Miss Denham sitting in cold grandeur in Mrs. Parker's drawing-room to be kept from silence by the efforts of others, to Miss Denham at Lady Denham's elbow, listening and talking with smiling attention or solicitous eagerness, was very striking—and very amusing—or very melancholy, just as satire or morality might prevail.—Miss Denham's character was pretty well decided with Charlotte.

Sir Edward's required longer observation. He surprised her by quitting Clara immediately on their all joining and agreeing to walk, and by addressing his attentions entirely to herself.—Stationing himself close by her, he seemed to mean to detach her as much as possible from the rest of the party and to give her the whole of his conversation. He began, in a tone of great taste and feeling, to talk of the sea and the sea shore—and ran with energy through all the usual phrases employed in praise of their sublimity,[5] and descriptive of the *undescribable* emotions they excite in the mind of sensibility.[6]—The terrific[7] grandeur of the ocean in a storm, its glassy surface in a calm, its gulls and its samphire,[8] and the deep fathoms of its abysses, its quick vicissitudes, its direful deceptions, its mariners tempting it in sunshine and overwhelmed by the sudden tempest, all were eagerly and fluently touched;—rather commonplace perhaps[9]—but doing very well from the lips of a handsome Sir Edward,—and she could not but think him a man of feeling[10]—till he began to stagger her by the number of his quotations,[11] and the bewilderment of some of his sentences.—

"Do you remember," said he, "Scott's beautiful lines on the sea?—Oh! what a description they convey!—They are never out of my thoughts when I walk here.—That man who can read them unmoved must have the nerves of an assassin![12]—Heaven defend me from meeting such a man un-armed."[13]—

"What description do you mean?"—said Charlotte. "I remember none at this moment, of the sea, in either of Scott's poems."[14]—

"Do not you indeed?—Nor can I exactly recall the beginning at this moment.—But—you cannot have forgotten his description of woman.—

'Oh! Woman in our hours of ease'[15]——

Delicious! Delicious!—Had he written nothing more, he would have been immortal. And then again, that unequalled, unrivalled address to parental affection—

> 'Some feelings are to mortals given
> With less of earth in them than heaven' &c.[16]

But while we are on the subject of poetry, what think you Miss Heywood of Burns's lines to his Mary?[17]—Oh! there is pathos to madden one!—If ever there was a man who *felt*, it was Burns.—Montgomery has all the fire of poetry,[18] Wordsworth has the true soul of it[19]—Campbell in his pleasures of hope has touched the extreme of our sensations—'Like angel's visits, few and far between'.[20] Can you conceive any thing more subduing, more melting, more fraught with the deep sublime than that line?—But Burns—I confess my sense of his pre-eminence Miss Heywood.—If Scott *has* a fault, it is the want of passion.—Tender, elegant, descriptive—but *tame.*[21]—The man who cannot do justice to the attributes of woman is my contempt.—Sometimes indeed a flash of feeling seems to irradiate him—as in the lines we were speaking of—'Oh! Woman in our hours of ease'—. But Burns is always on fire.—His soul was the altar in which lovely woman sat enshrined, his spirit truly breathed the immortal incense which is her due.—"

"I have read several of Burns's poems with great delight," said Charlotte as soon as she had time to speak, "but I am not poetic enough to separate a man's poetry entirely from his character;—and poor Burns's known irregularities greatly interrupt my enjoyment of his lines.—I have difficulty in depending on the *truth* of his feelings as a lover. I have not faith in the *sincerity* of the affections of a man of his description. He felt and he wrote and he forgot."[22]

"Oh! no no—" exclaimed Sir Edward in an extasy. "He was all ardour and truth!—His genius[23] and his susceptibilities might lead him into some aberrations.—But who is perfect?—It were hyper-criticism, it were pseudo-philosophy[24] to expect from the soul of high toned genius, the grovellings of a common mind.—The coruscations[25] of talent, elicited by impassioned feeling in the breast of man, are perhaps incompatible with some of the prosaic decencies of life;—nor can you, loveliest Miss Heywood—(speaking with an air of deep sentiment)—nor can any woman be a fair judge of what a man may be propelled to say, write or do, by the sovereign impulses of illimitable ardour."

This was very fine;—but if Charlotte understood it at all, not very moral—and being moreover by no means pleased with his extraordinary stile of compliment, she gravely answered,

"I really know nothing of the matter.—This is a charming day. The wind I fancy must be southerly."

"Happy, happy wind, to engage Miss Heywood's thoughts!—"

She began to think him downright silly.—His chusing to walk with her, she had learnt to understand. It was done to pique Miss Brereton. She had read it, in an anxious glance or two on his side—but why he should talk so much nonsense, unless he could do no better, was unintelligible.—He seemed very sentimental, very full of some feelings or other, and very much addicted to all the newest-fashioned hard words—had not a very clear brain she presumed, and talked a good deal by rote.—The future might explain him further—but when there was a proposition for going into the library she felt that she had had quite enough of Sir Edward for one morning, and very gladly accepted Lady Denham's invitation of remaining on the Terrace with her.—

The others all left them, Sir Edward with looks of very gallant despair in tearing himself away, and they united their agreeableness—that is, Lady Denham, like a true great lady, talked and talked only of her own concerns, and Charlotte listened—amused in considering the contrast between her two companions.—Certainly, there was no strain of doubtful sentiment, nor any phrase of difficult interpretation, in Lady Denham's discourse. Taking hold of Charlotte's arm with the ease of one who felt that any notice from her was an honour, and communicative, from the influence of the same conscious importance or a natural love of talking, she immediately said in a tone of great satisfaction—and with a look of arch sagacity—

"Miss Esther wants me to invite her and her brother to spend a week with me at Sanditon House, as I did last summer.—But I shan't.—She has been trying to get round me every way, with her praise of this, and her praise of that; but I saw what she was about.—I saw through it all.—I am not very easily taken in my dear."

Charlotte could think of nothing more harmless to be said, than the simple enquiry of—"Sir Edward and Miss Denham?"—

"Yes, my dear. *My young folks*, as I call them sometimes, for I take them very much by the hand. I had them with me last summer about this time, for a week; from Monday to Monday; and very delighted and thankful they were.—For they are very good young people my dear. I would not have you think that I *only* notice them for poor dear Sir Harry's sake. No, no; they are very deserving themselves, or trust me, they would not be so much in *my* company.—I am not the woman to help any body blindfold.—I always take care to know what I am about and who I have to deal with, before I stir a finger.—I do not think I was ever over-reached in my life; and that is a good deal for a woman to say that has been married twice.—Poor dear Sir Harry (between ourselves) thought at first to have got more. —But (with a bit of a sigh) he is gone, and we must not find fault with the dead. Nobody could live happier together than us—and he was a very honourable man, quite the gentleman of ancient family.—And when he died, I gave Sir Edward his gold watch.—"

She said this with a look at her companion which implied its right to produce a great impression—and seeing no rapturous astonishment in Charlotte's countenance, added quickly—

"He did not bequeath it to his nephew, my dear—it was no bequest. It was not in the will. He only told me, and *that* but once, that he should wish his nephew to have his watch; but it need not have been binding, if I had not chose it.—"

"Very kind indeed! very handsome!"—said Charlotte, absolutely forced to affect admiration.—

"Yes, my dear—and it is not the *only* kind thing I have done by him.—I have been a very liberal friend to Sir Edward. And poor young man, he needs it bad enough;—for though I am *only* the *dowager*[26] my dear, and he is the *heir*, things do not stand between us in the way they commonly do between those two parties.—Not a shilling do I receive from the Denham estate. Sir Edward has no payments to make *me*. He don't stand uppermost, believe me.—It is *I* that help *him*."

"Indeed!—He is a very fine young man;—particularly elegant in his address."—

This was said chiefly for the sake of saying something—but Charlotte directly saw that it was laying her open to suspicion by Lady Denham's giving a shrewd glance at her and replying—

"Yes, yes, he is very well to look at—and it is to be hoped some lady of large fortune will think so—for Sir Edward *must* marry for money.—He and I often talk that matter over.—A handsome young fellow like him, will go smirking and smiling about and paying girls compliments, but he knows he *must* marry for money.—And Sir Edward is a very steady young man in the main, and has got very good notions."

"Sir Edward Denham," said Charlotte, "with such personal advantages may be almost sure of getting a woman of fortune, if he chuses it."—

This glorious sentiment seemed quite to remove suspicion. "Aye my dear—that's very sensibly said," cried Lady Denham. "And if we could but get a young heiress to Sanditon! But heiresses are monstrous scarce! I do not think we have had an heiress here, or even a co,[27] since Sanditon has been a public place. Families come after families, but as far as I can learn, it is not one in an hundred of them that have any real property, landed or funded.[28]— An income perhaps, but no property. Clergymen may be, or lawyers from town, or half pay officers,[29] or widows with only a jointure.[30] And what good can such people do anybody?—except just as they take our empty houses—and (between ourselves) I think they are great fools for not staying at home. Now, if we could get a young heiress to be sent here for her health—(and if she was ordered to drink asses' milk I could supply her)—and as soon as she got well, have her fall in love with Sir Edward!"—

"That would be very fortunate indeed."

"And Miss Esther must marry somebody of fortune too—she must get a rich husband. Ah! young ladies that have no money are very much to be pitied!—But—" after a short pause—"if Miss Esther thinks to talk me into inviting them to come and stay at Sanditon House, she will find herself mistaken.—Matters are altered with me since last summer you know—. I have Miss Clara with me now, which makes a great difference."

She spoke this so seriously that Charlotte instantly saw in it the evidence of real penetration and prepared for some fuller remarks—but it was followed only by—

"I have no fancy for having my house as full as an hotel. I should not chuse to have my two housemaids' time taken up all the morning, in dusting out bed rooms.—They have Miss Clara's room to put to rights as well as my own every day.—If they had hard places, they would want higher wages.—"

For objections of this nature, Charlotte was not prepared, and she found it so impossible even to affect sympathy, that she could say nothing.—Lady Denham soon added, with great glee—

"And besides all this my dear, am I to be filling my house to the prejudice of Sanditon?—If people want to be by the sea, why don't they take lodgings?—Here are a great many empty houses—three on this very terrace; no fewer than three lodging papers staring us in the face at this very moment, Numbers 3, 4 and 8. 8, the corner house, may be too large for them, but either of the two others are nice little snug houses, very fit for a young gentleman and his sister.—And so, my dear, the next time Miss Esther begins talking about the dampness of Denham Park, and the good bathing always does her, I shall advise them to come and take one of these lodgings for a fortnight.—Don't you think that will be very fair?—Charity begins at home you know."—

Charlotte's feelings were divided between amusement and indignation—but indignation had the larger and the increasing share.—She kept her countenance and she kept a civil silence. She could not carry her forbearance farther; but without attempting to listen longer, and only conscious that Lady Denham was still talking on in the same way, allowed her thoughts to form themselves into such a meditation as this:—

"She is thoroughly mean. I had not expected any thing so bad.—Mr. Parker spoke too mildly of her.—His judgement is evidently not to be trusted.—His own good nature misleads him. He is too kind hearted to see clearly.—I must judge for myself.—And their very *connection* prejudices him.—He has persuaded her to engage in the same speculation—and because their object in that line is the same, he fancies she feels like him in others.—But she is very, very mean.—I can see no good in her.—Poor Miss Brereton!—And she makes every body mean about her.—This poor Sir Edward and his sister,—how far nature meant them to be respectable I can not tell,—but they are *obliged* to be mean in their servility to her.—And I am mean too, in giving her my attention, with the appearance of coinciding with her.—Thus it is, when rich people are sordid."—

Chapter 8

The two ladies continued walking together till rejoined by the others, who as they issued from the library were followed by a young Whilby running off with five volumes[1] under his arm to Sir Edward's gig—and Sir Edward, approaching Charlotte, said, "You may perceive what has been our occupation. My sister wanted my counsel in the selection of some books.—We have many leisure hours, and read a great deal.—I am no indiscriminate novel-reader. The mere trash of the common circulating library, I hold in the highest contempt.[2] You will never hear me advocating those puerile emanations which detail nothing but discordant principles incapable of amalgamation, or those vapid tissues of ordinary occurrences from which no useful deductions can be drawn.[3]—In vain may we put them into a literary alembic;—we distil nothing which can add to science.[4]—You understand me I am sure?"

"I am not quite certain that I do.[5]—But if you will describe the sort of novels which you *do* approve, I dare say it will give me a clearer idea."

"Most willingly, fair questioner.[6]—The novels which I approve are such as display human nature with grandeur—such as shew her in the sublimities of intense feeling—such as exhibit the progress of strong passion from the first germ of incipient susceptibility to the utmost energies of reason half-dethroned,—where we see the strong spark of woman's captivations elicit such fire in the soul of man as leads him—(though at the risk of some aberration from the strict line of primitive obligations[7])—to hazard all, dare all, achieve all, to obtain her.—Such are the works which I peruse with delight, and I hope I may say, with amelioration. They hold forth the most splendid portraitures of high conceptions, unbounded views, illimitable ardour, indomptible[8] decision—and even when the event is mainly anti-prosperous to the high-toned machinations[9] of the prime character, the potent, pervading hero of the story, it leaves us full of generous emotions for him;—our hearts are paralized—. 'Twere pseudo-philosophy to assert that we do not feel more enwrapped by the brilliancy of his career, than by the tranquil and morbid[10] virtues of any opposing character. Our approbation of the latter is but eleemosynary.[11]—These are the novels which enlarge the primitive capabilities of the heart, and which it cannot impugn the sense, or be any dereliction of the character, of the most anti-puerile man, to be conversant with."—

"If I understand you aright—" said Charlotte—"our taste in novels is not at all the same."

And here they were obliged to part—Miss Denham being too much tired of them all, to stay any longer.—The truth was that Sir Edward, whom circumstances had confined very much to one spot, had read more sentimental novels than agreed with him. His fancy had been early caught by all the impassioned and most exceptionable parts of Richardson's;[12] and such authors as have since appeared to tread in Richardson's steps, so far as man's determined pursuit of woman in defiance of every opposition of feeling and convenience is concerned,[13] had since occupied the greater part of his literary hours, and formed his character.—With a perversity of judgement, which must be attributed to his not having by nature a very strong head, the graces, the spirit, the ingenuity, and the perseverance, of the villain of the story outweighed all his absurdities and all his atrocities with Sir Edward. With him, such conduct was genius, fire and feeling.—It interested and inflamed him; and he was always more anxious for its success and mourned over its discomfitures with more tenderness than could ever have been contemplated by the authors.—Though he owed many of his ideas to this sort of reading, it were unjust to say that he read nothing else, or that his language were not formed on a more general knowledge of modern literature.[14]—He read all the essays, letters, tours and criticisms of the day[15]—and with the same ill-luck which made him derive only false principles from lessons of morality, and incentives to vice from the history of its overthrow, he gathered only hard words and involved sentences from the style of our most approved writers.—

Sir Edward's great object in life was to be seductive.—With such personal advantages as he knew himself to possess, and such talents as he did also give himself credit for, he regarded it as his duty.—He felt that he was formed to be a dangerous man—quite in the line of the Lovelaces.[16]—The very name of Sir Edward, he thought, carried some degree of fascination with it.—To be generally gallant and assiduous about the fair, to make fine speeches to every pretty girl, was but the inferior part of the character he had to play.—Miss Heywood, or any other young woman with any pretensions to beauty, he was entitled (according to his own views of society) to approach with high compliment and rhapsody on the slightest acquaintance; but it was Clara alone on whom he had serious designs; it was Clara whom he meant to seduce.—Her seduction was quite determined on. Her situation in every way called for it. She was his rival in Lady Denham's favour, she was young, lovely and dependant.—He had very early seen the necessity of the case, and had now been long trying with cautious assiduity to make an impression on her heart, and to undermine her principles.—

Clara saw through him, and had not the least intention of being seduced—but she bore with him patiently enough to confirm the sort of attachment which her personal charms had raised.—A greater degree of discouragement indeed would not have affected Sir Edward—. He was armed against the highest pitch of disdain or aversion.—If she could not be won by affection, he must carry her off. He knew his business.—Already had he had many musings on the subject. If he *were* constrained so to act, he must naturally wish to strike out something new, to exceed those who had gone before him—and he felt a strong curiosity to ascertain whether the neighbourhood of Tombuctoo might not afford some solitary house adapted for Clara's reception;[17]—but the expence alas! of measures in that masterly stile was ill-suited to his purse, and prudence obliged him to prefer the quietest sort of ruin and disgrace for the object of his affections, to the more renowned.—

Chapter 9

One day, soon after Charlotte's arrival at Sanditon, she had the pleasure of seeing, just as she ascended from the sands to the Terrace, a gentleman's carriage with post horses standing at the door of the hotel, as very lately arrived, and by the quantity of luggage taking off, bringing, it might be hoped, some respectable family determined on a long residence.—

Delighted to have such good news for Mr. and Mrs. Parker, who had both gone home some time before, she proceeded for Trafalgar House with as much alacrity as could remain, after having been contending for the last two hours with a very fine wind blowing directly on shore; but she had not reached the little lawn, when she saw a lady walking nimbly behind her at no great distance; and convinced that it could be no acquaintance of her own, she resolved to hurry on and get into the house if possible before her. But the stranger's pace did not allow this to be accomplished;— Charlotte was on the steps and had rung, but the door was not opened, when the other crossed the lawn;—and when the servant appeared, they were just equally ready for entering the house.—

The ease of the lady, her "How do you do Morgan?—" and Morgan's looks on seeing her, were a moment's astonishment—but another moment brought Mr. Parker into the hall to welcome the sister he had seen from the drawing room, and she was soon introduced to Miss Diana Parker.

There was a great deal of surprise but still more pleasure in seeing her.—Nothing could be kinder than her reception from both husband and wife. "How did she come? and with whom?—And they were so glad to find her equal to the journey!—And that she was to belong to *them*,[1] was a thing of course."

Miss Diana Parker was about four and thirty, of middling height and slender;—delicate looking rather than sickly; with an agreeable face, and a very animated eye;—her manners resembling her brother's in their ease and frankness, though with more decision and less mildness in her tone. She began an account of herself without delay—thanking them for their invitation, but "*that* was quite out of the question, for they were all three come, and meant to get into lodgings and make some stay."—

"All three come!—What!—Susan and Arthur!—Susan able to come too!—This was better and better."

"Yes—we are actually all come. Quite unavoidable.—Nothing else to be done.—You shall hear all about it.—But my dear Mary, send for the children;—I long to see them."—

"And how has Susan borne the journey?—and how is Arthur?—and why do not we see him here with you?"—

"Susan has borne it wonderfully. She had not a wink of sleep either the night before we set out, or last night at Chichester,[2] and as this is not so common with her as with *me*, I have had a thousand fears for her—but she has kept up wonderfully—had no hysterics[3] of consequence till we came within sight of poor old Sanditon—and the attack was not very violent—nearly over by the time we reached your hotel—so that we got her out of the carriage extremely well, with only Mr. Woodcock's assistance—and when I left her she was directing the disposal of the luggage and helping old Sam uncord the trunks.—She desired her best love, with a thousand regrets at being so poor a creature that she could not come with me. And as for poor Arthur, he would not have been unwilling himself, but there is so much wind that I did not think he could safely venture,—for I am *sure* there is lumbago hanging about him—and so I helped him on with his great coat and sent him off to the Terrace, to take us lodgings.—Miss Heywood must have seen our carriage standing at the hotel.—I knew Miss Heywood the moment I saw her before me on the Down.—My dear Tom I am glad to see you walk so well. Let me feel your ancle.—That's right; all right and clean. The play of your sinews a *very* little affected;—barely perceptible.—Well—now for the explanation of my being here.—I told you in my letter, of the two considerable families I was hoping to secure for you—the West Indians, and the seminary."[4]—

Here Mr. Parker drew his chair still nearer to his sister, and took her hand again most affectionately as he answered "Yes, yes;—how active and how kind you have been!"—

"The West Indians," she continued, "whom I look upon as the *most* desirable of the two—as the best of the good—prove to be a Mrs. Griffiths and her family. I know them only through others.—You must have heard me mention Miss Capper, the particular friend of *my* very particular friend Fanny Noyce;—now, Miss Capper is extremely intimate with a Mrs. Darling, who is on terms of constant correspondence with Mrs. Griffiths herself.—Only a *short* chain, you see, between us, and not a link wanting. Mrs. Griffiths meant to go to the sea, for her young people's benefit—had fixed on the coast of Sussex, but was undecided as to the where, wanted something private, and wrote to ask the opinion of her friend Mrs. Darling.—Miss Capper happened to be staying with Mrs. Darling when Mrs. Griffiths's letter arrived, and was consulted on the question; *she* wrote the same day to Fanny Noyce and mentioned it to her—and Fanny, all alive for *us*, instantly took up her pen and forwarded the circumstance to me—except as to *names*—which have but lately transpired.—There was but *one* thing for *me* to do.—I answered Fanny's letter by the same post and pressed for the recommendation of Sanditon. Fanny had feared your having no house large enough to receive such a family.—But I seem to be spinning out my story to an endless length.—You see how it was all managed. I had the pleasure of hearing soon afterwards by the same simple link of connection that Sanditon *had been* recommended by Mrs. Darling, and that the West Indians were very much disposed to go thither.—This was the state of the case when I wrote to you;—but two days ago—yes, the day before yesterday—I heard again from Fanny Noyce, saying that *she* had heard from Miss Capper, who by a letter from Mrs. Darling understood that Mrs. Griffiths has expressed herself in a letter to Mrs. Darling more doubtingly on the subject of Sanditon.—Am I clear?—I would be anything rather than not clear."—

"Oh! perfectly, perfectly. Well?"—

"The reason of this hesitation, was her having no connections in the place, and no means of ascertaining that she should have good accommodations on arriving there;—and she was particularly careful and scrupulous on all those matters more on account of a certain Miss Lambe, a young lady (probably a niece) under her care, than on her own account or her daughters'.—Miss Lambe has an immense fortune—richer than all the rest—and very delicate health.—One sees clearly enough by all this, the *sort* of woman Mrs. Griffiths must be—as helpless and indolent, as wealth and a hot climate are apt to make us. But we are not all born to equal energy.—What was to be done?—I had a few moments' indecision;—whether to offer to write to *you*,—or to Mrs. Whitby to secure them a house?—but neither pleased me.—I hate to employ others, when I am equal to act myself—and my conscience told me that this was an occasion which called for me. Here was a family of helpless invalids whom I might essentially serve.—I sounded Susan—the same thought had occurred to her.—Arthur made no difficulties—our plan was arranged immediately, we were off yesterday morning at six—, left Chichester at the same hour to day—and here we are.—"

"Excellent!—Excellent!—" cried Mr. Parker.—"Diana, you are unequalled in serving your friends and doing good to all the world.—I know nobody like you.—Mary, my love, is not she a wonderful creature?—Well—and now, what house do you design to engage for them?—What is the size of their family?[5]—"

"I do not at all know—" replied his sister—"have not the least idea;—never heard any particulars;—but I am very sure that the largest house at Sanditon cannot be *too* large. They are more likely to want a second.—I shall take only one however, and that but for a week certain.—Miss Heywood, I astonish you.—You hardly know what to make of me.—I see by your looks, that you are not used to such quick measures."—

The words "Unaccountable officiousness!—Activity run mad!"—had just passed through Charlotte's mind—but a civil answer was easy.

"I dare say I do look surprised," said she—"because these are very great exertions, and I know what invalids both you and your sister are."

"Invalids indeed.—I trust there are not three people in England who have so sad a right to that appellation.—But my dear Miss Heywood, we are sent into this world to be as extensively useful as possible, and where some degree of strength of mind is given, it is not a feeble body which will excuse us—or incline us to excuse ourselves.—The world is pretty much divided between the weak of mind and the strong—between those who can act and those who can not—and it is the bounden duty of the capable to let no opportunity of being useful escape them.—My sister's complaints and mine are happily not often of a nature, to threaten existence *immediately*—and as long as we *can* exert ourselves to be of use to others, I am convinced that the body is the better for the refreshment the mind receives in doing its duty.—While I have been travelling, with this object in view, I have been perfectly well."—

The entrance of the children ended this little panegyric on her own disposition—and after having noticed and caressed them all, she prepared to go.—"Cannot you dine with us?—Is not it possible to prevail on you to dine with us?" was then the cry; and *that* being absolutely negatived, it was "And when shall we see you again? and how can we be of use to you?"—and Mr. Parker warmly offered his assistance in taking the house for Mrs. Griffiths.—

"I will come to you the moment I have dined," said he, "and we will go about together."—

But this was immediately declined.—

"No, my dear Tom, upon no account in the world shall you stir a step on any business of mine.—Your ancle wants rest. I see by the position of your foot, that you have used it too much already.—No, I shall go about my house-taking directly. Our dinner is not ordered till six—and by that time I hope to have completed it. It is now only half past four.—As to seeing *me* again to day—I cannot answer for it; the others will be at the hotel all the evening, and delighted to see you at any time, but as soon as I get back I shall hear what Arthur has done about our own lodgings, and probably the moment dinner is over shall be out again on business relative to them, for we hope to get into some lodgings or other and be settled after breakfast tomorrow.—I have not much confidence in poor Arthur's skill for lodging-taking, but he seemed to like the commission.—"

"I think you are doing too much," said Mr. Parker. "You will knock yourself up. You should not move again after dinner."

"No, indeed you should not—" cried his wife, "for dinner is such a mere *name* with you all, that it can do you no good.—I know what your appetites are."—

"My appetite is very much mended I assure you lately. I have been taking some bitters of my own decocting,[6] which have done wonders. Susan never eats—I grant you—and just at present *I* shall want nothing; I never eat for about a week after a journey—but as for Arthur, he is only too much disposed for food. We are often obliged to check him."—

"But you have not told me anything of the *other* family coming to Sanditon," said Mr. Parker as he walked with her to the door of the house—"the Camberwell seminary; have we a good chance of *them*?—"

"Oh! certain—quite certain.—I had forgotten them for the moment, but I had a letter three days ago from my friend Mrs. Charles Dupuis which assured me of Camberwell. Camberwell will be here to a certainty, and very soon.—*That* good woman (I do not know her name) not being so wealthy and independent as Mrs. Griffiths—can travel and chuse for herself.—I will tell you how I got at *her*. Mrs. Charles Dupuis lives almost next door to a lady, who has a relation lately settled at Clapham, who actually attends the seminary and gives lessons on eloquence and belles lettres[7] to some of the girls.—I got that man a hare[8] from one of Sidney's friends—and he recommended Sanditon—without *my* appearing however—Mrs. Charles Dupuis managed it all."—

Chapter 10

It was not a week since Miss Diana Parker had been told by her feelings, that the sea air would probably in her present state be the death of her, and now she was at Sanditon, intending to make some stay, and without appearing to have the slightest recollection of having written or felt any such thing.—It was impossible for Charlotte not to suspect a good deal of fancy in such an extraordinary state of health.—Disorders and recoveries so very much out of the common way, seemed more like the amusement of eager minds in want of employment than of actual afflictions and relief. The Parkers were no doubt a family of imagination and quick feelings—and while the eldest brother found vent for his superfluity of sensation as a projector,[1] the sisters were perhaps driven to dissipate theirs in the invention of odd complaints.—The *whole* of their mental vivacity was evidently not so employed; part was laid out in a zeal for being useful.—It should seem that they must either be very busy for the good of others, or else extremely ill themselves.

Some natural delicacy of constitution in fact, with an unfortunate turn for medicine, especially quack medicine,[2] had given them an early tendency, at various times, to various disorders;—the rest of their suffering was from fancy, the love of distinction and the love of the wonderful.—They had charitable hearts and many amiable feelings—but a spirit of restless activity, and the glory of doing more than anybody else, had their share in every exertion of benevolence—and there was vanity in all they did, as well as in all they endured.—

Mr. and Mrs Parker spent a great part of the evening at the hotel; but Charlotte had only two or three views of Miss Diana posting[3] over the Down after a house for this lady whom she had never seen, and who had never employed her. She was not made acquainted with the others till the following day, when, being removed into lodgings and all the party continuing quite well, their brother and sister and herself were entreated to drink tea with them.—They were in one of the Terrace houses—and she found them arranged for the evening in a small neat drawing room, with a beautiful view of the sea if they had chosen it,—but though it had been a very fair English summer-day, not only was there no open window, but the sopha and the table and the establishment[4] in general was all at the other end of the room by a brisk fire.—

Miss Parker—whom, remembering the three teeth drawn in one day, Charlotte approached with a peculiar degree of respectful compassion—was not very unlike her sister in person or manner—though more thin and worn by illness and medicine, more relaxed in air, and more subdued in voice. She talked however, the whole evening, as incessantly as Diana—and excepting that she sat with salts[5] in her hand, took drops[6] two or three times from one, out of the several phials already at home on the mantlepiece, and made a great many odd faces and contortions, Charlotte could perceive no symptoms of illness which she, in the boldness of her own good health, would not have undertaken to cure, by putting out the fire, opening the window, and disposing of the drops and the salts by means of one or the other.

She had had considerable curiosity to see Mr. Arthur Parker; and having fancied him a very puny, delicate-looking young man, the smallest very materially of not a robust family, was astonished to find him quite as tall as his brother and a great deal stouter—broad made and lusty[7]—and with no other look of an invalid, than a sodden[8] complexion.—Diana was evidently the chief of the family; principal mover and actor;—she had been on her feet the whole morning, on Mrs. Griffiths's business or their own, and was still the most alert of the three.—Susan had only superintended their final removal from the hotel, bringing two heavy boxes herself, and Arthur had found the air so cold that he had merely walked from one house to the other as nimbly as he could,—and boasted much of sitting by the fire till he had cooked up a very good one.—

Diana, whose exercise had been too domestic to admit of calculation, but who, by her own account, had not once sat down during the space of seven hours, confessed herself a little tired. She had been too successful however for much fatigue; for not only had she by walking and talking down a thousand difficulties at last secured a proper house at eight guineas per week[9] for Mrs. Griffiths; she had also opened so many treaties with cooks, housemaids, washerwomen and bathing women,[10] that Mrs. Griffiths would have little more to do on her arrival, than to wave her hand and collect them around her for choice.—Her concluding effort in the cause had been a few polite lines of information to Mrs. Griffiths herself—time not allowing for the circuitous train of intelligence which had been hitherto kept up,—and she was now regaling in the delight of opening the first trenches[11] of an acquaintance with such a powerful discharge of unexpected obligation.

Mr. and Mrs. Parker and Charlotte had seen two post chaises crossing the Down to the hotel as they were setting off—a joyful sight—and full of speculation.—The Miss Parkers and Arthur had also seen something;—they could distinguish from their window that there *was* an arrival at the hotel, but not its amount. Their visitors answered for two hack-chaises.[12]—Could it be the Camberwell seminary?—No—No.—Had there been a third carriage, perhaps it might; but it was very generally agreed that two hack chaises could never contain a seminary.—Mr. Parker was confident of another new family.—

When they were all finally seated, after some removals to look at the sea and the hotel, Charlotte's place was by Arthur, who was sitting next to the fire with a degree of enjoyment which gave a good deal of merit to his civility in wishing her to take his chair.—There was nothing dubious in her manner of declining it, and he sat down again with much satisfaction. She drew back her chair to have all the advantage of his person as a screen,[13] and was very thankful for every inch of back and shoulders beyond her pre-conceived idea.

Arthur was heavy in eye as well as figure, but by no means indisposed to talk;—and while the other four were chiefly engaged together, he evidently felt it no penance to have a fine young woman next to him, requiring in common politeness some attention—as his brother, who felt the decided want of some motive for action, some powerful object of animation for him, observed with considerable pleasure.—Such was the influence of youth and bloom[14] that he began even to make a sort of apology for having a fire.

"We should not have one at home," said he, "but the sea air is always damp. I am not afraid of anything so much as damp.—"

"I am so fortunate," said Charlotte, "as never to know whether the air is damp or dry. It has always some property that is wholesome and invigorating to me.—"

"*I* like the air too, as well as anybody can," replied Arthur; "I am very fond of standing at an open window when there is no wind,—but unluckily a damp air does not like *me*.—It gives me the rheumatism.—You are not rheumatic I suppose?—"

"Not at all."

"That's a great blessing.—But perhaps you are nervous."

"No—I believe not. I have no idea that I am."—

"*I* am very nervous.—To say the truth—nerves[15] are the worst part of my complaints in *my* opinion.—My sisters think me bilious, but I doubt it.—"

"You are quite in the right, to doubt it as long as you possibly can, I am sure.—"

"If I were bilious," he continued, "you know wine would disagree with me, but it always does me good.—The more wine I drink (in moderation) the better I am.[16]—I am always best of an evening.—If you had seen me today before dinner, you would have thought me a very poor creature.—"

Charlotte could believe it—. She kept her countenance however, and said—

"As far as I can understand what nervous complaints are, I have a great idea of the efficacy of air and exercise for them,—daily, regular exercise;—and I should recommend rather more of it to *you* than I suspect you are in the habit of taking.—"

"Oh! I am very fond of exercise myself,"—he replied—"and mean to walk a great deal while I am here, if the weather is temperate. I shall be out every morning before breakfast—and take several turns upon the Terrace, and you will often see me at Trafalgar House."—

"But you do not call a walk to Trafalgar House much exercise?—"

"Not as to mere distance, but the hill is so steep!—Walking up that hill, in the middle of the day, would throw me into such a perspiration![17]—You would see me all in a bath, by the time I got there!—I am very subject to perspiration, and there cannot be a surer sign of nervousness.—"

They were now advancing so deep in physics,[18] that Charlotte viewed the entrance of the servant with the tea things as a very fortunate interruption.—It produced a great and immediate change. The young man's attentions were instantly lost. He took his own cocoa[19] from the tray,—which seemed provided with almost as many tea-pots &c as there were persons in company, Miss Parker drinking one sort of herb-tea[20] and Miss Diana another—and turning completely to the fire, sat coddling and cooking it to his own satisfaction and toasting some slices of bread, brought up ready-prepared in the toast rack—and till it was all done, she heard nothing of his voice but the murmuring of a few broken sentences of self-approbation and success.—When his toils were over however, he moved back his chair into as gallant a line as ever, and proved that he had not been working only for himself, by his earnest invitation to her to take both cocoa and toast.—She was already helped to tea—which surprised him—so totally self-engrossed had he been.—

"I thought I should have been in time," said he, "but cocoa takes a great deal of boiling.—"

"I am much obliged to you," replied Charlotte—"but I *prefer* tea."

"Then I will help myself," said he.—"A large dish of rather weak cocoa every evening agrees with me better than anything."—

It struck her however, as he poured out this rather weak cocoa, that it came forth in a very fine, dark coloured stream—and at the same moment, his sisters both crying out—"Oh! Arthur, you get your cocoa stronger and stronger every evening"—, with Arthur's somewhat conscious reply of "*Tis* rather stronger than it should be tonight"—convinced her that Arthur was by no means so fond of being starved as they could desire, or as he felt proper himself.—He was certainly very happy to turn the conversation on dry toast, and hear no more of his sisters.—

"I hope you will eat some of this toast," said he, "I reckon myself a very good toaster; I never burn my toasts—I never put them too near the fire at first—and yet, you see, there is not a corner but what is well browned.—I hope you like dry toast.—"

"With a reasonable quantity of butter spread over it, very much"—said Charlotte—"but not otherwise.—"

"No more do I"—said he, exceedingly pleased.—"We think quite alike there.—So far from dry toast being wholesome, *I* think it a very bad thing for the stomach. Without a little butter to soften it, it hurts the coats of the stomach.[21] I am sure it does.—I will have the pleasure of spreading some for you directly—and afterwards I will spread some for myself.—Very bad indeed for the coats of the stomach—but there is no convincing *some* people.—It irritates and acts like a nutmeg grater.—"

He could not get the command of the butter however, without a struggle, his sisters accusing him of eating a great deal too much, and declaring he was not to be trusted;—and he maintaining that he only ate enough to secure the coats of his stomach;—and besides, he only wanted it now for Miss Heywood.—Such a plea must prevail; he got the butter and spread away for her with an accuracy of judgement which at least delighted himself; but when her toast was done, and he took his own in hand, Charlotte could hardly contain herself as she saw him watching his sisters, while he scrupulously scraped off almost as much butter as he put on, and then seize an odd moment for adding a great dab just before it went into his mouth.—Certainly, Mr. Arthur Parker's enjoyments in invalidism were very different from his sisters'—by no means so spiritualized.—A good deal of earthy dross[22] hung about him. Charlotte could not but suspect him of adopting that line of life, principally for the indulgence of an indolent temper—and to be determined on having no disorders but such as called for warm rooms and good nourishment.—In one particular however, she soon found that he had caught something from *them*.—

"What!" said he—"Do you venture upon two dishes of strong green tea[23] in one evening?—What nerves you must have!—How I envy you.—Now, if *I* were to swallow only one such dish—what do you think its effect would be upon me?—"

"Keep you awake perhaps all night"—replied Charlotte, meaning to overthrow his attempts at surprise, by the grandeur of her own conceptions.—

"Oh! if that were all!—" he exclaimed.—"No—it would act on me like poison and entirely take away the use of my right side, before I had swallowed it five minutes.—It sounds almost incredible—but it has happened to me so often that I cannot doubt it.—The use of my right side is entirely taken away for several hours!"

"It sounds rather odd to be sure"—answered Charlotte coolly—"but I dare say it would be proved to be the simplest thing in the world, by those who have studied right sides and green tea scientifically[24] and thoroughly understand all the possibilities of their action on each other."—

Soon after tea, a letter was brought to Miss Diana Parker from the hotel.—"From Mrs. Charles Dupuis"—said she.—"Some private hand.[25]"—And having read a few lines, exclaimed aloud, "Well, this is very extraordinary! very extraordinary indeed!—That both should have the same name.—Two Mrs. Griffiths!—This is a letter of recommendation and introduction to me, of the lady from Camberwell—and *her* name happens to be Griffiths too."—

A few lines more however, and the colour rushed into her cheeks, and with much perturbation she added— "The oddest thing that ever was!—a Miss Lambe too!—a young West Indian of large fortune.—But it *cannot* be the same.—Impossible that it should be the same."—

She read the letter aloud for comfort.—It was merely to "introduce the bearer, Mrs. Griffiths from Camberwell, and the three young ladies under her care, to Miss Diana Parker's notice.—Mrs. Griffiths being a stranger at

Sanditon, was anxious for a respectable introduction—and Mrs. Charles Dupuis therefore, at the instance of the intermediate friend, provided her with this letter, knowing that she could not do her dear Diana a greater kindness than by giving her the means of being useful.—Mrs. Griffiths's chief solicitude would be for the accommodation and comfort of one of the young ladies under her care, a Miss Lambe, a young West Indian of large fortune, in delicate health."—"It was very strange!—very remarkable!—very extraordinary," but they were all agreed in determining it to be *impossible* that there should not be two families; such a totally distinct set of people as were concerned in the reports of each made that matter quite certain. There *must* be two families.—Impossible to be otherwise.—"Impossible" and "Impossible", was repeated over and over again with great fervour.—An accidental resemblance of names and circumstances, however striking at first, involved nothing really incredible—and so it was settled.—

Miss Diana herself derived an immediate advantage to counterbalance her perplexity. She must put her shawl over her shoulders, and be running about again. Tired as she was, she must instantly repair to the hotel, to investigate the truth and offer her services.—

Chapter 11

It would not do.—Not all that the whole Parker race could say among themselves, could produce a happier catastrophe[1] than that the family from Surry and the family from Camberwell were one and the same.—The rich West Indians, and the young ladies' seminary had all entered Sanditon in those two hack chaises. The Mrs. Griffiths who, in her friend Mrs. Darling's hands, had wavered as to coming and been unequal to the journey, was the very same Mrs. Griffiths whose plans were at the same period (under another representation) perfectly decided, and who was without fears or difficulties.—All that had the appearance of incongruity in the reports of the two, might very fairly be placed to the account of the vanity, the ignorance, or the blunders of the many engaged in the cause by the vigilance and caution of Miss Diana Parker. *Her* intimate friends must be officious like herself, and the subject had supplied letters and extracts and messages enough to make everything appear what it was not.—

Miss Diana probably felt a little awkward on being first obliged to admit her mistake. A long journey from Hampshire taken for nothing—a brother disappointed—an expensive house on her hands for a week—must have been some of her immediate reflections, and much worse than all the rest must have been the sort of sensation of being less clear-sighted and infallible than she had believed herself.—No part of it however seemed to trouble her long. There were so many to share in the shame and the blame, that probably when she had divided out their proper portions to Mrs. Darling, Miss Capper, Fanny Noyce, Mrs. Charles Dupuis and Mrs. Charles Dupuis's neighbour, there might be a mere trifle of reproach remaining for herself.—At any rate, she was seen all the following morning walking about after lodgings with Mrs. Griffiths—as alert as ever.—

Mrs. Griffiths was a very well-behaved, genteel kind of woman, who supported herself by receiving such great girls and young ladies, as wanted either masters for finishing their education, or a home for beginning their displays.[2]—She had several more under her care than the three who were now come to Sanditon, but the others all happened to be absent.—Of these three, and indeed of all, Miss Lambe was beyond comparison the most important and precious, as she paid in proportion to her fortune.—She was about seventeen, half mulatto,[3] chilly and tender, had a maid of her own, was to have the best room in the lodgings, and was always of the first consequence in every plan of Mrs. Griffiths.—

The other girls, two Miss Beauforts, were just such young ladies as may be met with, in at least one family out of three, throughout the kingdom; they had tolerable complexions, shewy figures, an upright decided carriage and an assured look;—they were very accomplished and very ignorant, their time being divided between such pursuits as might attract admiration, and those labours and expedients of dexterous ingenuity, by which they could dress in a stile much beyond what they *ought* to have afforded; they were some of the first in every change of fashion—and the object of all, was to captivate some man of much better fortune than their own.—

Mrs. Griffiths had preferred a small, retired place, like Sanditon, on Miss Lambe's account—and the Miss Beauforts, though naturally preferring anything to smallness and retirement, yet having in the course of the spring been involved in the inevitable expence of six new dresses each for a three days' visit, were constrained to be satisfied with Sanditon also, till their circumstances were retrieved. There, with the hire of a harp for one, and the purchase of some drawing paper for the other,[4] and all the finery they could already command, they meant to be very economical, very elegant and very secluded; with the hope, on Miss Beaufort's side, of praise and celebrity from all who walked within the sound of her instrument, and on Miss Letitia's, of curiosity and rapture in all who came near her while she sketched—and to both, the consolation of meaning to be the most stylish girls in the place.—The particular introduction of Mrs. Griffiths to Miss Diana Parker, secured them immediately an acquaintance with the Trafalgar House family, and with the Denhams;—and the Miss Beauforts were soon satisfied with "the circle in which they moved in Sanditon" to use a proper phrase, for every body must now "move in a circle",[5]—to the prevalence of which rotatory[6] motion, is perhaps to be attributed the giddiness and false steps of many.—

Lady Denham had other motives for calling on Mrs. Griffiths besides attention to the Parkers.—In Miss Lambe, here was the very young lady, sickly and rich, whom she had been asking for; and she made the acquaintance for Sir Edward's sake, and the sake of her milch asses. How it might answer with regard to the baronet remained to be proved, but as to the animals, she soon found that all her calculations of profit would be vain. Mrs. Griffiths would not allow Miss Lambe to have the smallest symptom of a decline,[7] or any complaint which asses' milk could possibly relieve. "Miss Lambe was under the constant care of an experienced physician;—and his prescriptions must be their rule—" and except in favour of some tonic pills, which a cousin of her own had a property in,[8] Mrs. Griffiths did never deviate from the strict medicinal page.—

The corner house of the Terrace was the one in which Miss Diana Parker had the pleasure of settling her new friends, and considering that it commanded in front the favourite lounge[9] of all the visitors at Sanditon, and on one side, whatever might be going on at the hotel, there could not have been a more favourable spot for the seclusions of the Miss Beauforts. And accordingly, long before they had suited themselves with an instrument, or with drawing paper, they had, by the frequency of their appearance at the low windows upstairs,[10] in order to close the blinds, or open the blinds, to arrange a flower pot on the balcony, or look at nothing through a telescope,[11] attracted many an eye upwards, and made many a gazer gaze again.—A little novelty has a great effect in so small a place; the Miss Beauforts, who would have been nothing at Brighton, could not move here without notice;—and even Mr. Arthur Parker, though little disposed for supernumerary exertion, always quitted the Terrace in his way to his brother's by this corner house, for the sake of a glimpse of the Miss Beauforts—though it was half a quarter of a mile round about, and added two steps to the ascent of the hill.

Chapter 12

Charlotte had been ten days at Sanditon without seeing Sanditon House, every attempt at calling on Lady Denham having been defeated by meeting with her beforehand. But now it was to be more resolutely undertaken, at a more early hour, that nothing might be neglected of attention to Lady Denham or amusement to Charlotte.—

"And if you should find a favourable opening my love," said Mr. Parker (who did not mean to go with them)—"I think you had better mention the poor Mullins's situation, and sound her ladyship as to a subscription for them.[1]—I am not fond of charitable subscriptions in a place of this kind—it is a sort of tax upon all that come—yet as their distress is very great and I almost promised the poor woman yesterday to get something done for her, I believe we must set a subscription on foot—and therefore the sooner the better,—and Lady Denham's name at the head of the list will be a very necessary beginning.—You will not dislike speaking to her about it, Mary?—"

"I will do whatever you wish me," replied his wife—"but you would do it so much better yourself. I shall not know what to say."—

"My dear Mary," cried he, "it is impossible you can be really at a loss. Nothing can be more simple. You have only to state the present afflicted situation of the family, their earnest application to me, and my being willing to promote a little subscription for their relief, provided it meet with her approbation."—

"The easiest thing in the world"—cried Miss Diana Parker, who happened to be calling on them at the moment—. "All said and done, in less time than you have been talking of it now.—And while you are on the subject of subscriptions Mary, I will thank you to mention a very melancholy case to Lady Denham, which has been represented to me in the most affecting terms.—There is a poor woman in Worcestershire, whom some friends of mine are exceedingly interested about, and I have undertaken to collect whatever I can for her.[2] If you would mention the circumstance to Lady Denham!—Lady Denham *can* give, if she is properly attacked—and I look upon her to be the sort of person who, when once she is prevailed on to undraw[3] her purse, would as readily give ten guineas as five.[4] And therefore, if you find her in a giving mood, you might as well speak in favour of another charity which I, and a few more, have very much at heart—the establishment of a charitable repository at Burton on Trent.[5] —And then,—there is the family of the poor man who was hung last assizes at York,[6] though we really *have* raised the sum we wanted for putting them all out,[7] yet if you *can* get a guinea from her on their behalf, it may as well be done.—"

"My dear Diana!" exclaimed Mrs. Parker.—"I could no more mention these things to Lady Denham—than I could fly."—

"Where's the difficulty?—I wish I could go with you myself—but in five minutes I must be at Mrs. Griffiths'—to encourage Miss Lambe in taking her first dip. She is so frightened, poor thing, that I promised to come and keep up her spirits, and go in the machine[8] with her if she wished it—and as soon as that is over, I must hurry home, for Susan is to have leeches at one o'clock, which will be a three hours' business,[9]—therefore I really have not a moment to spare—besides that (between ourselves) I ought to be in bed myself at this present time, for I am hardly able to stand—and when the leeches have done, I dare say we shall both go to our rooms for the rest of the day."—

"I am sorry to hear it, indeed; but if this is the case I hope Arthur will come to us."—

"If Arthur takes my advice, he will go to bed too, for if he stays up by himself, he will certainly eat and drink more than he ought;—but you see Mary, how impossible it is for me to go with you to Lady Denham's."—

"Upon second thoughts Mary," said her husband, "I will not trouble you to speak about the Mullins's.—I will take an opportunity of seeing Lady Denham myself.—I know how little it suits you to be pressing matters upon a mind at all unwilling."—

His application thus withdrawn, his sister could say no more in support of hers, which was his object, as he felt all their impropriety and all the certainty of their ill effect upon his own better claim.—

Mrs. Parker was delighted at this release, and set off very happy with her friend and her little girl, on this walk to Sanditon House.—It was a close, misty morning, and when they reached the brow of the hill, they could not for some time make out what sort of carriage it was, which they saw coming up. It appeared at different moments to be everything from the gig to the phaeton,—from one horse to four; and just as they were concluding in favour of a tandem,[10] little Mary's young eyes distinguished the coachman and she eagerly called out, "'Tis Uncle Sidney mama, it is indeed." And so it proved.—Mr. Sidney Parker driving his servant in a very neat carriage was soon opposite to them, and they all stopped for a few minutes.

The manners of the Parkers were always pleasant among themselves—and it was a very friendly meeting between Sidney and his sister in law, who was most kindly taking it for granted that he was on his way to Trafalgar House. This he declined however. "He was just come from East Bourne, proposing to spend two or three days, as it might happen, at Sanditon—but the hotel must be his quarters.—He was expecting to be joined there by a friend or two."—The rest was common enquiries and remarks, with kind notice of little Mary, and a very well-bred bow and proper address to Miss Heywood on her being named to him—and they parted, to meet again within a few hours.—

Sidney Parker was about seven or eight and twenty, very good-looking, with a decided air of ease and fashion, and a lively countenance.—This adventure afforded agreeable discussion for some time. Mrs. Parker entered into all her husband's joy on the occasion, and exulted in the credit which Sidney's arrival would give to the place.

The road to Sanditon House was a broad, handsome, planted approach[11] between fields, and conducting at the end of a quarter of a mile through second gates into the grounds, which though not extensive had all the beauty and respectability which an abundance of very fine timber[12] could give.—These entrance gates were so much in a corner of the grounds or paddock, so near one of its boundaries, that an outside fence was at first almost pressing on the road—till an angle *here*, and a curve there threw them to a better distance. The fence was a proper park paling in excellent condition; with clusters of fine elms, or rows of old thorns following its line almost every where.[13]—*Almost* must be stipulated—for there were vacant spaces—and through one of these, Charlotte, as soon as they entered the enclosure, caught a glimpse over the pales of something white and womanish in the field on the other side;—it was a something which immediately brought Miss Brereton into her head—and stepping to the pales, she saw indeed—and very decidedly, in spite of the mist—Miss Brereton seated, not far before her, at the foot of the bank which sloped down from the outside of the paling and which a narrow path seemed to skirt along;—Miss Brereton seated, apparently very composedly—and Sir Edward Denham by her side.—

They were sitting so near each other and appeared so closely engaged in gentle conversation, that Charlotte instantly felt she had nothing to do but to step back again, and say not a word.—Privacy was certainly their object.—It could not but strike her rather unfavourably with regard to Clara;—but hers was a situation which must not be judged with severity.—She was glad to perceive that nothing had been discerned by Mrs. Parker; if Charlotte had not been considerably the tallest of the two, Miss Brereton's white ribbons might not have fallen within the ken of *her* more observant eyes.—Among other points of moralising reflection which the sight of this tete a tete produced, Charlotte could not but think of the extreme difficulty which secret lovers must have in finding a proper spot for their stolen interviews.—Here perhaps they had thought themselves so perfectly secure from observation!—the whole field open before them—a steep bank and pales never crossed by the foot of man at their back—and a great thickness of air, in aid.—Yet, here, she had seen them. They were really ill-used.—

The house was large and handsome; two servants appeared, to admit them, and every thing had a suitable air of property and order.—Lady Denham valued herself upon her liberal establishment, and had great enjoyment in the order and importance of her style of living.—They were shown into the usual[14] sitting room, well-proportioned and well-furnished;—though it was furniture rather originally good and extremely well kept, than new or showy—and as Lady Denham was not there, Charlotte had leisure to look about, and to be told by Mrs. Parker that the whole-length portrait of a stately gentleman, which, placed over the mantlepeice, caught the eye immediately, was the picture of Sir Harry Denham—and that one among many miniatures in another part of the room, little conspicuous, represented Mr. Hollis.—Poor Mr. Hollis!—It was impossible not to feel him hardly used; to be obliged to stand back in his own house and see the best place by the fire constantly occupied by Sir Harry Denham.

Jane Austen on Fiction

To Mrs. Hunter of Norwich[1]

Miss Jane Austen begs her best thanks may be conveyed to Mrs. Hunter of Norwich for the Threadpaper[2] which she has been so kind as to send her by Mr Austen,[3] & which will be always very valuable on account of the spirited sketches (made it is supposed by Nicholson or Glover[4]) of the most interesting spots, Tarefield Hall, the Mill, & above all the Tomb of Howard's wife,[5] of the faithful representation of which Miss Jane Austen is undoubtedly a good judge having spent so many summers at Tarefield Abbey the delighted guest of the worthy Mrs. Wilson.[6] Miss Jane Austen's tears have flowed over each sweet sketch in such a way as would do Mrs. Hunter's heart good to see; if Mrs. Hunter could understand all Miss Jane Austen's interest in the subject she would certainly have the kindness to publish at least 4 vols more about the Flint family, & especially would give many fresh particulars on that part of it which Mrs. H. has hitherto handled too briefly; viz, the history of Mary Flint's marriage with Howard.[7]

Miss Jane Austen can not close this small epitome of the miniature abridgment of her thanks & admiration without expressing her sincere hope that Mrs. Hunter is provided at Norwich with a more safe conveyance to London than Alton can now boast, as the Car of Falkenstein which was the pride of that Town was overturned within the last 10 days.[8]

line 9: 'Hall' deleted before 'Abbey'.

Letters on Fiction to Anna Lefroy

PS to a letter from Mrs Austen, ?mid-July 1814[1]
?Chawton to Steventon[2]

My dear Anna—I am very much obliged to you for sending your MS. It has entertained me extremely, all of us indeed; I read it aloud to your G. M.—& A^{t} C.[3] —and we were all very much pleased.—The Spirit does not droop at all. Sir Tho:—Lady Helena, & St Julian are very well done—& Cecilia continues to be interesting inspite of her being so amiable.—It was very fit that you should advance her age. I like the beginning of D. Forester very much—a great deal better than if he had been very Good or very Bad.—A few verbal corrections were all that I felt tempted to make—the principal of them is a speech of St Julians to Lady Helena—which you will see I have presumed to alter.—As Lady H. is Cecilia's superior, it w^{d} not be correct to talk of her being introduced; Cecilia must be the person introduced—and I do not like a Lover's speaking in the 3^{d} person;—it is too much like the formal part of Lord Orville,[4] & I think is not natural. If you think differently however, you need not mind me.—I am impatient for more—& only wait for a safe conveyance to return this Book.[5]—Yours affec^{ly}, J. A.

Wednesday 10–Thursday 18 August 1814
Chawton to Steventon

My dear Anna

I am quite ashamed to find that I have never answered some questions of yours in a former note.—I kept the note on purpose to refer to it at a proper time, & then forgot it.—I like the name "Which is the Heroine?" very well, & I dare say shall grow to like it very much in time—but "Enthusiasm"[6] was something so very superior that every common Title must appear to disadvantage.—I am not sensible of any Blunders about Dawlish. The Library was particularly pitiful & wretched 12 years ago, & not likely to have anybody's publication.[7]—There is no such title as Desborough—either among the Dukes, Marquisses, Earls, Viscounts or Barons.[8]—These were your enquiries. —I will now thank you for your Envelope, received this morning.—I hope M^{r}. W. D. will come. —I can readily imagine M^{rs}. H. D. may be very like a profligate Young Lord—I dare say the likeness will be "beyond every thing".[9]—Your Aunt Cass:—is as well pleased with S^{t}. Julian as ever. I am delighted with the idea of seeing Progillian again.

Wednesday 17.—We have just finished the 1st. of the 3 Books I had the pleasure of receiving yesterday; I read it aloud—& we are all very much amused, & like the work quite as well as ever.—I depend upon getting through another book before dinner, but there is really a great deal of respectable reading in your 48 Pages.[10] I was an hour about it. —I have no doubt that 6 will make a very good sized volume.—You must be quite pleased to have accomplished so much.—I like Lord P. & his Brother very much;—I am only afraid that Lord P.—'s good nature will make most people like him better than he deserves.—The whole Portman Family are very

Chawton Wednesday Aug: 10.

My dear Anna

I am quite ashamed to find that I have never answered some questions of yours in a former note. — I kept the note on purpose to refer to it at a proper time, & then forgot it. — I like the name "Which is the Heroine?" very well, & I dare say shall grow to like it very much in time — but "Enthusiasm" was something so very superior that every common Title must appear to disadvantage. — I am not sensible of any Blunders about Dawlish. The Library was particularly pitiful & wretched 12 years ago, & not likely to have any body's publication. — There is no such Title as Desborough — either among the Dukes, Marquisses, Earls, Viscounts or Barons. — These were your enquiries. — I will now thank you for your Envelope, received this morning. — I hope Mr W. D. will come. — I can readily imagine Mrs H. D. may be very like a profligate young Lord — I dare say the likeness will be "beyond every thing." Your Aunt Cass: is as well pleased with St Julian as ever. I am delighted with the idea of seeing Progillian again.

Wednesday 17. — We have just finished the 1st of the 3 Books I had the pleasure of receiving yesterday; I read it aloud — & we are all very much amused, & like the work quite as well as ever. — I depend upon getting

4 Jane Austen to Anna Lefroy, 10–18 August 1814. The conclusion of the postscript is written upside down between the address and the beginning of the letter. Note the neatness of the writing and lack of correction.

good—& Lady Anne, who was your great dread, you have succeeded particularly well with.—Bell Griffin is just what she should be.—My Corrections have not been more important than before; —here & there, we have thought the sense might be expressed in fewer words—and I have scratched out Sir Tho: from walking with the other Men to the Stables &c the very day after his breaking his arm—for though I find your Papa did walk out immediately after his arm was set, I think it can be so little usual as to appear unnatural in a book—& it does not seem to be material that Sir Tho: should go with them.—Lyme will not do. Lyme is towards 40 miles distance from Dawlish & would not be talked of there.—I have put Starcross indeed.[11]—If you prefer Exeter, that must be always safe.[12]—I have also scratched out the Introduction between Lord P. & his Brother, & Mr. Griffin. A Country Surgeon (dont tell Mr. C. Lyford) would not be introduced to Men of their rank.[13]—And when Mr. Portman is first brought in, he wd. not be introduced as the Honble—That distinction is never mentioned at such times;—at least I beleive not.[14]—Now, we have finished the 2d. book—or rather the 5th.—I do think you had better omit Lady Helena's postscript; —to those who are acquainted with P. & P. it will seem an Imitation.[15]—And your Aunt C. & I both recommend your making a little alteration in the last scene between Devereux F. & Lady Clanmurray & her Daughter. We think they press him too much—more than sensible Women or well-bred Women would do. Lady C. at least, should have discretion enough to be sooner satisfied with his determination of not going with them.—I am very much pleased with Egerton as yet—. I did not expect to like him, but I do; & Susan is a very nice little animated Creature—but St. Julian is the delight of one's Life. He is quite interesting.—The whole of his Break-off with Lady H. is very well done.—

Yes—Russel Square is a very proper distance from Berkeley St.[16]—We are reading the last book.—They must be two days going from Dawlish to Bath; They are nearly 100 miles apart.[17]

Thursday. We finished it last night, after our return from drinking tea at the Gt House.[18]—The last chapter does not please us quite so well, we do not thoroughly like the Play; perhaps from having had too much of Plays in that way lately.[19]—And we think you had better not leave England. Let the Portmans go to Ireland, but as you know nothing of the manners there, you had better not go with them. You will be in danger of giving false representations.[20] Stick to Bath & the Foresters.[21] There you will be quite at home.—Your Aunt C. does not like desultory novels, & is rather fearful yours will be too much so, that there will be too frequent a change from one set of people to another, & that circumstances will be sometimes introduced of apparent consequence, which will lead to nothing.—It will not be so great an objection to me, if it does. I allow much more Latitude than she does—& think Nature & Spirit cover many sins of a wandering story—and People in general do not care so much about it—for your comfort. I should like to have had more of Devereux. I do not feel enough acquainted with him.—You were afraid of meddling with him I dare say.—I like your sketch of Lord Clanmurray, and your picture of the two poor young girls enjoyments is very good.—I have not yet noticed[22] St Julian's serious conversation with Cecilia, but I liked it exceedingly;—what he says about the madness of otherwise sensible Women, on the

lines 3–4: 'They are nearly 100 miles apart.' A later addition, with a full stop after 'Bath' adjusted to a semicolon, and 'apart' squeezed above line at end of line. // lines 15–16: 'of' deleted; 'from one set of' inserted above line.

subject of their Daughters coming out, is worth it's weight in gold.—I do not see that the language sinks.—Pray go on.

Yours very affec:[ly] J. Austen

[Postscript]

Twice you have put Dorsetshire for Devonshire. I have altered it.—M[r] Griffin must have lived in Devonshire; Dawlish is half way down the County.—

Friday 9 – Sunday 18 September 1814
Chawton (to Steventon?)

My dear Anna

We have been very much amused by your 3 books, but I have a good many criticisms to make—more than you will like.—We are not satisfied with M[rs] F.'s settling herself as Tenant & near Neighbour to such a Man as Sir T. H. without having some other inducement to go there; she ought to have some friend living thereabouts to tempt her. A woman, going with two girls just growing up, into a Neighbourhood where she knows nobody but one Man, of not very good character, is an awkwardness which so prudent a woman as M[rs] F would not be likely to fall into. Remember, she is very prudent;—you must not let her act inconsistently.—Give her a friend, & let that friend be invited to meet her at the Priory, & we shall have no objection to her dining there as she does; but otherwise, a woman in her situation would hardly go there, before she had been visited by other Families.—I like the scene itself, the Miss Lesleys, Lady Anne, & the Music, very much.—Lesley <u>is</u> a noble name.[23] —Sir T. H. you always do very well; I have

line 20: 'not' inserted above line.

only taken the liberty of expunging one phrase of his, which would not be allowable. "Bless my Heart."—It is too familiar & inelegant.[24] Your G. M. is more disturbed at Mrs. F.'s not returning the Egertons visit sooner, than anything else. They ought to have called at the Parsonage before Sunday.[25]—

You describe a sweet place, but your descriptions are often more minute than will be liked. You give too many particulars of right hand & left.—

Mrs. F. is not careful enough of Susan's health;—Susan ought not to be walking out so soon after Heavy rains, taking long walks in the dirt. An anxious Mother would not suffer it.—I like your Susan very much indeed, she is a sweet creature, her playfulness of fancy is very delightful. I like her as she is <u>now</u> exceedingly, but I am not so well satisfied with her behaviour to George R. At first she seemed all over attachment & feeling, & afterwards to have none at all; she is so extremely composed at the Ball, & so well satisfied apparently with Mr. Morgan. She seems to have changed her Character. —You are now collecting your People delightfully, getting them exactly into such a spot as is the delight of my life;—3 or 4 Families in a Country Village is the very thing to work on—& I hope you will write a great deal more, & make full use of them while they are so very favourably arranged.[26] You are but <u>now</u> coming to the heart & beauty of your book; till the heroine grows up, the fun must be imperfect—but I expect a great deal of entertainment from the next 3 or 4 books, & I hope you will not resent these remarks by sending me no more.—We like the Egertons very well, we see no Blue Pantaloons, or Cocks & Hens;[27]—there is nothing to <u>enchant</u> one certainly in Mr. L. L.—but we make no objection to him, & his inclination to like Susan is pleasing.—The Sister is a good contrast—but the name of Rachael is as much as I can bear.—They are not so much like the Papillons[28] as I expected. Your last chapter is very entertaining—the conversation on Genius &c. Mr. St. J.—& Susan both talk in character & very well.—In some former parts, Cecilia is perhaps a little too solemn & good, but upon the whole, her disposition is very well opposed to Susan's—her want of Imagination is very natural.—I wish you could make Mrs. F. talk more, but she must be difficult to manage & make entertaining, because there is so much good common sense & propriety about her that nothing can be very broad. Her Economy & her Ambition must not be staring.—The Papers left by Mrs. Fisher is very good.—Of course, one guesses something.—I hope when you have written a great deal more you will be equal to scratching out some of the past.[29]—The scene with Mrs. Mellish, I should condemn; it is prosy & nothing to the purpose—& indeed, the more you can find in your heart to curtail between Dawlish & Newton Priors, the better I think it will be.—One does not care for girls till they are grown up.—Your Aunt C. quite enters into the exquisiteness of that name. Newton Priors is really a Nonpareil.—Milton wd. have given his eyes to have thought of it.[30]—Is not the Cottage taken from Tollard Royal?[31]—

Sunday 18.th—I am very glad dear Anna, that I wrote as I did before this sad Event[32] occurred. I have now only to add that your G. Mama does not seem the worse now for the Shock.—I shall be very happy to receive more of your work, if more is ready; & you write so fast, that I have great hopes Mr. D.[33] will come freighted back with such a Cargo as not all his Hops or his Sheep could equal the value of.

Your Grandmama desires me to say that she will have finished[34] your Shoes tomorrow & thinks they will look very well;—and that she depends upon seeing you, as you promise,

line 6: 'good' deleted; 'natural.' written above.

before you quit the Country, & hopes you will give her more than a day.—Yrs: affec:ly

J. Austen

Wednesday 28 September 1814
Chawton to Steventon

My dear Anna

I hope you do not depend on having your book back again immediately. I keep it that your G: Mama may hear it—for it has not been possible yet to have any public reading. I have read it to your Aunt Cassandra however—in our own room at night, while we undressed—and with a great deal of pleasure. We like the first chapter extremely—with only a little doubt whether Ly Helena is not almost too foolish. The matrimonial Dialogue is very good certainly.—I like Susan as well as ever—and begin now not to care at all about Cecilia—she may stay at Easton Court as long as she likes. —Henry Mellish I am afraid will be too much in the common Novel style—a handsome, amiable, unexceptionable Young Man (such as do not much abound in real Life) desperately in Love, & all in vain. But I have no business to judge him so early. —Jane Egerton is a very natural, comprehendable Girl—& the whole of her acquaintance with Susan, & Susan's Letter to Cecilia, very pleasing & quite in character.—But Miss Egerton does not entirely satisfy us. She is too formal & solemn, we think, in her advice to her Brother not to fall in love; & it is hardly like a sensible Woman; it is putting it into his head.—We should like a few hints from her better.—We feel really obliged to you for introducing a Lady Kenrick, it will remove the greatest fault in the work, & I give you

line 29: 'I' inserted above line.

credit for considerable forbearance as an Author in adopting so much of our opinion. —I expect high fun about Mrs. Fisher & Sir Thomas. —You have been perfectly right in telling Ben of your work, & I am very glad to hear how much he likes it.[35] His encouragement & approbation must be quite "beyond everything". —I do not at all wonder at his not expecting to like anybody so well as Cecilia at first, but shall be surprised if he does not become a Susan-ite in time.—Devereux Forester's being ruined by his Vanity is extremely good; but I wish you would not let him plunge into a "vortex of Dissipation". I do not object to the Thing, but I cannot bear the expression;—it is such thorough novel slang—and so old, that I dare say Adam met with it in the first novel he opened.[36]—Indeed I did very much like to know Ben's opinion.—I hope he will continue to be pleased with it, I think he must—but I cannot flatter him with there being much Incident. We have no great right to wonder at his not valueing the name of Progillian. That is a source of delight which he hardly ever can be quite competent to.—Walter Scott has no business to write novels, especially good ones.—It is not fair.—He has Fame & Profit enough as Poet, and should not be taking the bread out of other people's mouths. —I do not like him, & do not mean to like Waverley if I can help it—but I fear I must.[37]—I am quite determined however not to be pleased with Mrs. West's Alicia de Lacy, should I ever meet with it, which I hope I may not.[38]—I think I can be stout against any thing written by Mrs. West.—I have made up my mind to like no Novels really, but Miss Edgeworth's,[39] Yours & my own.—

What can you do with Egerton to increase the interest for him?—I wish you cd. contrive something, some family occurrence to draw out his good qualities more—some

line 24: 'be' inserted above line.

distress among Brothers or Sisters to releive by the sale of his Curacy—something to [take] him mysteriously away, & then heard of at York or Edinburgh—in an old great Coat.— I would not seriously recommend any thing Improbable, but if you c^{d}. invent something spirited for him, it w^{d}. have a good effect.—He might lend all his Money to Captn. Morris—but then he w^{d}. be a great fool if he did. Cannot the Morrises quarrel, & he reconcile them? —Excuse the liberty I take in these suggestions. —

. . .

Your affect^{te}. Aunt J. Austen

Wednesday 30 November 1814[40]
London, Hans Place, to Hendon[41]

My dear Anna

I have been very far from finding your Book an Evil I assure you; I read it immediately—& with great pleasure. I think you are going on very well. The description of D^{r}. Griffin & Lady Helena's unhappiness is very good, just what was likely to be.—I am curious to know what the end of them will be: The name of Newton-Priors is really invaluable! —I never met with anything superior to it.—It is delightful.—One could live upon the name of Newton-Priors for a twelvemonth.— Indeed, I do think you get on very fast. I wish other people of my acquaintance could compose as rapidly.[42]—I am pleased with the Dog scene, & with the whole of George & Susan's Love; but am more particularly struck with your serious conversations &c.—They are very good throughout.—S^{t}. Julian's History was quite a surprise to me; You had not very long known it yourself I suspect—but I have no objection to make

line 2: 'take' assumed; missing because of hole in paper. // line 3: 'in an old great Coat.' inserted above line.

to the circumstance—it is very well told—& his having been in love with the Aunt, gives Cecilia an additional Interest with him. I like the Idea:—a very proper compliment to an Aunt!—I rather imagine indeed that Neices are seldom chosen but in compliment to some Aunt or other. I dare say Ben was in love with me once, & w$^{d.}$ never have thought of <u>you</u> if he had not supposed me dead of a Scarlet fever.—Yes, I was in a mistake as to the number of Books. I thought I had read 3 before the 3 at Chawton;[43] but fewer than 6 will not do.—I want to see dear Bell Griffin again.—Had not you better give some hint of S^{t}. Julian's early [history in the beginning of your story?][44]

line 5: 'or other' added at end of line.

Plan of a Novel,[1] according to hints from various quarters.[2]

Scene to be in the Country, Heroine the Daughter of a [a]Clergyman,[3] one who after having lived much in the World had retired from it, & settled on a Curacy, with a very small fortune of his own.—He, the most excellent Man that can be imagined, perfect in Character, Temper & Manners— without the smallest drawback or peculiarity to prevent his being the most delightful companion to his Daughter from one year's end to the other.[4]—Heroine a [b]faultless Character herself,[5]—perfectly good, with much tenderness & sentiment, & not the [c]least Wit—very highly [d]accomplished, understanding modern Languages & (generally speaking) everything that the most accomplished young Women learn,[6] but particularly excelling in Music—her favourite pursuit— & playing equally well on the Piano Forte & Harp—& singing in the first stile.[7] Her Person, quite beautiful— [e]dark eyes & plump cheeks.—Book to open with the description of Father & Daughter— who are to converse in long speeches, elegant Language— & a tone of high, serious sentiment.—The Father to be

[a] Mr. Gifford
[b] Fanny Knight
[c] Mary Cooke.
[d] Fanny K.
[e] Mary Cooke

line 1: 'only child' deleted; 'Daughter' inserted above line.
line 6: 'doing infinite good in his Parish, a Blessing to everybody connected with him, &' deleted before 'without'.
line 16: '& Harp—' inserted above line.
line 20: 'who are' inserted above line.

induced, at his Daughter's earnest request, to relate to her the past events of his Life.[8] This Narrative will reach through the greatest part of the 1st. vol.—as besides all the circumstances of his attachment to her Mother & their Marriage, it will comprehend his going to sea as [f]Chaplain to a distinguished Naval Character about the Court, his going afterwards to Court himself, which introduced him to a great variety of Characters & involved him in many interesting situations,[9] concluding with his opinion of the Benefits to result from Tythes being done away, & his having buried his own Mother (Heroine's lamented Grandmother) in consequence of the High Priest of the Parish in which she died, refusing to pay her Remains the respect due to them.[10] The Father to be of a very literary turn, an Enthusiast in Literature, nobody's Enemy but his own[11]—at the same time most zealous in the discharge of his Pastoral Duties, the model of an [g]exemplary Parish Priest.—The heroine's friendship to be sought after by a young Woman in the same Neighbourhood, of [h]Talents & Shrewdness, with light eyes & a fair skin, but having a considerable degree of Wit, Heroine shall shrink from the acquaintance.[12]—From this outset, the Story will proceed, & contain a striking variety of adventures. Heroine & her Father never above a [i]fortnight together in one place, he being driven from his Curacy by the vile acts of some totally unprincipled & heart-less young Man, desperately in love with the Heroine, & pursueing her with unrelenting passion[13]—no sooner settled in one Country of Europe than they are necessitated to quit it & retire to another[14]—always

[f] Mr. Clarke.

[g] Mr. Sherer.

[h] Mary Cooke

[i] Many Critics

line 11: 'own' inserted above line.

line 26: 'driven' inserted above line.

making new acquaintance, & always obliged to leave them. —This will of course exhibit a wide variety of Characters—but there will be no mixture; the scene will be for ever shifting from one Set of People to another—but all the [j]Good will be unexceptionable in every respect—and there will be no foibles or weaknesses but with the Wicked, who will be completely depraved & infamous, hardly a resemblance of Humanity left in them.[15]—Early in her career, in the progress of her first removals, Heroine must meet with the Hero—all [k]perfection of course[16]—& only prevented from paying his addresses to her, by some excess of refinement.[17]—Wherever she goes, somebody falls in love with her, & she receives repeated offers of Marriage—which she always refers wholly to her Father, exceedingly angry that [l]he sh[d] not be first applied to.—Often carried away by the anti-hero,[18] but rescued either by her Father or the Hero—often reduced to support herself & her Father by her Talents, & work for her Bread; —continually cheated & defrauded of her hire, worn down to a skeleton, & now & then starved to death.[19]—At last, hunted out of civilised Society, denied the poor Shelter of the humblest Cottage,[20] they are compelled to retreat into Kamschatka[21] where the poor Father, quite worn down, finding his end approaching, throws himself on the Ground, & after 4 or 5 hours of tender advice & parental Admonition to his miserable Child, expires in a fine burst of Literary Enthusiasm,[22] intermingled with

[j] Mary Cooke.

[k] Fanny Knight.

[l] M[rs] Pearse of Chilton-Lodge.

line 3: 'but there will be no mixture;' inserted above line.
line 4: 'but' inserted above line.
line 6: 'and' inserted above line.
line 8: 'Mortal' deleted; 'Humanity' inserted above line.
line 11: '& only' inserted above line.

Invectives against Holders of Tythes. —Heroine inconsolable for some time—but afterwards crawls back towards her former Country—having at least 20 narrow escapes of falling into the hands of Anti-hero—& at last in the very nick of time, turning a corner to avoid him, runs into the arms of the Hero himself,[23] who having just shaken off the scruples which fetter'd him before, was at the very moment setting off in pursuit of her.—The Tenderest & completest Eclaircissement takes place, & they are happily united. — Throughout the whole work, Heroine to be in the most [m]elegant Society & living in high style. The name of the work not to be [n]Emma—but of the same sort as [o]S & S. and P & P.[24]

[m] Fanny Knight
[n] Mrs. Craven
[o] Mr. H. Sanford

CORRECTIONS AND EMENDATIONS

p. 226 line 16	Harp——	Harp—
p. 229 line 1	again Holder's	against Holders

Opinions of *Mansfield Park*

"We certainly do not think it as a whole, equal to P. & P. — but it has many & great beauties. Fanny is a delightful Character! and Aunt Norris is a great favourite of mine. The Characters are natural & well supported, & many of the Dialogues excellent.—You need not fear the publication being considered as discreditable to the talents of it's Author." F. W. A.[1]

Not so clever as P. & P. — but pleased with it altogether. Liked the character of Fanny. Admired the Portsmouth Scene.—Mr. K.[2] —

Edward & George.[3]—Not liked it near so well as P. & P.—Edward admired Fanny—George disliked her.—George interested by nobody but Mary Crawford.—Edward pleased with Henry C.—Edmund objected to, as cold & formal.—Henry C.'s going off with Mrs. R—at such a time, when so much in love with Fanny, thought unnatural by Edward.—

Fanny Knight.[4]—Liked it, in many parts, very much indeed, delighted with Fanny;—but not satisfied with the end—wanting more Love between her & Edmund—and could not think it natural that Edmd. shd. be so much attached to a woman without Principle like Mary C.—or promote Fanny's marrying Henry.—

Anna[5] liked it better than P.& P.—but not so well as S. & S.—could not bear Fanny.—Delighted with Mrs. Norris, the scene at Portsmouth, & all the humourous parts.—

line 10: 'near' inserted above line.

Mrs. James Austen,[6] very much pleased. Enjoyed Mrs. Norris particularly, & the scene at Portsmouth. Thought Henry Crawford's going off with Mrs. Rushworth, very natural.—

Miss Clewes's[7] objections much the same as Fanny's.—

Miss Lloyd[8] preferred it altogether to either of the others.—Delighted with Fanny.—Hated Mrs. Norris.—

My Mother—not liked it so well as P. & P.—Thought Fanny insipid.—Enjoyed Mrs. Norris.—

Cassandra—thought it quite as clever, tho' not so brilliant as P. & P.—Fond of Fanny.—Delighted much in Mr. Rushworth's stupidity.—

My Eldest Brother[9]—a warm admirer of it in general.—Delighted with the Portsmouth Scene.

Edward[10]—Much like his Father.—Objected to Mrs. Rushworth's Elopement as unnatural.

Mr. B. L.[11]—Highly pleased with Fanny Price—& a warm admirer of the Portsmouth Scene.—Angry with Edmund for not being in love with her, & hating Mrs. Norris for teazing her.—

Miss Burdett[12]—Did not like it so well as P. & P.

Mrs. James Tilson[13]—Liked it better than P. & P.

Fanny Cage[14]—did not much like it—not to be compared to P. & P.—nothing interesting in the Characters—Language poor.—Characters natural & well supported—Improved as it went on.—

Mr. and Mrs. Cooke[15]—very much pleased with it—particularly with the manner in which the Clergy are treated.—Mr. Cooke called it "the most sensible Novel he had ever read."—Mrs. Cooke wished for a good Matronly Character.—

line 2: 'Thought' inserted above line.

Mary Cooke[16]—quite as much pleased with it, as her Father & Mother; seemed to enter into Lady B.'s character, & enjoyed Mr. Rushworth's folly. Admired Fanny in general; but thought she ought to have been more determined on overcoming her own feelings, when she saw Edmund's attachment to Miss Crawford.—

Miss Burrel[17]—admired it very much—particularly Mrs. Norris & Dr. Grant.—

Mrs. Bramstone[18]—much pleased with it; particularly with the character of Fanny, as being so very natural. Thought Lady Bertram like herself.—Preferred it to either of the others—but imagined that might be her want of Taste—as she does not understand Wit.—

Mrs. Augusta Bramstone[19]—owned that she thought S & S.—and P. & P. downright nonsense, but expected to like MP. better, & having finished the 1st vol.— flattered herself she had got through the worst.

The families at Deane[20]—all pleased with it.—Mrs. Anna Harwood delighted with Mrs. Norris & the green Curtain.

The Kintbury Family[21]—very much pleased with it;—preferred it to either of the others.—

Mr. Egerton the Publisher[22]—praised it for it's Morality, & for being so equal a Composition.—No weak parts.

Lady Rob: Kerr [23] wrote—"You may be assured I read every line with the greatest interest & am more delighted with it than my humble pen can express. The excellent delineation of Character, sound sense, Elegant Language & the pure morality with which it abounds, makes it a most desirable as well as useful work, & reflects the highest honour &c. &c.— Universally admired in Edinburgh, by all the wise ones.— Indeed, I have not heard a single fault given to it."—

line 25: 'pleasure' deleted; 'interest' written above. // line 28: 'very' deleted; 'most' written above.

Miss Sharpe[24]—"I think it excellent—& of it's good sense & moral Tendency there can be no doubt.—Your Characters are drawn to the Life—so very, very natural & just—but as you beg me to be perfectly honest, I must confess I prefer P & P."—

M^{rs}. Carrick.[25]—"All who think deeply & feel much will give the Preference to Mansfield Park."

M^{r}. J. Plumptre.[26] — "I never read a novel which interested me so very much throughout, the characters are all so remarkably well kept up & so well drawn, & the plot is so well contrived that I had not an idea till the end which of the two w^{d}. marry Fanny, H. C. or Edm^{d}. M^{rs}. Norris amused me particularly, & Sir Thos. is very clever, & his conduct proves admirably the defects of the modern system of Education."—M^{r}. J. P. made two objections, but only one of them was remembered, the want of some character more striking & interesting to the generality of Readers, than Fanny was likely to be.—

Sir James Langham & M^{r}. H. Sanford,[27] having been told that it was much inferior to P. & P.—began it expecting to dislike it, but were very soon extremely pleased with it—& I beleive, did not think it at all inferior.—

Alethea Bigg.[28]—"I have read MP. & heard it very much talked of, very much praised, I like it myself & think it very good indeed, but as I never say what I do not think, I will add that although it is superior in a great many points in my opinion to the other two Works, I think it has not the Spirit of P & P., except perhaps the Price family at Portsmouth, & they are delightful in their way."—

Charles[29]—did not like it near so well as P. & P.—thought it wanted Incident.—

line 16: 'striking' inserted above line. // after line 28: 'M^{rs}. Maling—(Lady Mulgrave's mother) delighted with it; read it through in a day & a half.—' deleted.

Mrs. Dickson.[30]—"I have bought M P.—but it is not equal to P. & P.—

Mrs. Lefroy[31]—liked it, but thought it a mere Novel.—

Mrs. Portal[32]—admired it very much—objected cheifly to Edmund's not being brought more forward. —

Lady Gordon[33] wrote "In most novels you are amused for the time with a set of Ideal People whom you never think of afterwards or whom you the least expect to meet in common life, whereas in Miss A-s works, & especially in MP. you actually live with them, you fancy yourself one of the family; & the scenes are so exactly descriptive, so perfectly natural, that there is scarcely an Incident a conversation, or a person that you are not inclined to imagine you have at one time or other in your Life been a witness to, born a part in, & been acquainted with."

Mrs. Pole[34] wrote, "There is a particular satisfaction in reading all Miss A—s works—they are so evidently written by a Gentlewoman—most Novelists fail & betray themselves in attempting to describe familiar scenes in high Life, some little vulgarism escapes & shews that they are not experimentally acquainted with what they describe, but here it is quite different. Everything is natural, & the situations & incidents are told in a manner which clearly evinces the Writer to belong to the Society whose Manners she so ably delineates." Mrs. Pole also said that no Books had ever occasioned so much canvassing & doubt, & that everybody was desirous to attribute them to some of their own friends, or to some person of whom they thought highly.—

Adml. Foote[35]—surprised that I had the power of drawing the Portsmouth-Scenes so well.—

Mrs. Creed[36]—preferred S & S. and P & P.—to Mansfield Park.

line 3: '&' deleted before 'but'.

Opinions of *Emma*

Captn. Austen.[1]—liked it extremely, observing that though there might be more Wit in P&P—& an higher Morality in MP—yet altogether, on account of it's peculiar air of Nature throughout, he preferred it to either.

M^{rs}. F. A.[2]—liked & admired it very much indeed, but must still prefer P. & P.

Mrs J. Bridges[3]—preferred it to all the others.

Miss Sharp[4]—better than MP.—but not so well as P. & P.—pleased with the Heroine for her Originality, delighted with M^{r}. K—& called M^{rs}. Elton beyond praise.—dissatisfied with Jane Fairfax.

Cassandra—better than P. & P.—but not so well as M. P.—

Fanny K.[5]—not so well as either P. & P. or MP.—could not bear <u>Emma</u> herself.— M^{r}. Knightley delightful.—Should like J. F.—if she knew more of her —

M^{r}. & M^{rs}. J. A.[6]—did not like it so well as either of the 3 others. Language different from the others; not so easily read.—

Edward[7]—preferred it to M P.—<u>only</u>.— M^{r}. K. liked by every body.

Miss Bigg[8]—not equal to either P & P.—or MP.—objected to the sameness of the subject (Match-making) all

lines 17–18: 'Language . . . read.—' added below line.

through.—Too much of Mr. Elton & H. Smith. Language superior to the others.—

My Mother—thought it more entertaining than MP. —but not so interesting as P. & P.—No characters in it equal to Ly Catherine & Mr. Collins.—

Miss Lloyd[9]—thought it as clever as either of the others, but did not receive so much pleasure from it as from P. & P.—& MP.—

Mrs. & Miss Craven[10]—liked it very much, but not so much as the others.—

Fanny Cage[11]—liked it very much indeed & classed it between P & P.—& MP. —

Mr. Sherer[12]—did not think it equal to either MP—(which he liked the best of all) or P & P.—Displeased with my pictures of Clergymen.—

Miss Bigg[13]—on reading it a second time, liked Miss Bates much better than at first, & expressed herself as liking all the people of Highbury in general, except Harriet Smith—but cd. not help thinking her too silly in her Loves.

The family at Upton Gray—all very much amused with it.—Miss Bates a great favourite with Mrs. Beaufoy.[14]

Mr. & Mrs. Leigh Perrot[15]—saw many beauties in it, but cd not think it equal to P. & P.—Darcy & Elizth had spoilt them for anything else.—Mr. K. however, an excellent Character; Emma better luck than a Matchmaker often has.—Pitied Jane Fairfax—thought Frank Churchill better treated than he deserved.—

Countess Craven[16]—admired it very much, but did not think it equal to P & P. — which she ranked as the very first of it's sort.—

lines 1–2: 'Language . . . others.—' added. // line 3: 'M' written over 'P'. // line 6: 'thought it' added above line.

Mrs. Guiton[17]—thought it too natural to be interesting.

Mrs. Digweed[18]—did not like it so well as the others, in fact if she had not known the Author, could hardly have got through it.

Miss Terry[19]—admired it very much, particularly Mrs. Elton.

Henry Sanford[20]—very much pleased with it—delighted with Miss Bates, but thought Mrs. Elton the best-drawn Character in the Book.—Mansfield Park however, still his favourite.

Mr. Haden[21]—quite delighted with it. Admired the Character of Emma.—

Miss Isabella Herries[22]—did not like it—objected to my exposing the sex in the character of the Heroine—convinced that I had meant Mrs. & Miss Bates for some acquaintance of theirs—People whom I never heard of before.—

Miss Harriet Moore[23]—admired it very much, but M. P. still her favourite of all.—

Countess Morley[24]—delighted with it.—

Mr. Cockerell[25]—liked it so little, that Fanny wd. not send me his opinion.—

Mrs. Dickson[26]—did not much like it—thought it very inferior to P. & P.— Liked it the less, from their being a Mr. and Mrs. Dixon in it.—

Mrs. Brandreth[27]—thought the 3d vol: superior to anything I had ever written—quite beautiful!—

Mr. B. Lefroy[28]—thought that if there had been more Incident, it would be equal to any of the others.—The Characters quite as well drawn & supported as in any, & from being more everyday ones, the more entertaining.—Did not like the Heroine so well as any of the others. Miss Bates excellent, but rather too much of her. Mr.

and Mrs. Elton admirable & John Knightley a sensible Man.—

Mrs. B. Lefroy[29]—rank'd Emma as a composition with S & S.—not so Brilliant as P. & P—nor so equal as M P.—Preferred Emma herself to all the heroines.—The Characters like all the others admirably well drawn & supported—perhaps rather less strongly marked than some, but only the more natural for that reason.— Mr. Knightley Mrs. Elton & Miss Bates her favourites.—Thought one or two of the conversations too long.—

Mrs. Lefroy[30]—preferred it to M P—but liked M P. the least of all.

Mr. Fowle[31]—read only the first & last Chapters, because he had heard it was not interesting.—

Mrs. Lutley Sclater[32]—liked it very much, better than M P—& thought I had "brought it all about very cleverly in the last volume."—

Mrs. C. Cage[33] wrote thus to Fanny—"A great many thanks for the loan of Emma, which I am delighted with. I like it better than any. Every character is thoroughly kept up. I must enjoy reading it again with Charles. Miss Bates is incomparable, but I was nearly killed with those precious treasures! They are Unique, & really with more fun than I can express. I am at Highbury all day, & I ca'nt help feeling I have just got into a new set of acquaintance. No one writes such good sense & so very comfortable.

Mrs. Wroughton[34]—did not like it so well as P. & P.—Thought the Authoress wrong, in such times as these, to draw such clergymen as Mr. Collins & Mr. Elton.

Sir J. Langham[35]—thought it much inferior to the others.—

Mr. Jeffrey[36] (of the Edinburgh Review) was kept up by it three nights.

Miss Murden[37]—certainly inferior to all the others.

Capt. C. Austen[38] wrote—"Emma arrived in time to a moment. I am delighted with her, more so I think than even with my favourite Pride & Prejudice, & have read it three times in the Passage."

Mrs. D. Dundas[39]—thought it very clever, but did not like it so well as either of the others.

Poems and Charades

Poems

'This little bag'

This little bag I hope will prove
To be not vainly made—
For, if you thread & needle want
It will afford you aid.

And as we are about to part
T'will serve another end,
For when you look upon the Bag
You'll recollect your freind.
Jan:ry 1792.

'Miss Lloyd has now sent to Miss Green'[1]

Miss Lloyd has now sent to Miss Green,
As, on opening the box, may be seen,
Some yards of a Black Ploughman's Gauze,[2]
To be made up directly, because
Miss Lloyd must in mourning appear—
For the death of a Relative dear—[3]
Miss Lloyd must expect to receive
This license to mourn & to grieve,
Complete, e're the end of the week—
It is better to write than to speak—

'Happy the Lab'rer'

Miss J. Austen

Happy the Lab'rer in his Sunday Cloathes!—
In light-drab coat,[1] smart waistcoat, well-darn'd Hose

And hat upon his head to Church he goes;—
As oft with conscious pride he downward throws
A glance upon the ample Cabbage rose[2]
Which stuck in Buttonhole regales his nose,
He envies not the gayest London Beaux.—
In Church he takes his seat among the rows,[3]
Pays to the Place the reverence he owes,
Likes best the Prayers whose meaning least he knows,
Lists to the Sermon in a softening Doze,
And rouses joyous at the welcome close.—

'Oh! M.r Best'

Oh! M.r Best, you're very bad
  And all the world shall know it;
Your base behaviour shall be sung
  By me, a tuneful Poet.—

You used to go to Harrowgate
  Each summer[1] as it came,
And why I pray should you refuse
  To go this year the same?—

The way's as plain, the road's as smooth,
  The Posting[2] not increased;
You're scarcely stouter[3] than you were,
  Not younger Sir at least.—

If e'er the waters were of use[4]
  Why now their use forego?
You may not live another year,
  All's mortal here below.—

It is your duty M.r Best
  To give your health repair
Vain else your Richard's pills[5] will be,
  And vain your Consort's care.—

But yet a nobler Duty calls
  You now towards the North.

Arise ennobled—as Escort
Of Martha Lloyd stand forth.

She wants your aid—she honours you
With a distinguish'd call.
Stand forth & be the friend of her
Who is the friend of all.—

Take her, & wonder at your luck
In having such a Trust.
Her converse sensible & sweet
Will banish heat & dust.—

So short she'll make the journey seem
You'll bid the Chaise stand still.
T'will be like driving at full speed
From Newb'ry to Speen Hill.—[6]

Convey her safe to Morton's wife[7]
And I'll forget the past,
And write some verses in your praise
As finely & as fast.

But if you still refuse to go
I'll never let you rest,
But haunt you with reproachful song
Oh! wicked Mr. Best!—

J.A.
Clifton 1806

'See they come'

See they come, post haste[1] from Thanet,[2]
Lovely Couple, side by side;

stanza 6 line 3: 'Escort' written over another word or words (possibly 'the friend'). // stanza 10 line 1: 'Decide(?) to go to Harrowgate' deleted; 'Convey her safe to Morton's wife' inserted above line, and a black line added for the full length of the line to divide it from the previous stanza. // stanza 11 line 2: 'Oh! wicked Mr. Best' deleted; 'I'll never let you rest,' added below deleted line.

They've left behind them Richard Kennet[3]
With the Parents of the Bride![4]

Canterbury they have passed through;
Next succeeded Stamford-bridge;
Chilham village they came fast through;[5]
Now they've mounted yonder ridge.

Down the hill they're swift proceeding,
Now they skirt the Park around;
Lo! the Cattle[6] sweetly feeding,
Scamper, startled at the sound!

Run, my Brothers,[7] to the Pier gate![8]
Throw it open, very wide!
Let it not be said that we're late
In welcoming my Uncle's Bride!

To the house the chaise[9] advances;
Now it stops—They're here, they're here!
How d'ye do, my Uncle Francis?
How does do your Lady dear?

On Sir Home Popham's sentence—April 1807.

Of a Ministry pitiful, angry, mean,[1]
A Gallant Commander the victim is seen;
For Promptitude, Vigour, Success—does he stand
Condemn'd to receive a severe reprimand![2]
To his Foes I could wish a resemblance in fate;
That they too may suffer themselves soon or late
The Injustice they warrant—but vain is my spite,
They cannot so suffer, who never do right.—

To Miss Bigg previous to her marriage, with some pocket handfs. I had hemmed for her.—

Cambrick![1] with grateful blessings would I pay
The pleasure given me in sweet employ:—

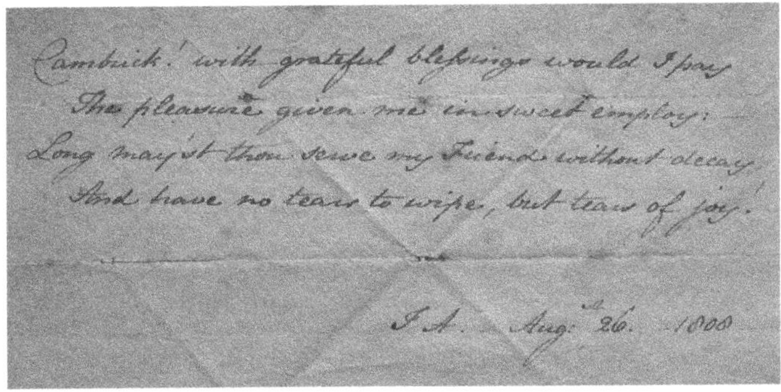
Cambrick! with grateful blessings would I pay
The pleasure given me in sweet employ:
Long may'st thou serve my Friend without decay
And have no tears to wipe, but tears of joy!
J. A. Aug: 26. 1808

5 Poem 'To Miss Bigg', with the fold-marks in the paper clearly visible.

Long may'st thou serve my Friend without decay,
And have no tears to wipe, but tears of joy!
J. A.—Aug:st 26.—1808—

On the same occasion—but not sent.—

Cambrick! Thou'st been to me a Good,
And I would bless thee if I could.
Go, serve thy Mistress with delight,
Be small in compass, soft & white;
Enjoy thy fortune, honour'd much
To bear her name[2] & feel her touch;
And that thy worth may last for years,
Slight be her Colds & few her Tears!—

To the memory of Mrs. Lefroy, who died Dec:r 16.—my birthday.—written 1808.—

The day returns again, my natal day;
What mix'd emotions with the Thought arise!
Beloved friend, four years have pass'd away
Since thou wert snatch'd forever from our eyes.—

The day, commemorative of my birth
Bestowing Life & Light & Hope on me,
Brings back the hour which was thy last on Earth.
Oh! bitter pang of torturing Memory!—

Angelic Woman! past my power to praise
In Language meet, thy Talents, Temper, Mind,
Thy solid Worth, thy captivating Grace!—
Thou friend & ornament of Humankind!—

At Johnson's death,[1] by Hamilton t'was said,
"Seek we a substitute—Ah! vain the plan,
No second best remains to Johnson dead—
None can remind us even of the Man."[2]

So we of thee—unequall'd in thy race
Unequall'd thou, as he the first of Men.
Vainly we search around thy vacant place,
We ne'er may look upon thy like again.

Come then fond Fancy, thou indulgent Power,—
—Hope is desponding, chill, severe to thee!—
Bless thou, this little portion of an hour,
Let me behold her as she used to be.

I see her here, with all her smiles benign,
Her looks of eager Love, her accents sweet.
That voice & Countenance almost divine!—
Expression, Harmony, alike complete.—

I listen—'tis not sound alone—'tis sense,
'Tis Genius,[3] Taste, & Tenderness of soul.
'Tis genuine warmth of heart without pretence
And purity of Mind that crowns the whole.

She speaks; 'tis Eloquence—that grace of Tongue
So rare, so lovely!—Never misapplied
By <u>her</u> to palliate Vice, or deck[4] a Wrong,
She speaks & reasons but on Virtue's side.

Her's is the Energy of soul sincere.
Her Christian Spirit, ignorant to feign,

Seeks but to comfort, heal, enlighten, chear,
Confer a pleasure, or prevent a pain.—

Can ought enhance such Goodness?—Yes, to me,
Her partial favour from my earliest years
Consummates all.—Ah! Give me yet to see
Her smile of Love—the Vision disappears.

'Tis past & gone—We meet no more below.
Short is the Cheat of Fancy o'er the Tomb.
Oh! might I hope to equal Bliss to go!
To meet thee Angel! in thy future home!—

Fain would I feel an union in thy fate,
Fain would I seek to draw an Omen fair
From this connection in our Earthly date.
Indulge the harmless weakness—Reason, spare.—

J.A.

'Alas! poor Brag, thou boastful Game!'[1]

"Alas! poor Brag,[2] thou boastful Game!—What now
avails thine empty name?—
Where now thy more distinguish'd fame?—My day is
o'er, and Thine the same.—
For thou like me art thrown aside, At Godmersham,
this Christmas Tide;
And now across the Table wide, Each Game save
Brag or Spec: is tried."—
"Such is the mild Ejaculation, Of tender hearted
Speculation."—[3]

'My dearest Frank'

Chawton,[1] July 26.—1809.—

My dearest Frank,[2] I wish you joy
Of Mary's safety with a Boy,
Whose birth has given little pain
Compared with that of Mary Jane.—[3]

May he a growing Blessing prove,
And well deserve his Parents Love!—
Endow'd with Art's & Nature's Good,
Thy name possessing with thy Blood,
In him, in all his ways, may we
Another Francis William see!—[4]
Thy infant days may he inherit,
Thy warmth, nay insolence of spirit;—
We would not with one fault dispense
To weaken the resemblance.
May he revive thy Nursery sin,
Peeping as daringly within,
His curley Locks but just descried,
With "Bet, my be not come to bide."—[5]
   Fearless of danger, braving pain,
And threaten'd very oft in vain,
Still may one Terror daunt his Soul,
One needful engine[6] of Controul
Be found in this sublime array,
A neighbouring Donkey's aweful Bray.
So may his equal faults as Child,
Produce Maturity as mild!
His saucy words & fiery ways[7]
In early Childhood's pettish days,
In Manhood, shew his Father's mind
Like him, considerate & kind;
All Gentleness to those around,
And eager only not to wound.
   Then like his Father too, he must,
To his own former struggles just,
Feel his Deserts with honest Glow,
And all his self-improvement know.—
A native fault may thus give birth
To the best blessing, conscious worth.—[8]

   As for ourselves, we're very well;
As unaffected prose will tell.—
Cassandra's pen will paint our state,

The many comforts that await
Our Chawton home, how much we find
Already in it, to our mind;
And how convinced that when complete
It will all other Houses beat
That ever have been made or mended,
With rooms concise, or rooms distended.[9]
You'll find us very snug next year,
Perhaps with Charles & Fanny[10] near,
For now it often does delight us
To fancy them just over-right[11] us.—
J.A.

'In measured verse'

1

In measured verse[1] I'll now rehearse
The charms of lovely Anna:
And, first, her mind is unconfined
Like any vast savannah.[2]

2

Ontario's lake[3] may fitly speak
Her fancy's ample bound:
Its circuit may, on strict survey
Five hundred miles be found.

3

Her wit descends on foes and friends
Like famed Niagara's Fall;[4]
And travellers gaze in wild amaze,
And listen, one and all.

4

Her judgment sound, thick, black, profound,
Like transatlantic groves,[5]
Dispenses aid, and friendly shade
To all that in it roves.

5

If thus her mind to be defined
America exhausts,
And all that's grand in that great land
In similes it costs—

6

Oh how can I her person try
To image and portray?
How paint the face, the form how trace
In which those virtues lay?

7

Another world must be unfurled,
Another language known,
Ere tongue or sound can publish round
Her charms of flesh and bone.

'I've a pain in my head'

I've a pain in my head[1]
Said the suffering Beckford,
To her Doctor so dread.
Oh! what shall I take for't?

Said this Doctor so dread,
Whose name it was Newnham.[2]
For this pain in your head,
Ah! what can you do Ma'am?

Said Miss Beckford, Suppose
If you think there's no risk,
I take a good Dose
Of calomel,[3] brisk.—

What a praise-worthy notion.
Replied Mr. Newnham.
You shall have such a potion,
And so will I too Ma'am.—

Feby. 1811.—

On the marriage of Mr. Gell of East Bourn to Miss Gill.—[1]

Of Eastbourn, Mr. Gell
   From being perfectly well
Became dreadfully ill
   For the Love of Miss Gill.
So he said with some sighs
   I'm the slave of your i.s
Ah! restore if you please
   By accepting my e.s.

'I am in a dilemma'

"I am in a Dilemma, for want of an Emma,"
"Escaped from the Lips, Of Henry Gipps."—

'Between Session & Session'[1]

"Between Session & Session"
   "The just[2] Prepossession"[3]
"May rouse up the Nation["][4]
"And the Villainous Bill"
"May be forced to lie still"[5]
"Against Wicked Men's will."[6]

'When stretch'd on one's bed'

   When stretch'd on one's bed
   With a fierce-throbbing head
Which precludes alike Thought or Repose,
   How little one cares
   For the grandest affairs
That may busy the world as it goes!—

   How little one feels
   For the Waltzes & reels[1]
Of our dance-loving friends at a Ball!

How slight one's concern
To conjecture or learn
What their flounces or hearts may befall.

How little one minds
If a company dines
On the best that the Season affords!
How short is one's muse
O'er the Sauces & Stews,
Or the Guests, be they Beggars or Lords! —

How little the Bells,
Ring they Peels, toll they Knells
Can attract our attention or Ears! —
The Bride may be married,
The Corse[2] may be carried,
And touch nor our hopes nor our fears.

Our own bodily pains
Ev'ry faculty chains;
We can feel on no subject beside.
'Tis in health & in Ease
We the Power must seize
For our friends & our Souls to provide.

Oct[r] 27. 1811.

J.A

stanza 2 lines 4–6 'How little one thinks [?] / Of the S[illegible] or the Stinks [?] / Which pervade the Assembly all.' deleted; 'How slight one's concern / To conjecture or learn / What their flounces or hearts may befall.' inserted. // stanza 4 line 3 'catch' deleted; 'attract' written above line. // after stanza 4 stanza cancelled – it may have originally read:

For ourselves and our pains (?)
Ev'ry faculty chains.
We can feel on no subject beside.
'Tis for Health & for Ease
The Time present (?) to seize
For their Friends & their Souls to provide.

'Camilla, good humoured, & merry, & small'

Camilla, good humoured, & merry, & small
For a Husband was at her last stake;[1]
And having in vain danced at many a Ball
Is now happy to jump at a Wake.[2]

'When Winchester races[1] first took their beginning'

When Winchester races first took their beginning
It is said the good people forgot their old Saint[2]
Not applying at all for the leave of S^t: Swithin
And that William of Wykham's[3] approval was faint.

The races however were fix'd and determin'd
The company met & the weather was charming
The Lords & the Ladies were sattin'd & ermin'd
And nobody saw any future alarming.

But when the old Saint was informed of these doings
He made but one spring from his shrine[4] to the roof
Of the Palace which now lies so sadly in ruins[5]
And then he address'd them all standing aloof.

Oh, subjects rebellious, Oh Venta[6] depraved
When once we are buried you think we are dead
But behold me Immortal.—By vice you're enslaved
You have sinn'd & must suffer.—Then further he said

These races & revels & dissolute measures[7]
With which you're debasing a neighbouring Plain[8]
Let them stand—you shall meet with your curse in your pleasures
Set off for your course, I'll pursue with my rain.

Ye cannot but know my command o'er July.
Henceforward I'll triumph in shewing my powers,
Shift your race as you will it shall never be dry
The curse upon Venta is July in showers.

Charades

1.
When my 1st is a task to a young girl of spirit
And my second confines her to finish the piece
How hard is her fate! but how great is her merit
If by taking my whole she effect her release!

Jane

2.
Divided, I'm a Gentleman
In public Deeds and Powers
United, I'm a Man who oft
That Gentleman devours.

Jane

3.
You may lie on my first, by the side of a stream,
And my second compose to the Nymph you adore
But if when you've none of my whole, her esteem
And affection diminish, think of her no more.

Jane.

2. line 3 'Man who oft' deleted, 'Monster who' added above the line, in pencil in another hand.

Appendices

APPENDIX A

Transcription of 'The Watsons'

[f.1r]

in   in Surry*

THE first winter assembly of the Town of ~~L.~~ D. — ^ was to be held on Tuesday

it was

Octr. y^{e} 13th, & ~~was~~ generally expected to be a very good one; a long list of Country

Families was confidently run over as sure of attending, & sanguine hopes

were entertained that the Osbornes themselves would be there. —

The Edwardes' invitation to the Watsons followed of course. The Edward's

were people of fortune who lived in the Town & kept their Coach; the

Watsons inhabited a village about 3 miles distant, were poor & had no close

carriage; & ever since there had been Balls in the place, the former ~~had~~

dress

were accustomed to invite the Latter to ^ dine & sleep at their House,

~~for~~ on every monthly return throughout the winter. — On the present

as only two of M^{r}. W.'s children were at home, & one was always necessary ~~to him~~ as

occasion, ~~one only of the Family in Stanton Parsonage could profit by~~

companion to himself, for he was sickly †& had lost his wife, one only could profit by

the kindness of their friends; Miss Emma Watson ~~was to make her first~~

* First 'r' in 'Surry' written over 's'.   † letter crossed out before '&'.

who was very recently returned to her family from the care of an Aunt who had
~~public appearance in the Neighbourhood; & Miss Watson drove her~~
brought her up, was to make her first public appearance in the Neighbourhood; — &

her eldest Sister, whose delight in a Ball was not lessened by a ten years Enjoyment,[*] had
~~& all her finery in the old chair to D. on the important morning of the~~

some merit in chearfully
~~her eldest sister, who had kindly~~ undertaking[†] to drive her & all her finery in
~~Ball; without being able to stay & share the pleasure herself, because~~

the old Chair to D. on the important morn^{g}. —
~~her Father who was an Invalid could not be left to spend the Even^{g}.~~

~~alone~~
[f.1v] As they splashed along the dirty Lane Miss Watson thus instructed &

it be
cautioned her inexperienc'd sister. — "I dare say ~~you~~ will ~~have~~ a very good

hardly
Ball, & among so many officers, you will ~~not~~ ^ want partners. You

and
will find M^{rs}. Edwards' maid very willing to help you, ~~but~~ ^ I would ~~re~~ =

advise
= ~~commend~~ you to ask Mary Edwards's opinion if you are at all at a loss

for she has a very good Taste. — If M^{r}. E. does not lose his money at

Cards, you will stay as late as you can wish for;[‡] ~~& hav~~ if he does, he

will hurry you home perhaps — but you are sure of some comfortable

Soup. — I hope you will be in good looks — . I should not be sur-

[*] 'Enjoyment' written over another word (illegible).
[†] 'undertaking' written over 'undertook t'.
[‡] semicolon written over comma.

-prised if you were to be thought one of the prettiest girls in the room,

Tom
~~&~~ there is a great deal in Novelty. Perhaps ~~Charles~~ Musgrave may ~~ad:~~
take notice of you — but I would advise you by all means not to

every
give him any encouragement. He generally pays attention to ^ ~~any~~
new girl, but he is a great flirt & never means anything serious."

"I think I have heard you speak of him before, said Emma. Who is he?"
"A young Man of very good fortune, quite independant, & remark:
:ably agreable, an universal favourite wherever he goes. Most of the
girls hereabouts are in love with him, or have been. I beleive I
am the only one among them that have escaped with a whole heart,
and yet I was the first he paid attention to, when he came into this
Country, six years ago; and very great attention indeed did he pay me.
Some people say that he has never seemed to like any girl so well

behaving in a particular way to an
Since, tho' he is always ^ ~~philandering with~~ one or ^ other." —
"And how came <u>your</u> heart to be the only cold one? — " said Emma smiling.
"There was a reason for that — replied Miss W. changing colour. — I have not been
very well used Emma among them, I hope you will have better luck." —
"Dear Sister, I beg your pardon, if I have unthinkingly given you pain." —
"When first we knew Tom Musgrave, continued Miss W. without seeming to hear

of the name of Purvis
her, I was very much attached to a young Man — ~~a neighbour~~ — ~~& he to~~

a particular friend of Robert's, who used to be with us a great deal.
~~me. Perhaps you may see him to-night. His name is Purvis & he has the~~

Every body thought it would have been a Match." A sigh accompanied
~~Living of Alford about 14 miles off. We were very much attached to~~

in silence —
~~each other~~ these words, which Emma ~~would have~~ respected ~~too much to urge~~

~~continue~~ after a short pause, went on — .
~~the subject; further~~; ; but her Sister ~~had pleasure in the communication~~
^

"You will naturally ask why it did not take place, & why he is married to

another Woman, while I am still single. — But you must ask him — not

me — you must ask Penelope. — Yes Emma, Penelope was at the bottom of it

[f.2v] all. — She thinks everything fair for a Husband; I trusted her, she set him against

gaining
me, with a veiw of ~~getting~~ him herself & it ended in his discontinuing his visits
^

soon after
& ^ marrying somebody else. — Penelope makes light of her conduct, but <u>I</u> think

such Treachery very bad. It has been the ruin of my happiness. I shall never

love any Man as I loved Purvis. I do not think Tom Musgrave should be

named with him in the same day. — " "You quite shock me by what you

say of Penelope — said Emma. Could a sister do such a thing? — Rivalry,

Treachery between Sisters! — I shall be afraid of being acquainted with

her — but I hope it was not so. Appearances were against her" — "You

There is nothing she w^{d} not do to get* married — she
do not know Penelope. — ~~She w^{d} not deny it herself, she makes no secret of~~
^

* 'get' written over 'be'.

would as good
~~wishing to marry~~ as tell you so herself. — Do not trust her with any secrets
^
of your own, take warning by me, do not trust her; she has her good

qualities, but she has no Faith, no Honour, no Scruples, if she can pro:

I wish with all my heart she was well married.
:mote her own advantage. — ~~I wish she were well married with all my~~

I declare I had rather have her well-married than myself." —
~~heart; when once she is, she will be a very worthy character~~ — ~~but till then~~
^
"Than yourself! — yes I can suppose so. A heart, wounded like yours

can have little inclination for Matrimony." — "Not much indeed —

but you know we must marry. — I could do very well single for my
own part —

[Booklet] 1

[f.3r] A little company, & a pleasant Ball now &

then, would be enough for me, if one could

be young for ever, but my Father cannot

provide for us, & it is very bad to grow old

I have lost
& be poor & laughed at. — ~~Penelope is now~~

it is true
Purvis, but very few people marry their first

Loves. I should not refuse a man because he

was not Purvis — . Not that I can ever quite

forgive Penelope." — Emma shook her head

in acquiescence. — "Penelope however has had

her Troubles — continued Miss W. — She was

sadly disappointed in Tom Musgrave, who

afterwards transferred his attentions from me

to her, & whom she was very fond of; — but

never means anything

he ~~meant nothing~~ serious, & when he had

trifled with her long enough, he began to

slight her for

~~take notice of~~ Margaret, & poor Penelope
^

was very wretched — . And since then, she

has been trying to make some match at

Chichester

~~Southampton~~; she wont tell us with whom,

but I beleive it is a rich old Dr. Harding,

Uncle to the friend she goes to see; — & she

taken a vast about him

has ~~had a monstrous~~ deal of trouble & given
^ ^

up a great deal of Time to no purpose

as yet. —

[f.3v] the other day,

When she went away she said it should be
^

the last time. ~~of trial~~. — I suppose you did

particular Chichester

not know what her Business was at ~~South:~~

nor guess at the that

~~:ampton — you did not suspect~~ object ~~that~~

could from Stanton

~~could~~ take her away, ~~from home~~ just

as you were coming home after so many

had not

years absence." — "No indeed, I ~~should never~~

the

~~have~~ smallest suspicion of it. I considered her

engagement to Mrs. Shaw just at that time

as very unfortunate for me. I had hoped

to be able to

to find all my Sisters at home; ~~I wished to~~

immediate

make an friend of each." — "I suspect the Dr.

Asthma.

to have had an attack of the ~~Gout~~, — & that

she was hurried away on that account —

the Shaws are quite on her side. — At least

I believe so — but she tells me nothing. She

professes to keep her own counsel; she says,

& truly enough, that "Too many Cooks spoil

the Broth." — "I am sorry for her anxieties,

said Emma, — but I do not like her plans
or her opinions. I shall be afraid of her. —
She must have too masculine & bold a temper. —
To be so bent on Marriage — to pursue a Man merely
for the sake of Situation — is a sort of thing that
[f.4r] shocks me; I cannot understand it. Poverty
is a great Evil, but to a woman of Education &
feeling it ought not, it cannot be the great:
=est. — I would rather be Teacher at a school
(and I can think of nothing worse) than marry
a Man I did not like. — " "I would rather do
any thing than be Teacher at a school — said
her Sister. I have been at school, Emma,
& know what a Life they lead; you never
have. — I should not like marrying a disa:
:greable Man any more than yourself, —
but I do not think there are many very
disagreable Men; — I think I could like
any goodhumoured Man with a com:
:fortable Income. — I suppose my aunt
brought you up to be rather refined."
"Indeed I do not know. — My Conduct must

tell you how I have been brought up.
I am no judge of it my self. I cannot com:
:pare my aunt's method with any other
persons, because I know no other." —
"But I can see in a great many things
that you are very refined. I have observed
it ever since you came home, & I am
[f.4v] afraid it will not be for your happiness.
Penelope will laugh at you very much."

"That will not be for my happiness I am
sure. — If my opinions are wrong, I must
~~endeavour to~~ correct them — if they are a:
:bove my Situation, I must endeavour to
conceal them. — But I doubt whether Ridi=
=cule, — Has Penelope much wit?" —
"Yes — she has great spirits, & never cares
what she says." — "Margaret is more gen:
especially
:tle I imagine?" — "Yes — ^ in company; she
is all gentleness & mildness when anybody
is a little fretful & perverse
is by. — But she ~~has a good deal of spirit~~ a:

creature! — she
:mong ourselves. — Poor ~~Margaret~~ is possessed

with the notion of Tom Musgrave's being

more
seriously in love with her, than he ever
^
was with any body else, & is always ex:

:pecting him to come to the point. This

within this twelvemonth
is the second time ^ that she has gone to

spend a month with Robert & Jane

on purpose to egg him on, by her ab=

:sence — but I am sure she is mistaken,

& that he will no more follow her to

[f.5r] now
Croydon ^ than he did last March. — He will

never marry unless he can marry some-

=body very great; Miss Osborne perhaps,

or something in that stile. — " "Your ac:

:count of this Tom Musgrave, Elizabeth,

gives me very little inclination for his

acquaintance." "You are afraid of him,

I do not wonder at you."
~~& well you may~~. — "No indeed — I dislike

& despise him." — "Dislike & Despise Tom

Musgrave! No, that you never can.

I defy you not to be delighted with him

if he takes notice of you. — I hope he will

dance with you — & I dare say he will,

unless the Osbornes come with a large

party, & then he will not speak to any

body else. — " "He seems to have most

engaging manners! — said Emma. — Well,

we shall see how irresistable Mr. Tom

& I

Musgrave ^ find each other. — I suppose

I shall know him as soon as I enter the

Ball-room; — he must carry some of

his Charms in his face." — "You will not

find him in the Ball room I can tell

you,

[f.5v] you will go early that Mrs. Edwards may

get a good place by the fire, & he never

&

comes till late; If the Osbornes are coming,

Passage

he will wait in the ~~Tea-room~~, & come in

with them. — I should like to look in

upon you Emma. If it was but a good day

with my Father, I w^{d}. wrap myself up, &
James should drive me over, as soon as
I had made Tea for him, &* I should be
with you by the time the Dancing began."
"What! would you come late at night
in this Chair?" — "To be sure I would. —
There, I said you were very refined; — &
<u>that</u>'s an instance of it. — " Emma for a
made no answer —
moment ~~was silenced~~ — at last she said —
^
"I wish Elizabeth, you had not made a point
of my going to this Ball, I wish you were
going instead of me. Your pleasure would
be greater than mine. I am a stranger here,
& know nobody but the Edwardses, — my
Enjoyment therefore must be very doubtful.
Yours among all your acquaintance w^{d}.
be certain. — It is not too late to change.
[f.6r] Very little apology c^{d}. be requisite to the
Edwardes, who must be more glad of your
sh^{d}.
company than of mine, & I ~~shall~~ most
^

* 'him, &' written over 'him. —'.

not
readily return to my Father; & should ^ be
at all afraid to drive this quiet old Creature,
home.
Your Cloathes I would undertake to find
means of sending to you." — "My dearest Emma
cried Eliz: warmly — do you think I would
do such a thing? — Not for the Universe —
but I shall never forget your goodnature
in proposing it. ~~What a sweet temper~~ You
sweet temper indeed!
must have a ^ — I never met with any thing
like it
~~so kind~~.! — And w^{d} you really give up the
Ball, that I might be able to go to it! — Be:
:leive me Emma, ~~I shall never forget the~~
~~kindness of the proposal. But~~ I am not so
that comes to.
selfish as ~~to accept it~~ ^. No, tho' I am nine
years older than you are, I would not be
the means of keeping you from being
seen. — You are very pretty, & it would be
very hard that you should not have as fair
a chance as we have all had, to make

your fortune. — No Emma, whoever stays

at home this winter, it sha'nt be you.

[f.6v] I am sure I sh^{d}. never have forgiven the

person who kept me from a Ball at 19."

Emma expressed her gratitude, & for a few min:

:utes they jogged on in silence. — Elizabeth

first spoke. — "You will take notice who

Mary Edwards dances with." — "I will remem:

her partners know
:ber ~~their names~~ if I can — but ~~do~~ you ~~wish me~~
^

they will be all strangers
~~particularly to observe them~~ to me." "Only
^

Hunter,
observe whether she dances with Capt. ~~Carr~~

have my fears in
more than once; I ~~am rather afraid of~~ that
^

quarter. Not that her Father or Mother like

it is all
officers, but if she does you know, ~~all the~~

over with
~~worse for~~ poor Sam. — And I have promised
^

to write him word who she dances with."

"Is Sam. attached to Miss Edwardes ?" —

not
"Did ^ you know <u>that</u>?" — "How should I know

Shropshire
it ? — How should I know in ~~Devonshire~~, ^ what

of that nature in Surry ?
is passing ^ ~~in Sussex?~~ — It is not likely that

such delicacy
circumstances of ~~so delicate a nature~~ should

communication
make any part of the scanty ~~Correspondence~~

you & me for the last 14
which passed between ~~us for a dozen~~ ^ years;"

"I wonder I never mentioned it when I

wrote. Since you have been at home, I

have been so busy with my poor Father
& our great wash

[Booklet] 2

[f.7r] that I have had no leisure to tell you

anything — but indeed I concluded you knew

it all. — He has been very much in love with

her these two years, & it is a great disappoint:

:ment to him that he cannot always get away

to our Balls — but Mr Curtis wo'nt often

spare him, & just now it is a sickly time at

Guilford"
~~Dorking~~. — "Do you suppose Miss Edwardes
inclined to like him — ?" "I am afraid not: you
know she is an only Child, & will have at
least ten thousand pounds." — "But still she
may like our Brother." "Oh! no — . The Edwardes
look much higher. Her Father & Mother w[d].
never consent to it. Sam is only a Surgeon
you know. — Sometimes I think she does
like him. But Mary Edwardes is rather
prim & reserved; I do not always know what
she w[d]. be at." — "Unless Sam feels on sure
grounds with the Lady herself, It seems a
pity to me that he should be encouraged
to think of her at all." — "A young Man
must think of somebody. said Eliz: — & why
should not he be as lucky* as Robert, who
six
has got a good wife & ~~four~~ thousand pounds?"
^

[f.7v] "We must not all expect to be individually lucky
replied Emma. The Luck of one member
of a Family is Luck to all. — " "Mine is all

* 'c' of 'lucky' written over another letter (illegible).

to come I am sure — said Eliz: giving another
sigh to the remembrance of Purvis. — I have
been unlucky enough, & I cannot say much
for you, as my Aunt married again so fool:
=ishly.* — Well — you will have a good Ball
I dare say. The next turning will bring us
to the Turnpike. You may see the Church
& White Hart
Tower over the hedge, ^ the ~~Town Hall~~ ^ is
close by it. — I shall long to know what you
think of Tom Musgrave." Such were the
last audible sounds of Miss Watson's voice,
before they passed thro' the Turnpike gate
& entered on the pitching of the Town —
the jumbling & noise of which made far:
:ther Conversation most thoroughly undesira:
heavily
:ble. — The old Mare trotted ~~stupidly~~ ^ on,
wanting no direction of the reins to take
the right Turning, & making only one
Blunder, in proposing to stop at the Mil:
leners,

* 'hly' in '=ishly' written over other letters (illegible).

[f.8r] before she drew up towards Mr. Edward's

door. — Mr. E. lived in the best house in the

place, if Mr. Tomlinson
Street, & the best in the ~~Town, if~~ the Banker

newly erected ~~one~~
might be indulged in calling his ~~new House~~
^
House with a Shrubbery & sweep
at the end of the Town ^ in the Country, ~~which~~
^

~~however was not often granted~~. — Mr. E.s

was higher than most of its neighbours
House ~~was of a dull brick colour, & an high~~

with ~~two~~ windows on each side the door, ~~&~~
~~Elevation, a flight of stone steps to the Door~~

~~five~~ the windows guarded by ~~a chain & green~~
~~& two windows flight of stone steps with~~

posts & chain, the door approached
~~white posts, & a chain, divided~~ by a flight of

stone steps. — "Here we are — said Eliz: —

as the Carriage ceased moving — safely ar:

:rived; — & by the Market Clock, we have been

only five & thirty minutes coming. — which

I think is doing pretty well, tho' it would be

nice
nothing for Penelope. — Is not it a ~~prett~~
^
Town ? — The Edwards' have a noble house

you see, & They live quite in stile. ~~I assure~~

~~you~~. The door will be opened by a Man

with

in Livery ~~&~~ a powder'd head, I can tell you."
^

Emma had seen the Edwardses only

one morn^g. at Stanton, they were therefore

all but Strangers to her, & tho' her spirits

were by no means insensible to the

[f.8v] expected joys of the Evening, she felt a little

thought

uncomfortable in the ~~idea~~ of all that was
^

to

~~fo~~ precede them. Her conversation with
^

too some very

Eliz. ~~had~~ giving* her ~~many~~ unpleasant feel:

with respect to her own family; had†

=~~x~~ ings, ~~to add to the awkwardness of so~~

~~other~~

made‡ her more open to ~~any~~ disagreable im:

~~slight an acquaintance to the consciousness~~

~~& in particular to~~

from any other cause, rushing into Intimacy on

~~of~~:pressions, ~~of the awkwardness~~ of so slight an ac:

& increased her sense of the awkwardness

* 'ing' written over 'e' in 'giving'.

† 'had' written over '&'.

‡ 'a' in 'made' written over another letter (illegible).

:quaintance. ~~seemed a serious Evil~~. — There was
nothing in the manners of M^rs. or Miss Edwardes
change
to give immediate ~~dissipation~~ to these Ideas; — the
^
tho' had a reserved
Mother ~~was~~ a very friendly woman, ~~but of rather~~
^
air, & a great
~~formal aspect, &~~ deal of formal Civility — & the
a of 22
daughter, ~~the~~ genteel looking girl, with her hair
^ ^
very
in papers, seemed ~~as was~~ naturally to have caught
something of the Stile of the Mother who had brought
Emma
her up. — ~~She~~ was soon left to know what they
^
could be, by Eliz.'s being obliged to hurry away —
& some very, very languid remarks on the pro:
:bable Brilliancy of the Ball, were all that
broke at intervals a silence of half an hour
before they were joined by the Master of the
&
house. — M^r. Edwards had a much easier, more
communicative air than the Ladies of the Family;
came
he was fresh from the Street, & he ~~entered~~ ready
^

[f.9r] to tell whatever might interest. — After a cordial
reception of Emma, he turned to his daughter with
"Well Mary, I bring you good news. — The Osbornes
will certainly be at the Ball to night. — Horses for
two Carriages are ordered from the White Hart, to be

by 9
at Osborne Castle ~~at 8~~." — "I am glad of it — observed
^

our
M^{rs}. E., because their coming gives a credit to ~~the~~

Assemblies
~~Ball~~. The Osbornes being known to have been
^
at the first Ball, will dispose a great many peo:

more than they deserve
:ple to attend the second. — It is ~~not very reasonable~~,
^
for in fact they add nothing to the pleasure of the
Evening, they come so late, & go so early; — but Great

have always their charm."
People ~~must always be the vogue, & Little ones~~

~~are very fond of looking at~~
~~love to be infatuated by them~~ — M^{r}. Edwards
^ ^
proceeded to relate every other little article of news
which his morning's lounge had supplied him with,
& they chatted with greater briskness, till M^{rs}. E.'s
moment for dressing arrived, & the young Ladies
were carefully recommended to lose no time. —

Emma was shewn to a very comfortable apart:
:ment, & as soon as M^{rs}. E.'s civilities could leave
her to herself, the happy occupation, the first
Bliss of a Ball began. — The girls, dressing
in some measure together, grew unavoidably
better acquainted; Emma found in Miss E. —

[f.9v] the shew of
~~the appearance of~~ good sense, a modest unpre:
^
:tending mind, & a great wish of obliging — &
when they returned to the parlour where M^{rs}. E.
respectably
was sitting ~~safely~~ attired in one of the two Sattin
^
gowns which went thro' the winter, & a new
Cap from the Milliners, they entered it with much
easier feelings & more natural smiles than they
had taken away. — Their dress was now to be
examined; M^{rs}. Edwards acknowledged herself
of
too old-fashioned to approve every modern
^
extravagance however sanctioned — & tho' com:
:placently veiwing her daughter's good looks, w^{d}.
give but a qualified admiration; & M^{r}. E.
not less satisfied with Mary, paid some Com:

:pliments of good humoured Gallantry to Emma

at her expence. — The discussion led to more

gently*

intimate remarks, & Miss Edwardes ~~obs~~ asked
^

Emma if she were not often reckoned very

like her youngest brother. — Emma thought

she could perceive a faint blush accompany

the question, & there seemed something still

more suspicious in the manner in which

Mr. E. took up the subject. "— You are

paying Miss Emma no great compliment

[f.10r] I think Mary, said he hastily — . Mr. Sam.

Watson is a very good sort of young man, &

I dare say a very clever Surgeon, but ~~to~~

his

~~compare a young Lady to a Man whose~~ com:

has been rather too

:plexion ~~is pretty~~ much exposed to all weathers,
^

to make a likeness to him very flattering."

had

Mary apologized in some confusion. "She ~~did~~ not

thought

~~think~~ a strong ~~degree of~~ Likeness at all incom:
^

* 'gen' in 'gently' written over other letters (illegible).

:patible with very different degrees of Beauty. —
There might be resemblance in Countenance;
& the complexion, & even the features be very
unlike." — "I know nothing of my Brother's
Beauty, said Emma, for I have not seen him
7 ~~but let him be ever~~
since he was ~~ten~~ years old — ~~& if you do not~~
~~so plain, I have you know, I have no right to refuse~~
~~tell me that he is plain therefore~~
~~being like him~~ but my father reckons us alike."
"Mr. Watson! — cried Mr. Edwardes, Well, you
astonish me. — There is not the least likeness in
Yr. brother's
the world; ~~his~~ eyes are grey, yours are brown,
He has a long* face, & a wide mouth.
~~& every feature is different~~ — My dear, do <u>you</u>
perceive the least resemblance?" — "Not the
least. — Miss Emma Watson puts me very much
in mind of her eldest Sister, & sometimes I see
a look of Miss Penelope — & once or twice there
has been a glance of Mr. Robert — but I
[f.10v] cannot perceive any likeness to Mr. Samuel."
"I see the likeness between her & Miss Watson,

* 'long' written over another word, possibly 'broad'.

very strongly* — I am
replied M[r] E. — , ~~it is very strong~~ — but ~~for the~~

not sensible of the† others. ~~I cannot see~~
~~life of me I cannot any of the others that~~

~~any other~~ — I do not much think she is
~~you fancy. No. I am sure there is no likeness~~

like
~~between her, &~~ any of the Family but Miss

Watson; but I am very sure there is no re:

:semblance between her & Sam." —

This matter was settled, & they went to Dinner. —

"Your Father, Miss Emma, is one of my oldest

friends — said M[r] Edwardes, as he ~~poured~~ helped

drawn round the fire
her to wine, when they were ~~set in for their~~

to enjoy their to
Desert, — We must drink his better health. —
^ ^

It is a great concern to me I assure you that

he should be such an Invalid. — I know no:

:body who likes a game of cards in a social

does; very
way, better than he ~~is~~; — & few people that play
^

a ~~better~~ fairer rubber. — It is a thousand pities

* 'ly' in 'strongly' written over 'one'. † 'the' written over 'any'.

that he should be so deprived of the pleasure.

For* now
We have a quiet little Whist club that meets
^
three times a week at the White Hart, & if he

how much he
c^{d}. but have his health, ~~I think he~~ w^{d}. enjoy

it." ~~very much~~. "I dare say he would Sir — & I

wish with all my heart he were equal to it."

"Your Club w^{d}. be better fitted for an Invalid, said

M^{rs}. E. if you did not keep it up so late." — This

[Booklet] 3

[f.11r] was an old greivance. — "So late, my dear, what

are you talking of; cried the Husband with sturdy

pleasantry — . We are always at home before

midnight. They would laugh at Osborne Castle

to hear you call <u>that</u> late; they are but just

rising from dinner at midnight." — "That is

calmly
nothing to the purpose. — retorted the Lady ~~gravely~~.
^
The Osbornes are to be no rule for us.

better two
You had meet every night, & break up ~~your~~
^
hours sooner."

* 'For' written over 'now'.

~~party at ten, than~~ so far, the subject was very

so
often carried; — but Mr. & Mrs. Edwards were ^ wise

as
~~enough~~ never to pass that point; & Mr. Edwards

now
turned to something else., — He* had lived ~~long~~
^

enough
~~sufficiently~~ long ^ in the Idleness of a Town to

having
become a little of a Gossip, & ~~he had~~ some

~~the~~
curiosity to know more of the ~~marriage of that~~

Circumstances of
~~Aunt with whom~~ his young Guest ~~had been used~~
^

began
~~to reside~~, than had yet reached him, he ~~ob:~~

with
~~:served to her~~, "I think Miss Emma, I remem:

very well I am
:ber your Aunt ^ about 30 years ago; ~~one of the~~

in the old
pretty sure I danced with her ~~at Wiltshire's~~

rooms at Bath, the year before I married — .

* 'He' written over 'th'.

She was a very fine woman then — but like

other people I suppose she is grown somewhat

older since that time. — I hope she is likely

to be happy in her second choice."

[f.11v] "I hope so, I beleive so, Sir — said Emma in some

"M^{r}. Turner had not been dead a great while I think?

agitation." — ~~M^{r}. "Her name was Turner~~ —

"About 2 years Sir." "I forget what her name is now?"

~~I forget what it is now~~. — "O'brien." "Irish!

Ah! I remember — & she is gone to settle in Ire:

:land. — I do not wonder that you should not wish

to go with her into <u>that</u> Country Miss Emma — .

but it must be a great deprivation to her,

poor Lady! — After bringing you up like a

Child of her own." — "I was not so ungrateful

Sir, said Emma warmly, as to wish to be any

where but with her. — It did not suit them,

it did not suit Capt. O'brien that I sh^{d}. be

of the party." — "Captain! — repeated M^{rs}. E

~~drawing up~~ the Gentleman is in the army then"?

"Yes Ma'am." — "Aye — there is nothing like

your officers for captivating the Ladies,

Young or old. — There is no resisting a Cockade

my dear." — "I hope there is." — said Mrs. E.

gravely,
with a quick glance at her daughter; — and
^

had just
Emma ^ recovered from her own perturbation

~~just~~ in time to see a blush on Miss E.'s

in
cheek, & ~~to~~ remembering* what Elizabeth had

said of Capt. Hunter, to wonder & waver

between his influence & her brother's. —

"Elderly Ladies should be careful how they make

[f.12r] choice.
a second ~~match~~." observed Mr. Edwardes.—

Carefulness — Discretion —
"~~The Caution~~ ^ should not be confined to Elderly
choice, ~~marriage~~
Ladies, or to a second ~~connection~~ added his wife.

It is quite as necessary to young Ladies in their

replied he
first ~~choice~~." — "Rather more so, my dear — ^

because young Ladies are likely to feel the

effects of it longer. When an old Lady plays

the fool, it is not in the course of nature

that she should suffer from it many years."

* 'ing' added at the end of 'remember'.

Emma drew her hand across her eyes — &

M^{rs}: Edwards on perceiving it, changed the

subject to one of less anxiety to all. —

With nothing to do but to expect the hour

of setting off, the afternoon was long to the

two young Ladies; & tho' Miss Edwards was

rather discomposed at the very early hour

which her mother always fixed for going,

that early hour itself was watched for with

some eagerness. — The entrance of the Tea things

at 7 o'clock was some releif — & luckily M^{r}:

& M^{rs}: Edwards always drank a dish ex:

:traordinary, & ate an additional muffin

when they were ~~to~~ going to sit up late, which

wished for

lengthened the ceremony ~~to~~ almost to the ~~desirable~~

moment. At a little before 8, the Tomlinsons

[f.12v] carriage was heard to go by, which was the

to

constant signal for M^{rs}: Edwards ^ order~~ing~~ hers

to the door; & in a very few minutes, the party

were transported from the quiet ~~&~~ warmth of

a snug parlour, to the bustle, noise & draughts

of air of the broad Entrance-passage of an Inn. —

Mrs Edwards carefully guarding her own dress,

while she attended with
~~& watching over the~~ yet greater solicitude to

the proper security of her young Charges' shoulders

& Throats, led the way up the wide staircase,

while no sound of a Ball but the first, ~~tuning~~

Scrape of one violin, blessed the ears of her fol:

:lowers, & Miss Edwards on hazarding the

anxious enquiry of whether there were many

~~yet~~ yet ~~as she knew she should~~
people ^ come ^ was ~~only~~ told, by the Waiter
as she knew she should,
that Mr Tomlinson's family were in the room."

In passing along a short gallery to the As:

in ~~Candle~~-lights
:sembly-room, brilliant ^ before them ~~with~~

~~Candles,~~ They were accosted by a young

a morning dress &
Man in ^ Boots, who was standing in the

apparently
doorway of a Bedchamber, ~~seemingly~~ on

purpose to see them go by. — "Ah! M^{rs} E —

how do you do ? — How do you do Miss E. ? —
he cried, with an

[f.13r] easy ~~familiarity~~ air; — You are determined to

The candles

be in good time I see, as usual. — ~~We shall~~

are but this moment lit — "~~& I am waiting~~
~~have an a famous Ball.~~ — ~~The Osbornes are~~

"I like to get a good seat ~~assure you of~~ by the
~~certainly coming, I can answer for that; I~~

fire you know, M^{r}. Musgrave". replied M^{rs}. E.
~~was with L^{d}. Osborne this morn^{g}.~~ —

"I am this moment going to dress, said he —

I am waiting for my stupid fellow. — We

shall have a famous Ball, The Osbornes are

certainly coming; you may depend upon <u>that</u>

for I was with L^{d}. Osborne this morn^{g}. —"

The party passed on — M^{rs}. E's sattin gown swept

to the fire

along the clean floor of the Ball-room, ~~where~~

place at the upper end, where while
one party only were formally seated, ~~& a~~
∧

were together

three or four Officers lounging ~~about, &~~
∧

~~backwards & forwards~~

passing in & out from the adjoining card-

room. — A very stiff meeting between these

near neighbours ensued — & as soon as they were

placed low
all duely ~~seated~~ again, Emma in the ~~quiet~~
^ ^
whisper which became the solemn scene,

~~observed~~
said
~~said~~ to Miss Edwardes, "The gentleman we
^

then.
passed in the passage, was Mr Musgrave, ~~was~~

~~it?~~ — He is reckoned remarkably agreable I un:

:derstand. — " Miss E. answered hesitatingly — "Yes —

— he is very much liked by many people. — But we

are not very intimate." — "He is rich, is not he?" —

[f.13v] "He has about 8 or 900£ a year I beleive. — He

came into possession of it, when he was very young,

& my Father & Mother think it has given him

rather an unsettled turn. — He is no favourite with

appearance
them." — The cold & empty ~~air~~ of the Room &
^

demure
the ~~solemn~~ air at one end of it
^
~~began soon to~~ of the small cluster of Females
^

soon
began ~~now~~ to give ~~a~~way; the inspiriting sound
^
of other Carriages was heard, & continual accessions

of portly Chaperons, & strings of smartly-dressed

~~giggling~~

girls were received, with now & then a fresh,
^

Gentleman Straggler,

~~straggling Man,~~ who if not enough in Love

~~creature~~

~~with any fair She~~, to station himself near any,
^ ^

fair Creature

seemed glad to escape into the Card-room. —
^

Among the increasing numbers of Military

Men, one now made his way to Miss Edwards,

with an air of Empressément, which decidedly

said to her Companion "I am Capt. Hunter." —

& Emma, who could not but watch her at

rather distressed, but

such a moment, saw her looking ~~rather shy~~

by no* means

~~than~~ displeased, & heard an engagement formed
^

for the two first dances, which made her think

~~poorly~~ Sam's a hopeless

~~ill of~~ her Brother~~'s chances~~ case. —
^ ^

Emma in the mean while was not unob:

:served, or unadmired herself. — A new face

* 'by no' written over 'but not'.

& a very pretty one, could not be slighted —

[f.14r] party
her name was whispered from one ^ to another,
& no sooner had the signal been given ~~for be:~~
~~:ginning~~, by the Orchestra's striking up a fa:
which seemed to call the young men to
:vourite air, ~~& the young to put all the young~~
their duty, & people the centre of the room,
~~people in motion~~, ^ than she found herself en:
:gaged to dance with a Brother officer, introduced
by Capt. Hunter. — Emma Watson was not
more than of the middle* height — well made
& plump, with an air of healthy vigour. — Her
skin was very brown, but clear, smooth and
which with
glowing — ; ~~and she had~~ a lively Eye,
~~brightened with a fine colour~~ a sweet smile,
gave
& an open Countenance, ~~she had~~ beauty to
that beauty
attract, & expression to ~~engage~~ make ~~it seem~~
improve
~~greater~~ ^ on acquaintance. — Having no reason

Even^{g}.

* 'ing' deleted at the end of 'middle'.

to be dissatisfied with her partner, the ~~Ball~~
began very pleasantly to her; & her feelings
perfectly coincided with the re-iterated ob:
:servation of others, that it was an excellent
not quite
Ball. — The two first dances were ~~nearly~~
over, when the returning sound of Carriages
after a long interruption, called general
notice, & "the Osbornes are coming, the
Osbornes are coming" — was repeated round
the room. — After some minutes of extraor:
:dinary bustle without, & watchful curiosity
[f.14v] within, the important Party, preceded by the
attentive Master of the Inn to open a door which
was never shut, made their appearance. They
consisted of Ly. Osborne, her son L[d]. Osborne, her
daughter Miss Osborne; Miss Carr, her daughter's
friend, M[r]. Howard formerly Tutor to L[d]. Osborne,
now Clergyman of the Parish in which the Castle
a
stood, M[rs]. Blake, ~~his~~ widow-sister who lived
^
with him, her son a fine boy of 10 years old,
& M[r] Tom Musgrave; who ~~had~~ probably

imprisoned within his own room, had

been listening in bitter impatience to the
^
sound of the Music, for the last half hour.

In their progress up the room, they paused

almost immediately behind Emma, to receive

the Compt^s. of some acquaintance, & she heard

had made a

Ly. Osborne observe that they ~~were xxxxx~~*
^
point of coming early for the gratification

of M^rs. Blake's little boy, who was uncommonly

fond of dancing. — Emma looked at them all

chiefly

as they passed — but ~~her eyes~~ & with most interest
^
on Tom Musgrave, who was certainly a genteel,

good looking young man. — Of the females, Ly.

had by

Osborne ~~was the~~ much the finest person; — tho'

all

nearly 50, she was very handsome, & had ~~quite~~
^
Dignity

the ~~air of a Woman~~ of Rank. —

[Booklet] 4

[f.15r] L^d. Osborne was a very fine young man;

* illegible.

Coldness, of
but there was an air of, ^ Carelessness, even of

Awkwardness about him, which seemed to

speak him out of his Element in a Ball room.

He came in fact only because it was judged

for him Borough
expedient ^ to please the ~~Town~~ ^ — he was not

he
fond of Women's company, & ^ never danced. —

M[r]. Howard was an* ~~very~~ agreable-looking

a
Man, ^ little more than Thirty. —

At the conclusion of the two Dances, Emma found

herself, she knew not how, seated amongst the

Osborne Set; & she was immediately struck

with the fine Countenance & animated ges:

:tures of the little boy, as he was standing

before his Mother, wondering when they

be surprised
should begin. — "You will not ~~wonder~~ ^ at

Charles's impatience, said M[rs]. Blake, a

lively pleasant-looking little Woman of 5 or

her
6 & 30, to a Lady who was standing near, ^

* 'n' added after 'a' in 'an'.

when you know what a partner he is

to have. Miss Osborne has been so very

kind as to promise to dance the two 1st

dances with him." — "Oh! yes — we have been

[f.15v] engaged this week. cried the boy. & we are

to dance down every couple." — On the other side

of Emma, Miss Osborne, Miss Carr, & a party

engaged lively

of young Men were standing ^ in very ~~fluent~~ ^

soon afterwards

consultation — & ~~after a short time~~ ^ she saw

the smartest officer of the Sett, walking off

to the Orchestra to order the dance, while

Miss Osborne passing before her, to her

little expecting Partner hastily said — "Charles,

I beg your pardon for not keeping my engagement,

~~to you~~, but I am going to dance these two dances

with Col^{n}. Beresford. I know you will excuse me,

& I will certainly dance with you after Tea."

she

And without staying for an answer, ^ turned

again to Miss Carr, & in another minute was

begin the Set.

led by Col. Beresford to ~~the top of the room~~ ^.

in it's happiness
If the poor little boy's face had been interesting
^
~~in it's happiness~~ to Emma, it was infinitely more

under
so ~~in~~ this sudden reverse; — he stood the picture
^
of disappointment, with crimson'd cheeks, quivering
lips, & eyes bent on the floor. His mother, stifling

mortification
her own ~~angry feelings~~, tried to sooth his, with
^
the prospect of Miss Osborne's second~~ary~~ promise;
[f.16r] but tho' he contrived to utter with an effort of
Boyish Bravery "Oh! I do not mind it" — it was very
evident by the unceasing agitation of his features
that he minded it as much as ever. — Emma
did not think, or reflect; — she felt & acted — .
"I shall be very happy to dance with you Sir, if

holding out her hand
you like it." said she, with the most unaffected
^
in one moment restored to
goodhumour. — The Boy ~~was again all xxxxx~~*

looked joyfully at his Mother
all his first delight — ~~wanted no farther solicitation~~;
And ~~instantly~~ stepping forward with an honest &
~~& with a Thank you, as honest as his smiles,~~

* illegible; possibly 'made as'.

Simple
Thank you M'aam was instantly ready
^ ~~held out his hand in a hurry to~~ to attend his

Thankfulness
new acquaintance. — The ~~gratitude~~ of Mrs. Blake

look, most expressive
was more diffuse; — with a ~~truly gratified look~~
^

&
of ~~astonishment~~ unexpected pleasure, ~~she of~~ lively
^

Gratitude
~~Thankfulness~~, she turned to her neighbour with
^

of
repeated & fervent acknowledgements ~~for~~ so great
^

& condescending a kindness to her boy. — Emma

could assure her
with ~~great~~ perfect truth ~~assured Mrs. B.~~ that she
^

could not be giving greater pleasure than she

felt herself — & Charles being provided with his

gloves & charged to keep them on, they joined

the Set which was now rapidly forming,

nearly
with ^ equal complacency. — It was a Partner:

:ship which cd. not be noticed without surprise.

It gained her a broad stare from Miss Osborne & Miss

[f.16v] Carr as they passed her in the dance. "Upon my

word Charles you are in luck, (said the former as
she turned him,) you have got a better partner
the happy
than me — " to which ^ Charles answered "Yes." —
Tom Musgrave who was dancing with Miss
inquisitive
Carr, gave her, ~~she perceived~~, many ^ glances; &
after a time under pretence of talking
Ld Osborne himself came & ~~spoke to her partner~~
^
to Charles, stood to look~~ing~~[*] at his partner. —
~~for the sake of looking at her~~. — Tho' rather
distressed by such observation, Emma could not
repent what she had done, so happy had it made
both the boy & his Mother; the latter of whom
continually making
was ~~continually taking every~~ opportunity[†] of
~~more than civilly, of warmly~~ addressing her
with the warmest civility. — Her little partner she
found, tho' bent cheifly on dancing, was not
unwilling to speak, when her questions or re:
:marks gave him any thing to say; & she
learnt, by a sort of inevitable enquiry that

[*] 'to' inserted in space between 'stood' and 'look~~ing~~'.
[†] 'y' written over 'ies' at the end of 'opportunity'.

& their Mama
he had two brothers & a sister, that they ^ all lived

with his Uncle at Wickstead, that his Uncle

taught him Latin, that he was very fond of

riding, & had a horse of his own given him by

& already
L^{d}: Osborne; ^ that he had been out once ^ with

[f.17r] L^{d}: Osborne's Hounds." — At the end of these Dances

Emma found they were to drink tea; — Miss E.

gave her a caution to be at hand, in a manner

which convinced her of M^{rs}: E.'s holding it very

~~veiw~~
important to have them both ~~within a yard~~

close to her
~~of her~~ ^ when she moved into the Tearoom;

& Emma was accordingly on the alert to gain

her always
~~the~~ ^ proper station. It was ^ the pleasure of the

company ~~always~~ to have a little bustle &

refresh:
croud when they thus adjourned for ~~what~~

The Tea room was a small room within the Card room,
:ment; — & in passing thro' the ~~Cardroom where~~
~~nine out of ten had no inclination~~

latter, where

the passage was straightened by Tables, M^{rs}. E.
^

hemmed

& her party were for a few moments ~~unable to~~

in   It happened

~~proceed~~. ~~Emma saw herself~~ close by Lady Os:
^

M^{r}. Howard who belonged to it

:borne's Cassino Table; ~~& saw at the same time~~
^

spoke to his Nephew; & Emma on perceiving

herself the object of attention ~~to~~ both to Ly. O. & him,

~~that both Lady & Gentleman were~~ had just turned
^

to avoid seeming to hear

away her eyes in time, ~~when she heard~~ her young

companion   aloud

~~partner~~ delightedly whisper ~~in a very audible~~
^   ^

~~Mr. H~~.

~~voice to his Uncle~~ — "Oh! Uncle, do look at my
^

~~To her great releif~~

partner. She is so pretty!" As* They were imme:

however,   was hurried off ~~from~~

:diately in motion again ~~&~~ Charles ~~left his Uncle~~
^   ^

without being able to receive his Uncle's suf:

:frage. — On entering the Tea room, in which

[f.17v]   prepared

two long Tables were ~~set out~~, L^{d}. Osborne was
^

* 'As' written over '—'.

quite alone as if re:

to be seen ~~seated~~ at the end of one, ~~away from~~

=treating as far as he could from the

~~everybody else, as if to enjoy his own Thoughts~~.

Ball, to enjoy his own thoughts, & gape without

restraint. — Charles instantly pointed him out

to Emma — "There's Lord Osborne — ~~he cried~~ —

~~But To this~~

Let you & I go & sit by him. — ~~Emma could~~

said Emma laughing

"No, no, ^ you must sit with my

~~not quite agree to this, & Charles at any rate~~

~~party~~ friends." ~~easily overruled —~~

~~very happy, was contented to sit where she chose;~~

~~& when she soon afterwards~~

~~& she ^ saw L^{d}. Osborne so soon afterwards driven~~

~~a party, she did not~~

~~away by the approach of others, that she c^{d}.~~

~~xxxxx,~~* ~~that how very unwelcome~~

~~fail to remark~~† ~~that they should probably have~~

~~not imagine the ^ Companionableness of either~~

~~been very little welcome themselves were at all~~

~~Charles or herself would have given his Ld~~:

~~to his taste~~.

~~:ship much~~ Charles was now free enough to

* illegible. † 'remark' written over another word, possibly 'observe'.

hazard a few questions in his turn. "What o'clock
was it? — " ~~almost~~ "Eleven." — "Eleven! — And I am
not at all sleepy. Mama said I should be a:
:sleep before ten. — Do you think Miss Osborne
will keep her word with me, when Tea is over?"

she
"Oh! yes. — I suppose so." — tho' ~~Emma~~ felt that

no better reason to give than that
she had ~~nothing to guide her beleif, but~~ Miss

had not
Osborne's ~~having broken~~ kept it before. —
"When shall you come to Osborne Castle?" — "Never,
probably. — I am not acquainted with the family."
[f.18r] "But you may come to Wickstead & see Mama,
& she can take you to the Castle. — There is a
monstrous curious stuff'd Fox there, & a Badger —
any body would think they were alive. It is
a pity you should not see them." —

On rising from ~~the~~ Tea ~~Tables~~, there was again
a scramble for the pleasure of being first out

which happened to be one or two
of the room, ~~and it was~~ increased by ~~some~~ of the

just the players
Card parties having broken up & ~~their members~~

move
being disposed to ~~come~~ exactly the different
^
way. Among these was Mr. Howard — his Sister

were they within
leaning on his arm — & no sooner ~~had they met~~

reach of
~~them~~ Emma, than Mrs. B. calling her notice by
^
a friendly touch, said "Your goodness to Charles,

my dear
Miss Watson, brings all his family upon you.
^
Give me leave to introduce my Brother — Mr. H."

Emma curtsied, the gentleman bowed — made

a hasty request for the honour of her hand in

the two next dances, to which as hasty an af:

:firmative was given, & they were immediately

in opposite directions.
impelled ~~different ways~~. — Emma was very
^
well pleased with the circumstance; — there was

a quietly-chearful, gentlemanlike air in Mr. H.

suited her —
which ~~she liked greatly approved~~ — & in a few
^
minutes afterwards, the value of her Engagement

[f.18v] increased in the Card room
~~rose~~ when as she was sitting somewhat screened
^ ^
by a door, she heard Ld. Osborne, who was lounging

~~with Tom Musgrave~~ on a vacant Table near

Tom

her, ~~say~~ call ^ Musgrave towards him & say,

Why do not you that beautiful

"~~Musgrave, when~~ dance with ^ Emma Watson? —

her —

I want you to dance with ~~that girl —~~ & I will

come & stand by you." — ~~She is a beautiful crea:~~

on it

determining this

~~:ture~~." "I was ~~thinking of being~~ ^ very moment

I'll be introduced

~~to be introduced, to her~~ my Lord; ^ & dance with

her directly. — " "Aye do — & if you find she does

to,

not want much Talking ^ you may intro:

:duce me by & bye." — "Very well my Lord — .

If she is like her Sisters, she will only want to

be listened to. — I will go this moment. I

her

shall find ^ in the Tea room. That stiff old M^{rs}

E. has never done tea." — Away he went —

Ld Osborne after him — & Emma lost no

exactly

~~directly~~ the

time in hurrying from her corner, ~~into the~~
^
other way, forgetting in her haste that she
left Mrs. Edwardes behind. — "We had quite
lost you — said Mrs. E. — who followed her with
Mary, in less than five minutes. — If you
prefer this room to the other, there is no reason
why you should not be here, but we had
better all be together." Emma was saved
[Booklet] 5
[f.19r] the Trouble of apologizing, by their being
joined at the moment by Tom Musgrave, who
requesting Mrs. E. aloud to do him the honour
of presenting him to Miss Emma Watson, left
that good Lady without any choice in the busi:
:ness, but that of testifying by the coldness of her
manner that she did it unwillingly. The
honour of dancing with her, was solicited without
loss of time — & Emma, however she might
like to be thought a beautiful girl by Lord
or Commoner, was so little disposed to favour
Tom Musgrave himself, that she had consi:
:derable satisfaction in avowing her prior

Engagement. — He was evidently surprised & dis:
:composed. — The stile of her last partner had pro:
beleive
:bably led him to ~~suppose~~ ^ her not overpowered
with
~~by~~ ^ applications. — "My little friend Charles Blake,
he cried, must not expect to engross you the
whole evening. We can never suffer this —
It is against the rules of the Assembly — & I am
sure it will never be patronised by our good
she
friend here Mrs. E.; ~~who~~ is by much too
nice a judge of Decorum to give her
license to such a dangerous Particularity." —
[f.19v] "I am not going to dance with Master Blake Sir."
a little
The Gentleman ~~quite~~ ^ disconcerted, could only
hope he might be more fortunate another
time — & seeming unwilling to leave her, tho'
his friend Ld. Osborne was waiting in the Door=
=way for the result, as Emma ~~saw~~ with some
perceived, make civil
amusement — he ~~soon soon~~ began to ^ enquiries
after her family. — "How comes it, that we have

not the pleasure of seeing your Sisters here this
Evening? — Our Assemblies have been used to be
so well treated by them, that we do not know
this neglect.
how to take ~~their absence~~." — "My eldest Sister
∧
is the only one at home — & she could not leave
"Miss Watson the only
my Father — " ~~said Emma with civil~~ one at
∧
home! — You astonish me! — It seems but
the day before yesterday that I saw them
all three in this Town. But I am afraid I
have been a very sad neighbour of late. I
hear dreadful complaints of my negligence
& I confess
wherever I go, — It is a shameful length
∧
of time since I was at Stanton. — But
now endeavour to
~~I feel that~~ I shall ~~soon~~ make myself
∧
amends for the past." — Emma's calm curt:
:sey in reply ~~to all this gallantry~~ must have
[f.20r] struck him as very unlike the ~~gratitude of her~~
~~Sisters~~ encouraging warmth he had been used to
receive from her Sisters, & gave him probably the
novel sensation of doubting his own influence, & of

bestowed.
wishing for more attention than she ~~gave~~. —
^

being
The dancing now recommenced; Miss Carr ~~was~~
^

impatient to call, everybody was required to

stand up — & Tom Musgrave's curiosity was ap:

on seeing — Mr: come forward & claim
:peased, ~~by seeing~~ Howard ~~come to claim his~~
^

Emma's hand
~~partner.~~ — "That will do as well for me" — was

when his friend carried
Ld: Osborne's remark, ~~when answering his friend's~~

him the news —
~~communication~~; — & he was continually at Ho:

two
:ward's Elbow during the dances. — The frequency
^

of his appearance there, was the only unpleasant

part of her engagement, ~~to Emma~~, the only ob:

:jection she could make to Mr: Howard. — In

himself, she thought him as agreable as he

topics
looked; tho' chatting on the commonest ~~matt~~
^

sensible way
he had a~~n easy~~, unaffected, ~~& unpretending man~~:
^

:~~ner which~~ of expressing himself, which made

them all worth hearing, & she only regretted

that he had not been able to make his

pupil's Manners as unexceptionable as his

own. — The two dances seemed very short,

& she had her partner's authority for considering

[f.20v] them so. — At their conclusion the Osborne &

their Train
~~Party~~ were all on the move. "We are off
^

at last, said his Lordship to Tom ~~Musgrave~~ —

How much longer do <u>you</u> stay in this Heavenly

place? — till Sunrise?" — "No. faith! my Lord,

quite I assure you — ~~out~~
I have had ^ enough of it; ^ I shall not ^ ~~stay~~

shew myself
~~your party~~ here again when I have had the
^

Ly. her
honour of attending ~~Miss~~ Osborne to ~~the~~ Carriage.
^

I shall retreat* in as much secrecy as possible

corner of
the most remote ~~room in~~ the House,† where I shall
to ~~my own room, where I have ordered~~
^

order a Barrel of Oysters, & be famously snug."

"Let us see you soon at the Castle; & bring me

* 'ea' in 'retreat' written over other letters (illegible).
† 'House' written over another word (illegible).

she
word ~~if you can~~, how ~~Emma Watson~~ ^ looks
by daylight." — Emma & M^rs^. Blake parted
as old acquaintance, & Charles shook her by
at least
the hand & wished her "good bye" ^ a dozen times.
From Miss Osborne & Miss Carr she received
like
something ~~of~~ ^ a jirking curtsey as they passed
even
her; ^ Ly. Osborne gave her a look of com:
actually
:placency — & his Lordship ^ came back after
the others were out of the room, to "beg her
pardon", & look ~~fo~~ in the window seat behind
her for the* gloves which were visibly com:
[f.21r] :pressed ~~at the same moment~~ in his hand. —
As Tom Musgrave was seen no more, we
may suppose his plan to have succeeded, &
imagine him mortifying with his Barrel of
Oysters, in dreary solitude — or gladly assisting
Bar
the Landlady in her ~~little parlour~~ to make
fresh Negus for the ~~D~~ happy Dancers above.

* 'the' written over 'his'.

Emma could not help missing the party,

some respects
by whom she had been, tho' in ~~such various~~

unpleasantly,
~~ways so much~~ distinguished, & the two Dances
^
which followed & concluded the Ball, were

rather flat, in comparison with the others. —

M^r. E. having play'd with good luck, they were

some of the last in the room — "Here we are,

back again I declare — said Emma sorrowfully,

as she walked into the ~~Edwards's~~ Dining room,

where the Table was prepared, ~~for supper~~, & the neat

~~neat~~
~~where the Cloth was~~ Upper maid was lighting
^
the Candles — "My dear Miss Edwards — how

at an end!
soon it is ~~over~~! — I wish it could all come
^
A great deal of kind pleasure was
over again! — " ~~They all~~ expressed ~~their pleasure~~
^
in her having enjoyed the Even^g. so much —

as warm as herself,
& M^r. Edwards was ~~particularly earnest in praising~~

in praise of the fullness, brilliancy
~~the excellence of the meeting~~ & spirit of the
^ ^
meeting

[f.21v] tho' as he had been fixed the whole time at

the same
~~one~~ Table in the same Room, with only one
^
change of Chairs, it might have seemed a matter

scarcely perceived.
~~of little concern~~ ~~known to him~~. — But he had
^

4
won ~~5~~ rubbers out of 5, & every thing went well.
^
His daughter felt the advantage of this gratified

state of mind, in the course of the remarks &

retrospections which now ensued, over the wel=

=come Soup. — "How came you not to dance with

either of the Mr. Tomlinsons, Mary? — said her Mother.

"I was always engaged when they asked me."
"I thought you were to have stood up with Mr..

James, the two last dances; Mrs. Tomlinson

I
told me he was gone to ask you — & ~~you~~ had
^
heard you say
~~told me~~ two minutes before that you were not
^
engaged. — " "Yes — but — there was a mistake —

I had misunderstood — I did not know I was

— I thought it had been for the
engaged, ~~till Capt. Hunter assured me~~ 2 Dances
^

after, if we staid so long — but Capt. Hunter

assured me it was for those very Two. — " —

"So, you ended with Capt. Hunter Mary, did you?

said her Father. And who did you begin with"?

was repeated, in a very humble tone —
"Capt. Hunter." "Hum! — That is being constant

however. But who else did you dance with?"

"Mr.. Norton, & Mr.. Styles." "And who are they?"

a cousin "And who is
"Mr Norton is ~~friend~~ of Capt. Hunter's". — ~~&~~ Mr.. Styles?
^

[f.22r] ~~is~~ "One* of his particular friends." — "All in the

same Rgt added Mrs E. — Mary was surround:

:ed by Red coats the whole Eveng. I should have

been better pleased to see her dancing with some

of our old Neighbours I confess. — " "Yes, yes,

we must not neglect our old Neighbours — . But

if these Soldiers are quicker than other people in

a Ball room, what are young Ladies to do?"

their engaging themselves
"I think there is no occasion for ~~Engagements~~
^

so many Dances beforehand, Mr.. Edwards." —

"No — perhaps not — but I remember my dear

* 'O' written over 'o' in 'One'.

when you & I did the same." — M^{rs}. E. said

no more, & Mary breathed again. — A great deal

of goodhumoured pleasantry followed — & Emma

went to bed in charming spirits, her head full

of Osbornes, Blakes & Howards. —

The next morn^{g}. brought a great many visi:

way of the
:tors. It was the place always to call on M^{rs}. E.
∧

on
the morn^{g}. after a Ball, & this neighbourly
∧

~~now~~ in the present instance
inclination was increased by a general spirit
∧

on Emma's account, as
of curiosity ~~to see the girl who~~ Everybody
∧

wanted to look again at the girl who had been

admired the night before by L^{d}. Osborne — .

Many were the eyes, & various the degrees of

approbation with which she was examined.

[f.22v] Some saw no fault, & some no Beauty — . With

some her brown skin was the annihilation of

grace, & others could
every~~thing good looking wh~~ never be persuaded

that she were half so handsome as Eliz: Watson

had been ten years ago. — The morn^{g}. passed quiet:

:ly away in discussing the merits of the Ball with

all this* succession of Company — & Emma was

by finding & considering
at once astonished ~~to find~~ it Two o'clock, ~~and~~
^ ^

that she had heard
~~no Chair come for~~ nothing of her Father's Chair.

After this discovery she had walked twice examine
~~Twice had she walked~~ to the window to ~~look for~~
^

the street, &
~~it~~ — ~~& she~~ was on the point of asking leave to
^

ring the bell & make enquiries, when the

light sound of a Carriage driving up to the

door set her heart at ease. She stepd again to

the window — but instead of the convenient tho'†

~~too long~~
Family Equipage perceived
very un-smart ~~conveyance she expected~~ a neat
^

was
Curricle. — ~~In two minutes~~ Mr. Musgrave ~~entered~~
^

shortly afterwards
~~the room~~ announced; — & Mrs. Edwards put on

her very stiffest look
~~a stiffer look than usual~~ at the sound. — Not
^

however
at all dismayed by her chilling air, ~~however~~
^

* 'is' written over 'e' in 'this'. † 'tho'' written over 'but'.

he paid* his Comp:ts. to each of the Ladies with

no unbecoming Ease, & continuing to address

Emma, presented her a note, which he had "the

to

honour of bringing from her Sister; But ^ which he

observe ~~xxxx~~† that a verbal postscript

must ~~(added, will not comment~~ from himself
^
wd. be requisite." —

[Booklet] 6

[f.23r] The note, which Emma was beginning to read

rather <u>before</u> M:rs Edwards had entreated her

to use no

~~not to stand on any~~ ceremony, contained a few
^

lines from Eliz: importing that their Father

in consequence of being unusually well had taken

the sudden resolution of attending the visitation

his Road lay quite wide from

that day, & that as ~~he had therefore tak different~~
^

R. come

~~way,~~ it was impossible for her to ~~be fetched~~ home
^

till the following morng., unless the Edwardses

w:d send her which was hardly to be expected, or

* 'paid' written over another word, possibly 'found'.

† 'observe' written over another word (illegible); another short word (illegible) crossed out after it.

she c^{d} meet with any chance conveyance, or
did not mind walking so far. — She had scarcely
run her eye thro' the whole, before she found her:
:self obliged to listen to Tom Musgrave's farther
account. "I received that note from the fair
hands of Miss Watson only ten minutes ago,
said he — I met her in the village of Stanton,
whither my good Stars prompted me to turn
at that moment
my Horses heads — she was ^ in quest of a
Errand
person to employ on the ~~Embassy,~~ ^ & I was
fortunate enough to convince her that she
could not find a more willing or speedy
Messenger than myself — . Remember, I say
nothing of my Disinterestedness. — My reward
[f.23v] is to be the indulgence of conveying you to
Stanton in my Curricle. — Tho' they are not
bring
written down, I ~~have~~ ^ your Sister's orders for
the same. — " Emma felt distressed; she
did not like the proposal — she did not wish
terms
to be on ~~any degree~~ of intimacy with the Pro:

fearful of encroaching on the
:poser — & yet ~~without assistance from the~~
^
as well as wishing to go home
Edwardes', ~~she could not avoid going home~~ her:
^
:self, she was at a loss how entirely to decline
what he offered — . M^{rs}. E. continued silent,
either not understanding the case, or waiting
to see how the young Lady's inclination lay.
Emma thanked him — but professed herself
very unwilling to give him so much trouble.
"The Trouble was of course, Honour, Pleasure,
Delight. What had he or his Horses to do?" —
Still she hesitated. "She beleived she must beg
leave to decline his assistance — She was rather
~~fearful~~ afraid of the sort of carriage — . The
distance was not beyond a walk. — " — M^{rs}. E.
was silent no longer. She enquired into the
particulars — & then said "We shall be extremely
happy Miss Emma, if you can give us the
[f.24r] pleasure of your company till tomorrow — but
if so
you can not conveniently do ~~it~~, our Carriage
^
is quite at your Service, & Mary will be pleased

with the opportunity of seeing your Sister." —

longed
This was precisely what Emma had ~~wished~~

most
& she accepted the offer ~~very~~ thankfully;
for, ~~but without at all expecting~~ —

acknowledging that as Eliz: was entirely alone
~~Eliz. being quite alone~~, it was her wish to
^
return home to dinner. — The plan was

warmly opposed by their visitor. "I cannot

suffer it indeed. I must not be deprived of

the happiness of escorting you. I assure you

there is not a possibility of fear with my

Horses. You might guide them yourself.

<u>Your Sisters</u> all know how quiet they are;

none of them the smallest
They have ~~no~~ scruple in trusting themselves
^
with me, even on a Race-Course. — Beleive

me — added he lowering his voice — <u>You</u> are quite

safe, the danger is only <u>mine</u>." — Emma

was not more disposed to oblige him for

all this. — "And as to M^rs. Edwardes' carriage

being used the day after a Ball, it is a thing

quite out of rule I assure you — never heard

of before — the old Coachman will look
as black as his Horses — . Won't he

[f.24v] Miss Edwards?" — No notice was taken. The
Ladies were silently firm, & the gentleman
found himself obliged to submit. —
"What a famous Ball we had last night! —
he cried, after a short pause. How long did
you keep it up, after the Osbornes & I went
away?" — "We had two dances more." —
"It is making it too much of a fatigue I
think, to stay so late. — I suppose your Set was
not a very full one." — "Yes, quite as full
as ever, except the Osbornes. There seemed no
vacancy anywhere —
~~room for anybody more~~ — & everybody danced
^
with uncommon spirit to the very last." —
Emma said this — against
~~said Emma~~ — tho' her conscience. — "Indeed!
^ ^
perhaps I might have looked in upon you a:
:gain, if I had been aware of as much; — for
I am rather fond of dancing than not. —
Miss Osborne is a charming girl, is not she?"
"I do not think her handsome." replied Emma,

to whom all this was cheifly addressed. "Perhaps
she is not critically handsome, but her Manners
Fanny
are delightful. And ~~Miss~~ Carr is a most inte:
:resting little creature. You can imagine
nothing more naive or piquante; & what
[f.25r] do you think of Ld. Osborne Miss Watson?"
That even, tho'
"He would be handsome ~~if~~ he were not a
^ ^
Lord — & perhaps — better bred; more desirous of
pleasing, & shewing himself pleased in a right
place. —" "Upon my word, you are severe
upon my friend! — I assure you Ld. Osborne
is a very good fellow." — "I do not dispute his
virtues — but I do not like his careless air." —
"If it were not a breach of confidence, replied
Tom with an important look, perhaps I might
be able to win a more favourable opinion
of poor Osborne. —" Emma gave him no En:
:couragement, & he was obliged to keep his
friend's secret. — He was also obliged to put
an end to his visit — for Mrs. Edwards' having
ordered her Carriage, there was no time to

be lost on Emma's side in preparing

for it. — Miss Edwards[*] accompanied

it was Dinner hour at

her home, but as ~~Eliz: was just sitting~~

Stanton

~~down to dinner~~, staid with them only a

few minutes. — "Now my dear Emma,

Miss W.

said ~~Eliz~~:, as soon as they were alone, you must

talk to me all the rest of the day, without stopping,

[f.25v] or I shall not be satisfied. But first of all Nanny

shall bring in the dinner. Poor thing! — You

will not dine as you did yesterday, for we

have nothing but some fried beef. — How nice

Mary Edwards looks in her new pelisse! — And

now tell me how you like them all, & what

I am to say to Sam. I have begun my Letter,

Jack Stokes is to call for it tomorrow, for his

Uncle is going within a mile of Guilford the[†]

next day. — "

~~friday or Saturday~~ Nanny brought in the dinner;

~~soon sent away~~

[*] 'war' in 'Edwards' written over other letters (illegible).
[†] 'the' written over another word, possibly 'on'.

~~& was not detained to wait~~. — "We will wait upon

continued Eliz:
ourselves, & then we shall lose no time. — And
^

so, you would not come home with Tom Mus:

:grave?" — "No. You had said so much against

him that I could not wish either for the

the use of his
obligation, or the Intimacy which ~~his bringing~~

Carriage
~~me home~~ must have created — . I should not
^

even
have liked the appearance of it." — "You did
^

very right; tho' I wonder at your forbearance,

& I do not think I could have done it myself. —

He seemed so eager to fetch you, that I could

not say no, tho' it rather went against me to

be throwing you together, so well as I knew

[f.26r] his Tricks; — but I did long to see you, & it was

clever Besides —
a ~~nice~~ way of getting you home; ~~&~~ it wont
^ ^

do to be too nice. — Nobody could have thought

of the Edwards' letting you have their Coach, —

after the Horses being out so late. — But what

am I to say to Sam?" — "If you are guided by

me, you will not encourage him to think of

Miss Edwards. — The Father is decidedly against

him, the Mother shews him no favour, & I doubt

Mary

his having any interest with ~~her~~. She danced

twice with Capt. Hunter, & I think shews him

in general as much Encouragement as is con:

:sistent with her disposition, & the circumstances

she is placed in. — She once mentioned Sam, &

certainly with a little confusion — but that was

perhaps ~~solely~~* merely

~~most likely~~ oweing to the consciousness of his
^

come to

liking her, which may very probably have ~~reached~~

knowledge." yes

her — "Oh! dear! — she has heard enough of that
^ ^

Poor Sam! — ~~It very~~ He

from us all. ~~Yes, she knows well~~ is out of
^

luck as well as other people. — For the life of

me Emma, I cannot help feeling for those

that are cross'd in Love. — Well — now begin,

* 'solely' written over 'only', then struck through.

& give me an account of every thing as it
happened. — " Emma obeyed her — & Eliz: listened
[f.26v] with very little interruption till she heard of M^r^ H.
as a partner. — "Dance with Mr H. — Good Heavens!

Why —
You don't say so! — He is quite one of the great &
^
Grand ones; ~~is not he?~~ — Did not you find him very
high? — " "His manners are of a kind to give me
much more Ease & confidence than Tom Musgraves."
"Well — go on. I should have been frightened out
of my wits, to have had anything to do with

set."
the Osborne's — Emma concluded her narration. —
^
"And so, you really did not dance with Tom M.
at all? — But you must have liked him, you
must have been struck with him altogether." —
"I do not like him, Eliz: — . I allow his person
& air to be good — & that his manners to a certain
point — his address rather — is pleasing. — But I

On the contrary, he seems
see nothing else to admire in him. — ~~He is~~ very
^ ^
vain, very conceited, absurdly anxious for Distinc:

absolutely
:tion, & contemptible in some of the measures he
^

takes for becoming so. — There is a ridiculous:

:ness about him that entertains me — but his

company ~~emotion~~ other* agreable Emotion."
gives me no ~~other pleasure~~. —
^ ^ ^

"My dearest Emma! — You are like nobody else

It is well Margaret ~~w~~ is not by. —
in the world. — ~~Do not let Margaret hear suc~~h

You ~~that's all~~ — do not offend me tho' I hardly know
~~words; she would never forgive you~~
^

how to beleive you. But Marg^{t}. w^{d} never forgive
such words." ~~xxxxx~~†

[Booklet] 7

[f.27r] "I wish Marg^{t}. could have heard him profess

his ignorance of her being out of the Country; —

he declared it seemed only two days since he had

seen her. — " "Aye — that is just like him. &

yet this is the Man, she will fancy so desperately

in love with her. — He is no favourite of mine,

as you well know, Emma; — but you must

think him agreable. Can you lay your hand on

your heart, & say you do not?" — "Indeed I can.

Both Hands; &‡ spread to their widest extent. — "

* 'other' written over 'than'.
† word crossed out (illegible).
‡ '&' written over '—'.

"I should like to know the Man you <u>do</u> think
agreable." "His name is Howard." "Howard! Dear me.
I cannot think of <u>him</u>, but as playing cards with
Ly Osborne, & looking ~~very~~ proud. — I must own
                                                            can
however that it <u>is</u> a releif to me, to find you ~~are~~
speak as you do, of
~~not infatuated by~~ Tom Musgrave; ~~for~~ my
                    ^
          did misgive
heart ~~misgave~~ me that you would like him
            ^
too well. You talked so stoutly beforehand,
that I was sadly afraid your Brag would be
                                                  & that
punished. — I only hope it will last; — ~~But~~
   he will not come on
~~if he should come~~ to pay you much attention;
            ^   ^
it is a hard thing for a woman to stand against
the flattering ways of a Man, when he is bent
upon pleasing her. — " As their quietly-sociable
[f.27v] little meal concluded, Miss Watson could not
help observing how comfortably it had passed.
"It is so delightful to me, said she, to have Things
going on in peace & goodhumour. Nobody can
tell how much I hate quarrelling. Now, tho'

we have had nothing but fried beef, how

everybody

good it has all seemed. — I wish ~~poor Margt.~~

were

~~loved~~ as easily satisfied as you — but poor Margt.

is very snappish, & Penelope ~~say~~ owns she had

rather have Quarrelling going on, than nothing

at all." — Mr. Watson returned in the Evening,

not the worse for the exertion of the day, &

consequently pleased with what he had done,

& glad to talk of it, over his own Fireside. —

Emma had not foreseen any interest to herself

in the occurrences of a Visitation — but when

she heard Mr. Howard spoken of as the Preacher,

& as having given them an excellent Sermon,

she could not help listening with a quicker

Ear. — "I do not know when I have heard a

continued Mr. W.

Discourse more to my mind — or one better deli:

=vered. — He reads extremely well, with great

very

& in a~~n~~ impressive manner;

propriety & at the same time without any The:

own, I do not
:atrical grimace or violence. — I ~~have an abhor:~~
^
like ~~I cannot~~
~~:rence of~~ much action in the pulpit — ~~& of the~~
I do not like ~~endure~~ the

[f.28r] artificial
studied air & ^ inflexions of voice, which your
very popular & most admired Preachers generally
have. — A simple delivery is much better calcu:
:lated to inspire Devotion, & shews a much
better Taste. — M^r. H. read like a Scholar & a
gentleman." — "And what had you for dinner
Sir? —" said his eldest Daughter. — He related the
Dishes & told what he had ate himself. "Upon the
whole, he added, I have had a very comfortable
day; my old friends were quite surprised to see
me amongst them — & I must say that everybody
& seemed to feel
paid me great attention, ~~as an Invalid~~ for
^
me as an Invalid. — They would make me sit
near the fire, & as the partridges were pretty high,
D^r. Richards would have them sent away to
the other end of the Table, that they might
not offend M^r. Watson — which I thought very

kind of him. — But what pleased me as much

as anything was M^{r}. Howard's attention; —

There ~~are~~ is a pretty steep flight of steps up to

quite

the room we dine in — which do not agree

walked by me from the

with my gouty foot — & Mr Howard ~~would~~
^

bottom to the top, & would

make me take his arm. — It struck me as
^

[f.28v] very becoming in so young a Man, but I am

I never

sure I had no claim to expect it; for ~~excep~~t
^

saw him before in my Life. — By the bye,

he enquired after one of my Daughters, but

I do not know which. I suppose you know

among yourselves." —

---

at

On the 3^{d}. day after the Ball, as Nanny five
^

minutes before three, ~~the dinner hour at Stanton~~,

was beginning to bustle into the parlour with

she was suddenly

the Tray & the Knife-case, ~~two gentlemen on~~
^

called to
~~Horseback~~ the front door, by the sound of as
^
smart a rap as the end of a riding-whip c^{d}.

tho' charged by ~~pause of curiosity on~~
give — & ~~after a short exercise of wonder &~~
^
~~the part~~ Miss.W. to let nobody in, re:
~~Curiosity of the Miss Watsons, they were~~
^
:turned in half a minute, with a look of

awkward parlour
dismay, to hold the door open for L^{d}. Osborne
^ ^
& Tom Musgrave. — The Surprise of the young

Ladies may be imagined. No visitors would

a
have been welcome at such moment; but
^
as these —
such visitors ~~were~~ such a one as L^{d}. Osborne
^
at least, a nobleman & a stranger, was

really distressing. — He looked a little embar:

on
:rassed himself, — as, ~~after~~ being introduced by
^
his
[f.29r] easy, voluble friend, he muttered something

of doing himself the honour of waiting on

M^{r}. Watson. — Tho' Emma could not but take

the compliment of the visit to herself, she was

very far from enjoying it. She felt all the

inconsistency of such an acquaintance with

the very humble stile in which they were

& having
obligedto live; In ^ her Aunts' family ~~she had~~

was
been used to many of the Elegancies of Life, ~~&~~

~~she could not without some mortification~~
~~she had not quite philosophy enough to be~~
~~consider~~ fully sensible of all that must be open

to the ridicule of Richer people in her present

Of
home. — ~~From~~ ^ the pain of such feelings, Eliz:

knew very
~~was free~~ ^ little; — her simpler Mind, or juster

reason saved her from such mortification —

& tho' shrinking under a general sense
~~& she wished them away more from a sense~~

she
of Inferiority, ^ felt no ~~peculiar~~ particular
~~of Convenience than of Shame~~ ^ Shame. —

the Gentlemen
Mr. Watson, as ~~they~~ had already heard from

Nanny, was not well enough to be down

stairs; — ~~the gentlemen~~, With* much concern

* 'W' written over 'we'.

they
took their seats — Ld. Osborne near Emma,
^
& the convenient Mr. Musgrave in high
spirits at his own importance, on the other
side of the fireplace with Elizth. — He was at no
loss for words; — but when Ld. Osborne had hoped
not caught
that Emma had ~~taken no~~ cold at the Ball,
^
[f.29v] time
he had nothing more to say for some ~~minutes~~,
^
& could only gratify his Eye by occasional
fair
glances at his neighbour. — Emma was not
^
inclined to give herself much trouble for his
Entertainment — & after hard labour of mind,
remark
he produced the ~~question~~ of it's being a very
^
fine day, & followed it up with the question
of, "Have you been walking this morning?"
"No, my Lord. We thought it too dirty." "You
should wear half-boots." — After another pause,
"Nothing sets off a neat ancle more than a
looks
half-boot; nankin galoshed with black ~~have~~

well
~~a~~ very ~~good air~~. ∧ — Do not you like Half-boots?
"Yes — but unless they are so stout as to ~~lo~~ in:
are not fit for
:jure their beauty, they ~~have not advantage in~~ ∧
~~the deep dirt of~~ country walking. — " "Ladies
should ride in dirty weather. — Do you ride?"
"No my Lord." "I wonder every Lady does
not. ~~ride~~. — A woman never looks better
than on horseback. — " "But every woman
may not have the inclination, or the means."
"If they knew how much it became them, they
would all have the inclination — & I fancy
Miss Watson — when once they had the in:
:clination, the means w^{d} soon follow." —
[f.30ar] *"Your Lordship thinks we always have our own
way. — <u>That</u> is a point on which Ladies & Gentle^{n}
have long disagreed — But without pretending to
decide it, I may say that there are some circum:
:stances which even <u>Women</u> cannot controul. —
will my Lord,
Female Economy ~~may~~ ∧ do a great deal ∧ but it cannot

* beginning of section inserted from additional sheet in ms.

turn a small income into a large one." — L^{d}. Osborne

was silenced. Her manner had been neither sententious

its' mild

nor sarcastic, but there was a something in ~~what she~~

seriousness, as well as in the words themselves

~~said~~ which made his Lordship think; — and when he

^

a degree of considerate

addressed her again, it was with ^ ~~courteous~~ propriety, to:

:tally unlike the half-awkward, half-fearless stile

It was a new thing with him

of his former remarks. — ~~You have not been long in~~

to wish to please a woman; it was the first time that

~~this Country I understand. I hope you are pleased with~~

he had ever felt in

~~it~~ — ~~the delicate~~ what was due to a woman, ~~his equal~~

Emma's situation.

~~in Education~~, — But as he wanted neither Sense

nor a good disposition, he did not feel it without

effect.

~~resolving on the necessary effort~~ — "You have not been

in the tone of a Gentle^{n}.

long in this Country I understand, said he ^ I hope you

are pleased with it." — He was rewarded by a*

[f.30r] ~~I am to suppose~~

"~~You mean a compliment of course my Lord, said~~

^

* end of inserted section.

~~can~~ ~~define~~

~~Emma bowing, tho' I do not exactly understand it."~~

^ ^

~~Lord Osborne laughed rather awkwardly~~ — ~~& then said~~

~~"Upon my Soul, I am a bad one for Compliments.~~

~~I wish I knew more of the 'such things' matters~~ —

~~Nobody can be a worse hand at it than myself.~~" —

^

~~not~~

~~and after some minutes silence~~ — ~~added, "Can you~~

^

~~give me a lesson Miss Watson on the art of paying~~

~~Comp^{ts}~~ — ~~I should be very glad to learn." I want~~

~~A cold monosyllable & grave look from Emma~~

~~very much to know how to please the Ladies~~ —

~~repressed the growing~~

~~one Lady at least~~ ~~freedom of his manner.~~

^

~~He had too much sence, not to take the hint~~ —

~~& when he spoke again, it was with a degree~~

~~was not often at~~

~~of courteous propriety which he had never used~~

^

~~employing.~~

~~before the trouble of using~~. ~~He was rewarded~~

full

by a gracious answer, & a more liberal veiw

^

of her face than she had yet bestowed. ~~on him~~.

Unused to exert himself, & happy in contem:

then some
:plating her, he ^ sat in silence for ~~about five~~ ^
minutes longer, while Tom Musgrave was chatter:
=ing to Elizth., till they were interrupted by Nanny's
half
approach, who ~~putting~~ opening the door & putting
in her head, said "Please Ma'am, Master wants
to know why he be'nt to have his dinner." —

hitherto
The Gentlemen, who had ^ disregarded every
symptom, however positive, of the nearness of that
Meal, now jumped up with apologies, while
[f.30v] called ~~loudly~~ briskly
Elizth. ~~was calling~~ ^ after Nanny "to tell Betty
to take up the Fowls." — "I am sorry it happens
goodhumouredly
so — she added, turning ^ towards Musgrave — but
you
^ know what early hours we keep. — " Tom had
nothing to say for himself, he knew it very well,
& such honest simplicity, such shameless Truth
parting Compt^{s}.
rather bewildered him. — L^{d}. Osborne's ^ took some
his inclination ~~his rea:~~
time, ~~to pay his parting Compt^{s}. to Emma; the~~

for speech
~~:diness at words~~ seeming to increase with the
^
shortness of the term for indulgence. — He recom:

:mended Exercise in defiance of dirt — spoke

begged that his Sister
again in praise of Half-boots — ~~wanted her to~~
^
might be Emma
allow'd ~~his sister~~ to send ~~her~~ the name of her Shoe
^ ^

My Hounds
=maker — & concluded with saying, "~~I shall~~

will be hunting this Country next week — I be:

:leive they will throw off at Stanton Wood on

at 9 o'clock. — I mention this, in hopes of y[r]. being
Wednesday — ~~I hope you will be~~ drawn out
^ ^

~~Everybody allows~~
to see what's going on. — ~~Nobody can be in:~~

~~that there is not so fine a sight in the world~~
~~:different to the glorious sounds~~

~~a pack of Fox-~~
~~as a pack of Hounds in full cry. I am sure you~~

~~delighted~~
~~will be pleased to hear the first Burst~~ — ~~if we~~
^

~~but~~
~~can find there as I dare say we shall~~. — If the
^

pray do us the honour of giving us your good wishes
morning's tolerable, ~~do not be kept at home~~ —
in person."

[Booklet] 8

[f.31r] The Sisters looked on each other with astonish:

=ment, when their visitors had withdrawn.

"Here's an unaccountable Honour! cried Eliz:

at last. Who would have thought of Ld Osborne's

coming to Stanton. — ~~I wish he would give~~

~~my poor Father a Living, as he makes such a~~

~~to be sure~~

~~point of coming to see him. But Mr Howard~~

~~of that kind sort~~ ~~L^{d} O is~~

~~will have everything he has to give. He has~~
^ ^

~~very~~ He is very

~~a~~ handsome; ~~young man~~ — but Tom Musgrave
^

smartest & Man

looks all to nothing, the most fashionable ~~Man~~
^ ^

of the two. I am glad he did not say anything to

w^{d} had talk to such a

me; I ~~should~~ not have ~~liked~~ to ~~to have had~~
^

great man for the world.

~~to speak to him~~. Tom was very agreable, was
^

But him ask

not he? — Did you hear ~~leave her~~ where Miss
^ ^

Penelope & Miss Marg^{t}. were, when he first came

It

in? — ~~He~~ put me out of patience. — I am glad
^

Nanny had not laid the Cloth however, it w^{d}

— just
have looked so awkward; — ~~just~~ the Tray did
^
not signify. — " To say that Emma was not

flattered by Ld Osborne's visit, would be to as:

:sert a very unlikely thing, & describe a very

odd young Lady; but the gratification was

[f.31v] His coming ~~of~~ was a
~~was~~ by no means unalloyed; ~~for the~~ sort of no:

which ~~welcome~~ might please her vanity, but ~~e^{d}~~
:tice ~~though agreable to her vanity, was not soothing~~
^
~~not be welcome~~
did not ~~rather~~ suit
~~to her pride to~~ her pride, & she w^{d} rather have known
^
that he wished the visit without presuming to

make it, than have seen him at Stanton. —

feelings
Among other unsatisfactory ~~reflections~~ it ~~had~~ once
^
why
occurred to her to wonder ~~that~~ M^{r}. Howard had
^
not taken the same privilege of coming, &

accompanied his Lordship — but she was willing

to suppose that he had either known nothing

about it, or ~~that~~ had* declined any share in

* 'had' written over 'he'.

carried

a measure which ~~had~~ quite as much Imper:

in it's form Mr. W. was very far

:tinence as Good breeding. ~~in it.~~ — — . ~~When~~

from being delighted, when he — a little

~~Mr.Watson~~ heard what had passed; ~~he expressed~~

~~no~~ peevish under immediate pain, & illdisposed* to

replied —

be pleased, he only ~~said~~ — "Phoo! Phoo! — What occa:

Ld. O.'s coming. 14

:sion could there be for ~~it~~. I have lived here ~~twelve~~

years without being noticed by any of the family.

It

~~This~~ is some foolery of that idle fellow T. Musgrave.

I cannot return the visit. — I would not if I could."

And when T. Musgrave was met with again,

he was commissioned with a message of excuse

-sufficient

to Osborne Castle, on the too-~~reasonable~~ plea of

Mr. Watson's infirm~~ity~~ state of health. —

[f.32r] A week or ten days rolled quietly away ~~after~~

after this visit,

~~this visit, at Stanton Parsonage~~ before any

new bustle arose to interrupt even for half a

* 'ill' written over 'in' in 'illdisposed', with 'to' squashed in at the end of the line.

day, the tranquil & affectionate intercourse of the
mutual
two Sisters, whose ^ regard ~~for each other~~ was in:
of each other
:creasing with the intimate knowledge ^ which
such intercourse produced. — The first circum:
in
:stance to break ^ on this serenity, was the receipt
of a letter from Croydon to announce the speedy
return of Margaret, & a visit of two or three days
from M^{r}. & M^{rs}. Robert Watson who undertook
& wished to see their Sister Emma.
to bring her home ^ — It was an expectation to
fill the thoughts of the Sisters at ~~home~~ Stanton, &
busy ~~time~~ hours
to ~~employ~~ ^ the ~~Corporeal powers~~ ^ of one of them
at least — for as Jane had been a woman of
fortune, the preparations for her entertain:
:ment were considerable, & as Eliz: had at all
times more good will than method in her
she
guidance of the house, ^ could make no change
An absence of 14. years
without a Bustle. — ~~Emma had not heard~~
had made all her Brothers & Sisters

~~anything of Margaret to make~~ Strangers to

Emma, but in her expectation of Margaret

there was more than the awkwardness of such

heard

an alienation; she had ^ things which made

[f.32v] her dread her return; & the day which brought

the party to Stanton seemed to her the probable

almost

conclusion of ^ all that had been comfortable

in the house. — Robert Watson was an Attorney

at Croydon, in a good way of Business; ~~&~~

very well satisfied with himself for the

same, & for having married the only daughter

attorney

of the ~~man~~ ^ to whom he had been Clerk, with

a fortune of six thousand pounds. — M^{rs}. Robt.

was not less pleased with herself for having

had that six thousand pounds, & for being

now in possession of a very smart house in

Croydon, where she gave ~~as~~ genteel parties, &

wore fine Cloathes. — In her person there was

nothing remarkable; her manners were pert

& conceited. — Margaret was not without beauty;

she had a slight, pretty figure, & rather wanted
but the sharp & anxious
Countenance than good features; — ~~the~~ expression
^
made her beauty
of her face, ~~sharp & anxious~~ in general ~~hxx~~* little
^
long-absent
felt. — On meeting her Sister, as on every occa:
^
manner was all
:sion of shew, her ~~smiles were very~~ affection
^
& her voice all gentleness; continual smiles
being her constant
~~distinguished her~~
& a very slow articulation ~~were her constant~~
~~had~~ resource
~~were what she always recoursed to~~ when de:
^ ^
:termined on pleasing. —

[f.33r] She was now so "delighted to see dear, dear Emma"
she could hardly speak a word in a minute.
that ~~the words seemed likely never to end~~. —
^
"I am sure we shall be great friends" — she ob:
:served, with much sentiment, as they were sitting
together. — Emma scarcely knew how to answer
a proposition — . &
such ~~an observation~~; the manner in which it
^

* letters crossed out (illegible).

was spoken, she could not attempt to equal.

Mrs R. W. eyed her with much familiar curi:

:osity & Triumphant Compassion; — the loss

of the Aunt's fortune was uppermost in her

at the moment of

mind, ~~& in her husband's on meeting her~~

& she cd. not but feel how much better it

meeting; — ~~they had not been ten minutes toge:~~

^

was to be the daughter of a gentleman of ~~easy~~

~~:ther before the latter shewed that it was~~

property in Croydon, than the neice of an

threw herself away on

old woman who ~~gave all her money to~~ an

^

Captain

Irish ~~officer.~~ — Robert was carelessly kind, as

became a prosperous Man & a brother; more in:

Post-Boy

:tent on settling with the ~~Postboy Driver~~, in:

advance

:veighing against the Exorbitant ~~rise~~ in Posting,

^

& pondering over a doubtful halfcrown, than

on welcoming a Sister, who was no longer likely

to have any property for him to get the di:

:rection of. — "Your road through the village

is infamous, Eliz:; said he; worse than ever it was.

[f.33v] By Heaven! I would endite it if I lived near

Surveyor
you. Who is ~~Overseer~~ now?" — There was a little
^

neice
~~nephew~~ at Croydon, to be fondly enquired after

by the kind-hearted Elizabeth, who regretted very

her
much ~~his~~ not being of the party. — "You are

her
very good — replied ~~his~~ Mother — & I assure you

very Augusta
it went ^ hard with ~~John~~ ^ to have us come away

her say we were only
without ~~him~~. I was forced to ~~send him out a~~

going to Church & promise her
~~walking, & promise not~~ ^ to come back for ~~him~~

directly. — But you know it would not do, to

her her as
bring ~~him~~ without ~~his~~ maid, & I am ~~very~~ par:

as ever her
:ticular ^ in having ~~him~~ ^ properly attended to."

"Sweet little Darling! — cried Marg^t^. — It quite

her "Then
broke my heart to leave ~~him~~. — " ^ Why was

her
you in such a hurry to run away from ~~him~~"?

cried M^{rs}. R. — You are a sad shabby girl. — I have

been quarrelling with you all the way we came,

have not I? — Such ~~as~~ a visit as this, I never

heard of! — You know how glad we are to have

— if it be
any of you with us, for months together. —
^

&
I am sorry, ~~she added~~ (with a witty smile) we
^

have not been able to make
~~you have found~~ Croydon ~~so dis~~agreable this
^

Autumn." — "My dearest Jane — do not over=
=power

[f.34r] me with your Raillery. — You know what in:

Spare me, I entreat you —
:ducements I had to bring me home.* — ~~but~~ I am
^

no match for your arch sallies." — "Well, I only

beg you will not set your Neighbours against

the place. — Perhaps Emma may be tempted to go

back with us, & stay till Christmas, if you do'nt

put in your word." — Emma was greatly obliged.

"I assure you we have very good society at

Croydon. — I do not much attend the Balls, they

* '.' written over ','.

are rather too mixed, — but our parties are very se=

seven
=lect & good. — I had ~~nine~~ Tables last week in my
^
~~two~~ Drawingroom. — Are you fond of the Country?

How do you like Stanton?" — "Very much" — re:

:plied Emma, who thought a comprehensive

answer, most to the purpose. — She saw that

her Sister in law despised her immediately. — M^{rs}.

indeed home Emma
R. W. was wondering what sort of a ~~place she~~ c^{d}.
^ ^ ^
possibly
have been used to in Shropshire, & setting it down
^
as certain that the Aunt could never have had

six thousand pounds. — "How charming Emma

is! — " whispered Marg^{t}. to M^{rs}. Robert in her most

languishing tone. — Emma was quite distress'd

by such behaviour; — & she did not like it better

~~5 minutes afterwards~~ when she heard Marg^{t}. 5 minutes
afterwards say
~~on overhearing Marg^{t}. saying~~ to Eliz: in a sharp

accent
quick ~~tone~~, totally unlike the first — "Have you
^
[f.34v] to Chichester?
heard from Pen. ~~lately~~ since she went ~~away~~. —

I had a letter the other day. — I do'nt find she is
likely to make any thing of it. I fancy she'll
come back "Miss Penelope" as she went. — " —
Such, she feared would be Margaret's common voice,
when the novelty of her own appearance were
over; the tone of artificial Sensibility was not
recommended by the idea. — The Ladies were in:
:vited upstairs to prepare for dinner. "I hope
you will find things tolerably comfortable Jane" —
said Eliz.th as she opened the door of the spare-bed=
=chamber. — "My good Creature, replied Jane, use
no ceremony with me, I intreat you. I am one
of those who always take things as they find
them. I hope I can put up with a small apart:
:ment for two or three nights, without making
a peice of work. I always wish to be treated
now
quite "en famille" when I come to see you — &
^
I do hope you have not been getting a great
dinner for us. — Remember we never eat
rather quickly
Suppers." — "I suppose, said Marg.^{t} to Emma,
^
You & I are to be together; Eliz.th always

takes care to have a room to herself." —

"No — Eliz.th gives me half her's." — "Oh! —

(in a soften'd voice, & rather mortified to find
that she was not ill used)

[Booklet] 9

[f.35r] "I am sorry I am not to have the pleasure

of your company — especially as it makes me

nervous to be much alone." —

Emma was the first of the females in the

on entering it
parlour again; ^ she found her brother ~~there~~

alone. — "So Emma, said he, you are quite

the Stranger at home. It must seem odd enough

to you to be here. — A pretty peice of work your

Aunt Turner has made of it! — By Heaven!

a woman should never be trusted with money.

said
I always ~~thought~~ ^ she ought to have settled

as soon as her Husband died."
something on you, ~~when she took you away.~~ ^"

"But that would have been trusting <u>me</u> with

money, replied Emma ~~smiling~~, & <u>I</u> am a wo:

~~placed~~
:man too. — " "It might have been ^ secured to

your* ~~after~~ future use, ~~in Trust~~, without your

having any power over it now. — What a blow

it must have been upon you! — To find yourself,

~~probable~~

instead of ~~being~~ Heiress of 8 or 9000£, sent back
^

a weight upon your family, without a six:

:pence. — I hope the old woman will smart for it."

"Do her —

"~~I beg you~~ not ~~to~~ speak disrespectfully of ~~my~~
^

~~Aunt, Brother~~ She was very good to me; &† If

she has made an imprudent choice, she will

suffer more from it herself, than I can possibly do."

[f.35v] "I do not mean to distress you, but you know

every body must think her an old fool. —

[f.35ar]) ‡I thought Turner had been reckoned an extra=

=ordinary sensible, clever Man. — How the Devil

came he to ~~leave~~ make such a will?" — "My

Uncle's Sense is not at all impeached in my o:

:pinion, by his attachment to my Aunt. She

had been an excellent wife to him. The most

Liberal & enlightened minds are always the most

* 'r' added to 'you' in 'your'.
† '&' written over '—'.
‡ beginning of section inserted from additional sheet in ms.

confiding. — The event has been unfortunate,

if possible
~~for me,~~ but my Uncle's memory is endeared to
^

me by such a proof of tender respect for my

Aunt." — "That's odd sort of Talking! — He

might have provided decently for his widow,

every thing that he had to dispose of, or any part of it
without leaving ~~it all~~ at her mercy." — "My
^

Aunt may have erred — said Emma warmly —

she <u>has</u> erred — but my Uncle's conduct was

faultless. I was her own Neice, & he left to

self
her the power & the pleasure of providing for
^

me." — "But unluckily she has left the pleasure

&
of providing for you, to your Father without
^

the power. — That's the long & the short of the

business. After keeping you at a distance from

such a
your family for ~~14 years~~ length of time as must
^

among us
do away all natural affection & breeding you
^

up (I suppose) in a superior stile, you are

returned upon their hands without a sixpence."

"You know, replied Emma struggling with her
tears, my Uncle's melancholy state of health. —
He was a greater Invalid than my father. He c^{d}.
not leave home." "I do not mean to make you cry. —
said Robt. rather softened — & after a short silence,
by way of changing the subject, he added —*
[f.35v contd.] — "I am just come from my Father's room, he
seems very indifferent. It will be a sad break-
-up when he dies. Pity, you can none of you
get married! — You must come to Croydon as
well as the rest, & see what you can do there. —
I beleive if Marg^{t}. had had a thousand or fifteen

man

hundred pounds, there was a young ^ who w^{d}. have
thought of her." Emma was glad when they were
joined by the others; it was better to look at her

Robert, who

Sister in law's finery, than listen to ~~her brother~~ ^ — .
had equally ~~mortified~~ irritated & greived her. —
M^{rs}. Robert exactly as smart as she had been at
her own party, came in with apologies for her
dress — "I would not make you wait, said she,

* end of inserted section.

so I put on the first thing I met with. — I am
afraid I am a sad figure. — My dear Mr. W. — (to her
husband) you have not put any fresh powder
in your hair." — "No — I do not intend it. — I think
there is powder enough in my hair for my wife
& Sisters." — "Indeed you ought to make some
alteration in your dress before dinner when
tho'
you are out visitting, ~~if~~ you do not at home."
"Nonsense. — " "It is very odd you should not like
to do what other gentlemen ~~too~~ do. Mr. Marshall &
[f.36r] Mr. Hemmings change their dress every day of their
Lives before dinner. And what was the use of my
putting up your last new Coat, if you are never
to ~~pu~~ wear it." — "Do be satisfied with being fine
yourself, & leave your husband alone." — To put an
end to this altercation, & soften the evident vexation
(tho' in no Spirits to make such nonsense easy)
of her Sister in law, Emma, ^ began to admire her
gown. — It produced immediate complacency. —
"Do you like it? — said she. — I am very happy. — It
excessively
has been ~~very much~~ ^ admired; — but sometimes I think

the pattern too large. — I shall wear one tomorrow

that I think you will prefer to this. — Have you

seen the one I gave Margaret?" —

Dinner came, & except when M[rs]. R. looked at

her husband's head, she continued gay & flippant,

on

chiding Eliz[th]. for the profusion ~~of~~ the Table,

the entrance of

& absolutely protesting against ~~having~~ the roast
^

Turkey — which formed the only exception to "You

see your dinner",. ~~brought in~~ — "I do beg & en:

:treat that no Turkey may be seen to day. I am

really frightened out of my wits with the number

of dishes we have already. Let us have no Turkey

I beseech you." — "My dear, replied Eliz. the Turkey

as

is roasted, & it may just as well come in, ~~&~~ stay

Besides in

in the Kitchen. If it is cut, I am hopes my Father
^ ^

may be tempted to eat a bit, for it is rather a
favourite dish."

[f.36v] "You may have it in my dear, but I assure

you I sha'nt touch it." —

M[r]. Watson had not been well enough to join the

party at dinner, but was prevailed on to come down
& drink tea with them. — "I wish we may be able
to have a game of cards tonight," said Eliz. to M^{rs}. R.
after seeing her father comfortably seated in his
arm chair. — "Not on my account my dear, I beg.
You know I am no card player. I think a snug
chat infinitely better. I always say Cards are
very well sometimes, to ~~help~~ break a formal
circle, but one never wants them among friends."
"I was thinking of its' being something to amuse
my father, answered Elizth. — if it was not disa:
:greable to you. He says his head won't bear
Whist — but perhaps if we make a round
game he may be tempted to sit down with
us." — "By all means my dear Creature. I am
quite at your service. Only do not oblige me
to chuse the game, that's all. <u>Speculation</u> is
the only round game at Croydon now, but I
can play any thing. — When there is only one
or two of you at home, you must be quite at
why do not you
a loss to amuse him — ~~but you must~~ get him

[f.37r]

at
to play ^ Cribbage? — Margaret & I have ~~always~~
played at Cribbage, most nights that we have
not been engaged." — A sound like a distant Carriage
caught;
was at this moment ~~heard~~; every body listened, ~~&~~
^
it ~~grew~~ became* more decided; it certainly drew
nearer. — It was an unusual sound in Stanton
at any time of the day, for the village was on
very
no public road, & contained no gentleman's family
^
but the Rector's. — The wheels rapidly approached; —
in two minutes
the general expectation was answered; they stopped
^
beyond a doubt at the garden gate of the Parsonage.
"Who could it be? — it was certainly a postchaise. —
creature to be She
Penelope was the only ~~person~~ thought of. ~~as tolerably~~
^
unexpected
~~likely~~ might perhaps have met with some ~~sudden~~
^
opportunity of returning." — A pause of suspense
~~upon~~ ~~gravel~~ ,
distinguished, first along the paved
ensued. — ~~Foot~~Steps† were ~~heard ascending the paved~~
^ ^

* 'be' in 'became' written over 'm'. † 'S' in 'Steps' written over 's'.

Footway which le~~a~~d under the windows of the

house ~~from the gate~~ to the front door, & then

within

~~in~~ the passage. They were the Steps of a man.

^

It could not be Penelope. It must be Samuel. —

displayed

The door opened, & ~~shewed~~ Tom Musgrave in*

^

the wrap of a Travellor. — He had been in

London & was now on his way home, & he

had come half a mile out of his road merely

to call for ten minutes at Stanton. He loved

[f.37v] to take people by surprise, with sudden visits

at extraordinary seasons; & in the present in:

:stance ~~he~~ had had the additional motive of be:

:ing able to tell the Miss Watsons, whom he de:

:pended on finding sitting quietly employed

after tea, that he was going home to an 8

however,

o'clock dinner. — As it happened ^ he did not

give

~~create~~ more surprise than he received, when in:

^

little

:stead of being shewn into the usual ^ Sitting room,

* 'in' written over '—'.

a foot larger each way than the other
the door of the best parlour was thrown open,

he
& beheld a circle of smart people whom he c^{d}

not immediately recognise ~~sollem~~ arranged with

all the honours of visiting round the fire,

& Miss Watson sitting at the best Pembroke

with
Table, ~~making~~ the best Tea things before her.

stood
He ~~stopt, for~~ a few seconds, in silent amaze:

:ment. — "Musgrave!" — ejaculated Margaret in

a tender voice. — He recollected himself, & came

such
forward, delighted to find ~~himself~~ a circle of

Friends, & blessing his good fortune for the

unlooked-for Indulgence. — He shook hands

with Robert, bowed & smiled to the Ladies, &

did every thing very prettily; but as to any

particularity of address or Emotion towards

who closed observed him, perceived nothing that did
Margaret, Emma ~~discerned no more than~~

not justify Eliz.'s opinions
~~she had expected, tho~~ tho' Margaret's modest

[f.38r] smiles imported that she meant to take the
visit to herself. — He was persuaded without
much difficulty to throw off his great coat,
"For
& drink tea with them. Whether he dined at 8
as
or 9, he observed, was a matter of very little
^
and ~~took~~ without seeming to
consequence." — ~~He did not seem to avoid the~~
turn away from
seek, he did not ~~avoid~~ the chair close* to
^
~~seat by~~ Margaret which she was assiduous
^
thus
in providing him. — She had secured him
^
from her Sisters — but it was not immediately
in her power to preserve him from her Brother's
claims, for as he came avowedly from London,
ago,
& had left it only 4. hours ~~back~~, the last cur:
^
:rent report as to public news, & the general
understood,
opinion of the day must be ~~enquired into~~, before
^
let
Robert could ~~yeild~~ his attention be yeilded
^

* 'close' written over another word (illegible).

& ~~or~~ important demands
to the less national, ~~more domestic enquiries~~
^
of the Women. — At last however he was at liber:

spoke
:ty to hear Margaret's soft address, as she ~~feared~~

her fears of his having
~~he must have~~ had a most terrible, cold, dark
^
dreadful Journey. — "Indeed you should not have

set out so late. — " "I could not be earlier, he replied.

~~Horse Guards~~
I was detained chatting at the Bedford, by a friend.

~~of Lord Osbornes.~~ — All hours are alike to me. —

How long have you been in the Country

Miss Marg^{t}.?" — "~~He~~ We came only this ~~very~~

morn^{g}. — My kind Brother & Sister brought me

home this very morn^{g}. — 'Tis singular is not it?"

[f.38v] "You were gone a great while, were not you?

a fortnight I suppose?" — "You may call a

fortnight a great while M^{r}. Musgrave, said M^{rs}.

Robert smartly — but we think a month very

little. I assure you we bring her home at the

end of a month, much against our will."

"A month! have you really been gone a

Month! 'tis amazing how Time flies. — "

"You may imagine, said Marg^{t}. in a sort of

what are my Sensations

Whisper, ~~how great my enjoyment,~~ in finding

^

myself once more at Stanton, ~~in the bosom of~~

~~my Family.~~ You know what a sad visitor

I make. — And I was so excessively impatient

to see Emma; — I dreaded the meeting, & at

the same time longed for it. — Do not you

comprehend the sort of feeling?" — "Not at all,

cried he aloud. I could never dread a meeting

with Miss Emma Watson, — or any of her Sisters."

It was lucky that he added that finish. —

~~"Oh! you Creature!" was Margaret's reply.~~ — "Were

you speaking to me? — " said Emma, who had

caught her own name. — "Not absolutely — he

answered — but I was thinking of you, — as many

at

at a greater distance are probably doing ~~like:~~

this

~~wise~~ moment. — Fine open weather Miss

^

Emma! — Charming season for Hunting."

[Booklet] 10

[f.39r] "Emma is delightful, is not she? — whispered Marg^{t}.
I have found her more than answer my warmest
hopes. — Did you ever see any thing more perfectly
beautiful? — I think even you must be a convert
to a brown complexion." — He hesitated; Margaret
was fair herself, & he did not particularly want
to compliment her; but Miss Osborne & Miss Carr
was likewise fair, & his devotion to them carried
the day. "Your Sister's complexion, said he at last,
a dark complexion can
is as fine as ~~the hue of her ski~~ be, but I still
^
profess my preference of a white skin. You
my model for
have seen Miss Osborne? — She is ~~very fair~~. —
a truly
~~Miss Osborne~~ feminine complexion, & she is
^
Is she fairer than me?" —
very fair." — "~~She is about as fair as I am, I~~
Tom made no reply. — "Upon my
~~think.~~" —— ~~Instead of making any reply, Tom~~
Honour Ladies, said he, giving a glance over
highly endebted to your
his own person, I am ~~most fervently ashamed~~

Condescension for admitting me, in such

Dishabille

~~a state~~ into your Drawingroom. I really did
^

~~unsuitably~~

unfit to be here

not consider how ~~unfit~~ I was ~~to for your pre:~~
^ ^

~~:sence~~, or I hope I should have kept my dis=

=tance. Ly. Osborne would tell me that I

were growing as careless as her son, if she saw

me in this condition." — The Ladies were not

stealing

wanting in civil returns; &* Robert Watson ~~took~~
^

[f.39v] a ~~slight~~ veiw of his own head in an opposite

said

glass, — ~~and he~~ with equal civility, ~~said~~, "You can:
^

:not be more in dishabille than myself. — We

got here so late, that I had not time even to

fresh

put a little powder in my hair." — Emma
^

could not help entering into what she supposed

at that moment.

her Sister in law's feelings ~~must be on this oc:~~

~~casion~~. — When the Tea things were removed,

* '&' written over '—'.

old
Tom began to talk of his Carriage — but the ^ Card

being set out, & with
Table ~~was placed~~ ^ The fish & counters ~~&~~ ^ a tolerably

from the beaufit
clean pack brought forward ^ by Miss Watson,

the general voice was so urgent with him to join

agreed to
their party, that he ~~would~~ ^ allow himself an:

:other quarter of an hour. ~~in their~~ Even Emma

was pleased that he would stay, for she was be:

~~circle~~
party
:ginning to feel that a family ~~party~~ ^ might be the

&
worst of all parties; ^ the others were delighted. —

"What's your Game?" — cried he, as they stood

round the Table. — "Speculation I beleive, said

Eliz.th — My Sister recommends it, & I fancy we

all like it. I know you do, Tom." — "It is the

only round game played at Croydon now, said

M^{rs}. Robert — we never think of any other. I

am glad it is a favourite with you.." — "Oh! me!

cried Tom. Whatever you decide on, will be

[f.40r] a favourite with <u>me</u>. — I have had some pleasant

hours ~~enough~~ at Speculation in my time — but

I have not ~~played at~~ been in the way of it now for

a long while. — Vingt-un is the game at Os:

:borne Castle; I have played nothing but Vingt-

-un of late. You would be astonished to hear the

noise we make there. — The fine old, Lofty Drawing

-room rings again. Ly. Osborne sometimes de=

=clares she cannot hear herself speak. — Ld. Osborne

famously

enjoys it ~~amazingly~~ &[*] he makes the best Dealer

without exception that I ever beheld[†] —

~~in the world~~ — such quickness & spirit! he[‡] lets

their cards.

nobody dream over ~~it~~. — I wish you could see

^

over draw himself his own

him ~~deal himself~~ on both cards — it is

^ ^

worth any thing in the World!" — "Dear me! —

cried Marg^{t}. why should not we play at vingt un? —

a

I think it is much better game than Speculation.

^

I cannot say I am very fond of Speculation."

[*] '&' written over '—'.

[†] 'beh' in 'beheld' written over other letters, possible 'saw'.

[‡] 'he' written over '—'.

offered
~~said~~
Mrs. Robert ~~withdrew~~ not another word in sup:
^

She was quite vanquished, & the
:port of the game. — ~~Osborne Castle carried it~~,
^ ^

~~Croydon~~ fashions of Osborne — the
~~even in her estimation~~ Castle carried it over ~~those~~
^

fashions ~~most~~
of Croydon. — ~~T. Musgrave was a very useful ad:~~
^ ^

~~:dition; without him, it would have been a~~

[f.40ar] *"Do you see much of the Parsonage-family at the

as
Castle, Mr. Musgrave? — " said Emma, ~~while~~ they were
^

they are
taking their seats. — "Oh! yes — almost always there.
^

Mrs. Blake is a nice little goodhumoured Woman,

She & I are ~~gre~~ sworn friends; & Howard's a very

Gentlemanlike good sort of fellow! — You are not

forgotten I assure you by any of the~~m~~ party. I fancy

you must have a little Cheek-glowing now &

Miss Emma.
then Were not you rather warm last Sa:
^

:turday about 9 or 10 o'clock in the Eveng — ?

* beginning of section inserted from additional sheet in ms.

I will tell you how it was. — I see you are dieing

Howard L^{d}. Osborne —"
to know. — Says ~~Ld Osborne~~ ^ to ~~Howard~~ — —

called on
At this interesting moment he was ~~interrupted~~ ^ by

the others, to regulate the game & determine some dis:

:putable point; & his attention was so totally engaged

& afterwards by the course of the game
in the business ^ as never to revert to what he had been

saying before; — & Emma ~~could not remind him~~, tho'

dared
suffering a good deal from Curiosity, ~~could~~ not

remind him. — He proved a very useful addition

~~to~~ at their Table; without him, it w^{d} have been a*

[f.40r contd.] ~~must~~
could
party of such very near relations as ~~xx~~† have

felt little maintained little
~~deadened the~~ ^ Interest, & perhaps ~~even impaired the~~

complaisance, ~~of the players~~ but his presence

gave variety & secured good manners. — He

[f.40v] in fact
was ^ excellently qualified to shine at a round

* end of inserted section. † letters illegible.

& ~~seldom~~ few situations made him
Game; ~~he never~~ appear~~ed~~ to greater advantage.

He played with Spirit, & had a great deal ~~He played with Eagerness~~ —
~~than when assisting at one. & He talked much~~ —

to say, with no wit himself, c[d] sometimes
^ & tho' ~~without wit, sometimes said a lively thing~~

make use of the wit of an absent friend; & had

a lively way of ~~saying~~ retailing a commonplace,

~~did~~ had great
or saying a mere nothing, that ~~was abundantly~~

effect
~~useful~~ ^ at a Card Table. The ways, & good Jokes

ordinary
of Osborne Castle were now added to his ^ means

of Entertainment; he repeated the smart sayings

one Lady
of ~~Miss Osborne~~, detailed the oversights of ~~Miss~~

another, even
~~Carr~~, ^ & indulged them ^ with a copy of L[d]

Osborne's stile of overdrawing himself on both

cards. — The Clock struck nine, while he

was thus agreably occupied; & when Nanny came

in with her Master's Bason of Gruel, he had

the pleasure of observing to M[r] Watson that

while
he should leave him at supper, ~~as~~ ^ he went

home to dinner himself. — The Carriage was

ordered to the door — & no entreaties for his staying

avail, — for he well knew, that
longer c[d]. now ~~prevail; — if he staid, he knew~~

if he staid less than
he must sit down to supper in ^ ten minutes —
^

been long
which to a Man whose* ~~must~~ heart had† ^ fixed on

was
calling his next meal a Dinner, ~~must be~~ ^ quite‡
~~a very late dinner, was~~ ^ insupportable. —

to go,
On finding him determined ^ Marg[t].. began to wink

[f.41r] & nod at Eliz[th] to ask him to dinner for the

following day; & Eliz. at last not able to resist

hints, which§ her own more than
~~& from her~~ ^ hospitable, social temper ~~not above~~

half-seconded
~~half wishing~~, gave the invitation. "Would he

give Rob[t]. the meeting, they sh[d]. be very happy."

* 'se added to 'who' in 'whose'.
† 'had' written over 'was'.
‡ 'quite' written over 'was'.
§ 'ich' in 'which' written over other letters (illegible).

"With the greatest pleasure" — was his first re:

"That is

:ply. In a moment afterwards —if I can possibly
^

here

get ~~home~~ in time — but I shoot with Ld Osborne,
^

must not engage —— You will not

& therefore ~~cannot positively answer — In another~~
^ ^

think of

~~moment —~~ me unless you see me." — And so, he
^

departed, delighted with the uncertainty in which

left

he had ~~placed~~ it. —
^

———

Marg^{t}. in the joy of her heart under circum:
:stances, which she chose to consider as peculi:
:arly propitious, would willingly have made
a confidante of Emma when they were alone
for a short time the next morn^{g}; & had pro:
:ceeded so far as to say — "The young man who
was here last night my dear Emma & returns
to day, is more interesting to me, than perhaps
you may be aware — " but Emma pretend:
:ing to understand nothing extraordinary in
the words, made some very inapplicable reply,

ran away
& jumping up, ~~made her escape~~ from a sub:

:ject which was odious to her feelings. ——

As Marg^{t}: would not allow a doubt to be

[f.41v] repeated
~~entertained~~ of Musgrave's coming to dinner,
^

preparations were made for his Entertainment

much exceeding what had been ~~done~~ deemed ne:

:cessary the day ~~f~~ before; ~~for M^{rs}. Robert~~ — and

taking the office of Superintendance intirely from her

~~xxxxxx~~*
~~superseding all Eliz.'s cares usual cares, she~~
^
Sister, ~~for the occasion~~, she herself
was half the morning in the Kitchen directing
^ ^

indifferent Cooking, & anxious
& scolding. — After a great deal of ~~Cooking, &~~
^ ^

Suspense however
~~waiting~~, they were obliged to sit down without

their Guest. — T. Musgrave never came, & Marg.

under
was at no pains to conceal her vexation ~~or~~
^

the disappointment, or
repress the peevishness of her Temper —. The
^

Peace of the party for the remainder of that

* illegible letters deleted.

day, & the whole of the next, which com:

:prised the length of Robert & Jane's visit,

was continually invaded by her fretful dis:

attacks. —

:pleasure, & querulous ~~altercations~~. — Eliz. was
^

usual Marg^{t}.

the object of both. ~~She~~ had just respect enough
^ ^

for her B^{r}. & S$^{r's}$ opinion, to behave properly

by <u>them</u>, but Eliz. & the maids c^{d}. never do

whom

anything right — & Emma, ~~found the~~ she
^

seemed no longer to think about, found the

continuance of the ~~even shorter lived~~ beyond her

~~affec~~^{te} gentle voice ~~more short lived even than~~
^

calculation ~~breif~~ short. Eager ~~Glad~~

~~she had expected.~~ — ~~Delighted~~ to be as little
^ ^

~~each evens~~

~~glad to~~

delighted with the alternative of

among them as possible, Emma was ~~xxxxxxxx~~*
^

~~xxxxx~~†

~~prefer & invita propose in attending her Father for~~

~~take Eliz.'s usual place with in their Father's room~~,
^ ^

* illegible letters deleted. † illegible letters deleted.

above: &

sitting ~~upstairs~~, with her father, ~~who~~ warmly entreated
^

[f.42r] to be his constant Comp:^{n} each eveng. — as

~~was confined both days to his room~~ — & Eliz.
^

~~who~~

loved company of any kind too well, not to

~~when~~ at all risks

prefer being below ~~while she c^{d} beleive persuaded~~
^

~~to believe it no sacrifice on Emma's part~~

as to

She had rather talk of Croydon ~~with~~ Jane,
^ ^

every

with ~~all the~~ interruption~~s~~ of Marg^{t}.'s perverse:
^

:ness, than sit with only her father, who

frequently c^{d} not endure Talking at all,

the affair

~~it~~ was ~~soon~~ so settled, as soon as she could be
^

persuaded to beleive it no sacrifice on her

the Exchange

Sister's part. — To Emma, ~~it~~ was ~~a~~ most accep:

:table, & delightful~~, releif~~. ~~He~~ Her father, if ill,

little more than &, being a man

required ~~only~~ gentleness & silence; ~~if able to~~

of Sense & Educa~~being~~tion, was if able to converse,

~~converse, as he was a man of Education &~~
^

a welcome
~~Taste, he was a pleasing~~ companion. —
^

In his chamber, Emma was at peace from the

mortifications
dreadful ~~Evils~~ of unequal Society, & family
^

Discord — from the immediate endurance of

low-minded Conceit,
Hard-hearted prosperity, ~~mean-spirited Self-suffic:~~
^

~~and a~~ folly, engrafted
:~~iency~~, & wrong-headed ~~ill-disposed~~ on an un:
^

still
:toward Disposition. — She suffered from them
^

in the Contemplation
~~only in~~ of their existence; in memory & in pros:
^

ceased to be
:pect, but for the moment, she ~~had a pause~~
^

effects. was
tortured by their ~~effusions~~. — She ~~could~~ at leisure,
^ ^

tho' her ~~perhaps~~
she could read & think, — ~~Her~~ situation was
^ ^

hardly
~~not~~ such as to make reflection very soothing.
^

[f.42v] Evils arising from the loss of her Uncle
The ~~misfortunes which her Uncle's death had~~
^

neither
~~brought on her~~, were ~~every day~~ trifling, nor
^

likely to lessen; & when Thought had been

in contrasting

freely indulged, ~~when~~ the past & the present,

^

the

~~had been contrasted, the dissipations~~ employment

of mind, the dissipation of unpleasant ideas

reading ~~Books~~

which only ~~reading~~ could produce, made her

^

a book. ~~fall~~

thankfully turn to ~~them~~. — ~~The sink in her~~

^ ^

The &

~~fortunes, the~~ change in her home society stile

^ ^

~~Mrs Turner's~~

the death of one friend & the

of Life ~~had~~ in consequence of ~~her Aunt's~~ impru:

~~of another, had indeed been materialy~~

~~the infatuation~~ of another had indeed been striking.

:dence, ~~had been great and greivous~~. — From being

^ ^

the first object of Hope & Solicitude to an Uncle

who had formed her mind with the care of a

Parent, & of Tenderness to an Aunt whose a:

:miable temper had delighted to give her every

indulgence, from being the Life & Spirit of

a ~~whole~~ House, where all had been comfort &

Elegance, & the expected ~~Inh~~ Heiress of an easy

become of importance

Independance, she was ~~reduced to a House~~

those, whose affection she

to no one, a burden on ~~an already too full~~
^

c[d]. not expect, an addition in an House, already over:
~~House where she was felt as an Intruder, a Stranger~~

surrounded by inferior minds

:stocked, with
~~among those~~ little chance of domestic ~~enjo~~
^

as little

comfort, & ~~no~~ hope of ~~a~~ future support. — It was

for

well for her that she was naturally chearful; —

might

the Change had been such as ~~to~~ have plunged
^
~~as it was a change which~~ weak spirits ~~must~~

~~gloom~~ in

~~have into wretchedness &~~ Despondence. —

[Booklet] 11

[f.43r] She was very much pressed by Robert &

Jane to return with them to Croydon, &

had some difficulty in getting a refusal

accepted; as they thought too highly of their

offer

own kindness & situation, to suppose the~~y~~
^

advantageous
could appear in a less ~~favourable~~ light to
^
anybody else. — Eliz.th gave them her interest,
tho' evidently against her own, in privately
urging Emma to go — "You do not know what
you refuse Emma — said she — nor what you
have to bear at home. — I would advise you
by all means to accept the invitation; there
at
is always something lively going on ^ Croydon,
You will be in company almost every
day, & Robt & Jane will be very kind to
you. ~~It is a pity you should not go.~~ — As
off
for me, I shall be no worse ^ without you,
than I have been used to be; but poor
Marg.$^{ts'}$ disagreable ways are new to <u>you</u>,
you
& they would vex you more than ^ think
for, if you stay at home. — " Emma was of
esteem
course un-influenced, except to greater ~~affection~~
^
for Eliz.th, by such representations — & the Visitors
departed without her. —

APPENDIX B

Transcription of 'Sanditon'

[f.1r] **Jany. 27. — 1817.** **1**

A Gentleman & Lady travelling from Tun-

bridge towards that part of the Sussex

Coast which lies between Hastings &

being induced by Business to quit
E. Bourne, ~~were on quitting~~ the high

~~toil~~ attempt a very rough Lane,
road, & ~~toiling up a very long steep hill~~

were
~~through a rough Lane~~, overturned in

half rock, half sand.
toiling up its' long ascent. ^ The accident

happened just beyond the only Gentleman's

a
House near the Lane — ~~the~~ House, which

first take
their Driver on being ^ required to ~~turn~~ that

Direction,
~~way,~~ had conceived to be necessarily their

object, & had with most unwilling Looks

by —.

been constrained to pass ~~two minutes~~

He had grumbled & shaken his Shoulders

~~before grumbling~~ so much indeed, ~~& looking~~

and pitied & cut

~~so black, & pitying & cutting~~ his Horses so

sharply

~~much~~, that he might have been open to

the suspicion of overturning them on pur:

not his Masters

:pose (especially as the Carriage was ~~not~~

had

the Gentleman's own) if the road ^ not

considerably

indisputably ~~& evidently~~ become ~~much~~

worse than before, as soon as the

premises of the said House were

expressing ~~saying~~ with a

~~passed~~ left behind — ~~as Bad as it had~~

most intelligent ~~and seeming~~

portentous

~~been before the change seemed to say,~~ ^

countenance

^ that beyond it no wheels but cart

could safely proceed.
wheels ~~had ever thought of proceeding~~.*

[f.1v] The severity of the fall was broken

by their slow pace & the narrowness

of the Lane, & the ~~Travellors~~

~~beleived found themselves at first~~

~~only shaken & bruised~~ Gentleman

having scrambled out & helped

out his companion, they neither

at first
of them ^ felt more than shaken

& bruised. But the Gentleman had

in the course of the extrication

soon
sprained his foot — & ^ becoming

sensible of it ~~in a few moments,~~

in a few moments
was obliged ^ to cut short, both his

remonstrance to the Driver & his

to his wife & himself —
~~Self~~ congratulations — & sit down

on the bank, unable to stand. —

* '~~She was become~~ that Loveliness was complete.' at bottom of page.

"There is something wrong here, said
he — putting his hand to his ancle —
But never mind, my Dear — (looking
up at her with a smile) — It c^{d} —
not have happened, you know, in
[f.2r] a better place. — Good out of Evil — . The
very thing perhaps to be wished for.
We shall soon get releif. — There, I
fancy lies my cure" — pointing to the*
neat-looking end of a Cottage, ~~appearing~~
which was seen ~~peeping out from among~~

among wood
~~wood, and~~† romantically situated ^ on a
high Eminence at some little Distance —
"Does not that promise to be the
very place? — " His wife fervently hoped
it was — but stood, terrified & anxious,

neither
~~& not~~ able to do or suggest anything —
& receiving her first real comfort
from the sight of several persons

* 'the' written over 'a'. † '~~and~~' written over something illegible.

now coming ~~from~~ to their assistance.

had
The accident ~~having~~ been discerned
from a Hayfield adjoining the
House they had passed — & the persons
who approached, were a well-looking
Hale, Gentlemanlike Man, of middle age,
the Proprietor of the Place, who happened
to be among his Haymakers at the
time, & three or four of the ablest
of them summoned to attend their
Master — to say nothing of all the
rest of the field, Men, Women &
[f.2v] Children — not very far off. —
Mr. Heywood, such was the name
of the said Proprietor, advanced
with a very civil salutation —
~~& very~~ — much concern for the
accident — some surprise at any
body's attempting that road in a
assistance.
Carriage — & ready offers of ~~service~~.
~~in any way~~ His courtesies were

received with Goodbreeding &

one or two of
gratitude & while ^ the Men lent

their help to the Driver in getting

the Carriage upright again, the

Travellor said — "You are extremely

obliging Sir, & I take you at your

word. — The injury to my Leg is

I dare say very trifling, but it

best
is always ~~better to~~ in these cases

to have a Surgeon's opinion without

loss of time; & as the road does

[f.3r] a
not seem at present in ~~the best~~ ^

favourable
~~possible~~ state for my getting up

to his house myself, I will thank

you to send off one of these good
People for the Surgeon." "The Surgeon

Sir! — replied Mr Heywood — I am afraid

you will find no Surgeon at hand here,

but I dare say we shall do very well

him.
without ~~any~~." — "Nay Sir, ~~his Partner~~

if <u>he</u> is not in the way his Partner

rather
will do just as well — or ^ better — . I

w[d]. rather see his Partner indeed —

prefer the attendance of
I would ~~have~~ ^ his Partner. ~~by prefer~~:

can
~~:ence~~. — One of these good people ~~will~~ be

with him
~~there~~ in three minutes I am sure.

I need not ask whether I see the

House; (looking towards the Cottage).

for
^ Excepting your own, we have passed

none in this place, which can be

the Abode of a Gentleman." —

M[r]. H. looked very much astonished

& replied — "What Sir! are you expecting

to find a Surgeon in that Cottage? —

we have neither Surgeon nor Partner

[f.3v] in the Parish I assure you." —

"Excuse me Sir — replied the other.

I am sorry to have the appearance

though
of contradicting you — but ~~either~~

from the extent of the Parish or

some other cause you may not be

Stay —
aware of the fact, — Can I be

mistaken in the place? — Am I not

in Willingden? — Is not this Willingden?"

"Yes Sir, this is certainly Willingden."

"Then Sir, I can bring proof of your

whether you may know it or not.
having a Surgeon in the Parish — ^ Here

Sir — (taking out his Pocket book —) if

you will do me the favour of casting

your eye over these advertisements,

which I cut out myself from the

Morning Post & the Kentish Gazette,

only yesterday morn^{g}. in London —
^ I think you will be convinced that

I am not speaking at random. You

will find it an advertisement Sir,

a
of the dissolution of ^ Partnership

in the Medical Line — — in your

own Parish — extensive Business — unde:

:niable Character — respectable references —

wishing to form a separate Establishment

[f.4r] — you will find it at full length Sir” —

offering him the two little oblong

with a good humoured smile

extracts. — “Sir — said Mr. Heywood ^ — if

you were to shew me all the Newspapers

that are printed in one week throughout

the Kingdom, you ~~yo~~ wd. not persuade

me of there being a Surgeon in ~~this~~

for having ~~have~~ ~~Sir~~

~~Parish~~ Willingden, — ~~having~~ ^ lived here ^

ever since I was born, Man & Boy ~~Sir~~

~~and never heard before~~ I think

57 years, ~~without ever hearing of the~~

I must have <u>known</u> at least

~~existence~~ of such a person, ~~before~~. — ~~I~~

~~therefore~~

~~think~~ I may venture ~~at least~~ to say

~~at least~~

^ that he has not <u>much Business</u>; — ~~Though~~

To
~~to~~ ^ be sure, if Gentlemen were to be
often attempting this Lane in Post-
-chaises, it might not be a bad spe:
:culation for a Surgeon to get a House
at the top of the Hill. — But as to
Sir
that Cottage, I can assure you ^ that
it is in fact — (inspite of its spruce air
at this distance* —) as indifferent a
double Tenement as any in the Parish,
and that
^ My Shepherd lives at one end, & three
old women at the other." He took
peices
the ~~bits~~ of paper as he spoke — & having
[f.4v] looked them over, added — "I beleive I
can explain it Sir. — Your mistake is
in the place. — There are two Willing:
:dens in this Country — & your adver:
:tisements refer to the other — which
is Great Willingden, or Willingden Abbots,

* 'i' written over 'a' in 'distance'.

& lies 7 miles off, on the other side

of Battel — quite down in the Weald.

And we Sir — (speaking rather proudly)

are not in the Weald." — "Not down

in the Weald I am sure Sir, replied

the Traveller, pleasantly. It took us

half an hour to climb your Hill. —

Well Sir — I dare say it is as you say

& I have made an abominably stupid

Blunder. — All done in a moment; —

the advertisements did not catch my

last
eye till the ^ half hour of our being

when was ~~being~~ in the
in Town — ; ^ everything* ~~in~~ ^ hurry &

confusion which always attend a

One is never
short stay there — ~~Nothing~~ able to be

anything
complete~~d~~ ^ in the way of Business

you know and
^ till the Carriage is at the door — ^ ~~I~~

* the first 'e' in 'everything' written over '&'.

accordingly satisfying
~~satisfied~~ myself with a breif enquiry,

& finding we were actually to pass

[f.5r] within a mile or two of a Willingden

I
sought no farther. — My Dear — (to his
^
wife) I am very sorry to have brought

Scrape.
you into this ~~awkward Predicament~~. But

do not be alarmed about my Leg. It gives

me no pain while I am quiet, — and as

soon as these good people have succeeded

in setting the Car^ge. to rights & turning

the Horses round, the best thing we

can do will be to measure back our

steps into the Turnpike road & proceed

to Hailsham, & so Home, without at:

:tempting anything farther. — Two

hours take us home, from Hailsham —

And when once at home, we have our

you know. — own
remedy at hand. — A little of our ^ Bracing

Sea Air will soon set me on my feet

again. — Depend upon it my Dear, it is exactly a case for the Sea. Saline ^air & im: :mersion will be the very thing. — My Sensations tell me so already." — In a most friendly manner Mr Heywood here interposed, entreating them not to think of proceeding till the ancle had been examined, & some refresh= =ment taken, & very cordially pressing [f.5v] them to make use of his House for both purposes. — "We are always well stocked, said he, with all the common remedies for Sprains & Bruises — & I will answer for the pleasure it will give my wife & daughters to be of ~~use to Service~~ service to you & this Lady, in every way in their power. — " A twinge or two, in trying to move his foot disposed the Travellor to think rather more as he had done at first of the benefit of immediate assistance — & consulting his wife in the few words of "Well my Dear, I beleive

it will be   for us — "
~~we had~~ better ~~accept this kind offer~~" —

~~he~~ turned again to M^{r}. H — & said —

"Before we accept your Hospitality Sir,

in order
— & ^ to do away any unfavourable im:

:pression which the sort of wild goose —

— chase you find me in, may have

rise to —
given ^ — allow me to tell you who

we are. My name is Parker. — M^{r}.

Parker of Sanditon; — this Lady, my wife

home
M^{rs}. Parker. — We are on our road ^ from

London; — My name perhaps — tho' I

am by no means the first of ~~the~~ my

Family, holding Landed Property in the

Parish of Sanditon, may be unknown

[f.6r] at this distance from the Coast — but

itself —
Sanditon ^ — everybody has heard of Sanditon,

— the favourite — for a young & rising Bathing-

the favourite Spot
–place, certainly ~~the most favourite~~ of all

that are to be found along the ~~favourite~~

Coast of Sussex; the most favoured by Nature,

promising to be
& ~~consequently;~~ the most ~~likely to be~~ chosen

by Man." — "Yes — I have heard of Sanditon.

replied Mr. H. — Every five years, one hears of

some new place or other starting up by the

Sea, & growing the fashion. — How they can

the wonder!
half of them be filled, is ~~amazing to me!~~

<u>Where</u> People can be found with Money

or
~~&~~ Time to go to them! — Bad things for

a — sure to
~~any~~ Country; — ^ raise the price of Provisions

as
& make the Poor good for nothing ^ — I dare

say you find, ~~it so~~ Sir." "Not at all Sir,

not at all — cried Mr. Parker eagerly.

Quite the contrary I assure you. — A

common idea — but a mistaken one.

It may apply to your large, overgrown

Places, like Brighton, or Worthing, or

East Bourne — but not to a small

Village like Sanditon, precluded by

experiencing
its size from ~~feeling~~ any of the evils

[f.6v] of Civilization, while the growth of

Nursery
the place, the Buildings, the ~~laying~~

Grounds
~~out Gardens~~, the demand for every thing,

& the sure resort of the very best Company,

those* regular, steady, private Families

who
of thorough Gentility & Character, ~~excite~~

are a blessing every where, excite and
~~not only~~ the industry of the Poor ^ ~~but~~

diffuse comfort & improvement among

sort
them of every ~~kind~~. — No Sir, I assure

you, Sanditon is not a place — "

"I do not mean to take exceptions to

any ~~one~~ place in particular Sir, an:

:swered Mr. H. — I only think our Coast

* 'those' written over 'the'.

is too full of them altogether — But
had we not better try to get you" —
"Our Coast too full" — repeated Mr. P. —
totally
On that point perhaps we may not
^
disagree; — At least there are <u>enough</u>.
Our Coast is abundant enough; it demands
no more. — Everybody's Taste & every
body's finances may be suited — And
those good people who are trying to
add to the number, are in my
opinion excessively absurd, & ~~I have~~
must soon
~~no doubt will~~ find themselves ~~in~~
^
[f.7r] ~~the end~~ — the Dupes of their own
fallacious Calculations. — Such a
place as Sanditon Sir, I may say was
wanted, was called for. — Nature had
marked it out — had spoken in most
intelligible Characters — The finest, purest
Sea Breeze on the Coast — acknowledged
to be so — Excellent Bathing — fine hard

Sand — Deep Water 10 yards from the Shore

— no Mud — no Weeds — no slimey rocks —

Never was there a place more palpably

designed by Nature for the resort of

the Invalid — the very Spot which

Thousands seemed in need of — The

most desirable distance from London!

One complete,

~~A~~ measured mile nearer than East

^

Bourne. Only conceive Sir, the ad:

saving a whole Mile,

:vantage of ~~that~~, in a long Journey.

But Brinshore Sir, which I dare

say you have in your eye — the

attempts of two or three speculating

People about Brinshore, this last

year, to raise that paltry Hamlet,

lying, as it does

~~situated~~ between a stagnant marsh,

a bleak Moor

& the constant effluvia of a ridge

^

of putrifying Sea weed,* can end in

* 'weed' written over 'wed'.

nothing but their own Disappointment.

[f.7v] What in the name of Common Sense

is to <u>recommend</u> Brinshore? — A

most insalubrious Air — Roads pro:

:verbially detestable — Water Brackish

beyond example, impossible to get a

good dish of Tea within 3 miles

of the place — & as for the Soil —

it is so cold & ungrateful that it

~~pro~~ yeild

can hardly be made to ~~grow~~ ^ a

Cabbage. — Depend upon it Sir, that

this is a faithful Description of

Brinshore — not in the smallest

degree exaggerated — & if you have

heard it differently spoken of —"

"Sir, I never heard it spoken of

in my Life before, said Mr. Heywood.

I did not know there was such a

place in the World." — "You did

not! — There my Dear — (turning with

exultation to his Wife) — you see how

it is. So much for the Celebrity of

Brinshore! — This Gentleman did not

know there was such a place in

Why, in truth Sir, I fancy
the World. — ~~I fancy Sir~~ ^ we may

apply to Brinshore, that[*] line~~s~~ of

the Poet Cowper in his description

[f.8r] of the religious[†] Cottager, as opposed

to Voltaire — "<u>She</u>, never heard of half

a mile from home." — "With all my

Heart Sir — Apply any Verses you like

to it — But I want to see something applied

to your Leg — & I am sure by your Lady's

is of my opinion
countenance that she ^ quite ~~agrees with~~

& thinks —
~~me in thinking~~ it a pity to lose any

more time — And here come my Girls to

speak for themselves & their Mother.

~~(turning round towards~~ (two or three

* 'that' written over 'those'.
† 'o' in 'religious' written over illegible letter.

~~who~~ followed
genteel looking young women ^ ~~attended~~

now seen
by as* many Maid Servants, were ^

issueing from the House) — I began to

wonder the Bustle should not have

reached <u>them</u>. — A thing of this kind

soon makes a Stir in a lonely place

like ours. — Now Sir, let us see

how you can be best conveyed into

the House." — The young Ladies approached

every thing that
& said ~~& did what~~ was proper to

recommend
~~enforce~~ their Father's offers; & in an un:

:affected manner calculated to make

[f.8v] the Strangers easy — and as Mrs: P—

was exceedingly anxious for releif — and

her Husband by this time, not much

less disposed for it — a very few

Civil Scruples were enough — especially

the Carriage being now set up, was

* 'as' written over 'm'.

as ~~it was now ascertained that the~~

Discovered to have received such Injury
~~Carriage was so much injured~~ on the

fallen side as to be unfit for present

therefore
use. — Mr. Parker was ^ carried into the

House, & his Carriage wheeled off to

a vacant Barn. —

Chapter 2. ——

The acquaintance, thus oddly begun,*

was neither short nor unimportant.

For a whole fortnight the Travellors were
~~The Parkers were the Guests of the~~

fixed at Willingden; Mr. P.'s ~~being~~
~~Heywoods a fortnight~~;† ~~The~~ sprain ~~was~~

proving him
^ too serious for ~~Mr. Parker to be sooner~~

~~able~~ to move sooner. — He had fallen

into very good hands. The Heywoods

were a thoroughly respectable family,

& every possible attention was paid

* 'un' in begun' written over other letters illegible.
† ';' written over '.'.

in the kindest & most unpretending

manner, to both Husband & wife.

[f.9r] He was waited on & nursed, & she

cheared & comforted with ~~equal goodwill~~

unremitting kindness — and as every

~~act &~~ office of Hospitality & friendliness

was received as it ought — as there was

not more good will on one side than

Gratitude on the other — nor any

deficiency of generally pleasant manners

on
~~in~~ either, they grew to like each other

in the course of that fortnight, ex:

:ceedingly well. — Mr Parker's Character

unfolded.
& History were soon ~~made known.~~

All that he understood of himself, he

for he was ~~being~~
readily told, ~~was he was~~ very open:
^ ^
:hearted; — & where he might be him=

conversation
=self in the dark, his* ^ was still giving

* 'his' written over 'he'.

information ~~unconsciously,~~ to such of

the Heywoods as could observe. —

By such he was perceived to be an

Enthusiast; — ~~in~~ on the subject of

Sanditon, a complete Enthusiast. —

Sanditon, — the success of Sanditon as a

small, fashionable Bathing Place was

the object, for which he seemed to live.

[f.9v]

quiet

A very few years ago, & it had been a ^

~~simple~~

^ Village ~~interesting only~~ of no ~~consideration~~

~~inhabited by one Family of consequence,~~

~~his own, of secondary~~ pretensions; but some

some

natural advantages in its position & ~~some~~

accidental circumstances having suggested

Land Holder

to himself, & the other principal ~~Proprietor~~

becoming

~~of the Land~~, the probability of its' ~~being~~

a profitable Speculation, they* had engaged

in it, & planned & built, & praised & puffed,

* 'they' written over something else, probably 'he'.

& raised it to a Something of ~~note~~ young

Renown —
~~notoriety~~, and Mr. Parker could now think

of very little besides. — The Facts, which

in more direct communication, he

laid before them were that he was

about 5 & 30 — had been married, —

very happily married 7 years — &

had 4 sweet Children at home; —

of a respectable
that he was ~~no Profession~~ Family,

& easy though not large fortune; — no

Profession — succeeding as eldest son to

the Property which 2 or 3 Generations

had been holding & accumulating be:

:fore him; — that he had 2 Brothers

2
& ^ Sisters — all single & all indepen:

former
:dant — the eldest of the two ~~Brothers~~

[f.10r] indeed
~~in fact~~, by collateral Inheritance, quite

as well provided for as himself. — His

object in quitting the high road, to hunt

for an advertising Surgeon, was also

plainly stated; — it had not proceeded

his

from any intention of spraining ~~an~~

ancle or doing himself any other Injury

for the good of such Surgeon — nor

(as M^{r}. H. had been apt to suppose)

from any design of entering into Part:

:nership with him — ; it was merely

in consequence of a wish to establish

some medical Man at Sanditon,

which the nature of the Advertisement

induced him to expect to accomplish

in Willingden. — He was convinced that

the advantage of a medical Man at

hand w^{d}. very materially promote

the rise & prosperity of the Place — w^{d} —

prodigious

in fact tend to bring a ~~great~~ influx;

— nothing else was wanting. He had

strong reason to beleive that one family

last year

had been deterred ^ from trying Sanditton

on that account — & probably very
many more — and his own Sisters
who were sad Invalids, & whom he
[f.10v] was very anxious to get to Sanditon
this Summer, could hardly be expected
to hazard themselves in a place where
they could not have immediate
medical advice. — Upon the whole, Mr. P.
was evidently an amiable, family-man,
fond of Wife, Childn, Brothers & Sisters —
& generally kind-hearted; — Liberal, gentle:
:manlike, easy to please; — of a sanguine
turn of mind, with more Imagination
than Judgement. And Mrs. P. was as
evidently a gentle, amiable, sweet tempered
Woman, the properest wife in the World
for a Man of strong Understanding, but
not of capacity to supply the cooler re:
:flection which her own Husband some:
:times needed, & so entirely waiting to
be guided on every occasion, that
whether he were risking his Fortune

remained
or spraining his Ancle, she ~~was~~ equally
^
useless. — Sanditon was a second wife
& 4 Children to him — hardly less Dear —
& certainly more engrossing. — He could
talk of it for ever. — It had indeed
not only those of
the highest claims; — Birth place, Property,
^
and
Home, — it was ~~also~~ his Mine, his Lottery,

[f.11r] his Occupation
his Speculation &* his Hobby Horse; his Hope
^
& his Futurity. — He was extremely desirous
of drawing his good friends at Willingden
and
thither; his endeavours in the cause, were
^
as grateful & disinterested, as they were
warm. — He wanted to secure the promise
of a visit — to get as many of the Family
own
as his house w^d contain, to follow him
^
to Sanditon as soon as possible — and
healthy as they all undeniably were —
foresaw that every one of them w^d be

* '&' written over ','.

benefited by the sea. ~~air~~ — He held it indeed

as certain, that no person c[d]. be really well,

no person, (however upheld for the present

by fortuitous aids of exercise & spirits* in

a semblance of Health) could be really

in a state of secure & permanent Health

without spending at least 6 weeks by

the Sea every year. — The Sea Air & Sea

nearly

Bathing together were ~~almost~~ infallible,

~~in every disorder~~ one or the other of

them being a match for every Disorder,

~~In cases~~ of the Stomach, the Lungs or the

Blood; ~~they were equally sovereign~~;

They were

~~They were~~ anti-spasmodic, anti-pul:

anti-bilious

:monary, anti-sceptic ^ & anti-rheumatic.

Nobody could catch cold by the Sea,

Nobody wanted appetite by the Sea,

[f.11v] Nobody wanted Spirits, Nobody

~~nor c[d] the most obstinate Cougher re:~~

* closing parenthesis deleted.

wanted Strength.

~~:tain a cough there 4 & 20 hours~~. — They

were healing, softing, relaxing — forti:

seemingly

:fying & bracing — just as ~~wh~~ was
^

wanted — sometimes one, sometimes the

other. — If the Sea breeze failed, the Sea-

Bath was the certain corrective; — & where

Bathing disagreed, the Sea Breeze alone

evidently

was ~~palpably~~ designed by Nature for the

cure. — His eloquence however could

not prevail. M^{r} — & M^{rs} H — never left

home. Marrying early & having a very

numerous Family, ~~they~~ their movements

long

had been ~~very long~~ limitted to one
^

small circle; & they were older in

Habits than in Age. — Excepting

two Journeys to London in the year,

to receive his Dividends, Mr H. went

no farther than his feet or his well-

could carry

-tried old Horse ~~conveyed~~ him, and

Mrs. Heywood's Adventurings were
only now & then to visit her Neigh:
old
:bours, in the ^ ~~ol~~ Coach which had
been new when they married &
eldest
fresh lined on their ^ Son's coming of
age 10 years ago. ——

[f.12r] They had very pretty Property — enough,
had their family been of reasonable
Limits to have allowed them a very
gentlemanlike Share of Luxuries & Change —
enough for them to have indulged in a
an occasional
new Carriage & better roads, ~~a Summer~~
month
~~occasionally~~ at Tunbridge Wells, & ~~a~~
and
symptoms of the Gout ~~to make~~ a Winter
at Bath; — but the maintenance, Edu:
:cation & fitting out of 14 Children de:
:manded a very quiet, settled, careful
course of Life — & ~~forbidding~~ obliged them
to be stationary & healthy at Willingden.

What Prudence had at first enjoined,
was now rendered pleasant by Habit.
They never left home, & they had a gra:
:tification in saying so. — But very far
from wishing their Children to do the
same, they were glad to promote their
getting out into the World, as much
as possible. They staid at home, that
their Children might get out; — and while
making that home extremely comfortable,
welcomed every change from it which
give useful connections or
could ~~lead them into respectable Company~~.
respectable acquaintance to Sons or Daughters.
[f.12v] When Mr. & Mrs. Parker therefore ceased
from soliciting a family-visit, and
bounded their veiws to carrying back
Daughter
one ~~young Lady~~ with them, no diffi:
:culties were started. It was gene[r]al plea:
:sure & consent. — Their invitation was
to Miss Charlotte Heywood, a very
pleasing young woman of two & twenty,

the eldest of the Daughters at home, &

under her Mother's directions
the one, who ~~in acting for her Mother,~~

had been particularly useful & obliging

to them; ~~&~~ who had attended them most,

& knew them best. — Charlotte was to

go, — with excellent health, to bathe

& be better if she could — to receive

every possible pleasure which Sanditon

could be made to supply by the

gratitude
~~grateful feelings~~ of those she went
^

with — & to buy new Parasols, new

for her Sisters &
Gloves, & new Broches, ~~& every thing else~~

~~that~~ herself at the Library, ~~there~~, which

Mr. P. was anxiously wishing to support. —

All that Mr. Heywood himself could be

persuaded to promise was, that he would

send ~~go by~~
~~recommend~~ everyone to Sanditon, who
^

asked his advice, & that nothing should

[f.13r] ever induce him (as far the future

could be answered for) to spend even

5 Shillings
~~one night~~ at Brinshore. —

Chapter 3.

Every Neighbourhood should have a

Great Lady. — The great Lady of Sanditon,

was Lady Denham; & in their Journey

from Willingden to the Coast, M^r. Parker

gave Charlotte a more detailed account

of her, than had been called for before. —

She had been necessarily often mentioned

at Willingden, — for being his Colleague in

speculation, Sanditon itself could not be

talked of long, without the introduction

of Lady Denham & that she was a very

rich old Lady, who had buried two Hus:

:bands, who knew the value of Money,

was very much looked up to & had

facts
a poor Cousin living with her, were ^

already well known, but some further

her history
particulars of ~~names & places~~, & ~~some~~

her
~~hints of~~ ^ Character ~~(though given with~~
~~the* light touch of a very friendly hand)~~
~~were~~ served to lighten the tediousness of

Hill
a long ~~Pull~~, ^ or a heavy bit of road,

and to give the visiting Young
[f.13v] Lady a suitable Knowledge of the Person
~~wh~~ with whom she might now expect to
be daily associating. — Lady D. had been a
rich Miss Brereton, born to Wealth but
not to Education. Her first Husband had
been a M^r. Hollis, a man of considerable Pro:
:perty in the Country, of which a large share
of the Parish of Sanditon, with Manor &
Mansion House made a part. He had been
~~quite~~ an elderly Man when she married
him; — her own age about 30. — Her motives
for such a Match could be little understood
at the distance of 40 years, but she had so

* '~~the~~' written over '~~a~~'.

well nursed & pleased M^{r}. Hollis, that at his
death he left her everything — all his Estates,[*]
& all at her Disposal. After a widowhood
of some years, she had been induced to
marry again. The late Sir Harry Denham,
of Denham Park in the Neighbourhood of
Sanditon had succeeded in removing her
& her large Income to his own Domains,
but he c^{d}. not succeed in the veiws of
permanently enriching his family, which[†]
were attributed to him. She had been too
wary to put anything out of her own
Power — and when on Sir Harry's Decease
she returned again to her own House
[f.14r] at Sanditon, she was said to have made
this boast to a friend "that though she
had got nothing but her Title from the
Family, still she had given nothing
for it." — For the Title, it was to be supposed
that she had married — & M^{r}. P. acknowledged

[*] 'E' of 'Estates' written over 'P'.
[†] 'which' written over another word, possibly 'while'.

there being just such a degree of value for

her conduct

it apparent now, as to give ~~it~~ ^ that na:

:tural explanation. "There is at times

said he — a little self-importance — but it

is not offensive; — & there are moments,

there are points, when her Love of Money

greatly

is carried ~~much~~ ^ too far. But she is a good-

-natured Woman, a very goodnatured Woman.

a chearful, independant, valuable
character.

— a very obliging, friendly Neighbour; ~~to us~~ —

may entirely

and her faults ~~are to~~ ^ be ~~cheifly~~ ^ imputed

her

to ~~the~~ ^ want of Education. She has good

natural Sense, but quite uncultivated. —

She has a fine active mind, as well as

a fine healthy frame for a Woman of 70,

& enters into the improvement of Sanditon

truly admirable —

with a spirit ~~which one admires~~ — though

now & then, a Littleness <u>will</u> appear.

She cannot look forward quite as I would

have her — & takes alarm at a trifling

present expence, without considering

what returns it will make her in
a year or two.

[f.14v] now &

That is — we think differently, we ~~see~~

then, see

things differently, ~~now & then~~ Miss H. —
^

you know

Those who tell their own Story ^ must be

listened to with Caution. — When you see

us in contact, you will judge for your:

:self." — Lady D. was indeed a great

wants of Society —

Lady beyond the common ~~Social order~~

for she had many Thousands a year to

bequeath, & three distinct sets of People

to be courted by; her own relations,

who might very reasonably wish for

her Original Thirty Thousand Pounds among

them, the legal Heirs of Mr Hollis, who

must hope to be more endebted to her

he had allowed them to
sense of Justice than ~~they c^d^~~ be to <u>his</u>,
and those Members of the Denham Family,
whom her 2^d^ Husband had hoped to make
a good Bargain for. — By all of these,
or by Branches of them, she had no doubt
been long, & still continued to be, well
attacked; — and of these* three divisions, M^r^ P.
did not hesitate to say that Mr Hollis'
~~Cous~~ Kindred were the <u>least</u> in favour
& Sir Harry Denham's the <u>most</u>. — The former
he beleived, had done themselves irreme:
:diable harm by expressions of very
unwise & unjustifiable resentment at
the time of Mr. Hollis's death; — the
[f.15r] Latter, to the advantage of being the rem:
:nant of a Connection which she certainly
valued, joined those of having been known
to her from their Childhood & of being
at hand to preserve their
always ~~able by their vicinity, to~~ interest

* 'these' written over 'the'.

by reasonable attention. Sir Edward, the

present Baronet, nephew to Sir Harry, re:

:sided constantly at Denham Park; & M^r P —

had little doubt, that he & his Sister Miss D —

who ~~always~~ lived with him, w^d. be ~~very~~

principally remembered in her Will.

He sincerely hoped it. — Miss Denham had a

very small provision — & her Brother was a

poor Man for his rank in Society. "He is a

warm friend to Sanditon — said Mr Parker —

& his hand w^d be as liberal as his heart,

he

~~if he~~ had ^ the Power. — He would be a noble

Coadjutor! — As it is, he does what he

can — & is running up a tasteful little

Cottage Ornèe, on a strip of waste Ground

Lady D. has granted him — ,

~~he holds under Lady D~~ — , which I have

we shall

no doubt ~~will~~ have many a Candidate

for, before the end even of <u>this</u> Season".

Till within the last twelvemonth, Mr P. had

considered Sir Edw: as standing without a

the fairest
rival, as ~~being~~ having ~~a very fair~~ chance of
succeeding to the greater part of all that
she had to give — but there was now
[f.15v] another person's claims to be taken into the
account, those of the young female relation,
whom Lady D. had been induced to receive
into her Family. After having always
protested against any such addition, ~~depre:~~
~~:cating the idea of a Companion, defying &~~
and long & often enjoyed
*~~enjoying~~ the repeated defeats she had
given to every attempt of her relations ~~on~~
~~that head, she had been~~ to introduce this
young Lady, or that young Lady as a Compa:
:nion at Sanditon ~~Hall~~ House, she had brought
back with her from London last Michaelmas
a Miss Brereton, who bid fair by her
merits to vie in favour with Sir Edward,†
& to ~~restore~~ secure for herself & her family
that share of the accumulated Property

* two illegible letters scored through.
† 'ard' of 'Edward' written over other letters (illegible).

which they had certainly the best right

to inherit. — Mr. Parker spoke warmly

of Clara Brereton, & the interest of his

story increased very much with the

Character.

introduction of such a ~~young Woman~~.

Charlotte listened with more than amuse:

:ment now; — it was solicitude & Enjoyment,

as she heard her ~~delineated~~ described ~~(and~~

~~not with~~ to be lovely, amiable, gentle,

unassuming, conducting herself uniformly

with great good sense, & evidently gaining

by her innate worth, on the affections

of her Patroness. — Beauty, Sweetness,

[f.16r] Poverty & Dependance, do not want

the imagination of a Man to operate upon.

With due exceptions — Woman feels for

promptly &

Woman very ^ compassionately. He gave

the particulars which had led to Clara's ad:

:mission at Sanditon, as no bad exemplification

of that mixture of Character, that union of

Littleness with Kindness with Good Sense

with even Liberality which he saw in Lady
D. — After having avoided ~~being in~~ London
& principally very
for many years, ^ on account of these ^ Cousins
~~there resident there,~~ who were continually
& whom she was
writing, inviting & tormenting her, ~~she had~~
determined to keep at a Distance, she had
there
been obliged to go ~~there~~ ^^ last Michaelmas
with the certainty of being detained at least
a fortnight. — She had gone to an Hotel — living
by her own account, as prudently as possible,
reputed
to defy the ~~proverbial~~ expensiveness of such
calling
a home, & at the end of three Days ~~called~~
for her Bill, that she might judge of
her state. — Its' amount was such as deter:
not
:mined her on staying ^ another hour in
all the
the House, & she was preparing in ~~great~~
anger & perturbation which a beleif of very
gross imposition there, & an ignorance of

where to go for better usage, to leave the

Hotel at all hazards, when the Cousins,

the politic & lucky Cousins, who seemed

a

always to have ^ spy on her, introduced

themselves at this important moment,

persuaded

& learning her situation, ~~induced~~ her to

for the rest of her stay

accept such a home ^ as their humbler

[f.16v] a

house in ^ very inferior part of London, c^{d}

offer. ~~for the rest of her stay~~. — She went;

was delighted with her welcome & the

hospitality & attention she received from

every body — found her good Cousins the B —

beyond her expectation

~~were~~ ^ worthy people — & finally was impelled

by a personal knowledge of their narrow

Income & pecuniary difficulties, to invite one

of the girls of the family to pass the Winter

with her. The invitation was to one, for six

months — with the probability of another

being then to take her place; — but in

selecting the one, Lady D. had shewn the
good part of her Character — for passing by
the actual daughters of the House, she had
chosen Clara, a Neice — , more helpless &
more pitiable of course than any — &
dependant on Poverty — an additional Bur:
:then on an encumbered Circle — & one, who
had been so low in every worldly veiw, as with
all her natural endowments & powers, to have

a
been preparing for ^ situation little better than
a Nursery Maid. — Clara had returned with

merit ~~sweetness~~
her — & by her good sense & ~~unpretending manners~~
had now, to all appearance secured a very strong
hold in Lady D.'s regard. The six months had long
been over — & not a syllable was breathed of
any change, or exchange. — She was a general

steady conduct
favourite; — the influence of her ~~good Judgement~~
& mild, ~~unassuming,~~ gentle Temper was felt by
everybody. The prejudices which had met her at
first in some quarters, were all dissipated. She

was felt to be worthy of Trust — to be the very

companion who w^d^. guide & soften Lady D — who

w^d^. enlarge her mind & open her hand. — She was as

thoroughly amiable as she was lovely — & since

having
~~she had~~ had the advantage of their Sanditon Breezes,
^

~~she was become~~ that Loveliness was
complete.*

[f.17r] [Booklet 2]

Chapter 4.

"And whose very snug-looking Place is

this?" — said Charlotte, as in a sheltered Dip

close
within 2 miles of the Sea, they passed ~~in~~
^

by
~~front of~~ a moderate-sized house, well fenced

Orchard
& planted, & rich in the Garden, ~~Ground~~ &

Meadows
~~Orchards~~ which are the best embellishments

such a
of ~~such any~~ Dwelling. "It seems to have as
^

many comforts about it as Willingden." —

* line written at bottom of f.1r. See p. 383.

old
"Ah! — said Mr. P. — This is my ∧ House — the house
of my Forefathers — the house where I & all
my Brothers & Sisters were born & bred —
& where my own 3 eldest Children were
born — where Mrs. P. & I lived till within
the last 2 years — till our new House
was finished. — I am glad you are pleased
with it. — It is an honest old Place — and
Hillier keeps it in very good order. I have
you know
given it up ∧ to the Man who occupies the
cheif of my Land. <u>He</u> gets a better House
by it — & I, a rather better situation! —
Hill
one other ~~ascent~~ brings us to ~~the heart~~
— modern Sanditon —
~~of~~ Sanditon ∧ — ~~we shall soon catch the~~
~~roof of my new house; my real home,~~ —
a beautiful Spot. — Our Ancestors, you know
always built in a hole. — Here were we,
pent down in this little contracted Nook,
without Air or Veiw, only one mile &

[f.17v] 3 q^{rs}. from the noblest expanse of Ocean

between the Southforeland & the Land's end,

&

without the smallest advantage from it.
^

You will not think I have made a

bad exchange, when we reach Trafalgar

House — which by the bye, I almost wish

I had not named Trafalgar — for Waterloo

is more the thing now. However, Waterloo

is in reserve — & if we have encouragement

a

enough this year for ~~the~~ little Crescent to

be ventured on — (as I trust we shall.) ~~&~~

~~a Crescent is a building that always takes —)~~

then, we shall be able to call it Waterloo

joined to the

Crescent — & the ~~very~~ name ~~will give us~~

~~choice of Lodgers~~. — form of the Building, which

always takes, will give us the command

In a good Season

of Lodgers —. We sh^{d}. have more applications
^

than we could attend to." — "It was always

a very comfortable House — said M^{rs}. Parker —

at it
looking ^ through the back window with ~~a great~~

~~deal of~~ something like the fondness of regret. —

And such a nice Garden — such an ex:

:cellent Garden." "Yes, my Love, but that

we may be said to carry with us. — It

supplies us, as before, with all the fruit &

in fact
vegetables we want; & we have all the

comfort of an excellent Kitchen Garden,

the constant Eyesore of or the
without ~~having~~ ^ its formalities;* ~~as an Eyesore~~,

yearly nuisance of its
~~or its occasional~~ ^ decaying vegetation. —

Who can endure a Cabbage Bed in October"?

[f.18r] ~~and~~
"Oh! dear — yes. — We are quite as well off

ever we were —
~~here~~ for Gardenstuff as ~~we used to be~~ — for

if it is forgot to be brought at any time, we

can always buy what we want at

Sanditon-House. — The Gardiner there, is

glad enough to supply us — . But it was a

* 'ies' written over 'y' at the end of 'formalities'.

nice place for the Children ~~f~~ to run about

in. So Shady in Summer!" "My dear, we

on the Hill

shall have shade enough ^ & more than enough

~~about us~~ in the course of a very few years — ;

The Growth of my Plantations is a general

~~my Plantations astonish everybody by their~~

astonishment.

~~Growth~~. ^ In the mean while we have the

Canvas Awning, which gives us the most

complete comfort within doors — & you

can get a Parasol at Whitby's for little

Mary at any time, or a large Bonnet at

Jebbs' — And as for the Boys, I must say

I w^{d}. rather <u>them</u> run about in the

Sunshine than not. I am sure we agree

my dear, in wishing our Boys to be as

hardy as possible." — "Yes indeed, I am sure

we do — & I will get Mary a little Parasol,

her as proud as can be

which will make ~~her so proud! — It will~~

How Grave she will walk

~~be delightful to see her walking~~ about

and
with it, ~~so gravely. She will~~ fancy her:
:self quite a little Woman. — Oh! I have
not the smallest doubt of our being a
great deal better off where we are now.
If we any of us want to bathe, ~~now~~, we
have not a q.ͬ of a mile to go. — But you
[f.18v] know, (still looking back) one loves to
look at an old friend, at a place where
one has been happy. — The Hilliers did
not seem to feel the Storms last Winter
at all
~~as we did~~. — I remember seeing M.ʳˢ Hillier
those
after one of ~~our~~ dreadful Nights, when <u>we</u>
had been literally rocked in our bed, and
she did not seem at all aware of the
Wind being anything more than common."
"Yes, yes — that's likely enough. <u>We</u> have all
the Grandeur of the Storm, with less real
with
danger, because the Wind meeting ^ nothing
to oppose or confine it around our House,
simply rages & passes on — while down

in ~~this Pit~~, this Gutter — nothing is known

of the state of the Air, below the Tops of

the Trees — and the Inhabitants may be

one

by ~~any~~

taken totally unawares, ~~if one~~ of those

which should do more mischief

dreadful Currents ~~should pour through~~

in a when they do arise

~~the~~ Valley, ~~which do more mischeif~~

than an open Country ever ~~knows~~

experiences in the heaviest Gale. — But my

dear Love — as to Gardenstuff; — you were

saying that any accidental omission is

supplied in a moment by Ly D.'s Gardiner —

~~get~~

but it occurs to me that we ought to ~~deal~~

~~with all our~~ go else where upon such oc:

Stringer

:casions — & that old ~~Salmon~~ & his son have

a higher claim. I encouraged him to set up —

& am afraid he does not do very well — that is,

[f.19r] there has not been time enough yet. — He will

beyond a doubt

do very well — but at first it is Up hill work;

^

and therefore we must give him what

Help
~~encouragement~~ we can — & when any Vegetables

or fruit happen to be wanted, — & it will

often wanted,
not be amiss to have them ~~forgotten~~, to have

something or other forgotten most days; —

Just to have a nominal supply you know,

that poor old Andrew may not lose his daily

Job — but in fact to buy the cheif of our con:

:sumption of ~~old~~ the Stringers. — " "Very well

be
my Love, that can ^ easily done — & Cook

will be satisfied ~~I hope~~ — which will be a

great comfort, for she is always complaining

& says
of old Andrew now, ^ he never brings her

what she wants. — There — now the old House

is quite ~~out of~~ left behind. — What is it, your

Brother Sidney says about its' being a Hospital?"

"Oh! my dear Mary, merely a Joke of his.

He pretends to advise me to make a Hospital of it.

He pretends to laugh at my Improvements.

Sidney says any thing you know. He has

always said what he chose ~~of his eldest~~

~~B^r. & to his Eldest B^r. &~~ of & to us, all.

Most Families have such a member among
~~A young Man of Abilities & Address, &~~

them I beleive Miss Heywood. — There is a
~~general. ease of manner Miss H. — who says~~

privileged by superior abilities or
spirits

someone in most families ~~who is privileged~~
^

~~anything~~ In ours, it is Sidney; who is a
to say anything. — ~~Sidney is~~ ^ very clever

and with great powers of pleasing. —
Young Man, ^ — ~~very lively, very pleasant~~ —

He lives too to be settled;
~~living very~~ much in the World ~~— & liked~~

that is his only fault. — ~~I wish we may~~
~~by everybody. I should~~
He is here & there & every where. I wish we may

[f.19v] get him to Sanditon. I should like to

have you acquainted with him. — And

fine thing
it would be a ~~credit to~~ for the Place! — Such
^

a young Man as Sidney, with his neat

equipage & fashionable air, — You & I

Mary, know what effect it might have:"

Many a respectable Family, many a careful

Mother, many a pretty Daughter, might it

secure us, to the prejudice of E. Bourne &

Hastings." — They were now approaching the

real

Church & ^ village of ~~original~~ Sanditon, which

Hill

stood at the foot of the ~~Down~~ they were

afterwards to ascend — a Hill, whose side

was covered with the Woods & enclosures

and Height ended in

of Sanditon House ~~but~~ whose ~~Top was~~ an

where the new Build^{gs}: might soon be looked for.

open Down ~~overlooking the Sea~~. A branch

winding more obliquely

only, of the Valley, ~~wound~~ ^ towards the

gave

Sea, ~~giving~~ a passage to an inconsiderable

formed

Stream, & ~~forming~~ at its mouth, a 3^{d}

Habitable Division, in a small cluster

of Fisherman's Houses. — The Village

contained little more than Cottages, but

the Spirit of the day had been caught, as

delight

Mr P. observed with ~~great pleasure~~ to

Charlotte, & two or three of the best of

them were smartened up with a

white Curtain & "Lodgings to let" — , and

farther on, in the little Green Court of

an old Farm House, ~~were actually~~ two

[f.20r] Females in elegant white were actually to

be seen with their books & camp stools —

and in turning the corner of the Baker's

shop, the sound of a Harp might be heard

upper

~~from~~ through the ~~open~~ Casement. — Such

Blissful

sights & sounds were highly ~~exhilarating~~ to

Mr P. — Not that he had any personal

concern in the success of the Village itself; for

considering it as too remote from the Beach,

he had done nothing there — but it was a

most valuable proof of the increasing

fashion of the place altogether. If the

might

village could attract, the Hill ~~must~~ be

nearly full. — He anticipated an amazing
Season. — At the same time last year,
(late in July) there had not been a single
Lodger in the Village! — nor did he remem:
during Summer
:ber any ^ the whole ~~Season~~, excepting one
family of children who came from London
and
for sea air after the hooping Cough, ~~but~~
would not let them be
whose Mother ~~c^{d} not bear to have them~~
the Shore
nearer ^ for fear of their tumbling in. —
"Civilization, Civilization indeed! — cried
M^{r} P — , delighted — . Look my dear Mary —
William
Look at ~~old~~ Heeley's windows. — Blue
Shoes, & nankin Boots! — Who w^{d} have
at a Shoemaker's
expected such a sight ^ in old Sanditon! —
This is new within the Month. There was no blue Shoe when
we passed this way a month ago. —
Glorious indeed! — Well, I think I <u>have</u>
done something in my Day. — Now, for
[f.20v] our Hill, our health-breathing Hill. —"

In ascending, they passed the Lodge-Gates

of Sanditon House, & saw the top of the

House itself among its Groves. It was the

former Days
last Building of ~~old erection~~ in that line

of the Parish. A little higher up, the Mo:

:dern began; & in crossing the Down, a

Prospect House, a Bellevue Cottage, & a Denham

Place were to be looked at by Charlotte

with the calmness of amused Curiosity, &

~~to be watched~~
~~by Mr. Parker their d~~ by Mr. P. with the
∧

eager eye which hoped to see scarcely any

empty houses. — More Bills at the Window

calculated
than he had ~~reckoned~~ on; — ~~fewer~~ and a

smaller shew of company on the Hill — Fewer

Carriages, fewer Walkers. He had fancied

it just the time of day for them to be

all returning from their Airings to dinner

But
— ~~but there were the Sands~~ — the Sands

& the Terrace   and the
^always attracted some — Tide must be

                                -Tide now.
flowing — about half ~~in~~. — He longed to

                                at
be on the Sands, the Cliffs, ^ his own House,

                                at once.
& every where out of his House ^ His Spirits

                                he
rose with the very sight of the Sea & ^ c^{d} —
almost feel his Ancle getting stronger already. —
Trafalgar House on the most elevated spot

on the Down was a light   standing
~~of any, was an~~ ^ elegant Building, ~~separated~~
~~from the Down only by a~~ in a small

          a   round
Lawn with ^ very young plantation~~s over~~ ^ it,

[f.21r] about
~~not~~ an hundred yards from the brow
of ~~the Cliff, — which was~~ a steep, but not

very
^ lofty Cliff — and the nearest to it, of every

                                short
Building, excepting one ^ row of smart-
-looking Houses, called the Terrace, with

a broad walk in front, aspiring to be
the Mall of the Place. In this row were
the best Milliner's shop & the Library —
a little
~~a small space~~ detached from it, the Hotel
& Billiard room — Here began the Descent
to
to the Beach, & ^ the Bathing Machines — &
this was therefore the favourite spot for
Beauty & Fashion. — At Trafalgar House,
rising at a little distance behind the Terrace,
The Travellors were safely set down, & all
was happiness & Joy between Papa & Mama &
their Children; while Charlotte having received
possession of her apartment, found amusement
ample, venetian
enough in standing at her ^ window, & looking
over the miscellaneous foreground of un:
:finished Buildings, waving Linen, & tops
of Houses, to the Sea, dancing & sparkling
in Sunshine & Freshness.
~~under a Sunshiny breeze.~~ —

<u>Chapter 5.</u>

When they met before dinner, Mr P.
was looking over Letters. — "Not a Line
from Sidney ! — said he. — He is an idle
fellow. — I sent him an account of my
[f.21v] accident from Willingden, & thought
he would have vouchsafed me an
But
answer. — ^ Perhaps it implies that he is
I trust it may.
coming himself. — ~~Not unlikely~~. — But
here is a Letter from one of my Sisters.
<u>They</u> never fail me. — Women are the only
Correspondents to be depended on. — Now
Mary, (smiling at his Wife) — before I
open it, what shall we guess as to the
state of health of those it comes from —
say
or rather what wd Sidney ~~guess~~ ^ if he
were here? — Sidney is a saucy fellow, Miss
H. — And you must know, he will have
it there is a good deal of Imagination in

two
my ^ Sisters' complaints — but it really is

not so — or very little — They have wretched

frequently
health, as you have heard us say & are

subject to a variety of very serious
~~at times martyrs to very dreadful~~ Dis=

=orders. — Indeed, I do not beleive they

know what a day's health is; — & at

the same time, they are such excellent

useful Women & have so much energy

of character that, where any Good is

to be done, they force themselfes on ex:

:ertions which to those who do not

thoroughly know them, have an extra:

:ordinary appearance. — But there is

really no affectation about them. They have

[f.22r] only weaker constitutions & stronger

minds than are often met with, either

separate or together. — And our Youngest

B^{r}. — who lives with them, & who is

much
not ^ above 20,* I am sorry to say, is almost

* '20' written over '22'.

as great an Invalid as themselves. — He is
so delicate that he can engage in no Pro:
:fession, ~~which is most unfortunate~~. —
Sidney laughs at him — but it really is
no Joke — tho' Sidney often makes me
laugh at them all inspite of myself. —
Now, if he were here, I know he w^{d}. be
offering odds, that either Susan, Diana
w^{d}. appear by this letter to have
or Arthur ~~had~~ been at the point of death
^
within the last month. —" Having run his
eye over the Letter, he shook his head &
began — :
~~observed~~ "No chance of seeing them at
^
Sanditon I am sorry to say. — A very in:
:different account of them indeed. Seriously,
a <u>very</u> indifferent account. — Mary, you
will be quite sorry to hear how ill they
have been & are. — Miss H., if you will
give me leave, I will read Diana's
Letter aloud. — I like to have my friends
acquainted with each other — & I am
afraid this is the only sort of acquaintance

accomplishing
I shall have the means of ~~bringing~~

between you.
~~about~~; — And I can have no scruple on

shew
Diana's account — for her Letters ~~describe~~

[f.22v] her exactly as she is, the most active,

friendly, warmhearted Being in existence,

& therefore must give a good impression."

He read. — "My dear Tom, We were all

at
much greived ~~by~~ your accident, & if

you had not described yourself as fallen

into such very good hands, I sh^{d}. have

been with you at all hazards the day

after the rec^{pt}. of your Letter, though

it found me ~~hardly able to crawl from~~

~~my~~ suffering
~~the Bed to the Sofa.~~ under a more
^

severe attack than usual of my old

& hardly able to crawl from my Bed to the Sofa.
greivance, Spasmodic Bile . — But how
^

were you treated? — Send me more Particu:

:lars in your next. — If indeed a simple

Sprain, as you denominate it, nothing
w^{d}. have been so judicious as Friction,
Friction by the hand alone, supposing
it could be applied <u>instantly</u>. — Two
years ago I happened to be calling on M^{rs}
Sheldon when her Coachman sprained
his foot as he was cleaning the Carriage
& c^{d}. hardly limp into the House — but
use
by the immediate ~~application~~ of Friction
steadily
alone, ~~well~~ persevered in, (& I rubbed
six
his Ancle with my own hand for ~~4~~
Hours without Intermission) — he was
well in three days. — Many Thanks my
[f.23r] dear Tom, for the kindness with respect
to us, which had so large a share in
bringing on your accident — But pray:
never run into Peril again, in looking
for an Apothecary on our account, for
had you the most experienced Man in his
Line Settled at Sanditon, it w^{d}. be no

recommendation to us. We have entirely
done with the whole Medical Tribe.
We have consulted Physician after Phy^{n} —
in vain, till we are quite convinced
that they can do nothing for us & that we
must trust to our own knowledge of our
own wretched Constitutions for any releif. ~~to~~
~~be obtained.~~ — But if you think it ad:
:visable for the interest of the Place, to
get a Medical Man there, I will un:
:dertake the commission with pleasure,
& have no doubt of succeeding. — I ~~know~~
~~where to apply~~ could soon put the ne:
:cessary Irons in the fire. — As for getting
to Sanditon myself, it is quite an Im:
:possibility. I greive to say that I dare
not attempt it, but my feelings tell
me too plainly that in my present
State, the Sea air w^{d}. probably be the
death of me. — And neither of my dear
Companions will leave me, or I w^{d} —
[f.23v] promote their going down to you for a

fortnight. But in truth, I doubt whether

Susan's nerves w^{d}. be equal to the effort.

She has been suffering much from the

10

Headache and Six Leaches a day for ~~the~~

days together so
~~last week have~~ releived her ~~a~~ ^ little

that we* thought it right to change our

measures — and being convinced on exa:

:mination that much of the Evil lay

in her Gum, I persuaded her to attack

accordingly
the disorder there. She has ^ had 3 Teeth

drawn ~~accordingly~~, & is decidedly better,

but her Nerves are a good deal deranged.

She can only speak in a whisper — and

fainted away twice this morning

trying to suppress ~~coughing.~~ a cough.
on poor Arthur's ~~sneezing~~ ^ He, I am

happy to say is tolerably well — tho'

more languid than I like — & I fear

for his Liver. — I have heard nothing

* 'we' written over 'I'.

of Sidney since your being together in Town,

but conclude his scheme to the I. of Wight

has not taken place, or we should have

seen him in his way. — Most sincerely

do we wish you a good Season at Sandi:

:ton, & though we cannot contribute to

your Beau Monde in person, we are

doing our utmost to send you Company

worth having; &* think we may

safely reckon on securing you two

[f.24r] one

large Families, ~~that of~~ a rich West Indian

Girls

from Surry, the other, a most respectable ^

Boarding School, or Academy, from Camber:

:well. — I will not tell you how many

People I have employed in the business

But

— Wheel within wheel. — ^ Success more than

repays. — Yours most affec[ly] — &c"

as he ~~concluded~~

"Well — said Mr P. — ~~having finished & re:~~

* '&' written over '—'.

finished ~~it.~~ — Though I dare say
~~:folded his Letter — I suppose if~~ Sidney ~~w^d^ —~~

~~to laugh at~~
extremely entertaining
might find something ~~very amusing~~ in

& make us laugh for half an hour together
this Letter I declare I ~~can see nothing in~~

by myself, can see nothing ~~either~~
in either
it — but what is very pitiable or very
^ ^
creditable. — With all their sufferings, you

in
perceive how much they are occupied ~~for~~

~~advancing~~ promoting
the Good of others! — So anxious for Sanditon!
^
Two large Families — One, for Prospect House

probably, the other, for N.º 2. Denham

Place — or the end house of the Terrace, —

extra
& Beds at the Hotel. — I told you my
^
Sisters were excellent Women, Miss H — ."

"And I am sure they must be very

extraordinary ones. — said Charlotte. I am

~~quite~~ astonished at the chearful style of

the Letter, considering the state in which

both Sisters appear to be. — Three Teeth

drawn at once! — ~~It is really~~ frightful! —

Your Sister Diana seems almost as ill as possible,

but those 3 Teeth of your Sister Susan's, are

[f.24v] more

~~most~~ distressing ~~to one's imagination~~ than

all the rest. — " "Oh! — they are so used to the

operation — to every operation — & have such

Fortitude! — " " Your Sisters know what they

are about, I dare say, but their Measures

seem to touch on Extremes. — I feel that in

any illness, I should be so anxious for Pro:

:fessional advice, so very little venturesome

for myself, or any body I loved! — But then,

we have been so healthy a family, that I

can be no Judge of what the habit of self-

own

-doctoring may do. — " " Why to ~~say~~ the truth,

said M^{rs}. P. — I do think the Miss Parkers

carry it too far sometimes — & so do you

my Love, you know. — You often think they

w^{d}. be better, if they w^{d}. leave themselves

more alone — & especially ~~p~~ Arthur. I

know you think it a great pity they sh^{d} give him such a turn for being ill. — " " Well, well — my dear Mary — I grant you, it is unfortunate for poor Arthur, that, at his time of Life he sh^{d} be encouraged to give way to Indisposi= =tion. It is bad; — it is bad that he should be fancying himself too sickly for any Profession — & sit down at 1 & 20, ~~idle & indolent~~, on the interest of his own little Fortune, without any idea of attempting to ~~the slightest plan~~ improve it, or ~~any prospect~~ of engaging in [f.25r] any occupation that may be of use to himself or others. — But let us talk of pleasanter things. — These two large Families are just what we wanted — But — here is something at hand, plea: :santer still — Morgan, with his "Dinner on Table." —

Chap: 6.

The Party were very soon moving

after Dinner. Mr P. could not be satis:
:fied without an early visit to the
Library, & the Library Subscription book,
&
& Charlotte was glad to see as much, as
quickly as possible, where all was new.
They were out in the very quietest part
of a Watering-place Day, when the im:
Business
:portant ^ of Dinner or of sitting after Dinner
was going on in almost every inhabited
Elderly
Lodging; — here & there a solitary ^ Man
might be seen, who was forced to move
early & walk for health — but in
general, it was a thorough pause of
Company, it was Emptiness & Tranquil:
&
:lity on the Terrace, the Cliffs, ^ the
Sands. — The Shops were deserted — the
Straw Hats & pendant Lace seemed left
the House
to their fate both within ^ & without,

[f.25v] and Mrs Whilby at the Library was

her room
sitting in ~~the little~~ inner ~~parlour~~, reading

one of her own Novels, for want of

employment.
~~something better to do.~~ — The List of

Subscribers was but commonplace. The

Lady Denham, Miss Brereton, Mr & Mrs P —

Sir Edw: Denham & Miss Denham, whose

names might be said to lead off the

Season, were followed by nothing better

than ~~such as these.~~ — Mrs Mathews —

Miss Mathews, Miss E. Mathews, Miss H.

Brown*
Mathews. — Dr & Mrs ~~Henderson~~ — Mr

Richard Pratt. — ~~M~~ Lieut: Smith RN.

Capt: Little, — Limehouse. — Mrs Jane Fisher.

Miss Fisher. Miss Scroggs. — Rev: Mr Hankins.†

Mr Beard — Solicitor, Grays Inn. — Mrs Davis.

& Miss Merryweather. — Mr P. could not

the List
but feel that ~~it~~ ^ was not only ~~a List~~

* 'Brown' written over other letters (illegible).
† 'Hankins' written over 'Hankin' i.e. 's' added later.

without Distinction, but less numerous

than he had hoped. It was but July

however, & August & September were

the Months; — And besides, the promised

large Families from Surry & Camberwell,

were -ready consolation.
~~was~~ an ever-~~present source of Joy.~~ —

without delay
M^rs. Whitby came forward ~~immediately~~

from her Literary recess, delighted to see

M^r. Parker again, whose manners re:

:commended him to every body, & they

were fully occupied in their various

[f.26r] Civilities & Communications, while Charlotte

having added her name to the List ~~with all~~

~~becoming alacrity~~ as the first offering to the

busy in
success of the Season, was ~~proceeding to~~

further
some immediate purchases for the ^ good of

Everybody, as soon as Miss Whitby could be

hurried down from her Toilette, with all her

smart Trinkets
glossy Curls & ~~ornamented Comb's~~ to wait

on her. — The Library of course, afforded every

thing; all the useless things in the World

that c^{d}. not be done without, & among so

many pretty Temptations, & with so much

good will for M^{r}. P. to encourage Expenditure,

Charlotte began to feel that she must check

she reflected
herself — or rather ~~began to feel~~ that at two

& Twenty there c^{d}. be no excuse for her

for her
doing otherwise — & that it w^{d}. not do ^ to be

very
spending all her Money the ^ first Evening.

She took up a Book; it happened to be a
~~of her arrival~~ ~~A~~ vol: of <u>Camilla</u>. ~~happened~~

~~to lie on the Counter~~. She had not <u>Camilla's</u>

Youth, & had no intention of having her

so, she turned from the
Distress, — ~~The Gl~~ Drawers of rings & Broches

~~must be resisted~~ repressed farther solici:

:tation & paid for what she bought. —

For her particular gratification, they were

then to take a Turn on the Cliff — but

as they quitted the Library they were met

[f.26v] by two Ladies whose arrival made an
alteration necessary, Lady Denham & Miss
Brereton. — They had been to Trafalgar House,
& ~~had~~ been thence
~~whence they were~~ directed ^ to the Library,
& though ~~her having walked a good mile~~
~~was~~ Lady D. was a great deal too active
to regard the walk of a mile as anything
requiring rest, & talked of going home again
directly, the Parkers knew that to be pressed
into their House, & obliged to take her
Tea with them, would suit her best, — &
therefore the stroll on the Cliff gave way
to an immediate return home. — "No, no,
said her Ladyship — I will not have you hurry
your Tea on my account. — I know you
like your Tea late. — My early hours are not
to put my Neighbours to inconvenience.
No, no, Miss Clara & I will get back to
our own Tea. — We came out with no
other Thought. — We wanted just to see
you & make your
~~our good Neighbours, & be~~ ^ sure of ~~their~~

being really come — , but we get back to

our own Tea." — She went on however

towards Trafalgar House & took possession

very quietly —

of the Drawing room ~~without any other~~

~~species of opposition~~ without seeming to

hear a word of Mrs. P.'s orders to the Ser:

:vant as they entered, to bring Tea directly.

Charlotte was fully consoled for the loss

[f.27r] of her walk, by finding herself in company

with those, whom the conversation of the

morng had given her a great curiosity

She observed them well.

to see. ^ — Lady D. was of middle height, stout,

upright & alert in her motions with a shrewd

&

eye, ^ ~~a~~ self-satisfied air — but not an un:

:agreable Countenance — & tho' her manner

was rather downright & abrupt, as of a

being free-spoken

person who valued herself on ~~free speaking~~,

there was a goodhumour & cordiality ~~in~~

about her —

~~it~~ — ^ a civility & readiness to be acquainted

of
with Charlotte herself, & a heartiness ~~and~~

welcome
~~interest~~ towards her old friends, which ~~was~~
^
was inspiring the Good will, she seemed to

feel; — And as for Miss Brereton, her ap:

:pearance so completely justified Mr. P.'s

praise that Charlotte thought she had never

beheld a more lovely, or more Interesting

young Woman. — Elegantly tall, regularly

handsome, with great delicacy of complexion

&
& soft Blue Eyes, a sweetly modest~~y~~ yet
^
naturally graceful~~ness of~~ * Address, Charlotte

in
could see her only the† most perfect re:
^
whatever Heroine might
:presentation of ~~all the most beautiful~~

~~& bewitching Heroines~~ be most beautiful

& bewitching, in all the numerous vol:s

on
they had left behind them ~~in~~ Mrs. Whilby's

* 'ly' added to 'sweet' and 'ly' added to 'natural' so that 'sweet modesty . . . naturally graceful of Address' becomes 'sweetly modest . . . naturally graceful Address'.
† 'the' written over letters (illegible).

shelves. — Perhaps it ~~was from~~ might be partly

[f.27v] oweing to her having just issued from

a Circulating Library — but she c^{d} not

separate the idea of a complete Heroine

from Clara Brereton. Her situation with

Lady Denham so very much in favour of

it! — She seemed placed with her on pur:

Such

:pose to be ill-used. — ^ Poverty & Dependance

such

joined to ^ Beauty & Merit, seemed to leave

no choice in the business. — These feelings

were not the result of any spirit of Ro:

:mance in Charlotte herself. No, she was

a very sober-minded young Lady, suffici:

:ently well-read in Novels to supply her

Imagination with amusements, but not

at all unreasonably influenced by them;

first

& while she pleased herself ~~in~~ the ^ 5 minutes

with fancying the Persecutions which <u>ought</u>

be the Lot of

to ~~await~~ ^ the interesting Clara, especially

in the form of the most barbarous conduct

on Lady Denham's side, she found no re:
:luctance to admit from subsequent ob:
:servation, that they appeared to be on
very comfortable Terms. — She c^{d} see
nothing worse in Lady Denham,~~'s~~ than the
sort of oldfashioned formality of always calling
her Miss Clara — nor anything objectionable
in the degree of observance & attention which
Clara paid. — On one side it seemed protecting
[f.28r] kindness, on the other grateful & affectionate
respect. — The Conversation turned entirely
upon Sanditon, its present number of Visitants
& the Chances of a good Season. It was evi:
:dent that Lady D. had more anxiety, more
fears of loss, than her Coadjutor. She wanted
to have the Place fill faster, & seemed to have
many harassing apprehensions of the
Lodgings being in some instances under-
-let. — Miss Diana Parker's two* large Families
were not forgotten. "Very ~~very~~ good, very good,
said her Ladyship. — A West Indy Family

* 'two' written over other letters (illegible).

& a school. That sounds well. That will
spend
bring Money." — "No people ~~are said~~ more
freely, I beleive, than W. Indians." observed
Mr. Parker. — "Aye — so I have heard — and
fancy
because they have full Purses, ~~think~~ themselves
equal, may be, to your old Country Families.
But
~~And~~ then, they who scatter ~~about~~ their
Money so freely, never think of whether
they may not be doing mischeif by
raising the price of Things — And I have
heard that's very much the case with
your West=ingines — and if they come
among us to raise the price of our ne:
:cessaries of Life, we shall not much
thank them Mr. Parker." — "My dear Madam,
they can only raise the price of con:
[f.28v] :sumeable Articles, by such an extraordinary
Demand for them & such a diffusion of
Money among us, as must do us more
Good than harm. — Our Butchers & Bakers

& Traders in general cannot get rich without

bringing Prosperity to us. — If they do not

gain, our rents must be insecure — & in

proportion to their profit must be ours even:

:tually in the increased value of our Houses."

"Oh! — well. — But I should not like to

have Butcher's meat raised, though — & I

shall keep it down as long as I can. —

Aye — that young Lady smiles ~~at me~~ I see; —

I dare say
She thinks me a odd* sort of a Creature,
^

~~may be~~ — but she will come to care a:

:bout such matters herself in time. Yes,

yes, my Dear, depend upon it, you will

be thinking of the price of Butcher's meat

in time — tho' you may not happen

to have quite such a Servants Hall ~~full~~

to feed, as I have. — And I do beleive

those are best off, that have† fewest

Servants. — I am not a Woman of Parade,

* 'o' of 'odd' written over another letter (illegible).
† 'ha' of 'have' written over other letters (illegible).

as
all the World knows, & if it was not
^
for what I owe to poor Mr Hollis's me:
:mory, I should never keep up Sanditon
House as I do; — it is not for my own
pleasure. — Well Mr Parker — and the
other is a Boarding school, a French
[f.29r] Boarding School, is it? — No harm in
that. — They'll stay their six weeks. — And
out of such a number, who knows but some
may be consumptive & want Asses milk —
& I have two Milch asses at this present
time. — But perhaps the little Misses may
hurt the Furniture. — I hope they will have
a good sharp Governess to look after
them." — Poor Mr Parker got no more
~~thanks~~ credit from Lady D. than he had
from his Sisters, for the object which had
taken him to Willingden. "Lord! my dear
Sir, she cried, how could you think of
such a thing? I am very sorry you met
with your accident, but upon my word you

deserved it. — Going after a Doctor! —
Why, what sh^{d} we do with a Doctor here?
It w^{d} be only encouraging our Servants
& the Poor to fancy themselves ill, if there
was a D^{r} at hand. — Oh! pray, let us
have none of the Tribe at Sanditon.
We go on very well as we are. There
is the Sea & the Downs & my Milch-
asses — & I have told Mrs Whilby that
if any body enquires for a Chamber-
-House, they may be supplied at a fair
rate — (poor Mr Hollis's Chamber Horse,*
as good as new) — and what can
[f.29v] People want for more? — Here have I
lived 70 good years in the world & never
took Physic above twice — and never
saw the face of a Doctor in all my Life,
on my <u>own</u> account. — And I verily
my
beleive if ^ poor dear Sir Harry had never
seen one neither, he w^{d} have been

* the 'r' in 'Horse' written over another letter (possibly 'u').

alive now. — Ten fees, one after an:
:other, did the Man take who sent
<u>him</u> out of the World. — I beseech you
Mr Parker, no Doctors here." —
The Tea things were brought in. — "Oh! my
dear Mrs Parker — you should not indeed —
Why would you do so? — I was just upon
the point of wishing you good Evening.
But since you are so very neighbourly, I
       & I
beleive Miss Clara ^ must stay". —

<u>Chapter 7.</u>

The popularity of the Parkers brought them
some visitors the very next morning; —
    them
amongst ~~others~~, Sir Edwd Denham & his
Sister, who having been at Sanditon H —
drove on to pay their Compliments; &
the duty of Letter-writing being accomplished,
    settled with Mrs P. — in
Charlotte was ^ ~~in~~ the Drawing room ~~when~~
~~they came~~ in time to see them all. —

The Denhams were the only ones to excite
particular attention. Charlotte was glad
to complete her knowledge of the family
by an introduction to them, & found them,
[f.30r] the better half at least — (for while single
the Gentleman may sometimes be thought
the better half, of the pair) — not unworthy
notice. — Miss D. was a fine young woman,
but cold & reserved, giving the idea of
one who felt her consequence with Pride
& her Poverty with Discontent, & who was
immediately gnawed by the want of an
handsomer Equipage than the simple Gig
in which they travelled, & which their
Groom was leading about still in her
sight. — Sir Edw[d]. was much her superior
in air & manner; — certainly handsome,
but yet more to be remarked for his
very good
~~pleasing~~ address & wish of paying at:
:tention & giving pleasure. — He came
into the room remarkably well, talked

much — & very much to Charlotte, by
whom he chanced to be placed — & she
soon perceived that he had a ~~very~~ fine
Countenance, a most pleasing gentleness
of voice, & a great deal of Conversation.

She
~~Charlotte~~ liked him. — Sober-minded as
^
she was, she thought him ~~very~~ agreable,

suspicion
& did not quarrel with the ~~notion~~ of his

<u>would</u> arise,*
finding her equally so, which ~~might be~~
~~implied~~ from his evidently disregarding
his Sister's motion to go, & persisting in
[f.30v] his station & his discourse. — I make no
apologies for my Heroine's vanity. — If there
are young Ladies in the World at her time

~~simple~~ dull of Fancy
of Life, more ~~Dull of Mind~~ & more ~~ind~~ careless
of pleasing, I know them not, & never wish
to know them. — At last, from the low
French windows of the Drawing room which

* 'i' written over 'o' in 'arise'.

commanded the road & all the Paths across

the Down, Charlotte & Sir Edw: as they sat,

could not but observe Lady D. & Miss B. walking

by — & there was instantly a slight change

in Sir Edw:'s countenance — with an anxious

glance after them as they proceeded — ~~and~~

followed by an early proposal to his Sister —

merely
not ~~only~~ ^ for moving, but for walking

altogether
on together to the Terrace — which ^ gave

an hasty turn to Charlotte's fancy, cured

her of her halfhour's fever, & placed her in

a more capable state of judging, when

Sir Edw: was gone, of <u>how</u> agreable

he had actually been. — "Perhaps there

was a good deal in his air & Address;

him no harm."
And his Title did ~~not hurt him~~."

She was very soon in his company again.

The first object of the Parkers, when their

House was cleared of morn^{g}. visitors

was to get out themselves; — the Terrace

was the attraction to ~~th~~ all; — Every body who walked, must begin with the Terrace, [f.31r] & there, seated on one of the two Green Benches by the Gravel walk, they found the united Denham Party; — but though united in the Gross, very distinctly divided again — the two superior Ladies being at one end of the bench, & Sir Edw: & Miss B. at the other. — Charlotte's first glances told her that Sir Edw:'s air was that of a Lover. — There could be no doubt of his Devotion to Clara. — How Clara received it, was less obvious — but she was inclined to think not very favourably; for tho' sitting thus apart with him (which probably she might not have been able to prevent) her air was calm & grave. — That the young Lady at the other end of the Bench was doing Penance, was indubitable. The difference in Miss Denham's countenance, the change from Miss Denham sitting in cold Grandeur in M^{rs}. Parker's Draw^{g}-

-room to be kept from silence by the
efforts of others, to Miss D. at Lady D.'s
Elbow, listening & talking with smiling
attention or solicitous eagerness, was very
striking — and very amusing — or very me:
:lancholy, just as Satire* or Morality
might prevail. — Miss Denham's Character
was pretty well decided with Charlotte.
[f.31v] Sir Edward's required longer Observation.
He surprised her by quitting Clara
immediately on their all joining & a:
:greeing to walk, & ~~devoting himself~~
by
~~entirely~~ ^ addressing his attentions entirely
Stationing himself
to herself. — ^ Close by her ~~side~~, he seemed
to mean to detach her as much as
to
possible from the rest of the Party & ^ give
her the whole of his Conversation. He
began, in a tone of great Taste & Feeling,
to talk of the Sea & the Sea shore — &

* 'a' in 'Satire' written over another letter (illegible).

ran with Energy through all the usual
Phrases employed in praise of their Sub:
:limity, & descriptive of the undescribable
Emotions they excite in the Mind of
Sensibility. — The terrific Grandeur of
the Ocean in a Storm, its glassy sur:
:face in a calm, it's Gulls & its Samphire,
& the deep fathoms of it's Abysses, it's
quick vicissitudes, it's direful Deceptions,
it's Mariners tempting it in Sunshine
& overwhelmed by the sudden Tempest,
all were eagerly & fluently touched; —
rather commonplace perhaps — but doing
very well from the Lips of a handsome
Sir Edward, — and she c^{d}. not but think
him a Man of Feeling — till he began to
[f.32r] stagger her by the number of his Quo:
:tations, & the bewilderment of some of
his sentences. — "Do you remember, said he,
Scott's beautiful Lines on the Sea? — Oh! what
a description they convey! — They are never
out of my Thoughts when I walk here. —

That Man who can read them unmoved
must have the nerves of an Assassin! —
Heaven defend me from meeting such
a Man un-armed —". "What description
do you mean? — said Charlotte. I remember
none at this moment, of the Sea, in either
of Scott's Poems. —". "Do not you indeed? —
— Nor can I exactly recall the beginning
at this moment — But — you cannot
have forgotten his description of Woman. —
"Oh! Woman in our Hours of Ease" ——
Delicious! Delicious! — Had he written
nothing more, he w^{d}. have been Immortal.
And then again, that unequalled, unrivalled
Address to Parental affection —

"Some feelings are to Mortals given
With less of Earth in them than Heaven" &c

But while we are on the subject of Poetry,
what think you Miss H. of Burns Lines
to his Mary?" —

Oh! ^"there is^ Pathos ~~that~~ ^to^ madden~~s~~ one! — If ever

there was a Man who <u>felt</u>, it was Burns. —
Montgomery has all the Fire of Poetry,
Wordsworth has the true soul of it —
[f.32v] Campbell in his pleasures of Hope has
touched the extreme of our Sensations —
"Like Angel's visits, few & far between".
Can you conceive any thing more sub:
:duing, more melting, more fraught with
the deep Sublime than that Line? — But
Burns — I confess my sense of his Pre-e:
:minence Miss H. — If Scott <u>has</u> a fault,
it is the want of Passion. — Tender, Elegant,
Descriptive — but <u>Tame</u>. — The Man who
cannot do justice to the attributes of Woman
is my contempt. — Sometimes indeed a flash
of feeling seems to irradiate ~~Scott~~ him — as in
the Lines we were speaking of — "Oh! Woman
in our hours of Ease" — . But Burns is
always on fire. — His Soul was the Altar
in which lovely Woman sat enshrined,
his Spirit ^truly breathed the immortal Incence

which is her Due. — " "I have read several
of Burn's Poems with great delight, said
Charlotte as soon as she had time to speak,
but I am not poetic enough to separate
a Man's Poetry entirely from his Cha:
:racter; — & poor Burns's known Irregu:
:larities, greatly interrupt my enjoyment
of his Lines. — I have* difficulty in depending
on the Truth of his Feelings as a Lover.
I have not faith in the sincerity of the
affections of a Man of his Description. He
felt & he wrote & he forgot." "Oh! no
[f.33r] no — exclaimed Sir Edw: in an extasy.
He was all ardour & Truth! — His Genius
& his Susceptibilities might lead him into
some Aberrations — But who is perfect? — It were
Hyper-criticism, it were Pseudo-philosophy to
expect from the soul of high toned Genius, the
grovellings of a common mind. — The Corusca:
:tions† of Talent, ~~of~~ elicited by impassioned

* 'h' in 'have' written over another letter, possibly 'a'.
† 'u' in 'Coruscations' written over another letter, possibly 'a'.

feeling in the breast of Man, are perhaps
incompatible with some of the prosaic
Decencies of Life; — nor can you, loveliest
Miss Heywood — (speaking with an air
of deep sentiment) — nor can any Woman
be a fair Judge of what a Man may be
propelled to say, write or do, by the sove:
:reign impulses of illimitable ardour."
This was very fine; — but if Charlotte un:
:derstood it at all, not very moral — &
being moreover by no means pleased with
his extraordinary stile of compliment, she
gravely answered "I really know nothing
of the matter. — This is a charming day.
The Wind I fancy must be Southerly."
"Happy, happy Wind, to engage Miss Hey:
:wood's Thoughts! — " She began to think
him downright silly. — His chusing to
had learnt to understand.
walk with her, she ~~could comprehend~~.
^
It was done to pique Miss Brereton. She
had or two on
~~could~~ read it, in an anxious glance ~~of~~
^

his side —
~~two of Sir Edwards~~ — but why he sh^{d}
[f.33v] talk so much Nonsense, unless he could
do no better, was un-intelligible. — He seemed
very sentimental, very full of some Feelings
or other, & very much addicted to all the
newest-fashioned hard words — had not a
very clear Brain she presumed, & talked
a good deal by rote. — The Future might
explain him further — but when there was
a proposition ~~of~~ for going into the Library
she felt that she had had quite enough of
Sir Edw: for one morn^{g}, & very gladly ac:
:cepted Lady D.'s invitation of remaining
on the Terrace with her. — The others all
left them, Sir Edw: with ~~some~~ looks of
very gallant despair in tearing himself away,
& they ~~were to~~ united* their agreeableness —
that is, Lady Denham like a true great
Lady, talked & talked only of her own con:
:cerns, & Charlotte listened — ~~deriving con~~:

* 'd' of 'united' added at the end of the word.

amused in considering
:~~siderable amusement from~~ the contrast
^
~~of~~ between her two companions. — Certainly,

strain of
there was no ^ doubtful Sentiment, nor
any phrase of difficult interpretation in

discourse.
Lady D's ~~manner of talking~~. Taking hold
of Charlotte's arm ~~immediately~~ with the

felt ~~herself doing~~
ease of one who ~~had been long used to~~
that any notice from her was an Honour,
~~consider her honour by any notice she be:~~
:~~stowed~~ & communicative, from the in:
:fluence of the same conscious Importance

[f.34r] or a natural
~~& a~~ love of talking, she immediately said
^
in a tone of great satisfaction — & with a
look of arch sagacity — "Miss Esther wants me
to invite her & her Brother to spend a week
with me at Sanditon House, as I did last
Summer — But I sha'nt. — She has been trying

every way,
to get round me ^ with her praise of this,

& her praise of that; but I saw what she
was about. — I saw through it all. — I am
not very easily taken-in my Dear."
Charlotte c^{d}. think of nothing more harmless
to be said, than the simple enquiry of — "Sir
Edward & Miss Denham?" — "Yes, my Dear.
My young Folks, as I call them sometimes,
for I take them very much by the hand.
with me
I had them ^ last Summer, about this time,
for a week; from Monday to Monday; and
very delighted & thankful they were. — For
they are very good young People my Dear.
I w^{d}. not have you think that I only
notice them, for poor dear Sir Harry's
sake. No, no; they are very deserving them:
:selves, or trust me, they w^{d}. not be so
much in my Company. — I am not the
Woman to help any body blindfold. — I
always take care to know what I am
about & who I have to deal with, before
I stir a finger. — I do not think I was

ever over-reached in my Life; & That is
a good deal for a woman to say that
has been married twice. — Poor dear Sir
[f.34v] Harry (between ourselves) thought at first
to have got more — But (with a bit of
a sigh) He is gone, & we must not ~~rip~~
find fault with Nobody could
~~up the faults of~~ the Dead. ~~We lived per:~~
live happier together than us —
~~:feectly happy together~~ — & he was a very
honourable Man, quite the Gentleman of
ancient Family. — And when he died, I gave
Sir Edwd his Gold Watch. — " She said this
with a look at her Companion which implied
its' right to produce a great Impression — &
Charlottes
seeing no rapturous astonishment in ~~her~~ ^
countenance, added quickly — "He did not
bequeath it to his Nephew, my dear — It was
no ~~legal~~ bequest. It was not in the Will.
He ~~had~~ only told me, & <u>that</u> but once, that
he sh^{d}. wish his Nephew to have his Watch;

it
but ~~that~~ ^ need not have been binding, if I
had not chose it. — " "Very kind indeed!
very Handsome!" — said Charlotte, absolutely
forced to affect admiration. — "Yes, my
dear — & it is not the <u>only</u> kind thing I
have done by him. — I have been a very
liberal friend to Sir Edwd. And poor young
bad
Man, he needs it ^ enough; — For though I
am <u>only</u> the <u>Dowager</u> my Dear, & he is
the <u>Heir</u>, things do not stand between us
in the way they commonly do between
those two parties. — Not a shilling do I
receive from the Denham Estate. Sir
Edw: has no Payments to make <u>me</u>.
He don't stand uppermost, beleive me. —
It is <u>I</u> that help <u>him</u>." "Indeed! — He

[f.35r] a
is ^ very fine young Man; — particularly Elegant
in his
^ Address." — This was said cheifly for the sake
directly saw
of saying something — but Charlotte ~~imagined~~

that
it was laying her open to suspicion by
^
Lady D's giving a shrewd glance at her &
replying — "Yes, yes, he is very well to look
at — & it is to be hoped some Lady of large
fortune will think so — for Sir Edw
must marry for Money. — He & I often
talk that matter over. — A handsome young
fellow like him, will go smirking & smiling
about & paying girls compliments, but
he knows he must marry for Money. —
And Sir Edw: is a very steady young Man
in the main, & has got very good notions."
"Sir Edw: Denham, said Charlotte, with such
personal Advantages may be almost sure
of getting a Woman of fortune, if he chuses
quite
it." — This glorious sentiment seemed ^ to
to remove suspicion. "Aye my Dear —
That's very sensibly said* cried Lady D —
And if we c^{d}. but get a young Heiress to S!

* beginning of section originally written in pencil.

But Heiresses are monstrous scarce! I do not
think we have had an Heiress here, or even a
Co — since Sanditon has been a public place.
Families come after Families, but as far as I
can learn, it is not one in an hundred of them
real Landed or Funded.
that have any ^ Property, — ^ An Income perhaps, but
no Property. Clergymen may be, or Lawyers from
Town, or Half pay officers, or Widows with only a
And
Jointure. ~~Now~~ what good can such people do
[f.35v] anybody? — except just as they take our
empty Houses — and (between ourselves) I think
they are great fools for not staying at home.
Now, if we could get ~~get~~ a young Heiress
to be sent here for her health — (and if she
was ordered to drink asses milk I could supply
her) — and as soon as she got well, have her
fall in love with Sir Edward!" — "That would be
very fortunate indeed." "And Miss Esther
must marry somebody of fortune too — She
must get a rich Husband. Ah! young Ladies

that have no Money are very much to be
pitied! — But — after a short pause — if
Miss Esther thinks to talk me into inviting
them to come & stay at Sanditon House, she
will find herself mistaken. — Matters are altered
with me since last Summer you know — .
I have Miss Clara with me now, which
makes a great difference." She spoke this
so seriously that Charlotte* instantly saw in
it the evidence of real penetration & ~~was~~
prepared for some fuller remarks — but it
was followed only by — "I have no fancy for
having my House as full as an Hotel.
I should not chuse to have my 2 Housemaids
Time taken up all the morn^{g}, in dusting
~~the~~ ^out Bed rooms. — They have Miss Clara's
room to put to rights as well as my own
every day. — If they had hard Places, they would
want Higher wages. — " For objections of
[f.36r] this Nature, Charlotte was not prepared,

* end of section originally written in pencil.

& she found it so impossible even to
affect simpathy, that she c^{d}. say no:
:thing. — Lady D. soon added, with great
glee — "And besides all this my Dear, am I
to be filling my House to the prejudice of
Sanditon? — If People want to be by the
Sea, why dont they take Lodgings? — Here are
a great many empty Houses — 3 on this very
Terrace; no fewer than three Lodging Papers
staring us in the face at this very mo:
:ment, Numbers 3, 4 & 8. 8, the Corner House
may be too large for them, but ~~3 or 4~~
either of the two others are nice little
snug Houses, very fit for a young Gentleman
& his Sister — And so, my dear, the next
time Miss Esther begins talking about the
Dampness of Denham Park, & the Good
Bathing always does her, I shall advise them
to come & take one of these Lodgings for
a fortnight. — Don't you think that will
be very fair? — Charity begins at home you
know." — Charlotte's feelings were divided

between amusement & indignation — but

indignation had the larger & the increasing

share. — She kept her Countenance & she kept

a civil Silence. She could not carry her

but
forbearance farther; ~~&~~ without attempting to

& only conscious that Lady D. was still talking
listen longer, ~~while Lady D. still talked~~ on in

the same way, allowed her Thoughts to form

[f.36v] themselves into such a Meditation as

thoroughly mean.
this. — "She is ~~much worse than I expected~~ —

I had not expected anything so bad.
~~meaner~~ — ~~a great deal meaner. She is~~

~~very mean.~~ — Mr. P. spoke too mildly of

her. — ~~His own kind Disposition makes him~~

~~judge too well of others.~~ His Judgement is

~~always~~
evidently not ^ to be trusted. ~~in his opinion of~~

~~others &~~ — His own Goodnature misleads him ~~in~~

j~~udging of others~~. He is too kind hearted to see

clearly. — I must judge for myself. — And their

very <u>connection</u> prejudices him. — He has

persuaded her to engage in the same

Speculation — & because their object in that

Line
~~respect~~ is the same, he fancies she feels

like him in others. — But she is very, very

mean. — I can see no Good in her. — Poor

Miss Brereton! — And she makes every body

mean about her. — This poor Sir Edward

& his Sister, — how far Nature meant them

not
to be respectable I can ^ tell, — but they are

obliged to be Mean in their Servility to

her. — And I am Mean too, in giving

her my attention, with the appearance

of coinciding with her. — Thus it is, when

Rich People are Sordid." —

Chapter 8.

The two Ladies continued walking together

till
~~by~~ rejoined by the others, who as they
^

issued from the Library were followed by

a young Whilby running off with 5 vols.

under his arm to Sir Edward's Gig —

[f.37r] and Sir Edw: approaching Charlotte, said

has been our
"You may perceive what ~~we have been~~

occupation.
~~doing~~. My Sister wanted my counsel in the

selection of some books. — We have many lei:

:sure hours, & read a great deal. — I am no

indiscriminate Novel-Reader. The mere Trash

of the common Circulating Library, I hold in

the highest contempt. You will never hear

me advocating those puerile Emanations

which detail nothing but discordant Prin:

:ciples incapable of Amalgamation, or

those vapid tissues of ordinary occurrences

from which no useful Deductions can be

drawn. — In vain may we put them into

a literary Alembic; — we distil nothing

which can add to Science. — You understand

me I am sure?" "I am not quite certain

But
that I do. — ^ If you will describe the sort

I dare say
of Novels which you <u>do</u> approve, ^ it will

~~probably~~ give me a clearer idea." "Most
willingly, Fair Questioner. — The Novels
which I approve are such as display Hu:
:man Nature with Grandeur — such as
shew her in the Sublimities of intense
Feeling — such as exhibit the progress of
strong Passion from the first Germ of
incipient
Susceptibility to the utmost Energies of
^
Reason half-dethroned, — where we see
[f.37v] the strong Spark of Woman's Captiva:
:tions elicit such Fire in the Soul of
Man as leads him — (though at the risk
of some aberration~~s~~ from the strict line of
Primitive Obligations) — to hazard all, dare
atcheive
all, ~~encounter~~ all, to obtain her. — Such are
delight
the Works which I peruse with ~~ardour~~, &
I hope I may say, with Amelioration. They
hold forth the most splendid Portraitures
of high Conceptions, Unbounded Veiws, illi:

indomptible
:mitable ardour, ~~unconquerable~~ Decision — and

even where the Event is mainly anti-pros:

high-toned Machinations of the
:perous to the ^ prime Character, the potent,

pervading Hero of the Story, it leaves us

full of Generous Emotions for him; — our

Hearts are paralized — . T'were Pseudo-

-Philosophy to assert that we do not feel

more enwraped by the brilliancy of his Career,

than by the tranquil & morbid Virtues

any opposing character.
of ~~his Rival.~~ Our approbation of the

but
Latter is ^ Eleemosynary. — These are

the Novels which enlarge the primitive

Capabilities of the Heart, & which it cannot

impugn the Sense or be any Dereliction

anti-puerile
of the character, of the most ~~sagacious~~ ^ Man,

to be conversant with." —

"If I understand you aright — said Charlotte—

our taste in Novels is not at all the same."

And here they were obliged to part — Miss

D. being too much tired of them all, to

stay any longer. —

[f.38r] whom Circumstances had confined very much to one spot

The truth was that Sir Edw: ^ had read more

sentimental Novels than agreed with him.

His fancy had been early caught by all

the impassioned, & most exceptionable parts

since

of Richardsons; & such Authors as have ^ appeared

to tread in Richardson's steps, so far as Man's

determined pursuit of Woman in defiance

opposition of feeling & convenience

of every ~~thing~~ ^ ^ is concerned, had since oc=

:cupied the greater part of his literary

hours, & formed his Character. — With a

perversity of Judgement, which must be

attributed to his not having by Nature

a very strong head, the Graces, the Spirit,

of the

the Ingenuity, & the Perseverance, ~~of the~~

~~which were the usual~~ Villain of the Story

outweighed all his absurdities & all his

Atrocities with Sir Edward. With him,

such Conduct was Genius, Fire &

Feeling. — It interested & inflamed him;

was more anxious for its

& he ^ always ~~wished it better~~ ^ Success

~~than it c^{d}. ever have~~ & mourned over

its Discomfitures with more Tenderness

than c^{d}. ever have been contemplated

by the Authors. — Though he owed

many of his ideas to this sort of

reading, it were unjust to say that

he ~~owed his~~ read nothing else, or

were

that his Language ~~was~~ not formed

on a more general knowledge of

[f.38v] modern Literature. — He read all the

Essays, Letters, Tours & Criticisms of

the day — & with the same ill-luck

which made him derive only false Prin:

:ciples from Lessons of Morality, & incen:

:tives to Vice from the History of it's

overthrow, he gathered only hard words

& involved sentences from the style of

~~the~~ our
~~our~~ most approved writers. —
^

Sir Edw:'s great object in life was to be

seductive. — With such personal advan:

:tages as he knew himself to possess, &

such Talents as he did also give himself

credit for, he regarded it as his Duty. —

He felt that
He was formed to be a dangerous Man —
^

— quite in the line of the Lovelaces. —

The very name of Sir Edward he thought, carried some
degree of fascination with it. —
To be generally gallant & assiduous about

the fair, to make fine speeches to every

pretty Girl, was but the inferior part

of the character he had to play. — Miss

Heywood, or any other young Woman

any
with ~~some~~ pretensions to Beauty, he
^

was entitled (according to his own

~~mistaken~~ veiws of Society) to approach

with high Compliment & Rhapsody

on the slightest acquaintance; but

alone
it was Clara ^ on whom he had serious
designs; it was Clara whom he meant
to seduce. — Her seduction was quite
[f.39r] determined on. Her Situation in every
way called for it. She was his rival in
Lady D.'s favour, she was young, lovely
& dependant. — He had very early seen
the necessity of the case, & had now been
long trying with cautious assiduity to
make an impression on her heart, and
to undermine her Principles. — Clara saw
through him, & had not the least inten:
:tion of being seduced — but she bore
with him patiently enough to confirm
the sort of attachment which her personal
Charms had raised. — A greater degree of
discouragement indeed would not have
affected Sir Edw: — . He was armed a:
:gainst the highest pitch of Disdain or
Aversion. — If she could not be won

by affection, he must carry her off.
He knew his Business. — Already had
he had many Musings on the subject.
If he were constrained so to act, he must
naturally wish to strike out something
new, to exceed those who had gone
before him — and he ~~wd have~~ felt a
strong ascertain
~~some~~ curiosity to ~~know~~ whether the
neighbourhood of Tombuctoo might
not afford some ~~desola~~ solitary House
adapted for Clara's reception; — but
[f.39v] the Expence alas! of Measures in that
masterly style was ill-suited to his
Purse, & Prudence obliged him to pre=
=fer the quietest ~~st~~ sort of ruin & dis:
:grace for the object of his affections,
to the more renowned. —

Chapter 9.

One day, soon after Charlotte's arrival at
Sanditon, she had the pleasure of seeing
just as she ascended from the Sands to

the Terrace, a Gentleman's Carriage with
Post Horses standing at the door of the
Hotel, as very lately arrived, & by the
quantity of Luggage taking off, bringing
,it might be hoped, some respectable family
determined on a long residence. —
Delighted to have such good news for
Mr. & Mrs. P., who had both gone home
some time before, she proceeded for
Trafalgar House with as much alacrity
having been
as could remain, after ~~being~~ contending
for the last 2 hours with a very fine
wind blowing directly on shore; but
she had not reached the little Lawn, when
she saw a Lady walking nimbly be:
:hind her at no great distance; and
could be
convinced that it ~~was~~ no acquaintance
^
of her own, she resolved to hurry on &
[f.40r] if possible
get into the House ^ before her. ~~if possible~~.
But the stranger's pace ~~was too brisk~~

did not allow

~~for~~ ^ this to be accomplished; — Charlotte

was on the steps & had rung, but the

when

door was not opened, ~~as~~ the other crossed

the Lawn; — and when the Servant appeared,

they were just equally ready for entering

the House. — The ease of the Lady, her

"How do you do Morgan? — " & Morgan's

a moment's

Looks on seeing her, were ~~beginning to~~

astonishment —

~~astonish Charlotte~~ — but another mo:

:ment brought M^{r}. P. into the Hall

to welcome the Sister he had seen

from the Draw^{g}. room, & she was

soon introduced to Miss Diana Parker.

~~much~~ ~~xxxxx~~

a great deal of but

There was ~~great astonis~~ surprise ~~&~~

~~a~~ still more Nothing

~~great~~ pleasure in seeing her. — ~~How~~

c^{d}. be kinder than her reception from both Husband
and Wife.
"How did* she come? & with whom? — And

they were so glad to find her equal

that
to the Journey! — And ^ she was to be:

:long to <u>them</u>, was a thing of course."

Miss Diana P. was about 4 & 30,

delicate looking
of middling† height & slender; — ~~but rather~~

rather
~~delicate~~ ^ than ~~absolutely~~ sickly; ~~in her~~

with an agreable face, & a very animated

resembling
eye; — ~~and~~ her manners ~~resembled~~ her

Brother's in their ease & frankness,

with
though ~~there was~~ more decision &

[f.40v] less mildness in her Tone. She began

without delay
an account of herself ~~as soon as they were~~

~~in the Drawing room~~ — Thanking them for

their Invitation, but "<u>that</u> was quite out

of the question, for they were all three

* '"How did' written over another, shorter word or part-word (illegible).
† 'middling' written over 'middle'.

come, & meant to get into Lodgings & make

some stay." — "All three come! — What! — Susan

& Arthur! — Susan able to come too! — This

better & better."

was ~~a great increase of the Happiness! —~~ "

"Yes — we are actually all ~~here~~ come. Quite

Nothing else to be done.

unavoidable. — ~~A case of Necessity.~~ — You

shall hear all about it. — But my dear

Mary, send for the Children; — I long to

see them." — "And how has Susan born

the Journey? — & how is Arthur? — & why

do not we see him here with you?" —

"Susan has born it wonderfully. She

had not a wink of sleep either the night

before we set out, or last night ~~which~~

and as

~~we spent~~ at Chichester, ~~but~~ ^ this is Not*

so

common with her ~~that~~ as with me, I
^

have had a thousand fears for her —

wonderfully.

* 'N' of 'Not' written over another letter (illegible).

but she has kept up ~~charmingly~~ — . ~~She~~

had
~~and~~ no Hysterics of consequence till we
^

within sight of the attack
came ~~to~~ poor old Sanditon — and ~~they were~~

was not very violent — ~~quite over~~ nearly over
~~quite subsided~~ by the time we reached
^

your Hotel — so that we got her out of

the Carriage extremely well, with only

M^{r}. assistance
~~young~~ Woodcock's ~~help~~ — & when I left her

the Disposal of
she was Directing ~~where all~~ the Luggage

Sam
~~sh^{d}. be carried~~, & helping old ~~Hannah~~
^

~~unf~~ uncord the Trunks. — She desired
her best love,

[f.41r] [Booklet 3]

March 1st. 2

with a thousand regrets at ~~her~~ being so

poor a creature that she c^{d}. not come

with me. And as for poor Arthur, he

unwilling
w^{d}. not have been ~~afraid for~~ himself,

but there is so much Wind that I did

not think he c^{d}. safely venture, — for

I am <u>sure</u> there is Lumbago hanging

about so I
~~over~~ him — and ~~therefore~~ helped him

on with his great Coat & sent him off

the Terrace, to
to ^ take us Lodgings. — Miss Heywood

must have seen our Carriage standing

at the Hotel. ~~I am sure~~ — I knew Miss

Heywood the moment I saw her before

on
me ~~in~~ ^ the ~~field~~ Down. — My dear Tom

I am glad to see you walk so well.

Let me feel your ancle. — That's right;

all right & clean. The play of your

affected;
Sinews a <u>very</u> little ~~stiffened;~~ — barely

perceptible. — Well — now for the

explanation of my being here. — I told

you in my Letter, of the two considerable

Families, I was hoping to secure for

you — the West Indians, & the Se:

:minary. — " Here M^{r}. P. drew his Chair

still nearer to his Sister, & took her

hand again most affectionately as he

[f.41v] answered "Yes, Yes; — How active & how

kind you have been!" — "The Westindians,

she continued, whom I look upon as

the most desirable of the two — as the

the Good —

Best of ~~two Excellent~~ — prove to be a

know

Mrs. Griffiths & her family. I ~~have only~~

them only

~~heard of them~~ through others. — ~~My friend~~

You must

~~Fanny Noyce~~ — ~~I dare say you~~ have

heard me mention Miss Capper, the

particular friend of my very particular

friend Fanny Noyce; — now, Miss Capper

is extremely intimate with a Mrs

Darling, who is on terms of constant

correspondence with Mrs. Griffiths her:

only

:self. — ~~But~~ a short chain, you see,

between us, & not a Link wanting.

Mrs. G. meant to go to the Sea, for her

Young People's benefit — had fixed on

the coast of Sussex, but was undecided

where

as to the ~~Spot~~, wanted something Pri:

:vate, & wrote to ask the opinion of

her friend Mrs. Darling. — Miss Capper

happened to be staying with Mrs. D.

when Mrs. G.'s Letter arrived, & was

on

consulted ~~as to~~ the question; she wrote

the same day to Fanny Noyce and

mentioned it to her — & Fanny all alive

[f.42r] for us, instantly took up her pen &

forwarded the circumstance to me — ex:

:cept as to ~~th~~ Names — which have but

There

lately transpired. — ~~The~~ was but one

^

thing for me to do. — I answered Fanny's

Letter by the same Post & pressed for the

recommendation of Sanditon. Fanny had

feared your having no house large e:

to receive

:nough ~~for~~ such a Family. — But I seem

to be spinning out my story to an

endless length. — You see how it was all
managed. I had the pleasure of hearing
simple
soon afterwards by the same ~~connecting~~
of connection
link ^ that Sanditon had been recom:
:mended by Mrs. Darling, & that the
Westindians were very much dis:
:posed to go thither. — This was the
case
state of the ~~question~~ when I wrote
to you; — but* two days ago; — yes, the
day before yesterday — I heard again
from Fanny Noyce, saying that she had
heard from Miss Capper, who by a
Letter from Mrs. Darling understood
that Mrs. G. — has expressed herself
in a letter to Mrs. D. more doubtingly
on the subject of Sanditon. — Am I
[f.42v] clear? — I would be anything rather
than not clear." — "Oh! perfectly, perfectly.
Well?" — "The reason of this hesitation,

* 'b' in 'but' written over 'B'.

was her having no connections in the

place, & no means of ascertaining that she

should have good accomodations on ar:

there; —

:riving ^— and she was particularly care:

:ful & scrupulous on all those matters

more on account of a certain Miss Lambe

a young Lady (probably a Neice) under her

care, than on her own account ~~than~~ or

her Daughters. — Miss Lambe has an im:

:mense fortune — richer than all the

rest — & very delicate health. — One sees

all

clearly enough by ^ this, the sort of woman

M^rs. G. must be — as helpless & indo:

:lent, as Wealth & a Hot Climate are

us.

apt to make ~~the English~~ But we are

not all born to equal Energy. — What was

to be done? — I had a few moments

indecision; — ~~By~~ whether to offer to

or to

write to you, — ^ to M^rs. Whitby~~? But~~

secure them a House? — but neither

pleased me. — I hate to employ others,

am equal

when I ~~ought~~ to act myself — and my

conscience told me that this was an

[f.43r] me.

occasion which called for ~~my Exertions~~.

Here was a family of helpless Invalides

whom I might essentially serve. — I

sounded Susan — the same Thought had

occurred to her. — Arthur made no diffi:

:culties — our plan was arranged imme:

:diately, we were off yesterday morn^{g}.

left Chichester

at 6 — , ^ at the same hour to day — &

here we are. — " "Excellent! — Excellent! —

cried Mr Parker. — Diana, you are une:

& doing Good to all the World.

:qual'd in serving your friends ^ — I know

nobody like you. — Mary, my Love, is not

she a wonderful Creature? — Well — and

now, what House do you design to

engage for them? — What is the Size

of their family?" — "I do not at all

know — replied his Sister — have not

the least idea; — never heard any par:

:ticulars; — but I am very sure that

the largest house at Sanditon cannot

be <u>too</u> large. They are more likely

to want a second. — I shall take only

one however, & that, but for a week

certain. — Miss Heywood, I astonish

you. — You hardly know what to

make of me. — I see by your Looks, that

[f.43v] quick

you are not used to such ~~hasty~~ mea:

:sures." — ~~The part of the story which~~

~~most~~ ~~to~~

~~was really astonishing Charlotte most, she~~
^ ^

~~xx~~

~~could not~~ ~~noticed, she had just given it~~
^

~~to herself~~ The* words ~~of~~ "Unaccountable

had

officiousness! — Activity run mad!" — ~~but~~

mind

just passed through Charlotte's ~~brain~~ — ~~and~~

* 'T' of 'The' written over 't'.

~~she could only give one explanation of~~

~~collecting her Thoughts, she replied~~ —
~~the Amazement which she c^{d}. easily~~

~~"I dare say I look surprised, for I feel so,~~
~~beleive to be painted in her face~~.— but

~~that~~ a civil answer was easy. "I dare

do
say I ^ look surprised, said she — because

these are very great exertions, & I know

what Invalides
~~that~~ both You & Your Sister are." ~~sad~~

~~Invalides"~~
~~sufferers as to Health~~ "Invalides indeed. —

I trust there are not three People in

England who have so sad a right to that

appellation.
~~name~~! — But my dear Miss Heywood,

we are sent into this World to be as

extensively useful as possible, & where

some degree of Strength of Mind is given,

it is not a feeble body which will ex:

:cuse us — or ~~which will~~ incline us to

excuse ourselves. — ~~Howe~~ The World is

pretty much divided between the

Weak of Mind & the Strong — between

those who can act & those who can

not

~~act~~ ^ & it is the bounden Duty of the

no opportunity of ~~doing~~

Capable to let ~~none of their faculties~~

being useful ~~Good~~, escape them.

[f.44r] ~~be wasted~~. — My Sister's Complaints &

mine are happily not often of a

Nature, to threaten Existence immedi:

:ately — & as long as we can exert

ourselves to be of use of others, I am

convinced that the Body is the better,

for the refreshment the Mind receives

in doing its' Duty. — While I have been

travelling, with this object in veiw,

I have been perfectly well." — The en:

:trance of the Children ended this little

panegyric on her own Disposition — &

after having noticed & caressed them

all, — she prepared to go. — "Cannot you

dine with us? — Is not it possible to

prevail on you to dine with us?"

was then the cry; and that being

absolutely negatived, it was "And

when shall we see you again? and

how can we be of use to you?" —

warmly offered his assistance

and Mr. P. ~~particularly urged for~~

in taking the house for Mrs. G. — "I

will come to you the moment I have

dined, said he, & we will go about

together." — But this was immediately

declined. — "No, my dear Tom, upon

no account in the World, shall you

[f.44v] of mine.

stir a step on any business ^ — Your

Ancle wants rest. I see by the position

of your foot, that you have used it too

much already. — No, I shall go about

my House-taking directly. Our Dinner

is not ordered till six — & by that time

I hope to have completed it. It is now

only ½ past 4. — As to seeing me again

to day —

~~this Even^{g}~~ — I cannot answer for it;

the others will be at the Hotel all the

Even^{g}, & delighted to see you at any time,

but as soon as I get back I shall hear

what Arthur has done about our own

Lodgings, & probably the moment

Dinner is over, shall be out again

on business relative to them, for we

some ~~other~~ Lodgings or other
hope to get into ~~them~~ & be Settled
^

after breakfast tomorrow. — I have

not much confidence in poor Arthur's

skill for Lodging-taking, but he seemed

the commission.
to like ~~to undertake it~~. — " "I think

you are doing too much, said M^{r}. P.

You will knock yourself up. You

sh^{d}. not move again after Dinner."

"No, indeed you should not —
~~"Oh! as to your Sisters Dinner~~ cried

for Dinner is such a
his wife, ~~that's never anything more~~

mere
~~than a~~ <u>name</u> with you all, that

[f.45r] it can do you no good. — I know what your appetites are." — "My appetite is very much mended I assure you lately. I have been taking some Bitters of my own decocting, which have done wonders.

I grant you —
Susan never eats — & just at present I̲ shall want nothing; I never eat for about a week after a Journey — but as

~~eats xxxxxxxx.* We~~
for Arthur, he ~~is much more likely to~~
is only too much disposed for Food. We are often
~~eat too much than too little on~~ obliged to check him." — "But you have not told me anything of the other Family coming to Sanditon, said Mr. P. as he walked with her to the door of the House — the Camberwell Seminary; have we a good chance of them? — "

"Oh! Certain — quite certain. — I had forgotten them for the moment, but I had a letter 3 days ago from my

* word illegible; R.W. Chapman suggested 'enormously'.

friend Mrs Charles Dupuis which
assured me of Camberwell. Camberwell
will be here to a certainty, & very
soon. — That good Woman (I do not
know her name) not being so weal:
:thy & ~~so~~ independant as Mrs G. —
can travel & chuse for herself. —
I will tell you how I got at her.
Mrs Charles Dupuis lives almost
next door to a Lady, who has a
[f.45v] relation lately settled at Clapham,
who actually attends the Seminary
~~& attends some of the girls of the~~
and gives lessons on Eloquence and
~~Seminary, to give them lessons in~~
~~Poetry &~~ Belles Lettres to some of the
Girls. — I got that Man a Hare from
one of Sidney's friends — and he re:
:commended Sanditon; — Without my
however
appearing ^ — Mrs Charles Dupuis managed
it all." —

Chapter 10.

It was not a week, ~~ago~~ since Miss
Diana Parker had been told by her
feelings, that the Sea Air wd. probably
in her present state, be the death of her,
and now she was at Sanditon, intending
to make some Stay, & without appearing
to have the slightest recollection of
having written or felt any such thing. —
It was impossible for Charlotte not to
suspect a good deal of fancy in such
an extraordinary state of health. —
Disorders & Recoveries so very much out
of the common way, seemed more like
the amusement of eager minds in
want of employment than of actual
afflictions & releif. The Parkers, were
[f.46r] no doubt a family of Imagination &
quick feelings — and while the eldest
Brother found vent for his superfluity
of sensation ~~in~~ as a Projector, the Sisters
were perhaps driven to dissipate theirs

in the invention of odd complaints. ~~for~~

~~themselves~~. — The whole of their mental

vivacity was evidently not so employed;

a Zeal for

Part was laid out in ~~the love of~~ being

useful. — It should seem that they

must either be very busy for the Good

or others, or else extremely ill themselves.

Some natural delicacy of Constitution

in fact, with an unfortunate turn

for medecine, especially quack Medecine,

an early at

had given them ~~a~~ ^ tendency ~~to~~ ^ various

times, to various Disorders; — the rest of

their Suffering
^ was from Fancy, the love of Distinction

& the love of the Wonderful. — They had

charitable
~~benevolent~~ hearts & many amiable

a spirit restless

feelings — but ~~the disease~~ of ^ activity,

& the glory of doing more than any

-body else, had their share in every

Benevolence —
exertion of ~~Health, as well as in every inaction of Sickness~~ — and there was Vanity in all they did, as well as in all they endured. —

M^{r}. & M^{rs}. P. spent a great part of
[f.46v] the Even^{g}. at the Hotel; but Charlotte had only two or three veiws of Miss Diana posting over the Down after a House for this Lady whom she had never seen, & who~~se~~ had never employed her. She was not made acquainted with the others till the following day, when, being removed into Lodgings & all the party continuing quite well, their Brother & Sister & herself were entreated to drink tea with them. — They were in one
she found them
of the Terrace Houses — & ^ arranged for the Even^{g}. in a small neat Drawing room, with a beautiful veiw of the Sea if they had chosen it, — but though it had been

a very fair English Summer-day, — not
^

only was there no open window, but

the

the Sopha & ^ Table, & the Establishment

in general was all at the other end

of the room by a brisk fire. — Miss P—

whom, remembering the three Teeth

drawn in one day, Charlotte approached

a peculiar degree

with ~~the sort~~ ^ of respectful Compassion,

was not very unlike her Sister in

person or manner — tho' more thin

& worn by Illness & Medecine, more

relaxed in air, & more subdued in voice.

[f.47r] She talked however, the whole Evening

as incessantly as Diana — & excepting* that

she sat with salts in her hand, took

Drops two or three times from one, out

the several at home

of ~~many~~ ^ Phials already ~~domesticated~~

on the Mantlepeice, — & made a great

many odd faces & contortions, Charlotte

* 'ing' added to 'except'.

symptoms
could perceive no ~~signs~~ ^ of illness which
she, in the boldness of her own good
health, w^{d}. not have undertaken to
cure, by putting out the fire, opening
the Window, & disposing of the Drops
the
& ^ Salts by means of one or the other.

considerable
She had had ~~great~~ curiosity to see
him
M^{r}. Arthur Parker; & having fancied ^ a
very puny, delicate-looking young Man,
the smallest very materially of not a
robust Family, was astonished to find
him quite as tall as his Brother & a
great deal Stouter — Broad made &
Lusty — and ~~excepting~~ with no other
look of an Invalide, than a sodden
complexion. — Diana was evidently
the cheif of the family; principal
mover & actor; — she had been on her
Feet the whole morning, on M^{rs}. G.'s

business or their own, & was still
the most alert of the three. — Susan
[f.47v] had only superintended their final
removal from the Hotel, bringing two
heavy Boxes herself, & Arthur had found
the air so cold that he had merely
walked from one House to the other as
much
nimbly as he could, — & boasted ~~most~~ of
^
sitting by the fire till he had cooked up
a very good one. — Diana, whose exercise
had been too domestic to admit of cal:
:culation, but who, by her own account,
had not once sat ~~for~~ down during the
space of seven hours, confessed herself
a little tired. She had been too suc:
:cessful however for much fatigue;
for not only had she by walking &
talking down a thousand difficulties
at last secured a proper House at 8$^{G.}$
also
p^{r}. week for Mrs G. — ; she had ^ opened
so many Treaties with Cooks, Housemaids,

Washerwomen & Bathing Women, that
Mrs. G. would have little more to do
on her arrival, than to wave her
hand & collect them around her for
Choice. — Her concluding effort in the
cause, had been a few polite lines of
Information to Mrs. G. herself — time
not allowing for the circuitous train of
been
intelligence which had ^ hitherto kept up, —
[f.48r] and she was now regaling in the delight
of ~~what she had done~~ opening the first
Trenches of an acquaintance with such a
powerful discharge of unexpected obligation.
Mr. & Mrs. P. — & Charlotte had seen two
Post chaises crossing the Down to the Hotel
as they were setting off, — a joyful sight —
& full of speculation. — The Miss Ps — & Arthur
seen
had also ~~distinguished~~ something; ~~of the~~
~~matter from their window;~~ — they could
from their window
distinguish ^ that there <u>was</u> an arrival

its
at the Hotel, but not ~~the~~ ^ amount. ~~of it.~~
Their visitors answered for two Hack-
-Chaises. — Could it be the Camberwell
Seminary? — No — No. — Had there been
a 3^{d} carriage, perhaps it might; but
it was very generally agreed that two
Hack chaises could never contain a
Seminary. — Mr P. was confident of
another new Family. — When they
some removals to
were all finally seated, after ~~looking~~ ^
look
^ at the Sea & the Hotel, Charlotte's place
next
was by Arthur, who was sitting ~~close~~
to the Fire with a degree of Enjoyment
which gave a good deal of merit to
civility in wishing her to take his
his ~~polite civil offer offering her his own~~
Chair. — There was nothing dubious in
[f.48v] her manner of declining it, & he sat down
much
again with ~~great~~ satisfaction. She

drew back her Chair to have all the ad:

his Person as

:vantage of ~~him for~~ a Screen, & was

^

very thankful for every inch of Back &

Shoulders beyond her pre-conceived idea.

Arthur was heavy in Eye as well as figure,

~~He had in every respect a heavy Look~~

but by no means

~~yet was not~~ indisposed to talk; — and

cheifly

while the other 4 were ~~very much~~

he

engaged together, evidently felt it no

^

~~with greatly agreable~~

penance to have ~~a good-looking Girl~~

a fine young Woman

next to him, requiring in common

^

Politeness some attention — as his B^{r},

~~gr~~

~~observed with much pleasure~~ who felt

decided

the ~~great~~ want of some motive for action,

Powerful object him

~~of~~ some~~thing source~~ of animation for ~~Arthur~~,

observed with ~~no in~~considerable pleasure. —

Such was the influence of Youth & Bloom

began even to make
that he ~~made~~ a sort of apology for having
^
a Fire. "We sh^{d}. not have one at home,

said he, but the Sea air is always damp.

I am not afraid of anything so much

as Damp. — " "I am so fortunate, said C.

as never to know whether the air is damp

or dry. It has always some property that

& invigorating to
is wholesome ~~for~~ me. — " "I like the air
^
well
too, as ~~much~~ as anybody can; replied

Arthur, I am very fond of standing at

[f.49r] an open window when there is no Wind —

but unluckily a Damp air does not like

me. — It gives me the Rheumatism. — You

are not rheumatic I suppose? — " "Not at all."

"That's a great blessing. — But perhaps you

are nervous." "No — I beleive not. I have

no idea that I am." — "I am very nervous. —

To say the truth —
~~In my own opinion~~ Nerves are the worst

in <u>my</u> ~~own~~ opinion
part of my Complaints ^ . — My Sisters think
me Bilious, but I doubt it. — " "You are
quite in the right, to doubt it as long as
you possibly can, I am sure. — " "If I
were Bilious, he continued, you know
Wine w^{d}. disagree with me, but it
always does me good. — The more Wine
I drink (in moderation) the better
I am. — I am always best of an
Even^{g}. — If you had seen me to day
thought ~~found~~
before Dinner, you w^{d}. have ^ ~~thought~~ ^
me a very poor creature. — " Charlotte
could beleive it — . She kept her countenance
however, & said — "As far as I can un:
:derstand what nervous complaints are,
I have a great idea of the efficacy
of air & exercise for them, — daily,
regular Exercise; — and I should re:
:commend rather more of it to <u>you</u>
than I suspect you are in the habit
of taking. — " "Oh! I am very fond of

[f.49v] exercise myself — he replied — & mean to

walk
~~take~~ a great deal while I am here, if

the Weather is temperate. I shall be

out every morning before breakfast — &

take several turns upon the Terrace,

& you will often see me at Trafalgar

House." — "But you do not call a walk

to Traf: H. much exercise? — " "Not, ~~in~~

as to the Hill is so steep!
mere distance, but ~~there is such a steep~~
^
~~Hill to get up to it~~! — Walking up that

Hill, in the middle of the day, would throw

me into such a Perspiration! — You would

see me all in a Bath, by the time I got

there! — I am very subject to Perspiration,

~~which~~ and there cannot be a surer sign

of Nervousness. — " They were now advancing

so deep in Physics, that Charlotte ~~th~~

veiwed the entrance of the Servant with

the Tea things, as a very fortunate Inter:

:ruption. — It produced a great & imme:

:diate change. The young Man's attentions

were instantly lost. He took his own
Cocoa ~~Pot~~ from the Tray, — which seemed
provided with almost as many Tea-
-pots &c as there were persons in com:
=pany, Miss P. drinking one sort of Herb-
-Tea & Miss Diana another, & turning
completely to the Fire, sat coddling &
cooking it to his own satisfaction &

[f.50r] brought up
toasting some Slices of Bread, ^ ready-
-prepared in the Toast rack — and till it
was all done, she heard nothing of his

the murmuring of
voice but ~~in a faint murmur, &~~ a

self-
few broken sentences of ^ approbation ~~of his~~

& success
~~own Doings & prosperity~~. — When his Toils
were over however, he moved back his

into as gallant a Line as ever,
Chair ~~with quite as much Gallantry as~~
~~before~~ & proved that he had not been working
only for himself, by his earnest invitation
to her to take both Cocoa & Toast. —

She was already helped to Tea — which
surprised him — so totally self-engrossed had
he been. — "I thought I should have been in
time, said he, but Cocoa takes a great
deal of Boiling. — " "I am much obliged to
you, replied Charlotte — but I prefer Tea."
"Then I will help myself, said he. — A
rather
large Dish of weak Cocoa every evening
agrees with me better than anything." —
It struck her however, as he poured
out this rather weak Cocoa, that it came
very
forth in a fine, dark coloured stream —
and at the same moment, his sisters
both crying out — "Oh! Arthur, you get
your Cocoa stronger & stronger every
Even^{g}" — , with Arthur's somewhat cons:
:cious reply of "Tis rather stronger
than it should be tonight" — convinced
[f.50v] by no means
her that Arthur was ~~not~~ so fond
of being starved as they could desire,

or as he felt proper himself. — He was

certainly
~~evidently~~ very happy to turn the conversa:

of
tion on dry Toast, & hear no more ~~from~~ his
^
sisters. — "I hope you will eat some of this

Toast, said he, I reckon myself a very good

Toaster; I never burn my Toasts — I never

put them too near the Fire at first — &

yet, you see, there is not a Corner but

what is well browned. — I hope you like

dry Toast. — " "With a reasonable quantity

of Butter spread over it, very much — said

Charlotte — but not otherwise. — " "No more

exceedingly
do I — said he ~~very much obliged~~ pleased —

there.
We think quite alike ~~upon that sub:~~

~~:ject~~. — So far from dry Toast being wholesome,

a thing
I think it ~~is~~ very bad for the Stomach.
^ ^
Without a little butter to soften it, it

hurts the Coats of the Stomach. I am

sure it does. — I will have the pleasure

of spreading some for you directly — &

afterwards I will spread some for my:

:self. — Very bad indeed for the Coats of

the Stomach — but there is no convincing

<u>some</u> people. — It irritates & acts like a

nutmeg grater. — " ~~It was rather amusing~~

~~to see~~ He could not get the command

[f.51r] ~~Glass~~

of the Butter ^ however, without a

accusing

struggle; His Sisters ~~accused~~ him of eating

a great deal too much, & declaring* he was

and

not to be trusted; — ^ he maintaining† that

he only eat enough to secure the Coats

of his Stomach; — & besides, he only wanted

it now for Miss Heywood. — Such a plea

must prevail, he got the butter & spread

away for her with an accuracy of Judge:

:ment which at least delighted himself;

* 'ing' written over 'ed' in 'declaring'.
† 'ing' written over 'ed' in 'maintaining'.

her Toast
but when ~~that~~ was done, & he took his

own ~~Toast~~ in hand, Charlotte c^{d} hardly

herself
contain ~~himself~~ as she saw him watching
^

his Sisters, while he scrupulously scraped

almost
off ^ as much butter as he put on, &

then seize an odd moment for adding

a great dab just before it went into

his Mouth. — Certainly, Mr Arthur P.'s

enjoyments in Invalidism were very

different from his Sisters — by no means

so spiritualized. — A good deal of Earthy*

Dross Charlotte could not but suspect him
hung about him. ~~He seemed of having~~†
^

of adopting principally
~~chosen~~ that line of Life, ~~cheifly~~ for the

indulgence of an indolent Temper — & to

be determined on having no Disorders

but such as called for warm rooms

& good Nourishment. — In one particular

* 'y' added to 'Earthy'.
† '~~of having~~' written over '~~to have~~'.

however, she soon found that he had

[f.51v] caught something from them. — "What! said

he — Do you venture upon two dishes of

strong Green Tea in one Even^{g}? — What

Nerves you must have! — How I envy

you. — Now, if I were to swallow only one

such dish — what do you think it's effect

would be upon me? — " "Keep you awake

perhaps all night" — replied Charlotte, mean:

:ing to overthrow his attempts at Surprise, by

the Grandeur of her own Conceptions. — "Oh!

if that were all! — he exclaimed. — No — it

act on me like Poison and

w^{d} entirely take away the use of my

right side, before I had swallowed it 5

sounds almost incredible —

minutes. — It ~~is a sort of thing hardly to~~

~~be believed~~ — but it has happened to me

~~several~~ so often that I cannot doubt it. —

~~three times~~. — The use of my right Side is

entirely taken away for several hours!"

^

"It sounds rather odd to be sure — answered

Charlotte coolly — but I dare say it would

be proved to be the simplest thing in the
World, by those who have studied right
sides & Green Tea scientifically & thoroughly
understand all the possibilities of their
action on each other." — ~~Very~~ Soon* after
Tea, a Letter was brought to Miss D. P —
from the Hotel. — "From M^{rs}. Charles Dupuis —
said she. — some private hand." — And having
read a few lines, exclaimed aloud "Well,
[f.52r] this is very extraordinary! very extraordi:
:nary indeed! — That both should have
the Same Name. — Two M^{rs}. Griffiths! — This
is a Letter of recommendation & introduction
to me, of the Lady from Camberwell — &
<u>her</u> name happens to be Griffiths too." —

and
A few lines more however, ~~brought~~ the

rushed
colour ^ into her Cheeks, & with ~~a good~~

much
~~deal of~~ ^ Perturbation she added — "The oddest
thing that ever was! — a Miss Lambe too! —

* 'S' written over 's' in 'Soon'.

a young Westindian of large Fortune. — But
it cannot be the same. — Impossible that
it should be the same." — She read the Letter
aloud for comfort. — It was merely to "intro:
:duce the Bearer, M^{rs}. G. — from Camberwell,
& the three young Ladies under her care,
to Miss D. P — 's notice. — M^{rs}. G. — being a
stranger at Sanditon, was anxious for a
respectable Introduction — & M^{rs}. C. Dupuis
therefore, at the instance of the interme:
:diate friend, provided her with this Letter,
knowing that she c^{d}. not do her dear
Diana a greater kindness than by giving
her the means of being useful. — M^{rs}
G.'s cheif solicitude w^{d}. be for the
accomodation & comfort of one of the young
Ladies under her care, a Miss Lambe,
a young W. Indian of large Fortune, in
[f.52v] delicate health." — "It was very strange! —
very remarkable! — very extraordinary"
but they were all agreed in determing it
to be impossible that there should not be

two Families; ~~totally seperate & distinct~~ such a totally distinct set of people as were concerned in the reports of ~~them~~ ^each^ made that matter quite certain. There <u>must</u> be two Families. — Impossible to be otherwise. "Im: :possible" & "Impossible", was repeated over & over again with great fervour. — An accidental resemblance of Names & circum: :stances, however striking at first, involved nothing really incredible — and so it was settled. — Miss Diana herself derived an immediate ~~Good~~ ^advantage^ to counterbalance her Perplexity. She must put her shawl over her shoulders, & be running about again. Tired as she was, she must instantly repair to the Hotel, to investigate the truth & offer her Services. —

Chapter 11.

It would not do. — Not all that the whole

race
Parker ~~family~~ could say among themselves,

c^{d}. produce a happier catastrophée than

that
the Family from Surry & the Family
^
were
from Camberwell ~~being~~ one & the

same. — The rich Westindians, & the

young Ladies Seminary had all entered

[f.53r] Sanditon in those two Hack chaises.

The M^{rs}. G. who in her friend M^{rs}. Darling's

hands, had wavered as to coming & been

unequal to the Journey, was the very same

M^{rs}. G. whose plans were at the same

period an
~~time~~ (under ^ other representation~~s~~) perfectly

decided, & who was without fears or

difficulties. — All that had the appearance

of Incongruiety in the reports of the two,

might very fairly be placed to the account

blunders
of the Vanity, the Ignorance, or the ~~mistakes~~

~~of some~~ of the many engaged in the cause

by the vigilance & caution of Miss Diana

P — . <u>Her</u> intimate friends must be officious

like herself, & the subject had supplied

Letters & Extracts & Messages enough to

make appear what it was not.
~~throw~~ everything ~~into confusion~~. —

Miss D. probably felt a little awkward

on being first obliged to admit her mis:

:take. A long Journey from Hampshire

taken for nothing — a Brother disap:

expensive
:pointed — an[*] ^ House on her hands for a

week, must have been some of her

immediate reflections — & much worse

than all the rest, must have been the

sort of sensation of being less clear-

-sighted & infallible than she had ~~supposed.~~

beleived herself. — No part of it however

seemed to trouble her long. There

were so many to share in the shame

[f.53v] & the blame, that probably when

she had divided out their proper

* 'n' added in 'an'.

portions to M^{rs}. Darling, Miss Capper,

M^{rs}. C. D's

Fanny Noyce, M^{rs}. C. Dupuis & ~~her~~

mere

Neighbour, there might be a ~~very~~

of reproach

trifle ^ remaining for herself. — At any

all following

rate, she was seen ^ the ~~next~~ morn^{g}

walking about after Lodgings with M^{rs}

G. — as alert as ever. — M^{rs}. G. was a

very well-behaved, genteel kind of

Woman, who supported herself by ~~giving~~

receiving such

~~a home to~~ ^ great girls & young Ladies,

as

~~who~~ wanted either Masters for finishing

their Education, or a home for beginning

their Displays. — She had several more

under her care than the three who were

now come to Sanditon, but the others

all happened to be absent. — Of these

three, & indeed of all, Miss Lambe was

beyond comparison the most important

& precious, as she paid in proportion
to her fortune. — She was about 17, half-
mulatto, chilly & tender, had a maid
of her own, was to have the best room
in the Lodgings, & was always of the
first consequence in every plan of Mrs:
G. — The other Girls, two Miss Beauforts
[f.54r] were just such young Ladies as may
be met with, in at least one family
out of three, throughout the Kingdom;
they had tolerable complexions, shewey
figures, an upright decided carriage &
an assured Look; — they were very accom:
:plished & very Ignorant, their time
such
being divided between ~~the~~ pursuits* ~~of~~
~~what~~ as might attract ~~general~~ admiration,
& those Labours & Expedients of dexterous
Ingenuity, by which they could dress
in a stile much beyond what they
ought to have afforded; they were

* 's' added to 'pursuits'.

some of the first in every change of
fashion — & the object of all, was to
captivate some Man of much better
fortune than their own. — Mrs. G.
had preferred a small, retired place, like
Sanditon, on Miss Lambe's account —
and the Miss Bs — , though naturally
                                Smallness &   yet
preferring anything to ^ Retirement, ^ having
in the course of the Spring
been involved in ~~some~~ the inevitable
                                        each
expence of six new Dresses ^ for a three
days visit, were constrained to be
satisfied with Sanditon also, till their cir:
:cumstances were retreived. There, with
the hire of a Harp for one, & the purchase
of some Drawing paper for the other
[f.54v] & all the finery they could already com:
:mand, they meant to be very econo:
                                        secluded
:mical, very elegant & very ~~retired~~; with
the hope on Miss Beaufort's side, of praise

from
& celebrity ~~with~~ all who walked within
the sound of her Instrument, & on Miss
Letitia's, of curiosity & rapture in all
who came near her while she sketched —
and to Both, the consolation of meaning
to be the most stylish Girls in the
Place. — The particular introduction
of M^{rs}. G. to Miss Diana Parker, secured
them immediately an acquaintance with
the Trafalgar House-family, & with the
Denhams; — and the Miss Beauforts were
soon satisfied with "the Circle in which
in Sanditon"
they moved ^ to use a proper phrase,
for every body must now "move in a
to
Circle", — ^ the prevalence of which rototory
Motion, is perhaps to be attributed the
Giddiness & false steps of many. —
Lady Denham had other motives for
calling on M^{rs}. G. besides attention to
the Parkers. — In Miss Lambe, here was

the very young Lady, sickly & rich,

been asking for;
whom she had ~~wanted~~, & she made

the acquaintance for Sir Edward's sake,

[f.55r] & the sake of her Milch asses. How

it might answer with regard to the

Baronet, remained to be proved, but

soon
as to the Animals, she ^ found that all

be
her calculations of Profit w^{d}. ~~fail her.~~

vain. Mrs G. would not allow Miss L.

to have the smallest symptom of a De:

:cline, or ~~to have~~ any complaint which

Asses milk c^{d}. possibly releive. "Miss L.

was under the constant care of an ex:

~~could therefore~~
:perienced Physician; — ~~& if M^{rs}. G. ever~~

~~xxx~~* and his Prescriptions must be their

rule — "and except in favour of some

Tonic Pills, which a Cousin of her own

* illegible, possibly 'nee'- to begin 'needed'.

had a Property in, M^{rs}. G. did never deviate from the strict medecinal page. — The corner house of the Terrace was the one in which Miss D. P. had the pleasure of settling her new friends, & considering that it commanded in front the favourite Lounge of all the Visitors at Sanditon, & on one side, whatever might be going on at the Hotel, there c^{d}. not have been a more favourable spot for the seclusions of the Miss Beauforts.

[f.55v] accordingly
And ~~indeed~~, long before they had suited themselves with an Instrument, or ^with Drawing paper, they had, by the fre: :quency of their appearance at the low Windows upstairs, in order to close the blinds, or open the Blinds, to arrange a flower pot on the Balcony, or look at nothing through a Telescope, attracted

an

many ^ eye upwards, & made many a Gazer

gaze again. — A little novelty has a

great effect in so small a place; the

Miss Beauforts, who w^{d} have been nothing

at Brighton, could not move here

without ~~being~~ noticed; — and even M^{r}

Arthur Parker, though little disposed ~~by~~

~~habit~~ for supernumerary exertion, al:

quitted

:ways ~~went out at this end of~~ the

way his Brothers

Terrace, in his ~~walk~~ to ~~Trafalgar H~~.

by this corner House, for the sake of

a glimpse of the Miss Bs — , though

round-

it was ½ a q^{r} of a mile - ^ about, &

added two steps to the ascent of the

Hill.

Chap: 12.

Charlotte had been 10 days at Sanditon

without seeing Sanditon House, every

[f.56r] attempt at calling on Lady D. having

been defeated by meeting with her

beforehand. But now it was to be more
resolutely undertaken, at a more early
hour, that nothing might be neglected of
attention to Lady D. or amusement to
Charlotte. — "And if you should find a
favourable opening my Love, said Mr P.
(who did not mean to go with them) —
better
I think you had ^ mention the poor
Mullins's situation, & sound her Lady:
:ship as to a subscription for them. — I
am not fond of charitable subscriptions
in a place of this kind — It is a sort
of tax upon all that come — Yet as
their distress is very great & I almost
promised the poor Woman yesterday to
get something done for her, I beleive
we must set a subscription on foot
~~for them —~~ & therefore the sooner the
better, — & Lady Denham's name at the
head of the List will be a very
necessary beginning. — You will

not dislike speaking to her about it,

Mary? — " "I will do whatever you

[f.56v] wish me, replied his wife — but you

would do it so much better yourself.

I shall not know what to say." — "My

dear Mary, cried he, it is impossible you

be a

can ^ really ~~be~~ at ~~any~~ loss. Nothing can

more

be ^ simple. You have only to state the

present afflicted situation of the family,

earnest

their ^ application to me, & my being

willing to promote a little subscription

for their releif, provided it meet with

her approbation." — "The easiest thing in

the World — cried Miss Diana Parker who

happened to be calling on them at the

moment — . All said & done, in less

time that you have been talking

of it now. — And while you are on the

subject of subscriptions Mary, I will

thank you to mention a very melan:

:choly case to Lady D, which has been
represented to me in the most affecting
terms. — There is a poor Woman in
Worcesteshire, whom some friends of
mine are exceedingly interested about,
& I have undertaken to collect whatever
I can for her. If you w^d^. mention
the circumstance to Lady Denham! —
[f.57r] Lady Denham <u>can</u> give, if she is
properly attacked — & I look upon her
to be ^the^ sort of Person who, when once she
~~can be~~ ^is^ prevailed on to undraw her Purse,
would as readily give 10 ^Gs^ as 5. — And
therefore, if you find her in a Giving
mood, you might as well speak in
favour of another Charity which I & a
few more, have very much at heart —
the establishment of a Charitable Repository
at Burton on Trent. — And ~~as to~~ then, —
there is the family of the poor Man
who was hung last assizes at York,

tho' we really have raised the Sum

all

we wanted for putting them ^ out,

yet if you can get a Guinea from

her on their behalf, it may as well

be done. — " "My dear Diana! exclaimed

M^{rs}. P. — I could no more mention

these things to Lady D. — than I c^{d}

fly." — "Where's the difficulty? — I

wish I could go with you myself —

but in 5 minutes I must be at M^{rs}

G. — to encourage Miss Lambe in taking

her first Dip. She is so frightened, poor
Thing,

[f.57v] that I promised to come & keep up her

Spirits, & go in the Machine with her if

she wished it — and as soon as that is

~~all~~ over, I must hurry home, for Susan

at one oclock

is to have Leaches ~~today~~ ^ which will be

a three hours business, — therefore I really

have not a moment to spare — besides

that (~~besides~~ between ourselves) I ought

to be in bed myself at this present time,
for I am hardly able to stand — and
when the Leaches have done, I dare say we
shall both go to our rooms for the rest
to hear it,
of the day." — "I am sorry ~~for this~~ indeed;
if this is the case
but ^ I hope Arthur will come to us." — "If
Arthur takes my advice, he will go to
bed too, for if he stays up by himself,
he will certainly eat & drink more
than he ought; — but you see Mary,
how impossible it is for me to go with
you to Lady Denham's." — "Upon second
thoughts Mary, said her husband, I will
not trouble you to speak about the
Mullins's. — I will take an opportu:
:nity of seeing Lady D. myself. — I
know how little it suits you to
be pressing matters upon a Mind at
[f.58r] all unwilling." — <u>His</u> application thus
withdrawn, his Sister could say no more

in support of hers, which was his object,

as he felt all their* impropriety ~~of them~~ &

all the certainty of their ill effect upon

his own better claim. — M^{rs}. P. was delighted

at this release, & set off very happy with

her friend & her little girl, on this walk

to Sanditon House. — It was a close,

misty morn^{g}, & when they reached the

not

brow of the Hill, they could ^ for some

time make out what sort of Carriage

it was, which they saw coming up. ~~it~~.

It appeared at different moments to be

every thing from the Gig to the Pheaton, —

from one horse to 4; & just as they

were concluding in favour of a Tandem,

little Mary's young eyes distinguished

the Coachman & she eagerly called out,

"T'is Uncle Sidney Mama, it is indeed."

And so it proved. — M^{r}. Sidney Parker

driving his servant in a very neat

* 'ir' added to 'the'.

Carriage was soon opposite to them, &
they all stopped for a few minutes.
The manners of the Parkers were always
it was
pleasant among themselves — & ~~in the~~
~~p~~ a very friendly meeting between Sidney
[f.58v] most kindly
& his Sister in law, who was ^ taking it for
granted that he was on his way to
Trafalgar House. This he declined however.
"He was just come from Eastbourne, pro:
:posing to spend two or three days, as
it might happen, at Sanditon — but the
Hotel must be his Quarters — He was ex:
:pecting to be joined there by a friend
or two." — The rest was common enquiries
& remarks, with kind notice of little
Mary, & a very well-bred Bow & proper
address to Miss Heywood on her being
named to him — and they parted, to
meet again within a few hours. —
Sidney Parker was about 7 or 8 & 20,

with a decided air
very good-looking ~~with a & very much the~~

of Ease & Fashion, and a
~~Man of fashion in his air~~

lively countenance. — This adventure

afforded agreable discussion for some time.

M^{rs}. P. entered into all her Husband's

joy on the occasion, & exulted in the

credit which Sidney's arrival w^{d}. give

road
to the place. The ~~approach~~ to Sanditon

~~by~~
H. was ~~at first only~~ ^ a broad, hand:

approach
:some, planted ~~road~~ ^ between fields, ~~of~~

~~about a q^{r}. of a mile's length~~,& conducting

at the end of a q^{r}. of a mile
~~but ending in about a q^{r}. of a mile~~

through second Gates not
into the Grounds, which though ^ extensive
^

[f.59r] ~~were~~ had all the Beauty & Respectability

which an abundance of very fine Timber

These Entrance Gates were so much in a corner
could give. — ~~They were so narrow at~~

of the Grounds or Paddock, so near one of its Boundaries
an
~~the Entrance~~, that ~~one~~ ^ outside fence
was at first almost pressing on the
here
road — till an angle ~~in one~~, & a curve
there threw to
~~in the other gave~~ them ^ a better distance.
The Fence was a proper Park paling in
clusters ~~rows~~ of fine
excellent condition; with ~~vigorous~~ ^ Elms,
rows of line
or ^ old Thorns ~~& Hollies~~ following its ~~course~~
almost every where. — Almost must be
stipulated — for there were ~~intervals~~ vacant
spaces — & through one of these, Charlotte
as soon as they entered the Enclosure,
over the pales
caught a glimpse ^ of something White &
Womanish ~~over the pales,~~ in the field
on the other side; — it was a something
which immediately brought Miss B. into
her head — & stepping to the pales, she
decidedly inspite of
saw indeed — & very ~~distinctly~~, ~~though~~

the Mist;

~~at some distance before her~~ Miss B —

seated, not far before her, at the foot of

the ~~sloping~~ bank which sloped down

from the outside of the Paling & ~~at~~

Path

which a narrow ~~track~~ seemed to

^

skirt along; — Miss Brereton seated,

apparently very composedly — & Sir

[f.59v] E. D. by her Side. — They were sitting

so near each other & appeared so closely

engaged in gentle conversation, that Ch —

instantly felt ~~that~~ she had nothing to

do but to step back again, & say not

a word. — Privacy was certainly their ob:

her

:ject. — It could not but strike rather

^

unfavourably with regard to Clara; —

must

but hers was a situation which ~~ought~~

not ~~to~~ be judged with severity. — She

was glad to perceive that nothing ~~of it~~

discerned If Charlotte

had been ~~seen~~ by M^{rs}. Parker. ~~she~~ had

^

not been
considerably the tallest of the two, ~~or~~
^
Miss B.'s white ribbons might not have
fallen within the ken of her more ob:
:servant eyes. — Among other points of
moralising reflection which the sight
of this Tete a Tete produced, Charlotte
c^{d}. not but think of the extreme dif:
:ficulty which secret Lovers must have
in finding a proper spot for their stolen
Interveiws. — Here perhaps they had
perfectly
thought themselves so secure from
^
observation! — the whole field open be:
:fore them — a steep bank & Pales
never crossed by the foot by Man
at their back —
~~behind them~~ — and a great thickness
[f.60r] of air, in aid. — Yet here, she had
seen them. They were really ill-used.
~~by her~~. — The House was large & hand:
:some; two Servants appeared, to admit

them, & every thing had a suitable air
of Property & Order. — Lady D. valued her:
:self upon her liberal Establishment,
order and the
& had great enjoyment in ^ Importance
of her style of living. — They were shewn
into the usual sitting room, well-pro:
:portioned & well-furnished; — tho' it was
Furniture rather originally good & extremely
well kept, than new or shewey — and
as Lady D. was not there, Charlotte had
leisure to look about, & to be told by
Mrs. P. that the whole-length Portrait
stately
of a ~~portly~~ ^ Gentleman, which placed
over the Mantlepeice, caught the eye
immediately, was the picture of Sir H.
Denham — and that one among many
miniatures in another part of the
represented
room, little conspicuous, ~~was~~ Mr
Hollis. — Poor Mr. Hollis! — It was
impossible not to feel him hardly

used; to be obliged to stand back in

own House

his ~~room~~ ^ & see the best place by the

[f.60v] fire constantly occupied by Sir H. D.

March 18.

APPENDIX C

'Sir Charles Grandison'

Samuel Richardson's long and popular novel *Sir Charles Grandison* (1753–4) maintained its popularity to the end of the eighteenth century, reaching its eighth edition in 1796, and prompted a number of abridgements by other authors. *The History of Little Grandison*, by M. Berquin, published in English translation (from the original French) in 1791, makes no attempt to copy the novel except in the name of the title character and his conspicuous virtue even as a child. However, both *The History of Sir Charles Grandison and the Hon. Miss Byron, in which is included the Memoirs of a Noble Italian Family* (?1780, 87 pages) and *The History of Sir Charles Grandison* (1789, 10th edition in 142 pages, 1798) attempt to reproduce a relatively comprehensive account of its complex plot, while devoting most attention to the courtship of Sir Charles and Harriet Byron.

The Austen play concentrates entirely on the Harriet Byron plot, the whole 'Italian' section of the novel being represented only by a passing reference to the Lady Clementina (in the novel a serious rival to Harriet for Sir Charles's hand in marriage), and most of the sub-plots hardly mentioned. The Harriet plot, however, is neatly rendered: in Act 1 she goes missing after the masquerade; Act 2 shows the wicked Sir Hargrave Pollexfen attempting to force her into marriage; in Acts 3 and 4, after her rescue by Sir Charles, she meets his family, including his lively sister Charlotte; and Act 5 resolves the action with a double wedding. Scene, character and even turn of phrase very closely follow those of Richardson. For example the play, like the published narrative abridgements, renders in detail one of the most famous scenes in the novel, the attempted forced marriage (vol.1, letter 29): the circumstances of the abduction, the Awberrys, the clergyman and the candles are directly as in Richardson. So is the clergyman's dramatic opening of the wedding service and Harriet's spirited response of 'no dearly beloveds' (though this detail is scored through in the play manuscript) and her dashing the prayerbook out of his hand, the squeezing of Harriet in the door and 'So, I hope you have killed me', and the removal in 'a long cloak' ('a capuchin' in the novel, and in the draft of the manuscript, scored through) by candlelight. The one incident not in Richardson – the throwing of the prayer book in the fire and Mrs Awberry's acknowledgement that no other is readily available – 'improves' Richardson insofar as it provides a practical motivation (lacking in the novel) for the wedding service being abandoned, and must also have held a particularly comic appeal for the Austens, brought up in parsonages and rectories as sons and daughters of the clergy.

Other Richardsonian details reappear in the play: not only the family relationships, which are accurately represented, but the debate about public and private marriage (vol. 4, letters 14, 15), reference to Mr Selby's trouble with his 'Dame' (vol. 6, letter 43) and Charlotte's unusual description of a baby as a 'marmouset' (vol. 7, letter 2). Many of the liveliest parts of the dialogue directly echo Richardson. In the play Sir Charles tells Charlotte, 'I will not be bribed into liking your wit'; in the novel he tells Harriet that 'Beauty shall not bribe me on your side, if I think you wrong in any point that you submit to my judgement' (vol. 3, letter 14), and Harriet comments of Charlotte 'See . . . how high this dear flighty creature bribes! But I will not be influenced, by her bribery, to take her part' (vol. 4, letter 27).

What is less reminiscent of Richardson is the constant establishment in the play of precise times of day (especially mealtimes) which the characters keep insisting upon, and a number of clumsily static exchanges ('Will you accompany us? / Lord L., will you? / Certainly. / Yes, we will go . . .' (Act 3)). It is possible that these are Austen in-jokes about Richardson, or about other plays, or about their own family (as the reference to Lucy and Nancy having had colds – a perennial Austen illness – almost certainly is) but it looks more like clumsiness or inexperience in directing characters.

Overall, it is likely that the play could offer a competent script for theatrical performance by a family who knew well the novel on which it was based, and were ready to be entertained by an abridgement of its main plot. There is nothing in it, however, which signals the kind of creative engagement with Richardson that might have increased the comedy, satire or drama of the original.

Quotations from Richardson's novel are taken from Samuel Richardson, *The History of Sir Charles Grandison*, 7 vols. (1753–4). The transcription of the play has been made from the manuscript omitting some pencil revisions in another hand which seem to have been made after the time of composition. Some very minor adjustments to punctuation and layout have been made in the cause of consistency of presentation and very obvious errors have been corrected. Significant textual revisions are noted at the foot of the relevant page.

Sir Charles Grandison
or
The happy Man,
a Comedy

Dramatis Personae

Men	Women	
Sir Charles Grandison	Milliner	Harriot Byron
Sir Hargrave Pollexfen	Sally	Miss Jervois
Lord L.	Mrs Selby	Lady L.
Lord G.	Miss Selby	Miss Grandison
Mr Reeves	Miss Ane Selby	Mrs Reeves
Mr Selby	Bridget	Mrs Auberry
Mr Beacham	Jenny	Miss Auberry
		Miss Sally

ACT THE FIRST.

Scene the First. *Mr. Reeve's House. Enter Mrs. Reeves & the Milliner at different doors.*

MRS. R. So, you have brought the dresses, have you?

line 17: JA wrote 'a Comedy in'; another hand completed the phrase (erroneously) in pencil, '6 Acts'.

MIL. I have brought the young Lady's dress, & Mistress says you may depend upon having yours this Evening.

MRS. R. Well, tell her to be sure & bring it. But let us see the dress that is come.

She takes the Bandbox out of the Milliner's hands.

MIL. Have you any other commands Madam?—

MRS. R. No. you may go. Miss Byron & I will come to morrow & pay you.

Exit Milliner.

Come, I will see whether she has made it right. Oh! but here is Miss Byron coming. I think it is but fair to let her see it first.

Enter Miss Byron with a work bag on her arm.

MRS. R. Here my dear, here is your dress come. I hope it will fit, for if it does not she will hardly have time to alter it.

MISS B. We will take it up stairs if you please & look at it, for Mr. Reeves is coming, & we shall have some of his Raillery.

Exeunt in an hurry.

Enter Mr. Reeves.

MR. R. So, for once in a way I have got the coast clear of Dresses & Band boxes; & I hope my wife & Miss Byron will continue to keep their Millinery in their own rooms, or any where so as they are not in my way. Why, if I had not had a little spirit the other day I should have had them in my own study.——

Enter Sally.

SALLY. Do you know where Miss Byron is Sir?—

MR. R. She is up in her own room I beleive.—

Sally curtseys & go[es] off.—

MR. R. Sally, Sally.—

Re-enter Sally.

line 17: 'for so many people employ her & these fashionable Milliners these sort of people are not very expeditious. / Miss Byron unlocks the Bandbox & takes out the Dress' deleted after 'alter it'.

SALLY. Sir—

MR. R. Tell Thomas to bring out the Bay horse.

SALLY. Yes Sir.

Exit Sally.

MR. R. Well, I must go & get on my boots—& by that time the horse will be out.—

Scene 2d *Mr. Reeves' house.*

Mr. Reeves entering in a great hurry at one door, & running out at the other, calls behind the Scenes.—

John, run all over London & see if you can find the Chairman or Chair that took Miss Byron. You know what number it was.—Thomas, run for Dr. Smith directly.

He comes in again in great agitation.

Enter Bridget.

BRID. Mistress is rather better Sir, & begs you will send for Dr. Smith.

MR. R. I have, I have.

Exit Bridget, exit Mr. Reeves at different doors.—calls behind the Scenes—

William, run to Mr. Greville's Lodgings & if he is at home—Stop William, Come in here:—

(*He comes in again, takes out his writing box & writes a note in great haste.*)

Here William is a note. Carry it to Mr. Greville's—

Exit William.

Enter Thomas

THOS. Dr. Smith, Sir.

MR. R. Shew him up stairs to your Mistress.

Enter John.

JOHN. I cannot find either the Chair or the Chairman Sir and Wilson is not come within Sir.

MR. R. Well, she must be carried out into the country I think.—You go to Paddington & tell Thomas to go to Hampstead, & see if you can find her, & I will go to Clapham.

Exit Mr. Reeves.

ACT THE SECOND.

Scene1st *Paddington—. The curtain draws up & discovers Miss Byron, Mrs. Awberry.*

MRS. A. But my dear young Lady, think what a large fortune Sir Hargrave has got, & he intends you nothing but marriage—

MISS B. Oh! Mrs. Awberry, do you think I can marry a man whom I always disliked & now hate? Is this not your House? Cannot you favour my Escape?—

MRS. A. My dear Madam that is impossible without detection. You know Sir Hargrave is here & there & everywhere.

MISS B. My dear Mrs. Awberry you shall have all the money in this purse if you will release me.—

Sir Hargrave bursts into the room.

SIR H. Mrs. Awberry I see you are not to be trusted with her, you are so tender-hearted. And you Madam!—

He snatches the purse out of her hand & flings it on the ground. He goes to the door & calls

Mr — —We are ready.—

Enter a Clergyman & his Clerk.

SIR H. Miss Awberry you will be Bridemaid if you please.—

He takes hold of Miss Byron's hand.

Now Madam, all your purses will not save you.—

The Clergyman takes a book out of his pocket. Miss Byron screams & faints away. Miss Sally Awberry runs in.

MISS. A. Sally, Sally, bring a glass of water directly.

Mrs. Awberry takes out her Salts & applies them to Miss Byron's nose.—

SIR H. I wish Women were not quite so delicate, with all their faints and fits!—

line 1: the following section deleted: 'Act the 2d. Scene the 1st. / Paddington [Colnebrook deleted]. / [Enter Miss Grandison & Miss Byron deleted.] Mrs. Awberry's Parlour. Enter Miss Byron, [pushed deleted] dragged in by Sir Hargrave Pollexfen. Mrs. Awberry & her two daughters. Sir Hargrave brings Miss Byron a seat. Miss Awberry goes to a closet & takes out a long cloak, attempts to put it round Miss Byron.—'

Miss Byron revives. Miss Sally returns with a glass of water & offers it to Miss Byron who drinks some.

MRS. A. What a long time you have been Child! If she faints again I shall send your Sister.—

SALLY. (*aside*) I am glad of it.—

SIR H. Come Sir, we will try again.—

Takes hold of Miss Byron's hand, Miss Awberry goes behind her.

CLERGN: *reads*. Dearly beloved—

She dashes the book out of his hand.—

CLERGN: *picking it up again* — Oh! my poor book!

SIR H. Begin again Sir, if you please. You shall be well paid for your trouble.

CLERGN: *reading again* / Dearly Beloved—

Miss Byron snatches the book out of his hand & flings it into the fire, exclaiming

Burn, quick, quick.—

The clergn runs to the fire & cries out

Oh! Sir Hargrave you must buy me another.—

SIR H. I will Sir, & twenty more if you will do the business.—Is the book burnt?—

MRS. A. Yes Sir—& we cannot lend you one in its place, for we have lost the key of the closet where we keep our Prayerbooks.

SIR H. Well Sir, I beleive we must put it off for the present. And if we are not married in this house we shall be in mine in the Forest.

CLERGN: Then I may go Sir I suppose. Remember the Prayer book.—

SIR H. Yes Sir.

Exit Clergyman & his Clerk.

SIR H. I shall be very much obliged to you Mrs. A. if you & the young Ladies will go out of the room for an instant. I will see if I cannot reason with this perverse girl.—

MRS. A. Here Deb & Sal, come out.

Exeunt Mrs & Miss A s.

line 10: 'MISS B. I see no Dearly Beloveds here, & I will not have any.—' deleted before 'She dashes'.

MISS B. Oh! do not leave me alone with him, let me go out too.

She runs to the door. Sir H. follows her. She gets half way through the door, & he in shutting it squeezes her. She screams & faints. He carries her away in his arms to a Chair, & rings the bell violently.

Enter Mrs. A. & her daughters

SIR H. Bring some water directly.

Both the daughters go out. Miss Byron revives, & exclaims

So, I hope you have killed me at last.

Re-enter Miss Awberry with the water. Sir Hargrave takes the glass & gives it to Miss B.

MISS B. No I thank you. I do not want anything that can give me life.

SIR H. Well Miss Awberry you had better get out the Cloak. It is four o'clock & she may as well die in my house as in yours.

MRS. A. Shall I order the Chariot Sir?—

SIR H. If you please Ma'am.

Miss A. takes a long Cloak out of a Closet and attempts to put it round Miss B.—Miss B. struggles.

SIR H. I will put it on Miss Awberry if she will not let you.

He puts it on.

SIR H. Will you help me lead her down stairs Miss Awberry?

MISS A. Yes Sir.

They both take hold of Miss B.—Enter Sally Awberry.

SALLY. Can I be of any service Sir?—

SIR H. You may hold the Candle.

Sally takes the Candle, Exeunt.—

ACT THE THIRD.

Scene 1. *Colnebrook—*

Enter Miss Grandison & Miss Byron.

MISS B. And where is this brother of yours to whom I am so much endebted.

line 20: 'Capuchin' deleted; 'long' written above.

MISS G. Safe in St. James's Square I hope.—But why my dear will you continue to think yourself so much endebted to him, when he only did his duty?

MISS B. But what must he have thought of me in such a dress?—Oh! these odious Masquerades!

MISS G. La! my dear, what does it signify what he thinks? He will understand it all in time. Come if your stomach pains you, you had better go to bed again.

MISS B. No, it does not pain me at all. But how kind it was in my cousin Reeves to come & see me.

MISS G. Yes he is a very nice Man. I like him very much. He disputes charmingly,—I thought he would have got the better of me.—Well but my dear Harriet, you have had a letter today. How does my Grandmama Shirley do, & my Uncle & Aunt Selby and my Cousins Lucy & Nancy?

MISS B. They are all very well I thank you, & my Grandmama thinks herself under the greatest obligation to Sir Charles for being both her & his Harriet's Deliverer, for if he had not rescued me, she would have died of a broken heart.—

MISS G. Well really I am very glad he saved you for both your sakes. My brother is a charming Man. I always catch him doing some good action. We all wish him to be married but he has no time for Love.—At least he appears to have none. For he is constantly going about from one place to another. But what for, we cannot tell. And we have such a high respect for him that we never interfere in his affairs. —I will return in a minute. I am going to fetch my work bag.

Exit Miss G.—

MISS B. What an odd Brother is this! If he is so fond of them, why should he wish them not to know his affairs?—

Re-Enter Miss G.

line 29: 'Nor do we ever express a wish to know, for we are sure that were they ever so important if he thought we wished to be acquainted with them he would tell us.' deleted after 'affairs'. // line 33: 'I wish I had such a brother' deleted after 'affairs?—'.

MISS G. What is the matter Harriet? What makes you so dull Child?—I shall take care not to leave you by yourself again in an hurry, if on my return I am to find these gloomy fits have taken hold of you. Come, I will play you your favourite tune Laure & Lenze.

MISS B. I was thinking of Sir Hargrave Pollexfen. But be so good as to play my tune.

MISS G. I will directly.

She goes to the Harpsichord & plays—After she has done playing she comes to Miss B. & says

Come, it is time for you to go to bed. It is 4 o'clock & you have been up ever since 12.

Exeunt.

Curtain draws up & discovers Miss G. reading in the Library.

MISS G. Well I think this book would suit Harriet. But here is Sir Charles come home I beleive. I will go & see. Oh! here he is.—

Enter Sir Charles. She goes to him. He takes hold of her hand.

SIR C. No more colds I hope my dear Charlotte—but above all, how does our lovely Charge do?

MISS G. Oh! Much better. She got up at 12, & I have but just sent her to bed.

SIR C. When do you expect Lord & Lady L.?—

MISS G. This Evening, about six or seven o'clock.

SIR C. Indeed! I am very glad of it.

Enter Jenny.

JEN. Miss Byron would be glad to speak with you Ma'am.

MISS G. Very well, I will come to her.

SIR C. How is your Cold Jenny?

JEN. Quite well I thank you Sir.

Curtsies & exit.

MISS G. You will excuse me for a minute Sir Charles. I must obey my summons.

Exit.

SIR C. Certainly. Well I must go & speak to Frederic.

Exit.—

Scene 3.— *Curtain draws up & discovers Lord & Lady L. & Sir Charles & Miss G. at Tea.—*

SIR C. So my Lord, you have heard of our new Sister?

LORD L. Yes Sir Charles, and Miss G. by her description of her, has made me long to see her.—

MISS G. Frederic,—Take this to Sir Charles.— (*holding some Tea.*)

SIR C. I hope you will not be disappointed when you see her.— I might say *We*, for I have hardly seen her yet.

MISS G. I hope you do not think of me a flatterer Sir Charles.

SIR C. Certainly not my dear Charlotte.

LADY L. I assure you Charlotte can flatter sometimes.

MISS G. Oh! For shame Caroline I thought you knew better than to tell tales. Lord L. will you have any more tea?

LORD L. No I thank you Charlotte.

LADY L. But Charlotte how do we come by our new Sister? I have not heard that yet.

MISS G. Well, we will go & take a walk in the Garden & talk about it. Frederic you may take away. Come Caroline make haste, or the fit will be off.—Gentlemen, will you accompany us?—

SIR C. Lord L. will you?

LORD L. Certainly.

SIR C. Yes, we will go Charlotte.—

MISS G. Come, make haste the fit is almost off.

Exeunt.

ACT THE FOURTH.

Scene 1. *Colnebrook. Curtain draws up & discovers Sir C. & Miss G., Lord L. & Miss B.—*

MISS G. What an impudent fellow Lord G., is to make you wait so Sir Charles.—Oh! he is a poor creature.

SIR C. Have patience my dear Charlotte. Something most likely has detained him.

MISS G. Indeed Sir Charles, you are too forgiving. If he were to serve to me so, he would not get into favour for some time.—What say you Harriot?—

MISS B. Indeed Miss G. you are too severe.—Besides, as Sir Charles says, something may detain him; & it is a different thing making a Lady wait on a Gentleman. But here ought to be an end of your severity, for the object of it I beleive is come. I hear him in the Hall.

Enter Lord G.

LORD G. I am afraid I have been making you wait Gentlemen.

MISS G. Well, you need not be afraid any longer, for you certainly have.

SIR C. Fye Charlotte!—I do not think that was the civillest thing in the world to say.

LORD G. I hope I have not offended you Madam.

MISS G. Yes you have, for making my dear brother wait.

SIR C. I will not be bribed into liking your wit Charlotte.—But where is Caroline all this while?—

MISS G. She is gone out in her Chariot with Emily—but I wonder Sir Charles you did not enquire after your *favourite* Sister before.

LORD L. I am sure Miss G. you cannot reproach your brother with partiality. But Sir Charles is it not time for us to go out riding?—If it is not, I am sure Miss G. might have spared her severity on Lord G.

SIR C. I assure you Lord L. that I had not forgot it, but I think it is too late to go out now. It is 3 o'clock. Now Charlotte hold your tongue. I am sure some raillery is coming out.

He rings the bell.

MISS G. I will not hold my tongue Sir Charles.

SIR C. Then Charlotte if you speak, do not let us have any severity.

MISS G. Very well, I will be good. Harriot, what is the matter, Child? You look languid. I will ring the bell for some Broth for you.

SIR C. Spare yourself that trouble my dear Charlotte, I have just rung it.

Enter Frederic

SIR C. Bring some sandwiches & a bason of broth Frederic.

Exit Frederic.

MISS G. Harriot, should you like your broth up in your own room better?—

MISS B. If you please.

MISS G. Well, we will take it up with us.

Enter Frederic with the Sandwiches & the Broth. He sets it down upon the Table. Exit Fred.—Miss G. takes the broth.

MISS G. Come Harriot.—

Exit Miss B. & Miss G.

Sir C. hands the Sandwiches.

SIR C. How long Caroline has been gone! I hope no more Sir Hargrave Pollexfens have run away with her & Emily.—

Enter Lady L. Miss G. & Miss J. Lord L. goes to meet her, takes her hand & leads her to a Sopha.

MISS G. Lord! What a loving Couple they are.

SIR C. Charlotte, hold your tongue.

LORD L. And where have you been to my dear Caroline?

LADY L. Only shopping. But Charlotte where is Miss B?

MISS G. Very safe in her own room. I always send her away when she gapes.

LADY L. Poor Creature! I hope she does not gape too often. But seriously Charlotte, is she worse or better?—

MISS G. Law! Lady L. you are so afraid I shall not take care of her.—Why, she is just as she is always is—languid at 3 o'clock. I beleive it is because Lord G. always comes about at that time; & she is so sorry to see her poor Charlotte plagued so!—

MISS JERVOIS. Dear Miss G. who plagues you? I am sure Lord G does not.

MISS G. Emily you do not know anything of the matter. You must hold your tongue till it is your turn to be called upon.—

MISS J. Well Miss G. I think it is you who teaze him, but he will certainly get the better of you at last. He did once you know. And I do not know what you mean by its being my turn to be called upon.

MISS G. Why, when it is your turn to be married. But you had better not get on Lord G.'s side; you will be worsted certainly. But come is not it time to dress? (*looks at her watch*) Dear me! It is but four.

LORD L. You need not say "But" Charlotte, for you know we are to dine at 1/2 after 4. to day.

MISS G. Indeed my Lord, my Lady did not tell me so. Well, I will pardon her this time. Come then Let us go, if it is time.

Exeunt Ladies.

LORD L. What an odd girl is Charlotte. But you must not despair Lord G. I beleive she likes you tho' she wont own it. I hope Miss Byron when she is recovered will have a little influence over her.

SIR C. Indeed I hope so too. Miss Byron is a charming young woman. I think from what I have seen of her, her mind is as complete as her person. She is the happy medium between Gravity & over liveliness. She is lively or grave as the occasion requires.

LORD G. Indeed she is a delightful young woman, & only Miss G. can equal her. I do not mean any offence to Lady L.

LORD L. Indeed my Lord I do not take it as such. Caroline is grave, Charlotte is lively, I am fond of gravity, you most likely are fond of Liveliness.

Enter a Footman

FOOTMAN. Dinner is on Table my Lord.—

LORD L. Very well.

Exit Footman

Enter Lady L. Miss G. Miss B. & Miss J.

LORD L. Dinner is upon Table my dear Caroline.

LADY L. Indeed. Come Harriet & all of you.—

Exeunt.

ACT THE FIFTH.

Scene 1. *Library at Colnebrook[.] Sir Charles & Mr. Selby.*

MR. S. But my dear Sir Charles my neice is but 18. I never will allow her to marry till she is 22. I shall take her back into Northamptonshire if you have done nothing but put such notions into the girl's head. I had no notion of my Harriet's coming to this. And besides Sir C. I never will allow her to marry you till Lady Clementina della Porretta is married.—

SIR C. Mr. Selby that has been my objection for some time to making my proposals to Miss B. But yesterday I received some Letters from Italy in which they have great hopes of Lady Clementina's being soon persuaded to marry. She wishes me in the same letter to set her the example by marrying an English woman. I admire Miss Byron very much, but I will never marry her against your consent. And if you had not told me she was 18, I should have thought her quite as much as 22. I do not mean by her looks but by her prudence.

MR. S. Upon my word you are a fine fellow, you have done away all my objections, & if you can get Harriot's consent you have mine. I hope she will not be nice, for if she do not get a husband now, she never may for she has refused all the young Gentry of our Neighbourhood. And as to her fortune I will tell you plainly she has no more than 14,000£.

SIR C. As to her fortune it is no object to me. Miss Byron herself is a Jewel of inestimable value. Her understanding more than makes up for want of fortune. And now if we can bring Lord G. & my Sister Charlotte together we shall have a double wedding. But I am afraid Charlotte is too lively for matrimony.

MR. S. Oh! Yes, your sister is a fine girl, only she is too nice about an husband. Adsheart! I hope you wo'nt have such a plague with my Harriot, as I had with my Dame Selby. Well, but it is three o'clock. I will go & break it to her. Sir Charles, you may come & stay at the door till you are admitted, you know.

Exeunt.—

line 29: 'As sure as two & two make four' deleted and 'Oh! Yes,' inserted above line.

Scene 2. *Drawing room. Lady L. Miss G. Miss B. & Miss J.*

MISS G. There is something monstrous frightful to be sure my dear Harriot in marrying a man that one likes.

LADY L. My dear Charlotte, you overpower Harriot with your Raillery.—I dare say you will feel the same fright when you marry Lord G.—

MISS G. I will tell you what Lady L.—To tell you a secret I am not likely to marry Lord G.—for I want to be married at home, & my brother will not consent to it.

MISS J. Oh! fye! Miss Grandison, I wonder how you could think of it!

MISS B. Indeed Charlotte, I am of Emily's opinion. Are not you Lady L.?

LADY L. Certainly. And I know my brother will let as few people be by at the Ceremony as possible.

MISS G. I see you are all joined in concert against me; but before I give up, I will take the liberty to chuse how many people I like to be by.—

LADY L. I am sure Harriot will not object to that. Shall you Harriot?—

MISS B. Oh! not at all. Indeed I wish myself to have but few people by. Lord Bless me! I do beleive here are my Aunt & Cousins come.

MISS G. I suppose Mrs. Reeves has brought her Marmouset with her.

Enter Mr. & Mrs. Reeves, Mrs. Selby, Lucy & Nancy.—

MISS BYRON *rising & meeting Mrs. Selby.* Oh! how do you do, my dear Aunt?—How does my Grandmama do?—

MRS. S. She is pretty well my Love, & she would have come, but she thought the Journey too long for her to undertake.

MISS B. Lucy & Nancy are you quite rid of your colds? And Mrs. Reeves!—I did not expect this favour.—Let me introduce you all to my friends.—

She introduces them.

MISS G. Mrs. Reeves, have you not brought your Baby?—

MR. R. No, she would not take that liberty. I wanted her to do it, because I knew you would excuse it. Miss Byron, where are the Bridegrooms?—

LADY L. I will go & call them, & my Lord.—

Exit Lady L.

MISS B. Lucy, were the roads very good?—

LUCY. Indeed they were very good[.]

MR. R. Yes, our ponies went on fast enough.

MISS G. Did you ride Sir?

MR. R. No Ma'am, we came in our phaeton, & the Selbys in their Coach.—

Enter Lady L.—with the 4 Gentlemen. She introduces them.

MR. S. Mrs. Selby, here is the Bridegroom of your Harriot. Adsheart! we shall have a double marriage, as sure as two—& two—make four. And here is the other Bridegroom.

(*pointing to Lord G.*)

MISS G. Yes, that is my Man sure enough. I wish, I had a better one to shew you. But he is better than he was.

SIR C. Fye! Charlotte, I am sure you have nothing to complain of in Lord G. And if you will make a good wife, I will answer for it he will a Husband.—And I hope you will be as happy, as I promise myself Miss Byron & I shall be.—And I hope she will have no reason to lament having chosen me for her Husband.—

The Curtain Falls.

APPENDIX D

Prayers

Evening Prayer—

Give us grace, Almighty Father, so to pray, as to deserve to be heard, to address thee with our Hearts, as with our Lips. Thou art every where present, from Thee no secret can be hid; may the knowledge of this, teach us to fix our Thoughts on Thee, with Reverence & Devotion that we pray not in vain.—

Look with Mercy on the Sins we have this day committed, & in Mercy make us feel them deeply, that our Repentance may be sincere, and our Resolutions stedfast of endeavouring against the commission of such in future.—Teach us to understand the sinfulness of our own Hearts, and bring to our knowledge every fault of Temper and every evil Habit in which we may have indulged to the dis-comfort of our fellow-creatures, and the danger of our own Souls.—May we now, and on each return of night, consider how the past day has been spent by us, what have been our prevailing Thoughts, words and Actions during it, and how far we can acquit ourselves of Evil. Have we thought irreverently of Thee, have we dis-obeyed thy Commandments, have we neglected any known Duty, or willingly given pain to any human Being?—Incline us to ask our Hearts these questions Oh! God, and save us from deceiving ourselves by Pride or Vanity.

Give us a thankful sense of the Blessings in which we live, of the many comforts of our Lot; that we may not deserve to lose them by Discontent or Indifference.

Be Gracious to our Necessities, and guard us, and all we love, from Evil this night. May the sick and afflicted, be now, & ever thy care; and heartily do we pray for the safety of all that travel by Land or by Sea, for the comfort & protection of the Orphan & Widow, & that thy pity may be shewn, upon all Captives & Prisoners.

Above all other blessings Oh! God, for ourselves, & our fellow-creatures, we implore Thee to quicken our sense of thy Mercy in the redemption of the World, of the Value of that Holy Religion in which we have been brought up, that we may not, by our own neglect, throw away the Salvation Thou hast given us, nor be Christians only in name.—Hear us Almighty God, for His sake who has redeemed us, & taught us thus to pray.—

Our Father which art in Heaven &c.

Almighty God! Look down with Mercy on thy Servants here assembled & accept the petitions now offer'd up unto thee.

Pardon Oh God! the offences of the past day. We are conscious of many frailties; we remember with shame & contrition, many evil Thoughts & neglected duties, & we have perhaps sinned against Thee & against our fellow-creatures in many instances of which we have now no remembrance.—Pardon Oh God! whatever thou hast seen amiss in us, & give us a stronger desire of resisting every evil inclination & weakening every habit of sin. Thou knowest the infirmity of our Nature, & the temptations which surround us. Be thou merciful, Oh Heavenly Father! to Creatures so formed & situated.

We bless thee for every comfort of our past and present existence, for our health of Body & of Mind & for every other source of happiness which Thou hast bountifully bestowed on us & with which we close this day, imploring their continuance from Thy Fatherly Goodness, with a more grateful sense of them, than they have hitherto excited. May the comforts of every day, be thankfully felt by us, may they prompt a willing obedience of thy commandments & a benevolent spirit towards every fellow-creature.

Have mercy Oh gracious Father! upon all that are now suffering from whatsoever cause, that are in any circumstance of danger or distress—Give them patience under every affliction, strengthen, comfort & relieve them. To Thy goodness we commend ourselves this night beseeching thy protection of us through its darkness & dangers. We are helpless & dependant; graciously preserve us—For all whom we love & value, for every Friend & connection, we equally pray; However divided & far asunder, we know that we are alike before Thee, & under thine Eye. May we be equally united in Thy Faith & Fear, in fervent devotion towards Thee, & in Thy merciful Protection this night. Pardon Oh Lord! the imperfections of these our Prayers, & accept them through the mediation of our Blessed Saviour, in whose Holy Words, we farther address thee;

Our Father

Father of Heaven! whose goodness has brought us in safety to the close of this day, dispose our Hearts in fervent prayer.

Another day is now gone, & added to those, for which we were before accountable. Teach us Almighty Father, to consider this solemn Truth, as we should do, that we may feel the importance of every day, & every hour as it passes, & earnestly strive to make a better use of what Thy Goodness may yet bestow on us, than we have done of the Time past.

Give us Grace to endeavour after a truly christian Spirit to seek to attain that temper of Forbearance & Patience, of which our Blessed Saviour has set us the highest Example, and which, while it prepares us for the spiritual Happiness of the life to come, will secure to us the best enjoyment of what this World can give. Incline us Oh God! to think humbly of ourselves, to be severe only in the examination of our own conduct, to consider our fellow-creatures with kindness, & to judge of all they say & do with that Charity which we would desire from men ourselves.

We thank thee with all our hearts for every gracious dispensation, for all the Blessings that have attended our Lives, for every hour of safety, health & peace, of domestic comfort & innocent enjoyment. We feel that we have been blessed far beyond any thing that we have deserved; and though we cannot but pray for a continuance of all these Mercies, we acknowledge our unworthiness of them & implore Thee to pardon the presumption of our desires.

Keep us oh! Heavenly Father from Evil this night.—Bring us in safety to the beginning of another day & grant that we may rise again with every serious & religious feeling which now directs us.

line 23: handwriting changes after '& do'.

May thy mercy be extended over all Mankind, bringing the Ignorant to the knowledge of thy Truth, awakening the Impenitent, touching the Hardened.—Look with compassion upon the afflicted of every condition, assuage the pangs of disease, comfort the broken in spirit.

More particularly do we pray for the safety and welfare of our own family & friends wheresoever dispersed, beseeching Thee to avert from them all material & lasting Evil of Body or Mind; & may we by the assistance of thy Holy Spirit so conduct ourselves on Earth as to secure an Eternity of Happiness with each other in thy Heavenly Kingdom. Grant this most merciful Father, for the sake of our Blessed Saviour in whose Holy Name & Words we further address Thee.

Our Father &c.

APPENDIX E

Poems attributed to Jane Austen

'Sigh Lady Sigh'

The poem is written in pencil, in a hand similar in some respects to that of Jane Austen, across two pages of Ann Murry, *Mentoria: or, The Young Lady's Instructor* (1778, second edn 1780), including the title page. The lines seem to be original, but authorship is impossible to verify. The book was owned by Jane Austen in the 1790s and given by her to Anna Lefroy in 1801. It is now owned by the Jane Austen Memorial Trust at Chawton Cottage. See Introduction, p. cxxvii.

Sigh Lady sigh, hide not the tear thats stealing
Down thy young face now so pale & cheerless
Let not thy heart be blighted by the feeling
That presses on thy soul, of utter loneliness.

In sighs suppress & grief that's [ever?] weeping
Beats slow & mournfully [a mourning?] heart
A heart oer which decay & death are creeping
In which no sunshine can a gleam impart.

Thou art not desolate, tho' left forsaken
By one in whom thy very soul was bound
Let Natures voice thy dreary heart awaken
Oh listen to the melodies around.

For Summer her pure golden tress is flinging
On woods & glades & silent gliding streams

line 11: 'be blighted by' inserted in place of '[be only with?]'. // line 13: 'grief' written over another word (illegible).

With joy the very air around is ringing
Oh rouse thee from those mournful mournful dreams.

Go forth let not that voice in vain be calling
Join thy hearts voice to that which fills the air
For he who een a sparrow saves from falling
Makes <u>thee</u> an object of peculiar care.

'On the Universities'

The manuscript is held in the Henry W. and Albert A. Berg Collection at the New York Public Library and is in JA's hand. However, she must simply have copied out the poem, which appears in many collected volumes of verse and epigrams including in the 'Epigrams' section of the highly popular *Elegant Extracts: or Useful and Entertaining Pieces of Poetry, selected for the Improvement of Youth* (London: Charles Dilly, *c*.1789[?] and subsequent editions). See Introduction, pp. cxxvi–cxxvii.

No wonder that Oxford and Cambridge profound
In Learning and Science so greatly abound
Since some <u>carry</u> thither a little each day
and we meet with so few who <u>bring any away</u>.

line 2: 'melancholy' inserted above 'mournful mournful', presumably as an alternative.

APPENDIX F

Family poems

'Miss Lloyd has now sent to Miss Green'—Miss Green's reply—by Mrs Austen

[see pp. 243, 707–8]

I've often made clothes
For those who write prose,
But 'tis the first time
I've had orders in rhyme—.
Depend on't, fair Maid,
You shall be obeyed;
Your garment of black
Shall sit close to your back,
And in every part
I'll exert all my art;
It shall be the neatest,
And eke the completest
That ever was seen—
Or my name is not Green!

'Verses to rhyme with "Rose"'.—

[a group of four poems including one by JA, see pp. 243, 708–9]

M^rs^. Austen.

This morning I 'woke from a quiet repose,
I first rub'd my eyes & I next blew my nose.
With my stockings and shoes I then cover'd my toes
And proceeded to put on the rest of my cloathes.
This was finish'd in less than an hour I suppose;
I employ'd myself next in repairing my hose

'Twas a work of necessity, not what I chose;
Of my sock I'd much rather have knit twenty Rows.—
My work being done, I looked through the windows
And with pleasure beheld all the Bucks & the Does,
The Cows & the Bullocks, the Wethers & Ewes.—
To the Lib'ry each morn, all the Family goes,
So I went with the rest, though I felt rather froze.
My flesh is much warmer, my blood freer flows
When I work in the garden with rakes & with hoes.
And now I beleive I must come to a close,
For I find I grow stupid e'en while I compose;
If I write any longer my verse will be prose. —

Miss Austen

Love, they say is like a Rose;
I'm sure t'is like the wind that blows,
For not a human creature knows
How it comes or where it goes.
It is the cause of many woes,
It swells the eyes & reds the nose,
And very often changes those
Who once were friends to bitter foes. —
But let us now the scene transpose
And think no more of tears & throes.
Why may we not as well suppose
A smiling face the Urchin shows?
And when with joy the Bosom glows,
And when the heart has full repose,
'Tis Mutual Love the gift bestows.—

[then JA's poem]

Mrs. E. Austen

Never before did I quarrel with a Rose
Till now that I am told some lines to compose,
Of which I have little idea God knows!—
But since that the Task is assign'd me by those
To whom Love, Affection & Gratitude owes

A ready compliance, I feign would dispose
And call to befriend me the Muse who bestows
The gift of Poetry both on Friends & Foes.—
My warmest acknowledgements are due to those
Who watched near my Bed & soothed me to repose
Who pitied my sufferings shared in my woes,
And by their simpathy releived my sorrows.
May I as long as the Blood in my veins flows
Feel the warmth of Love which now in my breast glows,
And may I sink into a refreshing Doze
When I lie my head on my welcome pillows.

ABBREVIATIONS

Camilla	Frances Burney, *Camilla: or, A Picture of Youth*, 5 vols. (1796)
Chronology	Deirdre Le Faye, *A Chronology of Jane Austen and Her Family* (Cambridge: Cambridge University Press, 2006)
Cecilia	Frances Burney, *Cecilia: Or, Memoirs of an Heiress*, 5 vols. (1782)
Cookbook	Maggie Black and Deirdre Le Faye, *The Jane Austen Cookbook* (London: The British Museum Press, 1995)
Domestic Medicine	William Buchan MD, *Domestic Medicine: Or, A Treatise on the Prevention and Cure of Diseases by Regimen and Simple Medicines*, 17th edn (1800)
E	*Emma*
FR	Deirdre Le Faye, *Jane Austen: A Family Record*, 2nd edn (Cambridge: Cambridge University Press, 2004)
Gilson	David Gilson, *Jane Austen: Collected Articles and Introductions* (privately printed, 1998)
Grandison	Samuel Richardson, *The History of Sir Charles Grandison, in a Series of Letters*, 7 vols. (1753–4)

Guide to Watering Places	Anon.: *A Guide to All the Watering and Sea Bathing Places* (1803)
HRO	Hampshire Record Office
JA	Jane Austen
'Juv.'	'Juvenilia'
L	*Jane Austen's Letters*, collected and edited by Deirdre Le Faye (Oxford: Oxford University Press, 1995; paperback edn 1997)
'LS'	'Lady Susan'
Medical Guide	Richard Reece, *The Medical Guide, for the use of Clergy, Heads of Families, and Practitioners in Medicine and Surgery*, 12th edn (1817)
Memoir (1870)	James Edward Austen Leigh, *A Memoir of Jane Austen* (1870)
Memoir (1871)	James Edward Austen Leigh, *A Memoir of Jane Austen, second edition: To which is added Lady Susan, and Fragments of Unfinished Tales by Miss Austen* (1871)
MP	*Mansfield Park*
MW	*The Works of Jane Austen: vol. 6, Minor Works*, ed. R. W. Chapman (Oxford: Oxford University Press, 1954)
NA	*Northanger Abbey*
OED	*The Oxford English Dictionary* (on-line, 2008)
P	*Persuasion*
P&P	*Pride and Prejudice*
'S'	'Sanditon'
Self-Control	Mary Brunton, *Self-Control*, 2 vols. (1811)

Selwyn	David Selwyn, *Jane Austen: Collected Poems and Verse of the Austen Family* (Manchester: Carcanet Press, 1996)
S&S	*Sense and Sensibility*
TLS	*The Times Literary Supplement*
'W'	'The Watsons'

EXPLANATORY NOTES

LADY SUSAN

LETTER I

1 **Lady Susan**: there is no reference to 'Lady Susan' by this or any other title in documents which survive from JA's lifetime. The fair copy manuscript held in the Morgan Library, New York, comprising 158 folios of 198 mm × 160 mm, including two with the watermark 1805, has no title in JA's handwriting, though it is possible that a title page was discarded when the manuscript was bound in the late nineteenth century; the bound version has the title 'Lady Susan' on the front cover. Anna Lefroy, Caroline Austen and James Edward Austen Leigh all refer to the manuscript by the name of 'Lady Susan' in their correspondence over plans for the first publication of the text in the second edition of the *Memoir* (1871), and it was published with that title.

2 **Lady Susan Vernon**: Lady Susan's title, and in particular the use of her first name, indicates she is the daughter of a senior member of the British aristocracy, that is, a duke, marquess or earl. As such she continues to carry the title 'Lady' even if she marries a commoner.

3 **Langford . . . Churchill**: 'Churchill' and 'Langford' are common village names, and there is a village of Langford within two miles of a Churchill in Somerset to the west of Bath. Both may refer here to estates, however. JA used 'Churchill' in *E* for the name of the wealthy family whose daughter married Mr Weston and who raised the Westons' child Frank.

4 **sister**: sister-in-law, a common usage at the time.

5 **too much . . . state of mind**: as a way of giving formal expression to the natural state of grief in losing a spouse, a widow would spend a full year of deep or full mourning, leading a quiet life and wearing

nothing but black; in the next year of half- or second-mourning some public appearances would be permissible and the dress code would be relaxed. Mourning protocols for widowers were generally less restrictive, as is evident from the social activities of the recently bereaved Mr Elliot in *Persuasion*.

6 **retirement**: secluded home, far from the bustle of urban life.

7 **one of the best Private Schools in Town**: girls were often educated at home, by their mother or a governess, but some were sent to school, either for the educational and social benefits of a school education, or because they were not wanted at home. Private schools were usually small, and owned by the senior teacher; they would offer girls a curriculum usually including dancing, drawing, deportment and French, all skills of domestic and social use. Jane and Cassandra Austen attended The Abbey House School in Reading, 1785–6, and JA wrote in *E* of Mrs Goddard's school 'where a reasonable quantity of accomplishments were sold at a reasonable price, and where girls might be sent to be out of the way and scramble themselves into a little education, without any danger of coming back prodigies' (vol. 1, ch. 3). The social elite referred to London as 'town'.

8 **S. Vernon**: a formal signature was conventional even between close friends and relatives. JA frequently signed her letters to close relatives 'J.A.' but sometimes even to her sister Cassandra she signed 'J. Austen', particularly in adulthood.

LETTER 2

1 **proposals . . . Frederica**: Frederica, an unusual name in eighteenth-century England, became fashionable when Princess Frederica of Prussia (1767–1820) married the Duke of York, son of George III, in London in 1791. The event was widely reported, and prompted two anonymous novels: *Frederica, or the Memoirs of a young Lady* (1792), dedicated to the new Duchess, and *Frederica Risberg, a German Story* (1793). The Duchess lived a retired life and subsequent publicity for her was limited. 'Proposals' were an offer of marriage, with related financial settlements.

2 **romantic**: the word 'romantic' was shifting to its modern meaning at this time; Lady Susan's usage seems to acknowledge the older sense of fanciful and foolish.

3 **throwing her off**: disowning her, having nothing more to do with her. In *P&P* Mr Collins, hearing of Lydia's elopement with Wickham, advises Mr Bennet 'to throw off your unworthy child from your affection for ever, and leave her to reap the fruits of her own heinous offence' (vol. 3, ch. 6).

4 **No. 10 Wigmore St**: all the London addresses in 'Lady Susan' are located in the newly built streets on Portman estate land just north of Oxford Street. Wigmore Street, parallel with Oxford Street, contained houses for the gentry, and also, in the 1790s, a bookseller/circulating library, and a drapery shop.

5 **insupportable . . . Village**: what is 'insupportable' to Lady Susan was the reverse to JA in creative terms; in her comments on her niece Anna's novel in progress, JA, then working on *E*, wrote that 'You are now collecting your People delightfully, getting them exactly into such a spot as is the delight of my life;—3 or 4 Families in a Country Village is the very thing to work on' (9–18 September 1814, p. 220).

6 **good connections . . . pay**: board and education in private schools around London could cost between sixteen and thirty-five guineas a year, but one of the elite London schools could cost 100 guineas or more (more than £5,000 at early twenty-first century rates), plus extras such as an entrance fee and further charges for visiting teachers for specialist subjects. JA may have had in mind, for example, the smart school in Queen Square, Bloomsbury, sometimes called 'The Ladies' Eton', attended by Elizabeth Bridges, who married JA's brother Edward in 1791, run 'exclusively for the daughters of the nobility and gentry' (*FR*, p. 70).

LETTER 3

1 **spending the Christmas with you**: then as now, Christmas was regarded as a festival which families might spend together. JA, writing to Cassandra on 25 December 1798, wishes her sister a 'merry Christmas' and mentions that the family plan to dine with the James Austens at Deane, but otherwise records a normal

domestic and social routine. (*L*, pp. 30–31). Later, JA referred in verse to the card games popular at Godmersham at 'Christmas Tide' (17 January 1809, see p. 249). In *P*, Lady Russell, exhausted by the Musgroves' 'domestic hurricane', hopes to remember in future 'not to call at Uppercross in the Christmas holidays' (vol. 2, ch. 2).

2 **Staffordshire**: a part-rural, part-industrial county in the English Midlands, 150 miles north-west of London and considerably further from Churchill (see Letter 17, n. 5 below). JA's cousin Edward Cooper became rector of Hamstall-Ridware in Staffordshire in 1799. 'Staffordshire is a good way off,' JA wrote from Hampshire, 'so we shall see nothing more of them till, some fifteen years hence, the Miss Coopers are presented to us, fine, jolly, handsome, ignorant girls' (*L*, p. 37).

LETTER 4

1 **Coquette**: calculated flirt. Flirtatious behaviour was much frowned on throughout the eighteenth century and any literary coquette, unless a comic figure, would be subject to condemnation.

LETTER 5

1 **Dignity . . . Estate**: family property and estates were expected to be maintained by the holder and to pass, on his death, to his eldest son, thus maintaining a family's wealth and prosperity. Having to sell estates indicates financial mismanagement or the holder living beyond his means. Selling to a younger brother would have a clear advantage in keeping the estate in the family, though it might well add to the embarrassment of the seller.

2 **his name in a Banking House . . . money**: as a younger son of a gentleman with no prospect of inheriting the family estate, Charles has taken on a professional occupation, as a partner in a bank. Most banks of the time were privately owned and relatively small; while the partners could indeed make their fortunes they also had unlimited liability, so the risks were high. In 1801 JA's brothers Henry and Frank became 'named partners' in the banking house of Austen, Maunde & Austen. Henry's bank business failed in

1816 as a result of bad debts and the slump that followed cessation of the war with France, and he was declared bankrupt.

3 **sensibility**: refined and cultivated awareness of one's own feelings, a quality celebrated in the mid and late eighteenth century, though its excesses were much satirized, including by JA herself in her juvenilia: 'Alas! in the perusal of the following Pages your sensibility will be most severely tried,' writes Laura, 'Ah! . . . The Death of my Father my Mother, and my Husband though almost more than my gentle Nature could support, were trifles in comparison to the misfortune I am now proceeding to relate' ('Love and Freindship', 'Juv.', Volume the Second, p. 131).

4 **under cover to you**: within a letter addressed to Mrs Johnson. Envelopes were not yet used: the letter would be folded, sealed and addressed.

LETTER 6

1 **Symmetry . . . Grace**: what Sir Joshua Reynolds called 'the lore of symmetry and grace' (Sir Joshua Reynolds, 'The Art of Painting', line 592, in *Works*, 2 vols. (1797), vol. 2, p. 192) was widely regarded as a standard of beauty. Symmetry, the quality of being well proportioned, was particularly highly prized: early in *P&P* Darcy criticizes Elizabeth Bennet for 'more than one failure of perfect symmetry in her form' (vol. 1, ch. 6). Later in the same novel Miss Bingley condemns the fact that, among other failings, 'her complexion has no brilliancy' (vol. 3, ch. 3). According to Thomas Reid, 'The last and noblest part of beauty is grace, which consists of those motions, either of the whole body, or of a part or feature, which express the most perfect propriety of conduct and sentiment in an amiable character' (Thomas Reid, *Essays on the Intellectual Powers of Man* (1785), Essay 8, 'On Beauty', pp. 762–3).

2 **address**: manner of speaking, bearing in conversation.

3 **Springs . . . in town**: the main London social season for the aristocracy and gentry took place in the early months of the year, coinciding with the sitting of Parliament and ending when the warm weather of early summer encouraged people to return to their country estates; in the late eighteenth century George III's

birthday on 4 June formally marked the end of the season. In *S&S* Mrs Jennings, the Middletons, John and Fanny Dashwood and their various guests all meet at social events in London in the spring; and in *P* Sir Walter Elliot and his eldest daughter Elizabeth spend each spring in town until they can no longer afford to do so (vol 1, ch. 2).

4 **servants . . . better**: the pernicious effects of leaving children in the care of servants (who were almost certainly uneducated) were frequently mentioned in the eighteenth century. After some scathing criticisms of boarding schools, Mary Wollstonecraft argues that, if the mother cannot spare the time to educate her own children, they should be sent to school, 'for people who do not manage their children well, and have not large fortunes, must leave them often with servants, where they are in danger of still greater corruptions' (Mary Wollstonecraft, *Thoughts on the Education of Daughters* (1787), p. 60).

LETTER 7

1 **Edward St.**: the former name of the part of Wigmore Street lying between Marylebone Lane and Duke Street, and therefore effectively in the same street as Frederica's school.

2 **a perfect . . . Sciences**: as the rest of the paragraph makes clear, this does not mean the equivalent of a modern academic subject-based education, but, even so, Lady Susan is exaggerating. The acknowledged purpose of women's education was to enable them to be good wives; unofficially it was to give them the accomplishments that would enable them to get husbands. By the late eighteenth century, though parents were urged not to confine the education of their daughters to 'what is regarded as the ornamental parts of it' (Catharine Macaulay, *Letters on Education, with Observations on Religious and Metaphysical Subjects* (1790), p. 50), even radicals such as Mary Wollstonecraft stressed that 'The forming of temper ought to be the continual thought, and the first task of a parent or teacher' (*Thoughts on the Education of Daughters*, p. 61). In general, the education of girls followed the curriculum recommended in Mrs Chapone's popular *Letters on the Improvement of the Mind*: domestic economy to enable them to manage a home after marriage, and accomplishments such as 'Dancing and the knowledge

of the French tongue . . . To write a free and legible hand, and to understand common arithmetic' and, for girls with aptitude, music and drawing (Hester Chapone, *Letters on the Improvement of the Mind, Addressed to a Young Lady*, 2 vols. (1773), vol. 2, pp. 48–9, 115–20).

3 **she will not remain . . . thoroughly**: Mary Wollstonecraft was critical of the education a girl was likely to receive in a boarding school, even if she remained longer than Lady Susan anticipates for Frederica: 'few things are learnt thoroughly, but many follies contracted, and an immoderate fondness for dress among the rest' (*Thoughts on the Education of Daughters*, p. 58). At Elizabeth Bridges' school 'an old coach was kept propped up in a back room so that the girls could practise the art of getting in and out of it in a modest and elegant manner' (*FR*, p. 70). In *Cecilia*, Lady Honoria Pemberton is described as having received 'a fashionable education, in which her proficiency had been equal to what fashion made requisite; she sung a little, played the harpsichord a little, painted a little, worked a little, and danced a great deal' (vol. 3, bk 6, ch. 4).

4 **School . . . Frederica's age**: Frederica is sixteen, an age at which many girls would have finished their education and be taking a full part in adult social life. Harriet Smith has, at seventeen, been 'raised . . . from the condition of scholar to that of parlour-boarder' but she only remains at Mrs Goddard's school because she has nowhere else to go (*E*, vol. 1, ch. 3).

5 **uncomfortable till she does accept him**: Lady Susan here follows the same strategy as Sir Thomas Bertram in *MP*, who hopes to persuade Fanny Price into accepting Henry Crawford by sending her to spend time at her parents' small and noisy lodgings in Portsmouth (vol. 3, ch. 6).

6 **belied**: calumniated by false statements.

LETTER 8

1 **open weather**: mild weather, free of frost and fog, and therefore suitable for hunting.

2 **Sussex**: a rural county south of London, with an extensive coastline.

3 **hunting together**: the hunting season continued through to the end of March.

4 **send for his Horses immediately**: a gentleman keen on hunting would bring his own horses with him when making an extensive stay away from home during the hunting season. When Henry Crawford decides to stay at Mansfield 'another fortnight' during the winter months in order to make Fanny Price fall in love with him, his preparations involve sending for 'his hunters' (*MP*, vol. 2, ch. 6).

5 **Kent**: a rural county adjoining Sussex to the east, with a long coastline. Parts of Kent were well known to JA because the Knight family, who adopted her brother Edward, had extensive estates there, most of which Edward inherited; one of her earliest extant letters, dated 1 September 1796, was sent from Rowling in East Kent (*L*, p. 5).

6 **Delicacy**: delicate regard for her feelings.

LETTER 9

1 **entailed**: legally bound to be inherited by the eldest son.

LETTER 10

1 **platonic friendship**: a relationship intimate and affectionate, but not sexual, following the example of Plato. The phrase was often used in the fiction of the late eighteenth century, usually with scepticism: Jane West for example talks of 'the specious affectation of Platonic affection' (*A Tale of the Times*, 3 vols. (1799), vol. 3, ch. 36).

LETTER 12

1 **conduct . . . most interesting to your connections**: that is, because of his status as heir to family fortune and estates, Reginald's relatives have a legitimate interest in his conduct.

2 **absolute engagement**: firm commitment of marriage, which Reginald could break only at the cost of a public scandal and the loss of his good reputation. Edward Ferrars feels unable honourably

to break his engagement to Lucy Steele although it was formed secretly when he was a boy, Lucy may well have drawn him in, and his family is hostile (*S & S*, vol. 3, ch. 1).

3 **out of my power . . . Estate**: that is, because the estate is entailed. The same legal arrangement binds Mr Bennet in *P&P*, so that he cannot avoid the Longbourn estate being inherited by Mr Collins.

4 **distressing you during my Life**: that is, by withholding the allowance which will form Reginald's income until his father dies.

5 **intelligence**: information.

LETTER 13

1 **late**: recent.

LETTER 14

1 **candour**: openness of mind, freedom from malice or prejudice.

2 **economy**: management of expenses, or of her way of living more generally.

LETTER 15

1 **Shrubbery**: the gardens of most country estates of the period included a shrubbery, a private area close to the house, with paths spread with gravel for ease of walking, intersecting beds planted with ornamental trees and shrubs. In 'The Watsons' Mr Tomlinson's new house on the outskirts of the town can lay claim to being in the country – and therefore superior – partly because it has a 'shrubbery and sweep' (see 'W', p. 87). When he plans to let Kellynch Hall Sir Walter Elliot is 'not fond of the idea of my shrubberies being always approachable' (*P*, vol. 1, ch. 3).

LETTER 16

1 **Milkiness**: mildness, softness, gentleness, a usage now rare. Lady Susan may also be alluding to Lady Macbeth's well-known phrase, 'milk of human kindness' (*Macbeth*, Act 1, scene 5).

2 **elope**: run away (though without the modern implication of fleeing with a lover for the purposes of marriage).

3 **impertinent**: meddling with another person's private affairs, intrusive but not necessarily presumptuous or insolent.
4 **teizing**: pestering, irritating through persistence.
5 **incog**: slang abbreviation of the Latin 'incognito', meaning in a state of concealment or hidden identity. In *The Philosophy of Rhetoric*, 2 vols. (1776) George Campbell listed the term among a 'set of barbarisms' arising from 'the abbreviation of polysyllables, by lopping off all the syllables except the first, or the first and second'; Campbell concluded that this 'humour of abbreviating . . . seems hardly now to subsist amongst us' (vol. 1, pp. 428–9). However, the term 'incog.' continued to be widely used in novels, often to describe the arrival of a lover, in disguise, to be near his mistress. In the novel *Maria*, for example, Lord Newry humorously recalls the first time he fell in love – 'I gave my governor the slip . . . and flew to my beauteous queen, with whom I spent nine or ten days incog.' (Elizabeth Blower, *Maria: A Novel in Two Volumes* (1785), vol. 1, ch. 13).

LETTER 17

1 **Academy**: the word was used by learned bodies including the Royal Academy (founded in 1768) but more widely denoted a superior kind of school.
2 **at Tea**: tea was taken at the end of dinner, the main meal of the day usually eaten, in the country, around 4 or 5 in the afternoon. The separate meal of 'afternoon tea' was not introduced until later (see 'S', chs. 6, 10).
3 **pathetic**: full of pathos (here, of course, used ironically).
4 **neither so fair . . . Lady Susan's**: the concept of 'bloom', which denoted women's highest moment of health and beauty, is significant throughout JA's writings. 'A few years before, Anne Elliot had been a very pretty girl, but her bloom had vanished early,' she writes at the beginning of *P* (vol. 1, ch. 1), and the novel records the way in which Anne recovers her 'bloom' and her former lover Wentworth.
5 **a Thirty miles Journey**: at a normal travelling rate in a carriage of somewhere around six miles an hour this would take about

five hours, and would place Churchill in North Sussex, possibly somewhere around the small town of Crawley.

6 **small Pianoforté**: pianofortes had been introduced into England in the middle of the eighteenth century, and by the 1790s both grand pianos and smaller 'square' pianos were very common in genteel homes. There is, for example, room in the modest home of Mrs and Miss Bates for the 'very elegant looking instrument—not a grand, but a large-sized square pianoforté' which arrives from Broadwood's for Jane Fairfax (*E*, vol. 2, ch. 8).

7 **her eyes have no Brilliancy**: in *P&P* Mr Darcy is first attracted to Elizabeth Bennet by 'the beautiful expression of her dark eyes' (vol. 1, ch. 6). See also Letter 6, n. 1 above.

LETTER 19

1 **the stage**: stage-coaches offered a form of public transport; coaches 'go from different parts of London to all parts of the kingdom, almost every day', at a price of 3s. 1½d. per mile to sit inside the coach and a cheaper price to sit outside, with the coach driver (John Trusler, *The London Adviser and Guide: Containing Every Instruction and Information useful and necessary to Persons living in London and coming to reside there* (1790), p. 89). Respectable ladies, however, would not be expected to travel alone by stage-coach. In *NA* General Tilney's decision to send Catherine Morland home alone, even by the more private means of a post-chaise, a coach hired for individual use, is regarded as an insult (vol. 2, ch. 13).

LETTER 20

1 **Pelisses**: a pelisse is a long cloak, with armhole slits and a shoulder cape or hood, often made of a rich fabric; it was normal outerwear for gentlewomen around 1800.

2 **amiable**: with pleasing qualities and a friendly disposition. Such qualities were highly rated by JA. In *E* Mr. Knightley comments that Frank Churchill 'can be amiable only in French, not in English. He may be very "aimable," have very good manners, and be very agreeable; but he can have no English delicacy towards the feelings of other people: nothing really amiable about him' (vol. 1, ch. 18).

3 **Rattle**: a constant chatterer, a well-known social type in the life and literature of JA's time. In *Cecilia* the garrulous and thoughtless Lady Honoria Pemberton is described as a rattle (vol. 3, bk 6, ch. 4); and in *NA* James Morland considers his friend John Thorpe to be 'as good-natured a fellow as ever lived' despite being 'a little of a rattle' (vol. 1, ch. 7).

4 **Establishment**: material situation on marriage.

5 **invited himself . . . relation**: Sir James's inviting himself to stay with the Vernons, whom he has never met before, is an act of gross social impoliteness.

6 **distinguish**: recognize the (good) qualities of.

LETTER 21

1 **unspeakable great kindness**: an acceptable grammatical construction. The formal address of the merchants of Dublin to William Pitt paid tribute to his 'unspeakable great services' to his country (John Almon, *Anecdotes of the Life of the Right Honourable William Pitt, Earl of Chatham*, 3 vols., 3rd edn corrected (1793), vol. 3, p. 232).

2 **rather work for my bread than marry him**: in a similar way, in 'W', Emma Watson declares that 'I would rather be teacher at a school (and I can think of nothing worse) than marry a man I did not like' (p. 83). The sentiment was a conventional one in fiction, but was not usually tested.

LETTER 22

1 **no Solomon**: the Old Testament King Solomon was proverbial for his wisdom.

2 **keen**: operating like a sharp instrument, piercing, causing pain.

LETTER 23

1 **if you have . . . take it**: at a time when the post was expensive, and letters were paid for by the recipient at a rate per sheet of paper (unless a frank for free mail were provided by a Member of

Parliament), people regularly took the opportunity of having mail carried by their family, friends, neighbours and servants. In *P* Mary Musgrove is first angry because the Crofts, when they are to go to Bath, have not offered to carry a letter from her to her family there, and then delighted that the offer is made: 'I shall therefore be able to make my letter as long as I like' (vol. 2, ch. 6). See Conclusion, n. 1 below.

LETTER 24

1 **under par**: beneath the normal, expected standard or condition.
2 **Genius**: natural aptitude.
3 **warm**: ardent, excitable, prone to becoming heated.
4 **sensibly**: acutely, intensely to the senses.
5 **retribution**: in the older sense (becoming obsolete in the nineteenth century) of restitution, without any of the modern implication of punishment for evil done.

LETTER 25

1 **condescension**: gracious deference or submissiveness to an inferior.

LETTER 26

1 **unadvisable . . . at present**: the implication being that they might quarrel publicly or even fight a duel, either of which would cause a public scandal. Duelling was illegal in JA's time, but duels were occasionally fought in fact, and more often in fiction. In *S&S* Colonel Brandon reveals that he fought a duel with Willoughby after the latter had seduced and abandoned the daughter of Colonel Brandon's lost early love (vol. 2, ch. 9); however, in *P&P* Mrs Bennet's fears that her husband, in London searching for Wickham after his elopement with Lydia, 'will fight Wickham, wherever he meets him, and then he will be killed', are regarded by her family as 'terrific ideas' (vol. 3, ch. 5).

2 **going for his health . . . many weeks**: the natural mineral water from the springs of the spa town of Bath were seen as particularly effective for gout: 'Bath and its waters have formed the retreat of all gouty patients, when worn out and tired with the inefficacy of other medicines' (William Nisbet, *A Medical Guide for the Invalid, to the Principal Watering Places of Great Britain* (1804), p. 112). A course of treatment over several weeks was common. Gout, a very painful inflammation of the joints, was often seen as caused by overeating and overdrinking (see also 'W', n. 120).

3 **Drawing room-apartment . . . Upper Seymour St.**: a drawing-room apartment is a suite of rooms, possibly quite extensive, including a reception room for visitors; the term is still in use, particularly in Edinburgh, in describing apartments in Georgian buildings. Upper Seymour Street, developed in the late eighteenth century as part of the Portman Estate, runs westwards from fashionable Portman Square. Householders in the late eighteenth and early nineteenth centuries included General Paoli, who had fled to England after unsuccessfully defending Corsica against the French, and the poet Thomas Campbell (1777–1844), who is mentioned in 'S' (ch. 7).

4 **Title . . . Baronets**: baronet was a hereditary title, ranking above a knight. Baronets were technically regarded as commoners, and did not sit in the House of Lords; only the more senior titles – duke, marquess, earl, viscount and baron – were regarded as aristocracy.

LETTER 27

1 **for the benefit of Masters**: that is, to study with professional teachers of arts such as drawing and music. In *P&P* Lady Catherine tells Elizabeth Bennet that Mrs Bennet 'should have taken you to town every spring for the benefit of [drawing] masters'; later she comments that 'Miss Bennet would not play [the pianoforte] at all amiss, if she practised more, and could have the advantage of a London master' (vol. 2, chs. 6, 8).

2 **in Town this winter**: that is, for the social season which began after Christmas and was at its height between February and April (see Letter 6, n. 3 above).

LETTER 28

1 **the Lakes**: the Lake District in the North West of England became a popular tourist destination in the late eighteenth century as interest grew in sublime and picturesque locations; interest was focused by William Gilpin's *Observations Relative Chiefly to Picturesque Beauty, Made in the Year 1772, on Several Parts of England; particularly the Mountains, and Lakes of Cumberland and Westmoreland* (2 vols.), first published 1786 and frequently reprinted. Going to the Lake District was a substantial expedition for travellers from London, who would have to travel more than 200 miles to get there. In *P&P* the Gardiners' original plans to visit the Lake District are abandoned because Mr Gardiner can take no more than a month away from his business in London and 'that left too short a period for them to go so far, and see so much as they had proposed, or at least to see it with the leisure and comfort they had built on' (vol. 2, ch. 19).

LETTER 30

1 **Lady Susan to Mr. De Courcy**: by the conventions of the time an unrelated man and woman should only begin to correspond by letter once they were formally engaged to each other. In *NA* a correspondence between Catherine Morland and Henry Tilney has to be clandestine, until their engagement is sanctioned by his family (vol. 2, ch. 16). In *S&S* Elinor becomes convinced of Lucy Steele's claim to be engaged to Edward when she sees a letter to Lucy in Edward's handwriting – 'a correspondence between them by letter, could subsist only under a positive engagement' (vol. 1, ch. 22) – and she assumes that Marianne is engaged to Willoughby when she finds that Marianne is writing to him (vol. 2, ch. 4); in fact there is no engagement and the letters are a sign of Marianne's imprudence.

2 **imperiously**: by overmastering necessity.

3 **abroad**: in company, out of the home.

LETTER 33

1 **Eclaircissement**: clearing up of obscure matters. Originally a French theatrical term to denote a dramatic revelation, the word

was widely used in English with the more general meaning, despite the hostility of commentators: 'our language is in greater danger of being overwhelmed by an inundation of foreign words, than of any other species of destruction,' declared George Campbell; using 'eclaircissement' as his example, he pointed out that the additional disadvantage that 'a word may be very emphatical in the language to which it owes its birth . . . which, when it is transplanted into another language, loses its emphasis entirely' (*The Philosophy of Rhetoric*, vol. 1, pp. 412, 414).

2 **sure of you at 7**: that is, after the social events of the day, and before the likely late dinner hour, and subsequent evening entertainments, in fashionable London.

3 **manouvres**: imported from the French in the middle of the eighteenth century, the term 'manoeuvre' soon expanded from its original meaning of a strategic military movement, and by the 1790s was often used to describe calculated and adroit social positioning.

LETTER 37

1 **dismissed**: sent, disposed of.

LETTER 38

1 **such an extremity**: for a woman who found her enjoyments in the busy social round of London, the threat of living permanently on her husband's country estate, which might well be at some distance from any social centre, was a powerful one. Conversely it was generally regarded as a virtue for wives to be contented with a country existence, which involved responsibility for a household and contribution to the well-being of the local community, and not hanker after the social distractions of London.

2 **the Manwarings are to part**: a hugely significant step, at a period when divorce could only be obtained by Act of Parliament, and was available only to the very wealthy. Even if – as here – the woman was not at fault, she would suffer far more than the man in any formal separation or divorce, since her social position would be affected, and – her property or income having usually passed by

law to her husband – she would be entirely reliant upon others for her maintenance.

3 **no defying Destiny**: an ironic allusion to the usual novelistic reliance upon Providence to produce a happy ending to the heroine's vicissitudes.

CONCLUSION

1 **the Post office Revenue**: the cost of mail was paid by the recipient. Within London, until 1801, it cost one penny to receive a letter of a single sheet; outside London the charge was 3d. for a single sheet travelling up to fifteen miles, with higher rates for multiple sheets and longer distances. Post office traffic was expanding rapidly in the late eighteenth century and prices were gradually rising: net revenue, £398,373 in the decade 1784–93, rose by more than 50 per cent to £621,627 in the decade 1794–1803 (A. M. Ogilvie, 'The Rise of the English Post Office', *The Economic Journal*, 3.11 (September 1893), p. 453), Cyril H. Rock, *A Guide to the Collection Illustrating the History of the Post Office* (Tottenham: Tottenham Museum, 1938), p. 14.

2 **assistance to the State**: the postal service was operated through private enterprise, but fees were paid to the state.

3 **an Influenza**: sometimes called 'catarrh', influenza was, then as now, a highly infectious disease which could kill, and epidemics were much feared. There were major epidemics in England in 1782 and 1785, and another major outbreak in the autumn of 1794, 'vast numbers of Children, in particular, being affected with it; and it often . . . proving fatal among them' (J. Barker, *Epidemicks, or General Observations on the Air and Diseases from the Year 1740, to 1777, inclusive; and Particular Ones from that Time to the Beginning of 1795* (1795), p. 201).

4 **finessed**: brought or modified by finesse or delicate handling. The *OED* gives JA's phrase here as the first example of the use of the verb 'finesse' in this sense (though it erroneously cites the sentence as from 'The Watsons').

5 **Reginald's . . . lively**: JA returns in *MP* to the circumstance of a young man having to overcome his fascination for a sophisticated woman in favour of a quieter, more innocent girl who has loved

him throughout: 'exactly at the time when it was quite natural that it should be so, and not a week earlier, Edmund did cease to care about Miss Crawford, and became as anxious to marry Fanny, as Fanny herself could desire' (vol. 3, ch. 17).

THE WATSONS

1 **The Watsons**: the manuscript is untitled. The fragment was kept by Cassandra after JA's death, and was well known in the Austen family, but the title seems to have been first used by James Edward Austen Leigh, who chose 'The Watsons' when the work was published for the first time in the second edition of the *Memoir*, 'for the sake of having a title by which to designate it' (*Memoir* (1871), p. 295).

2 **The first winter assembly**: most provincial towns had a formal social season over the autumn and winter months. This would include a series of evening assemblies, held at local inns or assembly rooms, funded by subscriptions from those who planned to attend or who wished to patronize the event. They were usually four-weekly, to coincide with the full moon for ease of travel; extra events might take place in spring and autumn when better weather could be predicted. They provided an opportunity for families to meet together for dancing, playing cards and conversation, as well as courtship between the sons and daughters of local gentry. JA's early letters make frequent reference to her attendance at the assemblies at Basingstoke, the nearest substantial town to her home in Steventon. In *P&P* Elizabeth Bennet points out that her family will have a chance to meet Mr Bingley, the new occupant of Netherfield Park, at the assemblies in the local town of Meryton (vol. 1, ch. 2).

3 **town of D. in Surry**: this is generally assumed to be Dorking, the only substantial town in the county of Surrey of which the name begins with a D. Dorking is a market town thirty miles south of London; at the beginning of the nineteenth century it was on a main turnpike road, and JA would often have passed through the town on her journeys to and from her brother Edward and his family in Kent. Her cousin Eliza de Feuillide spent time there in the late 1790s, and in 1799 JA visited her godfather Rev. Samuel

Cooke and his family, who lived at Great Bookham, six miles north of Dorking (*FR*, p. 115); Box Hill, visited by the residents of the fictional Highbury, is just outside the town (*E*, vol. 3, ch. 7). JA was still undecided about the setting when she began 'The Watsons'. The original draft has 'L', which might possibly stand for Leatherhead, a smaller town in Surrey about ten miles north of Dorking and two miles from Great Bookham; but 'D.' is the first choice a few lines later.

4 **Tuesday October the 13th**: early–mid-October was a likely time for a series of winter assemblies to begin: in 1800 there was a Basingstoke ball on Thursday 2 October (*Chronology*, p. 244). Though it has been argued that JA often wrote to very specific timescales, and possibly with an almanack to hand (see for example Pat Rogers's discussion of dating *P&P*, in *Pride and Prejudice* (Cambridge: Cambridge University Press, 2006), pp. liii–lvii) she does not provide a date as precise as this for the actions of her published fictions. Much later in *P* she cites a date with personal significance, when recording that Mary Elliot married Charles Musgrove on her own birthday, (vol. 1, ch. 1) but there is no evidence of a personal connection here. 13 October fell on a Tuesday in 1795, 1801 and 1807.

5 **country families**: that is, the families of the gentry who would live on their estates outside the town.

6 **kept their coach**: keeping one's own coach or carriage was a very visible marker of substantial wealth. The cost of the carriage itself would be substantial: William Felton listed the cost of a 'plain coach' (which he recommended as an economical option where 'only one carriage is kept, and the use of it almost constantly required') as £105.9s. for the coach itself, and £133.9s. for 'extras' (William Felton, *A Treatise on Carriages, comprehending Coaches, Chariots, Phaetons, Curricles, Whiskies, &c*, 2 vols. (1796, vol. 2, pp. 33–4)); and the coach would also require horses to pull it and one or more servants to maintain and drive it. Rev. George Austen maintained a carriage for some time in the late 1790s, but in 1798 it had to be put into store because it had become too expensive to maintain (*FR*, pp. 105–6, 112). The Bennets in *P&P*, with an estate yielding £2,000 a year, keep a carriage, but the horses have to do double duty on farm work (vol. 1, ch. 7); in *E*, it is a matter

of interest to the Highbury community whether the prosperous local apothecary Mr Perry decides to set up his carriage (vol. 3, ch. 5).

7 **close carriage**: open-topped carriages had the disadvantages of exposing occupants to the weather, and making journeys uncomfortable. More substantial carriages and coaches were 'close', that is, with the seats covered by a wooden structure; the coachman would sit on a box in front of the closed part of the carriage to drive.

8 **The Edwardses . . . winter**: without a mature or married relative available to chaperone them the Watson girls would be reliant on another family to take them to the assembly. JA and Cassandra benefited from similar arrangements when they attended the assemblies at Basingstoke. On 1 November 1799 JA wrote to Cassandra, 'On wednesday morning it was settled that Mrs Harwood, Mary & I should go together, & shortly afterwards a very civil note of invitation for me came from Mrs Bramston . . . I might likewise have gone with Mrs Lefroy, & therefore with three methods of going, I must have been more at the Ball than anybody else.—I dined & slept at Deane' (*L*, pp. 52–3).

9 **an aunt who had brought her up**: in an age of large families, high mortality and emphasis on inheritance, it was common for wealthy childless couples to bring up a child of poorer relatives or relatives with large families of their own, and adopt him or her as their heir. JA's brother Edward was brought up by the wealthy Knight family, distantly related to his father, and became their heir. In *MP* Sir Thomas Bertram brings up his niece Fanny Price because the Prices are poor and have a large family.

10 **the old chair**: a chair – a 'rib chair, or Yarmouth cart' – was a very simple open carriage without springs or lining, usually with two wheels, and drawn by a single horse; it was about the most modest of carriages, even when new (Felton, *A Treatise on Carriages*, vol. 2, pp. 121–3, 184).

11 **lose his money at cards**: while the main focus of assemblies for young people was dancing, card tables were provided in a separate room for those men and women who chose not to dance. Various card games were played, and players might bet on the outcome of the games, but wagers would be modest.

12 **comfortable soup**: private balls might offer extensive refreshment – Mr Bingley feels it important for 'white soup' to be provided at the Netherfield ball (*P&P*, vol. 1, ch. 11) – but at public assemblies only light refreshments would be provided, so participants would eat before they went and after they came home. Soups were appropriate since they were easily prepared in advance from local ingredients, and after the exertions of a ball would be nourishing and warming, while not being too heavy on the digestion. A recipe book prepared by Martha Lloyd, who lived with Mrs Austen, Cassandra and JA in Southampton and Chawton, contains recipes for a number of different soups (see *Cookbook*).

13 **independent**: that is, in control of enough income to be self-supporting, rather than living on an allowance until he inherited property and funds on the death of his father. JA spelt the word 'independant'.

14 **country**: neighbourhood.

15 **behaving in a particular way to**: paying particular attention to. In her first extant letter JA writes of her flirtation with Tom Lefroy at the previous evening's ball: her friends, who were there, 'do not know how *to be particular*. I flatter myself, however, that they will profit by the three successive lessons which I have given them' (9 January 1796, *L*, p. 1).

16 **we must marry**: a sentiment prevalent throughout JA's writings and most eloquently expressed in connection with Charlotte Lucas in *P&P*, where marriage is described as 'the only honourable provision for well-educated women of small fortune, and however uncertain of giving happiness, must be their pleasantest preservative from want' (vol. 1, ch. 22).

17 **my father cannot provide for us**: Mr Watson's income as minister of the church will die with him. The construction 'my father', spoken by one sister to another, was quite normal: JA frequently refers to 'my mother' when writing to Cassandra (see for example 'my Mother began to suffer from the exercise', 27–28 October 1798, *L*, p. 16).

18 **very bad . . . laughed at**: the plight of genteel women with no fortune of their own who did not marry was unenviable: at best they might find a home with richer relatives; at worst they lived in outright poverty. Emma Woodhouse, heiress to £30,000, might

declare she will never marry: but Miss Bates, daughter of a clergyman's widow, provides an example of the plight of genteel women in reduced circumstances: 'She is poor,' Mr Knightley reminds Emma, 'she has sunk from the comforts she was born to; and, if she live to old age, must probably sink more. Her situation should ensure your compassion . . . You, whom she had . . . seen grown up from a period when her notice was an honour, to have you now . . . laugh at her, humble her' (*E*, vol. 3, ch. 7).

19 **very few . . . first loves**: In *S&S* Marianne Dashwood strongly disapproves of second attachments (vol. 1, ch. 11) until she learns from experience; in *P* Anne Elliot, having failed to enter into a second attachment, 'the only thoroughly natural, happy, and sufficient cure, at her time of life' (vol. 1, ch. 4), finds happiness with Wentworth, her first love, after all. In 1808 JA wrote to Cassandra that she would not have forgiven her acquaintance Lady Sondes for entering into a second marriage 'had her first marriage been of affection, or had there been a grown-up single daughter . . . but I consider everybody as having a right to marry *once* in their Lives for Love, if they can' (27 December 1808, *L*, p. 159).

20 **Chichester**: a cathedral city with a bustling market just inland from the south coast of England, about fifty miles from Dorking. JA originally wrote 'Southampton', a larger, more fashionable South coast town thirty miles west of Chichester. JA lived in Southampton 1806–1809.

21 **Stanton**: presumably a fictional village; a large number of places of this name are recorded in various parts of England, but none in Surrey.

22 **teacher at a school**: teaching was one of the few occupations open to educated women at the time, but it could be hard work for little income, and for a gentlewoman teaching in a school would involve even more loss of status than becoming a governess in a private house. Mary Wollstonecraft, who had experience of managing, and teaching in, a school, wrote in her account of the 'Unfortunate Situation of Females, fashionably educated, and left without a Fortune', that 'A teacher at a school is only a kind of upper servant, who has more work than the menial ones' (Wollstonecraft, *Thoughts on the Education of Daughters*, p. 71).

23 **I have been at school**: some girls were educated entirely at home and others attended school, for varying periods of time. JA and her sister Cassandra attended the Abbey House School 1785–6; the school was situated in Reading, about twenty-five miles north-east of their home in Steventon, and was run by Mrs La Tournelle (whose real name was Sarah Hackitt but who had been given the more exotic name by her employers when hired to teach a foreign language) (*FR*, pp. 50–2).

24 **refined**: in her 'Plan of a Novel' JA describes the hero, 'all perfection of course—& only prevented from paying his addresses to [the heroine], by some excess of refinement' (p. 228).

25 **Croydon**: a small market town about twenty miles north-east of Dorking, and about ten miles south of central London, on the main road from London to Brighton, and also on one of the possible routes between JA's early home Steventon and her brother Edward's Godmersham estate. On the way home from Godmersham in 1798 JA wrote to Cassandra that though their route was still undetermined 'I think we shall go to Staines through Croydon and Kingston, which will be much pleasanter than any other way' (24 October 1798, *L*, p. 15).

26 **a large party**: the gentry might well bring house guests, who could be numerous, to the local assembly. When the Austen sisters were staying with their brother Edward at Godmersham in Kent they went with him to the Ashford assembly (*FR*, p. 109). In *P&P* there is much speculation as to whether Mr Bingley, as the new occupant of Netherfield Park, will bring 'a large party' to the Meryton assembly (vol. 1, ch. 3).

27 **whether she dances . . . more than once**: by the etiquette of the time, dancing with the same partner more than once in an evening would be a mark of special favour. It is regarded in this light by Mrs Bennet in *P&P*, who is delighted that Mr Bingley dances twice with Jane: 'Only think of *that*, my dear; he actually danced with her twice,' she tells Mr Bennet (vol. 1, ch. 3).

28 **Not that her father or mother like officers**: a career in the army was regarded as a genteel occupation for younger, often impecunious, sons of the gentry. In the late 1790s and early 1800s, since England was at war with France, regiments on general alert in England were billeted in or near communities in the south of

England for short periods of time before moving on, and were inevitably seen as a disruptive element for eligible young women of the area. Commenting on a similar situation in Ireland, the Bishop of Limerick wrote: 'I walk'd out this evening to Parade, and every House in that Quarter, had all the Windows fill'd with Three Dress'd Caps in each, Like the Hot Roasted Pigs in Lubberland, with Knives and forks in their Back, crying come eat me' (Anthony Powell (ed.), *Barnard Letters 1778–1824* (London: Duckworth, 1928), p. 87). JA describes in *P&P* the effects on a small community of the temporary stay of a regiment of soldiers.

29 **Shropshire... Surry**: JA originally wrote 'Devonshire' – a county in the south west of England – before replacing it with the more distant Shropshire, more than 150 miles to the north west of Surrey, on the borders of Wales. In April 1805 JA wrote dismissively of 'some place in Shropshire' (*L*, p. 105). JA originally wrote 'Sussex' for 'Surry', which suggests she was still adjusting the location for her narrative. She had however by now fixed on 'D.' as the initial of the town, and there is no obvious town beginning with a 'D.' in Sussex, so perhaps this was just a slip.

30 **our great wash**: not the normal wash, but the much larger-scale enterprise that would take place in households in autumn and spring, and would cause considerable upheaval for several days. In April 1816 JA wrote in some embarrassment to her niece Caroline to explain why an invitation to Caroline's mother Mary Lloyd was for so short a time: 'we *must* wash before the G[odmersha]^{m} Party come & therefore Monday would be [the] last day that our House could be comfortable for her' (21 April 1816, *L*, p. 314). Elizabeth Watson probably would not be participating in the washing, but would be actively supervising the operation.

31 **Guilford**: a small market town about fifteen miles west of Dorking and about thirty miles south-west of London, more usually spelt Guildford even in JA's time. In 1801 the town only had about 2,500 permanent inhabitants but as the point where the main east–west and north–south coach roads crossed it attracted many travellers, and maintained three substantial coaching inns.

32 **ten thousand pounds**: either as dowry, to be given to her husband on marriage, or as inheritance on the death of her father, but in

either case a very significant fortune; a woman with this asset – which would normally become the property of her husband on marriage – could expect to attract a wealthy man. The 'rich' Emma Woodhouse, who will inherit £30,000, accepts that Mr Elton 'had not thrown himself away' in marrying a woman with a fortune 'of so many thousands as would always be called ten' (*E*, vol. 1, ch. 1, vol. 2, ch. 4).

33 **surgeon**: the profession of surgeon had begun in the eighteenth century in a very humble way, only splitting from the occupation of barber in 1745. By the late century surgeons were qualified men, trained locally through an apprenticeship arrangement, and licensed to perform operations. Though physicians were the most senior medical men, surgeons were seen as superior to apothecaries, who would dispense medicines and give general medical advice, and the establishment of the Royal College of Surgeons in 1800 gave them added professional status, but they were not high on the social scale. 'I have scratched out the Introduction between Lord P. & his Brother and Mr Griffin,' JA wrote to her niece Anna, who had asked her advice on a draft of a novel she was writing in 1814, 'A Country Surgeon . . . would not be introduced to Men of their rank' (see p. 217).

34 **turnpike**: a toll-gate, in the form of a barrier placed across the road, which would be lifted when a toll was paid. The name derives from a spiked barrier placed as a form of defence. Turnpike roads, the precursor of the modern toll roads, were common in the late eighteenth and early nineteenth centuries; the tolls paid for the roads' upkeep and therefore enabled the main travel routes to be kept in good condition. The turnpike road through Dorking was well established and this description is consistent with an approach to the town from the north.

35 **church tower . . . White Hart is close by it**: again details consistent with Dorking. A 1763 account stated that: 'The church is a plain stone building, and has a tower steeple, in which is a ring of eight small but tuneable bells, with a set of chimes' ('Some Account of the Parish of *Dorking* and its Environs', *Gentleman's Magazine*, May 1763). There is a 'White Hart' public house in Dorking but JA might have in mind the White Horse, a substantial coaching inn in the High Street, near the church.

36 **pitching**: a road surface made of cobblestones.
37 **milliners**: a shop which would sell a range of goods including ribbons and lace as well as hats.
38 **shrubbery and sweep**: a shrubbery is a small private garden near the house, with walks lined by shrubs and trees; a sweep is a driveway between the boundary of the grounds and the house itself, shaped in a half-circle to allow turning for carriages. Both signal that Mr Tomlinson, building on the edge of a country town, has recreated the features of a country estate.
39 **windows . . . flight of stone steps**: all features signalling a substantial town house: its height above the road would enable a degree of privacy from passers-by; the posts linked with chains would also prevent carts and carriages being parked directly outside the house. JA spent some time getting these details right, as is evident from the revisions to the manuscript (and see Introduction, p. lxv).
40 **market clock**: Dorking had been known from medieval times for its market, which was held on Thursdays.
41 **a man in livery with a powdered head**: more signs of status: the servants of the wealthy would wear a uniform, and their hair would be sprinkled with a scented powder made of fine flour or starch, in a fashion which had been popular in the second half of the eighteenth century for all classes but which by 1800 was retained largely for servants, and also provincial professional men such as the lawyer Robert Watson (see p. 124). Hair powder, along with many other domestic items, became subject to tax in the 1790s.
42 **hair in papers**: in order to introduce fashionable curls into the hair it was prepared by being twisted round pieces of soft paper, usually overnight.
43 **Horses . . . White Hart**: coaching inns kept horses which could be hired for use with privately owned carriages. In *P&P* Mrs Bennet remarks that the Hursts, visitors to Mr and Miss Bingley, have no horses of their own at Netherfield to pull their carriage (vol. 1, ch. 7).
44 **lounge**: stroll, leisurely walk.
45 **satin**: a luxurious silk fabric with a glossy surface, suitable for the light high-waisted ballgowns of the time. JA spelt 'sattin'.

46 **cap**: a mature woman such as Mrs Edwards might well have a quite substantial cap to cover her head, fastened with a pin.

47 **complexion . . . flattering**: a country surgeon would spend much of his time travelling to and from patients in villages, usually on horseback and therefore open to the weather. Describing the physical hardships facing men in the various professions, Mrs Clay talks of 'the physician . . . up at all hours, and travelling in all weather' (*P*, vol. 1, ch. 3). A sunburned or brown complexion in women was not much admired (see below, n. 68).

48 **Miss Watson**: Mr Edwards refers to Elizabeth; only the eldest sister would be given the title 'Miss Watson'.

49 **desert**: dessert would probably consist of dried fruit or sweets, and was quite often eaten away from the table.

50 **rubber**: a set of usually three games at whist.

51 **whist club . . . White Hart**: the Crown Inn at Highbury (a 'large and populous village almost amounting to a town') accommodates a whist club 'established among the gentlemen and half-gentlemen of the place', meeting weekly and including among its members Mr Elton the clergyman and Mr Perry the apothecary (*E*, vol. 1, ch. 1, vol. 2, ch. 6).

52 **rising from dinner at midnight**: Mr Edwards is exaggerating, but the timing of dinner was closely related to the status, and its length the capacity for leisure, of its participants. The Watsons themselves dine at 3 p.m. (see below). Dinner among genteel country families might take place at 4.30 or 5 p.m., as it does at the Mansfield vicarage when Fanny Price visits (*MP*, vol. 2, ch. 5). JA's own wealthy Kentish relatives would dine at 5 p.m., or later, finishing perhaps by 8 p.m., with a social evening to follow (*Cookbook*, p. 33).

53 **the old rooms at Bath**: the old or Lower Assembly Rooms, sometimes called 'Harrison's Rooms' after the original architect, were built in 1708 on Terrace Walk, in the centre of the town near the river. As Bath expanded a need grew for more assembly rooms, and the new or Upper Assembly Rooms, funded by subscription, were opened in 1771 in the newer, higher part of the city to the north. The two sets of rooms both flourished in the late eighteenth century but despite several attempts at renovations the Lower Rooms gradually lost favour, and when

they were extensively damaged by fire in 1820 they were replaced by a new building for the Bath Royal Literary and Scientific Institution (Michael Forsyth, *Bath* (New Haven and London: Yale University Press, 2004), pp. 207–8). In *NA* Mrs Allen and Catherine Morland attend their first ball in the Upper Rooms, but it is in the Lower Rooms that Catherine is introduced to Mr Tilney (vol. 1, ch. 3).

54 **Irish**: the Irish fortune-hunter was a stock figure in the literature of the period. In *Hermsprong*, a copy of which JA owned (Gilson, pp. 78–9), when Sir Philip Chestrum wishes to insult the novel's hero he accuses him of being 'an Irish fortune hunter; or some such take-in gentleman' (Robert Bage, *Hermsprong; or, Things as They Are Not*, 3 vols. (1796), vol. 2, ch. 23). Mrs Turner, as a widow with a substantial fortune under her own control, would be a very attractive marriage proposition; under the laws of the time, unless there was a legal agreement adjusting the arrangement, on marriage all her property would belong to her husband.

55 **that country Miss Emma**: among the English Ireland was considered a wild and outlandish spot. While we do not know in detail how 'The Watsons' was to continue (see Introduction, p. lxviii) it seems likely that JA would not have followed the O'Briens to Ireland: when advising Anna, who was writing a novel, JA wrote that 'we think you had better not leave England. Let the Portmans go to Ireland, but as you know nothing of the manners there, you had better not go with them. You will be in danger of giving false representations' (see p. 218). She took her own advice in *E*, where Jane Fairfax's friends the Dixons go to Ireland, but the narrative remains in Highbury.

56 **cockade**: a ribbon, knot of ribbons or rosette worn by a soldier as a badge of office; and, by extension, the soldier himself.

57 **ladies . . . second choice**: the widow making a foolish second match was a stock comic figure in fiction and drama; JA later challenged the stereotype in the figure of Lady Denham, who, having been left a fortune by her first husband Mr Hollis, gained rank with her second marriage to Sir Harry Denham but remained 'too wary to put anything out of her own power' and, widowed a second time, boasted 'that though she had *got* nothing but

her Title from the Family, still she had given nothing for it' ('S', ch. 3).

58 **the tea things**: tea was made where it was to be drunk. The teapot, tea (since there could be several kinds of tea, as in 'S' (see ch. 10), there could be several caddies), kettles or urn, cream jug, sugar bowl, cups and saucers for the tea itself, and crockery and cutlery for any accompanying food, were all brought into the room on a 'tea-board' by servants. The whole process constituted quite a 'ceremony', as mentioned below.

59 **a dish extraordinary**: an additional cupful of tea. Tea was then served in a very wide cup without a handle, and was often referred to as a 'dish'; it was permissible to drink tea from the saucer, presumably because the liquid would cool down more quickly that way.

60 **muffin**: small flat cake made from yeast batter, often eaten, split and toasted, with butter and/or jam at breakfast or at tea time.

61 **accosted**: addressed (without any sense of aggression).

62 **a morning dress and boots**: that is, his outdoor clothes as worn during the day, rather than the more formal dress which would be expected for the assembly.

63 **eight or nine hundred pounds a year**: a very comfortable income for a single man, and enough to maintain a family in a modestly genteel way. Mrs Jennings is confident that Lucy Steele should be able to marry Edward Ferrars on less: 'if Mrs. Ferrars would only allow him five hundred a-year, she would make as good an appearance with it as any body else would with eight . . . how snug they might live in such another cottage as yours—or a little bigger—with two maids and two men' (*S&S*, vol. 3, ch. 1). For Marianne Dashwood, in the same novel, £1,800 or £2,000 a year would be a 'competence' to live on, since she would want 'a proper establishment of servants, a carriage, perhaps two, and hunters'; whereas for Elinor, with less ambitious ideas, '*One* is my wealth' (*S&S*, vol. 1, ch. 17).

64 **chaperons**: married or elderly women who, for the sake of propriety and protection, conducted young unmarried women to public events.

65 **empressément**: an 'animated display of cordiality' (*OED*); both the word itself, and the use of the French term in connection

with Captain Hunter, suggest an element of artificiality and self-regard in his 'display'. In *Cecilia* Burney's Captain Aresby shows his foolish self-importance less obliquely by using French terms: 'I should be so unhappy as to commit any *faux pas* by too much *empressement*' (book 7, ch. 9).

66 **the two first dances**: by convention dances were arranged and performed in pairs; each pair of dances was regarded as a single dance for the purposes of choosing partners. Describing Mr Bingley's dancing at the Meryton assembly Mrs Bennet reports that 'the two third he danced with Miss King, and the two fourth with Maria Lucas, and the two fifth with Jane again, and the two sixth with Lizzy' (*P&P*, vol. 1, ch. 3).

67 **introduced by Captain Hunter**: a gentleman and lady could only dance if they had been formally introduced; the introduction could only be made by the master of ceremonies at the assembly, if one were present, or by someone who had already been introduced, however briefly, to both parties.

68 **brown . . . glowing**: pale skin was often regarded as more attractive than a deeper colour, since a brown skin was associated with manual labour outside the home. Attitudes were changing, however, in the light of the growing trend for wealthy people to make tourist expeditions. In *P&P* Miss Bingley criticizes Elizabeth Bennet for having 'grown so brown and coarse' but Mr Darcy points out she is only 'rather tanned,—no miraculous consequence of travelling in the summer' (vol. 3, ch. 3).

69 **the Osbornes . . . coming**: coincidentally or not (and satirically or not) JA's phrase recalls the popular song, 'The Campbells are coming', composed in 1715 to celebrate the victory of John Campbell, Duke of Argyll, over the Jacobite rebels in Scotland, and later the regimental march of the Argyll and Sutherland Highlanders.

70 **Lord Osborne**: indicating that Lady Osborne is a widow and her son has inherited the title.

71 **formerly tutor . . . castle stood**: the sons of aristocratic families were usually educated at home, at least in their early years, by a clergyman, who would be responsible for their moral as well as their academic training. Since such families would probably have the right to appoint ministers of parishes on their estates, it was

also common for the clergyman concerned to be rewarded with such an appointment.

72 **the Borough**: a borough was a town which sent representatives to Parliament; JA refers here to the senior group of (male) citizens who, in an era of very limited franchise, would control the election of a Member of Parliament for the town. Lord Osborne would not be wishing to stand for Parliament himself, since he would by right of his title be a member of the House of Lords, but he might well be nominating a candidate, and in any case there would be political advantage in being on good terms with the local electorate.

73 **dance down every couple**: dance right down the set, without pausing for rest. In the country dances of the period the dancers would stand in long lines of couples and during the dance would move gradually down the set as the dance figures caused the dancers to change places.

74 **the smartest officer . . . order the dance**: the first dance would usually be led off by the highest ranking lady present and her partner – in this case Miss Osborne would take her place at the top of the set for her first dance. The rules of precedence, involving marital as well as family status, were detailed and inflexible. When in *E* the much-postponed ball at the Crown eventually takes place, for the first dances 'Mr. Weston and Mrs. Elton led the way, Mr. Frank Churchill and Miss Woodhouse followed. Emma must submit to stand second to Mrs. Elton, though she had always considered the ball as peculiarly for her. It was almost enough to make her think of marrying' (vol. 3, ch. 2). There were also conventions concerning the order of dances but within these the lady at the top of the set would 'call', that is, determine which tune, and which dance figures, were to be offered, and her partner would convey these instructions to the musicians. For subsequent dances the duty of 'calling' passed to the second and third ranked ladies in turn. JA wrote to Cassandra in November 1800 that at the Basingstoke ball the night before she had, with her partner Mr Mathew, 'called the last' (20 November 1800, *L*, p. 60).

75 **not keeping my engagement**: insulting Charles by treating her engagement to dance with him as expendable in a way that would

have been unforgivable had he been an adult: once the woman accepted an invitation to dance, however far in advance of the event, the engagement must be kept. In *NA*, even when John Thorpe fails to arrive by the beginning of the dance for which he has arranged to partner Catherine Morland, she is not at liberty to accept Henry Tilney's invitation (vol. 1, ch. 8). Social conventions were, however, less strictly enforced than they had been a generation earlier: when Frances Burney's inexperienced heroine refuses one gentleman and then dances with another, she is accused of 'ill manners' and the incident forms the basis of an open quarrel between the two gentlemen concerned (Frances Burney, *Evelina: Or, A Young Lady's Entrance into the World* (1778), vol. 1, letter 11).

76 **Colonel Beresford**: the colonel is the commanding officer of the regiment, so probably the senior army officer present.

77 **after tea**: at assemblies there would usually be an interval in the dancing at which light refreshments were served.

78 **to begin the set**: the set would be the line of couples who would perform the dance as a group. In small gatherings there might only be one set; in larger gatherings the dancers would divide into several sets in order to provide manageable units. In *NA* Catherine, arriving on the dance floor late because of her partner's delay, finds herself entirely separated from her friend Isabella Thorpe, 'in different sets . . . separated from all her party, and away from all her acquaintance' (vol. 1, ch. 8).

79 **interesting**: affecting, touching. The word was important in sentimental fiction, indicating a sense of empathy and fine feeling which was much admired.

80 **Emma . . . acted**: JA has her later Emma Woodhouse act with similar impetuosity in a key moment of impulse, responding to Miss Bates on Box Hill, and using a very similar grammatical construction: 'Emma could not resist' (*E*, vol. 3, ch. 7).

81 **condescending**: stooping graciously from a position of dignity.

82 **gloves . . . keep them on**: men's ball attire included white gloves, which they were expected to wear through the dancing.

83 **complacency**: pleasure, with a more active sense of delight and enjoyment than usual usage now.

84 **as she turned him**: that is, as she took his hand or arm to swing around; the two would then return to their original places, or would use the turn as a way of moving up or down down the set.

85 **talking to Charles**: when the dancers were waiting to participate in the figures, short conversations with nearby non-dancers would be possible.

86 **Wickstead**: fictional; there is no village or substantial estate of that name recorded in Surrey.

87 **Latin**: competence in Latin, and also Greek, literature was still seen as an essential part of education for the sons of the aristocracy and gentry. From this they learned principles of grammar, oratory and rhetoric, together with a detailed understanding of the moral and philosophical issues discussed by classical thinkers and a literary appreciation of poetry and prose. Knowledge of the classics was also essential for entrance to the universities of Oxford and Cambridge, a degree from which was a requirement for entry to church ministry.

88 **he had been out . . . hounds**: aristocrats would keep and maintain a pack of hounds, especially trained for hunting purposes; since the fox-hunting season was unlikely to begin until November, (see below, n. 127), Charles is probably referring here to the more informal sport of cub-hunting, which took place officially for the purpose of training young hounds, and which could begin as early as late August.

89 **straitened**: JA wrote 'Straightened' but she must have meant 'made narrow'.

90 **cassino table**: cassino, or casino, is a card game for two players, though it can be played by three, or four in pairs, as is likely here. The numerical cards count at their pip values, and there are particular values to certain cards or combinations of cards; the object of the game is to collect points, and it requires a good memory and capacity for deduction. The table would be designated 'Lady Osborne's' because she would be the senior person in rank.

91 **suffrage**: approval, agreement.

92 **gape**: the older meaning of the word, 'yawn', which seems to be the meaning here, was gradually being superseded by the more modern 'stare in wonder'. When Lydia Bennet 'gaped' at the

sight of Mr Collins opening a volume of Fordyce's Sermons to read aloud, either meaning could have been intended (*P&P*, vol. 1, ch. 14).

93 **you must sit with my friends**: protocol required the gentleman dancing with a lady immediately before the interval to continue to accompany her, joining her party of friends and relatives rather than remaining with his own.

94 **lord or commoner**: commoners are people below the ranks of the peerage; the phrase 'lord or commoner', while an accurate description of Lord Osborne and Tom Musgrave, was often used in a general sense to denote the full range of men, from the highest to the lowest.

95 **against the rules of the assembly**: it is possible that the assembly, following the example of the major social centres such as Bath, has written rules of conduct and behaviour, but it is more likely that Tom is referring more figuratively – and humorously – to social conventions. In fact it was questionable whether an adult couple should dance two successive pairs of dances together: when in *NA* Isabella Thorpe tells James Morland that 'it would make us the talk of the place [the Upper Rooms in Bath], if we were not to change partners', he replies that 'in these public assemblies, it is as often done as not' (vol. 1, ch. 8). The conventions, however, might well be stricter at local assemblies.

96 **patronised**: supported, encouraged.

97 **nice**: in its older sense of precise or particular.

98 **particularity**: either particular distinction, or exception to the rule.

99 **sad**: unsatisfactory, inadequate.

100 **Miss Carr being impatient to call**: since Miss Osborne called the previous dance, the privilege moves to the next in order of rank, who is Miss Carr.

101 **barrel of oysters**: oysters were harvested off the south-east coast of England – Whitstable oysters, from the north Kent coast, were seen as particularly good – and were widely eaten; they were by no means a delicacy.

102 **a jerking curtsey as they passed her**: a significant acknowledgement of acquaintance, however reluctant. In *P* Elizabeth Elliot finally acknowledges Captain Wentworth with 'a slight

curtsy'; to Anne, this, 'though late and reluctant and ungracious, was yet better than nothing' (vol. 2, ch. 8).

103 **negus**: a drink made usually from fortified wine mixed with hot water, sweetened with sugar, and sometimes flavoured with spices; it was often served at balls as refreshment.

104 **upper maid**: a wealthy household such as the Edwards's would have a substantial number of servants. Housemaids would be responsible for the care of the rooms and the furniture, beginning with preparing the rooms early in the morning before family and guests were awake, and including scouring, cleaning and dusting. The upper maid would supervise the maids who carried out these tasks.

105 **red coats**: part of the distinctive uniform of the army, and generally recognized as a dangerous attraction to young ladies. In *P&P* Lydia's excited dreams of Brighton include the soldiers' camp, 'crowded with the young and the gay, and dazzling with scarlet' (vol. 2, ch. 18).

106 **curricle**: a light two-wheeled carriage drawn by two horses abreast, generally considered as fashionable for a young man to drive. The social-climbing John Thorpe claims that his gig is 'curricle-hung' (*NA*, vol. 1, ch. 7).

107 **visitation**: a meeting or gathering connected to a regular visit by a bishop or archdeacon to examine the affairs of the parish. As the daughter, sister and cousin of clergymen, JA must have been very familiar with such events.

108 **R.**: presumably this should be 'D.' if JA meant to write of Dorking. Linking this to the substitution of Guildford for Dorking as the location of Sam's work as surgeon (see p. 86), Chapman suggests that JA's original intention might have been to write of Dorking and Reigate (a town less than ten miles east of Dorking), for which she substituted Guildford and Dorking (*MW*, p. 460), though this would not account for the original 'L.' in the first line of the text.

109 **she was at a loss . . . offered**: Emma's dilemma here has some similarities with that of Catherine in *NA*: both young women are doubtful of the proprieties involved in taking carriage drives with young men to whom they are not related, and hope for guidance from those who are in a parental role. In *NA* Mr Allen

decides that no harm may have been done by a single journey, but to repeat it is 'not right' (vol. 1, ch. 13).

110 **dinner**: see n. 52.

111 **critically**: precisely; by the standards of critical judgement.

112 **pelisse**: a long cloak, with slits for armholes, and a shoulder-cape or hood, an essential item of clothing for genteel women of the period.

113 **letter . . . the next day**: at a time when 'The two chief defects of the postal service . . . were its insecurity and its expensiveness' – charges were dependent on the distance involved and the weight, that is the length, of a letter (double rates were payable on two-sheet letters, and four-fold rates on letters weighing an ounce), and were paid by the recipient – it was very common to send letters informally by travellers, as here (see Rock, *A Guide to the Collection*, pp. 12, 14). See 'Lady Susan', Letter 23, n. 1; Conclusion, n. 1.

114 **high**: lofty, arrogant.

115 **address**: way of speaking and behaving in social and formal situations.

116 **out of the country**: away from the neighbourhood.

117 **a discourse . . . better taste**: churchgoing was the norm in early nineteenth-century England and preachers seen as fashionable or 'popular' commanded a wide audience; the more extreme groups such as evangelicals or Methodists were particularly known for their fiery and dramatic oratory. The way in which sermons were delivered was a matter of study and debate, and JA here seems to support traditional arguments against new ideas. Hugh Blair's influential *Lectures on Rhetoric and Belles Lettres*, 2 vols. (1783), included a lecture on 'Eloquence of the Pulpit' which acknowledged the difficulty of getting the tone right in preaching – 'The Grave, when it is predominant, is apt to run into a dull uniform solemnity. The Warm, when it wants gravity, borders on the theatrical' – and warns against simply following the fashions set by popular preachers; he insists that the purpose of preaching is 'to give . . . at once, clear views, and persuasive impressions of religious truth'. He did not, however, approve of sermons being read rather than given from memory or expanded from notes: 'No discourse, which is designed to be persuasive,

can have the same force when read, as when spoken' (vol. 2, pp. 107, 105, 118).

JA returns to the subject of preaching in a discussion between the worldly Henry Crawford and the recently ordained Edmund Bertram in *MP*. Both agree that a 'clear manner, and good delivery', are important in preaching. But Henry Crawford's emphasis on the performance of the preacher 'who can touch and affect such an heterogeneous mass of hearers, on subjects limited, and long worn thread-bare in all common hands; who can say any thing new or striking, any thing that rouses the attention, without offending the taste, or wearing out the feelings of his hearers' is contrasted with Edmund Bertram's insistance on the purpose of the message being delivered: 'that distinctness and energy may have weight in recommending the most solid truths' and that 'there is more general observation and taste, a more critical knowledge diffused, than formerly' (vol. 3, ch. 3).

118 **dishes . . . himself**: a formal public dinner would include a large number of dishes, but not necessarily a large number of courses: there might be two courses at most, each offering a wide array of sweet and savoury dishes, which would be placed on the dining table. The host would supervise initial serving of soup and would carve the large joints of meat, after which diners would help themselves to the dishes they wished to eat; they were not expected to taste everything (*Cookbook*, pp. 11–12).

119 **the partridges were pretty high**: game birds such as partridge were generally hung for several days after being killed, in order for the meat to develop a stronger, richer flavour. As a result they could smell strongly, even unpleasantly. In 'The First Act of a Comedy' the cook's bill of fare includes '2 Ducks, a leg of beef, a stinking partridge, and a tart' ('Juv.', Volume the Second).

120 **gouty foot**: gout, now recognized as a form of arthritis, was a very common ailment, particularly among elderly and sedentary men; it 'generally makes its attack in the spring or beginning of winter . . . the patient is seized with a pain in his great toe, sometimes in the heel, and at other times in the ancle or calf . . . the pain increases, and fixing among the small bones of the foot, the patient feels all the different kinds of torture, as if the

part were stretched, burnt, squeezed, gnawed, or torn in pieces' (*Domestic Medicine*, p. 381).

121 **to bustle . . . knife-case**: that is, to make preparations for serving dinner, including setting out the cutlery. Knives would usually be kept in cases for protection.

122 **honour . . . Watson**: it was usual for a gentleman to call on his partner the morning – though not three days – after a ball, but Lord Osborne did not dance with Emma Watson, and his statement that he is 'waiting on' – making a formal visit to – Mr Watson creates social awkwardness, since the two have been neighbours for more than a decade without being on such terms.

123 **half-boots**: boots reaching well above the ankle, but not as far as the knee, and fastened by laces at the front. They were popular from the late eighteenth century. Emma Woodhouse wears half-boots for winter walking in the country (*E*, vol. 1, ch. 10).

124 **nankin galoshed with black**: nankin is a cloth originally made in Nanking, China, from a yellow variety of cotton. A galosh is a piece of leather running round the lower part of the boot above the sole. The boots would be fashionable, but not very practical.

125 **the means**: horses were expensive to buy – *The Times* of Monday 4 August 1800 advertised a Norfolk mare, 'warranted perfectly sound, and free from all vice', at twenty-four guineas, while other advertisements at around the same time offered horses at £30 or £40 – and ongoing expenses were also substantial. In *S&S*, there is consternation at the suggestion that Willoughby might give Marianne a horse; were she to accept the gift 'she must buy another for the servant, and keep a servant to ride it, and after all, build a stable to receive them' (vol. 1, ch. 12).

126 **female economy . . . large one**: 'female economy' usually meant domestic management or housewifery. Maria Edgeworth, in *Letters for Literary Ladies* (1795), defines it as 'the art of calculation, joined to the habit of order, and the power of proportioning our wishes to the means of gratifying them' (p. 69).

127 **next week . . . nine o' clock**: the fox-hunting season begins in November, so this will still be part of the 'cubbing' season (see n. 88 above). To 'throw off' was to free the hounds from their leashes, and so begin the hunt. By the early nineteenth century

9 a.m. was the usual time to begin the hunt; in the eighteenth century it had been earlier (see David Selwyn, *Jane Austen and Leisure* (London: The Hambledon Press, 1999), pp. 101–11).

128 **good wishes in person**: it was a country custom for local people to gather to see the hunt – which was a colourful and lively spectacle of horsemen, horses and hounds – begin, and to drink to its success with a 'stirrup cup', usually of port or sherry.

129 **a sort of notice . . . at Stanton**: there may be deliberate echoes here of a scene in Burney's *Evelina*, where the heroine is embarrassed, when staying with her socially inferior relatives, to find herself visited by a potential suitor of superior status (vol. 2, letter 16). The comedy of Evelina, her vulgar Branghton relatives with their equally vulgar lodger Mr Smith, and the visiting Sir Clement Willoughby, is much broader, but JA enjoyed it: her niece Caroline recalled that '*once* I knew her take up a volume of Evelina and read a few pages of Mr. Smith and the Brangtons and I thought it was like a play' (Caroline Austen, *My Aunt Jane Austen: A Memoir* (1867), in J.E. Austen-Leigh, *A Memoir of Jane Austen, And Other Family Recollections* ed. Kathryn Sutherland (Oxford: Oxford University Press, 2002), p. 174.

130 **impertinence in its form**: the Osbornes and the Watsons, despite being relatively near neighbours for years, have not been on social visiting terms, and this would have been the choice of the Osbornes, who as the socially superior family would have had to make the first visit. Lord Osborne's decision to visit now involves the Watsons in unnecessary and painful social worries about whether to return the visit as protocol would normally require.

131 **attorney at Croydon . . . pounds**: the profession of attorney, or solicitor, was a dignified one in local urban circles, though modest in terms of the social standards of the gentry. In *P&P* Mrs Bennet's father, an attorney in the local town of Meryton, had left her £4,000; her sister had married Mr Phillips, 'who had been a clerk to their father, and succeeded him in the business' (vol. 1, ch. 7), a connection which the Bingley sisters describe as 'low' (vol. 1, ch. 8).

132 **countenance**: appropriate demeanour, including, but not exclusively, facial expression.

133 **great friends . . . equal**: from her early writings JA satirized the phenomenon, frequent in sentimental novels, of young women becoming great friends immediately on meeting. In *NA* JA teases the reader about the immediate friendship of Catherine and Isabella which 'passed so rapidly through every gradation of increasing tenderness, that there was shortly no fresh proof of it to be given to their friends or themselves' (vol. 1, ch. 5).

134 **post-boy . . . posting**: Robert and his wife have evidently travelled 'post', that is, by hired carriage – they would probably have hired a carriage to take them to the nearest main posting inn, and then another to bring them to the Watsons' house – and so Robert needs to pay for the journey. The post-boy, or postilion, would ride on one of the horses to assist the carriage driver.

135 **doubtful halfcrown**: a half-crown was a coin worth two shillings and sixpence (there were eight half-crowns, or four crowns, in a pound). The counterfeiting of silver coins was a particular problem during the war years, because of the scarcity of raw silver (see Introduction, p. lxviii).

136 **road through the village . . . endite . . . now**: local roads were the responsibility of the parish through which they passed, and were maintained on the advice of a surveyor appointed for the purpose. To endite (now more usually spelt 'indict') is to bring a legal prosecution.

137 **Augusta . . . without her**: JA re-used the name 'Augusta' for Mrs Elton in *E*, a character in some respects reminiscent of Mrs Robert Watson. For JA's decision to give the Watsons a daughter rather than a son, see Introduction, p. lxvi.

138 **sad shabby**: slang terms of the period: 'sad' is deplorably bad; 'shabby' is a light criticism of someone for being less friendly or generous than hoped.

139 **visit . . . months together**: it was common for unmarried females, in particular, to make long visits to family members and friends. JA and Cassandra, together or separately, often visited their brothers, Edward in Kent and later Henry in London, and other relatives and friends, for weeks or even months at a time. Lady Susan makes an extended visit to her Vernon relatives, enabling the action of the novella to take place; Jane Bennet visits her

aunt and uncle the Gardiners for several months in *P&P*; Anne Elliot makes extended visits to her sister and brother in law Mary and Charles Musgrove in *P*.

140 **overpower . . . sallies**: Margaret's mannered vocabulary and turn of phrase are strongly reminiscent of the literature of sentiment which had been very popular in the second half of the eighteenth century, beginning with Samuel Richardson's *Sir Charles Grandison*, especially its frequent reference to 'raillery', a favourite Richardsonian expression. In the Austen family play, 'Sir Charles Grandison', Lady L. tells Charlotte Grandison, 'you overpower Harriot with your Raillery' (Act 5, scene 2, see Appendix C).

141 **balls . . . mixed**: that is, formal events open to a wide range of people, some of whom Mrs Watson clearly considers as her inferiors and therefore not socially desirable.

142 **seven tables**: that is, for cards. A table would normally seat four people, the usual number for whist.

143 **languishing**: JA, in using this clichéd term, associates Margaret with the sentimental females of fiction and drama. One of the heroines of Richard Sheridan's popular comedy *The Rivals* (1775) is named Lydia Languish.

144 **suppers**: with the dinner, the main meal of the day, eaten in the late afternoon or early evening, it was felt sufficient to offer a much more informal light hot or cold supper late in the evening (see *Cookbook*, p. 9).

145 **half hers**: it was quite common for adult unmarried daughters to share a bedroom, partly because of space requirements, which would be at a premium in large families. JA and Cassandra shared a bedroom even as adults, when they were both at home at Chawton.

146 **heiress . . . smart for it**: JA's juvenile heroine Laura declares Phillipa, who has married a fortune-hunter and disinherited her nephew as a result, to be 'a ridiculous old Woman whose folly in marrying so young a Man ought to be punished' ('Love and Freindship', Letter the 14th, 'Juv.', Volume the Second).

147 **The most liberal . . . confiding**: the idea that generous minds are the most trustful is an integral part of eighteenth-century

thought. Henry Fielding wrote of Abraham Adams that 'As he had never any Intention to deceive, so he never suspected such a Design in others' (Henry Fielding, *The History of the Adventures of Joseph Andrews, and of his Friend Mr. Abraham Adams*, 2 vols. (1742), book 1, ch. 3).

148 **indifferent**: in indifferent health.

149 **fresh powder in your hair**: see n. 41 above.

150 **putting up**: packing to bring.

151 **turkey . . . dinner**: meaning that the dishes to be offered at dinner were set out together on the dining table for participants to help themselves; evidently the turkey, as a particular luxury, was to be served separately. The lack of a second selection of dishes emphasizes the Watsons' simple style of living (*Cookbook*, pp. 11–12).

152 **a round game**: a game, usually of cards, in which any number of players could play individually, in contrast to games such as whist which required four people playing in pairs against each other.

153 **Speculation**: a round game at cards which involves the buying and selling of trump cards with 'fish' or counters, the player who possesses the highest trump in the round winning the pool. 'To play this game well, little more is requisite than recollecting what superior cards of that particular suit have appeared in the preceding deals, and calculating the probability of the trump offered proving the highest in the deal then undetermined' (*Hoyle's Games, Improved*, revised and corrected by Charles Jones (1800), p. 4). Because of its flexibility and simplicity, it was popular with families, and could be noisy. In *MP*, the Bertrams and their guests play a lively game of speculation: Fanny Price finds herself 'mistress of the rules of the game in three minutes' and only Lady Bertram needs Mr Crawford's continual advice on how to play (vol. 2, ch. 7).

154 **cribbage**: a card game, usually for two players, in which cards attract a varying number of points depending on the way they are collected and grouped; the points are registered by placing pegs in successive holes on a board. The first to reach the final hole, or 'peg out', wins the game. It is a relatively quiet game which requires some skill and concentration.

155 **postchaise**: a travelling carriage, with a closed body, usually seating two to four people and often used for the purposes of hire; the sound of one would suggest the possibility of people travelling from a distance.

156 **wrap**: an additional outer garment worn as a defence against wind or weather when travelling. The *OED* cites this sentence as the first example of this usage of the word.

157 **seasons**: in the general sense of 'occasions'.

158 **pembroke table**: a small table with a hinged drop-leaf on each side, and therefore particularly useful where space was limited because it could be pulled out and expanded and then folded away. The design became popular in the late eighteenth century. The Austens possessed more than one pembroke table at Steventon, but left them behind when they moved to Bath in 1801: 'the trouble & risk of the removal would be more than the advantage of having them at a place, where everything may be purchased' (3–4 January 1801, *L*, p. 68).

159 **the Bedford**: Bedford Coffee House, operating since the early eighteenth century on a site adjoining the Covent Garden Theatre. Its heyday was in the mid eighteenth century but it was still a popular meeting place decades later. In *NA* another young man aspiring to fashion, John Thorpe, claims to have met General Tilney 'for ever' at the Bedford (vol. 1, ch. 12). The manuscript of 'The Watsons' shows that JA contemplated replacing 'the Bedford' with 'Horse Guards', the guardhouse and general headquarters of the army two miles west of Covent Garden, but having written 'Horse Guards' above the line she deleted it and let 'the Bedford' stand.

160 **open**: mild, frost-free.

161 **dishabille**: informal dress, with a hint of carelessness in style.

162 **fish . . . tolerably clean pack**: small pieces of bone or ivory, sometimes though not always shaped like fish, were used instead of money or for keeping account in games of chance; counters, which came in various shapes and sizes, could be used in a similar way; the pack is of cards.

163 **beaufit**: an early spelling of buffet, a sideboard or sidetable; in *Waverley* (1814) Walter Scott refers to the 'old-fashioned

beaufet' in the dining room at Tully Veolan in mid eighteenth-century rural Scotland (ch. 10).

164 **Vingt-un**: vingt-et-un, also now known as Black Jack or pontoon, is a game of chance played with a full pack of cards by any number of players up to ten. The object of the game is to obtain a total of twenty-one points, or as near to it as possible, without exceeding it. The players bet on their prospects and the odds are very much in favour of the player who acts as dealer/banker. The game could certainly be noisy.

165 **overdraw himself on both his own cards**: if on receiving two cards a player holds a pair, he or she can split them and use each as the basis of two separate hands. Lord Osborne is here described as finding himself with more than twenty-one points – and therefore overdrawn and out of the game – on both the hands he is playing.

166 **basin of gruel**: JA wrote 'bason', using an eighteenth-century spelling outdated by the 1800s. Gruel was a light, liquid food chiefly consumed by invalids, made by boiling oatmeal in water or milk, sometimes with the addition of sugar or spices. In *E* 'another small basin of thin gruel as his own' is all that the valetudinarian Mr Woodhouse 'could, with thorough self-approbation, recommend' to his guests (vol. 1, ch. 3); though in fact the health merits of gruel were sometimes disputed: 'A very light supper is often necessary to amuse digestion . . . but gruels and suchlike are improper: they run into fermentation' (Thomas Trotter, *A View of the Nervous Temperament: Being a practical Enquiry into the increasing Prevalence, Prevention and Treatment of those Diseases commonly called Nervous* (1807), pp. 282–3).

167 **give Robert the meeting**: a formal invitation to Tom Musgrave to dine in honour of Robert, the visitor, but a homely grammatical construction: the uneducated Mrs Belfield, in Burney's *Cecilia*, under the false impression that Cecilia is attracted to her son, invites Cecilia to take tea with her, using a similar form: 'if you would only let one of your footmen just take a run to let me know when you'd come, my son would be very proud to give you the meeting' (book 6, ch. 1).

168 **shoot with Lord Osborne**: that is, join Lord Osborne in shooting game birds on the Osborne estate.

169 **heiress of an easy independence**: if Robert's assessment of Mrs Turner's wealth is correct, Emma could have expected to inherit about £8,000 or £9,000, a fairly modest sum in comparison to Emma Woodhouse's £30,000 but still enough, at the usual 5 per cent interest rate, to yield an annual income of £400–£450. With such an income she could have lived comfortably, if she remained unmarried, without being dependent on other members of the family for her subsistence, but the income would also have attracted a husband. Again, JA spelt 'independance'.

SANDITON

CHAPTER I

1 **Sanditon**: Sanditon (Sandy-town?) is a fictional resort on the south coast of England. Many such resorts had sprung up in the last decades of the eighteenth and the first decades of the nineteenth century, and 'Sanditon' does not seem to represent any particular one; for the suggestion that Sanditon might be based partly on the location around Bexhill in Sussex see Selwyn, *Jane Austen and Leisure*, pp. 57–8; Edmund Atkinson argues that Sanditon is Eastbourne ('Jane Austen and Sussex,' Jane Austen Society Report for the Year 1977, in *Collected Reports of the Jane Austen Society, 1976–1985* (Overton: Jane Austen Society, 1989), pp. 40–1).

2 **Tunbridge . . . East Bourne**: the town of Tonbridge is about thirty miles south of London, on one of the main coach roads to the south coast. The road divides at the spa town of Tunbridge Wells, with one branch of the road going south-east to Hastings, and the other south-west to Eastbourne, both towns about sixty miles south of Tonbridge on the south coast. JA spells 'Eastbourne' various ways, but usually as 'E. Bourne', or 'East Bourne', so the latter form is used here.

3 **cut**: struck with his whip.

4 **overturning**: carriage accidents were common in fact and in fiction. JA had taken early advantage of the comic and parodic possibilities involved: in 'Love and Freindship' an overturning carriage kills the two heroes Edward and Augustus, 'most elegantly attired but weltering in their blood' (Letter 13, 'Juv.', Volume the Second), and in *NA* Catherine Morland and Mr and

Mrs Allen travel to Bath without a single 'lucky overturn to introduce them to the hero' (vol. 1, ch. 2).

5 **not his master's**: JA wrote 'not his Masters' above the line though she did not delete the words they were intended to replace, 'the Gentleman's own'. Either formulation suggests that the travellers had hired horses, and a driver, to pull their own carriage, a common practice. In *P&P* the Hursts have their carriage at Netherfield Park, but no horses (vol. 1, ch. 7).

6 **seen romantically . . . at some little distance**: Mr Parker's attitude reveals him to be looking with a tourist's rather than a practical eye, and with ideas of beauty newly popular in the late eighteenth and early nineteenth century, with its fashion for the picturesque. William Gilpin, who did much to mould genteel taste in his accounts of his own travels, succinctly defined one of his favourite terms of high admiration, 'picturesque beauty', as 'that kind of beauty which *would look well in a picture*' and added 'Neither grounds laid out by art, nor improved by agriculture, are of this kind' (William Gilpin, *Observations on the Western Parts of England, relative chiefly to Picturesque Beauty* (1798), Section 35).

7 **proprietor . . . who happened to be among his haymakers**: haymaking normally takes place in July, so this places the opening of the novel in high summer. One of the earliest of JA's juvenile tales, 'Henry and Eliza', opens: 'As Sir George and Lady Harcourt were superintending the Labours of their Haymakers, rewarding the industry of some by smiles of approbation, and punishing the idleness of others, by a cudgel' ('Juv.', Volume the First).

8 **a surgeon's opinion**: surgeons were qualified medical men, trained and licensed to perform surgical operations. See 'W', n. 33.

9 **partner . . . well**: just as only a licensed surgeon could legally perform surgical operations, so only a licensed apothecary could dispense drugs, and it was therefore common for a surgeon and an apothecary to practise in partnership: Mr Parker may therefore be suggesting that his sprain only requires general care. Mr Parker's sister later assumes that the partner is an apothecary whom Mr Parker wishes to recruit for Sanditon (ch. 5). The Apothecaries Act had only recently (1815) introduced compulsory apprenticeships and formal qualifications for

apothecaries, raising their status as well as their likely level of competence.

10 **Willingden**: there is no village of this name in the immediate vicinity described here, but there is a village more commonly spelt Willingdon just inland from Eastbourne, which has a steep lane leading from the village to the Downs. At the beginning of the nineteenth century one of the main landowning families of the Eastbourne Willingdon was named Parker.

11 **Morning Post . . . Kentish Gazette . . . London**: the *Morning Post*, first published in 1772, and issued daily in London, was the most important newspaper for the monied and fashionable: it included, for example, lists of fashionable arrivals and departures not only in London but also in Bath, Weymouth, Cheltenham, Brighton and Ramsgate during their various social seasons. Any advertisement placed in it would be intended for a national or regional rather than for a local London audience. The *Kentish Gazette*, first published in 1768, came out twice weekly, with a catchment area of Kent and nearby counties including Sussex; in the 1810s it regularly carried advertisements by medical men: see, for example, on the front page of the issue for Tuesday, 9 April 1816: 'MR. ROBERTS, SURGEON, late R. N. begs to acquaint the Inhabitants of New Romney and the Vicinity, that he purposes practising Surgery, Midwifry, &c. &c.—'.

12 **post-chaises**: substantial four-wheeled travelling carriages, drawn by two or four horses, and able to carry up to four people.

13 **double tenement**: a house divided and let to two separate tenants or tenant families. In writing the *Memoir* of JA James Edward Austen Leigh reported sadly that the Austen house at Chawton 'has lost all that gave it its character. After the death of Mrs. Cassandra Austen, in 1845, it was divided into tenements for labourers' (*Memoir* (1871), p. 81).

14 **country**: county or local area.

15 **Great Willingden, or Willingden Abbots**: there is no village of either of these names in Kent, or near the Eastbourne Willingdon. However, 'Great' is a common prefix for English villages, and there are several 'Abbots' in the south of England, including Stanstead Abbots in Hertfordshire. In the medieval period, the

church of the Eastbourne Willingdon was in the care of abbots in France.

16 **Battle**: A small town eight miles inland from Hastings; the name is short for 'Battle Abbey' after the church built by William I of England to commemorate the Battle of Hastings (1066), which had been fought nearby; because of these associations Battle was a well-known spot. JA wrote 'Battel', a rare archaic form of the name.

17 **down . . . Weald**: the Weald is a stretch of southern England including portions of Sussex, Kent and Surrey, lying between two ranges of chalk uplands, known as the North and South Downs. It was formerly woodland ('weald' is the Old English word for 'forest') but by Austen's day it was mostly used for pasture.

18 **town**: London.

19 **turnpike road**: see 'W', n. 34.

20 **Hailsham**: a market town thirteen miles south-west of Battle and ten miles north of Eastbourne.

21 **Saline air and immersion**: then as now, sea air and salt water were both regarded as having healing properties, a belief supported by a range of enthusiastic treatises beginning with Sir John Floyer's *The Ancient Psychrolousia Revived; or, An Essay to prove Cold Bathing both Safe and Useful* (1702) and continuing throughout the eighteenth century. 'Were I to enumerate half the diseases which are every day cured by sea-bathing, you might justly say you had received a treatise,' writes Jery Melford (Tobias Smollett, *The Expedition of Humphry Clinker*, 3 vols. (1771), vol. 2, p. 136). 'Immersion' did not necessarily mean bathing in the sea: resorts often also offered sea-water baths. Worthing's sea-water bath, for example, was built in 1798 (John K. Walton, *The English Seaside Resort: A Social History, 1750–1914* (Leicester: Leicester University Press, 1983), p. 160).

22 **sensations**: instinctive feelings (rather than rational thought).

23 **well stocked . . . sprains and bruises**: according to William Buchan, whose opinions on domestic medicine guided many households of the period, safe remedies for sprains or strains might include 'poultices made of stale beer or vinegar and oatmeal, camphorated spirits of wine, Mindererus's spirit [a solution of ammonium acetate], volatile liniment, volatile aromatic spirit . . .

with the addition of brandy or spirit of wine'. Serious bruises could benefit from 'a poultice made by boiling crumbs of bread elder-flowers and camomile-flowers'. He adds that 'in some parts of the country the peasants apply to a recent bruise a cataplasm of fresh cow-dung', which has a good effect (*Domestic Medicine*, pp. 597, 582). Other remedies recommended for bruises included hartshorn, diluted by barley water, and for sprains 'Opodeldoc', a solution of Castile soap, diluted with camphor (Anon., *A Description of the Names and Qualities of those Medicinal Compositions contained in the Domestic Medicine Chests* (?1775), pp. 597, 3, 9, 13. Richard Reece's *Medical Guide* lists recommended contents of various kinds of medicine chest including a 'Family Dispensary' and a 'Ladies Dispensary' offered for sale at £5.10s.0d. pp. 3–5, xvii–xx).

24 **a young and rising bathing-place**: the development of seaside resorts was a natural extension to the eighteenth-century fashion for seeking a mix of medical attention and social occupation in spa towns such as Bath, Clifton and Tunbridge Wells. Brighton, and a small number of other resorts, were developing recognizable 'seasons' as early as the 1730s; but Dr Richard Russell's popular treatise on the medicinal uses of sea water (first published in English in 1752), and the subsequent move of London doctors to prescribe sea-bathing for their wealthy clients, meant that 'sea water followed spa water from the status of an uncertain fringe medicine to that of a sovereign remedy' (Walton, *English Seaside Resort*, pp. 11–12). As a result, in the later decades of the eighteenth and first decades of the nineteenth century a large number of sea resorts developed, often from fishing villages where there was already easy access to the sea. The main advantage of seaside over inland spa resorts, of course, was that bathing in the sea was enjoyable as well as medicinal: Tobias Smollett's fashionable young man, Jery Melford, writes to his friend that 'I love swimming as an exercise, and can enjoy it at all times of the tide . . . You and I have often plunged together into the Isis [at Oxford]; but the sea is a much more noble bath, for health as well as pleasure. You cannot conceive what a flow of spirits it gives, and how it braces every sinew of the human frame' (Smollett, *Humphry Clinker*, vol. 2, p. 136).

25 **all that are to be found along the coast of Sussex**: along the seventy miles or so of the Sussex coast, from Hastings in the east to Selsey in the west, large numbers of resorts had developed, many in the last years of the eighteenth century. Brighthelmston (which around 1800 became known more simply as Brighton) was the first to be developed, in the 1750s and 1760s, but other resorts soon followed, including Bexhill, Eastbourne itself, Seaford, Rottingdean, Hove, Worthing, Littlehampton and Bognor Regis. Most began as fishing villages and were still, in Austen's time, relatively small, though growing, centres of leisure and tourism. They had a clear advantage over resorts in other parts of England, in that, situated on the south coast, they had the best weather and a natural aspect towards the sun. 'In process of time, should the present taste continue, it is not improbable but that every paltry village on the Sussex coast which has a convenient beach for bathing will rise to a considerable town' (*Guide to Watering Places*, p. 202).

26 **some new place or other . . . growing the fashion**: see for example the *Guide*'s entry on Worthing: 'In a short space of time, a few miserable fishing huts and smugglers' dens have been exchanged for buildings sufficiently extensive and elegant to accommodate the first families in the kingdom' (*ibid.*, p. 390).

27 **money or time to go to them**: As with the inland spas in earlier decades, seaside resorts very soon developed from places where people went to improve their health, to social and holiday resorts; by the early nineteenth century increasing disposable income, and improving travel arrangements, meant that many more people had access to them. JA visited a number of seaside resorts on the south coast, including Worthing in 1805, for recreational rather than for health reasons. In *E* John Knightley has taken his family to the Essex resort of Southend on the recommendation of the family doctor 'for both sea air and bathing', to benefit the children's health; but it is also clearly a family holiday, to be enjoyed. The old-fashioned and ultra-cautious Mr Woodhouse responds that 'the sea is very rarely of use to any body. I am sure it almost killed me once'; but his doctor is reported as approving of Cromer, 100 miles or so further north, as 'the best of all the sea-bathing places. A fine open sea . . . and very pure air'

(vol. 1, ch. 12). In *P* the Musgrove/Wentworth party visit Lyme in November, simply sightseeing.

28 **raise the price . . . good for nothing**: Mr Heywood's argument here follows the influential economic thinking of Adam Smith: 'When the quantity of any commodity which is brought to market falls short of the effectual demand . . . the market price will rise more or less above the natural price' and one of the results might well be that 'the interest of the labourers . . . will prompt them to withdraw a part of their labour' (Adam Smith, *An Inquiry into the Nature and Causes of the Wealth of Nations*, 2 vols. (1776), vol. 1, bk 1, ch. 7).

29 **Brighton, or Worthing, or East Bourne**: Eastbourne was about twenty miles east and Worthing about fourteen miles west of Brighton. Brighton was in fact by far the largest and most popular of the three with fashionable tourists. The *Guide to Watering Places* lists Brighton as 'fashionable, elegant, and universally known', while Worthing is 'a desirable residence for those who really wish to enjoy the benefits of sea-bathing or air' and Eastbourne a 'delightful village' (pp. 70, 390, 54). At the beginning of the nineteenth century Eastbourne had about 1,700 inhabitants, and Worthing about 2,100, while Brighton recorded more than 7,000.

30 **nursery grounds**: the fields where vegetables and fruits were cultivated.

31 **private**: not maintaining a public position, and therefore not of the highest social status; but the word also carries an implication of domesticity and respectability, in contrast to fashion and display. In describing the features of the village of Rottingdean, four miles from Brighton, the *Guide to Watering Places* notes approvingly that it is 'chiefly filled by families who prefer retirement to the gaiety and bustle of Brighton' (p. 90).

32 **Such a place as Sanditon . . . long journey**: access from London was a strong selling point of tourist resorts. The *Guide to Watering Places* included a fold-in table of distances; among its twenty-nine entries, five are on the Sussex coast (Bognor, Brighton, East Bourne, Hastings and Worthing, listed as sixty-eight, fifty-four, sixty-three, sixty-four and fifty-nine miles from London respectively). Like other guides, it then lists distances from London

prominently in the description of each resort mentioned, to the extent of pointing out that while Brighton is only fifty-four miles from London by road, 'as the crow flies, it is not above forty-three' (p. 70).

33 **effluvia . . . sea weed**: the noxious and disgusting smells which Mr Parker claims are given off by the seaweed of Brinshore were regarded as more than just unpleasing: Buchan wrote of 'effluvia from putrid stagnating water' and 'vegetable effluvia' as causes of malignant fevers (*Domestic Medicine*, pp. 148, 195).

34 **insalubrious air**: the quality of the air by the sea could vary greatly, and was an important factor in considerations of health as well as aesthetic comfort. The Advertisement to the *Brighton New Guide* marks Brighton's advantages: 'The salubrity of the air, the excellent quality of the water, the pleasing, healthful, and convenient situation of the town' (Frederick Fisher, *Brighton New Guide; or, a Description of Brighthelmston and the Adjacent County*, 4th edn (1800), Advertisement). The *Guide to Watering Places* also makes a point of mentioning 'salubrity of air' as a recommendation for the Sussex resorts. See also n. 33 above.

35 **She, never heard of half a mile from home**: a line in 'Truth' (1782), a long poem by William Cowper (1731–1800), published in a volume of his verses so popular that there were at least seven further editions before his death. In the poem the early eighteenth-century writer, wit and iconoclast, Voltaire, is contrasted with a simple peasant woman:

> who weaves at her own door,
> Pillow and bobbins all her little store . . .
> Just knows, and knows no more, her bible true,
> A truth the brilliant Frenchman never knew . . .
> Oh happy peasant! Oh unhappy bard!
> His the mere tinsel, her's the rich reward;
> He prais'd perhaps for ages yet to come,
> She never heard of half a mile from home;
> He lost in errors his vain heart prefers,
> She safe in the simplicity of hers.
>
> (*Poems by William Cowper* (1782), pp. 89–90).

Readers might also have remembered the opening of the poem: 'Man on the dubious waves of error toss'd' until 'farewell all self-satisfying schemes, / His well-built systems, philosophic dreams' (p. 73), lines which could be associated with Mr Parker himself.

CHAPTER 2

1 **enthusiast**: in the usual modern sense of a person who is keen on some topic or cause, but carrying hints of the older meaning of visionary and self-deluded.

2 **speculation**: a commercial venture carrying the possibility of considerable profits, but also involving much risk. Just as there was a social gulf between the gentry, whose income derived from land, and the merchant classes whose income derived from trade, so to many of the gentry the idea of 'speculation' carried pejorative overtones. (The card game 'speculation', which depended entirely on chance, must have emphasized the link between trading and gambling.) Several of the new seaside resorts had expanded through speculative investment by particular individuals. See for example 'Bognor, or Hothampton . . . an extensive collection of brick-built villas, without any consistent plan as a whole, newly erected, and a favourite speculation of Sir Richard Hotham' (*Guide to Watering Places*, p. 58). Sir Richard Hotham (d. 1799), having made his money as a hatter and then as a merchant, invested heavily in Bognor in his last years, but Bognor failed to live up to its early promise. On the south coast in particular this was not untypical: the French wars together with expanding demand encouraged speculation, but most resorts had 'fragmented land ownership and . . . piecemeal development' and most failed (Walton, *English Seaside Resort*, pp. 110–14).

3 **puffed**: advertised, with exaggerated praise, a meaning which developed in the eighteenth century by extension from the earlier sense of to blow out or inflate. Mr Puff, in Richard Brinsley Sheridan's popular comedy, *The Critic* (1781), describes himself as 'a Practitioner in Panegyric, or to speak more plainly—a Professor in the Art of Puffing' (Act 1, scene 3).

4 **no profession**: normally the eldest son of a gentleman's family would inherit the family estate and its income on the death of his father; until that date he would expect an allowance, and

would not usually take on a profession. Younger sons, who could expect little or no such inheritance, would usually enter one of the professions considered as appropriate: the law, the Church, the army or the navy. In *S&S* Edward Ferrars, the elder son and therefore heir of his wealthy mother, feels idle because he has not had to take up a profession, and, when disinherited, turns with some relief to the Church (vol. 1, ch. 19).

5 **independent**: that is, possessing some form of individual inheritance, and therefore not reliant on other family members for their income. JA wrote 'independant', her usual spelling of the word.

6 **eldest . . . collateral inheritance**: that is, an inheritance from a relative with no direct heir, who might choose to benefit a younger son rather than leave his estate to someone unknown or already well provided for. The superlative form 'eldest' was often used in JA's time where the comparative would now be more normal: the phrase in fact refers to the elder of Mr Parker's two younger brothers.

7 **mine . . . lottery**: then as now, money was to be made from mining various substances from coal to gold: more generally, 'mine' suggests an abundant source of good things. A variety of lotteries operated successfully through the eighteenth century, including the State lottery, which ran from 1694 to 1826, offering cash prizes as large as £30,000 in reward for tickets costing at least £3 each (many gamblers bought only a share in a ticket). Lotteries were, however, always controversial and there was a new flurry of debate about the lottery in 1816. In April a letter to the *Gentleman's Magazine* declared lotteries to be 'an evil . . . pre eminently subversive of public morals, and . . . replete with effects at which Humanity shudders' as well as 'impolitic, and highly detrimental to trade' (vol. 86, p. 296). In June 1816 Parliament debated the future of the lottery and arguments were aired on both sides before the government, defending the lottery because the income could be used to fund major projects, defeated attempts to end the practice. JA's juvenile 'Edgar and Emma' includes among its characters Mr Willmott who 'possessed besides his paternal Estate, a considerable share in a Lead mine and a ticket in the Lottery' (Chapter the Second, Volume the First).

8 **hobby horse**: originally, a toy consisting of a long stick with a horse's head at one end, which was very popular with young children who could pretend to ride it, and so by extension both a favourite and a delusional pursuit or pastime. General Tilney's 'hobby-horse' is said to be his garden (*NA*, vol. 2, ch. 7). For any reader of Laurence Sterne's *Tristram Shandy* (1760–7) the word was inextricably associated with Tristram's Uncle Toby's obsession with re-enacting the siege of Namur (see for example vol. 1, ch. 24).

9 **futurity**: the usual meaning of the word is simply 'the future' or 'what will happen in the future' but JA seems to intend a stronger sense of confidence in future events.

10 **anti-spasmodic . . . anti-rheumatic**: JA is satirizing the medical jargon of the time, which specialized in 'anti-' words. Sedatives, most prominently laudanum, were the commonest remedy for spasms. 'Anti-pulmonary' seems to be a nonce-word to refer to remedies for diseases of the lungs, particularly consumption. Antiseptics were described by Watt (John James Watt, *Medical Dictionary*, 2nd edn (1813)) as 'medicines preventing animal putrefaction, and divided into Tonic Antiseptic . . . and Antispasmodic Antiseptics, as camphor' – it is impossible to be certain whether JA's spelling involved a deliberate allusion to Mr Parker's lack of scepticism. 'Anti-bilious' was an afterthought, added by JA above the line in the manuscript, possibly with her own illness in mind: on 24 January 1817 she wrote to her friend Alethea Bigg, 'I am more & more convinced that *Bile* is at the bottom of all I have suffered, which makes it easy to know how to treat myself' (*L*, pp. 326–7). Neither 'anti-pulmonary' nor 'anti-rheumatic' appear in *OED*.

In terms of the very broad salutary effects of sea air and sea-bathing, Dr Robert Squirrell advised that bathing could be used to advantage 'Whenever there are symptoms of universal debility, arising from depletion, or for want of due nourishment, such as flabbiness of the muscles, weariness over the whole body, a sense of fatigue, upon the slightest exertion of the muscular system, and many other symptoms . . . especially when the debility is the consequence of any disease, such as Indigestion, Gout, Fever, Jaundice, Dropsy, Hæmorrhages, Violent Evacuations, or any other disorder', as well as 'In all nervous diseases . . . as faintings, tremblings, depression of spirits, alarm on every trifling occasion, nervous head-ach, &c.' (R. Squirrell, MD, *An Essay on Indigestion and its Consequences . . . also Remarks on Sea or Cold Bathing . . . explaining the reason Why inspiring the Sea Air contributes more to the Recovery of Health than that of Cities and Inland Places* (1795), pp. 64–5).

11 **softing**: an unusual word, meaning becoming or growing soft; but possibly JA meant the more usual 'softening'. When Cassandra copied the manuscript she wrote 'softening'.

12 **sea-bath . . . corrective**: either bathing in the sea or immersing in a bath of sea water. See Chapter 1, n. 21, above.

13 **dividends**: clearly some of Mr Heywood's income derives from investments; at that time it would be advisable, if not essential, to go in person to the City or a London bank to collect dividend payments.

14 **old coach . . . years ago**: the Heywoods would have to be fairly wealthy in order to maintain their own coach, but a 'coach' rather than a 'carriage' carries overtones of a heavy and unfashionable vehicle. It would be common to acquire a new coach or carriage at the time of a marriage, and to mark an important family event by renewing the upholstery, but delaying this for more than twenty years, and then not renewing it for a decade since, indicates either a severe limit on funds or a carelessness of style and fashion or both. Relining, however – that is, renewing the cloth covering of the woodwork on the inside of the body of the carriage – was not cheap: Felton quotes £3 as the cost of the most basic work involved (William Felton, *The Supplement to the Treatise on Carriages* (1796), pp. 43–4).

15 **Tunbridge Wells . . . Bath**: both these spa towns were longer established than the newer seaside resorts. The medicinal properties of the spa waters of Tunbridge Wells had been discovered early in the seventeenth century, and the town had long attracted invalids. Bath had become pre-eminently popular early in the eighteenth century, especially as its waters were seen as particularly effective for use against gout (See 'LS', Letter 26, n. 2). Though both centres continued to attract invalids and tourists in the early nineteenth century, they no longer had quite the

fashionable cachet of earlier decades. In *P* Bath has a particular appeal for the socially conservative Lady Russell, and for the impoverished Sir Walter Elliot, and it attracts the Musgroves and Crofts for a visit, but the best it can offer socially is the ungracious Lady Dalrymple and her daughter.

16 **library**: the library at a spa or seaside resort would have a much wider function than simply serving as a repository for the loan of books. In the early years of the nineteenth century there were three circulating libraries in Brighton, where 'New publications of merit are constantly added to the catalogues; the daily papers are regularly laid on the reading-tables; magazines, reviews, and other pamphlets, are diligently procured for public use . . . Each library also has an extensive assortment of stationery, perfume, jewellry &c on constant sale; and the proprietors also let out musical instruments by the week, month or year'; more modest circulating libraries are recorded in Bognor, Eastbourne, Hastings and Worthing (*Guide to Watering Places*, pp. 78, 58, 64, 223, 390). In *P&P* Lydia Bennet sees, at the library at Brighton, 'such beautiful ornaments as made her quite wild' (vol. 2, ch. 19).

CHAPTER 3

1 **Lady Denham**: as the widow of the baronet Sir Harry Denham, Lady Denham is a rather modest 'great lady'. Lady Russell, 'the widow of only a knight . . . gave the dignity of a baronet all its due' (*P*, vol. 1, ch. 2), but baronet is the lowest of hereditary ranks. There is a Lady Denham in Hannah More's *Cœlebs in Search of a Wife* (1808), who bears some resemblance to JA's character, 'a dowager of fashion grown old in the trammels of the world', who behaves badly by her dependant granddaughter, and is opinionated and parsimonious (ch. 10).

2 **manor and mansion house**: In medieval times many rural settlements were structured as 'manors' containing the local church, houses and agricultural land, all within the ownership of the lord of the manor, who was responsible for maintaining the lawful behaviour of his tenants. In the early nineteenth century, though the lord of the manor no longer had formal responsibilities, the

term 'manor', often used in the phrase 'manor and mansion house' as here, continued to suggest extensive control over the village.

3 **all at her disposal**: somewhat unusually, Mr Hollis's property was not entailed on to male heirs and he had chosen to leave it to his widow without conditions. In 'W', Emma Watson's uncle had similarly left his property freely to his widow, and Emma is denied her expected inheritance on her aunt's remarriage.

4 **too wary . . . given nothing for it**: although when a woman married her property usually became part of her husband's estate and could be dealt with as he wished, a legal arrangement could be made at the time of the marriage by which the property remained her own. The widow of a baronet would keep her title unless she married again.

5 **her original thirty thousand pounds**: a substantial sum. In *S&S* Willoughby's bride, Miss Grey, with £50,000, is 'very rich' (vol. 2, ch. 8); in *E* Emma, heiress of £30,000, is considered as significantly wealthy (vol. 1, ch. 16).

6 **his rank in society**: Sir Edward Denham has inherited the title of baronet as his uncle's nearest male relative, and would normally be expected to own a substantial estate and play a leading role in local social and charitable activities.

7 **coadjutor**: helper.

8 **cottage ornée**: a mock-rustic detached house designed for the use of the gentry, and to be picturesque: the fashion had become established at least as early as the 1780s and continued well into the nineteenth century. John Papworth describes the 'cottage orné' as 'a new species of building . . . not the habitation of the laborious but of the affluent . . . in this age of elegant refinement, a mere cottage would be incongruous with the nature of its occupancy' (John B. Papworth, *Rural Residences, Consisting of a Series of Designs for Cottages, Decorated Cottages, Small Villas, and other Ornamental Buildings* (1818), p. 25). In *Ellinor: or the World as it Is*, the 'ancient piece of knight-errantry, the duke of Southernword', attempts to seduce the heroine by offering her 'a charming *cottage ornêe* in all the *studied simplicity* of fashionable elegance' – in this case the cottage is large enough to accommodate 'a suite of servants' (Mary Ann Hanway, *Ellinor: or the World As it Is* (1800), vol. 3, pp. 22, 25). JA wrote 'ornèe'.

9 **waste ground**: land not in productive use for pasture or growing crops.

10 **candidate . . . season**: the cottage is being built for letting, and Mr Parker is relying upon its being available before the end of the current 'season', which would probably be in October.

11 **companion**: it was common for wealthy families, and particularly wealthy women living alone, to take into their households a gentlewoman in poverty, perhaps a family member, to provide company and companionship in return for her keep. At a time when such gentlewomen had almost no respectable means of earning their own income this arrangement could be an enormous benefit; but there are many examples of the exploitation of the companion, who inhabited an uncomfortable position between employer and servants. Mary Wollstonecraft wrote of those poor women forced to be 'humble companion to some rich old cousin or . . . to live with strangers, who are so intolerably tyrannical, that none of their own relations can bear to live with them . . . It is impossible to enumerate the many hours of anguish such a person must spend. Above the servants, yet considered by them as a spy, and ever reminded of her inferiority when in conversation with the superiors. If she cannot condescend to mean flattery, she has not a chance of being a favorite . . . She is alone, shut out from equality and confidence . . . she must wear a cheerful face, or be dismissed' (*Thoughts on the Education of Daughters*, pp. 69–71). Among many literary examples are Laura Montreville in *Self-Control*, who spends several months as companion to her selfish and interfering aunt Lady Pelham, and Juliet Granville, who endures insult and ridicule as companion to Mrs Ireton in Frances Burney's *The Wanderer* (1814).

12 **Sanditon House**: JA originally wrote 'Sanditon Hall' but immediately corrected 'Hall' to 'House'. Perhaps she did not want to give Lady Denham's home too dignified and historic a sound, or perhaps she wished to keep the name consistent with her earlier reference to 'manor and mansion house'.

13 **Michaelmas**: the feast day of St Michael, 29 September, was one of the four 'quarter-days' of the year, on which regular legal and financial transactions took place; Lady Denham's visit to London

might have concerned her financial affairs, but the term may be used as a more general indicator of the time of year.

14 **hotel**: John Trusler descibed hotels as 'taverns or inns, under a new name, so called from the hotels in Paris, where you may be rather better accommodated than at the inns in and about London, but at a much greater expence' (*The London Adviser and Guide: Containing every Instruction and Information useful and necessary to persons living in London and coming to reside there* (1790), p. 158).

15 **nursery maid**: the nursery maid, whose task was to look after the young children of the family and keep their nursery clean, was among the lowest paid of the women servants, receiving perhaps £6 or £8 a year. She could be highly regarded within the family: in *P* the old nursery maid of the Musgrove family, who 'having brought up all the children . . . was now living in her deserted nursery to mend stockings, and dress all the blains and bruises she could get near her' (vol. 2, ch. 1), is in affectionate demand when Louisa is injured.

CHAPTER 4

1 **garden**: referring to fruit and vegetable gardens, rather than flowerbeds, which would form part of the pleasure gardens around a house.

2 **honest old place . . . land**: JA had alluded in *P* to the rapid changes taking place in early nineteenth-century social and domestic life, in describing the Musgroves who, 'like their houses, were in a state of alteration, perhaps of improvement. The father and mother were in the old English style, and the young people in the new' (vol. 1, ch. 5). Here, however, the alteration involves a complete change of residence, and there is an added dimension in that Mr Parker has handed over his house to his chief tenant, a gesture that would have been unthinkable for example between Mr Knightley and Robert Martin in the more established society of Highbury.

3 **South Foreland . . . End**: the full length of England's south coast from South Foreland near Dover in the east to Land's End at the tip of Cornwall to the west.

4 **in a hole . . . advantage from it**: the traditional reason for building settlements 'in a hole' would be for shelter and protection. Emma

Woodhouse, appreciating the traditional virtues of Mr Knightley's Donwell Abbey, praises 'its suitable, becoming characteristic situation, low and sheltered—its ample gardens stretching down to meadows washed by a stream, of which the Abbey, with all the old neglect of prospect, had scarcely a sight' (*E*, vol. 3, ch. 6). The siting of 'modern Sanditon' on the hilltop gives priority to views directly over the sea, which would indeed be beautiful but which would increase exposure to bad weather.

5 **Trafalgar . . . the thing now**: a shift in fashion also noted by Byron in *Don Juan* (1819): 'Nelson was once Britannia's god of war' but now 'There's no more to be said of Trafalgar / . . . Because the army's grown more popular' (Canto 1, stanza 4). At the Battle of Trafalgar, fought on 21 October 1805 off the coast of Cadiz, the combined French and Spanish fleets were defeated by the British under the command of Lord Nelson, effectively ending the naval war in Britain's favour. Its impact at home, enhanced by the news of Nelson's death on the day of the battle, was immense. In 1814 Napoleon was defeated, but escaped from imprisonment on Elba, and for a while it seemed as if he would re-establish himself as Emperor of France. However, the Anglo-Dutch army under the Duke of Wellington, assisted by the Prussians, defeated Napoleon on 18 June 1815 at the Battle of Waterloo. A Trafalgar Place was noted in Worthing in 1811. The Strand Bridge in London, begun in 1811, was renamed Waterloo Bridge in 1816 and formally opened in 1817. Another great nineteenth-century London landmark, Trafalgar Square, was only so named in 1830.

6 **Crescent**: an architectural design of terraced houses in a crescent shape, first used in the name of the Royal Crescent at Bath (built 1767–75) and very much associated with superior accommodation in spa towns: for example, crescents were built in the late eighteenth century in Clifton and Buxton, and Brighton's Royal Crescent was built 1798–1807. Given the nature of the design, crescents were often far from 'little': the Royal Crescent at Bath contains thirty large houses; the Royal Crescent at Cheltenham, which was built over the first three decades of the nineteenth century, was originally designed to provide two blocks of twelve houses, with a road

between, and eventually consisted of a single block of eighteen houses.

7 **formalities**: generally, outward form or appearance, but possibly referring more specifically to the vegetables, fruit trees etc. that would be planted in formal rows and squares. Late eighteenth-century ideas of the picturesque favoured the removal of unsightly details in the cause of providing a beautiful aspect.

8 **plantations**: areas planted with trees, with some suggestion of a commercial purpose. There is also an implied contrast between the need for Mr Parker to plant trees and the way in which woods nurtured over many generations form an integral part of a gentleman's landed estate.

9 **canvas awning**: evidently mounted against the windows of the house, this form of shelter had recently been adapted from its traditional use on board ship.

10 **parasol**: parasols had been introduced into Britain from south and south-east Asia, and were fashionable in the early nineteenth century for women to carry to protect the skin from sunshine and maintain a desirable paleness of complexion.

11 **grandeur of the storm**: with recent growing interest in the sublime, the mixture of beauty and terror exhibited by a storm at sea had begun to attract much aesthetic attention. George Carey, describing Margate as a watering place, recommended its 'pleasant look-out in the morning over the green ocean,—now a calm, now a breeze; and sometimes presenting itself with all its grandeur in a terrific storm' (George Saville Carey, *The Balnea: or, an Impartial Description of All the Popular Watering Places in England* (1799), pp. 5–6). Novelists and poets exploited the artistic possibilities of the sea-storm: in his most recent novel *The Antiquary*, which JA read on its publication in 1816, Walter Scott included a dramatic scene in which his heroine and her father are caught by a sudden storm as they walk home along the beach, and become stranded 'between two of the most magnificent, yet most dreadful objects of nature—a raging tide and an insurmountable precipice' (*The Antiquary* (1816), vol. 1, ch. 7).

12 **hospital**: hospitals, to enable invalids from outside the area of the resort to be cared for as they sought cures for their diseases, were usually established by charitable subscription or donation. The

developers of Flimflamton, the new resort in Thomas Skinner Surr's novel *The Magic of Wealth* (1815), are enthusiastic about a proposal for an infirmary to be erected alongside the marine baths (vol. 2, p. 202).

13 **improvements**: a word which JA had earlier used with a two-edged meaning: 'The Musgroves, like their houses, were in a state of alteration, perhaps of improvement' (*P*, vol. 1, ch. 5).

14 **equipage**: carriage, horses, and related accessories and servants.

15 **enclosures**: strictly speaking, enclosures were former common land, taken into private ownership and fenced off for cultivation, a process widespread from the mid eighteenth century, requiring Parliamentary approval. Henry Tilney talks to Catherine Morland of the 'inclosure' of forests along with 'waste lands, crown lands and government' (*NA*, vol. 1, ch. 14). But Mr Parker may be using the word in a general sense of 'enclosed land'.

16 **fisherman's houses**: most of the new resorts on the Sussex coast had been developed from fishing villages, which usually offered ready access to the sea. Such villages, however, often lay slightly inland, for purposes of protection, and the new resorts were built on the sea side of existing buildings.

17 **elegant white**: it was popular for young women to wear white in the early nineteenth century, combining fashion and the traditional associations with virgin simplicity. When a malicious onlooker scoffs at the simplicity of the dress of the heroine of *Self-Control* on a social occasion, Miss Bolingbroke responds, 'Pure, unadorned, virgin white . . . the proper attire of angels!' (ch. 27). Later in 'S', JA gives an impressionistic description of Clara Brereton as 'something white and womanish' (ch. 12).

18 **harp**: a very fashionable instrument, replacing, for some genteel young women, the square pianoforte which had dominated musical accomplishment in the late eighteenth century. Unlike the pianoforte, which required a stiff posture, the harp was 'calculated . . . to show a fine figure to advantage. The contour of the whole form, the turn and polish of a beautiful hand and arm, the richly-slippered and well-made foot on the pedal stops, the gentle motion of a lovely neck, and, above all, the sweetly-tempered expression of an intelligent countenance; these are shown at one glance, when the fair performer is seated unaffectedly, yet

gracefully, at the harp' ('A Lady of Distinction', *The Mirror of the Graces; or, The English Lady's Costume* (1811), p. 194). JA's niece Fanny Knight became proficient on the instrument. In April 1811 JA wrote to Cassandra of the 'great pleasure' she expected from hearing a professional harpist at a party she attended in London with Fanny (*L*, p. 180). In *MP* Mary Crawford's playing of a harp 'as elegant as herself' is associated both with her sophisticated London habits and with her sexual allure (vol. 1, ch. 7); in *E* Mrs Elton expresses her regret that Jane Fairfax could not offer proficiency in the harp as one of her skills as governess even in a provincial family (vol. 2, ch. 17). In 'Plan of a Novel' the 'very highly accomplished' heroine is said to play 'equally well on the Piano Forte & Harp', with '& Harp' inserted as an afterthought (see p. 226). In *P* the harp is an element in the modernizing of the Musgroves' old-fashioned parlour (given a 'proper air of confusion by a grand piano forte and a harp, flower-stands and little tables' (vol. 1, ch. 5)), but also a source of comfort for elderly Mrs Musgrove when depressed over thoughts of her dead son (vol. 1, ch. 6)

19 **after the hooping cough**: Whooping-cough, or chin-cough, was prevalent among children; it was always weakening, and could be fatal. As a 'spasmodic' disease it was treated with purgatives, opiates and tonics, but it was believed that one of the most effective remedies was a change of air – if possible to somewhere 'more pure and warm' (*Domestic Medicine*, pp. 284–8) – and a trip to the seaside was desirable to strengthen the patient in convalescence.

20 **Blue shoes . . . nankin boots**: from the 1790s blue shoes had become fashionable for women, replacing the more serviceable black shoes which had previously been worn. JA had previously made a joke of such a colour for shoes: 'Mama was so kind as to lend us a pair of blue Sattin Slippers, of which we each took one and hopped home from Hereford delightfully' ('A Tour through Wales—in a Letter from a young Lady—', 'Juv.', Volume the Second). JA has the 'fine gentleman' Lord Osborne recommend nankin boots to Emma Watson (see 'W', p. 115).

21 **health-breathing hill**: probably an allusion to a song attributed to George, Lord Lyttelton, which includes in the first of three stanzas the lines 'Adieu! thou sweet health-breathing hill, / Thou

canst not my comfort restore, / For ever adieu! my dear vill [*sic*], / My Lucy, alas! is no more'. The verses were reproduced in numerous collections of songs and glees from about 1780.

22 **Prospect House . . . Bellevue Cottage . . . Denham Place**: the new houses proclaim, by their names, either their exposed situation (which gives the view), or the achievement of contemporary speculators. Worthing offered a Prospect Place in 1811 and one of Brighton's new streets was named 'Bellevue'.

23 **bills at the window**: notices in the window advertising accommodation to let.

24 **just . . . dinner**: at a spa dinner, the main meal, would mark the dividing line between outdoor and healthy pursuits during the earlier part of the day and social events in the evening.

25 **Terrace . . . place**: the terrace was another form of building which came into fashion towards the end of the eighteenth century, much favoured by the new spa and seaside resorts: a terrace denoted a line of houses, attached to each other, and raised up from the natural street level in order to provide a wide walkway outside, as a formal promenade. A Gravel or Greville Terrace is recorded at Worthing by 1813, and a York Terrace a little later. A mall was originally an alley in which the game pall-mall (a form of putting) was played, but the term became used for a fashionable walk: 'the Mall' was a broad, tree-lined walk in St James's Park, London's most fashionable promenade space.

26 **milliner's shop**: a shop selling lace, ribbons, accessories and knick-knacks as well as hats.

27 **billiard room**: billiards were a popular entertainment among gentlemen, as is evident from the presence of billiard rooms in *MP* (vol. 1, ch. 13) and *NA* (vol. 2, ch. 8). They were a popular amenity even in the smaller new seaside resorts: in Eastbourne 'the appendage of billiard-tables' sat alongside the circulating library; in Hastings there was a billiard room over the library; at Lyme Regis, further west, an assembly-room, card-room and billiard table were all conveniently arranged under one roof (*Guide to Watering Places*, pp. 64, 223, 23).

28 **bathing machines**: even the smallest resorts would be provided with bathing machines to facilitate sea-bathing. Smollett's Jery Melford describes the bathing machines at Scarborough, when

they were a very new innovation in the 1770s, 'ranged along the beach, with all their proper utensils and attendants . . . Image to yourself a small, snug, wooden chamber, fixed upon a wheel-carriage, having a door at each end, and on each side a little window above, a bench below—The bather, ascending into this apartment by wooden steps, shuts himself in, and begins to undress, while the attendant yokes a horse to the end next the sea, and draws the carriage forwards, till the surface of the water is on a level with the floor of the dressing-room, then he moves and fixes the horse to the other end—The person within, being stripped, opens the door to the sea-ward, where he finds the guide ready, and plunges headlong into the water——After having bathed, he re-ascends into the apartment, by the steps which had been shifted for that purpose, and puts on his clothes at his leisure, while the carriage is drawn back again upon the dry land; so that he has nothing further to do, but to open the door, and come down as he went up . . . The guides who attend the ladies in the water, are of their own sex, and they and the female bathers have a dress of flannel for the sea; nay, they are provided with other conveniences for the support of decorum. A certain number of the machines are fitted with tilts, that project from the sea-ward ends of them, so as to screen the bathers from the view of all persons whatsoever' (*Humphry Clinker*, vol. 2, pp. 134–5).

29 **Venetian window**: a window with three openings, the central one being arched and larger than those on either side, a relatively recent innovation, designed to allow more light and air than earlier kinds of windows.

CHAPTER 5

1 **Women . . . depended on**: notable among JA's fictional correspondents is Lady Bertram, who 'rather shone in the epistolary line', having, partly 'from the want of other employment . . . formed for herself a very creditable common-place, amplifying style, so that a very little matter was enough for her' (*MP*, vol. 3, ch. 13). JA herself, and her sister Cassandra, were both keen letter-writers.

2 **spasmodic bile**: bile is the bitter fluid secreted by the liver; either an excess or an obstruction causes pain and nausea, in Diana's case in spasms.

3 **friction**: vigorous chafing or rubbing. In fact, the medical advice of the time rarely recommended friction for sprains or strains. William Nisbet recommends friction as one of several remedies for 'chronic' sprains (*The Clinical Pharmacopœia, or General Principles of Practice and Prescription* (1800), p. 206), but *The Family Physician* is more typical in recommending that 'The best remedy . . . is absolute rest, after applying a compress moistened in vinegar and water . . . If the sprain is moderate, a plunging of the part into cold water is excellent' (*The Family Physician; or, Advice with respect to Health, including Directions for the Prevention and Cure of Acute Diseases, Extracted from Dr. Tissot* (6th edn, corrected (1797), p. 158); see also ch. 1, n. 23 above).

4 **medical tribe**: a cliché description of a group of doctors, much used in eighteenth- and early nineteenth-century fiction, and also in popular medical tracts of the period.

5 **headache . . . together**: William Buchan advised that headaches could have a variety of different causes, one of which was 'excess of blood, or an hot bilious constitution'. In this case 'the application of leeches to the temples, and behind the ears, will be of service,' along with blistering the skin, gentle laxatives, or in stubborn cases, powerful purgatives (*Domestic Medicine*, pp. 354–5). The practice of applying leeches to suck blood from parts of the body regarded as having an excess of it had begun in classical times, and became more common as the nineteenth century advanced. Medicinal leeches were specifically bred for the purpose. The average leech spent fifteen minutes sucking about half a teaspoonful of blood.

6 **three teeth drawn**: a traumatic procedure, since there were no effective means of dulling the pain involved. A dentist of the time wrote that extraction was only used if all other ways of dealing with toothache failed: 'but,' he added, 'persons are in general terrified at the thoughts, and strive by all possible means to avoid it' – a response very understandable in the light of his account of everything that could go wrong, including extracting the wrong tooth (F. B. Spilsbury, *Every Lady and Gentleman their*

own Dentist, as far as the Operations Will Allow (1791), pp. 33–6). 'The poor girls and their teeth!' JA wrote to Cassandra on 16 September 1813, when her nieces Fanny, Marianne and Lizzy Knight came to London for dental treatment, 'poor Marianne had two taken out after all . . . When her doom was fixed, Fanny Lizzy and I walked into the next room, where we heard each of the two sharp hasty Screams' (*L*, p. 223). If the problem was indeed in Susan's gum, tooth extraction might well have been harmful: in such cases the pain 'seldom fails to be considerably aggravated by the distension of the socket of the jaw, and by that laceration of the gum which necessarily attends drawing the tooth' (Hugh Smythson, *The Compleat Family Physician, or Universal Medical Repository* (1781), ch. 11, 'Of the Tooth-Ache, and Fœtid Breath', p. 272).

7 **languid . . . liver**: it was believed that a sedentary or languid habit could be both cause and symptom of liver problems: 'The circulation in the liver being slow, obstructions in that organ can hardly fail to be the consequence of inactivity . . . loss of appetite, and a wasting of the whole body, seldom fail to be the consequences of a diseased state of the liver' (*Domestic Medicine*, p. 56).

8 **Isle of Wight**: the large island off the south coast of England, accessible from Southampton and Portsmouth, and visible from the towns and villages along the coast. Sidney is presumably travelling from London, and his route would therefore be through Hampshire, where the Parker sisters are later (ch. 11) said to live; one of the main coach routes from London to Southampton would travel through Winchester, sixteen miles from Chawton.

9 **beau monde**: the French phrase had been used since the early eighteenth century to describe the fashionable world, or society.

10 **families . . . a rich West Indian from Surry**: probably the family of an English merchant who had made his fortune in the West Indies, or an English gentleman who had been living on his West Indian plantations; because of the large profits to be made in trade from the West Indies, such families would be assumed to be very wealthy. Surrey, then a rural county, lies between London and the south coast.

11 **academy**: See 'LS', Letter 17, n. 1.

12 **Camberwell**: three miles south of the Thames, and now part of the conurbation of south London, Camberwell was in the early nineteenth century a country village in Surrey, within reach of the capital but offering healthier air and surroundings, and so a likely location for schools and hospitals as well as rural retreats for city dwellers.

13 **Wheel within wheel**: the reference is to the old saying, 'wheels within wheels', a complex network of influences and circumstances, not all of which are apparent. See Ezekiel, 1:16, describing a vision of four wheels containing the spirits of four winged creatures: 'their appearance and their work *was* as it were a wheel in the middle of a wheel'.

CHAPTER 6

1 **the library subscription book**: since every genteel visitor would be expected to subscribe to the library, the subscription book acted as a kind of social register.

2 **pendant lace**: this might denote a particular kind of lace designed to be draped around the body, hanging from the neck, or more generally any piece of lace hanging for display purposes.

3 **list . . . commonplace**: in Surr's satirical description of Flimflamton the narrator imagines a visitor reading the subscription book in the library and saying 'Any body here? Any fashion? Any High-flyers? Let's look in your book—No, all cits—all cockneys—your place will never do at this rate' (*The Magic of Wealth*, vol. 2, p. 244).

4 **The Lady Denham**: the prefix 'The' would normally be correct only if Lady Denham had been the widow of a peer rather than of a baronet, so either JA was suggesting that Sanditon was attempting to exaggerate Lady Denham's importance or she made a slip.

5 **whose names . . . lead off the season**: the resident gentry would naturally be the first names on the list, but significantly none of the visitors matches the residents in rank.

6 **Lieutenant Smith R. N.**: lieutenant was a very modest rank in the Royal Navy: JA's two naval brothers, Frank and Charles, were promoted from lieutenant to captain at the ages of twenty-four and twenty-five respectively. Smith is one of the most

commonplace of English surnames: Harriet Smith in *E* is 'the natural daughter of nobody knows whom' (vol. 1, ch. 8), while in *P* Mrs Smith's name prompts a tirade from the rank-conscious Sir Walter Elliot: 'A Mrs. Smith. A widow Mrs. Smith,—and who was her husband? One of the five thousand Mr. Smiths whose names are to be met with every where' (vol. 2, ch. 5).

7 **Captain Little,—Limehouse**: since Captain Little is not in the Royal Navy, it is likely that he is the captain of a merchant ship, lower in the naval hierarchy. Limehouse is an area on the north bank of the Thames, east of the City, containing a substantial part of London's bustling port facilities.

8 **solicitor, Grays Inn**: a lawyer in one of the Inns of Court in London, at the centre of the English legal system.

9 **August and September were the months**: the summer holiday season extended from May to October but was at its height in September. Walton quotes rates at William Stone's lodging house in Margate in 1787 as 2 guineas a week in May and June, 2 ½ guineas in July, 3 guineas in August, and 3 ½ guineas in September and early October, before falling away (*English Seaside Resort*, p. 18).

10 **literary recess**: possibly an allusion to Clara Reeve's popular novel *The Recess; or, a Tale of Other Times* (1785), a sensational account of the lives of the (fictional) twin daughters of Mary Queen of Scots, a historical figure whom JA greatly admired.

11 **her toilette**: the process of preparing her dress and appearance for public view.

12 **smart trinkets**: JA originally wrote 'ornamented Combs' but presumably, having already referred to Miss Whitby's glossy curls, she wished to vary the detail.

13 **Camilla's . . . Distress**: *Camilla: or, a Picture of Youth*, 5 vols. (1796) by Frances Burney. Camilla is just seventeen (bk 1, ch. 7) for the major part of the novel; her distresses include financial embarrassments through overspending a small allowance in the purchase of 'little keep-sakes' at the beginning of a visit to the fashionable spa of Tunbridge Wells (bk 6, ch. 2). JA had subscribed to *Camilla* on first publication, and commenting on the novel as a genre in *NA* (vol. 1, ch. 5, in lines probably drafted pre-1803) praised *Camilla*

alongside Burney's earlier *Cecilia* (1782) and Maria Edgeworth's *Belinda* (1801).

14 **stout**: strong, robust.

15 **interesting**: a popular adjective in the fiction of the period, with a stronger meaning than now, often used to indicate that something about the person being described has an air of mystery, or possibly a significant or unusual history which will inevitably be told during the course of the novel. It often has strong tender or sentimental undertones.

16 **address**: manner of speaking and conducting oneself generally towards other people.

17 **dependence . . . business**: many novels of the period showed genteel but impoverished heroines being ill treated by wealthy older women who were ostensibly offering them protection; see, for example, Emily St Aubert and Madame Cheron in Ann Radcliffe's *The Mysteries of Udolpho* (1794) and Laura Montreville and Lady Pelham in *Self-Control.*

18 **barbarous conduct on Lady Denham's side**: JA uses the hyperbolic 'barbarous' occasionally in her published works, as for example in Marianne Dashwood's emotionally fraught fears that someone 'may have been so barbarous to bely me' to Willoughby (*S & S*, vol. 2, ch. 7).

19 **visitants**: a form of the more usual 'visitors', becoming archaic in the early nineteenth century.

20 **No people spend more freely . . . than West Indians**: huge fortunes were to be made in the eighteenth and early nineteenth centuries by people who owned plantations, and traded goods such as sugar, produced by means of cheap slave labour; those who came back to Britain, or sent relatives to Britain, for education, leisure or retirement, were therefore likely to be very wealthy. People who lived in the West Indies were regarded as prone to temperamental and emotional extremes, from indolence on the one hand to passion on the other, because of the hot climate (a belief still prevalent when Charlotte Brontë wrote of mad Bertha Mason in *Jane Eyre* (1847)).

21 **West Indy . . . West-ingines**: not indigenous inhabitants, but Europeans who had settled in the West Indies. 'Indy' was a

common colloquial way of referring to India. The *OED* does not record the precise form 'West-ingines'; it cites 'S' as offering a variation of 'West Indian', using the spelling 'West-injines', as printed in Chapman's editions (*MW*, p. 392).

22 **diffusion of money . . . more good than harm**: the unstable market conditions which resulted from the end of the war with France in 1815 give this discussion between Lady Denham and Mr Parker a very contemporary resonance. Political economy was a popular subject for debate in the 1810s, but the phenomenon on which they express such different views had been influentially explored by Adam Smith in *The Wealth of Nations*; Smith was all in favour of the working of the marketplace, and concluded that even in case of a sudden increase in demand commodies would maintain their 'natural price': 'Different accidents may sometimes keep them suspended a good deal above it, and sometimes force them down even somewhat below it. But . . . [t]he whole quantity of industry annually employed in order to bring any commodity to market, naturally suits itself in this manner to the effectual demand' (Smith, *Wealth of Nations*, vol. 1, bk 1, ch. 7). His view was broadly endorsed by the well-informed Mrs B. in Jane Marcet's popularizing *Conversations on Political Economy* (1816), 'Of Money', p. 303. The word 'consumable' was an unusual one at the time; JA spelt it 'consumeable'.

23 **French boarding school**: that is, a boarding school run by a Frenchwoman, or a woman purporting to be French. In the 1780s JA and Cassandra attended such a school run by 'Mrs La Tournelle' (whose name was actually Sarah Hackitt (*FR*, p. 51)).

24 **asses' milk . . . milch asses**: asses' milk was considered to resemble human milk closely, and therefore to be superior to other milk. It was seen as particularly suitable for asthmatics and consumptives. Buchan advises that in cases of consumption 'Asses milk ought to be drank [*sic*], if possible, in its natural warmth, and by a grown person, in the quantity of half an English pint at a time . . . four times, or at least thrice a-day'; but he cautions that 'it cannot always be obtained; besides, it is generally taken in a very small quantity; whereas, to produce any effects, it ought to make a considerable part of the patient's diet' (*Domestic Medicine*, pp. 410, 179).

25 **governess**: teacher, particularly the chief teacher who might own the school (that is, the woman who governs the establishment).

26 **chamber horse**: an early exercise machine which simulated the experience of riding a horse. The word appears twice in this sentence; on the first occasion JA wrote 'chamber house', but 'chamber horse' is correct. In copying the manuscript, Cassandra wrote 'chamber horse'.

CHAPTER 7

1 **better half, of the pair**: 'better half' is still a colloquial term for spouse, almost exclusively used for a wife.

2 **gig**: a light two-wheeled open carriage able to carry two people and drawn by a single horse. It was a modest vehicle: in *NA* the aspiring John Thorpe owns a gig but insists that it is 'curricle-hung' (vol. 1, ch. 7).

3 **his station**: his position beside Charlotte.

4 **in the gross**: generally, in a general way.

5 **sublimity**: Edmund Burke defined the sublime: 'Whatever is fitted in any sort to excite the ideas of pain, and danger, that is to say, whatever is in any sort terrible, or is conversant about terrible objects, or operates in a manner analogous to terror, is a source of the *sublime*; that is, it is productive of the strongest emotion which the mind is capable of feeling' (Burke, *A Philosophical Enquiry into the Origin of our Ideas of the Sublime and the Beautiful*, 2nd edn (1757), 'With an introductory Discourse concerning Taste, and several other Additions', section 7, 'Of the Sublime'). Novelists and poets, particularly those within the Gothic tradition, wrote at length of mountains, lakes and seas as productive of this sublime terror, until the heightened rhetoric of the sublime became a cliché, ripe for comic or satiric treatment.

6 **sensibility**: in *A Sentimental Journey through France and Italy* Laurence Sterne, describing a moment of high sentiment, talks of tears: 'Maria let me wipe them away as they fell with my handkerchief.—then steep'd it in my own—and then in her's—and then in mine—and then I wip'd her's again—and as I did it, I felt such undescribable emotions within me, as I am sure could not be accounted for from any combinations of matter and

motion' (Laurence Sterne, *A Sentimental Journey through France and Italy, by Mr. Yorick*, 2 vols. (1768), vol. 2, pp. 172–3). The spelling 'undescribable' was still in the 1810s an acceptable alternative to the more usual 'indescribable': in the fourth canto of *Childe Harold's Pilgrimage* (published in 1818) Lord Byron leaves 'to learned fingers, and wise hands' to 'describe the undescribable' (canto 4, stanza 53). For 'sensibility' see 'LS', Letter 5, n. 3.

7 **terrific**: causing terror, dreadful, frightful, and thus closely related to ideas of the sublime (see n. 5 above).

8 **gulls . . . samphire**: samphire is an aromatic plant, growing in rocks by the sea, the fleshy leaves of which were gathered for culinary purposes. A traveller to the Isle of Wight made the association of both gulls and samphire with steep cliffs, describing the way in which local people suspended themselves in baskets to reach gulls' eggs, and pointing out a famous literary connection – 'A method not unlike that pursued by the gatherers of samphire, from the side of Dover Cliff, as described by Shakespeare, in his King Lear: / "—Half way down / Hangs one that gathers samphire;—dreadful trade! / Methinks, he seems no bigger than his head"' (John Hassell, *Tour of the Isle of White*, 2 vols. (1790), vol. 1, p. 168).

9 **all the usual phrases . . . rather commonplace perhaps**: Sir Edward's speech here is indeed reminiscent of a number of literary apostrophes to the sea. One by George Keate was published in *Sketches from Nature, Taken and Coloured in a Journey to Margate* (1779), extracted with the review of the book in the *London Magazine, or Gentleman's Monthly Intelligencer* (August 1779), and frequently quoted or anthologized thereafter, including in an account of Eastbourne in 1787. Keate begins 'Hail! thou inexhaustible source of wonder and contemplation!—Hail! thou multitudinous ocean!' and he goes on to admire the 'glorious' and 'aweful scenes' the ocean displays, 'Whether we view thee, when every wind is hush'd . . . or whether we behold thee in thy terrors!—when the black tempest sweeps thy swelling billows, and the boiling surge mixes with the clouds'. (Anon., *East-bourne; being a Descriptive Account of that Village, in the County of Sussex* (1787), pp. 10–11).

10 **man of feeling**: there may be a specific reference here to the popular novel *The Man of Feeling* (1771) by Henry Mackenzie, in which the eponymous hero, Harley, is so sensitive as to be debilitated from all meaningful action in the world. However, the sensitive and caring 'man of feeling' is a type familiar in many novels of the period, and the usage here does not necessarily suggest a debilitating extreme.

11 **number . . . quotations**: in *The Man of Feeling* Harley occasionally quotes poetry at moments of heightened emotion, but by the 1770s this was already conventional; Sarah Fielding's *The Countess of Dellwyn* (1759) was criticized for its heavy dependence on quotation. Several of JA's own characters allude to poetry, but the dangerous implications of using poetry to exaggerate the emotions are highlighted particularly in Anne Elliot's concern at the bereaved Captain Benwick's sustaining his grief-stricken state by wallowing in poetical emotion: 'she thought it was the misfortune of poetry, to be seldom safely enjoyed by those who enjoyed it completely' and 'ventured to recommend a larger allowance of prose in his daily study' (*P*, vol. 1, ch. 11).

12 **assassin**: a word much loved by Gothic novelists: Mrs Radcliffe, in the lurid opening scene of *The Italian*, depicts English tourists in an Italian church encountering a horrifying figure with 'an eye of uncommon ferocity', who turns out to be an assassin – 'assassinations are so frequent,' comments a local friar, 'that our cities would be half depopulated' if sanctuary were not offered to the perpetrators (Ann Radcliffe, *The Italian* (1797) vol. 1, ch. 1).

13 **meeting such a man un-armed**: gentlemen had stopped wearing swords well before the end of the eighteenth century, and would not usually carry knives or pistols so this is a figurative statement.

14 **in either . . . poems**: it is just possible that JA was using the word 'either' in the sense of 'any' but it is more likely that she was thinking of the two poems for which Walter Scott, the most popular poet of the period, was best known: *Marmion* (1808) and *The Lady of the Lake* (1810). In *P* the poetical Captain Benwick alludes to Scott and Byron as 'the first-rate poets' of the time, and tries to 'ascertain whether *Marmion* or *The Lady of the Lake* were to be preferred' (vol. 1, ch. 11). JA kept up to date with Scott's works and was conscious of his popularity. On first reading *Marmion*,

soon after its publication, she wrote, 'Ought I to be very much pleased with Marmion?—as yet I am not' (20–22 June 1808, *L*, p. 131), though her opinion may have changed later, since a friend remembered her reading it aloud, very well (HRO MS 23M93/66/2), and by 1813 she knew it well enough to parody two lines from it in a letter to Cassandra about *P & P* – 'I do not write for such dull elves / As have not a great deal of Ingenuity themselves' (*L*, p. 202). In neither *Marmion* nor *The Lady of the Lake* are there prominent lines on the sea, though in *Marmion*, during an account of a voyage, there is the near-couplet 'The whitening breakers sound so near / Where, boiling through the rocks they roar' (Walter Scott, *Marmion: A Tale of Flodden Field*, 3rd edn (1808), canto 2, verse 8). However, in his novel *The Antiquary*, which JA read shortly after publication, Scott wrote in highly atmospheric terms of Sir Arthur Wardour and his daughter caught by the tide (vol. 1, ch. 7).

15 **Oh! . . . ease**: Scott, *Marmion*, canto 6, verse 30. The quotation comes from a moment of high drama late in Scott's long narrative poem when the knight Marmion has been fatally wounded and the maiden, whose name in fact is Clara, comes to his aid:

> O, Woman! in our hours of ease,
> Uncertain, coy, and hard to please,
> And variable as the shade
> By the light quivering aspen made;
> When pain and anguish wring the brow,
> A ministering angel thou!—

16 **Some . . . &c.**: Walter Scott, *The Lady of the Lake: A Poem* (Edinburgh and London, 1810), canto 2, verse 22. The lines celebrate the selfless love of a father for his daughter:

> Some feelings are to mortals given,
> With less of earth in them than heaven;
> And if there be a human tear
> From passion's dross refined and clear,
> A tear so limpid and so meek,
> It would not stain an angel's cheek,
> 'Tis that which pious fathers shed
> Upon a duteous daughter's head!

17 **Burns's . . . Mary**: Robert Burns (1759–96) became famous in the late 1780s as a rustic genius. He wrote love poems to or about several different women, including 'Mary Morison', but 'his Mary' is likely to be Mary Campbell, known as 'Highland Mary', with whom he planned, for a brief, intense period before her sudden death in late 1786, to share his life. He wrote three poems to her, 'The Highland Lassie O' and 'Will ye go to the Indies, my Mary' in 1786, and, years later, an elegy that was much anthologized. R. H. Cromek told a romanticized version of Burns's continuing love for his lost Mary: 'The anniversary of *Mary Campbell's* death . . . awakened in the sensitive mind of *Burns* the most lively emotion . . . he wandered, solitary . . . His agitation was so great that he threw himself on the side of a corn stack, and there conceived his sublime and tender elegy—his address *To Mary in Heaven*' (*Reliques of Robert Burns, collected and published by R. H. Cromek* (1808), p. 238). The poem finishes

> O pale, pale now, those rosy lips
> I aft hae kiss'd so fondly;
> And clos'd for ay, the sparkling glance
> That dwalt on me sae kindly;
> And mouldering now in silent dust
> That heart that lo'ed me dearly!
> But still within my bosom's core
> Shall live my Highland Mary.
>
> (*Complete Poems and Songs of Robert Burns* (Glasgow: HarperCollins, 1995), pp. 645–6)

For a modern account of Burns and Mary Campbell see Ian McIntyre, *Dirt and Deity: A Life of Robert Burns* (London: HarperCollins, 1995), pp. 71–7; McIntyre describes the circumstances surrounding 'Highland Mary' as 'the most powerfully sentimental tradition in the Burns legend' (p. 73).

18 **Montgomery . . . poetry**: James Montgomery (1771–1854) was considered a dangerous radical in the 1790s, and was imprisoned for some of his political articles, but he later wrote romantic poetry including *The Wanderer of Switzerland* (1806), *The West Indies* (1807, accompanying a series of pictures published to commemorate the abolition of the slave trade) and *The World before*

the Flood (1812), on a biblical theme. He is nowadays best known for his hymns, including 'Angels from the Realms of Glory'.

19 **Wordsworth . . . it**: William Wordsworth (1770–1850) had by the 1810s outgrown the political radicalism that had coloured his early volume of poems, *Lyrical Ballads* (1798), written with Samuel Taylor Coleridge, and had consolidated his reputation as a poet with *Poems in Two Volumes* (1807) and *The Excursion* (1814).

20 **Campbell . . . between**: Thomas Campbell (1777–1844) is now best remembered for stirring poems such as 'Ye Mariners of England'. His first success was with 'The Pleasures of Hope', a lengthy meditation on hope in a world of war, tyranny and injustice, from which Sir Edward quotes here:

> Cease, every joy, to glimmer on my mind,
> But leave – oh! leave – the light of Hope behind;
> What though my winged hours of bliss have been,
> Like angel visits, few and far between;
> Her musing mood shall every pang appease,
> And charm – when pleasures lose the power to please!
>
> 'The Pleasures of Hope', Part 2, lines 221–6, in *The Pleasures of Hope; in two Parts, with Other Poems* (1799)

The poem was hugely popular, and was frequently reprinted in the first decades of the nineteenth century.

21 **Scott . . . want of passion . . . tame**: Scott reached his height of popularity as a poet around 1810; once Lord Byron's mature poems began to be published in the 1810s Scott's romantic tales of the English and Scottish past began to seem very tame in comparison with Byron's obsessive characters, exotic locations, racy situations, and pyrotechnic poetic style. The lack of reference to Lord Byron on Sir Edward's part is surprising; JA refers to 'the tenderest songs' of Scott and 'the impassioned descriptions of hopeless agony' of Byron in the discussion between Anne Elliot and Captain Benwick in *P* (vol. 1, ch. 11).

22 **poor Burns's . . . forgot**: reviewing one of the growing number of biographies of Burns in 1815 Alexander Peterkin commented that 'the personal character of the poet has, since his death, been in some measure inseparably blended with that of his writings' (*A Review of the Life of Robert Burns, and of the various Criticisms, on*

his Character and Writings (1815), pp. 37–8). Robert Heron wrote that Burns 'was even in the first years of his rising youth, an ardent lover: feeling the passion, not affected, light, and sportive'; but he was unable to withstand temptation, and spent 'Too many of his hours . . . in the tavern, in the brothel, on the lap of the woman of pleasure'. In enumerating Burns's strengths as a poet Heron emphasizes his 'native strength, ARDOUR, and delicacy of FEELINGS, passions and affections . . . He sings what he had himself beheld with interested attention,—what he had himself felt with keen emotions of pain or pleasure. You actually see what he describes: you more than sympathise with his joys: your bosom is inflamed with all his fire: your heart dies away within you, infected by the contagion of his despondency' (Robert Heron, *A Memoir of the Life of the Late Robert Burns* (1797), pp. 12–13, 27, 48–50). In *English Bards and Scotch Reviewers* (1809), Byron praised Burns among poets who 'Feel as they write, and write but as they feel' (line 817).

23 **genius**: the usual meaning of the word at the turn of the eighteenth–nineteenth centuries would be 'natural ability' or 'quality of mind', but the more modern meaning of a particular kind of intellectual power proceeding from divine or otherwise miraculous inspiration may also be intended here.

24 **hyper-criticism . . . pseudo-philosophy**: 'hyper-criticism' had been used since Dryden's time to mean excessive criticism, but usage was increasing in the 1810s and 1820s; according to the *OED*, this is the first recorded appearance of the compound 'pseudo-philosophy'.

25 **coruscations**: quivering flashes of light, originally describing atmospheric phenomena such as those coming from stars but occasionally used figuratively as here.

26 **dowager**: the widow of the previous owner.

27 **co**: that is, a co-, or joint-heiress.

28 **landed or funded**: among the aristocracy and gentry, financial status depended on land, and the income arising from it, or money invested in government stocks, or funds, rather than money earned.

29 **half pay officers**: officers in the army and navy who were not on active service, either because they were between assignments or

because they were unable to undertake active tasks, were reduced to what was usually termed half pay, though the actual rate for naval officers was slightly higher than half (Brian Southam, *Jane Austen and the Navy* (London and New York: Hambledon and London, 2000), p. 132).

30 **jointure**: that part of an estate specifically willed from a husband to a wife, to provide for her after his death; it would usually be a small proportion, since the main part of the estate would go to the heir, most often the eldest son.

CHAPTER 8

1 **five volumes**: possibly Burney's *Camilla*, which Charlotte had already seen on Mrs Whilby's counter and which consisted of five volumes altogether. Two of Burney's other novels, *Cecilia* (1782) and *The Wanderer* (1814), were published in five volumes, as were Charlotte Smith's *Ethelinde, or the Recluse of the Lake* (1789) and *Family Annals, or Worldly Wisdom* (1807) by Mrs Hunter of Norwich; most novels of the time were published in three or at most four volumes.

2 **trash . . . highest contempt**: although many circulating libraries carried a wide range of titles in fiction and non-fiction, circulating-library novels had been a byword for trash since well before Richard Sheridan had made comedy out of Lydia Languish's love of such novels in *The Rivals* ((1775), Act 1, scene 2). The Austens, however, found reading such novels an amusing pastime; JA's niece Anna Lefroy later recorded: 'It was my great amusement during one summer visit at Chawton to procure novels from a circulating Library at Alton, & after running them over to relate the stories to Aunt Jane . . . Greatly we both enjoyed it, one piece of absurdity leading to another, till Aunt Cassan[a] fatigued with her own share of laughter w[d]. exclaim, "How can you both be so foolish?" & beg us to leave off' (HRO MS 23M93/97/4/104).

3 **ordinary occurrences . . . drawn**: Sir Edward's declaration here forms a neat companion-piece to the famous description of the novel in *NA*, a work 'in which the greatest powers of the mind are displayed, in which the most thorough knowledge of human

nature, the happiest delineation of its varieties, the liveliest effusions of wit and humour are conveyed to the world in the best chosen language' (vol. 1, ch. 5). It also alludes to current debates about the purposes of fiction, and the nature of JA's own work. Through the eighteenth century novelists had claimed that their work offered a combination of instruction and entertainment (following Horace's dictum, 'dulce et utile'). Towards the end of the century two different strands of fiction developed, the Gothic, which aimed at outright entertainment through strong plots and exaggerated emotions, and the domestic (including for example Hannah More's *Cœlebs in Search of A Wife* (1808) and Maria Edgeworth's *Patronage* (1814)), which aimed to air moral issues through the presentation of day-to-day occurrences. JA's novels caused a puzzle by not falling into either category: for the reviewer in the *Gentleman's Magazine* (September 1816) *E* was 'amusing, if not instructive' (p. 249), while the novel's publisher, John Murray, worried that it wanted 'incident and Romance' (Samuel Smiles, *A Publisher and His Friends: Memoir and Correspondence of the Late John Murray, with an account of the Origin and Progress of the House, 1768–1843*, 2 vols. (1891), vol. 1, pp. 282–8).

4 **alembic . . . science**: an alembic is a glass vessel with a top, traditionally used for the distilling of chemicals, but acquiring a figurative meaning towards the end of the eighteenth century: for example, Edmund Burke in *Reflections on the Revolution in France* (1790) refers to 'the hot spirit drawn out of the alembick of hell, which in France is now so furiously boiling' (p. 135). There was increased interest in the various branches of science and technology in the early years of the nineteenth century. The modern meaning of the term 'science', however, did not develop until later in the nineteenth century; here, despite the scientific words elsewhere in the sentence, 'science' has its traditional meaning of general knowledge.

5 **You . . . do**: most of the individual words used by Sir Edward here are not in themselves clichés, but in the accumulation of such words, not all of them appropriate in context or even grammatically correct, he is copying the over-elaborations of the novels he claims to despise. JA may be remembering Sir Sedley Clarendel in *Camilla*, 'the least comprehensible person' the heroine had

ever known, who has a habit of circumlocution – when asked why he plays chess he replies that 'Those exquisite little moments we steal from any given occupation, for the pleasure of speculating in secret upon something wholly foreign to it, are resistless to deliciousness' (vol. 2, bk. 4, ch. 8 and vol. 2, bk. 3, ch. 12); but humour in elaborations of language had long been a literary convention. Mid-eighteenth-century examples include Fielding's Colonel Bath and Sheridan's Mrs Malaprop.

6 **fair questioner**: in Burney's *Camilla* the former governess Miss Margland, trying to cajole the pretty, vain and vacuous Indiana Lynmere, 'began a negociation with the fair questioner' (vol. 1, bk 2, ch. 13). *Camilla* is very far from the kind of novel Sir Edward says he admires.

7 **the strict line of primitive obligations**: 'primitive' here carries the meaning of 'original, basic', and the obligations would include upholding moral principles with friends, family and society.

8 **indomptible**: 'indomptable' is recorded in the *OED* as a variant on the more usual 'indomitable'.

9 **anti-prosperous . . . machinations**: 'anti-prosperous' is unrecorded as a word in the *OED*; 'high-toned machinations' casts a very favourable light on evil activities carried out by well-born villains. JA makes comedy of this in Mrs Morland's knowing 'so little of lords and baronets, that she entertained no notion of their general mischievousness, and was wholly unsuspicious of danger to her daughter from their machinations' (*NA*, vol. 1, ch. 2).

10 **morbid**: gloomy, brooding. Gothic novelists' praise of morbidity was satirized by Elizabeth Hamilton, who has her heroine Bridgetina Botherim asking her suitor 'What is become of that charming morbid excess of sensibility and tenderness, with which you then confessed the fervour of your fierce consuming flame?' (*Memoirs of Modern Philosophers*, 3 vols. (1800), vol. 2, ch. 13).

11 **eleemosynary**: given or received as an act of charity. The word was mostly used in legal documents and social commentaries, but it also appeared (often for comic effect) in fiction, including in *Tristram Shandy*, vol. 7 ch. 32, and in the famous opening to *Tom Jones*: 'An Author ought to consider himself, not as a Gentleman who gives a private or eleemosynary Treat, but rather as one who

keeps a public Ordinary, at which all Persons are welcome' (Henry Fielding, *The History of Tom Jones, A Foundling* (1749).

12 **the impassioned . . . Richardson's**: Samuel Richardson's three hugely successful novels, *Pamela* (1740), *Clarissa* (1747–8) and *Sir Charles Grandison* (1753–4), attracted controversy because of the propensity of the first two novels in particular to wallow in their vivid explorations of virtue under siege and in peril. *Clarissa*, which has particularly impressed Sir Edward, tells, at immense length and in the protagonists' own words, of the aristocratic hero Robert Lovelace's determination to seduce the virtuous Clarissa and her determination not to be seduced, despite soon finding herself in his power. The pursuit ends in rape and Clarissa's death, and Richardson clearly intended Lovelace's own subsequent death in a duel to be seen as an appropriate punishment for acts which could not be forgiven in this world. However, Lovelace, taking his place in a literary tradition of the (possibly) reformed rake, and endowed with wit, wealth, inventiveness and humour, proved a very attractive figure to readers, and many responses to the novel argued either that Clarissa should have forgiven him when he expressed repentance after the rape, or that she had only suffered because she had been too much of a prude in the first place.

13 **such authors . . . concerned**: Richardson's Lovelace was copied by a large number of novelists, including Richardson himself with the figure of Sir Hargrave Pollexfen in *Sir Charles Grandison*, and Frances Burney, with Sir Clement Willoughby in *Evelina* (1778). In the 1780s and 1790s the type received a new lease of life as it became caught up in arguments about the aristocracy in the context of ideas connected with the French Revolution. In most later novels Richardson's subtleties were replaced by a crude representation of a predatory male, who might appear appropriately within the pages of a melodramatic plot but who was completely out of place in a realistic representation of contemporary life, and who was therefore now out of date in all but Gothic and related fictions; the Lovelace-figure in *Self-Control*, Colonel Hargrave, while he is an increasing practical annoyance, and then threat, to the heroine, finally approaches a fascinating character-study of a very modern psychological obsession.

14 **modern literature**: literature from the eighteenth century, in contrast to the 'ancient' classical literature that still formed a large part of the reading particularly of men of the aristocracy and gentry.

15 **essays, letters, tours and criticisms of the day**: the eighteenth century had developed a fine tradition of non-fiction writing, beginning with the moral and instructive essays of Joseph Addison and Richard Steele, including in the *Tatler* (1709–11) and the *Spectator* (1711–14), both of which were in print in volume form throughout the century. A large number of journals, including the *Gentleman's Magazine*, offered regular articles, letters and criticism on a wide range of social, political and cultural issues, while collections of letters and essays were widely read. 'Tours' refers to the accounts of travels undertaken by young aristocrats on 'the grand tour', usually through the major capitals of western Europe, and also of increasingly popular general recreational tours within the UK and Europe.

16 **Lovelaces**: the aristocratic rake and seducer in *Clarissa* (see nn. 12–13 above) had become an iconic figure for later novel writers and novel readers. 'I know you have a hundred fancies about Colonel Scarsdale, and suppose that he is a sort of modern Lovelace,' Geraldine Verney writes to her sister in Charlotte Smith's *Desmond*, 'but, believe me, my Fanny, that character does not exist now; there is no modern man of fashion, who would take a hundredth part of the trouble that Richardson makes Lovelace take, to obtain Helen herself, if she were to return to earth' (Charlotte Smith, *Desmond*, 3 vols. (1792), vol. 2, pp. 214–15).

17 **carry her off . . . reception**: Sir Edward could be recalling any number of novels in which the heroine is abducted in this way, including *Self-Control*, in which the obsessive Colonel Hargrave has the heroine carried off to a hut in the wilds of Canada. JA was much amused by Brunton's novel, though she thought it a work 'without anything of Nature or Probability in it'. Little was known about Timbuktu, an ancient city on the southern edge of the African Sahara, and it was often used as the type of the most distant place imaginable. Mungo Park, in his account of

his travels in Africa, described the place as in the possession of a 'savage and merciless people, who allow no Christian to live there' (Mungo Park, *Travels in the Interior Districts of Africa*, 4th edn (1800), p. 302. Southam suggests that there was particular interest in Timbuktu in 1816–17 following the account of it in *The Narrative of Robert Adams* (1816), which was widely discussed in the papers and reviews (Brian Southam, *Jane Austen: A Students' Guide to the Later Manuscript Works* (London: Concord Books, 2007), p. 167). In fact Timbuktu was a centre of Muslim culture, with a famous library.

CHAPTER 9

1 **belong to them**: be their guests.

2 **Chichester**: a small cathedral city five miles inland from the south coast, and on the likely route from Hampshire, where the Parkers live (see ch. 11), to the south coast.

3 **hysterics**: hysterical fits or convulsions, associated rather with delicate fictional heroines than with real-life women taking a coach journey.

4 **seminary**: in the eighteenth century, a general synonym for school, but in the early nineteenth century particularly applied to a private school for young ladies. In *E* JA contrasts Mrs Goddard's 'real, honest, old-fashioned Boarding-school' with 'a seminary, or an establishment, or any thing which professed, in long sentences of refined nonsense, to combine liberal acquirements with elegant morality upon new principles and new systems – and where young ladies for enormous pay might be screwed out of health and into vanity' (vol. 1, ch. 3).

5 **family**: the household as a whole: that is, not only Mrs Griffiths and her daughters and niece, but also their servants.

6 **bitters . . . decocting**: bitters – either quinine ('Peruvian Bark', the powdered bark of the Cinchona tree) or bitter native herbs such as camomile and tansey – made into a medicine by boiling them down in water to a concentrate. Reece gives recipes for a number of decoctions, including Decoction of Peruvian Bark: 'Take of Peruvian bark bruised, one ounce; water, a pint and a quarter. Boil for ten minutes in a covered vessel, and strain

the liquor while hot' (*Medical Guide*, p. 71). Bitters were used against a wide range of ailments, including fevers and upset stomachs.

7 **belles lettres**: elegant or polite literature, including – according to Hugh Blair, the first Regius Professor of Rhetoric and Belles Lettres at the University of Edinburgh – the history, structure and style of language, the nature of literary language, and the study of examples from ancient and modern poetry and prose. It was usual for specialist teachers to visit schools to give occasional lessons, rather than teach full-time.

8 **I got that man a hare**: rabbits and hares usually bred on estate land and though they were not officially classed as game they were regarded as belonging to the owner of the land; they were unlikely therefore to be readily available in butchers' shops.

CHAPTER 10

1 **projector**: one who forms a project or enterprise; but the word could also pejoratively imply a misguided or foolish venturer, most famously in Jonathan Swift's Academy of Projectors on the Island of Laputa where one projector, 'of a meager Aspect, with sooty Hands and Face, his Hair and Beard long, ragged and singed in several places . . . had been eight Years upon a Project for extracting Sun-Beams out of Cucumbers' (*Gulliver's Travels* (1726), vol. 2, part 3, ch. 5).

2 **quack medicine**: a 'quack' was an ignorant pretender to medical skill, and there were many individuals who made a living out of the sale of various useless pills and potions with the claim that they could cure diseases and ailments. JA wrote 'medecine'.

3 **posting**: hurrying (alluding to the swift movement of the post-chaise).

4 **establishment**: arrangement, of the people and furniture.

5 **salts**: smelling salts, consisting usually of ammonium carbonate, used to combat faintness.

6 **drops**: a medicinal preparation taken in the form of drops of liquid. This would usually be either laudanum, an opiate, or elixir of vitriol: Buchan describes the latter as 'one of the best medicines which I know for hysteric and hypochondriac patients, afflicted

with flatulencies arising from relaxation or debility of the stomach and intestines' (*Domestic Medicine*, p. 733).

7 **stouter . . . lusty**: the modern meaning of 'stout' – plump, corpulent – was just coming into use in the early nineteenth century, and it is not clear whether JA intends this, or the earlier meaning of well- or strongly made; 'lusty' means large or substantial.

8 **sodden**: not, as now, looking as if soaked in water or alcohol, but rather characterized by heaviness, dullness, or want of vivacity.

9 **a proper house at eight guineas per week**: the equivalent of something approaching £500 a week at early twenty-first-century prices.

10 **bathing women**: women employed to assist bathers to change and get in and out of the sea or sea-water bath, sometimes called 'dippers' (see Chapter 4, n. 28).

11 **trenches**: a very unusual figurative use of the military term for the digging of hollows or ditches in the ground, reinforced by 'discharged' later in the sentence.

12 **post chaises . . . hack-chaises**: a 'hack' or 'hackney' chaise, like a post-chaise, was a coach available for hire.

13 **his person as a screen**: that is, Arthur's body acts as a firescreen, a common piece of furniture in the days of open fires, used to protect people from the direct heat of the fire.

14 **bloom**: see 'LS', Letter 17, n. 4.

15 **nervous . . . nerves**: Buchan wrote that 'Of all diseases incident to mankind, those of the nervous kind are the most complicated and difficult to cure. A volume would not be sufficient to point out their various appearances. They imitate almost every disease; and are seldom alike in two different persons, or even in the same person at different times' (*Domestic Medicine*, p. 420). At the same time symptoms of 'low spirits . . . and fickleness of temper' could be the result of self-indulgence or hypochondria, and the verdict of some doctors was brusque: '*Nervous* Disorders are the Diseases of the Wealthy, the Voluptuous, and the Lazy . . . mostly produced, and always aggravated, by *Luxury* and *Intemperance*', declared George Cheyne (*The English Malady: or, a Treatise on Nervous Diseases of All Kinds* (1733). p. 158). 'You have no compassion on my poor nerves,' complains Mrs Bennet. 'You

mistake me, my dear,' replies her husband. 'I have a high respect for your nerves. They are my old friends. I have heard you mention them with consideration these twenty years at least' (*P&P*, vol. 1, ch. 1).

16 **bilious . . . better I am**: for 'bilious' see Chapter 2, n. 10 above. If JA was still regarding her own complaint as arising from bile when she wrote this chapter, this could be a teasing defence of her own liking for wine: 'By the bye . . . I find many Douceurs in being a sort of Chaperon for I am put on the Sofa near the Fire & can drink as much wine as I like' (JA to Cassandra, 6–7 November 1813, *L*, p. 251).

17 **perspiration**: in fact, in most instances, perspiration was seen as health-giving rather than as a sign of illness: 'It is of so great importance to health, that few diseases attack us while it goes properly on; but when it is obstructed, the whole frame is soon disordered' (*Domestic Medicine*, p. 126); 'even the colliquative sweats attendant on pulmonary consumption or hectic fever are to be suppressed with the greatest caution' (*Medical Guide*, p. 384). Of course, then as now, overheating, and exercise by the unfit, could cause excessive perspiration.

18 **physics**: natural philosophy, the scientific study of human beings and of the laws that govern the human body.

19 **cocoa**: drinking chocolate made from the cacao (cocoa) bean, sweetened and flavoured. An advertisement published around 1790 for the patent cocoa made by Anna Fry and Son, of Bristol, claims cocoa is recommended by doctors as the best breakfast for 'such who have tender Habits, decayed Health, weak Lungs, or scorbutic Tendencies, being easy of Digestion, affording a fine and light Nourishment, and greatly correcting the sharp Humours in the Constitution'; the advertisement advises adding a little sugar and milk or cream. In fact cocoa was often regarded as a stimulant.

20 **herb-tea**: it was well-established that hot water flavoured with herbs such as camomile or tansey could have a variety of medicinal properties.

21 **coats . . . stomach**: 'coats' are the protective layers of membrane lining the stomach. Butter was seen as potentially harmful to health: 'Butter, though a good article of diet, may be used

too freely . . . To weak stomachs it is hurtful, even in small quantities, and when used freely, it proves prejudicial to the strongest.' Because it went rancid easily it upset the stomach, and bread without butter was recommended particularly for children (*Domestic Medicine*, pp. 662–3).

22 **earthy dross**: the original meaning of 'dross' was the scum thrown off from metals in the process of melting; more generally it was often used to mean impure materiality compared with a purer spirituality, 'common clay'. JA may be remembering Scott's description in *Waverley* of 'a man of earthly mould, after all; a good deal of dirt and dross about him' (vol. 2, ch. 19).

23 **green tea**: tea made from fresh leaves dried immediately after picking (in contrast to black tea, made from leaves fermented by being left in a humid atmosphere for several hours after picking). It was introduced to Britain in the mid seventeenth century. Its health effects were disputed (see n. 24 below).

24 **scientifically**: the joke has a basis in fact. A number of treatises were published in the eighteenth century considering the beneficial or otherwise qualities of tea, both black and green. In 1772, for example, John Lettsom described experiments he had made to monitor the effects of tea on animals, and case studies of human behaviour after taking large quantities of tea. He observed that green tea in particular was 'remarkably relaxing to many persons of tender and delicate constitutions', and had a depressive quality which in a person of melancholy disposition induced 'dejection and melancholy, with loss of memory, tremblings, a proneness to great agitation from the most trifling circumstances, and a numerous train of nervous ailments' (John Coakley Lettsom, *The Natural History of the Tea-Tree, with Observations on the Medical Qualities of Tea, and Effects of Tea-Drinking* (1772), pp. 40, 48). Buchan addressed concerns about the possible ill effects of tea by stating that the real problem was 'imprudent use of it', particularly drinking tea in the morning: 'If . . . persons, after fasting ten or twelve hours, drink four or five cups of green tea without eating almost any bread, it must hurt them. Good tea, taken in a moderate quantity, not too strong, nor too hot, nor drank upon an empty stomach, will seldom do harm' (*Domestic Medicine*, pp. 66–7).

25 **private hand**: a personal letter, delivered by private carrier.

CHAPTER II

1 **catastrophe**: the revolution that produces the resolution and conclusion of a dramatic piece; the denouement. JA wrote 'catastrophée'.

2 **beginning their displays**: that is, acquiring and learning how to show off the accomplishments of music, dancing and drawing which would assist in their gaining husbands.

3 **half mulatto**: a mulatto was the child of a black and a white person, in this context usually a female slave and a male slave-owner; more generally 'mulatto' could mean someone of mixed-race appearance. As half-mulatto, Miss Lambe would, strictly speaking, be a 'quadroon' or 'quarteroon', someone with one-quarter black blood. A mulatto or half-mulatto could be part of a wealthy slave-owner's family and could have a substantial inheritance: see for example 'Miss Swartz, the rich woolly-haired mulatto from St Kitts' (William Thackeray, *Vanity Fair* (1847), vol. 1, ch. 1; the novel is set in the 1810s).

4 **hire of a harp . . . other**: services which a good circulating library would offer: see for example the libraries at Brighton which offered 'an extensive assortment of stationery . . . and . . . let out musical instruments by the week, month or year' (*Guide to Watering Places*, p. 78).

5 **everybody . . . circle**: In *E* the upstart Mrs Elton advises Jane Fairfax to avoid employment 'in a family not moving in a certain circle, or able to command the elegancies of life'; she adds that 'with your superior talents, you have a right to move in the first circle' (vol. 2, ch. 17).

6 **rotatory**: JA spelled the word 'rototary' but Cassandra's copy has 'rotatory', which must be the word intended.

7 **a decline**: the term was used to describe, not merely a general failure of health, but a more specific disease, such as tuberculosis, in which the bodily strength gradually fails.

8 **tonic . . . in**: proprietary pills sold as a business in which people could invest – or have 'property' – in hopes of financial return. Reece's *Medical Guide* gives, among his Family Prescriptions, a recipe for tonic pills which involved mixing a concentrate of Peruvian bark with a preparation of iron, 'gul olibarum' and syrup; he

advises that three of these should be taken twice a day. His 'Ladies Dispensary' includes two boxes in a drawer for 'Ecphractic pill and Tonic pill' (pp. 63, xviii).

9 **lounge**: a place for strolling or lounging about.

10 **upstairs**: in Georgian houses the living-rooms were often on the first floor, with large or full-length windows through which the occupants could see and – as here – be seen, and a balcony outside.

11 **telescope**: the telescope had been introduced by Galileo in 1609 but the astronomical discoveries of William Herschel (1738–1822), knighted in 1816, and his sister Caroline, did much to make astronomy popular in the early years of the nineteenth century as a pastime for both men and women.

CHAPTER 12

1 **a subscription for them**: at a time when there was little organized poor relief much of the responsibility for assisting the poor was a matter of private charitable activity. A subscription was an arrangement whereby people signed up to make a specific contribution to a worthy cause, and the idea was that if prominent people lent their names to the subscription this would encourage others to contribute. In the hard times following the end of the war in 1815 the number of charitable subscriptions increased rapidly, and they were regarded with increasing ambivalence as a result.

2 **a poor woman . . . for her**: Worcestershire is a rural county to the north-west of London, about 100 miles from Hampshire, where Diana lives, and much further from the Sussex coast, a very long distance for charitable intervention, which was usually made on a local basis.

3 **undraw**: unfasten by pulling.

4 **ten guineas . . . five**: either would be a substantial sum in terms of charitable giving, the equivalent of about £600 or £300 today.

5 **charitable repository . . . Burton on Trent**: Burton on Trent was a manufacturing town of about 4000 inhabitants in the county of Staffordshire, about 200 miles north of the Sussex coast. The

charitable repository was the precursor of the modern-day charity shop, as a place where donated goods were sold for the benefit of the poor. Charitable repositories sometimes also offered schooling for the poor, and evidently some had facilities for lodging, probably above the shop: 'Mr and Mrs Chamberlayne are in Bath, lodging at the Charitable Repository,' JA wrote to Cassandra in January 1801, 'I wish the scene may suggest to Mrs C. the notion of selling her black beaver bonnet for the releif of the poor' (*L*, p. 74).

6 **hung . . . York**: Diana Parker's charitable objects are ever more distant; York is about 300 miles north of the south coast. The assizes were the court sessions, held periodically in each county of England, where lawyers who travelled from one session to the next tried civil and criminal cases. A large number of crimes still carried the death penalty, including forgery and theft of foods of relatively small value, and – particularly appropriate to York as a major staging post on the Great North Road between London and Edinburgh – robbing on the highway.

7 **putting them all out**: setting them up in apprenticeships or other ways of earning their own livings, which would require an initial premium to be paid on their behalf.

8 **dip . . . machine**: Miss Lambe is following general medical advice in the timing of her dip: 'Sea-Bathing should be used in general, in the morning before any food has been taken', or, if the constitution 'cannot bear it previous to a light breakfast . . . between breakfast and dinner, but not so soon after the first meal as to interfere with digestion' (Squirrell, *An Essay on Indigestion and Sea Bathing*, p. 66). On the general question of sea-bathing see ch. 1, nn. 21, 24 and 27, and ch. 4, n. 28.

9 **leeches . . . business**: applying leeches (JA spells 'leaches' throughout) was a delicate operation, the best way being 'by retaining them to the skin in a small wine glass, or the bottom of a large pill box, when they will, in general, in a little time, fasten themselves to the skin'. Once the leeches were removed pressure had to be applied to the wound, as leeches inject a blood-thinning agent with their bite and there was a risk that the flow of blood could not be stopped (James Parkinson, *Medical*

Admonitions addressed to families, respecting the practice of Domestic Medicine, and the Preservation of Health, 2 vols. (1799), vol. 2, pp. 487–9).

10 **gig . . . tandem**: a gig is a light two-wheeled carriage drawn by a single horse. A phaeton is a more substantial, but still not heavy, four-wheeled open carriage drawn by a pair of horses. A tandem is a two-wheeled vehicle drawn by two horses harnessed one behind the other. John Thorpe owns, and James Morland hires, a gig, which in each case carries two people in comfort (*NA*, vol. 1, ch. 7). Mrs Gardiner looks forward to driving round the park at Pemberley with Elizabeth in a 'low phæton, with a nice little pair of ponies' (*P&P*, vol. 3, ch. 10).

11 **planted approach**: the road leading to the house has been formally planted with trees on either side for an aesthetic effect that was becoming slightly outmoded by the 1810s.

12 **respectability . . . timber**: large quantities of mature trees were a valuable asset to a country estate, but took many decades to grow, and so their presence indicated good and thoughtful management by the owner of the estate over several generations; conversely the indiscriminate cutting down of timber was a very visible sign of bad or careless management of an estate. In *E* Emma looks with pride at the house and grounds of Mr Knightley's Donwell Abbey, including 'its abundance of timber in rows and avenues, which neither fashion nor extravagance had rooted up' (vol. 3, ch. 6). Strictly speaking, 'timber' denoted mature elm, oak and ash, but its more general meaning included any mature tree that was capable of being used for structural purposes.

13 **proper . . . elms . . . thorns . . . everywhere**: a paling was a solidly constructed fence with stakes driven into the ground, fixed to horizontal rails supported by posts, marking the boundaries of the park and keeping grazing animals secure within it; its presence is another sign of good management of the estate. Elm was one of the trees traditionally grown for its timber, and thorn was a prickly shrub traditionally grown in the English countryside.

14 **usual**: ordinary or everyday. There would be another sitting-room for use on formal occasions.

To Mrs. Hunter of Norwich

1 This spoof is reproduced in a letter of Anna Lefroy to her half-brother James Edward Austen Leigh in December 1864 HRO MS 23M93/97/4/104), which provides our copytext. In the 1860s James Edward was preparing material for the *Memoir*, and collecting information from various members of the family who had known JA. Anna described a summer visit at Chawton, when she had brought novels from the circulating library, and she and her aunt Jane had enjoyed ridiculing them. Among the novels was 'an exceedingly lengthy affair' written by Mrs Hunter of Norwich; 'there was no harm in the book, except that in a most unaccountable manner the same story about the same people, most of whom I think had died before the real story began was repeated 3 or 4 times over. A copy of the note written a few weeks afterwards, in reply to one from "Mrs Hunter" [presumably Anna herself], will give some idea of the state of the case'. And Anna then quotes the JA letter.

Deirdre Le Faye, in her edition of Jane Austen's letters, mentions that at least three other versions of this text exist. A draft of Anna Lefroy's letter was sold at Sotheby's in December 1977 and is in private hands. Anna's daughter Fanny Caroline copied the letter in her 'Family History' with a note saying she had given the original to her cousin Cholmley Austen Leigh (HRO MS 23M93/66/4/1), and also wrote it out on a separate piece of paper (now at the Morgan Library, New York). Both Fanny Caroline's versions include an extra sentence (see below) and other minor changes from the version Anna sent to James Edward. Anna and Fanny Caroline were probably both, therefore, copying direct from an original in JA's hand, which has apparently not survived.

The novel referred to in the anecdote is *Lady Maclairn, the Victim of Villany* (1806), in four volumes (by no means unusually long for the period), by Rachel Hunter (1754–1813), who identified herself on the title pages of this, and several other of her novels, as 'Mrs Hunter of Norwich'. Le Faye has tentatively dated the occasion as 29–31 October 1812 (as in *Letters*, but see Le Faye, 'Jane Austen: More Letters Redated', *Notes and Queries*, 236:3 (September 1991), pp. 306–8).

2 **Threadpaper**: strip of thin soft paper folded in creases in order to hold threads while keeping them separate from each other, a common household item at the time. Anna Lefroy wrote that as she related the circulating library stories to her aunt, JA 'sat busily stitching away at a work of charity' (Anna Lefroy to James Edward Austen Leigh, December 1864).

3 **Mr. Austen**: Anna's father, JA's eldest brother James.

4 **Nicholson or Glover**: Francis Nicholson (1753–1844) and John Glover (1767–1849), British artists best known at the time for their romantic landscapes. John Glover later emigrated to Australia and made a famous contribution to Australian art.

5 **Tarefield Hall . . . Howard's wife**: the first two are locations in the novel. Tarefield Hall (spelt Farefield Hall in volume 4) is a mansion originally in Dutch taste, but overlain with many different styles of architecture and decoration, and surrounded by 'a noble avenue of elms and horse-chestnuts' (vol. 1, p. 140); there is no single description of the mill, but the inside is presented as cosy and attractive. There is no reference to the tomb of Howard's wife, though Mrs Howard has died before the novel begins; it is possible that this is a deliberate mistake by JA.

6 **the worthy Mrs. Wilson**: the Wilsons are modest independent farmers, naturally kind and good-mannered, and living at Tarefield Abbey, now a farm with paying lodgers; Mrs Wilson's dairy and poultry yard are much admired. At this point in the account the two versions in Fanny Caroline Lefroy's hand contain an extra sentence, 'It is impossible for any likeness to be more complete.'

7 **the Flint family . . . Mary Flint's marriage with Howard**: part of the convoluted plot concerns Mary Flint, a great beauty, her marriage to Mr Howard, the local curate, her subsequent disinheritance and their deaths in undeserved poverty. Little is told about the marriage, in contrast to other family events; since both are virtuous characters their marriage would have presumably been exemplary.

8 **conveyance . . . days**: the distance from Norwich in the east of England, to London, was 112 miles, more than twice that between London and Alton, the market town a mile from Chawton. The coach that regularly travelled between Alton and London was

known as Collier's coach, or Falkner's coach, presumably after the current owner or driver. 'Collyer's daily coach with six horses was a sight to see,' wrote Caroline Austen (*My Aunt Jane Austen: A Memoir*, in J. E. Austen-Leigh, *A Memoir of Jane Austen and other Family Recollections* ed. Kathryn Sutherland (Oxford: Oxford University Press, 2002), p. 168; a vivid picture of one of its journeys painted during this period hangs in the museum in Alton. The fanciful phrase 'Car of Falkenstein' imitates the literary-Gothic language of the time: 'car' is an archaic word for carriage; Castle Falkenstein was a ruin in the Tyrol, and Matthew 'Monk' Lewis had recently entitled one of his tales 'The Lord of Falkenstein' (in *Romantic* Tales (1808)); the phrase as a whole is reminiscent of the titles of other Gothic novels such as *The Castle of Wolfenbach* (1793), mentioned in *NA* (vol. 1, ch. 6). Anna wrote in her letter of December 1864 to James Edward: 'The Car of Falkenstein, Collier's but at that time called Falkner's Coach, relates to some earlier nonsense' – possibly the 'few chapters . . . of a mock-heroic story . . . [with] no other foundation than their having seen a neighbour passing on the coach, without having previously known that he was going to leave home . . . written entirely by the Niece only under her [JA's] encouragement' described by Caroline (*My Aunt Jane Austen*, p. 172).

Letters on fiction to Anna Lefroy

At various times in the 1810s JA's nieces Anna and Caroline Austen, and her nephew James Edward Austen, were prompted by their aunt's success to write fiction of their own, and they all asked JA's views on their work. The most sustained attempt was Anna's in the summer and autumn of 1814. Between July and November she sent her draft chapters to JA, Cassandra and Mrs Austen for comment. Anna's marriage to Ben Lefroy in November 1814, and almost immediate pregnancy, interrupted her work, and the fragment was destroyed in the late 1820s (see Introduction, p. ci). JA's letters were preserved within the Lefroy family (that they were actively preserving the comments on fiction is evidenced by the fact that for the first letter only the postscript, containing the first comments on Anna's novel, survives), and were eventually given to St John's College Oxford, which a number of Austens, including Rev. George Austen and his eldest son, Anna's father James, had attended.

The letters are remarkable for their fluency: there are almost no additions or deletions, in contrast to the drafts of 'The Watsons' and 'Sanditon', where writing her own fiction, rather than commenting on her niece's, involved much revision.

1 **mid-July 1814**: the part-letter is undated, but it clearly begins the sequence. Deirdre Le Faye suggests the mid-July date (*L*, p. 266); for her detailed arguments see Deirdre Le Faye, 'Jane Austen: Some Letters Redated', *Notes and Queries*, 232:4 (December 1987), pp. 478–81.

2 **Chawton to Steventon**: Chawton Cottage, where Mrs Austen, Cassandra and JA lived with their friend Martha Lloyd, who was probably away at this time (*Chronology*, p. 484); the rectory at Steventon, the house where JA had been brought up, now occupied by her eldest brother James Austen and his family, including his eldest daughter Anna.

3 **Your G. M.—& A[t] C**: Anna's grandmother and Aunt Cassandra, JA's mother and sister.

4 **the formal part of Lord Orville**: Lord Orville is the hero of Frances Burney's hugely popular novel *Evelina* (1778). JA clearly knew the novel well, and quotes from it frequently in her correspondence. Lord Orville does not speak of himself in the third person but he does refer to the heroine in the third person, when speaking to her, as, for example, 'Must I now apologise to Miss Anville for the liberty of my interference?' (Volume 3, Letter 7).

5 **this Book**: the reference in these letters to Anna's manuscript arriving in 'books' suggests that, like JA herself, Anna was writing her novel on sheets of paper sewn or pinned to make booklets.

6 **"Which is the Heroine?" . . . "Enthusiasm"**: in the early years of the nineteenth century there was a vogue for one-word titles to indicate the moral nature of the novel, as, for example, with Mary Brunton's *Self-Control* (1811) and *Discipline* (1815) and Maria Edgeworth's *Ennui* (1809) and *Patronage* (1814). Titles posing a question were less common though they include Mary Meeke's *Which is the Man?* (1801) and Eleanor Sleath's *Who's the Murderer? or the Mystery of the Forest* (1802). Chapman suggests that the

title 'Enthusiasm' was perhaps given up on the discovery that Mme de Genlis had written *Les Voeux Temeraires ou L'Enthusiasme* (*L*, p. 434); an English translation, *Rash Vows: Or The Effects of Enthusiasm*, was published in 1799.

7 **Dawlish . . . publication**: Dawlish was a small resort on the picturesque Devon coast, and JA's comment here suggests that 'the Dawlish scheme' mentioned in her letter of 8–9 November 1800 (*L*, p. 56) as a prospect for 'next Summer', was carried out in 1802. In 1819 Gore's Library was included in a complimentary description of the 'elegant and commodious Rooms, which comprise a library, ball-room, billiard and reading rooms' (anon., *Scenery on the Southern Coast of Devonshire; Comprising Picturesque Views, at or near the Fashionable Watering Places, Sidmouth, Budleigh Salterton, Exmouth, Dawlish, Teignmouth, and Torquay* (1819), n.p.

8 **no such title as Desborough . . . Barons**: JA states the ranks of the aristocracy in descending order, and correctly points out that there was no such title as Desborough in the early nineteenth century.

9 **Mr W. D. . . . every thing**: members of the Digweed family, friends and neighbours of the Austens. William Francis Digweed, unmarried, lived at Steventon and was therefore a very near neighbour of Anna, who lived at the rectory there. His brother Harry Digweed and his wife, formerly Jane Terry, lived in Alton near Chawton; the frequent communications between the two branches of the family meant that Anna's manuscripts could be conveyed speedily and efficiently between Steventon and Chawton. JA was evidently fond of Mrs Digweed, but also enjoyed parodying her speech and mannerisms, and 'beyond everything' was a favourite phrase: in a letter of 23 June 1816 JA wrote to Anna: 'Mrs Digweed returned yesterday through all the afternoon's rain and was of course wet through, but in speaking of it she never once said "It was beyond everything," which I am sure it must have been' (*L*, p. 315).

10 **your 48 Pages**: if Anna was writing in home-made booklets in the same way as JA, as this suggests, her forty-eight pages compare with JA's eight-page booklets for 'W' and up to eighty-page booklets for 'S'.

11 **indeed**: the obvious word here is 'instead' but the word 'indeed' is as written.

12 **Lyme . . . safe**: Lyme is in fact forty-one miles east of Dawlish along the south coast, a long day's drive by early nineteenth-century coach. Starcross is four, and Exeter thirteen, miles north of Dawlish.

13 **A Country Surgeon . . . rank**: Charles Lyford (1778–1859) was a surgeon in Basingstoke, in partnership with his father John. Charles's cousin Giles King Lyford (1764–1837) practised as a surgeon in Winchester, and attended JA in her last illness in 1817 (*L*, p. 552).

14 **That distinction . . . not**: 'the Honourable' as a prefix to a name would indicate the son or daughter of a peer, but was only used on formal occasions. The rank-conscious Sir Walter Elliot refers to 'Our cousins, Lady Dalrymple and Miss Carteret' but takes care that their cards, giving more formal titles – 'the Dowager Viscountess Dalrymple, and the Hon. Miss Carteret' – are prominently displayed (*P*, vol. 2, ch. 4).

15 **postscript . . . Imitation**: there is no 'PS' in the letters in *P&P* to which this comment self-evidently refers. JA may refer to the device of conveying sudden plot developments mid-letter, as when, after giving news of day-to-day events 'the latter half' of Jane's letter to Elizabeth, 'which was dated a day later, and written in evident agitation', tells of Lydia's elopement (vol. 3, ch. 4); but this may be a more general reference to some part of the content of Anna's manuscript which seems to JA too reminiscent of something in *P&P*.

16 **Russel Square . . . Berkeley S^t^**: Berkeley Street, in fashionable Mayfair, is just under two miles west of Russell Square, a more modest address.

17 **Dawlish . . . apart**: Bath is 110 miles from Dawlish.

18 **the G^t^ House**: at Chawton. The house was owned by JA's brother Edward and was occupied at this time by JA's brother Frank and his family (*Chronology*, p. 486); it was only a short walk from the cottage where Mrs Austen, Cassandra and Jane were living.

19 **the Play . . . that way lately**: perhaps Anna had included scenes in which a performance of a play mirrored the relationships that

were developing between her characters, and JA saw this as too close an echo of the *Lovers' Vows* episode in *MP*. There were also play scenes in Burney's *The Wanderer* and Edgeworth's *Patronage* (both 1814).

20 **Ireland . . . representations**: in both *E*, which JA was writing in 1814, and the much earlier fragment 'The Watsons', Ireland is the 'offstage' location of characters whose removal there causes difficulties for Jane Fairfax and Emma Watson respectively. JA may well also have been conscious that Maria Edgeworth, one of the novelists she praised highly in *NA*, was of an Irish family and wrote knowledgeably and extensively of the Irish and Anglo-Irish gentry and peasantry.

21 **Stick to Bath & the Foresters**: the Austen family knew Bath well; JA had lived there 1801–6 and Anna had visited.

22 **noticed**: commented upon.

23 **Lesley is a noble name**: probably alluding to JA's own earlier use of the name in 'Lesley Castle' ('Juv.', Volume the Second). 'Leslie' was the ancient family name of a number of Scottish peers.

24 **"Bless my Heart" . . . inelegant**: the expression had been quite common in eighteenth-century fiction – it is used, for example, by Mrs Howe in Richardson's *Clarissa* ((1747–8), vol. 6, letter 64) – but by 1814 even Frances Burney, who had been out of England for more than a decade, saw it as associated with lower-class or very old-fashioned characters: in *The Wanderer* (1814) it is used by Mr Gooch, 'a hearty, cherry-cheeked dapper farmer' and the eccentric Mr Giles (vol. 3, bk 5, pp. 44, 66).

25 **returning . . . before Sunday**: the etiquette of making and returning visits was important. See for example 'The Watsons', where Lord Osborne's visit to Mr Watson creates concern because the visit cannot be returned; and the protocols of Harriet Smith visiting the Martins, and the Eltons' post-wedding visiting in *E* (vol. 2, chs. 5, 14).

26 **collecting your People . . . favourably arranged**: this often-quoted comment on the desirable circumstances for a fiction is precisely applicable among her published novels only to *E*, which JA was writing in autumn 1814.

27 **Blue Pantaloons . . . Cocks & Hens**: the tone of this comment suggests an in-joke, but the exact meaning is unclear. In the late

1790s blue pantaloons, deriving from military dress, were associated with fashionable pretension: in George Watson's *Cinthelia* (1797) the heroine's brother 'entered the room in a great coat and blue pantaloons, though the weather was warm' (vol. 1, p. 15); and John Moore described the would-be beau Mr Walker wearing blue pantaloons, 'as he is informed it is the present London mode of dress' (*Mordaunt* (1800), vol. 3, p. 318).

28 **the Papillons**: John Rawstorn Papillon (1763–1837) was rector of Chawton 1801–37; his unmarried sister Elizabeth lived with him as his hostess (*L*, pp. 560–1).

29 **scratching out some of the past**: following JA's own practice with *P & P*: on 29 January 1813 she wrote that she had 'lopt and cropt' the draft (*L*, p. 202).

30 **Newton Priors . . . thought of it**: Newton Priors is a fictional name, though there is a Newton Abbot in Devon; Chapman also noted a Newton Valence and Priors Dean in the Chawton neighbourhood (*L*, p. 436). JA herself created a Willingden Abbots in 'S' (ch. 1). She refers rather flippantly to the blindness of the seventeenth-century writer and radical John Milton.

31 **Tollard Royal**: a small village in South Wiltshire, the home of Ben Lefroy's sister Lucy and her husband Rev. Henry Rice. Anna had visited there in October 1813 (JA to Cassandra Austen, 12 October 1813, *L*, p. 233).

32 **this sad Event**: the death of Charles Austen's wife Fanny Palmer, JA's sister-in-law and Anna's aunt, on 6 September, following the birth of her fourth daughter on 31 August (*FR*, p. 216).

33 **M<u>r</u> D.**: William Digweed, see n. 9 above.

34 **finished**: put the finishing touches to: shoes were often ornamented with ribbons or other decorations, which were fixed by hand.

35 **Ben . . . likes it**: Anna was engaged to marry Ben Lefroy, a younger son of JA's old friend and mentor, 'Madam' Lefroy.

36 **"vortex of Dissipation" . . . opened**: the phrase was recorded as being used by Joseph Addison (1672–1719, see *Anecdotes, Memoirs, Allegories, Essays and Political Fragments, tending to amuse the Fancy, and Inculcate Morality, by Mr. Addison*, 12 vols. (1797), vol. 12, p. 121) but it became popular around 1770 and was indeed very widely used by novelists in the final decades of the

eighteenth century. JA never used the phrase herself, but she did refer to London and Brighton as 'haunts of Dissipation' in 'Lesley Castle' ('Juv.', Volume the Second, Letter the Fourth).

37 **Walter Scott . . . I fear I must**: Walter Scott's long poems on historical, often Scottish, subjects, including *The Lay of the Last Minstrel* (1805) and *The Lady of the Lake* (1810), had been a publishing sensation. His first novel, *Waverley, or 'Tis Sixty Years Since*, was published in July 1814 and four editions were called for before the end of the year. Mrs Austen wrote to Anna that *Waverley* 'has afforded me more entertainment than any Modern production (Aunt Janes excepted) of the novel kind that I have read for a great while' (25 December 1814, reproduced in Le Faye, 'Anna Lefroy and her Austen Family Letters', *Princeton University Library Chronicle*, 62.3, spring 2001 issue (2003)). Scott published his early novels anonymously, and his authorship was not acknowledged for some time, but JA evidently had no doubts about it.

38 **Mrs. West's . . . not**: Jane West (1758–1852) was a popular writer of moral and historical tales. *Alicia de Lacy: An Historical Romance* was published in June 1814.

39 **Miss Edgeworth's**: Maria Edgeworth (1767–1849) was one of the most highly respected novelists of the early nineteenth century. *Patronage*, her most ambitious novel, was published in January 1814, and two further editions were issued before the end of the year. Contemporary readers saw Edgeworth and JA as comparable: commenting on *MP* the Earl of Dudley wrote that JA 'has not so much fine humour as . . . Miss Edgeworth, but she is more skilful in contriving a story, she has a great deal more feeling, and she never plagues you with any chemistry, mechanics, or political economy, which are all excellent things in their way, but vile, cold-hearted trash in a novel' (Earl of Dudley to Mrs Helen Stewart, 11 August 1814: S. H. Romilly, *Letters to 'Ivy' from the first Earl of Dudley* (London: Longman, 1905), p. 250).

40 **30 November 1814**: for dating see Le Faye, *Notes and Queries*, 232.4 (December 1987), pp. 478–81.

41 **London . . . Hendon**: JA was staying with her brother Henry at 23 Hans Place. Anna and her new husband Ben Lefroy were living temporarily in Hendon in North London.

42 **other people . . . rapidly**: meaning herself, as she continued to work on *E* – though according to Cassandra's later record *E* had a relatively short period of composition, from 21 January 1814 to 29 March 1815. On 16 December 1816 JA wrote of' the little bit (two inches wide) of Ivory on which I work with so fine a Brush, as produces little effect after much labour' (*L*, p. 323).

43 **3 before the 3 at Chawton**: 'the 3 at Chawton' must be those booklets mentioned in the 10–18 August letter, when JA comments on reading the second book just sent 'or rather the 5th.'; it seems that JA had mistaken how many books she had seen before then.

44 **history . . . story**: the original letter ends mid-sentence, since a further page is missing. The concluding part of the sentence was given by Fanny Caroline in her 'Family History', either copying from an original now lost or creating a plausible end to the sentence with a note, 'The rest of the letter destroyed'.

Plan of a Novel, according to hints from various quarters

The original autograph manuscript is held at the Morgan Library, New York. A single sheet of paper is folded over to make four writing pages, each 233 mm × 187 mm, and the text ends about three-quarters of the way down the fourth page. This may not be the first draft of the 'Plan' but neither is it a fair copy in the way that 'Lady Susan' is, since there is evidence of authorial revision. The paper is watermarked 1813. Date of composition is not known; it is very likely to have been during or shortly after the exchange of correspondence November–December 1815 and March–April 1816 between JA and James Stanier Clarke, since this provided a major impetus for the 'Plan' (see Introduction, pp. ciii–civ, and explanatory notes below), though nothing in the 'Plan' directly refers to the March–April exchange of letters. After Cassandra Austen's death in 1845 the manuscript evidently came into the possession of Charles Austen's family since it was eventually sold on by his descendants in the 1920s (it is mentioned by Chapman in *TLS*, 14 January 1926 as one of a number of JA-related items 'recently dispersed'); around 1870 it was made available to James Edward Austen Leigh, who published it, in a slightly abbreviated and adapted form, in the second edition of the *Memoir* (1871).

Those named in the margin of the 'Plan'

JA includes as part of the 'Plan' fifteen marginal notes naming eight individuals and 'Many Critics', representing the sources of the 'hints from various quarters'; Austen Leigh refers to them as her 'advisers' (*Memoir* (1871), p. 119). In fact it is likely that some of the names bear a complex relationship to the relevant phrase or expression. JA's numbered links have been replaced by letters to avoid confusion with the explanatory notes.

M^r. Gifford: presumably William Gifford (1756–1826), chief reader for and associate of John Murray, who had become Austen's publisher for *E* (1815); Gifford read and admired *P&P*, and recommended *E*'s publication. There is no record of a meeting or correspondence between JA and Gifford, but given her interest in the practicalities of publishing her novels it is quite possible that they were in contact while *E* was going through the press in the autumn of 1815, or afterwards.

Fanny Knight: (1793–1882), the eldest daughter of JA's brother Edward, whose family had taken the name of Knight in 1812. JA advised Fanny on romantic dilemmas in 1814 and again in 1817. In late 1815, the time of the first letters in the James Stanier Clarke correspondence, Fanny was, like JA, staying with Henry Austen in London, and she was a guest for three weeks at the cottage at Chawton during May 1816.

Mary Cooke: (1781–post-1822), daughter of JA's godfather Rev. Samuel Cooke (1741–1820), whose wife Cassandra was first cousin to JA's mother. JA stayed with the Cookes at their home in Great Bookham, near Leatherhead in Surrey, in the summer of 1814 while she was writing *E* (*FR*, p. 213). See 'Opinions of *Mansfield Park*'.

M^r. Clarke: James Stanier Clarke (1766–1834), domestic chaplain and librarian to the Prince of Wales; he met JA in November 1815 when he showed her round the Prince's library at Carlton House, and was negotiator, on the Prince's behalf, for JA to dedicate *E* to him; his correspondence with JA, in which he suggested new topics for her writing, continued till April 1816. Caroline Austen later wrote that 'My aunt, soon after her visit to *him*, returned home, where the little adventure was talked of for a while with some interest, & afforded some amusement' (*My Aunt Jane Austen*, pp. 176–7). See Introduction, pp. ciii–civ.

M^{r}. Sherer: Rev. Joseph Sherer (1770–1824), vicar of Godmersham, the parish within which the Knights' main residence was located, from 1811 to 1824. JA wrote from Godmersham on 23–24 September 1813, after returning a visit from Mrs Sherer, that 'I like *Mr S.* very much' (*L*, p. 226); later that autumn, however, the Sherers moved to another of his parishes. Mr. Sherer was 'Displeased with my pictures of Clergymen' in *E* (see 'Opinions of *Emma*'), possibly the source of the reference to him in 'Plan'.

M^{rs}. Pearse of Chilton-Lodge: Anne (daughter of John Phillimore, a City of London merchant), wife of John Pearse (1760–1836), Director and then Governor of the Bank of England during the period 1790–1828. In 1800 Pearse had had Chilton Lodge built, in the village of Chilton Foliat, just a few miles from Kintbury, where the Austens' friends the Fowles and the Cravens (see 'M^{rs}. Craven' below) lived.

M^{rs}. Craven: Catherine (née Hughes), the second wife of Rev. John Craven (James Austen's uncle-in-law), a longstanding friend of the Austens, her name appearing frequently in the *Letters* from 1801 onwards. The Cravens lived at Chilton Foliat, and JA would probably have met them during her Kintbury visits. See 'Opinions of *Emma*'.

M^{r}. H. Sanford: Henry Sanford, friend and business associate of Henry Austen in London. In November 1814 JA wrote to Fanny Knight that 'Mr Sanford is to join us at dinner, which will be a comfort, and in the even^{g} . . . he shall tell me comical things & I will laugh at them, which will be a pleasure to both' (30 November 1814, *L*, p. 287). See 'Opinions of *Mansfield Park*' and 'Opinions of *Emma*'.

1 **Plan of a Novel**: Eaton Stannard Barrett's burlesque novel *The Heroine: Adventures of a Fair Romance Reader* was a great success on first publication in 1813, and further editions were published in 1814 and 1815. Barrett made changes on each occasion, and the

third edition – entitled *The Heroine, or, Adventures of Cherubina* – featured the heroine's comment that 'undoubtedly, certain events in the life of every heroine, are predestined; as their regular and unremitting recurrence fully proves. Of these events, the most prominent and indispensable, are: 1st. Her meeting with a hero. 2d. Her loving him, and his loving her. 3d. His rescuing her from peril, at a moment when she fancies him far away. 4th. Her finding every individual with whom she converses, implicated in her plot, and a friend, or a foe, or a near relation. 5th. If of mysterious origin, her being first reduced to extremities; then her discovering her family, and lastly, her attaining riches, rank, and marriage' (vol. 1, letter 4). JA read an earlier edition, which she much enjoyed as 'a delightful burlesque, particularly on the Radcliffe style' (2 March 1814, *L*, p. 256).

2 **according . . . quarters**: James Stanier Clarke encouraged JA to write a kind of fiction particularly to his taste – that is, either about his own past, or about royalty and court life – and recommended that she 'make all your friends send Sketches to help you' (21 December 1815, *L*, p. 307).

3 **Daughter of a Clergyman**: fictional heroines were often daughters of the clergy – see for example Frances Burney's Camilla Tyrold in *Camilla* (1796). None of JA's published novels by the time of the 'Plan' had such heroines, but Catherine Morland in what was eventually published as *NA*, and Emma Watson, in 'The Watsons', were both clergymen's daughters, as was JA herself.

4 **companion . . . the other**: while few novel heroines of the period have living mothers, idealized father-figures are very common; they are men of sensibility and intellectual abilities, usually either gentlemen withdrawn from the world after disappointments, or rural clergymen, or both. See for example Arabella's father the Marquis of — in Charlotte Lennox's *The Female Quixote* (1752), Evelina's guardian Rev. Villars in Frances Burney's *Evelina* (1778) and Laura Montreville's father in *Self-Control.*

5 **Heroine a faultless Character herself**: an accurate description of many novel heroines of the period, but not an ideal that JA followed in her own writing. Elizabeth Bennet confesses to Mr Darcy that 'my behavior to *you* was at least always bordering

on the uncivil, and I never spoke to you without rather wishing to give you pain than not' (*P&P*, vol. 3, ch. 18); Mr Knightley tells Emma that her behaviour to Miss Bates is 'unfeeling' and insolent', that she is 'acting wrong' (*E*, vol. 3, ch. 7). In commenting to Fanny Knight on her 'ideas of Novels and Heroines' JA wrote that 'pictures of perfection as you know make me sick and wicked' and that her new heroine, Anne Elliot, was 'almost too good for me' (23–25 March 1817, *L*, p. 335).

6 **very highly accomplished . . . learn**: it was felt inappropriate for young gentlewomen to learn the classical languages, but French and Italian were widely taught. Caroline Bingley suggests that in order to be considered accomplished, 'A Woman must have a thorough knowledge of music, singing, drawing, dancing, and the modern languages . . . and . . . she must possess a certain something in her air and manner of walking, the tone of her voice, her address and expressions', to which Darcy replies that 'to all this she must add yet something more substantial, in the improvement of her mind by extensive reading' (*P&P*, vol. 1, ch. 8).

7 **Music . . . first stile**: music had been the favoured pursuit of numerous heroines of novels since Charlotte Grandison's love of the piano in Richardson's *Sir Charles Grandison* (1753–4). More recently skill on the harp – admired partly for its sound and partly for the way in which the act of playing enhanced the beauty of the harpist – had been seen as particularly desirable. Emmeline, for example, entrances Delamere by her skill in singing to her own accompaniment on the harp (Charlotte Smith, *Emmeline: the Orphan of the Castle* (1788), vol. 1, ch. 14). Ellis, the heroine of Burney's *The Wanderer* (1814), plays and sings to professional standard, though she is overcome at the thought of using these skills in public to offset her poverty. The dazzling array of musical accomplishments of many heroines is parodied in Barrett's *The Heroine* when Cherubina sits down to play the harp despite knowing nothing about it: 'I suddenly recollected a heroine, who lived in an old castle, with only an old steward, his old wife, and an old lute; and who, notwithstanding, as soon as she stepped into society, played and sang, like angels, by intuition' (letter 26).

8 **The Father . . . his Life**: a typical, and of course implausible, way of introducing the idea of a tale within a tale, and flashback to the events of the previous generation, both very popular during the period, particularly, but not exclusively, in Gothic fiction. The device had been prevalent in the long French romances of the late seventeenth century, and had been satirized in Charlotte Lennox's *The Female Quixote* (1752).

9 **going to sea . . . situations**: Clarke had written, 'Carry your Clergyman to Sea as the Friend of some distinguished Naval Character about a Court—you can then bring foreward . . . many interesting Scenes of Character & Interest' (?21 December 1815, *L*, p. 307). Clarke had himself served as a naval chaplain 1794–9, initially under the captaincy of John Willett Payne, a friend of the Prince of Wales; he had been on the ship that had brought Princess Caroline of Brunswick to England to marry the Prince, and had later taken part in a number of skirmishes against the French. In 1799 he became domestic chaplain, and in 1805 librarian, to the Prince of Wales, and he became historiographer to the king in 1812 (see Chris Viveash, *James Stanier Clarke* (Winchester: Printed by Sarsen Press, 2006), esp. pp. 19–33).

10 **the Benefits . . . due to them**: 'shew dear Madam what good would be done if Tythes were taken away entirely, and describe him burying his own mother—as I did—because the High Priest of the Parish in which she died — did not pay her remains the respect he ought to do' (Clarke to JA, ?21 December 1815, *L*, p. 307). Tithes are the taxes due to the parish priest of the tenth part of the annual produce of the parish; the change which was recommended was not likely to be abolishing the tax, but allowing it to be commuted to a cash sum. Mrs Anne Clarke, James's mother, had died in 1802. At her funeral James 'rushed forward and accused the rector of the parish, Mathias D'Oyley, of not showing his mother's earthly remains the respect they demanded'. Rev. D'Oyley was apparently indignant and the congregation astonished, but James insisted that the rector leave the church, and he finished the funeral service himself (Viveash, *James Stanier Clarke*, p. 36). In publishing a version of the 'Plan' in the *Memoir* Austen Leigh omitted all reference to the incident.

11 **a very literary turn . . . his own**: Clarke had suggested that the 'English clergyman of the present day' about whom JA might write would be 'Fond of, & entirely engaged in Literature—no man's Enemy but his own' (16 November 1815, *L*, p. 297). Clarke was author of a series of publications on naval matters. The phrase 'nobody's Enemy but his own' has a long literary pedigree: most famous perhaps is Sophia Western's opinion that young Tom, 'tho' an idle, thoughtless, rattling Rascal, was no-body's Enemy but his own' (*Tom Jones*, Bk 4, ch. 5), but before Fielding the phrase had already been in use for more than a century, including the *Tatler*'s description of a gentleman 'who had good Humour to a Weakness, and was that Sort of Person, of whom it is usually said, He is no Man's Enemy but his own' (*Tatler*, No. 23, Tuesday 31 May to Thursday 2 June 1709). 'Enthusiasm' was a word often used of religious fervour, and is mentioned by Clarke in recommending JA to write about 'the Habits of Life and Character and enthusiasm of a Clergyman' (16 November 1815, *L*, p. 296).

12 **a young Woman . . . acquaintance**: while some heroines of the mid eighteenth century, such as Cynthia in Sarah Fielding's *Adventures of David Simple* (1744), could be praised for their wit, softer, more submissive heroines were later more admired. Charlotte Grandison's talent for 'raillery' is a double-edged quality, and is tamed by the responsibilities of wifehood and motherhood; later plots required a passive and persecutable female – Frances Burney's heroines, for example, most often respond to verbal or even physical aggression with shocked or helpless silence. Heroines were often very young, and worldly-wise women, as, for example, Mrs Arlbery or Mrs Berlinton in Burney's *Camilla* (1796), were regarded with suspicion. 'What a wicked sort of a sprite is a female wit,' declares Sir Sedley Clarendel in *Camilla*: 'breathing only in mischief! a very will'o'the-wisp, personified and petticoated, shining but to lead astray. Dangerous past all fathom!' (Bk 5, ch. 6).

13 **vile acts . . . unrelenting passion**: a frequent plot device of the time, the most notable examples being Delamere in *Emmeline*, who will not accept the heroine's rejection and eventually gets himself killed in a duel over her, and Hargrave in *Self-Control*,

who, piqued to obsession by the heroine's rejection of him, follows her wherever she goes, and abducts her to Canada.

14 **no sooner settled . . . retire to another**: Gothic fictions were often set in Italy or the south of France, and characters frequently travelled between continental countries; but the general theme of flight and pursuit common in novels of the period led to general restlessness of movement among characters.

15 **the Good . . . Humanity left in them**: the novels JA is burlesquing here depend for their effects on fast-moving plots, and characterization is usually very sketchy, so that the persecuted heroine meets evil after evil, until she is rescued by figures of idealized goodness. Violent Gothic villains have their equivalents, in the novels of Burney and others, in those who exercise social cruelties in more realistic contemporary contexts. In *NA* Catherine Morland grapples with the difference between Gothic characters and real personalities: 'Among the Alps and Pyrenees, perhaps, there were no mixed characters. There, such as were not as spotless as an angel, might have the dispositions of a fiend. But . . . among the English, she believed, in their hearts and habits, there was a general though unequal mixture of good and bad' (vol. 2, ch. 10). There had long been concern about the dangers of representing 'mixed' characters 'for the sake of following Nature', on the grounds that 'as we accompany them through their Adventures with Delight, and are led by Degrees to interest ourselves in their Favour, we lose the Abhorrence of their Faults' (Samuel Johnson, *Rambler*, 4 (1751)).

16 **all perfection of course**: inevitably a reference to Richardson's Sir Charles Grandison, frequently described as without fault, but also to a number of other idealized heroes in Gothic and domestic novels of the period.

17 **excess of refinement**: perhaps alluding particularly to Burney's heroes. In *Camilla* Edgar Mandelbert, encouraged by his tutor Dr Marchmont, delays proposing marriage to Camilla through the five volumes of the novel because he is not quite sure she will be a steady enough wife for him; in *Cecilia* (1782), Mortimer Delvile will not give up his family name and take up Cecilia's in order to marry her, as her father's will requires him to do in order for her to keep her fortune.

18 **anti-hero**: according to the *OED* the word is first used in Steele's essays *The Lover* (1715), though there it is spelt 'anti-heroe'; only in the reprint of the essays in 1789 and 1797 is the word spelt 'anti-hero' (Sir Richard Steele, *The Lover; to which is added The Reader* (1789), p. 37 and (1797), p. 8).

19 **often . . . starved to death**: the most obvious reference is Laura Montreville in *Self-Control*, who tries to earn money to support herself and her seriously ill father by selling her paintings, and goes without food herself in order to make sure her father has something to eat, so that when she faints 'The unfeeling landlady immediately expressed her opinion that Miss Montreville had died of famine' (ch. 17). Laura is not cheated and defrauded of her hire – indeed, attempts are made to pay her more than her paintings are worth in order to give her charitable assistance – but Ellis in *The Wanderer* finds it impossible to make her wealthy but unfeeling clients pay for harp lessons she has given them.

20 **hunted . . . humblest Cottage**: novelists enjoyed reducing their heroines to extremes of indigence before rescuing them to riches; see for example Burney's Cecilia in *Cecilia* and Ellis in *The Wanderer*.

21 **Kamschatka**: a remote area of present-day Russia, which was just beginning to become known in the West through accounts of voyages, including *A Compendious History of Captain Cook's Last Voyage* (1784), Jean Baptiste, Baron de Lesseps, *Travels in Kamtschatka, during the years 1787 and 1788* (English translation 1790), and Jean François de Galaup, comte de La Pérouse, *Voyage round the World* (English translation, 1798). The traveller Archibald Campbell follows his predecessors in painting a bleak picture of the country, the principal seaport 'nothing more than a miserable village' and the country around 'perfectly barren, and no cultivation of any kind is to be seen, except one or two gardens near the town'; travel is by sledge in the winter and in the summer by light boat, which can be lifted and carried over river rapids (Archibald Campbell, *Voyage round the World, from 1806 to 1812: in which Japan, Kamschatka, the Aleutian Islands, and the Sandwich Islands, were visited* (1815), pp. 35–9).

22 **The poor . . . Enthusiasm**: it frequently happens that the father dies while the father and daughter are in exile, and that the death

is accompanied by fine sentiments: see for example the death of St Aubert in Ann Radcliffe's *The Mysteries of Udolpho* (1795), vol. 1, ch. 7 and that of Captain Montreville in *Self-Control* (ch. 17).

23 **runs . . . Hero himself**: in *The Heroine* Cherubina talks of the hero's 'rescuing her from peril, at a moment when she fancies him far away' as one of the 'most prominent and indispensable' of the 'events in the life of every heroine [which] are predestined; as their regular and unremitting recurrence fully proves' (Letter IV).

24 **name . . . P&P**: that is, presumably, a title concerning moral qualities. Similar titles would include Mary Brunton's *Self-Control* and *Discipline* (1815), Maria Edgeworth's *Ennui* (1809) and *Patronage* (1814), and the first proposed title of the novel begun in 1814 by JA's niece Anna, 'Enthusiasm' – regarded by JA as 'something so very superior that every common Title must appear to disadvantage' (see p. 216).

Opinions of *Mansfield Park*

The manuscript descended through Charles Austen's branch of the family, and is now held in the British Museum. The paper is watermarked 1813. The 'opinions' were evidently collected in the months following publication of *MP* in May 1814: JA had earlier recorded in her letters a number of responses to *P&P*, and it seems likely that this prompted a more organized collection for her next novel. The reference to 'Anna' suggests that her opinion was written down before Anna married Ben Lefroy in November 1814 (in the 'Opinions of *Emma*' Anna is listed as 'Mrs. B. Lefroy'). It seems likely that JA stopped adding to her list in late November 1814: she recorded, probably on 24 November, that Mrs Creed's opinion (the last on the list), had been added; and on 26 November JA mentions a comment from Charles Haden which is not included on the list.

1 **F. W. A.**: JA's brother Frank Austen (1774–1865).

2 **Mr K.**: JA's brother Edward Knight (1767–1852, born Edward Austen, took the name Knight 1812).

3 **Edward & George**: JA's nephews, the two eldest of Edward Knight's six sons, born 1794 and 1795.

4 **Fanny Knight**: JA's niece, Edward Knight's eldest daughter (1793–1882). See 'Plan of a Novel', pp. 226–9.

5 **Anna**: JA's niece (1793–1872), daughter of James Austen, m. Benjamin Lefroy November 1814.

6 **M^{rs}. James Austen**: JA's eldest brother's second wife (1771–1843), born Mary Lloyd, sister of Martha (see below); JA often referred to her as Mrs James Austen or Mrs JA to distinguish her from another Mary, married to her brother Frank (Mrs FA). JA did not always find Mrs JA congenial, but appreciated her kindness later, during her last illness.

7 **Miss Clewes**: Miss Clewes was governess to Edward Knight's children from 1813 to 1820. When Miss Clewes was first appointed JA wrote that she 'seems the very Governess they have been looking for these ten years . . . And is not it a name for Edward to pun on?—is not a Clew a Nail?' (9 February 1813, *L*, p. 205).

8 **Miss Lloyd**: Martha Lloyd (1765–1843), sister of Mrs James Austen (above), lived with JA and her sister and mother from 1807, and continued to live with Cassandra after the deaths of JA and Mrs Austen until in 1828 she became Frank Austen's second wife.

9 **My Eldest Brother**: Rev. James Austen (1765–1819).

10 **Edward**: James Edward Austen (1798–1874), James and Mary's son, usually called Edward. He later took the surname 'Leigh' in order to inherit family estates and as James Edward Austen Leigh was author of the *Memoir* (1870, 1871).

11 **M^{r}. B. L.**: Benjamin Lefroy (1791–1829), son of JA's old friend Madam Lefroy, who married JA's niece Anna (see above) in November 1814.

12 **Miss Burdett**: probably Frances, the younger sister of Sir Francis Burdett, a radical MP of the time; 'I should like to see Miss Burdett very well, but that I am rather frightened by hearing that she wishes to be introduced to *me*' JA wrote on 24 May 1813 (*L*, p. 212), and 'Miss Burdett' is mentioned again in August 1814 as part of the Austens' social circle in London.

13 **M^{rs}. James Tilson**: Frances Sanford (1777–1823), wife of James Tilson, a partner with Henry Austen in the London bank of Austen, Maude and Tilson. The Tilsons met the Austens socially,

and Mrs Tilson's name first appears in JA's correspondence in 1808 (*L*, p. 571). She continued to correspond with JA through the 1810s and may have been the intended recipient of JA's last known letter on 28–29 May 1817 (*FR*, pp. 249–50 and *L*, pp. 343, 468).

14 **Fanny Cage**: cousin, contemporary (1793–1874) and close friend of Fanny Knight; she was brought up by her grandmother Lady Bridges, Edward Knight's mother-in-law, and spent a lot of time with the Knight family (*L*, p. 504).

15 **M^{r}. and M^{rs}. Cooke**: Rev. Samuel Cooke (1741–1820), rector of Cotsford, Oxfordshire, and vicar of Great Bookham, Surrey, godfather to JA; his wife Cassandra Leigh (1744–1826) was a first cousin of JA's mother, and a published author through *Battleridge, A Historical Tale founded on Facts* (1799). On 14 June 1814 JA wrote to Cassandra that Mr and Mrs Cooke 'admire Mansfield Park exceedingly. Mr Cooke said "it is the most sensible Novel he ever read"—and the manner in which I treat the Clergy, delights them very much' (*L*, pp. 508–9, 263).

16 **Mary Cooke**: daughter of Mr and Mrs Cooke (above). See 'Plan of a Novel'.

17 **Miss Burrel**: possibly a relative either of Peter Burrell, first Baron Gwydir (1754–1820), who married Lady Priscilla Bertie (1761–1828) – the Berties were friends of the Austens, and Lady Priscilla's uncle, the Duke of Ancaster, was godfather to Anna Lefroy – or of Litellus Burrell (1753–1827), an army staff officer and protégé of Warren Hastings, godfather of Henry Austen's wife Eliza.

18 **M^{rs}. Bramstone**: Mary Chute (1763–1822) married Wither Bramston in 1783; they later lived at Oakley Hall, Oakley, near Steventon, where George Austen was rector till 1805, and had known JA since her childhood (*L*, pp. 499–500, 507). 'Mrs Bramstone is the sort of woman I detest,' JA wrote to Cassandra on 24 January 1813 (*L*, p. 200).

19 **M^{rs}. Augusta Bramstone**: Augusta Bramston (1747–1819), Wither Bramston's sister, unmarried but accorded title of 'Mrs' as a matter of courtesy.

20 **The families at Deane**: the Harwood family had been living at Deane House, next to the church, for generations, and were friendly with the Austen family from the time when Rev. George Austen and his new wife lived in Deane parsonage 1764–8. Charles Harwood (1783–1855) and his family lived in a farmhouse near the village. 'Mrs Anna Harwood' refers to Betty Anna Maria Harwood (1751–1838), unmarried but accorded the courtesy title 'Mrs' (*L*, p. 599).

21 **The Kintbury Family**: Kintbury is a village in Berkshire, west of London, on the River Kennet. From 1798 its vicar was Fulwar Craven Fowle (1764–1840), the eldest of four brothers, all of whom had been pupils of Rev. George Austen at Steventon. His brother Tom Fowle had been engaged to Cassandra, but had died in 1797 before their marriage could take place. Fulwar was married to his first cousin Eliza Lloyd (1768–1839), sister of Martha and Mary (see above), and they had eight children. JA and Cassandra were in regular touch with the family, and are known to have visited Kintbury, though no visit is recorded in 1814 (*L*, pp. 524–5, 551).

22 **Mr. Egerton the Publisher**: Thomas Egerton had published JA's first three novels; he had bought the copyright of *P & P* but, either because he had less confidence in the next novel or because JA preferred not to sell the copyright, he issued *MP*, like *S & S*, at the author's cost. JA did not publish with him again; for her next novel, *E*, she moved to John Murray.

23 **Lady Rob: Kerr**: Mary Gilbert (1780–1861) married Lord Robert Kerr in 1806. In September 1813 JA wrote to Cassandra that their brother Henry, then in Scotland, had revealed her authorship of *P&P* to 'Lady Robert', who was 'delighted' with it, 'and really *was* so as I understood before she knew who wrote it' (15 September 1813, *L*, p. 340).

24 **Miss Sharpe**: Anne Sharp or Sharpe was governess to Edward Austen's children at Godmersham 1804–6, before resigning through ill health. She continued to correspond with both JA and Cassandra. On 3 November 1813 JA reported to Cassandra that she had had 'such sweet flattery from Miss Sharp!', presumably about *P&P*, and that 'She is an excellent kind friend'

(*L*, p. 250). Anne visited Chawton in June 1815, and one of JA's last extant letters, written on 22 May 1817, was to 'my dearest Anne' (*L*, p. 340).

25 **Mrs. Carrick**: mentioned in JA's letter of 3 November 1813, from Godmersham, as giving JA the information of being 'read & admired in Ireland too'. Le Faye suggests that she might be a friend of Henry's from the time of his military service in Dublin at the turn of the century, and just possibly Charity, daughter of Pierse Creagh of Dangan, Co. Clare, who married a Gerald Carrick (*L*, pp. 250, 505, private communication).

26 **Mr. J. Plumptre**: John Pemberton Plumptre (1791–1864). The Plumptres lived at Fredville in Kent, and were friendly with the Knights at nearby Godmersham. In 1814 Fanny Knight considered marrying Plumptre, but eventually decided against doing so partly because of his serious disposition and strict religious views (*L*, p. 563). Fanny sought JA's advice and letters survive from late 1814 in which JA discusses the pros and cons of the match, and more generally the importance of love in marriage (*L*, pp. 278–82, 285–7).

27 **Sir James Langham & Mr. H. Sanford**: Sir James Langham (1766–1833) and Henry Sanford, Henry Austen's friend and business associate (see 'Plan of a Novel'), were cousins.

28 **Alethea Bigg**: Alethea (1777–1847) and her sisters Elizabeth and Catherine had been friends of JA and Cassandra from girlhood. Their family home was Manydown Park, near Basingstoke, where JA and Cassandra often visited. It was here that their brother Harris Bigg-Wither proposed to JA in December 1802, though JA's decision to retract her acceptance did not harm the friendship with his sisters. In 1814 Alethea went to live with her now widowed sister Elizabeth Heathcote in the Cathedral Close at Winchester; JA visited them in December 1814, and they offered support when JA returned to Winchester in her final illness (*FR*, p. 221).

29 **Charles**: JA's youngest brother Charles Austen (1779–1852), a naval captain, a widower since September 1814.

30 **Mrs. Dickson**: possibly the same person mentioned in two JA letters of 1807, in which Mrs Dickson is described as undertaking

to send a christening dress for the first child of Frank Austen and Mary Gibson (8 January 1807, *L*, p. 115).

31 **Mrs. Lefroy**: Sophia, wife of John Henry George Lefroy, usually called George (1782–1823), eldest son of JA's old friend Madam Lefroy, and elder brother of Ben (see above). George succeeded his father as rector of Ashe, near Steventon, in 1806, and JA visited the Lefroys there in January 1815 (*FR*, p. 221).

32 **Mrs. Portal**: wife of William Portal (1755–1846), who owned Ashe Park, near Steventon (*L*, p. 564). JA visited the Portals just before visiting the Lefroys at Ashe in January 1815 (see above) (*FR*, p. 221).

33 **Lady Gordon**: Harriet Finch (d. 1821), wife of Sir Jenison Gordon (1748–1831), of Haverholm Priory, Lincolnshire. Her brother George Finch-Hatton owned Eastwell Park near Ashford, Kent, and Sir Jenison and Lady Gordon were there when JA visited while staying at Godmersham in August 1805 (*L*, pp. 106, 438, 502).

34 **Mrs. Pole**: possibly Felizarda, daughter of Richard Buller, who married Charles Pole, a director of the Bank of England 1796–1818, and therefore possibly a connection of Henry Austen. Another Richard Buller, son of Rev. William Buller, Bishop of Exeter, was one of George Austen's pupils in the 1780s, which might provide a family connection.

35 **Adml. Foote**: Edward James Foote (1767–1833), a naval officer and friend of Frank Austen from Southampton days. JA wrote to Cassandra on 7 January 1807 that he was 'good-humoured and pleasant' and 'gives us all the most cordial invitation to his house in the country' (*L*, p. 115). His marriage to Mary Patton in 1803 prompted James Leigh Perrot's epigram on their names (see p. 732).

36 **Mrs. Creed**: Catherine Herries, m. 1813 Henry Knowles Creed, possibly the same 'H. Creed' who was a neighbour of Henry Austen in Hans Place, Chelsea, in 1815. JA mentioned 'the Creeds of Hendon' dining in Hans Place on 17 October 1815, and afterwards pronounced them 'agreable People' (*L*, pp. 291, 293). In a letter to Anna, which Le Faye dates as probably 24 November 1814, JA wrote that 'Mrs Creed's opinion is gone down on my list' (*L*, pp. 282–3).

Opinions of *Emma*

The manuscript is held at the British Library, and the paper is watermarked 1813. *E* was published in December 1815, and it is likely that JA began to collect opinions of the novel shortly afterwards, as she had done with *MP*. In a letter of 20–21 February 1817 JA refers to receiving Mrs Cage's views (see n. 33 below), which suggests she was adding to her list at that date. There is still plenty of room on the last page of the manuscript for more 'opinions' – as it is, two more responses are recorded than for *MP*.

1 **Captn. Austen**: JA's brother Frank. See 'Opinions of *Mansfield Park*'.

2 **M^{rs}. F. A.**: Mary Gibson married Frank Austen in July 1806. She died in 1823 at the birth of their eleventh child.

3 **M^{rs}. J. Bridges**: Charlotte, younger daughter of successful barrister Sir Henry Hawley, married Rev. Brook John Bridges, brother of Edward Austen's wife Elizabeth, in 1810 (*L*, p. 501). Mrs. Bridges was at Godmersham when news reached Fanny Knight of JA's death in 1817.

4 **Miss Sharp**: Anne Sharp or Sharpe; see 'Opinions of *Mansfield Park*'.

5 **Fanny K.**: Fanny Knight; see 'Plan of a Novel'.

6 **M^{r}. & M^{rs}. J. A.**: JA's eldest brother James and his wife Mary. See 'Opinions of *Mansfield Park*'.

7 **Edward**: since his view is set down after that of James and Mary Austen, probably their son James Edward rather than JA's brother Edward or *his* son Edward Knight. See 'Opinions of *Mansfield Park*'.

8 **Miss Bigg**: see 'Opinions of *Mansfield Park*'.

9 **Miss Lloyd**: Martha Lloyd. See 'Opinions of *Mansfield Park*'.

10 **M^{rs}. and Miss Craven**: Rev. John Craven, uncle to the Lloyd sisters, Martha, Mary and Eliza, married Catherine Hughes in 1779; they lived at Barton Court near Kintbury. After his death in 1804 Mrs Craven lived in nearby Chilton Foliat and later Speen Hill. Her only daughter was Charlotte Elizabeth (1798–1877).

11 **Fanny Cage**: see 'Opinions of *Mansfield Park*'.

12 **Mr. Sherer**: Rev. Joseph Sherer, vicar of Godmersham. See 'Plan of a Novel'.

13 **Miss Bigg**: Alethea Bigg. See 'Opinions of *Mansfield Park*'.

14 **The family at Upton Gray . . . Mrs. Beaufoy**: John Hanbury Beaufoy (1762–1836) was Lord of the Manor of the village of Upton Grey, seven miles north of Chawton, 1800–25. His wife had been born Agnes Payne. The Beaufoys' son John Henry was killed at the Battle of Talavera in 1809; they had at least one other son, Charles, and a daughter Louisa. 'Family' could also include other relatives or members of the household.

15 **Mr. & Mrs. Leigh Perrot**: JA's maternal uncle James Leigh (1735–1817) added the name of Perrot in 1751 in order to inherit a family estate; he married Jane Cholmeley (1744–1836) in 1764 (*L*, pp. 549, 507). JA copied out at least one of his verses (see p. 732).

16 **Countess Craven**: Louisa Brunton (?1785–1860) was a professional actress until she married Lord Craven in 1807. Lord Craven was a distant cousin of the Lloyd sisters, Martha, Mary and Eliza, and his estate was at Ashdown Park near Kintbury, where Eliza (1768–1839) lived, having married her first cousin Rev. Fulwar Craven Fowle in 1788 (*L*, pp. 511–12, 551).

17 **Mrs. Guiton**: possibly the wife of J. Guiton of Little Park Place, near Fareham, Hants; these Guitons could have been friends of the Austens' Butler-Harrison cousins in Southampton and might have met the Austens in their Southampton days (Le Faye, private communication).

18 **Mrs. Digweed**: the Digweeds and the Terrys were neighbouring families to the Austens at Steventon. Harry Digweed (1771–1848) was married to the 'amiable and feather-brained' Jane Terry (1776–1860). They lived in Alton, near Chawton, in the 1810s, and Mrs Digweed spent much time with the Austen women. JA enjoyed mocking Mrs Digweed's expressions of speech: on 23 June 1816 she reported to Anna Lefroy that Mrs Digweed had got very wet in rain, but 'never once said "It was beyond everything," which I am sure it must have been' (*L*, p. 315).

19 **Miss Terry**: presumably Mary Terry, who after her sister Jane's marriage to Harry Digweed would be the eldest unmarried daughter of the Terry family of Dummer (*L*, p. 577).

20 **Henry Sanford**: see 'Plan of a Novel' and 'Opinions of *Mansfield Park*'.

21 **M^r. Haden**: Charles Haden (1768–1824) was doctor to the Austens in London from October 1815, and immediately became a social visitor: on 26 November JA wrote to Cassandra that 'Mr. H. is reading Mansfield Park for the first time & prefers it to P&P', a comment that presumably came too late for inclusion in 'Opinions of *Mansfield Park*'; she added that he brought 'good Manners & clever conversation' to their evening entertainment, and speculated light-heartedly about a possible flirtation with Fanny Knight (*L*, pp. 291, 301, 530, 531).

22 **Miss Isabella Herries**: a daughter (d. 1870) of Col. Charles Herries, of Cadogan Place, Sloane Street (*L*, p. 535). JA records dining with the 'Herrieses' – 'a large family party—clever & accomplish'd' – on 17 October 1815 (*L*, p. 291). Isabella's sister Catherine, who was married to Henry Creed, offered an opinion on *MP*.

23 **Miss Harriet Moore**: possibly a niece or granddaughter of one of Henry Austen's business friends in London (*L*, pp. 528, 557). In 1814 Harriet and her sister Eliza were on visiting terms at Henry's house in Henrietta Street, where JA was staying with her brother, and for a time JA saw Harriet as a possible wife for the recently widowed Henry (*L*, pp. 252, 271).

24 **Countess Morley**: Frances Talbot (1782–1857) m. 1809 John Parker, Lord Boringdon, created Earl of Morley in 1815. For a time some people believed her to have written *S&S* and *P&P* (*FR*, p. 207). JA sent her a copy of *E* on publication (*L*, p. 308). See *A Life of Mary Russell Mitford, Related in a Selection from her Letters to her Friends* (1870), vol. 1, p. 41, Rev. W. A. W. Jarvis, 'Jane Austen and the Countess of Morley', *Reports of the Jane Austen Society*, 4 (1986–95), pp. 6–14, 79, and Chris Viveash, 'Lady Morley and "the Baron so Bold"', *Persuasions*, 14 (1992), 53–6.

25 **M^r. Cockerell**: possibly the architect Samuel Pepys Cockerell (1753–1827), who had remodelled Daylesford House for Warren Hastings 1789–93, and could have had a connection with the Austens through Hastings's goddaughter Eliza, Henry Austen's wife. Le Faye suggests that Samuel Cockerell also had

property in Kent, which would explain why his views were conveyed through Fanny (private communication.)

26 **Mrs. Dickson**: see 'Opinions of *Mansfield Park*'.

27 **Mrs. Brandreth**: not yet identified, though possibly a relative of Henry Brandreth, a landowner of Houghton Hall, Ampthill, Bedfordshire.

28 **Mr. B. Lefroy**: Benjamin Lefroy, see 'Opinions of *Mansfield Park*'.

29 **Mrs. B. Lefroy**: married in November 1814, Anna was presumably by now fully established as Mrs Ben Lefroy and therefore merits a formal reference even from a friendly aunt.

30 **Mrs. Lefroy**: see 'Opinions of *Mansfield Park*'.

31 **Mr. Fowle**: see 'Opinions of *Mansfield Park*', 'the Kintbury family' and Lord Craven above.

32 **Mrs. Lutley Sclater**: Penelope Lutley-Sclater (?1752–1843), unmarried but given the courtesy title of 'Mrs', lived at Tangier Park, near Manydown and not far from Steventon.

33 **Mrs. C. Cage**: wife of Rev. Charles Cage (d.1848), brother to Lewis Cage, who had married the sister of JA's brother Edward's wife, and therefore a distant family connection of JA. Her name first appears in JA's extant letters in 1801. On 20–21 February 1817 JA wrote to Fanny Knight that 'I am very fond of Mrs C. Cage, for reasons good. Thank you for mentioning her praise of Emma &c' (*L*, p. 330).

34 **Mrs. Wroughton**: not yet identified. A Rev. Philip Wroughton is recorded as living at Woolley Park, Berks., not far from Newbury, so possibly known to JA through the Cravens and Fowles (Le Faye, private communication).

35 **Sir J. Langham**: see 'Opinions of *Mansfield Park*'.

36 **Mr. Jeffrey**: Francis Jeffrey (1773–1850), influential editor of the *Edinburgh Review* 1802–29. The *Edinburgh Review* was published by Archibald Constable, who had informal links with John Murray, the publisher of *E*, and JA may have heard of Jeffrey's response through John Murray or William Gifford.

37 **Miss Murden**: a relative of the Austens' friends the Fowles of Kintbury. Her mother was Christiana Fowle (1723–1808). She is mentioned in JA's first extant letter of January 1796. By 1808 she was living in straitened circumstances in Southampton; JA hopes for her comfort: 'at her age perhaps one may be as friendless

oneself, & in similar circumstances quite as captious' (28 December 1808, *L*, p. 161). Later she lived at Kintbury. She died in 1817.

38 **Capt. C. Austen**: JA's brother Charles. He had been sent a copy while serving in the Eastern Mediterranean (George Holbert Tucker, *A History of Jane Austen's Family* (Stroud: Carcanet, 1983), p. 187).

39 **M^rs. D. Dundas**: Janet Whitley Dundas, only daughter of Charles Dundas, MP for Berkshire 1794–1832, who, through his wife, inherited Barton Court near Kintbury, where the Austens' friends the Fowles lived. Janet married her cousin, naval captain James Deans, in 1808, and the couple took the married name of Deans-Dundas (*L*, p. 518).

POEMS

'This little bag'

Clergyman's widow Mrs Martha Lloyd, and her daughters Martha and Mary, became great friends of the Austens when they rented from Rev. George Austen the parsonage at Deane, a small village just north of Steventon, from 1789 to 1792. When they left Deane to move to Ibthorpe, about fourteen miles away to the west, JA made, and presented to Mary Lloyd, a 'housewife' ('huswife') or sewing kit – 'furnished with minikin needles and fine thread. In the housewife is a tiny pocket, and in the pocket is enclosed a slip of paper, on which, written as with a crow quill', is the poem (*Memoir* (1870), pp. 123–4). JA would have made the needlecase herself, as she did the handkerchiefs she later gave to Alethea Bigg (see 'To Miss Bigg', below): 'Her needlework both plain and ornamental was excellent, and might almost have put a sewing machine to shame,' commented James Edward Austen Leigh in the *Memoir* (1870), p. 123). The gift was a practical one, but Mary seems not to have used it – 'having been never used and carefully preserved, it is as fresh and bright as when it was first made' (p. 124). Mary married JA's brother James in 1797; their son, James Edward Austen Leigh, was the first to publish the poem.

The bag and its poem have remained in the hands of James Edward's direct descendants, the present owner being Mrs Freydis

Jane Welland. The bag is of cotton, possibly once white but now beige, with gold and black zigzag stripes. It unrolls to reveal a needle case of red (with one small needle still in it), giving the appearance of lips within which the slip of paper with the words is placed. In 1982 the then owner, Joan Austen-Leigh, wrote an article on the bag in *Country Life* (28 October 1982, p. 1323), which reproduced a picture of the bag and the poem, and described how the slip of paper, 51 mm × 77 mm in size, had been folded 'in accordian pleats' and doubled over to fit into the pocket of 26 mm × 13 mm. The slip of paper provides our copytext.

'Miss Lloyd has now sent to Miss Green'

This poem, and its reply from Mrs Austen taking Miss Green's part (see Appendix F), must have been written in late April/early May 1805. The Lloyd family were longstanding friends of the Austens (see note to 'This little bag' above), and in April 1805 Cassandra was visiting them at Ibthorpe to help nurse Mrs Lloyd in her final illness. Writing to her sister from Gay Street, Bath, where the Austens were then living, JA was evidently trying to sound cheerful: 'The Nonsense I have been writing . . . seems out of place at such a time; but I will not mind it, it will do you no harm, & nobody else will be attacked by it' (8–11 April 1805, *L*, p. 100). Mrs Lloyd, who had been failing in mind and body for some time, died on 16 April (*FR*, p. 148), and the poems must have been written shortly afterwards. It is not known whether they were kept by Mrs Austen and JA at Bath, or whether they were sent as more 'Nonsense' to try to cheer up Cassandra, who remained at Ibthorpe for some time after Mrs Lloyd's death, as well as Martha. They eventually came into the possession of Anna Lefroy (James Austen's daughter by his first wife Anne Mathew).

The original manuscript for the poems has not survived, but Anna included them in a book of notes on her family history, written probably between 1855 and 1870, known as the Lefroy MS. The Lefroy MS is now owned by descendants of Francis Austen: this provides our copytext. The poems were first published, from this source, in a letter from Deirdre Le Faye to the *TLS* on 20 February 1987, with 'See they come, post haste from Thanet' (see below), which was also included in the Lefroy MS. The title given in the Lefroy MS, 'Lines *supposed* to have been sent to an uncivil Dressmaker', was probably given by Anna, since most of the surviving original manuscripts of JA's poems are untitled, and so has not been used here.

1 **Miss Green**: evidently a professional dressmaker local to the Lloyds' home at Ibthorpe. It was usual for gowns to be made up professionally from material provided by the customer, and for mourning wear speed was essential.

2 **Ploughman's Gauze**: a fabric used for mourning gowns, probably a coarse kind of crape. Penelope Byrde describes crape, 'a type of silk gauze with a crimped surface which gave it a dull effect', as 'a distinctive mourning fabric much worn throughout the nineteenth century', though she talks of it as a fabric used rather for trimming than for gowns (Penelope Byrde, *Jane Austen Fashion: Fashion and Needlework in the Works of Jane Austen* (Ludlow: Excellent Press, 1999), p. 79).

3 **Miss Lloyd . . . Relative dear**: there were strict social rules about the clothes which should be worn after the death of relatives. On this occasion Martha, as daughter, would wear full black mourning. JA, who was a relative through the marriage of her brother to Mrs Lloyd's daughter, 'wore my crape sleeves to the Concert, I had them put in on the occasion; on my head I wore my crape & flowers' (21 April 1805, *L*, p. 103). When JA's sister-in-law Elizabeth died in October 1808 JA wrote to Cassandra that: '*I* am to be in Bombazeen & Crape, according to what we are told is universal *here* . . . *One* Miss Baker makes my gown, & the other my Bonnet' (15 October 1808, *L*, p. 148). In *P* Elizabeth Elliot is said to be 'wearing black ribbons' for the death of the wife of her father's heir, Mr William Elliot (vol. 1, ch. 1).

'Happy the Lab'rer'

This verse is one of a collection of four, the other three being by Mrs Austen, Cassandra and Edward's wife Elizabeth (1773–1808). JA's poem comes third in the group, in the copy of the manuscript that has survived. The three other poems are reproduced in Appendix F.

The poems are undated, though they must have been composed some time before October 1808 when Elizabeth Austen died suddenly shortly after the birth of her eleventh child: on hearing of Elizabeth's death JA wrote to CA 'of her great worth—of her solid principles, her true devotion, her excellence in every relation of Life' (13 October 1808, *L*, p. 147). They exist in a fair copy made by JA, under the heading 'Verses to rhyme with "Rose"', on a sheet of paper watermarked 1802, folded in half to make a booklet of four pages 256 mm × 200 mm in size which also contains the poems on Sir Home Popham and the two 'Miss Bigg' poems (see below). The paper is now in the possession of the Fondation Martin Bodmer, Geneva, and provides our copytext. For a discussion of issues of dating and composition see Introduction pp. cvii–cviii.

1 **light-drab coat**: a coat made of a light-brown cloth, much in fashion in the early nineteenth century.

2 **Cabbage rose**: a large, round, fully double rose with a strong scent and usually a deep pink colouring, developed by Dutch rose breeders as early as the seventeenth century. Its Latin name is *rosa centifolia*, the rose of a hundred petals.

3 **his seat among the rows**: in country churches a labourer, as well as people of higher social class, might have a specific pew or place officially or in practice designated for him. It would, however, be among the ordinary seating of the church – 'the rows' – rather than the enclosed box-pews reserved for prominent local families. In Godmersham church the Knights' box pew was raised high above the 'rows' where the ordinary parishioners sat.

'Oh! M[r]. Best'

JA, with her mother, sister and Martha Lloyd (since the death of her mother in April 1805 living with the Austen women) holidayed in Clifton, a popular spa village now a suburb of Bristol, in July 1806. JA was in high spirits: two years later she could still remember the 'happy feelings of Escape!' she had experienced in leaving Bath for Clifton (30 June–1 July 1808, *L*, p. 138). Evidently Martha was hoping to visit the Yorkshire spa town of Harrogate, two hundred miles north-east of Bristol; at the time it was felt inappropriate for a genteel woman to travel alone without a male escort – there are several references in JA's letters to the need to wait for a brother or nephew to escort her from one location to another – and so Mr Best's assistance would have been very welcome. Deirdre Le Faye, exploring possible connections of the poem with Newbury, has uncovered a Rev. Thomas Best as among the 'principal inhabitants' of the town at about this time, who could well be the person referred to.

The manuscript of the poem, in JA's hand and containing some textual corrections, was kept in the Austen family and is now in the possession of Mrs Damaris Jane Brix; this provides our copytext. It is untitled. The first three stanzas only were first published in William Austen-Leigh and Richard Arthur Austen-Leigh, *Jane Austen, Her Life and Letters: A Family Record* (London: Smith, Elder & Co., 1913), p. 70, and reproduced from that source in *MW*; the poem was first published in full in an article by Donald Greene in *Nineteenth-Century Fiction*, 30.3 (December 1975), from the manuscript, then in the possession of Mrs Joan Mason Hurley. Greene recorded that the poem was written on a single sheet of paper, with marks of a vertical fold producing two folios of 191 mm × 115 mm; the first six stanzas of the poem were written to the left of the fold, and the remaining stanzas, initials and date on the right. In addition, Mrs Hurley reported that the paper carried a watermark of 1808, which would suggest that the manuscript was a fair copy of the poem, made some time after the date of original composition, and that the corrections indicate that JA was still tinkering with wording. It has not been possible to verify the watermark, or the suggestion that the words 'To Martha' appear on the reverse side of the paper, as the poem is now encased in a frame.

1 **Harrowgate . . . summer**: Harrogate, like Clifton, was a spa town, offering a number of social attractions, including a theatre, billiard room and library, to entertain those who visited for their health. Each spa town had its own popular season; since it was in northern England it is not surprising that Harrogate's was in the summer: it began in May and finished, in fine seasons, as late as October (*Guide to Watering Places*, pp. 190–1).

2 **the Posting**: the costs of getting to Harrogate by means of hiring a carriage or post-chaise, including the teams of horses required for such a long journey.

3 **stouter**: more healthy.

4 **the waters were of use**: the waters of the 'Old Spa' had a metallic flavour, and were used as a general tonic. The waters of the sulphur wells, which were said to taste 'like rotten eggs and gunpowder', were taken to purge the system and were seen to be particularly useful in curing 'scurvy, scrofula, and cutaneous diseases' as well as 'worms . . . gout, jaundice, spleen, and green-sickness, and other disorders arising from obstructions'. They were also used externally, as an ointment or through immersion, against 'the diseases of the skin, and the cure of ulcers . . . as well as in removing old strains, aches, and paralytic disabilities' (*Guide to Watering Places*, pp. 188–9).

5 **Richard's pills**: no patent medicine officially known as 'Richard's pills' has been identified. JA had a dislike to the name of Richard – the clergyman Mr Morland is described as 'a respectable man, though his name was Richard' (*NA*, vol. 1, ch. 1) – and it is possible that this is an imaginary remedy.

6 **From Newb'ry to Speen Hill**: Newbury is a substantial town about fifteen miles north-east of the Lloyds' former home at Ibthorpe, and about ten miles east of Kintbury, home of the Austens' friends the Fowles; Mrs Craven, a widowed aunt of Martha Lloyd, lived in the village of Speen Hill, one mile west of Newbury, and the Lloyds and the Austens would have known the area well.

7 **Morton's wife**: it is not known who this Mr and Mrs Morton are, but in November 1812 JA asked Martha Lloyd for a Mr Morton's address in order to send him a turkey: 'It becomes now a sort of vanity in us not to know M[r] Morton's direction with any certainty' (29 November 1812, *L*, p. 197).

'See they come'

JA's fifth brother Frank, an officer in the Royal Navy, married Mary Gibson at St Lawrence's Church, Ramsgate, on the north Kent coast, on 24 July 1806, and the couple then spent their honeymoon at Godmersham Park, the home of JA's third brother Edward and his family, twenty-five miles inland. Edward's eldest daughter Fanny wrote in her diary for 29 July, 'I had a bit of a letter from Aunt Jane, with some verses of hers' – probably these, written to contribute to the festivities of the wedding, and to share the excitement of her niece, from whose point of view the lines are written (Centre for Kentish Studies U951. F24/1–69, 29 July 1806). JA was holidaying in Clifton, a spa near Bristol, with her mother, sister and Martha Lloyd, in late July, and the poem must have been written within days of 'Oh! Mr. Best' above.

There is no original manuscript extant. The only evidence for its existence is its inclusion in the Lefroy MS (see p. 707 above) as 'Lines written by Jane Austen for the amusement of a Niece (afterwards Lady Knatchbull) on the arrival of Captn. & Mrs. Austen at Godmersham Park soon after their marriage July 1806'; this provides our copytext though we have not reproduced the title, almost certainly added by Anna. The poem was first published in a letter from Deirdre Le Faye to the *TLS* of 20 February 1987, with the poem 'Miss Lloyd has now sent to Miss Green', also from the Lefroy MS.

1 **post haste**: with speed (mail coaches were supposed to travel at full gallop to deliver the post as soon as possible), and by post-chaise, a hired carriage.

2 **Thanet**: the area of north-east Kent containing Ramsgate, where the couple had married.

3 **Richard Kennet**: connected with Godmersham, possibly as a groom: Fanny Knight noted in her diary for 14 April 1804, 'I had a letter from Uncle F. by R. Kennett who brought home the Dun Poney' (*L*, p. 540). It may be that Edward Knight sent Richard Kennet with one of his own carriages to Ramsgate, for the newly married couple to drive back in, while Kennet made his own way home.

4 **the Parents of the Bride**: Mr and Mrs John Gibson of Ramsgate.

5 **Canterbury . . . through**: JA traces the then direct route from Ramsgate to Godmersham, via the city of Canterbury and the village of Chilham. The bridge is in fact Shalmsford Bridge; Anna Lefroy, unfamiliar with the route, may have misread JA's handwriting, and guessed Stamford Bridge, the name of a famous battle in

1066. Chilham village is very near Godmersham: the main coach road continued over a hill, and then carriages for Godmersham would leave the road to approach the house, in a sheltered dip.

6 **Cattle**: the older meaning of 'cattle' would include all animals out at pasture, including sheep and deer as well as cows. In her contribution to the 'Verses that rhyme with "Rose"' Mrs Austen talks of looking out of the window – possibly from Godmersham – and seeing 'all the Bucks & the Does, / The Cows & the Bullocks, the Wethers & Ewes' (see Appendix F). A contemporary picture of Godmersham shows mostly deer in the park (Nigel Nicolson, *Godmersham Park Kent, before, during and after Jane Austen's Time* (Alton: The Jane Austen Society, 1996), pp. 8–9).

7 **my Brothers**: by 1806 Fanny had five brothers: Edward (twelve), George Thomas (eleven), Henry (nine), William (eight) and Charles Bridges (three). A sixth, Brook John, was born in 1808.

8 **the Pier gate**: the main gate from the park to the stables, so called because it was hung from brick pillars or 'piers'. It had been put in place very recently; both gate pillars record the date of 1793 along with the initials of the then owner Thomas Knight, TCK.

9 **chaise**: either a hired carriage (a 'post-chaise', see above) or a carriage sent by Edward for the couple to return in privacy and style.

On Sir Home Popham's sentence—April 1807

Sir Home Popham, a highly successful, often controversial, naval officer with political ambitions (he was a Tory Member of Parliament 1804–12), had received plaudits in the summer of 1806 for his part in the daring capture of Buenos Aires from the Spanish. However, he was court-marshalled at Portsmouth between 6 and 11 March 1807 on the charge of achieving that success (which proved in any case to be temporary) only because he had left Cape Town unprotected by withdrawing his squadron from the Cape of Good Hope. The trial attracted much publicity in the national and local press, and opinion was vociferously divided. Popham was found guilty but many people saw his behaviour as vindicated, and Popham himself was described in the Austens' local newspaper as receiving 'the loud acclamations of the populace' (*Hampshire Chronicle*, 16 March 1807).

The Austens are generally regarded as Tory in political sympathies and so might have been expected to sympathize with Popham rather than with his accusers. Brian Southam has argued that JA might have had personal reasons for her hostility to the government that prosecuted Popham, and adds that Frank Austen may have known Popham personally (*Jane Austen and the Navy*, pp. 155–63). JA, with her mother and sister, had joined Frank and his wife Mary in shared lodgings in Southampton in March 1807, and so might well have been particularly interested in naval news at this time. Frank himself set sail for the Cape of Good Hope on 30 June 1807.

The poem appears in the Bodmer manuscript on the same page as the 'Miss Bigg' poems, and looks as if it were copied at the same time; since the first 'Miss Bigg' poem is precisely dated to 26 August 1808, it seems likely that JA made this copy at least sixteen months after composing the poem. The poem was first published in *Letters of Jane Austen*, ed. Lord Brabourne, 2 vols. (1884), vol. 2, p. 344, with the commentary 'In Jane Austen's handwriting, enclosed in the same Letter of 1807' as the 'Verses to Rhyme with Rose'.

1 **a Ministry, pitiful, angry, mean**: William Wyndham, Lord Greville, presided over the 'Ministry of all the Talents', a coalition government formed in February 1806 after the death of the previous Prime Minister William Pitt the Younger, and which aimed to include representatives of all parties, but which the Pittite Members of Parliament (including Popham) refused to join. The Ministry achieved the abolition of the slave trade with the Anti-Slave Trade Act of March 1807, but was otherwise characterized by confusion and general ineffectiveness, particularly in respect of foreign policy, and was generally unpopular.

2 **severe reprimand**: this was a serious punishment, but it fell short of disgrace; and had no visible negative effect on Popham's career since he was appointed Captain of the Fleet on an expedition against Denmark in July (despite the complaints of other senior officers). After a series of further expeditions he was promoted to rear-admiral, and he was knighted in 1815.

To Miss Bigg previous to her marriage, with some pocket handfs. I had hemmed for her.—

Members of the Bigg family, of Manydown Park, Wootton St Lawrence, a village about five miles from Steventon, were long-standing friends of the Austens; the friendship survived JA's retraction of her acceptance of a proposal of marriage from Harris Bigg-Wither in December 1802. Harris's fifth sister Catherine (1775–1848) married Rev. Herbert Hill (1749–1828) on 25 October 1808, and JA's poem was written and sent during the preparations for the wedding. JA was not optimistic about Catherine's marital prospects: 'tomorrow we must think of poor Catherine' she wrote to Cassandra on 24 October (*L*, p. 150). At thirty-five (the same age as JA herself) Catherine was a mature bride; the Rev. Hill, uncle of the poet Robert Southey, was nearly sixty; 'there is a melancholy disproportion between the Papa and the little children,' JA wrote to Cassandra after visiting the Hills in 1814, by which time Catherine was pregnant with her fourth child (2 September 1814, *L*, p. 274).

A gift of hand-embroidered handkerchiefs was not uncommon at the time, and JA was known as a skilled needlewoman (see above, 'This little bag'). Catherine was not the only recipient of gifts of handkerchiefs from JA in the autumn of 1808: 'I have just finished a Handkf. for Mrs James Austen, which I expect her Husband to give me an opportunity of sending to her ere long,' JA wrote to Cassandra (1 October 1808, *L*, p. 140).

Two manuscripts of the poem survive in JA's hand. The first is evidently the paper that was actually sent: it is a single sheet, 114 mm in height × 185 mm in width, many-folded, with the poem written on one side and 'Miss Bigg', as an address, on the other, all in JA's hand; the verses have no title. It is now owned by the Jane Austen Memorial Trust and provides our copytext, although we have included the title JA herself gave the poem when she copied it out later. The second is a fair copy, under the title given here, preserved in the Bodmer manuscript (see p. 709 above).

The two 'Miss Bigg' poems were both first published in the Brabourne *Letters* (1884), vol. 2, p. 344, under the same heading as the 'Sir Home Popham' verses (see p. 714 above).

Textual variants

	Chawton MS	Bodmer MS
line 2	employ: —	employ;
line 3	Friend	friend
line 4	tears to wipe, but tears	Tears to wipe, but Tears
	J. A.—Aug:[st] 26.—1808. —	No signature or date

1 **Cambrick**: a kind of fine white linen, originally made in Cambrai in France.

On the same occasion–but not Sent.—

JA evidently wrote two different sets of verses to accompany the handkerchiefs, and decided not to send this version. She kept it, however, and copied it out, with the sent version, on the sheet of paper now held at Fondation Martin Bodmer; this provides our copytext. The title is JA's.

1 **bear her name**: this suggests JA had embroidered Catherine's name or initials on the handkerchiefs.

To the memory of M[rs]. Lefroy, who died Dec:[r] 16.—my birthday.—written 1808.—

Mrs Anne Lefroy (born Anne Brydges 1749) was wife of George Lefroy, who became rector of the parish of Ashe, two miles northwest of Steventon, in 1783. Known as 'Madam Lefroy' and highly respected in her parish for her good works, she became a friend and mentor to the young JA. Her brother Egerton – later Sir Egerton Brydges – fourteen years younger than and greatly influenced by Madam Lefroy, wrote that she 'had an exquisite taste for poetry, and could almost repeat the chief English poets by heart, especially Milton, Pope, Collins, Gray, and the poetical passages of Shakespeare; and she composed easy verses herself with great facility . . . The charm of her first address was magical; her eyes were full of lustre; and the copiousness and eloquence of her conversation attracted all ears and won all hearts. It is probable that her conversation and example contributed greatly to my early bent to poetry . . . Mrs. Lefroy was a woman more brilliant, more spiritual, and more beaming with goodness, than I have ever elsewhere seen . . . She was spotless; and her heart was the seat of every affectionate and moral virtue'. He added that JA was 'very intimate with Mrs. Lefroy, and much encouraged by her' (Sir Egerton Brydges, *The Autobiography, Times, Opinions and Contemporaries of Sir Egerton Brydges*, 2 vols. (1834), vol. 1, p. 5 and vol. 2, pp. 40, 41).

On 16 December 1804 – JA's twenty-ninth birthday – Madam Lefroy went shopping in the local town of Overton and, meeting JA's brother James by chance, complained to him of the stupidity and sluggishness of her horse. On her way home, the horse bolted and she fell on to hard ground; she died a few hours later (*FR*, p. 145) and was buried at Ashe, with James officiating, on 21 December. The news must have spread very quickly to Bath, where JA was living with her family, and must have caused general shock.

These verses were evidently written on or around the fourth anniversary of her death in 1808. The copytext is JA's fair copy of the poem, written on both sides of a single sheet of paper 231 mm × 190 mm in size, now in the possession of the Dean and Chapter of Winchester Cathedral, to whom it was given in 1936 by Jessie Lefroy, one of Madam Lefroy's great-granddaughters.

The poem was reproduced in Sir Henry Lefroy's *Notes and Documents relating to the Family of Loffroy . . . by a Cadet* (1868), pp. 117–18, and was therefore the first example of JA's manuscript work to be published. It also appeared in the *Memoir* ((1870), pp. 76–8) but evidently from a different copytext, which was probably provided by Anna Lefroy (NPG, fo. 2), whose husband Ben was Madam Lefroy's son. It omits the fourth and fifth stanzas altogether, and contains other smaller variations from the Winchester manuscript. Emma Florence Austen (1851–1939), Charles Austen's granddaughter, sold a manuscript copy of the poem at Sotheby's on 3 May 1948; the present whereabouts of that version are unknown, but if the Sotheby's sale catalogue is correct in stating that its version of the manuscript contains all the Lefroy stanzas, and a significant correction in stanza 4 (see notes below), this may indicate it was earlier than the Winchester manuscript. David Gilson records two other manuscripts, which seem to have been copies made by Lefroy family members: the first appears at the end of a volume of memorabilia apparently put together by Christopher Edward

Lefroy (1785–1856), one of Madam Lefroy's sons; it now belongs to Miss Helen Lefroy. The second appeared in an album bearing the date of 11 November 1833 and the signature of 'Mrs Rice', that is, Lucy Jemima Lefroy (1779–1862), Madam Lefroy's daughter; it is said now to belong to one of her direct descendants. Both texts seem to be based on the Winchester manuscript (Gilson, pp. 42–5).

1 **At Johnson's death**: Dr Samuel Johnson, eminent sage and critic, died on 13 December 1784, at the age of seventy-five. His articles, essays and prayers were much admired in the late eighteenth century and beyond, and his reputation was further enhanced, and the facts of his life made more widely known, through the *Life of Johnson* by his acolyte James Boswell, published in 1791. Henry Austen, in the 'Biographical Notice' that accompanied the publication of *Northanger Abbey* and *Persuasion* in 1818, stated that Johnson was JA's 'favourite moral writer in prose' and the influence of Johnson on her prose style in particular has been widely discussed. JA owned a copy of his popular novel *Rasselas* (first published as *The Prince of Abissinia* in 1759).

2 **by Hamilton . . . the Man**: in his *Life of Johnson* Boswell quoted the words of 'an eminent friend' of Johnson, that 'He has made a chasm, which not only nothing can fill up, but which nothing has a tendency to fill up.—Johnson is dead.—Let us go to the next best.—There is nobody.—No man can be said to put you in mind of Johnson' (vol. 2, pp. 580–1). In the expanded third edition of the *Life* (1799) edited by Edmond Malone after Boswell's death, Malone identified the 'eminent friend' as 'The Late Right Hon. William Gerrard Hamilton'; the identification stands in subsequent editions. William Gerard Hamilton (1729–96) was Member of Parliament for a number of constituencies during his career, including Petersfield in Hampshire (the constituency in which Chawton was situated) 1754–61, and he held various ministerial appointments over the years.

According to the Sotheby's catalogue entry, in the version of the manuscript sold there on 3 May 1948 the words 'By Burke t'was finely said' are replaced by 'By Hamilton t'was said'. Edmund Burke (1729–97) was one of the most famous politicians and thinkers of his day and had in fact been Hamilton's assistant 1759–65. He was known to be a friend of Johnson's and may well be the 'eminent friend' referred to elsewhere in the *Life* (see for example Malone's note to the entry of Wednesday 19 May 1784) but his prominent role in the unsuccessful prosecution of Warren Hastings (1787–94), with whom the Austen family had personal connections and whom they held in great respect, would make any tribute from JA a startlingly generous one.

3 **Genius**: native intellectual quality of a superior kind.

4 **deck**: cover over with the aim of beautifying.

'Alas! poor Brag, thou boastful Game!'

The poem is contained in a letter JA wrote on 17–18 January 1809 to Cassandra, who was staying with their brother Edward and his family at Godmersham. It was written for the benefit of Edward's eldest son, also Edward (b. 1794). Cassandra had evidently earlier reported to JA that the family, choosing between two popular card games, brag and speculation, had preferred brag, and that young Edward had been prominent in the decision-making. JA wrote to Cassandra on 10–11 January 1809 that 'The preference of Brag over Speculation does not greatly surprise me I beleive, because I feel the same myself; but it mortifies me deeply, because Speculation was under my patronage;—& after all, what is there so delightful in a pair-royal of Braggers? it is but three nines, or three Knaves, or a mixture of them.—When one comes to reason upon it, it cannot stand its' ground against Speculation—of which I hope Edward is now convinced. Give my Love to him if he is' (*L*, pp. 163–4). In the 17–18 January letter JA offers this poem, which assumes that brag too will shortly be superseded, introducing it with the comment 'I have just received some verses in an unknown hand, & am desired to forward them to my nephew Edw[d]' (*L*, p. 167). Her next letter, on 24 January, continues: 'I am sorry my verses did not bring any return from Edward, I was in hopes they might—but I suppose he does not rate them high enough.—It might be partiality, but they seemed to me purely classical—just like Homer & Virgil, Ovid & Propria que Maribus' (*L*, p. 170). The Latin tag is taken, inaccurately, from the first lesson of the

Genders of Nouns in the widely used 'Eton Latin Grammar', *The Introduction to the Latin Tongue* printed at Eton by M. Pote and E. Williams in 1758 and frequently reprinted throughout the century: *Propria quæ maribus tribuuntur, mascula dicas; / Ut sunt Divorum*; *Mars* . . . (Proper names which are assigned to the male kind you may call masculines; as the names of the heathen gods; Mars . . .) (1798 edn, pp. 63, 119.)

The letter, which provides our copytext, was preserved by Cassandra and on her death in 1845 became the property of the elder Edward's daughter Fanny, by then Lady Knatchbull. It was first published by Lady Knatchbull's son, Lord Brabourne, in his edition of *Letters*, vol. 2, pp. 63–4. The letter is now held at the Morgan Library, New York.

1 **Alas . . . Game**: the opening phrase of the poem introduces a mild burlesque of the famous scene in *Hamlet* (Act 5, scene 1), in which Hamlet addresses the skull of the former court jester with the words, 'Alas! poor Yorick' and ponders on the effects of mortality partly through rhetorical questions: 'Where be your gibes now . . .?' Shakespeare's scene, like JA's poem, is much concerned with wordplay – 'Hum! This fellow might be in's time a great buyer of land, with his statutes, his recognizances, his fines, his double vouchers, his recoveries. Is this the fine of his fines, and the recovery of his recoveries, to have his fine pate full of fine dirt?' JA may have had the same scene in mind in her earlier 10–11 January letter, with the comment 'what is there so delightful in a pair-royal of Braggers? it is but three nines, or three Knaves, or a mixture of them'.

2 **Brag**: a card game designed for five to eight players, on which the modern game of poker is based. The players stake on the respective merit of their cards, which have values in specific combinations with names such as 'pair-royal' and 'pair-royal with bragger'. The name derives from the 'brag' or challenge given by one of the players to the rest to turn up cards equal in value to his or hers.

3 **Speculation**: a round game of cards, the chief feature of which is the buying and selling of trump cards, the player who possesses the highest trump in the round winning the pool. See 'W', p. 126 and n. 153.

'My dearest Frank'

JA, with her mother, sister and friend Martha Lloyd had lived with her brother Frank and his wife Mary Gibson in Southampton from 1806. In April 1807 Frank took command of HMS *St Albans*; in July 1809 he was with his ship nearing Canton in China, where he remained till March 1810. In April 1809 Mary, heavily pregnant, moved with her small daughter Mary Jane to Rose Cottage, Lenten Street, in the small, bustling town of Alton in Hampshire. On 7 July the Austen women moved in to their new home in Chawton, less than two miles from Alton, and on 12 July Mary gave birth to Frank's first son Francis William. JA's letter is a celebration both of the birth of the baby and of her own new home.

The letter, which contains no revisions, was preserved by Frank Austen and was given by his grandson Ernest Leigh Austen to the British Museum in 1930 (Add. 42180). It provides our copy-text. JA made a fair copy of the letter, which was preserved by Cassandra; on her death it went to her youngest brother Charles Austen, and it is now owned by the Jane Austen Memorial Trust and is kept at Chawton Cottage.

Textual variants:

	British Museum MS	Chawton MS
line 2	Boy,	boy,
line 3	pain	pain,
line 6	Love!—	Love!
line 17	His . . . descried,	(His . . . descried)
line 18	bide."—	bide."
line 19	Fearless	Fearless [no indentation]
line 21	Soul,	Soul
line 22	Controul	controul
line 24	neighbouring . . . Bray!	neigbouring . . . Bray!—
line 25	Child,	Child
line 26	mild!	mild,
line 28	days,	days
line 29	Manhood, . . . mind	Manhood . . . mind,
line 36	self-improvement	Self-improvement
line 39	well;	well,
line 40	tell.—	tell.
line 41	paint our state,	give our state
line 43	home,	home—
line 44	it, to our mind;	it to our mind,
line 45	complete	complete,
line 49	You'll . . . year,	You'll [indentation] . . . year;
line 50	near,	near—

The letter is written in rhymed tetrameters, one of the easiest of rhythms for domestic verse of this kind. It was used by Mrs Austen in her humorous lines on the Basingstoke assembly in 1799, beginning 'I send you here a list of all / The company who graced the Ball . . .' (Selwyn, pp. 29–30; *FR*, p. 115) and by James Austen in his memorial verses to JA, 'Venta! within thy sacred fane / Rests many a chief in battle slain' (Selwyn, pp. 48–50).

1 **Chawton**: Chawton Cottage had been JA's home for just two weeks, since she had moved in, with her mother, sister Cassandra and friend Martha Lloyd, on 7 July. The house had been provided by her brother Edward, who owned it along with other properties in the village, and was to be her home for the remaining eight years of her life. The move had been planned for several months: on 20 November 1808 JA wrote to Cassandra that 'there are six Bedchambers at Chawton . . . which is just what we wanted to be assured of' and also 'Garrets for Storeplaces' (*L*, p. 153), one of which was to be fitted up for the manservant they planned to employ. In the *Memoir* Austen Leigh described the Chawton house in some detail: it stood 'just where the road to Winchester branches off from that to Gosport. It was so close to the road that the front door opened upon it; while a very narrow enclosure, paled in on each side, protected the building from danger of collision with any runaway vehicle . . . it had been occupied by Mr. Knight's steward; but by some additions to the house, and some judicious planting and skreening, it was made a pleasant and commodious abode. Mr. Knight was experienced and adroit at such arrangements, and this was a labour of love to him. A good-sized entrance and two sitting-rooms made the length of the house . . . the large drawing-room window was blocked up and turned into a book-case, and another opened at the side which gave to view only turf and trees, as a high wooden fence and hornbeam hedge shut out the Winchester road, which skirted the whole length of the little domain. Trees were planted each side to form a shrubbery walk, carried round the enclosure, which gave a sufficient space for ladies' exercise . . . The house itself was quite as good as the generality of parsonage-houses then were, and much in the same style; and was capable of receiving other members of the family as frequent

visitors. It was sufficiently well furnished; everything inside and out was kept in good repair, and it was altogether a comfortable and ladylike establishment, though the means which supported it were not large' (*Memoir* (1871), pp. 80–1, expanded from a shorter description in 1870, pp. 104–5). Austen Leigh obtained much of this information from his sister Caroline: the description in *My Aunt Jane Austen* is very similar (Caroline Austen, *My Aunt Jane Austen: A Memoir* (1867), reproduced in J. E. Austen-Leigh, *A Memoir of Jane Austen and Other Family Recollections* ed. Kathryn Sutherland (Oxford: Oxford University Press, 2002), pp. 166–8). James Edward and Caroline's half-sister Anna Lefroy was more critical: she saw the house as 'small, & not very good' (Lefroy MS, np). By the time of Austen Leigh's *Memoir* the building had been turned into labourers' tenements; it has now been restored largely to its condition in JA's lifetime and is open to the public.

2 **Frank**: JA had already written verses to celebrate the wedding of her brother Frank ('See they come', above). His relationship with JA as expressed in their correspondence seems always to have been cordial. In July 1813 (in another letter to 'My dearest Frank') JA asked his permission to use the names of his ships in *Mansfield Park*, and from 1815 he was again living close to his sister, lodging with his family either in Chawton or in Alton. After Mary's death in 1823 he married Martha Lloyd; he became a rear-admiral in 1830, was made a Knight Commander of the Bath in 1837, a vice-admiral in 1838 and a full admiral in 1848. Just before his death in 1865, at the age of ninety-one, he became, by seniority, Admiral of the Fleet (see George Holbert Tucker, *A History of Jane Austen's Family* (1983; revised edn, Stroud: Sutton Publishing Ltd, 1998), pp. 165–79).

3 **Mary's . . . Mary Jane**: Mary had given birth to her first child, Mary Jane, in April 1807, while she was sharing lodgings with JA, Mrs Austen, Cassandra and Mary Lloyd in Southampton. Mary Jane's birth had been a very difficult one, and, along with concerns arising from that, there must have been strong family memories of Elizabeth Austen's death in childbirth in October 1808. Mary died in 1823 at the birth of her eleventh child.

4 **Thy name . . . see**: little Francis had been given the same names as his father, Francis William.

5 **Bet, my . . . bide**: something like, 'Bet isn't coming to stay', a shared reminiscence, in Hampshire dialect, from the Austens' childhood. 'Bet' is probably Elizabeth Littleworth, daughter of a cottager family in Steventon to whom Mrs Austen sent her babies for early nursing (*FR*, p. 19). Writing to Cassandra on 24 May 1813 about another brother, Henry, who was returning to Alton from London, JA commented that ' "he will not be come to bide", till after September' (*L*, p. 213).

6 **engine**: implement, mechanism.

7 **saucy words & fiery ways**: Frank was known as a precocious child: 'I have been told that Sir Francis Austen, when seven years old, bought on his own account . . . a pony for a guinea and a half; and after riding him with great success for two seasons, sold him for a guinea more' (*Memoir* (1871), p. 37).

8 **self improvement . . . conscious worth**: in the *Memoir* Frank is described as possessing 'great firmness of character, with a strong sense of duty, whether due from himself to others, or from others to himself . . . a strict disciplinarian . . . a very religious man . . . spoken of as "*the* officer who kneeled at church"' (*Memoir*, (1870) pp. 22–3).

9 **The many comforts . . . distended**: the Austen women had only been in the house for two weeks, and building work was probably still going on around them: records show that in 1809 Edward spent £45.19s.0d. on structural alterations and £35.6s.5d. on plumbing work for the cottage (*FR*, p. 175). They were clearly delighted to be in their own home after nearly ten years of temporary lodgings.

10 **Charles and Fanny**: at this point JA had not met her youngest brother's wife Fanny. Charles Austen (1779–1852) married Frances Palmer (1790–1814) in Bermuda in May 1807. They returned to England, with their two little girls, only in the summer of 1811. On that occasion Cassandra wrote to her cousin Phylly Walter that Charles 'is grown a little older . . . but we had the pleasure of seeing him return in good health & unchanged in mind. His Bermudan wife is a very pleasing little woman, she is gentle & amiable in her manners & appears to make him very

happy' (Deirdre Le Faye, *Jane Austen's 'Outlandish Cousin': The Life and Letters of Eliza de Feuillide* (London: British Library, 2002), pp. 169–70).

11 **over-right**: a Hampshire dialect word meaning directly opposite. The word is used by Mary Russell Mitford, another local author (her grandfather was at one time Rector of the parish of Ashe, which adjoined Steventon), in *Our Village*: 'he lived exactly over-right our house' (Mary Russell Mitford, *Our Village*, 4th series (1830), 'Early Recollections: The Cobbler over the Way').

'In measured verse'

There is no manuscript extant for this poem. It was included in the *Memoir* as one of the 'specimens . . . of the liveliness of mind which imparted an agreeable flavour both to her correspondence and her conversation' (*Memoir* (1870), pp. 115, 117–18); James Edward Austen Leigh saw it as 'nonsense' composed 'nearly extempore' (p. 118). His sister Caroline, discussing with him the possible contents of the *Memoir* as it was being compiled, had felt that this poem, as one in a small group of 'light nonsensical verses' '*might* take' (NPG, fos. 4–7). It has generally been assumed that 'Anna', described by Austen Leigh as 'a young friend, who really was clever and handsome', was Anna Lefroy, Austen Leigh's half-sister and JA's niece: it would be quite likely that Anna, an adviser on the *Memoir*, would prefer anonymity, and there are several other occasions where, through the general Victorian habit of discretion, Austen Leigh does not identify family members whose identities he must have known. However, Anna did not include the poem in the Lefroy MS in which she recorded several of JA's verses. Anna had been close to the Austens, particularly during her childhood and early adulthood. Her mother died when she was very small and once her father James married again and started a second family, she felt out of place, and spent a lot of time with Mrs Austen, JA and Cassandra; as she grew older her 'mercurial and excitable' character became apparent (*FR*, p. 191), and JA's letters sometimes express exasperation with her. There is no indication of the date of the poem, but it seems to be written about an adult rather than a child, which would place it in the Chawton years, after 1809, when Anna was sixteen, and before November 1814, when Anna married Ben Lefroy. In 1809 Anna was sent away to Godmersham, to prevent her from becoming attached to the Rev. Michael Terry, who was generally seen as unsuitable for her, and during the visit Fanny Knight wrote verses about her (Margaret Wilson, *Almost Another Sister: The Story of Fanny Knight, Jane Austen's Favourite Niece* (Maidstone: George Mann Books, 1998), pp. 34–5). Her parents relented, and allowed an engagement to take place; but Anna was in disgrace again in 1810 when she broke off the engagement. This time she was sent to Chawton to stay with her grandmother and aunts Cassandra and Jane, and it has been suggested (*FR*, p. 182) that the poem might have been written during this summer. It could as easily have been written on a later, less sensitive, occasion, perhaps in spring 1811, when JA was with Anna in London and wrote to Cassandra that she was 'quite an Anna with variations' (25 April 1811, *L*, p. 184), or early summer when Anna stayed with JA at Chawton for several weeks. Mary Brunton's novel *Self-Control*, which describes the abduction of the heroine to the exotic wilds of Canada, was published in March 1811 and JA read it some time after late April.

James Edward Austen Leigh wrote: 'I believe . . . that the fancy of drawing the images from America arose at the moment from the obvious rhyme which presented itself in the first stanza' (*Memoir* (1870), p. 118). In fact the same rhyme had recently been used by Robert Burns: one of his 'Songs' includes the lines

Ye monarchs tak the east and west,
  Frae Indus to Savannah!
Give me within my straining grasp,
  The melting form of Anna

(*Reliques of Robert Burns, collected and published by R. H. Cromek* (1808), p. 447)

The metre is the same as that of JA's poem, but JA's complex internal rhymes of lines 1 and 3 of the stanza are not attempted by Burns.

1 **measured verse**: that is, verse written in metre. In his *Defence of Poetry* (first printed 1595 and regularly reprinted thereafter) Sir

Philip Sidney differentiates between 'rhyme' and 'measured verse' (Sir Philip Sidney, *Defence of Poetry and Observations on Poetry and Eloquence*, new edn (1787), p. 47).

2 **savannah**: meadow or treeless plain, particularly associated with plains found in America. The phrase 'vast savannah' was a conventional one: the Duke de la Rochefoucault Liancourt in his *Travels through the United States of North America . . . in the years 1795, 1796 and 1797* 4 vols. (1799), wrote of 'those vast savannahs, which divide the enormous mass of water, that irrigates America' (vol. 1, p. 200) and James Thomson in *The Seasons* (1744) had earlier included it in a description of the (East) Indian landscape ('Summer', lines 685–6). The geographical inexactitude about savannahs was commonplace. Charlotte Smith's hero Orlando Somerive, sent to America with the British army, finds on the bank of the St Lawrence River 'an extensive Savannah, alive with cattle, and coloured with . . . a variety of swamp plants': *The Old Manor House* (1793), vol. 3, ch. 14.

3 **Ontario's lake**: Lake Ontario, with a shoreline length of 712 miles, is the smallest in surface area of the Great Lakes of North America. *The General Gazetteer: or Compendious Geographical Dictionary, originally written by R. Brookes, MD* (11th edn, with considerable additions and improvements, 1800), under 'Ontario' (np) describes the lake as having a circumference of 600 miles.

4 **Niagara's Fall**: Niagara Falls descend into Lake Ontario. 'I must repeat it again and again, that nothing can stand the test of comparison with the Falls of Niagara. Let no one expect to find here something pleasing, wildly beautiful or romantic; all is wonderfully grand, awful, sublime' (Duke de la Rochefoucault Liancourt, *Travels through the United States*, vol. 1, p. 398).

5 **thick, black, profound . . . transatlantic groves**: 'transatlantic' means pertaining to the region beyond the Atlantic; North American. JA may have in mind the description in *Self-Control* of Laura's experiences in Canada, though the shade there is far from 'friendly': 'The day dawned; and Laura perceived that, passing an open cultivated plain, she was pursuing her course towards woods impervious to the light. Dark and tangled they lowered over the stream, till

they closed around, and every cheerful object was blotted from the scene' (ch. 32).

'I've a pain in my head'

Maria Beckford was the daughter of Francis Beckford, of Basing Park, Hampshire (and a cousin of William Beckford (1759–1844), the author of the Gothic novel *Vathek* (1786)). Maria's sister Charlotte married John Middleton, and after Charlotte died in 1803 leaving several children Maria went to manage the household of her brother-in-law. Mr Middleton rented Chawton House 1808–13, and there are several references to 'Miss Beckford' in JA's letters 1811–14; on 25 April 1811 JA, then in London, wrote to Cassandra, that 'Poor Miss B. has been suffering again from her old complaint, & looks thinner than ever' (*L*, p. 183).

There are two manuscript versions of the poem extant. The version used as the copytext here is on exhibition at the City Museum, Winchester; it is written on a small sheet of paper about 139 mm × 95 mm, mounted on a card (so it is impossible to tell whether the paper is watermarked). As well as the date 'Feby. 1811' at the bottom of the poem the date of 'Jany. 1810' appears sideways to the right-hand side of the last stanza, suggesting that some other writing has been cut off.

A second version of the poem, written by JA on a single sheet of paper trimmed to a size of about 128 mm × 113 mm, and with twelve lines of what is apparently a longer riddle by 'C. Austen' – that is, Mrs Cassandra Austen, JA's mother – on the reverse side, is held in the private collection of Ms Sandy Lerner; it had long been in the possession of the Austen family, having been kept by Anna Lefroy (Gilson, p. 52). This version includes inverted commas round the speeches, and is signed 'Jane Austen', which suggests it might be a later, more formal, version, but it also repeats 'Ah!' rather clumsily, while the Winchester Museum version avoids the repetition with 'Oh!' in stanza 1. Unlike the Winchester Museum version, the Lerner version is not indented in lines 2 and 4 of each stanza. Neither version contains any corrections, and in both the poem is untitled.

Textual variants, with the copytext first:

	Winchester MS	Lerner MS
line 1	I've . . . head	"I've . . . head"
line 3	dread.	dread
line 4	Oh! . . . for't.	"Ah! . . . for't."
line 5	this	her
line 7	For	"For
line 8	Ma'am?	Ma'am?"
line 9	Beckford, Suppose	Beckford "Suppose
line 12	calomel, brisk.—	Calomel brisk."
line 13	What . . . notion.	"What . . .notion!"
line 14	Newnham,	Newnham
line 15	Ma'am—	Ma'am.

The poem also appears in the Lefroy MS which, although it varies from both autograph versions in some of its punctuation, is set out without indentation and has 'Oh!' in stanza 1, line 4, suggesting that it was taken from the Lerner version. This version has the title, 'Conversation, as it actually took place, in prose, between Miss Beckford (then of Chawton House) & Mr Newnham—Apothecary at Alton—', probably added by Anna Lefroy.

It appears as item 15 (d) in the list of Jane Austen memorabilia kept by the descendants of Charles Austen compiled by R. W. Chapman ('A Jane Austen Collection,' *TLS*, 14 January 1926).

1 **pain in my head**: headaches were clearly a perennial problem, exacerbated by bad lighting and limited use of spectacles, for which the recognized treatment, if the headache persisted, involved leeches to remove what was perceived as a harmful excess of blood in the head. There are frequent references to headaches in JA's letters. In October 1811 JA composed a verse about a headache of her own (see below, 'When stretch'd on one's bed').

2 **Newnham**: Mr Newnham, apothecary and surgeon, lived at Lansdowne House, 74 High Street, Alton (Jane Hurst, *Jane Austen and Alton* (privately printed, 2001, 2004), p. 6), in JA's time. He would need formal qualifications to be a surgeon, but was evidently also working as a general practitioner.

3 **calomel**: mercurous chloride, much used as a purgative in various medicinal preparations in the form of a yellowish white powder. Buchan's popular volume of domestic medicine advises that one to three grains of calomel should be used as an alterative (that is, a general remedy), and three to twelve grains as a purgative,

and he recommends calomel to treat a wide range of problems including smallpox, worms, dropsy, cataracts, ulcers and various sexual diseases (*Domestic Medicine*, xxx and passim).

On the marriage of M^{r}. Gell of East Bourn to Miss Gill.—

Two copies of the manuscript are extant. Both were preserved by the family of JA's youngest brother Charles Austen, and are listed by R. W. Chapman in 'A Jane Austen Collection,' *TLS*, 14 January 1926.

The first, which provides the copytext of the poem, is in the possession of Dr Park Honan. The lines are written on the verso of an irregularly trimmed piece of paper, extreme measurements about 130 mm × 117 mm, having on the recto a print of 'An interesting Scene from the Novel of / LOVE, MYSTERY, AND MISERY', a novel by the pseudonymous 'Anthony Frederick Holstein' (1810). Unusually for JA, the poem is given a title, which suggests the version may be a fair copy, though it could simply be a mock-announcement or reminder of the poem's source.

Another version of the poem is in the possession of the Roman Baths Museum, Bath and N. E. Somerset Council. The poem is written on the reverse side of a single folded sheet of paper, total dimensions 229 mm × 184 mm, which also contains the poem 'When stretch'd on one's bed' (see below); 'When stretch'd' is signed and dated 'Octr. 27.1811'. This copy of 'Mr Gell and Miss Gill' was probably written later than the Honan manuscript: the handwriting is neater and the poem is presented more formally, with inverted commas, and a longer title. The fourth page of the Honan version displays the words, 'For Captn Austen R.N.', and there are signs that the paper was further folded, to show the words on the outside. They are written in pencil and the handwriting might be either JA's or Cassandra's. It is possible that the manuscript was handed on to Charles Austen by Cassandra just before her death in 1845, when she was dividing up JA's papers (Charles was promoted to admiral in 1846).

The poem was first published in the *Memoir* (1870), p. 115, along with a version of the poem on Camilla Wallop (see below), as 'specimens . . . of the liveliness of mind which imparted an agreeable flavour both to her correspondence and her conversation'; the Bath version of the poem was also reproduced in facsimile. The version reproduced in the text of the *Memoir* differs from both manuscript versions in reproducing the poem in four lines rather than eight, and in other details including yet another way of making the pun – this time through 'iis' and 'ees' – and so it is possible that the source was a third manuscript, which may or may not have been written by JA herself or in her lifetime.

The variants between the two known manuscripts are as follows:

Honan MS: On the Marriage of M^{r}. Gell of East Bourn to Miss Gill.—

Bath MS: On reading in the Newspaper, the Marriage of "M^{r}. Gell of Eastbourne to Miss Gill."—

	Honan MS	Bath MS
line 6	I'm the Slave	"I'm the slave
line 6	i.s	eyes
line 7	Ah!	Oh!
line 8	e.s.—	ease."
	[none]	J. A.

Even lines are not indented in the Bath version.

1 **On the Marriage . . . Gill**: the whole Austen family had a quick appreciation of the potential of words and names for puns. Reporting the arrival of a new governess at Godmersham, Miss Clewes, JA wrote to Cassandra in February 1813 'is not it a name for Edward to pun on?' (9 February 1813 *L*, p. 205); and see 'Camilla Wallop' below. As the Bath version of the poem makes clear, the verse was prompted not by the marriage itself but by the notice of marriage in a newspaper. *The Hampshire Telegraph and Sussex Chronicle*, 25 February 1811 ('Price Sixpence Halfpenny') includes – not in fact in the 'Birth, Death, Married' column but prominently at the head of a miscellaneous column headed 'Sussex' (there is also one headed 'Hampshire') – 'Sussex, Saturday, February 23, 1811. On Saturday was married, Mr. Gell, of Eastbourn, to Miss Gill, of Well-street, Hackney'. It is likely that the poem was written when JA, who was at home at Chawton at this time, saw this or another announcement of the marriage. There is no indication that either of these individuals was known to JA, but the similarity of their

names offered an opportunity for the kind of wordplay that the Austens enjoyed.

The creation of a poem from a marriage announcement in a newspaper has a family precedent in a verse written by JA's uncle James Leigh Perrot 'on reading in a newspaper the marriage of Captain Foote to Miss Patten' (*Memoir* (1870), p. 55):—

Through the rough paths of life, with a patten your guard,
  May you safely and pleasantly jog.
May the knot never slip, nor the ring press too hard,
  Nor the *Foot* find the *Patten* a clog.'

The reproduction of JA's poem in four lines in the *Memoir* emphasizes the similarity with Leigh Perrot's verses. A copy of the poem, in JA's handwriting, survives in the Henry W. and Albert A. Berg Collection in the New York Public Library.

'I am in a dilemma'

This tiny poem forms part of a letter from JA, 30 April 1811 (*L*, pp. 185–7), from London where she was staying with her brother Henry, to Cassandra, who was at Godmersham with brother Edward and his family. Of all JA's poems, this one is most clearly a family in-joke, a result of gossip involving both Cassandra and Fanny, Edward's eldest daughter. The relevant section of the letter reads: 'Oh! yes, I remember Miss Emma Plumbtree's *Local* consequence perfectly' (punning on a connection between Emma and the local militia, based in Canterbury in 1811 and taking a large part in social life there), and then continues after the poem, 'But really, I was never much more put to it, than in contriving an answer to Fanny's former message. What is there to be said on the subject?—Pery pell—or pare pey?—or po.—or at the most, Pi pope pey pike pit' (the last phrases written in a joke language JA shared with Fanny, that of putting a 'p' in front of words; it probably means 'Very well—or are they? or no—or at the most, I hope they like it'). Emma Plumptre was a daughter of John Plumptre (*c.* 1760–1827), whose estate at Fredville was near Godmersham; the two families knew each other well socially, Emma and Fanny were friends and Emma's brother John was at about this time regarded as a possible husband for Fanny. Le Faye points out that Henry Gipps was presumably a member of the family running Gipps & Co., a banking firm in Canterbury from 1795 onwards (private communication). Southam notes that both Henry Gipps and Emma's brother John were officers in the East Kent Regiment of the local militia (*JA: A Students' Guide*, p. 207). Fanny wrote in her diary for 26 April 1811: 'Heard that E. P. is talked of for H Gipps!' (Centre for Kentish Studies, U951 F24/1–69, 26 April 1811). Fanny is clearly surprised, and the event may well have prompted a comment from Cassandra in the letter to which JA replied on 30 April. Emma became engaged to Henry in September 1811 and the two were married in 1812; Henry was ordained in 1815 and the couple moved later to Herefordshire.

While is possible that JA is recalling verses created on an earlier occasion, perhaps even by another member of the family, it is most likely that the verses were her own, composed for the letter. In November 1813 JA wrote to Cassandra that 'I saw M[r] Gipps last night—the useful M[r] Gipps, whose attentions came in as acceptably to us in handing us to the Carriage, for want of a better Man, as they did to Emma Plumptre.—I thought him rather a good looking little Man' (6 November 1813, *L*, pp. 252–3).

The letter with the poem in it became the property of Lady Knatchbull on Cassandra's death in 1845 and was inherited by her son, Lord Brabourne, who published it in *Letters of Jane Austen*, vol. 2, p. 97.

'Between Session & Session'

JA wrote these verses in the letter of 30 April 1811 which also contains 'I am in a dilemma' (see above). Both poems concern matters of interest to the family at Godmersham, in this case Edward Knight himself, since plans for the Weald of Kent canal allowed for it to cross the Godmersham estate. 'I congratulate Edward on the Weald of Kent Canal-Bill being put off till another Session, as I have just had the pleasure of reading. There is always something to be hoped from Delay.—' JA wrote in her letter, and then presented the verses in the form shown above. *The Morning Post* on Tuesday

30 April 1811 carried a notice reporting agreement reached at a General Meeting of the subscribers to the project, that 'it is now become advisable to postpone the further prosecution of the Bill until the ensueing Session' and a consequent resolution 'That the further prosecution of the Bill be for the present deferred, but that the same be resumed as early as possible in the next Session of Parliament'. The notice was reproduced in *The Times* of Wednesday 1 May.

The lines were first published in Lord Brabourne's *Letters*, vol. 2, p. 97.

In the late eighteenth and early nineteenth centuries a number of large projects were carried out to cut canals through the English countryside, with the aim of enabling trading and industrial traffic to move more efficiently. Proposals for such projects had to be approved by Parliament, and were generally supported by subscribers who anticipated a profit from their investments. An initial proposal for a twenty-eight-mile canal to link the Rivers Medway and Rother, with some collateral branches, running from near London to Wye near the south coast, thus transforming commercial transport routes between Kent and London, was first made in 1800 and an expanded scheme came to Parliament in 1811. The Bill passed its second reading – an intermediate stage of approval – on 22 April but was then withdrawn; and it was on reading of this that JA wrote her verses. Ironically, it seems that the Austens' hostility to the Bill was based on misleading information. 'Several . . . who voted against the second reading were, it was understood, induced to believe that the beautiful residences of Mr. Hatton, of Eastwell Park, and Mr. Austen of Godmersham Park, would be injured by the works: but the contrary is the fact, for it will not pass near these places by the distance of 3 or 4 miles', (*Maidstone Journal*, 20 February 1812, reproduced in *The Times*, 21 February 1812). The Bill was reintroduced in February 1812 and approved (Tony Singleton, 'The Weald of Kent Canal', *The Cranbrook Journal*, 15 (2004), p. 10 and private communication). The engineer John Rennie (1761–1821), who was responsible for the proposals, told a committee for the House of Lords in 1812 that 'it is without exception the finest piece of country to cut a canal through I ever saw'. However, the project was never carried out, possibly because sufficient capital could not be raised for it.

1 **Session**: Parliament usually met – that is, was in session – between January and July/August each year. In 1811 the session ended on 24 July, and the 1812 session began on 7 January.

2 **just**: previous editors have read the word as 'first'. As Southam points out, 'just' (a word also used by JA a few lines earlier in the same letter) looks more likely, and makes more sense of the phrase (*JA: A Students' Guide*, p. 208).

3 **Prepossession**: preconceived opinion, predisposition.

4 **the Nation**: public opinion had no direct authority over the small number of propertied men who were the only individuals eligible to vote for Members of Parliament in the early nineteenth century, but MPs were often lobbied by a wider constituency and could face riots if they persisted with very unpopular measures.

5 **lie still**: still be deferred or remain inactive.

6 **Wicked Men's will**: presumably the commercial interests seen to be promoting the Bill, and the MPs who supported them.

'When stretch'd on one's bed'

The copytext of the poem is a manuscript in the possession of the Roman Baths Museum, Bath and N. E. Somerset Council, which also contains the verses on Mr Gell and Miss Gill (see above). 'When stretch'd on one's bed' occupies the recto of one side of the sheet and the verso of the other.

This is the only extant version of the poem in JA's hand. It may be the original manuscript, since it contains extensive revisions; but in fact the poem looks as if it may have been written out as a fair copy, and then the author, having further thoughts, reworked half of one stanza and the whole of another, and made one or two other adjustments. The poem is untitled, and is dated 27 October 1811. At this date JA was probably at Chawton, awaiting publication of *S & S*: she had checked proofs of this novel in May, but it was only finally advertised for publication on 30 October.

The poem also appears in the Lefroy MS. It is similar to the Bath and N. E. Somerset Council version, but cannot have been copied from that manuscript because it provides the title, 'Lines written at Winchester by Jane Austen during her last illness', which can only have been written in ignorance of the date of 27 October 1811 on the Bath manuscript. It was first published in *MW*, pp. 447–8; this version derives from the Bath and N.E. Somerset Council text, though it does not reproduce the distinct layout of the stanzas, and there are minor differences in punctuation.

1 **Waltzes & reels**: aspects of the waltz, the new dance from Vienna in which men scandalously held their female partners in their arms, began to influence more traditional dancing from the turn of the century, but the waltz itself was only performed from about 1812 (Selwyn, pp. 167–8). Lord Byron, alert to the new fashion, wrote a facetious 'apostrophic hymn' to the waltz:

> Endearing Waltz!—to thy more melting tune
> Bow Irish jig and ancient rigadoon.
> Scotch reels, avaunt! and country-dance, forego . . .
>
> 'The Waltz' (1813), lines 109–11

The reel – a lively dance often associated with Scotland, usually danced by two couples facing each other and tracing figures of eight – was a much more traditional fixture at balls and assemblies.

2 **Corse**: a form of the word 'corpse' that was going out of even literary use by the early nineteenth century. In her copy Anna Lefroy spells the word 'Corps'.

'When Camilla, good humoured, & merry, & small'

Urania Catherine Camilla Wallop, evidently usually known as Camilla, and her mother, also Camilla, were longstanding friends of JA from Bath and Southampton: JA had noted with wry amusement the connection of the names of two naval ships – the *Urania* and the *Camilla* – with 'the Wallop race' as early as April 1805 (*L*, p. 101). *The Salisbury and Winchester Journal* for Monday 29 March 1813 reported that Camilla Wallop had married Rev. Henry Wake on 27 March 1813 at All Saints Church, Southampton. In fact JA had composed her poem several months previously: on 29–30 November 1812 she wrote from Chawton to Martha Lloyd that

'The 4 lines on Miss W. which I sent you were all my own, but James afterwards suggested what I thought a great improvement & as it stands in the Steventon edition' (*L*, pp. 196–7). Her comment raises the intriguing suggestion that James (who lived in the rectory at Steventon) was collecting family verses, perhaps to include in an album similar to the one which still survives containing family charades (see pp. 741–2).

There is no manuscript extant for the poem, but a version was preserved by James's daughter Anna Lefroy and written into the Lefroy MS under the inaccurate title 'On the marriage of Miss Camilla Wallop & the Revd Wake' (with a gap for his first name, which she evidently did not know). This may or may not be the version that contains James's 'great improvement' but it is the basis for our copytext, though without the title, which is clearly not authorial. Another version has survived, thanks to a Hampshire landowner Stephen Terry, who had long known the Austens and whose son had married Anna Lefroy's daughter; he wrote in his diary for 13 April 1860 that Anna – 'Mrs. Ben Lefroy' – had given him copies of some verses 'written by her very clever relation Jane Austen', and he quotes them: while lines 1 and 3 are identical with the version in the Lefroy MS, lines 2 and 4 are longer – 'For a husband, it happened, was at her last stake' and 'Is now very happy to jump at a Wake!' The poem was published in the *Memoir* (1870), p. 116, with the poem on the marriage of Mr Gell and Miss Gill (see above) in a version which was different again. Under the rather cumbersome title of 'On the marriage of a middle-aged Flirt with a Mr Wake, whom, it was supposed, she would scarcely have accepted in her youth', it offered a different first line – 'Maria, good-humoured, and handsome, and tall' – and the last four words in the fourth line were italicized, presumably to point up the pun. The substitution of the name 'Maria' – which has no connection with the prominent Wallop family – for 'Camilla' might have been a gesture of tact on Austen Leigh's part, or he may have been copying James's revisions made more than half a century earlier for much the same purpose. See *L*, p. 409 n. 7 and Gilson, pp. 47–8.

1 **at her last stake**: Urania Catherine Camilla Wallop was born on 23 November 1774 and was therefore celebrating her thirty-eighth

birthday in November 1812, a mature age for marriage. She married on 26 March 1813 and died on 31 December 1814.

2 **jump... Wake**: punning on 'jump' as a colloquial word for vigorous leaping, and 'jump at', graphically defined in *OED* as 'spring as a beast at a prey'. Rev. Henry. Wake was chaplain to the Marquis of Worcester and vicar of Mere in Wiltshire. In 1813 he became rector of Over Wallop in Hampshire, a living within the gift of the Earl of Portsmouth, a relative of his new wife; the 1851 Census recorded him still living there, at the age of eighty-one.

'When Winchester races first took their beginning'

JA wrote this poem on 15 July 1817 at 8 College Street, Winchester (sixteen miles from Chawton), where she had come with Cassandra in May to be attended by the respected surgeon Giles Lyford (*FR*, p. 248). Horse racing was a popular pastime in the late eighteenth and early nineteenth centuries, with a large number of local courses, and the Austen family often attended race meetings: JA's letters mention meetings at Newbury, Canterbury and Basingstoke, and it is quite possible that she had been to the races at Winchester, which usually took place in July, just before the meeting in Southampton. In October 1813 JA was solicitous of the effects of the weather on racegoers' enjoyment: 'Poor Basingstoke Races!—there seem to have been two particularly wretched days on purpose for them' (11 October 1813, *L*, p. 233). On 14 July 1817 the *Hampshire Chronicle and Courier* advertised the races to be run at the Winchester meeting forthcoming on 29–31 July, and related social events; JA could well have seen the advertisement, and, as so often before, been prompted by the newspaper to write light verse.

In his 'Biographical Notice' of December 1817 Henry Austen referred to the 'stanzas replete with fancy and vigour' which he thought had been composed just the day before her death. The reference did not appear in his expanded 1833 'Memoir of Miss Austen' and the verses clearly troubled the next generation of Austens (see Introduction, pp. xxxiii–xxxiv). The poem did not appear in the 1870 or 1871 *Memoir*, and was finally published in another family memoir, J. H. and E. C. Hubback's *Jane Austen's Sailor Brothers* (1906).

There is no manuscript in JA's hand extant – and indeed there may never have been one, if she dictated the poem, which is possible. Of two extant manuscripts from a period around 1817 one, in an unknown hand, might be the result of direct authorial dictation (see Introduction, pp. cix–cx). This version is written on a single sheet of paper about 210 mm × 185 mm, with the watermark G & R Munn 1816, and at the bottom of the second sheet appears, in another hand, the words, 'written July 15th 1817: by Jane Austen who died early in the morning [(1/2 past 4) inserted] of July 18th 1817 aged 41 y^{rs}'. It is now held in the Henry W. and Albert A. Berg collection at the New York Public Library.

Another manuscript is in the possession of the Jane Austen Memorial Trust at Chawton; it is a fair copy in Cassandra's hand; it is a single sheet of paper, folded into four pages about 236 mm × 196 mm, with a watermark of G PILE 1814. This version seems to have been the source of the poem as published by the Hubbacks. Anna Lefroy included the poem in the Lefroy MS, with the title 'Written at Winchester by Jane Austen, 1817'; although there are a few minor variations in punctuation it looks likely that Anna Lefroy copied from the Chawton rather than the Berg version of the poem. The Chawton version, which contains no errors and cancellations, provides our copytext, though we do not reproduce its title, 'Written at Winchester on Tuesday 15$^{th'}$ July 1817'.

1 **Winchester races**: horse races were held regularly in July, on a steeplechase course on flat ground at Worthy Down, about four miles north of Winchester. The course no longer exists as it did, but early nineteenth-century maps show an oval course, with a stand at the western end and a booth to the south.

2 **their old Saint**: Swithin was Bishop of Winchester from 852 until his death in 862, and afterwards was regarded as patron saint of the city. On 15 July 971 (later celebrated as St Swithin's Day) his body was moved from its first grave outside the cathedral to an indoor shrine. It was suggested that a massive storm on that

day prompted the popular belief that if it rained on St Swithin's Day the rain would continue for forty days: the following proverb continues to be popularly cited:

> St Swithin's day, if thou dost rain
> For forty days it will remain;
> St Swithin's day, if thou be fair
> For forty days 'twill rain nae mair.

3 **William of Wykham's**: William of Wykeham (1324–1404) was Bishop of Winchester from 1366 till his death. He became Chancellor of England, was the founder of New College, Oxford, and was patron of the remodelling of the great nave of Winchester Cathedral. He was also the founder of Winchester College, a prominent school through the early nineteenth century, when Edward Knight's sons attended it, and still flourishing today.

4 **his shrine**: in fact by 1817 St Swithin's shrine had been long demolished. There had been a splendid shrine in medieval times, frequently visited by pilgrims, but it was destroyed by agents of the Reformation in 1538.

5 **the Palace . . . in ruins**: the remains of Wolvesey Palace, the ancient residence of the Bishops of Winchester. A new palace had been built for the bishops in the late seventeenth century.

6 **Venta**: the Roman name for Winchester was Venta Belgarum, that is, the capital of the Belgari, the local Celtic tribe. Shortly after JA's death her eldest brother James, who had been too ill to attend her funeral, wrote a long poem beginning 'Venta! within thy sacred fane' which concludes with a handsome and heartfelt tribute to his sister, now buried in Winchester Cathedral (see Selwyn, pp. 48–50).

7 **races . . . measures**: then as now, races were accompanied by extensive betting and by a wide range of social events: the advertisements in the *Hampshire Chronicle and Courier* on 14 July include details of an assembly ball on 28 July ('Tickets, 5s.—Tea & Coffee included' – which doesn't sound very dissolute), and 'the Steward's Ball and Supper' on 30 July. Tom Bertram's participation, 'with a party of young men', in the pleasures of Newmarket races, assisted by 'a neglected fall and a good deal of drinking', brings on the illness that nearly kills him (*MP*, vol. 3, ch. 13).

8 **a neighbouring Plain**: Worthy Down, where the races were held.

CHARADES

The text of the three charades is taken from a small (111 mm × 85 mm) album containing seventy-seven leaves of gilt-edged paper of various colours, in a binding of maroon embossed leather gilt, which was preserved within the Austen family, and belonged more recently to R. W. Chapman; it is now owned by David Gilson. Some of the pieces contained in it, including these three, were first published, with a key giving solutions to all the charades except that by Rev. George Austen, in *Charades &c. written a hundred years ago by Jane Austen and her family* [Mary Augusta Austen-Leigh], London, with a preface dated 1895. The Gilson album (which is not paginated) contains, in a first section, forty-four charades written in a continuous sequence by what looks like the same hand, with authorship identified, but without solutions to the charades.

Only in the case of Jane Austen is authorship identified by a single name – 'Jane'; the other writers in this first section, identified by initials, are Rev. George and Mrs Cassandra Austen and James Leigh Perrot (JA's father, mother and uncle), JA's sister Cassandra, brothers James and Frank, James's son James Edward and daughters Caroline and Anna, and Anna's husband Ben Lefroy. After this section are a further forty-nine leaves of which eleven contain a variety of verses and other pieces, two dated 1859 and 1860, written in various hands; authorship is more varied and includes none of JA's generation.

The date of the album is unknown; the paper's watermark is nowhere complete, and may indicate 1807, or 1827 or 1837; it has been suggested that the binding may date from the 1840s (Gilson, p. 54). The charades must have been copied after 1814, since Anna Austen became Anna Lefroy (in the album 'I. A. E. L.' for Jane Anna Elizabeth Lefroy) in the November of that year, and before 1837, since James Edward Austen took the additional surname 'Leigh' in the February of that year, after the death of James Leigh Perrot's widow in late 1836, and thereafter signed himself 'J. E. A. L.' or 'I. E. A. L.' (as he does with some charades copied later into the volume, dated 1859 and 1860) rather than the 'I. E. A.' of the first group. The unusual attribution 'Jane' may indicate that Jane was a younger sister ('Miss Jane Austen' compared with 'Miss Austen' for Cassandra) or that there was a special importance about identifying her contributions, perhaps because she had died, which would date the album after July 1817.

Since no charade in the album is attributed to JA's brother Henry, part of the text of the 1895 printed edition, which includes charades by him, may derive from another family manuscript. R. W. Chapman mentioned his ownership of another manuscript collection partly in the hand of Cassandra (*Jane Austen: A Critical Bibliography* (Oxford: Clarendon Press, 1953), Item 31); the whereabouts of this manuscript are not now known.

The Austen family enjoyed composing, recording and circulating charades, which was at the time a popular domestic amusement: 'We admire your Charades excessively,' wrote JA at Chawton to Cassandra, who was staying with their brother James at Steventon, on 29 January 1813, 'but as yet have guessed only the 1st. The others seem very difficult. There is so much beauty in the Versification however, that the finding them out is but a secondary pleasure' (*L*, p. 202). In *E* (1815) JA describes Emma and Harriet Smith collecting riddles and charades, hoping to accumulate many more than the 300 achieved by Harriet's teacher Miss Nash (vol. 1, ch. 9). Sometimes the Austens' charades, like Emma's and Harriet's in *Emma*, were not original, but copied from other sources: one charade-poem long thought to be by JA was recently discovered to be the composition of the contemporary author Catherine Maria Fanshawe (Gilson, p. 60). However, since none of the charades in this section of the family album has been identified as copied from other sources, and since they are attributed to members of the family known to have written other original verse, it seems very likely that this is a collection of original charades created by the people identified, and that the three charades reproduced here were indeed written by JA.

Solutions: 1. Hemlock; 2. Agent; 3. Banknote